MW00562397

Praise for
Handbook of Response to Intervention in Early Childhood

"This is the right book at the right time. Two themes driving special education and early intervention today are 1) adoption of practices that are 'evidence-based,' and 2) use of multi-tiered systems of support such as RTI. Virginia Buysse and Ellen Peisner-Feinberg have recruited a set of chapters that integrate these themes while maintaining a clear focus on practical strategies for supporting young children."
—**Rob Horner, Ph.D.,** Professor, Special Education, University of Oregon

"Although much remains to be understood about how to conduct RTI in early childhood, the editors of this handbook have assembled a group of talented authors who collectively provide a very useful snapshot of what is currently known and unknown. This volume should be regarded as a touchstone for educators, researchers, and policymakers who hope to develop effective multi-tier systems of service delivery for young children and their families."
—**Doug Fuchs, Ph.D.,** Professor and Nicholas Hobbs Chair in Special Education and Human Development, Vanderbilt Kennedy Center, Vanderbilt University

"A remarkably clear and comprehensive overview of RTI that is framed specifically for early childhood audiences. The volume includes chapters from a who's who of the field who explicate overarching frameworks, describe how RTI guides instruction in varied content areas, and orient readers to state and federal practice. This much-needed volume is appearing at a critical time as the early childhood world is beginning to embrace principles of RTI."
—**David K. Dickinson, Ed.D.,** Professor, Department of Teaching and Learning, Vanderbilt University's Peabody College

"*Handbook of Response to Intervention in Early Childhood* brings together the current thinking and emerging evidence on RTI for all preschool age children, within the foundation of quality early childhood education and early childhood special education practices. This comprehensive compilation addresses both issues and opportunities in applying RTI to early settings and considers 'what it takes' from research, professional development, and administrative systems. This handbook represents where RTI in early childhood is now and provides direction for next steps in its evolution."
—**Bonnie Keilty, Ed.D.,** Adjunct Associate Professor, The City College of New York

Handbook of Response to Intervention in Early Childhood

Handbook of Response to Intervention in Early Childhood

edited by

Virginia Buysse, Ph.D.
Frank Porter Graham Child Development Institute
University of North Carolina at Chapel Hill

and

Ellen S. Peisner-Feinberg, Ph.D.
Frank Porter Graham Child Development Institute
University of North Carolina at Chapel Hill

·P A U L·H·
BROOKES
PUBLISHING C°®

Baltimore • London • Sydney

Paul H. Brookes Publishing Co.
Post Office Box 10624
Baltimore, Maryland 21285-0624
USA
www.brookespublishing.com

Typeset by Scribe, Philadelphia, Pennsylvania.
Manufactured in the United States of America by
Sheridan Books, Inc., Chelsea, Michigan.

Cover art ©iStockphoto.com/Terryfic3D.

Library of Congress Cataloging-in-Publication Data

Handbook of response to intervention in early childhood / edited by Virginia Buysse, Ph.D., Frank
   Porter Graham Child Development Institute, University of North Carolina at Chapel Hill, Chapel
   Hill, North Carolina and Ellen S. Peisner-Feinberg, Ph.D. Frank Porter Graham Child Development
   Institute, University of North Carolina at Chapel Hill Chapel Hill, North Carolina.
      pages   cm
   Includes index.
   ISBN-13: 978-1-59857-174-5
   ISBN-10: 1-59857-174-5
   1. Early childhood education—United States.   2. Response to intervention (Learning disabled
   children)   3. Learning disabled children—Education.   4. Remedial teaching.   5. Child develop-
   ment. I. Buysse, Virginia.

   LB1139.25.H347 2013
   372.21—dc23   2012049595

British Library Cataloguing in Publication data are available from the British Library.

2017   2016   2015   2014   2013

10   9   8   7   6   5   4   3   2   1

Contents

About the Editors

Virginia Buysse, Ph.D., Senior Scientist, Frank Porter Graham Child Development Institute, University of North Carolina at Chapel Hill, CB #8180, Chapel Hill, NC 27599-8180

Dr. Buysse is Senior Scientist at the Frank Porter Graham Child Development Institute at the University of North Carolina at Chapel Hill. In addition to directing a program of research on Recognition & Response, a model of response to intervention for prekindergarten, her research interests include innovations in professional development; models such as consultation, coaching, mentoring, and communities of practice that support professional development and program improvement; and educational practices and interventions that address the unique needs of diverse learners—those who have disabilities, who have learning difficulties, or who are dual language learners.

Ellen S. Peisner-Feinberg, Ph.D., Senior Scientist, Frank Porter Graham Child Development Institute, University of North Carolina at Chapel Hill, CB #8180, Chapel Hill, NC 27599-8180

Dr. Peisner-Feinberg is Senior Scientist at the Frank Porter Graham Child Development Institute at the University of North Carolina at Chapel Hill. Her background is in developmental psychology and public policy, and she has more than 20 years of research experience in early childhood education and program evaluation. Dr. Peisner-Feinberg has conducted numerous statewide and national research studies focused on the quality of early education programs and initiatives; the effects on children, especially dual language learners and children at risk; and quality improvement strategies.

Contributors

Reesha Adamson, M.A.
Doctoral Student of Special Education
University of Missouri
303 Townsend Hall
Columbia, MO 65211

Jason L. Anthony, Ph.D., Ed.S.
Associate Professor
University of Texas Health Science
    Center at Houston
7000 Fannin Street
Suite 2377
Houston, TX 77030

Michael A. Assel, Ph.D.
Associate Professor of Pediatrics
Children's Learning Institute
University of Texas Health Science
    Center at Houston
7000 Fannin Street
Suite 2300
Houston, TX 77030

Karen A. Blase, Ph.D.
Co-director
National Implementation Research
    Network
Senior Scientist
Frank Porter Graham Child
    Development Institute
University of North Carolina at Chapel
    Hill
CB# 8040
Chapel Hill, NC 27599

William H. Brown, Ph.D.
Professor and South Carolina
    Education Policy Fellow

Department of Educational Studies
University of South Carolina
820 Main Street
Columbia, SC 29208

Judith J. Carta, Ph.D.
Director of Early Childhood Research
Juniper Gardens Children's Project
Senior Scientist
Institute for Life Span Studies
Professor of Special Education
University of Kansas
444 Minnesota Avenue
Suite 300
Kansas City, KS 66101

Camille Catlett, M.A.
Co-principal Investigator
National Professional Development
    Center on Inclusion
Scientist
Frank Porter Graham Child
    Development Institute
University of North Carolina at Chapel
    Hill
CB #8185
Chapel Hill, NC 27599

Maureen A. Conroy, Ph.D.
Associate Director
Center for Excellence in Early
    Childhood Studies
Professor of Early Childhood Special
    Education, School Psychology, and
    Early Childhood Studies
University of Florida
Box 117050
Gainsville, FL 32611

Stephanie M. Curenton, Ph.D.
Adjunct Assistant Professor
Robert Wood Johnson Medical School
Institute for the Study of Child
    Development
Assistant Professor
Edward J. Bloustein School of Planning
    and Public Policy
Rutgers University
33 Livingston Avenue
New Brunswick, NJ 08901

Diane Trister Dodge, M.S.
Founder and President
Teaching Strategies, LLC
7101 Wisconsin Avenue
Suite 700
Bethesda, MD 20814

Michelle A. Duda, Ph.D.
Associate Director
National Implementation Research
    Network
Investigator
Frank Porter Graham Child
    Development Institute
University of North Carolina at Chapel
    Hill
CB# 8040
Chapel Hill, NC 27599

Barbrina Ertle, Ed.D.
Assistant Professor
Ruth S. Ammon School of Education
Adelphi University
Harvey Hall, Room 130
1 South Avenue
Post Office Box 701
Garden City, NY 11530

Edward G. Feil, Ph.D.
Senior Research Scientist
Oregon Research Institute
1715 Franklin Boulevard
Eugene, OR 97403

Angel Fettig, Ph.D.
Investigator
Frank Porter Graham Child
    Development Institute

University of North Carolina at Chapel
    Hill
CB# 8040
Chapel Hill, NC 27599

Dean L. Fixsen, Ph.D.
Senior Scientist
Frank Porter Graham Child
    Development Institute
University of North Carolina at Chapel
    Hill
CB# 8040
Chapel Hill, NC 27599

Lise Fox, Ph.D.
Co-director
Florida Center for Inclusive
    Communities
Professor of Child and Family
    Studies
Louis de la Parte Florida Mental
    Health Institute
University of South Florida
13301 Bruce B. Downs Boulevard
Room MHC 2116
Tampa, FL 33612

Andy J. Frey, Ph.D.
Associate Professor
Kent School of Social Work
University of Louisville
Louisville, KY 40292

Lynn S. Fuchs, Ph.D.
Nicholas Hobbs Professor of
    Special Education and Human
    Development
Vanderbilt University
Box 228, Peabody College
Nashville, TN 37203

Herbert P. Ginsburg, Ph.D.
Jacob H. Schiff Foundation Professor of
    Psychology and Education
Department of Human Development
Teachers College
Columbia University
525 West 120 Street
New York, NY 10024

Heather Smith Googe, Ph.D.
Doctoral Student in Early Childhood
  Education
The University of South Carolina
1530 Wheat Street
Columbia, SC 29208

Charles R. Greenwood, Ph.D.
Professor of Applied Behavioral Science
University of Kansas
Director
Juniper Gardens Children's Project
444 Minnesota Avenue
Suite 300
Kansas City, KS 66101

Fred Greer, Ph.D.
Research Assistant Professor
College of Education
Educational Studies Department
University of South Carolina–Columbia
235K Wardlaw Building
Columbia, SC 29033

Jennifer Grisham-Brown, Ed.D.
Professor
Interdisciplinary Early Childhood
  Education Program
Faculty Director
Early Childhood Laboratory School
  University of Kentucky
229 Taylor Education Building
Lexington, KY 40506

Shana J. Haines, M.S.
Research Assistant
Beach Center on Disability
Doctoral Candidate
Department of Special Education
University of Kansas
3136 Haworth Hall
1200 Sunnyside Avenue
Lawrence, KS 66049

Rena A. Hallam, Ph.D.
Associate Professor
Department of Human Development
  and Family Studies
University of Delaware
111 Alison Hall
Newark, DE 19716

Mary Louise Hemmeter, Ph.D.
Associate Professor
Department of Special Education
Vanderbilt University
Box 228, Peabody College
Nashville, TN 37203

Carly Hoffend, M.A.
Graduate Student
School of Education
University of North Carolina at Chapel
  Hill
CB# 3500
Chapel Hill, NC 27599

Heidi Hollingsworth, Ph.D.
Assistant Professor of Education
Program Coordinator
Early Childhood Education
Elon University
Campus Box 2105
Elon, NC 27244

Laura M. Justice, Ph.D.
Professor of Teaching and Learning
The Ohio State University
356 Arps Hall
1945 North High Street
Columbus OH 43210

Herman T. Knopf, Ph.D.
Associate Professor of Early Childhood
  Education
Department of Instruction and Teacher
  Education
University of South Carolina,
  Columbia
Yvonne & Schuyler Moore Child
  Development Research Center
1530 Wheat Street
Columbia, SC 29201

Steven E. Knotek, Ph.D.
Associate Professor
School of Education
University of North Carolina at Chapel
  Hill
CB# 3500
Chapel Hill, NC 27599

Doré R. LaForett, Ph.D.
Investigator
Frank Porter Graham Child
    Development Institute
University of North Carolina at Chapel
    Hill
CB #8180
Chapel Hill, NC 27599

Susan H. Landry, Ph.D.
Director and Founder
Children's Learning Institute
Executive Director
State Center for Early Childhood
    Development
Albert & Margaret Alkek Chair in
    Early Childhood
Michael Matthew Knight Professor
University of Texas Health Science
    Center at Houston
7000 Fannin Street
Suite 2318
Houston, TX 77030

Erica S. Lembke, Ph.D.
Associate Professor
Department of Special Education
University of Missouri
303 Townsend Hall
Columbia, MO 65211

Jim J. Lesko, Ed.D.
Director
Early Development and Learning
    Resources
Delaware Department of Education
401 Federal Street
Suite 2
Dover, DE 19901

Timothy J. Lewis, Ph.D.
Professor of Special Education
University of Missouri
303 Townsend Hall
Columbia, MO 65211

Ashley Lewis Presser, Ph.D.
Senior Research Associate
Education Development Center, Inc.
Center for Children and Technology
96 Morton Street, 7th Floor
New York, NY 10014

Amy McCart, Ph.D.
Research Associate Professor
Beach Center on Disability
University of Kansas
3136 Haworth Hall
1200 Sunnyside Avenue
Lawrence, KS 66045

Scott McConnell, Ph.D.
Professor of Educational Psychology
    and Child Psychology and Affiliate
Center for Early Education and
    Development
University of Minnesota
56 East River Road
Delivery Code 4101
Minneapolis MN 55455

Anita S. McGinty, Ph.D.
Clinical Speech-Language Pathologist
Research Scientist
Center for the Advanced Study of
    Teaching and Learning
Curry School
University of Virginia
2200 Old Ivy Way
Charlottesville, VA 22903

Tara McLaughlin, Ph.D.
Research Scientist
Center for Excellence in Early
    Childhood Studies
College of Education
University of Florida
Post Office Box 117050
1345 Norman Hall
Gainesville, FL 32611

Mary E. McLean, Ph.D.
Kellner Professor of Early Childhood
    Education
Professor
Department of Exceptional Education
University of Wisconsin–Milwaukee
671 Enderis Hall
2400 East Hartford Avenue
Milwaukee, WI 53211

Scott Methe, Ph.D.
Assistant Professor of Counseling and
    School Psychology
University of Massachusetts Boston

173 Wheatley Building
Boston, MA 02125

Barbara S. Mitchell, M.Ed.
Consultant
Missouri School-wide Positive
    Behavior Support Initiative
Doctoral Student in Special
    Education
University of Missouri
303 Townsend Hall
Columbia, MO 65211

Rollanda E. O'Connor, Ph.D.
Reading Specialist
Professor
Graduate School of Education
University of California at Riverside
1207 Sproul Hall
Riverside, CA 92521

Samuel L. Odom, Ph.D.
Director
Frank Porter Graham Child
    Development Institute
University of North Carolina at Chapel
    Hill
CB# 8180
Chapel Hill, NC 27599

Yi Pan, Ph.D.
Investigator Statistician
Frank Porter Graham Child
    Development Institute
University of North Carolina at Chapel
    Hill
CB# 8185
Chapel Hill, NC 27599

Kristie Pretti-Frontczak, Ph.D.
Professor
Department of Educational
    Foundations and Special Services
Kent State University
405 White Hall
Kent, OH 44242

M. Jamila Reid, Ph.D.
Research Affiliate
Psychology Department
University of Washington

Psychologist
Evidence Based Treatment Center of
    Seattle
316 NE 54th Street
Seattle, WA 98105

Thomas Rendon, M.B.A.
Iowa Head Start State Collaboration
    Office Coordinator
Iowa Department of Education
Grimes State Office Building
400 East 14th Street
Des Moines, IA 50319

Beth Rous, Ed.D.
Associate Professor
Educational Leadership Studies
University of Kentucky
111A Dickey Hall
Lexington, KY 40506

Susan R. Sandall, Ph.D.
Director
Professional Development and
    Applied Research Units
Associate Professor
Experimental Education Unit
University of Washington
Box 357925
Seattle, WA 98195

Jennifer M. Schaaf, Ph.D.
Investigator
Frank Porter Graham Child
    Development Institute
University of North Carolina at Chapel
    Hill
CB# 8180
Chapel Hill, NC 27599

Ilene S. Schwartz, Ph.D.
Professor of Special Education
Director
Haring Center for Applied Research
    and Training in Education
Experimental Education Unit
College of Education
University of Washington
Miller Hall, Box 353600
Seattle, WA 98195

Rune J. Simeonsson, Ph.D., M.S.P.H.
Professor of Education
School Psychology Program
Fellow
Frank Porter Graham Child
    Development Institute
University of North Carolina at Chapel
    Hill
CB# 3500
University of North Carolina
Chapel Hill, NC 27599

Patricia Snyder, Ph.D.
David Lawrence Jr. Endowed Chair in
    Early Childhood Studies
Professor of Special Education, Early
    Childhood Studies, and Pediatrics
University of Florida
1403 Norman Hall
Post Office Box 117050
Gainesville, FL 32611

Elena Soukakou, Ph.D.
Research Consultant
Frank Porter Graham Child
    Development Institute
University of North Carolina
Research Fellow
Oxford University
Wellington Square
Oxford
OX1 2JD
United Kingdom

Paul R. Swank, Ph.D.
Professor
Department of Pediatrics
University of Texas Health Science
    Center at Houston
7000 Fannin Street
Suite 2391
Houston, TX 77030

Kristina S. Ten Haagen, M.A.
Graduate Student
School Psychology Program
School of Education

University of North Carolina at Chapel
    Hill
CB# 3500
Chapel Hill, NC 27599

Ann Turnbull, Ed.D.
Co-director
Beach Center on Disability
Distinguished Professor
Department of Special Education
University of Kansas
3111 Haworth Hall
1200 Sunnyside Avenue
Lawrence, KS 66045

Amanda M. VanDerHeyden, Ph.D.
President
Education Research & Consulting, Inc.
102 Ashton Court
Fairhope, AL 36532

Carolyn Webster-Stratton, Ph.D.
Director
Parenting Clinic
Professor
School of Nursing
University of Washington
1411 8th Avenue West
Seattle, WA 98119

Pamela J. Winton, Ph.D.
Senior Scientist and Director of
    Outreach
Frank Porter Graham Child
    Development Institute
University of North Carolina at Chapel
    Hill
CB# 8185
Chapel Hill, NC 27599

Tricia A. Zucker, Ph.D.
Assistant Professor
University of Texas Health Science
    Center at Houston
7000 Fannin Street
Suite 2300
Houston, TX 77030

Foreword

Response to intervention (RTI) has exploded in the field of elementary education over the past decade. Implementation has lasted long enough that many of the flaws and imperfections are now clear. As is true for all innovations, more was promised than delivered. Nonetheless, in the view of many, RTI has been an extraordinary success for several reasons.

For the first time, teachers were provided with the experience of using (and often administering) efficient measures that were *psychometrically valid* to seriously inform their instruction. These data were used to determine which students needed additional small-group instruction and could be used to monitor whether these interventions were actually working. In that sense, RTI has slowly begun to change the professional school culture around assessment in a way that none of the other initiatives were able to do successfully.

In addition, screening has enabled students who need help with learning to read or becoming proficient in mathematics to receive that help. In the past, girls often failed to receive additional help when objective measures showed they needed it, in large part because teachers tended to provide extra help primarily to students who tended to engage in externalizing behaviors, the majority of whom are boys.

RTI also has been successful in establishing the type of serious substantive collaboration between classroom teachers and school psychologists and special educators that many have longed for and that was rarely accomplished with the various prereferral and collaborative consultation models of the past.

Based on the scope and quality of the excellent chapters in this volume on RTI in early childhood, the same potential exists in this field. In many respects, the field of early childhood education is an excellent venue for RTI in that many of the most troubling barriers that RTI faces in elementary and middle schools—lack of a time in the school day for individualized small-group instruction (without a student missing the instructional time for mathematics or science or music), concern with keeping the full class on schedule to meet the objectives in a mandated pacing chart—are far less pressing in this setting. Early childhood programs have a long history of learning centers and individualized small-group learning, and by and large there is not nearly as strong a press to "cover" grade- or age-level curriculum through whole-class instruction.

RTI emphasizes using assessments to provide instruction in areas related to literacy, language, and quantitative reasoning that are at the appropriate developmental level for a student. This has been a recurrent theme in early childhood education for well over a century. RTI has the potential to create and validate measures that are more efficient, and, most important, more easily usable by early childhood educators than those used in the past.

This volume presents several examples of efficient, psychometrically valid assessments that might be used in RTI. Many are in early stages of development. Readers may want to seriously consider some of the lessons learned from RTI in elementary education. First, universal screening measures seem to overidentify students, thus wasting precious resources in providing intensive support to children who would do fine with typical early childhood education. Second, progress-monitoring measures need to be validated with solid criterion measures that reflect contemporary standards for performance in cognitive or social domains. It is easy for developers to short-circuit this process, and results can lead to spurious evidence of progress.

On the other hand, readers should appreciate the sophistication that the authors bring to the various topics. Here are just a few examples. Assessments can only exist in an RTI system; merely implementing screening and progress-monitoring measures without a comprehensive system of RTI will not work. A comprehensive system provides clear guidelines for using screening data to form instructional groups or intervention groups and for monitoring student growth and instructional decision making. Although formative assessment is addressed, the role of formative assessment has yet to be established in RTI systems. An advantage of the type of general outcome measures described in several of the chapters is that they reflect goals independent of any specific curriculum.

Because of the importance of assessment in beginning an RTI system, I focus my comments on the chapters addressing assessment. However, this volume covers a wide range of other equally important topics including state and federal policy, advances in curriculum development and instructional strategies (including the important concept of embedded instruction), professional development, adjustments for English learners, as well as social aspects of early childhood education. I believe this comprehensive volume can help launch an exciting era of RTI in early childhood education. It intelligently builds on past successes and insights from developmental psychology to inform this new, vibrant field.

Russell Gersten, Ph.D.
Executive Director
Instructional Research Group
Los Alamitos, CA

To Bob, Katherine, Nick, Courtney, and Harper

and

To Tom and Aaron

*Whose constant love and encouragement
enabled us to accomplish a task of this scale
and realize our vision*

I

Introduction

Response to Intervention

Conceptual Foundations for the Early Childhood Field

Virginia Buysse and Ellen S. Peisner-Feinberg

Response to intervention (RTI) is a comprehensive and systematic approach for using assessment in instructional decision making that has captured the attention of educators, researchers, and policy makers (Burns & Gibbons, 2008; Eisenman & Ferretti, 2010; Glover & Vaughn, 2010; Haager, Klinger, & Vaughn, 2007; Jimerson, Burns, & VanDerHeyden, 2007; Pina & Eisenberg, 2009). The approach is gaining widespread acceptance in kindergarten through Grade 12 in the majority of states, with some evidence that these activities have begun to extend down to prekindergarten (pre-K), according to a recent report by the U.S. Department of Education (Bradley et al., 2011). RTI represents both an important current educational innovation being implemented in school districts throughout the United States and a mechanism for achieving broader educational reforms in the future. Indeed, no practice has generated as much recent attention as RTI for its ability to accommodate students with widely varying learning needs, including students who are high performing, students who are academically or behaviorally behind, and students who have specific learning disabilities in reading, writing, and math. With its emphasis on monitoring student progress in learning, RTI is a logical extension of both the evidence-based practice movement and more recent educational reforms focused on measuring teacher effectiveness in relation to student achievement (Sawchuk, 2012). At the same time, it is important to recognize that there is considerable variation in exactly how RTI is implemented in K–12 education, along with different perspectives among educators and scholars about the purpose and nature of RTI (Fuchs, Fuchs, & Stecker, 2010; see also Chapter 3 in this volume). Despite the widespread popularity of RTI in K–12, Fuchs and his colleagues noted its heavy demand on practitioners and the need for a comprehensive, coordinated service delivery system to implement RTI successfully (Fuchs, Fuchs, & Compton, 2012). These authors also advocated for a shift to something they referred to as "Smart RTI" in the future, which they defined as having three features: multistage screening to identify students at risk for learning difficulties, multistage assessment to determine appropriate levels of tiered instruction, and new roles for special educators focused on prevention as well as intervention.

The use of RTI to support learning and development for children prior to kindergarten has sparked widespread interest in early childhood (Greenwood et al., 2011). However, the early childhood field is at an early stage in understanding how RTI can complement existing practices for children from birth to age 5.

Furthermore, the field is only beginning to gather research evidence on RTI to guide its implementation and evaluate its effectiveness with this age group. A summary of eight listening sessions on RTI facilitated by the National Professional Development Center on Inclusion (NPDCI) revealed considerable variability in people's familiarity with this approach and their understanding of how it was designed to work in early childhood. (For more information, go to http://npdci.fpg.unc.edu/resources/articles/RTI-EC [NPDCI, 2012].) Many participants indicated that they had never heard of RTI, whereas others stated that although they understood RTI, their programs had not yet implemented the approach. Relatively few reported that programs in their communities had adopted RTI or had begun to implement the approach with children prior to kindergarten.

Despite being an unfamiliar practice to many who work with young children, RTI represents a major innovation in K–12 education—one that is having reverberating effects throughout the early childhood field (Greenwood et al., 2011). On the one hand, the innovation stems from the shift away from the traditional model of waiting until students fail repeatedly in the early grades before they are determined to be eligible for special education (i.e., the wait-to-fail or IQ-achievement discrepancy model) to one that involves intervening within the general education program as soon as students' learning difficulties become apparent (i.e., the early intervening or prereferral model). More broadly, RTI is now widely viewed as a way to improve teaching and learning for all students and is not limited to benefitting only those who receive special education or those who require additional instructional supports prior to referral for these services. The use of differentiated instruction based on demonstrated need disrupts the status quo in which general and special education have existed as separate systems—one serving the general population of students, the other serving students with identified disabilities, and both inadequately addressing the needs of students considered at risk for learning difficulties who fall somewhere between the two groups.

Just as in the public schools, there is a pressing need in the early childhood field to customize teaching and learning to address the needs of an increasingly diverse population of young children and families (Buysse & Wesley, 2010). The notion that general education teachers can apply targeted interventions derived largely from special education turns the traditional general-special education dichotomy on its head. Further evidence that RTI represents a disruptive innovation in K–12 education can be traced to the defining features that have been used to identify similar innovations in other fields, as identified by Christensen and his colleagues (Christensen, Horn, & Johnson, 2008). These features include the way RTI's assessment and instructional components fit and work together and its implementation in noncompeting contexts, often with grant funding for innovations outside traditional educational structures.

Although early childhood education is not as far along as the K–12 education field in adopting RTI, there are several reasons why the time is ripe for a comprehensive edited volume on this topic. First, the instructional principles that serve as the foundation for RTI are consistent with those widely acknowledged in early childhood, namely, the emphasis on high-quality curriculum and instruction and the importance of early intervening using research-based practices. Second, the world of practice has moved to embrace RTI and many early educators will not wait until all of the empirical evidence has been accumulated before implementing practices that are believed to improve early education for all children. The field needs a reliable source of information and research-based knowledge on RTI as practitioners begin to define and implement these practices in early childhood programs. Third, and perhaps most important, there is now a body of evidence on the effectiveness of RTI with school-age children and emerging evidence on its effectiveness for pre-K children (Burns, Appleton, & Stehouwer, 2005; Buysse & Peisner-Feinberg, 2009; Gersten et al., 2008, 2009).

One indication that the early childhood field is already moving in this direction is the widespread interest in tiered models of instruction, including the development of specific models such as Recognition & Response (R&R), the Pyramid Model, and Building Blocks (see Chapters 5, 6, 7, and 17), along with research-based tiered interventions linked to formative assessment tools developed by the Center for Response to Intervention in Early Childhood (CRTIEC; see Chapter 27). Organized by instructional intensity and matched to children's learning needs, these models collectively reflect some (if not all) of the defining components of RTI and indicate a commitment to help every child learn, including those with learning or behavioral difficulties, those with disabilities, and those from diverse cultural and linguistic groups (Chapters 22 and 23).

Another indicator of RTI's influence in early education can be found in guidance offered by a major professional organization suggesting that early educators rely more heavily on assessment data to improve instruction and better address children's academic learning needs (American Federation of Teachers, 2011). In a report published by the Rand Corporation, five approaches were identified for incorporating assessments of child functioning within state Quality Rating and Improvement Systems (QRISs), including two in which the purpose was defined as "to inform caregiving and instructional practice with individual children" (Zellman & Karoly, 2012, p. xiii). The fact that these recent recommendations reflect key tenets of RTI, but were not attributed to RTI, is perhaps a sign that RTI principles and practices are gaining wider traction and cachet in the field of early child care and education.

Both the widespread implementation of RTI throughout the nation and its more recent emergence as a promising practice for early childhood suggests that the approach warrants further serious consideration. At the same time, a number of questions about the use of RTI in early childhood have emerged within the field—what practices define RTI, who implements it, which children and families are affected, who benefits, and how does RTI fit within existing practices and programs?

The purpose of this text is to bring together the best thinking and current research-based knowledge on RTI to begin to address these questions. This chapter provides an overview of RTI and sets the stage for subsequent chapters focused on the assessment and instructional components, program-level supports, and the infrastructure that underpins an RTI approach. This volume attempts to bridge the gap between theory and practice by examining the current evidence base and practical strategies related to implementation, as well as offering recommendations for next steps and future directions. In this chapter, we outline the origins of RTI and define its key components, summarize the best available research evidence on RTI, and describe some of the challenges and issues related to implementation of RTI in early childhood.

ORIGINS OF RESPONSE TO INTERVENTION

The origins of tiered instructional approaches in early childhood can be traced directly to conceptual models of RTI for school-age students (National Center on Response to Intervention, 2010), and prior to that, to a classification model addressing primary, secondary, and tertiary prevention within public health (Chapter 2; see also Gresham [2011] for a comprehensive discussion on the history and origins of RTI). Figure 1.1 shows the parallel organizing frameworks for the public health prevention classification scheme and school-based RTI model. Organized by level of instructional intensity and representing a continuum of interventions and supports, RTI links students' formative assessment results with specific teaching and intervention strategies.

Although original conceptualizations of RTI focused on applications to academic learning, RTI applications show similarities in logic to models focused on positive behavior supports (PBS; also called positive behavior interventions and supports [PBIS] and schoolwide positive behavior support [SW-PBS]; Epstein, Atkins, Cullinan, Kutash, & Weaver, 2008; Malecki & Demaray, 2007; Sprague, Cook, Browning-Wright, & Sadler, 2008; Sugai, 2009). With its foundations in applied behavior analysis and its origins in developing alternative practices for students with significant disabilities within special education, the PBS approach has expanded in recent years to focus on the prevention and early detection of behavior problems among the general population of students served in public education and other contexts (e.g., juvenile justice). The National Center on

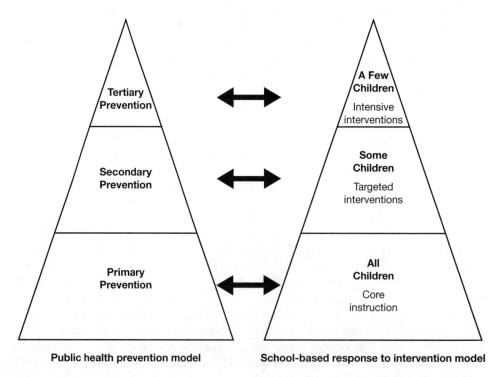

Public health prevention model   School-based response to intervention model

Figure 1.1. Conceptual frameworks for public health prevention and school-based response to intervention models.

Positive Behavioral Interventions and Supports (http://www.pbis.org; Sugai, 2009) has acknowledged the conceptual relationship between educational practices addressing behavior and academics within an integrated model as illustrated in a side-by-side comparison of PBS and RTI, although it has not indicated how such an integrated approach would be implemented within classrooms and programs. Figure 1.2 depicts a side-by-side comparison of RTI and PBS. An integrated RTI model in which teachers can screen for problems and provide tiered interventions to address both domains within the same framework ultimately would be most beneficial, because students often exhibit co-occurring difficulties in both academic learning and behavior, and teachers likely would find it difficult to implement multiple tiered models simultaneously. However, an integrated tiered approach has not been clearly specified in the literature, nor has an integrated approach been validated through research.

Federal policies explicitly addressing the use of RTI with children prior to kindergarten do not exist (Chapter 24). However, in 2010, the Office of Special Education Programs (OSEP) of the U.S. Department of Education issued informal guidance in a memorandum to state directors of special education on the use of RTI with 3- to 5-year-old children with respect to eligibility decisions, referrals for evaluation, and parental rights (http://www2.ed.gov/policy/speced/guid/idea/memosdcltrs/osep11-07rtimemo.pdf). The guidance from OSEP stemmed largely from confusion within Head Start about whether and how RTI should be used to determine eligibility for special education of individual children enrolled in Head Start programs. The OSEP guidance did not address broader questions about the use of RTI with children who may not be eligible for special education services but who potentially could benefit from an RTI approach prior to kindergarten.

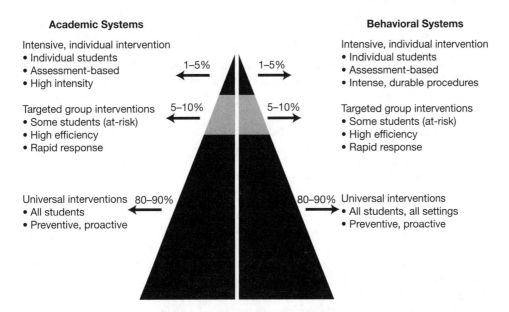

Figure 1.2. Integration of academic and social behavior: Three-tiered continuum of behavior support. (From G. Sugai, Center on Positive Behavioral Interventions & Supports; reprinted by permission.)

For school-age students in kindergarten through Grade 12, federal policies and a position statement published by the Council for Exceptional Children (2008), along with many other resources, guide the use of RTI in schools. The Individuals with Disabilities Education Improvement Act (IDEA) of 2004 (PL 108-446) includes two specific provisions on RTI. These provisions (Sections 613 [f][1] and 614[b][6]) allow local school districts to use RTI as an alternative method for identifying students with learning disabilities, and more important, state that students may be determined to have a specific learning disability on the basis of how they respond to research-based interventions (IDEA 2004).

SEC. 613. LOCAL EDUCATIONAL AGENCY ELIGIBILITY.

(f) EARLY INTERVENING SERVICES.—

(1) IN GENERAL.—A local educational agency may not use more than 15 percent of the amount such agency receives under this part for any fiscal year, less any amount reduced by the agency pursuant to subsection (a)(2)(C), if any, in combination with other amounts (which may include amounts other than education funds), to develop and implement coordinated, early intervening services, which may include interagency financing structures, for students in kindergarten through grade 12 (with a particular emphasis on students in kindergarten through grade 3) who have not been identified as needing special education or related services but who need additional academic and behavioral support to succeed in a general education environment.

SEC. 614. EVALUATIONS, ELIGIBILITY DETERMINATIONS, INDIVIDUALIZED EDUCATION PROGRAMS, AND EDUCATIONAL PLACEMENTS.

(b) EVALUATION PROCEDURES.—

(6) SPECIFIC LEARNING DISABILITIES.—

(A) IN GENERAL.—Notwithstanding section 607(b), when determining whether a child has a specific learning disability as defined in section 602, a local educational agency shall not be required to take into consideration whether a child has a severe discrepancy between achievement and intellectual ability in oral expression, listening comprehension, written expression, basic reading skill, reading comprehension, mathematical calculation, or mathematical reasoning.

(B) ADDITIONAL AUTHORITY.—In determining whether a child has a specific learning disability, a local educational agency may use a process that determines if the child responds to scientific, research-based intervention as a part of the evaluation procedures described in paragraphs (2) and (3).

PBS also is supported by specific policies within IDEA 2004. In the most recent reauthorization of IDEA, PBS was referenced multiple times (for a more comprehensive discussion, see Sanetti & Simonsen, 2011) as a way of improving the quality of behavior supports provided to all students enrolled in public education, with a particular focus on the importance of this improvement for students with disabilities. These provisions within IDEA on PBS address issues that range from funding, to the use of suspension and expulsion rates in evaluating its effects, to professional development and the role of teachers in implementing this approach.

DEFINING FEATURES OF A RESPONSE TO INTERVENTION APPROACH

Although a number of variations of the RTI model have been proposed (see Fuchs, Fuchs, & Compton, 2007; Marston, Muyskens, Lau, & Canter, 2003; Speece, Case, & Molloy, 2003; Vaughn & Fuchs, 2003; Vaughn, Linan-Thompson, & Hickman, 2003), RTI is generally based on three common components: 1) systematic assessment of students' level and rate of performance, 2) scientifically based core programs and interventions, and 3) carefully defined instructional decision-making criteria. RTI generally is conceptualized as a three-tier model that corresponds to the three levels of prevention within the public health framework: core instruction (primary prevention), targeted interventions (secondary prevention), and intensive, individualized interventions (tertiary prevention). The targeted interventions may be based on standardized treatments that have been validated through research, on a problem-solving process involving the systematic analysis of instructional variables on a case-by-case basis (Fuchs, Fuchs, & Stecker, 2010; Gresham, 2011), or, as recommended by Gresham (2007), a combination of the standard treatment and problem-solving approaches.

As mentioned previously, RTI is an emerging practice in early childhood and there are few policies and little information to guide its use with children prior to kindergarten. In response to this need, and with input from national experts and key stakeholders, the National Professional Development Center on Inclusion (NPDCI) released a concept paper in 2012 in which RTI in early childhood was closely aligned with broader RTI principles and the literature (NPDCI, 2012; see also Chapter 29). Figure 1.3 shows the continuum of instruction, interventions, and

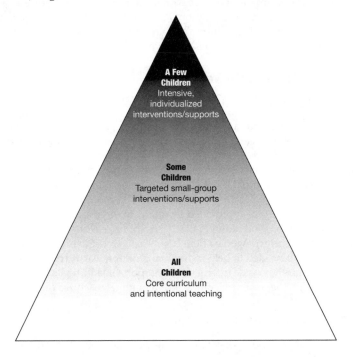

Figure 1.3. The continuum of instruction and interventions/supports within response to intervention in early childhood. (From National Professional Development Center on Inclusion [2012]. *Response to Intervention [RTI] in early childhood: Building consensus on the defining features.* Chapel Hill: University of North Carolina, Frank Porter Graham Child Development Institute; reprinted by permission.)

supports within a generic RTI model for early childhood as depicted in the NPDCI concept paper. The concept paper offered the following explanation for thinking about the meaning of RTI in early childhood:

> RTI is a framework that can be used in early childhood to help practitioners connect children's formative assessment results with specific teaching and intervention strategies. RTI is designed to improve instructional practices for all children and includes both foundational instructional practices as well as the provision of additional supports for children with varying learning needs such as children with learning difficulties, children with challenging behaviors, children who are dual language learners, and children with disabilities. The key components of an RTI approach in early childhood are: 1) formative assessment, 2) instruction and tiered interventions/supports, and 3) collaboration and data-based decision making. (NPDCI, 2012)

Formative Assessment

According to the NPDCI concept paper, assessment within RTI is defined as follows:

> Information is gathered on children's behavior and skills and used to inform instructional decisions. To guide decisions regarding the effectiveness of instruction and children's responsiveness to interventions, formative assessment should reflect measurable and relevant learning goals for young children. Universal screening and progress monitoring are particular types of formative assessment used within RTI. Universal screening involves gathering information periodically on *all* children in a classroom or program to monitor their development and learning, and to determine whether *some* children might need additional interventions to acquire key skills in academic learning or behavior regulation. Progress monitoring is designed to gather additional information on the children who receive targeted interventions to determine children's responsiveness to these interventions. (NPDCI, 2012)

Instruction and Tiered Interventions

NPDCI defined the instructional component as follows:

> An effective core curriculum and intentional teaching are the foundation of instructional practices for RTI in early childhood. Intentional teaching means the purposeful organization of the early learning environment and developmentally appropriate learning activities within a comprehensive curriculum to help children develop and acquire important skills. In RTI, the concept of intentional teaching is expanded to include targeted interventions for some children who require additional academic or behavioral supports, generally provided through small-group instruction, embedded instruction/interventions, or individualized scaffolding. Instructional strategies and behavioral supports are arranged by tiers from least to most intensive to show the level of adult involvement needed to help individual children learn. The targeted interventions for some children provide instructional supports in addition to those provided to all children through the core curriculum and intentional teaching. (NPDCI, 2012)

Collaboration and Data-Based Decision Making

Finally, NPDCI defined the decision-making processes within an RTI approach as follows:

> RTI includes methods that practitioners can use to collaborate with families, specialists, and others to plan and organize learning and behavioral supports and to assess

how well children are responding to them. Broader, system-level supports such as ongoing professional development, methods for gathering and reporting assessment results, and strategies for documenting and sharing information with families and others also are needed to support an RTI approach. (NPDCI, 2012)

EVIDENCE FOR THE EFFICACY OF RESPONSE TO INTERVENTION

There is little research available on the efficacy of RTI for children prior to kindergarten. However, there is mounting evidence on the efficacy of RTI for improving academic learning of school-age students. Collectively, research findings have indicated that RTI is particularly effective when implemented in the early grades, that it can yield positive learning outcomes, and that it can reduce the need for special education services. A meta-analysis of 24 studies involving school-age children offered evidence of the effects of RTI at both the child and the school level (Burns, Appleton, & Stehouwer, 2005). This meta-analysis concluded that students attending schools implementing RTI demonstrated greater growth in academic skills, more time on task, and better task completion, compared with those attending schools not implementing RTI. Two practice guides published under the auspices of the Institute of Education Sciences (IES), U.S. Department of Education, summarized the research evidence on the effects of RTI for improving the reading and mathematics skills of school-age students, and this information is summarized next.

The Efficacy of Response to Intervention for Improving Reading

With respect to the early primary grades, there is a growing body of evidence on RTI in reading, including the reliability and validity of specific screening and progress monitoring measures as well as data regarding the average growth rates used to gauge the effectiveness of tiered interventions. An IES practice guide summarized empirical support showing that universal screening in reading can aid in predicting children's future performance in this area and that progress monitoring can have a positive effect on teachers' instructional decision making (Gersten et al., 2008). The authors also found strong evidence for the effectiveness of Tier 2 small-group interventions in reading for elementary school students who were identified as at risk for learning difficulties in this area (i.e., scored below the benchmark on universal screening). In contrast, the evidence supporting differentiated reading instruction for all students at Tier 1 was reported to be low.

The Efficacy of Response to Intervention for Improving Skills in Mathematics

There also is a growing body of evidence on RTI in mathematics, including the reliability and validity of specific screening and progress monitoring measures as well as data regarding the average growth rates used to gauge the effectiveness of tiered interventions (Clarke, Gersten, & Newman-Gonchar, 2010; Foegen, Jiban, & Deno, 2007; Fuchs et al., 2005). An IES practice guide summarized empirical support showing that universal screening in math can aid in predicting children's future performance in this area and that progress monitoring can have a positive effect on teachers' instructional decision making (Gersten et al., 2009). The authors also found strong evidence for the effectiveness of targeted interventions in math for elementary students who were identified as at risk for learning difficulties in this area. The IES Practice Guide offered three recommendations regarding research-based practices to support RTI for improving skills in mathematics: 1) RTI should begin with high-quality instruction and universal screening for all students, with a focus on both prevention and early detection; 2) Tier 2 interventions for targeted children identified through screening should be systematic, explicit, and evidence-based; and 3) student responses to intervention should be measured to determine if adequate progress has been made and to make adjustments to instruction, if necessary.

The Efficacy of Positive Behavior Supports for Improving Social-Emotional Skills

Much of the early research on PBS involved descriptive or quasi-experimental studies involving very small samples of students with disabilities in special education settings (Sanetti & Simonsen, 2011). A few randomized controlled trials conducted in public schools with larger, more broadly representative samples showing positive effects for PBS in reducing recorded problem behaviors and increasing academic achievement have since been cited in the literature (Bradshaw, Reinke, Brown, Bevans, & Leaf, 2008, cited in Sanetti & Simonsen, 2011; Horner et al., 2009, cited in Sanetti & Simonsen, 2011), but additional studies are needed to establish the evidence base for this approach in both K–12 and early childhood education (Sanetti & Simonsen, 2011; see also Chapter 4). Unlike RTI, there is no research synthesis or IES practice guide on PBS available at this time. However, there is an IES practice guide that summarizes the research on the most common types of behavior problems encountered by teachers in public education (Epstein et al., 2008). The IES practice guide reported strong evidence showing that teachers should address these behavior problems by modifying the classroom environment to help students stay on task, teaching students the appropriate behaviors, and managing consequences to reinforce these "replacement" behaviors—all of which is consistent with several key practices within PBS.

THE STATE OF KNOWLEDGE ABOUT RESPONSE TO INTERVENTION IN EARLY CHILDHOOD

The early childhood field is only beginning to gather research evidence on RTI to guide its implementation and to evaluate its efficacy with children prior to kindergarten (Chapters 27 and 28). However, research-based knowledge on RTI in early childhood is expected to become more widely available in the next several years. In addition to the work being conducted by the Center for Response to Intervention in Early Childhood (CRTIEC), several research studies funded by IES (U.S. Department of Education) are underway to evaluate specific RTI applications in pre-K.

It is not surprising, then, that the literature on RTI prior to kindergarten is scant at best, and some of these publications reflect ideas that lack clarity or are inconsistent with broader RTI concepts. A search of the literature from 2006 to 2011 using search terms related to RTI and early childhood in Academic Search Premier, PsycArticles, and PsycINFO turned up only a handful of articles in peer-reviewed journals (e.g., Barnett, VanDerHeyden, & Witt, 2007; Bayat, Mindes, & Covitt, 2010; Buysse & Peisner-Feinberg, 2010; Fox, Carta, Strain, Dunlap, & Hemmeter, 2010;

Greenwood et al., 2011; Hemmeter, Ostrosky, & Fox, 2006; Jackson et al., 2009; Koutsoftas, Harmon, & Gray, 2009). Although this effort was not intended to be an exhaustive review of the literature on RTI in early childhood, the search results are one indication of the state of knowledge on this topic. All but one of the articles identified consisted of descriptions of particular models of RTI in early childhood or broader overviews or conceptualizations of how RTI is designed to work in pre-K; however, little congruity was evident among these various depictions of RTI. Perhaps as a sign of the interest on this topic and despite the limited research, the topic of RTI in early childhood is beginning to emerge in edited volumes and college textbooks and was featured prominently in many of the articles published in two special issues of the *NHSA Dialog*: one focused on language and literacy instruction, the other on behavioral supports (Frey, 2009; Smith, 2009).

Several models of RTI have become the most familiar and widely used RTI approaches in early childhood education (Greenwood et al., 2011). These are briefly described next; subsequent chapters in this book discuss them more fully. The Pyramid Model provides explicit guidance on classroom-wide practices that are foundational and prevention-oriented to address children's social-emotional development. It also includes targeted interventions that respond to more persistent needs of some children with respect to regulating behaviors, controlling impulses, focusing attention, and maintaining engagement in learning activities (Chapter 6). Another model called the Teaching Pyramid is part of a social-emotional curriculum called the *Incredible Years* (Chapter 17). Similar to the approach developed by Hemmeter and Fox (Chapter 6), the Incredible Years model includes foundational practices—such as building positive relationships, setting classroom rules, and teaching children emotional literacy skills—as well as more targeted interventions focused on decreasing inappropriate behaviors (e.g., using natural and logical consequences for behavior, creating individualized incentive systems). The Recognition & Response (R&R) model (Chapter 8) addresses academic learning (e.g., language, literacy, math) for young children with varying learning characteristics and includes all of the key RTI components (formative assessment, effective core instruction and research-based tiered interventions, and collaborative problem solving to support data-based decision making). The Center for Response to Intervention in Early Childhood (see Chapters 9 and 27) is developing evidence-based Tier 2 and Tier 3 interventions for language and literacy linked to specific universal screening and progress monitoring tools for use within an RTI framework in early childhood. Figures 1.4 and 1.5 depict these RTI models for use in early childhood.

Across all of these models, the primary emphasis is on helping early childhood educators organize the way in which they conduct assessments and deliver instruction and targeted interventions so as to respond effectively to children's learning and behavioral needs. In RTI, the formative assessment component differs from the way in which assessment typically is used in early childhood programs (Chapters 8, 9, 10, and 11). Unlike the way in which most standardized assessment tools currently are used in early childhood, assessment within an RTI context is designed to be conducted repeatedly throughout the school year and used to measure both *level* and *rate* of growth (i.e., how well a child performs at any given point and the amount of gain in learning over time). These assessments measure specific skills within key domains of behavior and learning that

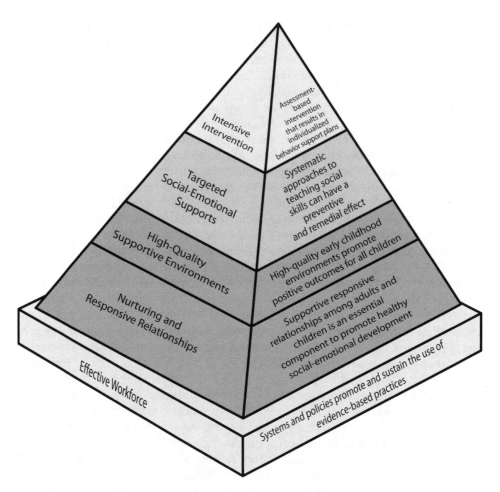

Figure 1.4. Conceptual framework for the Pyramid Model. (From Fox, L., Carta, J., Strain, P.S., Dunlap, G., & Hemmeter, M.L. [2010]. Response to intervention and the pyramid model. *Infants and Young Children*, 23, 3–13; reprinted by permission from http://csefel.vanderbilt.edu/)

predict later school adjustment and academic achievement when children enter kindergarten and the elementary grades.

Determining an appropriate assessment tool for use in universal screening and progress monitoring is a crucial decision in implementing an RTI approach to address academic learning in early childhood, and several tools are now available for this purpose. Unfortunately, as Gresham (2011) noted, there is no analogue for dependably measuring students' response to interventions in the area of social-emotional behavior in conjunction with PBS. Gresham's observation also applies to tiered models addressing social-emotional development in early childhood. However, several methods have been proposed to measure short-term changes in students' social-emotional behaviors in the context of PBS, and work is underway to adapt and validate some of these methods for use in early childhood.

The foundation of all tiered approaches involves providing a high-quality, effective core curriculum and intentional teaching of key school readiness skills, addressing both academics and social-emotional development (Chapters 13, 14, 15,

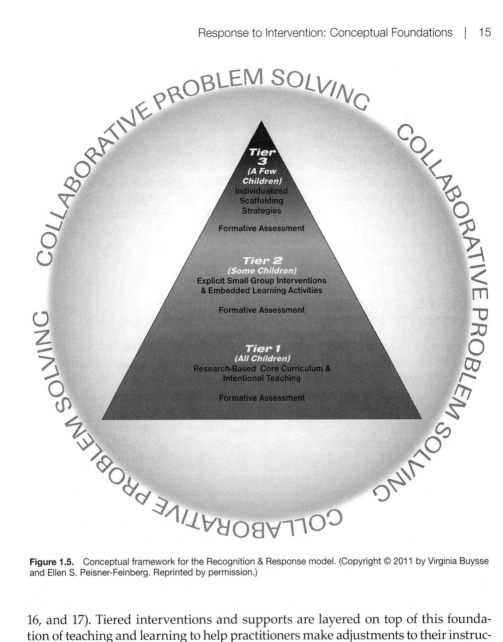

Figure 1.5.   Conceptual framework for the Recognition & Response model. (Copyright © 2011 by Virginia Buysse and Ellen S. Peisner-Feinberg. Reprinted by permission.)

16, and 17). Tiered interventions and supports are layered on top of this foundation of teaching and learning to help practitioners make adjustments to their instruction for *some* children who require additional supports to learn beyond the general curriculum and classroom activities provided for *all* children at Tier 1 (Chapter 18). In contrast to K–12 education, the early childhood field faces several significant challenges in implementing the instructional component of an RTI approach. As Greenwood and colleagues (2011) observed, there is far less consensus prior to kindergarten on what to teach and how to teach key skills than there is in K–12 education; this applies both to the foundational level of instruction (i.e., the core curriculum) and to the content and methods for the tiered interventions and supports. Whereas research-based core curricula and standardized, research-based interventions are widely available for use within an RTI context in K–12 education, these resources are limited or nonexistent in early childhood education, posing significant challenges for implementing RTI and establishing its efficacy prior to kindergarten. For example, the Preschool Curriculum Evaluation Research (PCER) initiative found that only 2 of 14 early childhood curricular interventions (one addressing language and literacy, the other mathematics) showed positive effects on child-level outcomes in the pre-K year (Preschool Curriculum Evaluation Research Consortium, 2008).

Efforts aimed at synthesizing research knowledge on academic learning in pre-K have been useful in identifying both foundational content and teaching and learning pathways to promote children's skill development in language, literacy, and mathematics (National Early Literacy Panel [NELP], 2008; Cross, Woods, & Schweingruber, 2009). These findings have reinforced the key principles of RTI— the use of a research-based core curriculum and the need to employ a variety of effective instructional methods at different levels of intensity, including small-group instruction and individualized scaffolding.

ISSUES RELATED TO IMPLEMENTING RESPONSE TO INTERVENTION IN EARLY CHILDHOOD

It is important to acknowledge that the use of RTI with children prior to kindergarten is an emerging practice. The results of one survey of state administrators from 46 states showed that only two states reported that RTI was being fully implemented in pre-K and only a few states reported having explicit statewide polices addressing the use of RTI in pre-K (Linas, Carta, & Greenwood, 2010, cited in Greenwood et al., 2011). Although RTI holds promise for supporting learning and development prior to kindergarten, additional research is needed to provide direct evidence of the efficacy of this approach with younger children and to guide its implementation in early child care and education programs. Because there are no specific provisions within federal legislation, nor policies or guidelines addressing the use of RTI prior to kindergarten, the field faces a number of significant implementation challenges. Next we highlight several issues that perhaps represent the most far-reaching challenges, but we also recognize that there are many others, including those that may be unique to particular states or regions.

Perhaps the most significant challenge that the early childhood field faces is the lack of consensus on the meaning of RTI. Greenwood et al. (2011) identified a number of myths in existence about RTI in early childhood, including that RTI is intended to replace special education and that it necessarily delays referral and eligibility for special education services. In the absence of both research knowledge and consensus wisdom on RTI in early childhood, publications on this topic sometimes contribute to the confusion by disseminating information that is inconsistent with an RTI approach. For example, the *Roadmap to Pre-K RTI* published in 2009 (Coleman, Roth, & West, 2009), though well-intentioned, described several models of RTI implementation that were poor exemplars of this approach (e.g., an example that confused outcome measures with formative assessment, an example that included only the foundational level of instruction but lacked tiered interventions).

As mentioned previously, the concept paper on RTI in early childhood published by NPCDI (2012) was intended to serve as an impetus to move the field forward in reaching agreement on the key concepts of RTI. However, as of 2012, there were no professional standards, guidelines, or consensus statements that define

RTI and broadly describe its use in pre-K. One indication that the early childhood field lacks consensus on components of RTI agreed upon in the broader literature is the confusion surrounding key concepts and terminology. Table 1.1 provides an explanation of concepts and terms related to RTI that are frequently misused within early childhood education. For example, *progress monitoring* and *universal screening*

Table 1.1. Key terms related to response to intervention (RTI) in early childhood

Terms	Explanation
Tiered and multitiered	These terms are used interchangeably within RTI and positive behavior interventions and supports (PBIS) to mean that an instructional or behavior support system is organized by levels of intensity.
Early intervening and early intervention	*Early intervening* within RTI means addressing student learning needs prior to referral for further diagnostic evaluation within special education; *early intervention* in early childhood refers to the Infant-Toddler Program for children birth to 3 with disabilities under Part C of the Individuals with Disabilities Education Improvement Act (IDEA) of 2004 (PL 108-446).
Instruction and intervention	*Instruction* refers to the general curriculum and intentional teaching that *all* children receive as the foundation of RTI; *interventions* refer to targeted instructional or behavioral supports that *some* children receive based on their learning needs as part of a tiered approach.
Learning difficulties and learning disabilities	*Learning difficulties* refer to students who have problems in acquiring key academic or behavioral skills (also referred to as being at risk for learning difficulties or disabilities), whereas *learning disabilities* refer to students who have an identified disability in academics or behavior requiring specialized services under IDEA.
Formative assessment	This term refers to assessment information that is gathered (typically by classroom teachers) on student behavior and skills to guide instructional decisions.
Universal screening and developmental screening	*Universal screening* is a type of formative assessment used within RTI that involves gathering information periodically on all students to determine whether some students need additional interventions. *Developmental screening* as part of a broader assessment system is used to determine whether a student needs further diagnostic assessment.
Progress monitoring	*Progress monitoring* is a type of formative assessment used within RTI to gather additional information on students who receive tiered interventions to determine their responsiveness to these interventions.
Curriculum-based measure and curriculum-based assessment	*Curriculum-based measures (CBMs)* are the basis of universal screening and progress monitoring within RTI. CBMs are brief measures of key skills that are linked to broad learning goals (but not to a particular curriculum), measure level and rate of growth, and predict later achievement. *Curriculum-based assessments* are linked to the learning goals of a specific curriculum.
General outcome measure	This term refers to CBMs in early childhood.
Small groups	*Small groups* within the context of RTI refers to explicit instruction provided to *some* students selected on the basis of their poor performance on specific skills. *Small groups* used more broadly in the context of early childhood represents planned classroom activities as part of foundational instruction that address broad curriculum goals appropriate for *all* students.
Problem-solving and support teams	*Problem-solving* and *support teams* within RTI or PBIS consist of teaching staff, specialists, parents, and administrators who support teachers in planning, implementing, and evaluating core instruction and targeted interventions at the classroom or program level.

are types of formative assessment that have very specific meanings in the context of RTI, but in early childhood education these terms are often used incorrectly (even by scholars and policy makers) to focus on different or more generic aspects of assessment (e.g., confusing universal screening with developmental screening, using progress monitoring to mean universal screening). Other terms such as curriculum-based measures and curriculum-based assessment with origins in K–12 education and special education have led to similar confusion in early childhood. Clearly, it is critical for the early childhood field to reach consensus on the defining features of RTI to create a common framework and shared meaning of key concepts that will serve as the basis for designing professional development and infrastructure supports for implementation.

Another challenge for the early childhood field is determining how RTI will work within existing contexts, including the fragmented nonsystem in which there are multiple programs and initiatives, funding streams, eligibility criteria, program standards, and quality and accountability frameworks (Chapter 25). This is the same challenge that any new educational innovation faces in the early childhood field. However, with respect to RTI, this problem is compounded by the pressing need for systemic supports for implementation (e.g., adoption at the programs versus classroom level, coordination between general and special education, integration with existing program practices, ongoing professional development and support for implementation, the allocation of time and resources for collaboration and problem solving) that will be more difficult to achieve in a field lacking systems-level cohesion. An important issue that the field must resolve in this regard is determining family involvement in the absence of procedural safeguards within RTI—methods of sharing information with families from diverse backgrounds and opportunities for families to participate in data-based decision making in collaboration with early childhood program staff (Chapter 20).

A third significant challenge to implementing RTI in early childhood programs concerns the lack of resources currently available to support this approach. In the context of school-age RTI, as mentioned previously, many more resources are available to support implementation, including technology-based assessment systems (e.g., AIMSweb, mCLASS assessment tools) and a range of validated formative assessment tools and intervention protocols for use within RTI (for information about these resources, see National Center on Response to Intervention, http://www.rti4success.org). Reaching consensus on the meaning of RTI in early childhood is an important initial step in articulating the field's collective wisdom on this topic, but to promote widespread adoption and implementation of RTI, the field needs additional resources to support its implementation on a broader scale. Despite emerging research knowledge on several widely familiar conceptual models of tiered instruction (e.g., the Pyramid Model, R&R), the early childhood field lacks experience with local implementation of RTI outside a research context. A future direction in this regard will be to translate existing conceptual models of RTI into practical implementation models that specify the particular instructional and assessment practices (including the specific tools and resources that can be used), and describe how these practices are implemented and evaluated, along with the necessary systems-level supports for ensuring that professionals are proficient in these practices (Chapter 26).

Some resources for implementing RTI in early childhood are available at this time. As previously mentioned, CRTIEC is developing formative assessment tools aligned with tiered interventions to address language and literacy skills for use within RTI (http://www.crtiec.org). Resources related to specific models of tiered instruction for early childhood (e.g., R&R, the Pyramid Model) are available on the developers' web sites (e.g., http://randr.fpg.unc.edu, http://csefel .vanderbilt.edu, http://www.challengingbehavior.org). Additional resources related to RTI more broadly are disseminated as part of national centers or initiatives (e.g., the National Center on Response to Intervention, the Center on Positive Behavioral Interventions and Supports, the RTI Action Network, the National Center for Learning Disabilities).

According to the NPDCI (2012) concept paper, RTI constitutes a set of related instructional practices, and as a result, a number of decisions must be made to support its implementation in early child care and education programs. Many of these decisions will need to be made at the program level, rather than by an individual classroom teacher, with input from key stakeholders such as administrators, practitioners, and families. NPDCI advises early childhood programs that elect to adopt RTI to establish an implementation team that will engage in a strategic planning process. Some of the important decisions that these teams will need to make are related to determining the context and scope of implementation (e.g., deciding whether to focus on academic learning, social-emotional development, or both; determining the age group of children with whom RTI will be used; choosing whether to implement RTI in a few sites versus more broadly across an entire system). Other decisions include identifying a valid formative assessment approach, determining benchmarks and cut points for decision making, selecting research-based curricula and interventions linked to curriculum goals and program standards, and specifying approaches for professionals and families to engage in collaboration and problem solving. In addition to these decisions, systemic supports are needed to ensure that RTI will be implemented appropriately and is beneficial for young children and families, according to the NPDCI concept paper. These infrastructure supports include providing ongoing professional development and support for implementing RTI, determining methods for sharing information about children's developmental progress with families and professionals, allocating resources related to using RTI, and making provisions for evaluating the implementation and effectiveness of RTI (Chapters 19, 20, and 21).

OVERVIEW OF THIS BOOK

Handbook of Response to Intervention in Early Childhood represents an ambitious undertaking: namely, to gather within a single volume all of the knowledge that exists on a topic that has attracted much attention in recent years. Although each chapter contributes important information on a particular aspect or component of RTI within early childhood, it is abundantly clear that collectively, the chapter contributors (and members of the field at large) are still working toward reaching consensus on a shared understanding of how RTI will function as an integrated system.

In Section I (which consists of this chapter), we presented the purpose for a comprehensive volume on RTI, the history and origins of RTI, and key contextual issues related to this approach in early childhood education. In Section II, scholars investigate more deeply the foundations of RTI by exploring its origins in public health models of prevention as well as school-age and pre-K models of RTI and PBS addressing academic learning and behavioral supports.

Section III focuses on the assessment component of RTI, with a particular emphasis on available formative assessment tools. The lead chapter offers guidance in creating an integrated assessment system in which formative assessment within RTI would comprise one component of an overall plan. Remaining chapters address content on formative assessment tools for use in early childhood RTI, such as the individual growth and development indicators (IGDIs) and the CIRCLE-Phonological Awareness Language and Literacy System (C-PALLS), as well as tools that can be used to assess behavioral skills and social-emotional development within an RTI or PBS framework. The authors of these chapters reflect the field's leading scholars in the area of formative assessment in the context of tiered approaches in early childhood.

Section IV addresses the instructional component of an RTI system. Written by scholars with expertise in curriculum and instruction, the chapters reinforce the importance of using an effective, comprehensive, core curriculum as the foundation of an RTI approach. Furthermore, the content covers key domains of school readiness in early childhood that can be addressed within RTI: language and literacy, mathematics, and social-emotional development. In addition, this section addresses the ways in which early educators can organize targeted interventions within tiers of an RTI system, drawing on research-based practices such as embedded interventions and individualized scaffolding strategies.

Sections V and VI focus on current and future systems-level supports related to implementing RTI in early childhood programs, with contributions by recognized scholars and practitioners in public policy and program administration, research, implementation science, and professional development. These chapters address the role of public policy and the need for adaptations of RTI for diverse learners, including young children with disabilities and those from diverse cultural and linguistic groups. Also included is information addressing consensus-building efforts, recommended practices from implementation science, next-generation innovations, and ways to build the evidence base for RTI through a systematic program of research.

RTI may offer one of the best opportunities in recent history for the early childhood field to ensure that every child served in an early care and education program, regardless of his or her learning needs, receives customized instruction supported by research-based knowledge and data-based decision making. This book is envisioned as an authoritative, reliable source of information for anyone interested in adopting RTI in early childhood education, yet it represents only an initial step at an early stage in building the evidence base for this educational innovation. Additional research, policies, and resources are needed to guide these practices in the future.

REFERENCES

American Federation of Teachers. (2011). *Right from the start: Transition strategies for developing a strong preK-3 continuum.* Washington, DC: Author. Retrieved from http://www.aft.org/pdfs/ece/rightfromthestart2012.pdf

Barnett, D.W., VanDerHeyden, A.M., & Witt, J.C. (2007). Achieving science-based practice through response to intervention: What it might look like in preschools. *Journal of Educational and Psychological Consultation, 17*(1), 31–54.

Bayat, M., Mindes, G., & Covitt, S. (2010). What does RTI (response to intervention) look like in preschool? *Early Childhood Education Journal, 37*, 493–500. doi: 10.1007/s10643-010-0372-6

Bradley, M.C., Daley, T., Levin, M., O'Reilly, R., Parsad, A., Robertson, A., & Werner, A. (2011). *IDEA National Assessment Implementation Study* (NCEE 2011-4027). Washington, DC: National Center for Education Evaluation and Regional Assistance, Institute of Education Sciences, U.S. Department of Education.

Burns, M.K., Appleton, J.J., & Stehouwer, J.D. (2005). Meta-analytic review of responsiveness-to-intervention research: Examining field-based and research-implemented models. *Journal of Psychoeducational Assessment, 23*, 381–394.

Burns, M.K., & Gibbons, K.A. (2008). *Implementing response-to-intervention in primary and secondary schools: Procedures to assure scientific-based practices.* New York, NY: Routledge.

Buysse, V., & Peisner-Feinberg, E. (2009). *Recognition & response: Findings from the first implementation study.* Retrieved from http://randr.fpg.unc.edu/sites/randr.fpg.unc.edu/files/KeyFindingsHandout.pdf

Buysse, V., & Peisner-Feinberg, E. (2010). Recognition & response: Response to intervention for pre-K. *Young Exceptional Children, 13*(4), 2–13.

Buysse, V., & Wesley, P.W. (2010). Program quality through the lens of disruptive innovation theory. In P.W. Wesley & V. Buysse (Eds.), *The quest for quality: Promising innovations for early childhood programs* (pp. 183–198). Baltimore, MD: Paul H. Brookes Publishing Co.

Christensen, C.M., Horn, B.B., & Johnson, C.W. (2008). *Disrupting class: How disruptive innovation will change the way the world learns.* New York, NY: McGraw-Hill.

Clarke, B., Gersten, R., & Newman-Gonchar, R. (2010). RTI in mathematics: Beginnings of a knowledge base. In T. Glover & S. Vaughn (Eds.), *The promise of response to intervention: Evaluating current science and practice* (pp. 187–203). New York, NY: Guilford Press.

Coleman, M.R., Roth, F., & West, T. (2009). *Roadmap to pre-K RTI: Applying response to intervention in preschool settings.* New York, NY: National Center for Learning Disabilities. Retrieved from http://www.RTINetwork.org

Council for Exceptional Children. (2008). *CEC's position on Response to Intervention (RTI): The unique role of special education and special educators.* Retrieved from http://www.cec.sped.org

Cross, C.T., Woods, T.A., & Schweingruber, H. (2009). *Mathematics learning in early childhood: Paths toward excellence and equity.* National Research Council; Committee on Early Childhood Mathematics, Center for Education, Division of Behavioral and Social Sciences and Education (Eds.). Washington, DC: The National Academies Press.

Eisenman, L.T., & Ferretti, R.P. (2010). Changing conceptions of special education [Special issue]. *Exceptional Children, 76*(3).

Epstein, M., Atkins, M., Cullinan, D., Kutash, K., & Weaver, R. (2008). *Reducing behavior problems in the elementary school classroom: A practice guide* (NCEE #2008-012). Washington, DC: National Center for Education Evaluation and Regional Assistance, Institute of Education Sciences, U.S. Department of Education. Retrieved from http://ies.ed.gov/ncee/wwc/publications/practiceguides

Foegen, A., Jiban, C., & Deno, S. (2007). Progress monitoring measures in mathematics: A review of the literature. *Journal of Special Education, 41*, 121–139.

Fox, L., Carta, J., Strain, P.S., Dunlap, G., & Hemmeter, M.L. (2010). Response to intervention and the pyramid model. *Infants and Young Children, 23*, 3–13.

Frey, A. (2009). Introduction: Positive behavior supports and interventions in early childhood education [Special section]. *NHSA Dialog, 12*(2), 71–74.

Fuchs, D., Fuchs, L.S., & Compton, D.L. (2007). Identifying reading disabilities by responsiveness-to-instruction: Specifying measures and criteria. *Learning Disabilities Quarterly, 27*, 216–227.

Fuchs, D., Fuchs, L., & Compton, D. (2012). SMART RTI: A next-generation approach to multilevel prevention. *Exceptional Children, 78*(3), 263–279.

Fuchs, D., Fuchs, L.S., & Stecker, P.M. (2010). The "blurring" of special education in a new continuum of general education placements and services. *Exceptional Children, 76*(3), 301–323.

Fuchs, L.S., Compton, D.L., Fuchs, D., Paulsen, K., Bryant, J.D., & Hamlett, C.L. (2005). The prevention, identification, and cognitive determinants of math difficulty. *Journal of Educational Psychology, 97*, 493–513.

Gersten, R., Beckmann, S., Clarke, B., Foegen, A., Marsh, L., Star, J.R., & Witzel, B. (2009). *Assisting students struggling with mathematics: Response to intervention (RTI) for elementary and middle schools* (NCEE 2009-4060). Washington, DC: National Center for Education Evaluation and Regional Assistance, Institute of Education Sciences, U.S. Department of Education. Retrieved from http://ies.ed.gov/ncee/wwc/publications/practiceguides/

Gersten, R., Compton, D.L., Connor, C.M., Dimino, J., Santoro, L., Linan-Thompson, S., & Tilly, W.D. (2008). *Assisting students struggling with reading: Response to intervention and multi-tier intervention for reading in the primary grades. A practice guide* (NCEE 2009-4045). Washington, DC: National Center for Education Evaluation and Regional Assistance, Institute of Education Sciences, U.S. Department of Education. Retrieved from http://ies.ed.gov/ncee/wwc/publications/practiceguides/

Glover, T.A., & Vaughn, S. (2010). *The promise of response to intervention: Evaluating current science and practice*: New York, NY: Guilford.

Greenwood, C.R., Bradfield, R., Kaminski, R., Linas, M., Carta, J.J., & Nylander, D. (2011). The response to intervention (RTI) approach in early childhood. *Focus on Exceptional Children, 43*(9), 1–22.

Gresham, F.M. (2007). Evolution of the response-to-intervention concept: Empirical foundations and recent developments. In S.R. Jimerson, M.K. Burns, & A.M. VanDerHeyden (Eds.), *Handbook of response to intervention: The science and practice of assessment and intervention* (pp. 10–24). New York, NY: Springer.

Gresham, F.M. (2011). Response to intervention: Conceptual foundations and evidence-based practices. In M.A. Bray & T.J. Kehle (Eds.), *The Oxford handbook of school psychology* (pp. 607–618). New York, NY: Oxford University.

Haager, D., Klinger, J., & Vaughn, S. (Eds.). (2007). *Evidence-based reading practices for response to intervention*. Baltimore, MD: Paul H. Brookes Publishing Co.

Hemmeter, M.L., Ostrosky, M., & Fox, L. (2006). Social and emotional foundations for early learning: A conceptual model for intervention. *School Psychology Review, 35*, 583–601.

Individuals with Disabilities Education Improvement Act (IDEA) of 2004, PL 108-446, 20 U.S.C. §§ 1400 *et seq.*

Jackson, S., Pretti-Frontczak, K., Harjusola-Webb, S., Grisham-Brown, J., & Romani, J.M. (2009). Response to intervention: Implications for early childhood professionals. *Language, Speech, and Hearing Services in Schools, 40*, 424–434.

Jimerson, S.R., Burns, M.K., & VanDerHeyden, A.M. (Eds.). (2007). *Handbook of response to intervention: The science and practice of assessment and intervention*. New York, NY: Springer.

Koutsoftas, A.D., Harmon, M.T., & Gray, S. (2009). The effect of tier 2 intervention for phonemic awareness in a response-to-intervention model in low-income preschool classrooms. *Language, Speech, and Hearing Services in Schools, 40*, 116–130.

Malecki, C.K., & Demaray, M.K. (2007). Social behavior assessment and response to intervention. In S.R. Jimerson, M.K. Burns, & A.M. VanDerHeyden (Eds.), *Handbook of response to intervention: The science and practice of assessment and intervention* (pp. 161–171). New York, NY: Springer.

Marston, D., Muyskens, P., Lau, M., & Canter, A. (2003). Problem-solving model for decision making with high-incidence disabilities: The Minneapolis experience. *Learning Disabilities Research & Practice, 18*, 187–200.

National Center on Response to Intervention. (2010, March). *Essential components of RTI: A closer look at response to intervention*. Washington, DC: U.S. Department of Education, Office of Special Education Programs. Retrieved from http://www.cldinternational.org/Articles/rtiessentialcomponents.pdf

National Early Literacy Panel. (2008). *Developing early literacy: Report of the National Early Literacy Panel*. Washington, DC: National Institute for Literacy.

National Professional Development Center on Inclusion. (2012). *Response to intervention (RTI) in early childhood: Building consensus on the defining features*. Chapel Hill: University of North Carolina, Frank Porter Graham Child Development Institute. Retrieved from http://npdci.fpg.unc.edu

National Professional Development Center on Inclusion. (2012). *Summary from listening sessions*. Chapel Hill: University of North Carolina, Frank Porter Graham Child Development Institute. Retrieved from http://npdci.fpg.unc.edu

Pina, A.A., & Eisenberg, N. (2009). Prevention and remediation of emotional and academic problems in youth [Special issue]. *Child Development Perspectives, 3*(1).

Preschool Curriculum Evaluation Research Consortium. (2008). *Effects of preschool curriculum programs on school readiness* (NCER 2008-2009). Washington, DC: National Center for Education Research, Institute of Education Sciences, U.S. Department of Education. Retrieved from http://ies.ed.gov/pubsearch/pubsinfo.asp?pubid=NCER20082009rev

Sanetti, L.M.H., & Simonsen, B. (2011). Positive behavioral supports. In M.A. Bray & J.J. Kehle (Eds.), *The Oxford handbook of school psychology* (pp. 647–665). New York, NY: Oxford University.

Sawchuk, S. (2012). Gates study offers teacher-effectiveness cues. *Education Week*. Retrieved from http://www.edweek.org/ew/articles/2010/12/10/15teach.h30.html

Smith, S. (2009). Introduction: Supporting struggling learners in preschool: Emerging approaches and opportunities. *NHSA Dialog, 12*(3), 185 –191.

Speece, D.L., Case, L.P., & Molloy, D.E. (2003). Responsiveness to general education instruction as the first gate to learning disabilities identification. *Learning Disabilities Research & Practice, 18*, 147–156.

Sprague, J., Cook, C.R., Browning-Wright, D., & Sadler, C. (2008). *Response to intervention for behavior: Integrating academic and behavior supports*. Palm Beach, FL: LRP Publications.

Sugai, G. (2009, May). *School-wide positive behavior support and response to intervention*. Storrs: University of Connecticut, OSEP Center on Positive Behavioral Interventions and Supports. Retrieved from http://pbis.org/common/pbisresources/presentations/Sugai_2009 rSWPBS_RtI%20final_May25_2009.pdf

Sugai, G. (2011, June). School climate and discipline: School-wide behavior support. Keynote presentation to and paper for the National Summit on Chered Implementation of IDEA. Washington, D.C.

Vaughn, S., & Fuchs, L.S. (2003). Redefining learning disabilities as inadequate response to instruction: The promise and potential problems. *Learning Disabilities Research & Practice, 18*, 137–146.

Vaughn, S., Linan-Thompson, S., & Hickman, P. (2003). Response to instruction as a means for identifying students with reading/learning disabilities. *Exceptional Children, 69*, 391–409.

Zellman, G.L., & Karoly, L.A. (2012). *Moving to outcomes: Approaches to incorporating child assessments into state early childhood quality rating and improvement systems*. Santa Monica, CA: RAND. Retrieved from http://www.rand.org/content/dam/rand/pubs/occasional _papers/2012/RAND_OP364.pdf

II

Foundations of
Response to Intervention
in Early Childhood

Prevention

A Public Health Framework

Rune J. Simeonsson and Yi Pan

Findings from the research literature and reports in the popular media agree on the increasing prevalence of physical and mental illness in the population. The field of medicine is responding by developing new medications, diagnostic procedures, and treatment regimens. The continued expansion of medical, pharmacological, and treatment innovations has contributed to significant reductions in mortality and morbidity and thereby reduced the prevalence and consequences of diseases and disorders. However, a fundamental challenge remains for public health to reduce the rate of new cases identified in the population. A rationale for focusing on reducing the incidence of new cases of disease and disorder can be made not only for the economic goal of reducing health care costs, but more important for the humanitarian goal of promoting the health and quality of life of individuals.

Reducing the incidence and prevalence of disease and disorder has been recognized as a national health priority in the policy document *Healthy People 2020* (U.S. Department of Health and Human Services [DHHS], 2010) and in its earlier version, *Healthy People 2010* (U.S. DHHS, 2000). These documents defined a comprehensive framework and specific national objectives to prevent diseases and promote health at the population level. For the 2000–2010 decade, population priorities included the prevention of heart disease, obesity, diabetes, and mental disorders (Wherrett & Daneman, 2011). Priorities specific to children included reducing premature death, developmental risks and disabilities, prenatal substance exposure, physical inactivity, insufficient nutrition for low-income children, mental illness, violence, and maltreatment against children (Daniels et al., 2005; Hahn et al., 2007; Miller, Kraus, & Veltkamp, 2005). For the 2010–2020 decade, the vision for national health has expanded significantly to include social determinants of health, including priorities related to physical and social environments in settings such as schools and communities (Koh et al., 2011). Endorsement of these national priorities indicates that promoting the health of a population requires a public health approach of primary prevention.

The need for primary prevention is based on the premise that the prevention of disease and disorder is not only more cost effective and efficient than treatment and intervention of health conditions, but that it increases the number of healthy life-years for an individual (Currie, 2010). Central to this premise is the underlying assumption that risk factors can be identified prior to the manifestation of a health condition and prevention measures should be implemented as early as possible. Although the timing of primary prevention will vary as a function of the specific disease, disorder, or health condition with onset in childhood, the challenge is to provide primary prevention early in development. Validation of the economic and individual health benefits of primary prevention for children's health is best illustrated by immunization programs for an infectious disease such as measles, in which the provision of vaccine in the first year of life protects the child from contracting the disease and promotes the child's health-related quality of life (Ehreth, 2003). The benefit to the individual child in terms of avoidance of suffering and enhanced well-being is paralleled by the economic benefits when the costs of diagnostic and comprehensive treatment programs are avoided. Beyond the example of measles immunization, the efficacy of primary prevention has been extended to a wide array of childhood diseases and disorders, with benefits to the child and health care services (Bass et al., 1993; Dehghan, Akhtar-Danesh, & Merchant, 2005; Wilson & Lipsey, 2007). The continuing implementation of primary prevention to reduce the incidence of health conditions in childhood, including developmental problems, is predicated on societal priorities and can be approached productively within the prevention framework to the extent that such conditions are identified. To that end, the purposes of this chapter are to 1) describe elements of an epidemiological framework of prevention, 2) apply a hierarchical-level prevention approach to developmental problems in childhood, and 3) identify implications of a prevention framework for the response to intervention initiative in special education.

PREVENTION: AN EPIDEMIOLOGICAL FRAMEWORK

The broad goals of public health are to promote the health of the population; reduce the need for diagnostic, curative, and therapeutic services; and reduce the need for corrective, remedial, and rehabilitative programs. These goals are in contrast with those of medical care, which focus on treating illness and disease of individual patients. Public health initiatives are thus focused on promoting the health and reducing the incidence of preventable health conditions in the population (Abraído-Lanza, Armbrister, Flórez, & Aguirre, 2006; Simeonsson, 1994). These initiatives are complementary in that any measure that promotes healthy functioning and development has the reciprocal benefit of preventing illness and problems of development. The basic premise of public health is that health of individuals can be promoted and illnesses can be prevented at the population level. An underlying assumption is that everyone in the population is at some risk for illness and health problems, but some individuals in the population are at differential risk for illness and disease due to genetic, environmental, or gene–environment interaction factors. Differential risk may also be associated with personal factors of age and gender in that the risks for specific problems are greater at different points in the life span, such as dementia with aging and unintentional injury during the early years of development. Although the dependent status of all children increases their vulnerability to some conditions, the risk for developmental problems is increased for some infants and children by factors intrinsic to the child as well as factors in the proximal and distal environment.

In order to implement effective health promotion and disease prevention programs, it is essential to identify the distribution of corresponding risk factors in the population. Central to the epidemiological approach are the goals of documenting the distribution of a defined health condition and identifying associated risk factors. These two documentation activities provide essential evidence for implementing a program of prevention. Documentation of the scope and magnitude of a health condition in the population is important in determining the need for, and potential efficacy of, preventing that particular health condition. Identification of subgroups of children at increased risk for health or developmental complications is necessary in order to initiate targeted prevention programs to remove risk factors and/or provide support and stimulation. A health condition or developmental problem that is rare and affects only a very small part of the population may present particular challenges for identification and the provision of primary prevention from a cost–benefit perspective (Vogt, Lafata, Tolsma, & Greene, 2004). On the other hand, more prevalent illnesses or health conditions, representing a significant burden of disease in the population, are a typical focus for primary prevention (Rockhill & Weed, 2006). An epidemiological approach is also necessary to identify risk factors that are precursors of an illness or health condition, yielding information about their nature and timing in the history of the condition (Abraído-Lanza et al., 2006). All this information is essential for planning when, in what form, and for whom a prevention program should be initiated.

Primary, Secondary, and Tertiary Prevention

The epidemiological approach provides evidence of preventable health conditions, who in the population is at elevated risk for these conditions, what prevention activities are indicated, and when they should be provided (Cummings, Koepsell, & Mueller, 1995). This evidence has formed the conceptual basis for prevention models corresponding to the sequence of procedures to reduce the incidence, prevalence, or complications of a health condition. The concept of preventing diseases was initially formalized in a proposal for primary and secondary prevention in the 1950s under the Commission on Chronic Illness (Gordon, 1983). A more complete classification model, adding the dimension of tertiary prevention, was proposed about a decade later by Caplan and Grunebaum (1967) and has been implemented widely since that time in public health to address a range of preventable conditions. Within this model, the aim of primary prevention is to reduce the incidence of a health condition (Benichou & Palta, 2004). Primary prevention activities eliminate or minimize risk factors for disease or illness and promote positive health behaviors. Perhaps the best example of primary prevention is immunization against infectious diseases and engagement in a healthy lifestyle (Dehghan et al., 2005; Ehreth, 2003).

Secondary prevention, on the other hand, focuses on reducing the prevalence of certain health conditions in the population (Silverman, 2003). Thus, the aim of secondary prevention is to reduce the number of individuals in the population who already have an identified disease or health condition. Prevention in this case takes the form of intervention and symptomatic treatment, and restoring the individual to a healthy state, if possible. For a specified childhood disease, secondary prevention can be a medical treatment to cure the disease and restore the child to health (Braswell et al., 1997; Daniels et al., 2005). Tertiary prevention activities are based on preventing complications of a chronic health condition. These activities strive to rehabilitate individuals with a diagnosed health condition and prevent or reduce complications of that condition (Wherrett & Daneman, 2011).

The primary, secondary, and tertiary prevention (PST) classification model described by Caplan and Grunebaum (1967) was defined in terms of preventing the manifestation of disease at its respective developmental stages. However, the model actually encompasses intervention in the form of treatment and rehabilitation of diagnosed conditions at the secondary and tertiary levels. Gordon (1983) proposed that the concept of prevention be restricted to "measures, actions or interventions that are practiced by or on persons who are not, at the time, suffering from any discomfort or disability due to the disease or condition being prevented" (p. 108). Building on this premise, he proposed defining primary prevention by a classification model of levels based on the segment of the population for whom preventive measures are provided. This classification model frames the concept of primary prevention into three levels that do not encompass the dimensions of treatment and rehabilitation defined in secondary and tertiary prevention, respectively.

Universal, Selected, and Indicated Prevention

Working within the framework of defining levels of primary prevention by the population to which measures are applied, Gordon (1983) proposed a classification of universal, selected, and indicated prevention (USI). In this expanded classification model of primary prevention, each level is defined by measures and activities directed toward population groups at different levels of risk for a health condition. The scope of prevention efforts is defined by a formulation of benefits relative to costs for addressing risk for disease in the population. The scope of prevention activities can thus range from universal efforts focused on everyone in the population to measures and activities directed to restricted subgroups in the population at increased levels of risk relative to secondary and tertiary prevention, as shown in Figure 2.1. The nature and scope of prevention at each level is defined by the calculus of level of risk and the benefit and cost of implementing prevention measures. Prevention at the universal level is based on the assumption that everyone in the population is at the same, average level of risk for a health condition and that

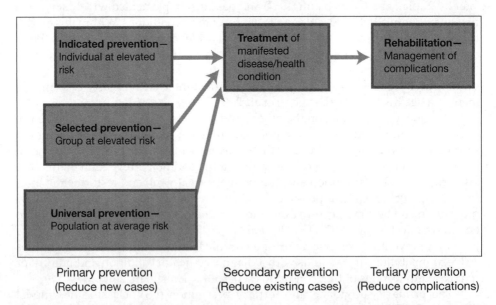

| Primary prevention | Secondary prevention | Tertiary prevention |
| (Reduce new cases) | (Reduce existing cases) | (Reduce complications) |

Figure 2.1. A comprehensive framework of universal, selected, indicated, secondary, and tertiary prevention. (*Source:* Simeonsson, 1994).

prevention efforts thus need to be directed toward everyone. Such efforts include programs to eliminate or reduce the risk for injury, as in requirements for seat-belt use when driving a car and vaccination of all children for preventable diseases of childhood (Huse, Meissner, Lacey, & Oster, 1994). They also include programs to promote nutrition, fitness, and dental health—for example, through fluoridation of the water supply (King & Rozier, 2008; Peters, Petrunka, & Arnold, 2003).

Selected primary prevention programs are directed at groups in the population at increased risk for a health condition on the basis of characteristics defining membership in a group rather than characteristics of an individual. In this case, prevention efforts can target groups who are at increased risk based on demographic characteristics such as age, gender, racial or ethnic identity, socioeconomic status, and occupation. Prevention measures are thus implemented for selected subgroups in the population, identified on the basis of shared membership in a group. For example, whereas vaccination of all children reflects universal prevention, vaccination programs that target only the elderly or others at increased risk for contracting an infectious illness are selected prevention programs (Rickert, Santoli, Shefer, Myrick, & Yusuf, 2006). The addition of folic acid to the diet of women of childbearing age is an example of selected prevention (van Beynum et al., 2010). Selected prevention identifies a population subgroup that is at increased risk, then calculates the ratio of cost to benefits of prevention efforts among members of the subgroup rather than the population at large.

In contrast to selected prevention efforts, indicated prevention is directed toward people who are manifesting individual risk factors for a health condition. Identifying individuals for indicated prevention requires evidence of risk factors, which may be documented through screening programs of the population. Identification of risk status for indicated prevention can also be based on routine screening and examinations in the school, workplace, or health care setting. Indicated prevention takes the form of measures and activities to reduce the role or impact of the risk factor in the manifestation of disease. Examples of indicated prevention are pharmacological management of hypertension and dietary control of elevated blood sugar and cholesterol levels (Greenwood-Robinson, 2002; Kinosian & Eisenberg, 1988). Because indicated prevention is based on identifying risk factors in the individual and providing measures at the level of the individual, the benefits come at a higher cost than in universal and selected prevention programs (McLaughlin, 2011). In that the increased risk status of these individuals is identified on the basis of actually manifesting risk factors of the disease, Gordon (1983) has suggested that indicated prevention corresponds to what was labeled "secondary prevention" in the earlier three-level model. However, he maintains that indicated prevention should be differentiated from the concept of treatment in that prevention is designed to control or reduce risk factors, whereas the concept of treatment in secondary conditions implies a therapeutic goal of managing illness or a health condition.

DEVELOPMENTAL PROBLEMS IN CHILDHOOD: A PREVENTION FRAMEWORK

Primary prevention has been an established public health approach to address physical as well as mental health conditions since its introduction in the middle of the 20th century (Offord, 1982). Over time, the approach has been implemented by other disciplines and extended to address chronic conditions associated with disability and to prevent secondary conditions and comorbidity (Simeonsson & McDevitt, 1999). The alarming increase of chronic childhood conditions such as obesity (Trost et al., 2003), developmental delay, autism, and attention-deficit/hyperactivity disorder (ADHD) (Boyle et al., 2011), and learning disabilities (Margai & Henry, 2003) makes it clear that the scope of these conditions cannot be addressed through secondary prevention alone. There is thus a growing need to implement a comprehensive prevention agenda to reduce the nature and severity of these conditions and to promote children's well-being. To this end, the implementation of a prevention approach can frame initiatives to prevent disorder and disability and promote the development and well-being of all children. In a broader sense, mandatory public education of all children can be seen as the prototypic universal prevention program for preventing illiteracy and promoting the full development of the child.

A prevention framework has been implicit in early intervention for young children at risk or with developmental delays to prevent or reduce disability later in development. The prevention framework has also been advanced as the rationale for a range of academic and psychological problems of children and youth, such as reading difficulties (Coyne, Kame'enui, Simmons, & Harn, 2004), character development (Miller et al., 2005), and bullying (Srabstein et al., 2008). Implementing a multilevel prevention framework requires that several sequential assumptions be considered. The first is that the manifestation of the targeted developmental problem or condition can be prevented. Second, if manifestation of the problem cannot be fully prevented, treatment or intervention needs to be provided with the goal of improving functioning to as typical or "normal" a state as possible. Third, for conditions or developmental problems in which functional improvement is limited, the focus is on supporting the child's capable level of functioning and preventing complications. Central to these assumptions is that in order to implement primary, secondary, or tertiary prevention, it is necessary to 1) operationally define the health condition or developmental problem of concern, and 2) identify risk factors associated with each level of prevention.

In order to implement a prevention framework, the child's developmental problem or health condition needs to be operationally defined—that is, practitioners specify the manifestation of the condition to be prevented. In many, if not most, cases with a significant biological etiology, this takes the form of a clinical diagnosis. Within the schematic of levels of prevention illustrated in Figure 2.1, the developmental problem or health condition is represented at the level of secondary prevention defining the focus for treatment. With reference to developmental problems defined by a medical or psychiatric condition, this would take the form of a diagnosis from the *International Classification of Diseases, Tenth Revision* (World Health Organization [WHO], 1992), such as mental retardation (F70-79), or *Diagnostic and Statistical Manual of Mental Disorders, Fourth Edition, Text Revision* (DSM-IV-TR; American Psychiatric Association, 2000), such as Autistic Disorder (299.00), respectively. In the context of special education in the United States, the developmental problem would take the form of 1 of 13 official categories listed in Individuals with Disabilities Education Improvement Act of 2004 (PL 108-446) such as visual, auditory, or motor impairment. Extending the focus to tertiary prevention, operationalizing the nature of complications of the developmental problem to be prevented could involve problems such as stereotypes or dependency.

Having operationalized the condition to be prevented and its complications, implementation of primary prevention initiatives requires the identification of risk factors associated with the disease or health condition. Diagnoses or categories, however, would not be the basis for defining target populations for universal, selected, and indicated prevention in that that the term *prevention* should be limited to initiatives "adopted by or practiced on persons not currently feeling the effects of a disease, intended to decrease the risk that that disease will afflict them in the future" (Gordon, 1983, p. 109).

To this end, identification of risk factors can be viewed within a perspective that a health condition or developmental problem has a natural history—factors can be identified prior to manifestation of the condition that are likely predictors of the condition. Because the nature and role of these risk factors are identifiable at different points in the history of a health condition, they define a causal chain for the history of that condition (Sackett, Haynes, Guyatt, & Tugwell, 1991). Identifying the causal chain of a health condition or developmental problem defines the sequence and timing in which risk factors are evident and indicates the critical points at which an associated prevention initiative can be more effective than if it were introduced at another point.

The derivation of a causal chain for a health condition is predicated on defining it in operational terms and examining its history to identify probable risk factors and the timing of their appearance. The generation of causal chains can be built both on a logical analysis of factors most likely predictive of a target condition and identification of risk factors from relevant research. Although the nature and time of emergence of risk factors in the natural history of a health condition varies from one condition to another, the points in time at which they are identifiable and their significance for initiation of prevention measures can be seen to follow the sequence shown in Figure 2.2. Within this sequence, it is assumed that there is some point at which there is a presumed onset of factors of significance in the history of the disease. However, the risk factors may not be evident or identifiable at that point.

The critical point here is for universal prevention in that specific risk factors are not known and everyone in the population is assumed to be at average risk.

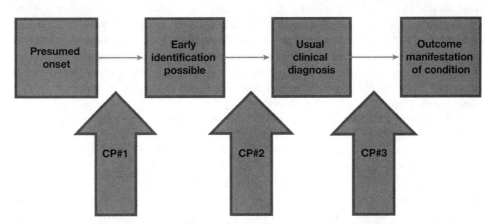

Figure 2.2. Identifying the critical points (CP) for prevention/intervention in the causal chain of a targeted condition. (*Key:* CP#1, universal prevention; CP#2, selected prevention; CP#3, indicated prevention.) (From Simeonsson, R.J. [1994]. Toward an epidemiology of developmental, educational, and social problems of childhood. In *Risk, resilience, and prevention: Promoting the well-being of all children* [p. 21]. Baltimore, MD: Paul H. Brookes Publishing Co.; adapted by permission.)

On this basis, universal prevention requires no identification because it is directed to all children within a defined population. For selected and indicated prevention, efforts would be directed toward identifying children based on group or individual risk characteristics rather than on a diagnosed condition. Such identification of risk always depends on the diagnosed developmental problem or condition of interest to be prevented and can range from biomarkers such as genetic traits (Caspi et al., 2002) or perinatal factors (van Bakel & Riksen-Walraven, 2002) to environmental or developmental indicators of poverty (Garmezy, 1991) or delayed acquisition of milestones (Luthar, 1991). At a later point, identification of one or more risk factors is possible, constituting a critical point for prevention. This critical point represents primary prevention in which the focus is preventing the manifestation of the disease and thereby reducing the incidence of the condition in the population. Further along the causal chain, the emergence of signs and symptoms of the disease allows clinical diagnosis of the health condition. This is the critical point for secondary prevention, in which the focus is to provide treatment to restore the person to a healthy state, thereby reducing the prevalence of the health condition in the population.

For situations that do not result in restoration of a developmental or chronic condition to a typical or normal state, the subsequent link in the natural history of the condition is the manifestation of complications. This is a critical point for tertiary prevention, in which clinical management and rehabilitation are designed to prevent or reduce complications and avoid further deterioration of the child's developmental status.

Causal chains provide a logical framework for identifying the nature and possible role of risk factors in determining developmental outcomes. Implementation of primary prevention requires not only conceptualizing a causal chain and identifying possible risk factors but also estimating the relative risk these factors pose for the manifestation of a developmental or chronic condition. In this case, relative risk can be defined as the differential vulnerability of a child for a developmental or health condition.

The strength of risk factors in defining the differential vulnerability of an individual for a condition is usually documented with two statistical tools: the odds ratio (OR) and relative risk (RR) indices. An OR provides an estimate of the strength of a risk factor and is commonly derived from analysis of data from retrospective studies involving cases with an identified health condition and controls without the condition. Derivation of the OR involves calculating the relationship of a health outcome with individuals' prior exposure or nonexposure to a specified risk factor.

The approach to derive OR can be illustrated with a recent study of early identification of developmental problems in young children. Giannoni and Kass (2010) reported a study on associations between participating children's withdrawal from the California Early Start (CES) program and subsequent diagnoses of developmental disability in a sample of 2,439 children. The CES is a statewide early intervention program that serves young children who are at high risk of developmental disabilities. In this sample, 472 children were later diagnosed with autism. Retrospective data indicated that 159 children left the service before completing the program, and of these 159 children, 49 were later diagnosed with autism. Of the 2,280 children who completed the CES program, 423 were later diagnosed with autism. The estimated risk for autism diagnosis was almost twice as likely (OR = 1.96) among children who withdrew from CES at the midpoint of the program as those who completed the program. In this case, the OR allows for an estimation of extent of risk based on available data. However, it does not provide the strength of the direct estimate calculated by the relative risk index.

In prospective studies, the strength of risk factors can be calculated directly in terms of a ratio of people exposed, or not exposed, to a specific risk factor. This can be illustrated hypothetically. Suppose data have been gathered prospectively on children in the CES program with the result that a subgroup received the diagnosis of autism. Among other measures collected is whether a child withdraws from CES before the program is completed. Derivation of the relative risk of exposure to a risk factor based on data from a cohort study involves calculating the ratio of the incidence of autism diagnosis in children who withdraw from the early intervention program to the incidence of autism diagnosis in children who complete the program. The relative risk for autism diagnosis is 1.59 times (RR = 1.59) for children who withdraw from CES compared with those who remain in the program. On the basis of this hypothetical example, the RR supports the premise that withdrawal from CES is a strong predictor for later autism diagnosis. The value of derived indices such as the OR and RR is that they provide evidence of the strength of a risk factor in the manifestation of a disorder or health condition and can therefore be used to define the focus for prevention efforts.

IMPLICATIONS FOR RESPONSE TO INTERVENTION

As previously noted, the application of a prevention framework has been extended beyond health and developmental problems of children to address behavioral, social, and academic problems. A significant extension has been to reading and learning difficulties in the form of the response to intervention (RTI) initiative in special education (Simmons et al., 2008). An associated purpose for applying a levels-of-prevention approach in education has been the prevention of specific learning disabilities, or SLD (Mastropieri & Scruggs, 2005). Although the goal of improving academic performance of young children through RTI has been seen as productive by Reschly (2005), he questions whether the initiative has demonstrated its effectiveness in preventing SLD.

Addressing this issue may be difficult given variability in the way in which the prevention framework has been implemented and the basis for its implementation under RTI. Although such variability in and of itself may not preclude demonstration of potential effectiveness of RTI, the fact that the manner of implementation does not correspond to the underlying assumptions of either PST or USI frameworks precludes interpretation within a levels-of-prevention framework. As defined earlier in this chapter, the underlying premise for defining levels of prevention within PST and USI frameworks is on the basis of population characteristics, not on the services that are provided. Specifically, given a preventable condition, the levels of prevention in PST are to prevent the condition in children without the condition (primary), reduce the number of those with the condition (secondary), and prevent complications in those with the condition (tertiary). In USI, prevention is focused on everyone without the condition (universal), on those at risk based on identification with a subgroup (selected) and those identified on the basis of individual risk factors (indicated).

A review of publications on RTI reveals variability in the application of prevention terminology of PST, USI, and combinations of both prevention frameworks without consistent adherence to specification of levels on the basis of population characteristics. Reviewing implementation issues related to the RTI model for identifying learning disabilities, Mastropieri and Scruggs (2005) concluded that "present conceptualizations of RTI are varied and ambiguous at best with respect to the specific roles of teachers and diagnosticians" (p. 525). Kamps and Greenwood (2005), for example, described intervention for students at risk for reading problems but did so using the language of secondary prevention. In another study, Kamps et al. (2008) similarly used the language of secondary and tertiary prevention for at-risk students. Fox and colleagues (2012), on the other hand, described universal, selected, and indicated prevention based on services provided rather than differentiated populations.

If studies of RTI choose to use the prevention language of PST or USI to reduce the incidence and prevalence of SLD, they should do so with adherence to the criteria specifying populations for associated levels of prevention. This is essential in order to interpret findings within the prevention framework and for generalization of findings across studies. To this end, it is essential that adoption of a prevention framework in studies of RTI to reduce the incidence and prevalence of SLD take into account the following considerations.

Problem Definition

First, it is important to define the problem, condition, or disorder of children to be prevented and to identify its scope. As described earlier, an operational definition of the problem or condition is the basis for specifying secondary prevention, usually in terms of a *DSM-IV-TR* diagnosis or IDEA category. The diagnosis or category of SLD, for example, serves as the basis for defining both precursors in the form of risk factors for primary prevention or consequences in terms of complications for tertiary prevention, as illustrated in Figure 2.1. Within the conceptual model of a causal chain, the operational definition of the problem constitutes the point at which the condition or disorder can be diagnosed or confirmed. Further, from the standpoint of scope, the problem condition should not be rare, but affect a significant part of the population of interest, as would be the case for SLD, in order to warrant primary prevention initiatives.

Differentiation of Risk

Having defined the target group of children with learning or reading disorders, children at increased risk for the problem condition need to be identified through screening. Are there logical indicators of risk factors, and what is the evidence for their strength as predictors of the problem condition? In the case of SLD, at what point is there an assumed onset of risk factors, and when in the history of the condition is there a critical point for possible identification through screening? Is there evidence for protective factors that may mitigate risk factors for manifestation of the condition, and how can they be identified? An example of defining risk is illustrated in a longitudinal study to prevent reading failure in kindergarten children (Simmons et al., 2008), in which risk status was operationalized in recognition of the variability of definitions found in other studies.

Targeting Prevention Level

Following identification of risk and protective factors and their relative strength in determining the manifestation of a problem condition, it is important to define the level at which the provision of prevention measures would be most cost-beneficial. That is, what is the level of prevention at which prevention efforts can be implemented most efficiently for the identified target population? Do potential learning problems of children warrant a universal prevention approach in which preventive measures are initiated for all children? Alternatively, are risk factors associated with membership in a subset of the population, such as children living in poverty? In this case, selected prevention is an efficient approach in that it does not require screening of the individual child. For situations in which children have been identified as at risk on the basis of screening but without manifesting the problem condition, preventive measures are implemented at the indicated level. Complementing the intent to implement prevention at the universal, selected, or indicated level on the basis of the strength and association of risk factors is the importance of identifying the resources that exist in the school and community for prevention measures at a particular level.

A final issue in the implementation of prevention programs is the importance of documenting their effectiveness (Hahn et al., 2007). A central task in terms of RTI initiatives to prevent learning disabilities is specifying how the outcomes of prevention efforts will be documented. Within the overall framework of universal, selected, and indicated prevention of SLD, the main outcome is reduction in the incidence of learning disabilities—that is, the number of new cases of children at risk for or with LD in the population. This broad outcome can be complemented with other outcomes specific to universal, selected, or indicated prevention in the form of children's acquisition of skills and improvement of functioning in major life areas. The *International Classification of Functioning, Disability and Health—Children and Youth version* (WHO, 2007) offers a framework and universal language for documentation of functional outcomes, such as attention, perception, and memory. In the contemporary expectation for evidence-based practice, such documentation is essential to demonstrate the scientific and economic logic of implementing primary prevention measures for children's developmental problems and documenting their benefit to the child and to society.

REFERENCES

Abraído-Lanza, A.F., Armbrister, A.N., Flórez, K.R., & Aguirre, A.N. (2006). Toward a theory-driven model of acculturation in public health research. *American Journal of Public Health, 96*(8), 1342–1346.

American Psychiatric Association. (2000). *Diagnostic and statistical manual of mental disorders* (4th ed., text rev.). Washington, DC: Author.

Bass, J.L., Christoffel, K.K., Widome, M., Boyle, W., Scheidt, P., Stanwick, R., & Roberts, K. (1993). Childhood injury prevention counseling in primary care settings: A critical review of the literature. *Pediatrics, 92*(4), 544–550.

Benichou, J., & Palta, M. (2004). Rates, risks, measures of association and impact. In W. Ahrens & I. Pigeot (Ed.), *Handbook of epidemiology* (pp. 91–156). New York, NY: Springer.

Boyle, C.A., Boulet, S., Schieve, L.A., Coehn, R.A., Blumberg, S.J., Yeargin-Allsopp, M., . . . Kogan, M.D. (2011). Trends in the prevalence of developmental disabilities in U.S. children, 1997–2008. *Pediatrics, 127*(6), 1034–1042.

Braswell, L., August, G.J., Bloomquist, M.L., Realmuto, G.M., Skare, S.S., & Crosby, R.D. (1997). School-based secondary prevention for children with disruptive behavior: Initial outcomes. *Journal of Abnormal Child Psychology, 25*(3), 197–208.

Caplan, G., & Grunebaum, H. (1967). Perspectives on primary prevention. *Archives of General Psychiatry, 17*, 331–346.

Caspi, A., McClay, J., Moffitt, T., Mill, J., Martin, J., Craig, I., et al. (2002). Role of genotype in the cycle of violence in maltreated children. *Science, 297*(5582), 851–854.

Coyne, M.D., Kame'enui, E.J., Simmons, D.C., & Harn, B.A. (2004). Beginning reading intervention as inoculation or insulin: First-grade reading performance of strong responders to kindergarten intervention. *Journal of Learning Disabilities, 37*(2), 90–104.

Cummings, P., Koepsell, T.D., & Mueller, B.A. (1995). Methodological challenges in injury epidemiology and injury prevention research. *Annual Review of Public Health, 16*(1), 381–400.

Currie, D. (2010). Country-by-country health rankings encourage community action. *The Nation's Health, 40*(3), 9.

Daniels, S.R., Arnett, D.K., Eckel, R.H., Gidding, S.S., Hayman, L.L., Kumanyika, S., et al. (2005). Overweight in children and adolescents: Pathophysiology, consequences, prevention, and treatment. *Circulation, 111*(15), 1999–2012.

Dehghan, M., Akhtar-Danesh, N., & Merchant, A.T. (2005). Childhood obesity, prevalence and prevention. *Nutrition Journal, 4*(24), 1–8.

Ehreth, J. (2003). The global value of vaccination. *Vaccine, 21*(7–8), 596–600.

Fox, L., Carta, J., Strain, P., Dunlap, G., & Hemmeter, M.L. (2012). Response to intervention and the pyramid model. *Infants & Young Children, 23*(1) 3–13.

Garmezy, N. (1991). Resiliency and vulnerability to adverse developmental outcomes associated with poverty. *American Behavioral Scientist, 34*(4), 416–430.

Giannoni, P.P., & Kass, P.H. (2010). Risk factors of children who exited from an early intervention program without an identified disability and returned with a developmental disability. *Research in Developmental Disabilities, 31*(3), 848–856.

Gordon, Jr., R. (1983). An operational classification of disease prevention. *Public Health Reports, 98*(2), 107–109.

Greenwood-Robinson, M. (2002). *Control diabetes in six easy steps*. New York, NY: St. Martin's Griffin.

Hahn, R., Fuqua-Whitley, D., Wethington, H., Lowy, J., Liberman, A., Crosby, A., . . . Dahlberg, L. (2007). The effectiveness of universal school-based programs for the prevention of violent and aggressive behavior: A report on recommendations of the Task Force on Community Preventive Services. *American Journal of Preventive Medicine, 56*(RR-7), 1–12.

Huse, D.M., Meissner, H.C., Lacey, M.J., & Oster, G. (1994). Childhood vaccination against chickenpox: An analysis of benefits and costs. *The Journal of Pediatrics, 124*(6), 869–874.

Individuals with Disabilities Education Improvement Act (IDEA) of 2004, PL 108-446, 20 U.S.C. §§ 1400 *et seq.*

Kamps, D., Abbott, M., Greenwood, C., Wills, H., Veerkamp, M., & Kaufman, J. (2008). Effects of small-group reading instruction and curriculum differences for students most at risk in kindergarten: Two-year results for secondary- and tertiary-level interventions. *Journal of Learning Disabilities, 41*(2), 101–114.

Kamps, D.M. & Greenwood, C.R. (2005) Formulating secondary level-reading interventions. *Journal of Learning Disabilities, 38*(6), 500–509.

King, R.S., & Rozier, R.G. (2008). School-based dental disease prevention and oral health education: Programs of the North Carolina oral health section. *North Carolina Medical Journal, 69*(6), 490–494.

Kinosian, B.P., & Eisenberg, J.M. (1988). Cutting into cholesterol. *The Journal of the American Medical Association, 259*(15), 2249.

Koh, H.K., Nowinski, J.M., & Piotrowski, J.J. (2011). A 2020 vision for educating the next generation of public health leaders. *American Journal of Preventive Medicine, 40*(2), 199–202.

Luthar, S. (1991). Vulnerability and resilience: A study of high-risk adolescents. *Child Development, 62*(3), 600–616.

Margai, F., & Henry, N. (2003). A community-based assessment of learning disabilities using environmental and contextual risk factors. *Social Science & Medicine, 56*, 1073–1085.

Mastropieri, M.A. & Scruggs, T.F. (2005). Feasibility and consequences of response to intervention: Examination of the issues and scientific evidence as a model for the identification of individuals with learning disabilities. *Journal of Learning Disabilities, 38*(6), 525–531.

McLaughlin, K.A. (2011). The public health impact of major depression: A call for interdisciplinary prevention efforts. *Prevention Science, 12*(4), 361–371.

Miller, T.W., Kraus, R.F., & Veltkamp, L.J. (2005). Character education as a prevention strategy in school-related violence. *The Journal of Primary Prevention, 26*(5), 455–466.

Offord, D.R. (1982). Primary prevention: Aspects of program design and evaluation. *Journal of the American Academy of Child Psychiatry, 21*(3), 225–230.

Peters, R.D.V., Petrunka, K., & Arnold, R. (2003). The better beginnings, better futures project: A universal, comprehensive, community-based prevention approach for primary school children and their families. *Journal of Clinical Child and Adolescent Psychology, 32*(2), 215–227.

Reschly, D.J. (2005). Learning disabilities identification: Primary intervention, secondary intervention, and then what? *Journal of Learning Disabilities, 38*(6), 510–515.

Rickert, D., Santoli, J., Shefer, A., Myrick, A., & Yusuf, H. (2006). Influenza vaccination of high-risk children: What the providers say. *American Journal of Preventive Medicine, 30*(2), 111–118.

Rockhill, B., & Weed, D. (2006). Increasing the contribution of epidemiology to the primary prevention of cancer. In D. Schottenfeld & J.F. Fraumeni Jr. (Ed.), *Cancer epidemiology and prevention* (pp. 1292–1303). New York, NY: Oxford University Press.

Sackett, D., Haynes, R., Guyatt, G., & Tugwell, P. (1991). *Clinical epidemiology: A basic science for clinical epidemiology.* Boston, MA: Little, Brown.

Silverman, M.M. (2003). Theories of primary prevention and health promotion. In T.P. Gullotta & M. Bloom (Ed.), *Encyclopedia of primary prevention and health promotion* (pp. 27–42). New York, NY: Kluwer Academic/Plenum Publishers.

Simeonsson, R.J. (1994). Promoting children's health, education, and well-being. In R.J. Simeonsson (Ed.), *Risk resilience and prevention: Promoting the well-being of all children* (pp. 3–12). Baltimore, MD: Paul H. Brookes Publishing Co.

Simeonsson, R.J., & McDevitt, L.N. (Eds.). (1999). *Issues in disability and health: The role of secondary conditions and quality of life.* Chapel Hill: University of North Carolina Press.

Simmons, D.C., Coyne, M.D., Kwok, O.M., McDonagh, S., Ham, B.A., & Kame'enui, E.J. (2008). Indexing response to intervention: A longitudinal study of reading risk from kindergarten through third grade. *Journal of Learning Disabilities, 41*(2), 158–173.

Srabstein, J., Joshi, P., Due, P., Wright, J., Leventhal, B., Merrick, J., et al. (2008). Prevention of public health risks linked to bullying: A need for a whole community approach. *International Journal of Adolescent Medicine and Health, 20*(2), 185–199.

Trost, S.G., Sirard, J.R., Dowda, M., Pfeiffer, K.A., & Pate, R.R. (2003). Physical activity in overweight and nonoverweight preschool children. *International Journal of Obesity, 27,* 834–839.

U.S. Department of Health and Human Services. (2000). *Healthy people 2010* (2nd ed.) Washington, DC: Office of the Assistant Secretary for Health.

U.S. Department of Health and Human Services. (2010). *Healthy people 2020.* Retrieved from http://www.healthypeople.gov/2020/about/DOHAbout.aspx

van Bakel, H., & Riksen-Walraven, J. (2002). Parenting and development of one-year-olds: Links with parental, contextual, and child characteristics. *Child Development, 73*(1), 256–273.

van Beynum, I.M., Kapusta, L., Bakker, M.K., Den Heijer, M., Blom, H.J., & de Walle, H.E.K. (2010). Protective effect of periconceptional folic acid supplements on the risk of congenital heart defects: A registry-based case–control study in the northern Netherlands. *European Heart Journal, 31*(4), 464–471.

Vogt, T.M., Lafata, J.E., Tolsma, D.D., & Greene, S.M. (2004). The role of research in integrated health care systems: The HMO research network. *The Permanente Journal, 10*(9), 643–648.

Wherrett, D.K., & Daneman, D. (2011). Prevention of type 1 diabetes. *Pediatric Clinics of North America, 58*(5), 1257–1270.

Wilson, S.J., & Lipsey, M.W. (2007). School-based interventions for aggressive and disruptive behavior: Update of a meta-analysis. *American Journal of Preventive Medicine, 33*(2), S130–S143.

World Health Organization. (1992). *International classification of diseases and related health problems* (10th rev.). Geneva, Switzerland: Author.

World Health Organization. (2007). *International classification of functioning, disability and health—Children and youth version.* Geneva, Switzerland: Author.

Responsiveness to Intervention in the Elementary Grades

Implications for Early Childhood Education

Rollanda E. O'Connor and Lynn S. Fuchs

The Individuals with Disabilities Education Improvement Act (IDEA) of 2004 (PL 108-446) encourages schools to adopt and implement multilevel prevention systems, known as responsiveness to intervention (RTI). The motivation for RTI stems, in part, from dissatisfaction with the traditional method for identifying students with learning disabilities (LD), which involves a discrepancy between a student's cognitive ability and achievement. Dissatisfaction stems from multiple causes, but one major problem is that the academic skill development of most students is insufficiently developed in the early grades, which makes it difficult to design test items that tap young students' potential for academic learning. For this reason, a discrepancy between cognitive ability and achievement takes years to accrue. This typically results in a long period of "waiting to fail" before students are deemed eligible for special education services, so that by the time they are identified, they manifest large achievement gaps that are difficult to narrow. The hope is that RTI may address the problems associated with this wait-to-fail model by integrating assessment and intervention within a multilevel prevention system in order to 1) provide a means for delivering earlier intervention outside the framework of special education, 2) reduce the inappropriate identification of students who have lacked strong instructional opportunities as students with LD, and 3) provide an alternative data source for LD identification by indexing a student's responsiveness to early intervention.

In this chapter, we consider the possibilities of RTI, as practiced in the primary grades, for informing early childhood education practice. We begin by explaining how RTI is typically used in the primary grades. Then we summarize some recent RTI studies at Grades 1 through 3 in reading and then in mathematics. In this description of studies, we focus largely on the intervention arm of RTI (rather than screening or progress monitoring, which belong to the assessment arm of RTI). We conclude by drawing implications for the design of RTI models in early childhood settings.

RESPONSE TO INTERVENTION AS PRESENTLY PRACTICED IN THE PRIMARY GRADES

Regardless of specific details, all models of RTI can be described using a catch-and-release metaphor. Measures that are sensitive to early development are used to identify (or catch) students whose skills fall below typical levels for the age and grade of the child. Next, children who are caught in this net receive intervention that is more specific and intensive than their general education instruction. Measures of progress are used on a regular schedule to release children who respond well to intervention, which indicates they are no longer at risk, and to consider alternatives for children who respond poorly.

For example, in many locales, schools use a three-level (or layered or tiered) approach for designing their RTI system to decrease or prevent learning difficulties. The first level, sometimes referred to as Tier 1 of the RTI prevention framework, comprises the instructional practices general educators conduct with all students: 1) the core instructional program, along with 2) classroom routines that provide opportunities for instructional differentiation, 3) accommodations that permit access to core instruction for all students, and 4) problem-solving strategies for addressing students' motivational problems that interfere with their ability to demonstrate the academic skills they possess. The major function of RTI assessment at this level is to identify students who are at risk of not responding to the general education program (i.e., to catch them) so that intervention with greater intensity may be allocated to these students. The assumption is that learning would suffer without such intervention and that intervention needs to be provided in a timely manner to circumvent severe, long-term academic difficulty. Assessment to identify risk for poor outcomes is typically accomplished using a brief screening test administered to all students (i.e., universally). A cutoff point is established, based on research for the specific test used, to classify students in terms of success versus failure on future important outcomes.

When screening reveals the need for more intensive intervention, those services, sometimes referred to as Tier 2, are provided. Typically, Tier 2 occurs in the form of small-group tutoring based on instruction that has been experimentally validated to improve academic outcomes. Tier 2 specifies instructional procedures, duration (typically 10–20 weeks of 20- to 45-minute sessions), and frequency (3 or 4 times per week). Schools design their RTI prevention systems so students receive just one or a series of Tier 2 small-group tutoring programs, depending on their responsiveness. At this level, the major purpose of assessment is to formulate sound conclusions about whether students have responded to tutoring. This is typically based on ongoing progress monitoring during tutoring, or assessment conducted at the end of tutoring, or a combination of progress monitoring and assessment of post-tutoring status. Schools use these assessment data to determine whether students should return to general education without additional support (i.e., be released) or instead receive additional validated small-group tutoring or more intensive intervention than is available with small-group tutoring.

Many schools struggle with how to conceptualize a third level of intervention that is more intensive than validated small-group tutoring. Fuchs, Fuchs, and Compton (2012) have suggested that this more intensive level of intervention, sometimes referred to as Tier 3, differs from validated small-group tutoring in two major ways. First, teachers set individualized year-end goals in instructional material that matches the student's needs. This material may or may not be the student's grade-appropriate curriculum. It may instead address foundational skills necessary for successful performance in grade-appropriate material and, in this way, create access to the general education curriculum and represent appropriate content standards (we return to this issue in the next section). Second, because the student has demonstrated insufficient response to both instruction in general education and validated small-group tutoring, the more intensive intervention is individualized. That is, the teacher begins with a more intensive version of a standard tutoring program (e.g., longer sessions, smaller group size) but does not presume it will foster adequate learning. Instead, assessment becomes a central feature of more intensive intervention, with ongoing progress monitoring used to quantify the effects of the student's program. For individualizing a student's instructional program, ongoing progress-monitoring data are summarized in terms of weekly rate of improvement (i.e., slope). When slope indicates that goal attainment is unlikely, the teacher experiments by modifying components of the teaching protocol and uses progress monitoring to assess the effects of those modifications. In this way, the teacher inductively designs an effective, individualized instructional program. A research program of randomized control trials demonstrates that this sort of data-based program development enhances outcomes on highly valued standardized achievement tests among special education students (for summaries, see Fuchs & Fuchs, 1998, or Stecker, Fuchs, & Fuchs, 2005). We note that some schools elect to provide Tier 3 services in the context of special education, whereas others choose to implement Tier 3 without special education.

SOME RECENT RESEARCH IN READING IN THE PRIMARY GRADES

The research base in reading development and intervention during the acquisition years of kindergarten through third grade is strong. Whereas early intervention in reading has a long and effective history, using children's response to early intervention as an indicator of potential disability is relatively new. In an exploratory study of effects for layered intervention, O'Connor (2000) began with professional development for eight kindergarten teachers in three schools to strengthen their implementation of instruction in phonemic awareness and letter-sound correspondence, thus improving the general education instructional environment. With each additional layer of intensity (i.e., professional development for general education kindergarten teachers, intensive intervention for students who responded poorly in Tier 2, continued intervention in first grade as needed), the number of children in the high-risk pool diminished. In comparison with historical controls (first-graders in the same schools the year prior to RTI implementation), the percentage of children who scored in the bottom quartile on standardized reading measures at the end of first grade dropped from 40 to 16. By second grade, fewer students were identified for remedial services with the RTI model (17%) than in historical control classes (36%). Nevertheless, the proportion of children identified for special education by the end of second grade did not change significantly.

Because students' responsiveness to instruction is related to the quality of that instruction, several research teams have considered how to improve the quality of instruction and practice opportunities in general education classes (Tier 1). One such model is classwide peer tutoring (Fuchs, Fuchs, Mathes, & Simmons, 1997; Greenwood, Delquadri, & Hall, 1989), which involves students working together in pairs on structured learning activities. Saenz, McMaster, Fuchs, and Fuchs (2007) reviewed nearly 20 years of research on Peer Assisted Learning Strategies (PALS; Fuchs et al., 1997), a system that was designed to improve the reading and mathematics development of students in kindergarten through sixth grade. In Reading PALS in kindergarten and first grade, teachers pair students to practice phonological awareness, decoding, word recognition, and fluency activities. With Reading PALS in Grades 2 through 5, students work on fluency- and comprehension-building activities. PALS has been shown to be an effective method for reducing rates of unresponsiveness within general education; this is the case across types of schools (including high-poverty schools) and for students with differing reading ability.

McMaster, Fuchs, Fuchs, and Compton (2005) extended this line of work to examine additional layers of the RTI model. In eight schools, they introduced Reading PALS to improve Tier 1 instruction. Following 7 weeks of this enhanced Tier 1, they selected students whose 7-week oral reading scores as well as their rate of oral reading progress were more than 0.50 standard deviation below the class average. They randomly assigned two thirds of these students to continue with PALS for another 7 weeks; the other third received 35 minutes of one-to-one tutoring by an adult, similar to O'Connor's (2000) first-grade Tier 2 intervention. Adult tutoring generated larger effects than PALS alone and reduced the proportion of students making minimal progress (50% in adult tutoring versus 80% in PALS). This lends more evidence in support of RTI models to reduce risk in first grade.

Other attempts to improve general class instruction (Tier 1) have shown similar positive effects. Blachman, Ball, Black, and Tangel (1994) provided professional development to kindergarten teachers and their assistants in early literacy skills, including activities to stimulate phonemic awareness and letter knowledge. Students in these classes ended the year with significantly stronger reading and spelling skills than students in the control classes. McCutchen and Berninger (1999) also used professional development of teachers to improve the Tier 1 learning environment and students' reading achievement.

Research that reports short-term outcomes (1–2 years) suggests that interventions can have strong effects on students' reading skills, regardless of whether these interventions occur in general or special education settings. Yet few studies monitor postintervention effects for more than a few months, and those that have tested maintenance one to 2 years later suggest declining effects over time. For example, Fuchs, Compton, Fuchs, Bryant, and Davis (2008) identified first-graders who responded poorly to general class instruction and randomly assigned them to 9 weeks of three-times-per-week small-group tutoring (Tier 2) or a control group without tutoring. Tier 2 intervention focused on sight words, letter-sound recognition, decoding, writing, and reading aloud. Toward the end of first grade, tutored students had improved more than those in the control group on a variety of measures, including standardized reading tests. At the end of second grade, however, the difference between children tutored or not tutored in first grade had narrowed.

A related question concerns RTI's impact on the prevalence of LD, which requires longer-term follow-up of RTI intervention effects. In a study that compared 4-year (end of third grade) outcomes for students who participated in a three-tier model of RTI against historical controls in the same schools prior to RTI, O'Connor, Fulmer, Harty, and Bell (2005) found overall differences of about 0.50 standard deviation favoring RTI. Because only 25% of students received Tier 2 or 3, they attributed this difference to improved teaching in Tier 1 (general education) classes, for which teachers received ongoing professional development. For students with LD in special education who received Tiers 2 and 3 prior to special education identification, outcomes were a full standard deviation higher than for LD students in the historical control. Reading rate and comprehension were also significantly higher. Nevertheless, the prevalence of LD dropped only slightly, and the authors cautioned that fourth grade accounts for nearly one third of all new cases of LD in the state where the study was conducted. So the authors anticipated that LD prevalence could remain unaffected by RTI as additional students were identified as LD during their fourth-grade year.

Because the research base for RTI in reading is strongest for Grades K–1, before most students with LD have been identified for special education historically, we do not yet know the extent to which RTI implementation may decrease the incidence of disability. Moreover, longitudinal studies show that over time "what counts as reading" changes. Skills that are relatively easy to teach, such as phoneme segmentation or decoding, give way to more complex forms of reading that require integration across several components, such as reading with prosody, sufficient rate, and comprehension (Schwanenflugel et al., 2006). Thus, when studies of RTI in kindergarten and first grade produce positive effects, we cannot necessarily conclude that RTI precludes risk for inadequate reading development.

O'Connor, Harty, and Fulmer (2005) demonstrated considerable movement across tiers in kindergarten through third grade, which was not always in the same direction. That is, students who grew slowly in Tier 1 were given intensive intervention in Tier 2, which improved their rate of growth. However, when some of these "successful" students returned to Tier 1, their rate of growth slowed such that months later or the following year, they again surfaced with risk. For this reason, Coyne, Kame'enui, Simmons, and Harn (2004) asked whether RTI offers inoculation (an injection of support that prevents disability) or insulin (regular injections that are required for continued good health). Their study, conducted in first-grade students, supported the theory of inoculation. Continuing this study into third grade, Simmons, Coyne, Kwok, McDonagh, Harn, and Kame'enui (2008) found that most of the students remaining in the study (i.e., less than half the original sample) continued to do well after they had shifted out of the high-risk category (i.e., were released).

By contrast, other work (O'Connor et al., 2005; Vaughn, 2003) has shown that whereas RTI serves as "inoculation" for some students, it functions as "insulin" for others by supporting stronger rates of growth than students show in Tier 1 alone. Moreover, how risk is measured plays a role in how responsiveness is defined. In Simmons et al.'s (2008) study, 78% of the third-graders who had earlier participated in Tier 2 and 3 interventions were considered good responders on isolated skills such as word recognition out of context; however, only 37% remained out of risk when a measure of reading connected text was used. It will be important to keep in mind that many students with LD are not identified until fourth grade or later— beyond the scope of the current research base in RTI.

Another issue in RTI involves shifting demographics of the United States, with increasing diversity in language and ethnicity in public schools. Some researchers have addressed this issue by comparing responsiveness to Tier 1 and 2 instruction for students who are English language learners (ELLs) versus native English speakers. When RTI was implemented in the primary grades, Linklater, O'Connor, and Palardy (2009) found no difference in growth across kindergarten on measures of early reading, and O'Connor, Bocian, Beebe-Frankenberger, and Linklater (2010) found no difference in response in kindergarten or first grade. Likewise, Lovett, De Palma, Steinbach, Temple, Benson, and Lacerenza (2008) found comparable response to Tier 2 intervention for third-graders, as did O'Connor, White, and Swanson (2007) for second- and fourth-graders who were ELLs versus native English speakers. In these studies, instruction was conducted in English. Linan-Thompson, Vaughn, Prater, and Cirino (2006), who assessed the effects of delivering Tier 2 intervention in English versus Spanish in first or second grade, found no effects for language of instruction; both intervention groups of Spanish-speaking ELLs outperformed control students.

In an ongoing longitudinal study of RTI's effects, O'Connor et al. (in press) are systematically varying whether students gain access to RTI in kindergarten or first grade and whether Tier 2 involves a standardized tutoring program or individualized tutoring based on students' reading performance assessments collected every 3 weeks. Compared with historical controls (students in the same schools who were in second grade as they implemented RTI in Grades K–1), RTI has improved end-of-Grade-2 outcomes significantly for students in the bottom third of each cohort. Initiating Tier 2 in kindergarten generates higher first-grade reading outcomes compared with waiting until first grade to begin Tier 2, and this advantage has been maintained through the end of second grade. In the five participating schools, 26%–49% of students are ELLs whose second-grade outcomes are comparable to those of native English speakers. Yet beginning Tier 2 in kindergarten has not reduced the prevalence of special education.

In considering this literature, it is important to note that differential attrition among high- and low-skilled children has plagued studies of RTI, raising questions about how to interpret apparent impacts. For example, O'Connor (2000) lost 29% of the sample over 2 years, and 20% of these students were among those most at risk. McMaster et al. (2005) reported 6% attrition across 7 weeks for low-skilled children versus 1% among average learners. Among 3- and 4-year studies of RTI's effects, the rate of attrition for the lowest-skilled students is alarming. Simmons et al. (2008) reported twice the attrition among students who received Tier 2 over those for whom general education was sufficient, and by the end of Grade 3 only 35% of the poor responders remained in the study. In our current work, only 53% of low-skilled kindergartners remained in the study schools at the end of third grade. When half of the high-risk sample leaves the study, how do we evaluate the effects of RTI on LD prevalence?

We also note that difficulty in accurately screening for students' risk status in the early grades may affect RTI outcomes, especially when the high-risk group that is followed over time was selected in kindergarten. During the reading acquisition years, the measures used in RTI models provide the means for identifying students as early as kindergarten who are having difficulty acquiring early literacy skills such as letter identification, letter-sound pairing, and phonemic blending and segmenting. Although these measures catch the majority of students who have reading difficulties during kindergarten and first grade, they err in two directions. First, these measures "catch" students who do not need early intervention. By overselecting students, the high proportion of students who respond well to Tier 2 may be due partly to including students who are not truly at risk for later reading problems. Second, as researchers follow children into later grades, it has become clear that our current measurement systems also miss some students at risk, specifically, students whose reading difficulties involve comprehension and developing automatic integration of lower-level skills (Catts, Adlof, & Weismer, 2006; Catts, Compton, Tomblin, & Bridges, 2012). Across the O'Connor and colleagues studies, about 20% of students identified for Tier 2 in first grade had scored as "typical readers" throughout the kindergarten screenings, and another 15% were identified with risk in second grade even though they had appeared to be making adequate progress in kindergarten and first grade. Kieffer (2010) reported that the proportion of students whose reading difficulties become apparent in third grade and later is especially high among ELLs.

Researchers are currently exploring whether the identification of risk can be improved within RTI. For example, Compton, Fuchs, et al. (2010) introduced a two-stage screening process in which brief universal screening is followed by short-term progress monitoring or more in-depth assessments for students who score poorly on the initial screen, and D. Fuchs et al. (2012) assessed the role of dynamic assessment as a second stage of screening. This research group's studies indicate that two-stage screening reduces false positive errors (i.e., the number of students identified with risk who would develop nicely without intervention beyond general education). Whether two-stage screening will improve sensitivity to "late emerging" reading difficulties, however, remains to be seen.

Although differential attrition and the kinds of errors associated with screening students into RTI represent important limitations to the research literature, advantages on reading outcomes have been found for early intervention across RTI studies. Whether RTI models decrease the prevalence of disability is open to question, because even the 3- and 4-year implementations of RTI have been too short to explore whether the somewhat lower incidence rates persist through sixth grade, by which time most students with LD have been identified. In the meantime, across studies the proportion of students who remain in the high-risk group despite participation in RTI models for 2 or more years hovers between 4% and 6%, which mirrors the national statistics for the prevalence of LD.

SOME RECENT RESEARCH INVOLVING MATHEMATICS IN THE PRIMARY GRADES

As in reading, research provides the basis for guarded optimism about the efficacy of Tier 2 small-group tutoring for preventing mathematics difficulty. In this section, we begin by illustrating efficacy using three large-scale randomized control trials. The first study investigated the effects of first-grade tutoring on multiple components of the curriculum (Fuchs et al., 2005); the second study focused on math facts tutoring for third-grade students (Fuchs et al., 2009); and the third study assessed the separate and combined effects of primary prevention and supplementary tutoring in the domain of word problems (Fuchs, Fuchs, et al., 2008).

Working in 41 first-grade classrooms in 10 schools, Fuchs et al. (2005) identified at-risk students and randomly assigned them to 16 weeks of Tier 2 small-group tutoring (three times per week) or control. Every tutoring session comprised two activities. The first was a 30-minute tutor-led lesson with explicit, interactive instruction. During the final 10 minutes of each tutoring session, students used a computer program to help them commit math facts to long-term memory. Based on measures of math concepts, procedural calculations, word problems, and math facts, findings supported the efficacy of tutoring as an added level of the prevention system to supplement the general education classroom program. The weekly rate of computation improvement for tutored students substantially exceeded that of the control group. This was also the case for word problems. On commercial tests of computation and concepts and application, results were even more impressive: Improvement for the tutored students exceeded not only that of control group peers but also that of not-at-risk classmates. Tier 2 tutoring therefore appeared efficacious. Yet, some patterns in the findings prompt caution about assuming that such tutoring inoculates at-risk learners from developing future difficulty in mathematics. The first cause for concern is the lack of universal response—as is typically the case even when results are substantial and statistically significant. It appears that approximately 5% of the general population may prove unresponsive to intervention even when this generally effective form of tutoring is provided to at-risk students. A second concern is that at the end of first grade, tutored students still performed below that of not-at-risk classmates on every measure. Even so, the performance gap had narrowed for the at-risk tutored students, while it had increased for the at-risk control children. So, Tier 2 tutoring enhanced the rate of math development beyond what would have occurred without tutoring, but the continued development of the students not-at-risk precluded the tutored children from catching up. The remaining performance gap suggests that, despite the efficacy of Tier 2 tutoring, some at-risk learners will require additional mathematics support in subsequent years.

Another potential concern is transfer. Mathematics, more than reading, is potentially complicated by the fact that school curricula are organized in strands within and across the grades, presumed to represent different component skills. In reading, measurement studies (e.g., Mehta, Foorman, Branum-Martin, & Taylor, 2005) provide the basis for five component reading skills: phonological awareness, decoding, fluency, vocabulary, and comprehension. Mathematics measurement studies are yet to be conducted, but the assumption, as reflected in the curriculum, is that many more component skills exist. For example, in primary school mathematics, curricular strands include concepts, numeration, measurement, basic facts, algorithmic computation, and word problems; in high school, strands include algebra, geometry, trigonometry, and calculus. It is unclear whether strengthening performance on one component skill can be expected to promote strong performance on other components, and a failure to produce strong performance across component skills would create additional challenges to dramatically reducing the need for ongoing, intensive support in mathematics.

Fuchs et al. (2009) addressed the issue of transfer from math facts to word problems in a randomized field trial that incorporated two tutoring conditions: one focused exclusively on math facts; the other focused primarily on word problems, although it allocated a small amount of time to foundational skills, including counting strategies to help students efficiently answer math facts (needed to solve word problems). Third-grade at-risk students were identified and randomly assigned to a control group or one of two Tier 2 tutoring conditions. In both active conditions, tutoring time was held constant at 20 to 30 minutes per session, with sessions held 3 times per week for 16 weeks. On math facts, both tutoring conditions effected superior improvement compared to the control group, with no significant difference between tutoring conditions. The comparability of outcomes for the two tutoring conditions was notable because math facts tutoring allocated dramatically more time to math facts over the 16-week intervention. In terms of procedural calculations, both tutoring conditions again produced superior outcomes compared with the control group. So, even without direct work on procedural calculations, math facts tutoring resulted in better outcomes on procedural calculations compared with the control group, indicating transfer. By contrast, there was no evidence of transfer to word-problem outcomes. Word-problem tutoring resulted in strong word-problem outcomes, compared with both contrasting conditions. With math facts improvement but in the absence of word-problem tutoring, however, students evidenced no word-problem improvement.

Results therefore suggest that intervention on one component of mathematics may not carry over to other components. This is problematic for RTI models because the mathematics curriculum routinely introduces new topics as students progress through school. For example, fractions, which do not comprise a major component of the curriculum in the primary grades, represent a strong focus in the intermediate grades. And whole-number logic may actually interfere with students' understanding of fractions (e.g., one eighth is not greater than one fourth, even though 8 is greater than 4; see Hecht, Vagi, & Torgesen, 2007). As this illustrates, RTI prevention activities in mathematics may present greater challenges to enduring effects than is the case in reading. And, as with any generally efficacious instructional intervention and as with Fuchs et al. (2005), not all students who received tutoring responded. For math facts tutoring, about 7% of the general population remained unresponsive on math facts outcomes; nearly 5% for word-problem tutoring on math facts outcomes; and nearly 4% for word-problem tutoring on word-problem outcomes.

A third randomized control trial, Fuchs, Fuchs, et al. (2008), also illustrates how generally efficacious mathematics intervention does not denote universal response, this time while considering how tutoring interacts with classroom instruction: If tutoring is differentially efficacious when combined with validated classroom instruction, then both levels of the prevention system are critical, and classroom instruction needs to be designed deliberately with at-risk students in mind, even when they receive tutoring. If, however, tutoring promotes comparable outcomes regardless of the classroom instructional context, then tutoring might occur as a replacement for, rather than as a supplement to, classroom instruction. Tutoring as a replacement for classroom instruction would make RTI prevention systems more feasible and efficient and would permit resources to be infused at the tutoring level.

Stratifying to represent classroom conditions in a balanced way in each school, in the 2008 study 40 classrooms were randomly assigned to control and 80 to validated word-problem instruction. All students participated in their classroom condition, but a representative sample of 1,200 students was selected to enter the study as research participants, from whom 288 were designated as at risk for poor word-problem outcomes. These at-risk students were assigned to validated tutoring or no tutoring, while stratifying by classroom condition. In this way, some at-risk students received no validated instruction (neither in their classrooms nor via tutoring), some received validated instruction in their classrooms but not via tutoring, some received validated instruction via tutoring but not in their classrooms, and some received validated instruction both in their classrooms and via tutoring. Results revealed an interaction between the two levels of the RTI prevention system: Tutoring was significantly and substantially more effective when it occurred in combination with validated classroom instruction than when tutoring occurred with conventional classroom instruction. This suggests that two levels are better than one level of prevention and indicates the importance of providing at-risk students validated instruction in the classroom and then supplementing that instruction with validated tutoring. We note, however, that in this study, the two levels of instruction were closely aligned, both addressing the same types of word problems at the same time and both relying on the same theoretical and operational approach to instruction. It is possible that when the two levels of instruction are less aligned, as is often the case, results may differ.

In terms of the present discussion, in which we consider the durability of prevention activities for long-term success with mathematics, it is also interesting to compare the performance of at-risk students with that of their not-at-risk peers. When at-risk students received validated tutoring, but with conventional classroom instruction, at-risk tutored students improved more than their not-at-risk classmates, narrowing the achievement gap. On the other hand, with two levels of the prevention system (i.e., validated classroom and tutoring), at-risk tutored students and not-at-risk peers achieved comparably, with the achievement gap remaining sizable. And as expected, when at-risk and not-at-risk students received the same, single level of validated classroom instruction, without tutoring for the at-risk learners, the achievement gap remained the same or grew. Together, findings indicate that validated Tier 2 tutoring is essential for at-risk learners. Without it, the gap between at-risk and not-at-risk students continues to widen, even when not-at-risk students suffer the disappointing effects of conventional problem-solving classroom instruction. Accordingly, results highlight the importance of validated word-problem instruction in the general education classroom and suggest that tutoring occur as a supplement to, not a replacement for, classroom instruction. When at-risk students receive tutoring combined with validated classroom instruction, their learning exceeds that of students who receive tutoring without validated classroom instruction. Even with these impressive results, however, Tier 2 tutoring did not ensure individual student response. Nearly 7% of the general population would be deemed unresponsive.

This set of studies is representative of a small but growing literature that relies on randomized control trials to assess the effects of RTI tutoring mathematics programs in the primary grades. Examples of additional studies include the following. Working with at-risk kindergarteners, Clarke et al. (2011) assessed the effects of ROOTS, a 50-lesson Tier 2 tutoring focused on whole number understanding (i.e., numeration to 20, counting, identifying and writing numbers to 20, counting from a number other than 1, reading and solving simple addition statements, understanding place value and model numbers to 20, and identifying quantities and numbers that are more, less, and equal). Tutoring occurred two to three times per week, for approximately 20 weeks. Small to medium effects, which meet the What Works Clearinghouse standards for showing a substantively important positive effect, favored ROOTS over the district's standard intervention practices on early number knowledge, calculations, and magnitude comparisons. However, only effects on magnitude comparisons were significant, because the unit of analysis was the classroom.

At first grade, Bryant et al. (2011) provided at-risk learners with tutoring four times per week for 19 weeks. Each session comprised 20 minutes of number knowledge tutoring and 4 minutes of practice. Tutored children improved significantly more than no-tutoring control students on simple arithmetic, place value, and number sequences. Tutoring did not, however, enhance word-problem outcomes. Also working at first grade, Fuchs, Geary, et al. (2011) randomly assigned at-risk children to control, number knowledge with math practice, and number knowledge tutoring with math games. Tutoring occurred three times per week for 16 weeks. In each 30-minute session, 25 minutes was designed to promote number knowledge and the remaining 5 minutes consisted of games or practice, depending on condition. Both forms of tutoring produced stronger learning than control on simple and complex arithmetic, number knowledge, and word problems, but practice was important. Students who received 5 minutes of practice per session improved significantly more on simple and more complex arithmetic than did children who played math games, and this difference was dramatic: The effect size for students who received practice was 0.87 compared with control; for games, the corresponding effect size was 0.51, and children who received practice, but not those who played games, improved more than low-risk classmates. Smith, Cobb, Farran, Cordray, and Munster (2011) evaluated Math Recovery (MR), in which tutors introduce tasks and have at-risk first-graders explain their reasoning, but without practice. Tutoring occurred four to five times per week, 30 minutes per session across 12 weeks, with a median number of 32 sessions delivered. At the end of first grade, effects favored MR over the control group on fluency with simple arithmetic, concepts and applications, quantitative concepts, and math reasoning, but effects were smaller than in other studies, perhaps due to the absence of practice. Comparisons are difficult, however, because this effectiveness study allowed fidelity to vary.

Together, studies on mathematics RTI, largely conducted at the primary level, provide the basis for conclusions about the power as well as the limitations of RTI in the area of mathematics. In terms of power across the three studies, results clearly demonstrate that students at risk for poor mathematics development suffer reliably and substantially less positive mathematics outcomes if left in the general education program without Tier 2 tutoring. Moreover, when at-risk students do not receive Tier 2 preventive tutoring services, the gap between their level of mathematics performance and those of not-at-risk classmates grows, making it increasingly difficult for these children to profit from classroom instruction. By contrast, at-risk students as a group, who receive high-quality tutoring, make progress toward catching up to their classmates and, for some of these children, the scaffolding provided through such short-term validated tutoring creates a strong foundation for them to experience long-term success with their mathematics schooling. Clearly, reliable screening of risk to identify students for 15–20 weeks of accurately implemented, validated Tier 2 tutoring is a valuable and important service.

At the same time, it is important to recognize the limitations of RTI for dramatically reducing the need for ongoing and more intensive services for some segments of the school population. First, each study illustrates that even with generally efficacious Tier 2 tutoring programs, we cannot expect all students to respond. The modal rate of unresponsiveness on the components of the curriculum targeted for intervention approximated 4% of the general population. This is similar to the prevalence of LD in the United States without RTI in place and when IQ-achievement discrepancy is used for identification. This rate of unresponsiveness, which is similar to the rate in reading, suggests the limitations of RTI preventive services for dramatically reducing the need for ongoing, intensive services. It is also important to consider, however, that the rate of unresponsiveness documented in these studies probably underestimates the actual percentage when RTI is practiced in the schools because, in these randomized control trials, fidelity of implementation for the validated tutoring procedures was ensured and because estimates of unresponsiveness were based on performance immediately following tutoring. In actual practice, fidelity of implementation is likely to be lower, with reduced effects. Also, as students continue in school the effects of tutoring can be expected to diminish, and without additional support some responders will reemerge with difficulty, as has been documented in the long-term studies of reading.

The second reason for caution is that each of these randomized control trials illustrates that even with efficacious tutoring programs, where students improve reliably and perform substantially better than control group at-risk students, the posttutoring mathematics achievement gap between tutored and not-at-risk students remains substantial. This prompts caution about whether at-risk students derive sufficient benefit from tutoring to transition back to general education with long-term mathematics success. The third issue concerns questions about transfer across components of the mathematics curriculum. As the studies illustrate, although transfer may occur from math facts tutoring to procedural calculations, there is no basis to presume that math facts tutoring enhances word-problem performance, even when those word problems require students to apply math facts to derive solutions. Transfer to other components of the curriculum, such as fractions and algebra, may be similarly challenging, creating the need for renewed focus on RTI as students face these major shifts in the mathematics curriculum.

IMPLICATIONS FOR EARLY CHILDHOOD

Research reveals that even with preschool education, children enter kindergarten with a wide range of reading and mathematics readiness skills, and this heterogeneity in performance challenges kindergarten teachers in addressing the needs of their students. The question is whether marrying assessment and intervention within an RTI system at the preschool level represents a reform that will enable early childhood education providers to prepare most, if not all, children for school entry. Across reading and mathematics at the primary grades, the research literature yields reasons for optimism as well as caution. On the one hand, relying on strong assessment for screening to identify risk for inadequate learning and for monitoring students' progress in response to intervention and joining these forms of assessment with validated Tier 2 tutoring has been shown to improve outcomes to an impressive extent. On the other hand, research to date suggests that validated Tier 2 small-group tutoring may not reduce the prevalence of LD or inoculate some of these students against future difficulty. RTI's strength may lie instead in the reduction of the proportion of students with low achievement in the general education system.

In addition, the context of early childhood education programs may raise additional challenges that need to be addressed as preschool RTI models are considered. First, early childhood settings are more variable than public schools in K–12, and emulate a range of characteristics, from private settings, to day care centers, to Head Start, and prekindergarten classes housed in elementary schools. These contexts affect instructional and social goals, and who teaches, which in turn influence the learning opportunities for students and the availability for training and technical support for teachers.

Across these early childhood contexts, not all teachers have received (or are required to receive) initial teacher preparation, and access to ongoing professional development may be limited for some teachers in early childhood settings. The strongest models of RTI in K–3 (e.g., Fuchs et al., 2008; O'Connor, Fulmer, et al., 2005) have demonstrated the importance of high-quality Tier 1 instruction for decreasing risk and augmenting the effects of validated Tier 2 intervention. Assessments for RTI models in K–3 have been studied and refined over the last 20 years; however, preschool screening measures with validated properties for the catch-and-release aspects of RTI are relatively new. As revealed in this research base, assessments for young children tend to have low reliability, and those spanning ages 3 to 5 tend to be less reliable for younger than for older children. Because reliability is related to the confidence we have in measures to do their job effectively, identifying children who could benefit from Tier 2 intervention and determining when they have grown sufficiently from intervention will be more problematic in preschool settings.

Moreover, useful progress measures must link to the skills children need to learn. Although teachers and researchers have come to some (although incomplete) agreement on academic content that is appropriate for students in kindergarten and first grade, along with defined desirable outcomes, early childhood settings often include a range of ages and expectations for children. These varying expectations may also lead to fewer defined outcomes with convergent professional opinion, which are essential for measuring the effects of an RTI model. Reading and mathematics have component features that enable measurement of distinct levels of outcome; in contrast, the major foci in most preschools are language and social development. Although standardized measures of language and social behavior exist and can be used to evaluate risk, the research base on monitoring progress in these areas represents another essential component of RTI as it is used in K–3 schooling, and is less defined for young children. As in K–3 RTI models, the growing diversity across the United States in culture and language will need to be considered as RTI measurement systems are evaluated in early childhood settings.

In all, developmental differences are large among young children who are considered "average," and these typical differences could make it difficult to differentiate degrees of risk. As early childhood educators keep these developmental differences in mind, clear expectations by age may be difficult to define and may even be deemed undesirable. Without clear definitions of risk across domains of learning central to early childhood education, models of RTI will lack substance. In the meantime, one potential benefit of considering RTI in early childhood is the invitation to notice the needs and progress of young children, which has always been a hallmark of excellent early childhood teaching. The notions of noticing need, providing instructional enhancements, and observing the effects of those enhancements may be universal to providing optimal learning environments.

REFERENCES

Blachman, B.A., Ball, E.W., Black, R.S., & Tangel, D.M. (1994). Kindergarten teachers develop phoneme awareness in low-income, inner-city classrooms. *Reading and Writing: An Interdisciplinary Journal, 6,* 1–18.

Bryant, D.P., Bryant, B.R., Roberts, G., Vaughn, S., Pfannenstiel, K.H., Porterfield, J., & Gersten, R. (2011). Early numeracy intervention program for first-grade students with mathematics difficulties. *Exceptional Children, 78,* 7–23.

Catts, H., Adlof, S., & Weismer, S. (2006). Language deficits in poor comprehenders: A case for the simple view of reading. *Journal of Speech, Language, and Hearing Research, 49,* 278–293.

Catts, H.W., Compton, D., Tomblin, J.B., & Bridges, M.S. (2012). Prevalence and nature of late-emerging poor readers. *Journal of Educational Psychology, 104,* 166–181.

Clarke, B., Baker, S., Smolkowski, K., Fien, H., Doabler, C., Cary, M.S., & Chard, D. (2011). *Testing the efficacy of a kindergarten Tier 2 intervention program.* Paper presented at the fall meeting of the Society for the Research on Educational Effectiveness, Washington, DC.

Compton, D.L, Fuchs, D., Fuchs, L.S., Bouton, B., Gilvert, J.K., Barquero, L.A., . . . Crouch, R.C. (2010). Selecting at-risk first-grade readers for early intervention: Eliminating false positives and exploring the promise of a two-stage gated screening process. *Journal of Educational Psychology, 102,* 327–340.

Coyne, M.D., Kame'enui, E.J., Simmons, D.C., & Harn, B.A. (2004). Beginning reading as inoculation or insulin: First-grade reading performance of strong responders to kindergarten intervention. *Journal of Learning Disabilities, 37,* 90–104.

Fuchs, D., Compton, D.L., Fuchs, L.S., Bryant, J., & Davis, G.N. (2008). Making "secondary intervention" work in a three-tier responsiveness-to-intervention model: Findings from the first-grade longitudinal reading study of the National Research Center on Learning Disabilities. *Reading and Writing, 21,* 413–436.

Fuchs, D., Fuchs, L.D., & Compton, D.L. (2012). Smart RTI, smart special education. *Exceptional Children, 78,* 263–279.

Fuchs, D., Fuchs, L.S., Mathes, P.G., & Simmons, D.C. (1997). Peer-assisted learning strategies: Making classrooms more responsive to diversity. *American Educational Research Journal, 34,* 174–206.

Fuchs, L.S., Compton, D.L., Fuchs, D., Paulsen, K., Bryant, J.D., & Hamlett, C.L. (2005). The prevention, identification, and cognitive determinants of math difficulty. *Journal of Educational Psychology, 97,* 493–513.

Fuchs, L.S., & Fuchs, D. (1998). Treatment validity: A unifying concept for reconceptualizing the identification of learning disabilities. *Learning Disabilities Research & Practice, 13,* 204–219.

Fuchs, L.S., Fuchs, D., Craddock, C., Hollenbeck, K.N., Hamlett, C.L., & Schatschneider, C. (2008). Effects of small-group tutoring with and without validated classroom instruction on at-risk students' math problem solving: Are two tiers of prevention better than one? *Journal of Educational Psychology, 100,* 491–509.

Fuchs, L.S., Geary, D.C., Compton, D.L., Fuchs, D., Schatschneider, C., Hamlett, C.L., . . . Changas, P. (2011). *Understanding and promoting at-risk learners' mathematics development in first grade: A randomized control trial.* Manuscript submitted for publication.

Fuchs, L.S., Powell, S.R., Seethaler, P.M., Cirino, P.T., Fletcher, J.M., Fuchs, D., . . . Zumeta, R.O. (2009). Remediating number combination and word problem deficits among students with mathematics difficulties: A randomized control trial. *Journal of Educational Psychology, 101,* 561–576.

Greenwood, C.R., Delquadri, J., & Hall, R.V. (1989). Longitudinal effects of classwide peer tutoring. *Journal of Educational Psychology, 81,* 371–383.

Hecht, S., Vagi, K.J., & Torgesen, J.K. (2007). Fraction skills and proportional reasoning. In D.B. Berch & M.M.M. Mazzocco (Eds.). *Why is math so hard for some children? The nature and origins of mathematical learning difficulties and disabilities* (pp. 121–132). Baltimore, MD: Paul H. Brookes Publishing Co.

Individuals with Disabilities Education Improvement Act (IDEA) of 2004, PL 108-446, 20 U.S.C. §§ 1400 *et seq.*

Kieffer, M. (2010). Socioeconomic status, English proficiency, and late-emerging reading difficulties. *Educational Researcher, 39,* 484–486.

Linan-Thompson, S., Vaughn, S., Prater, K., & Cirino, P.T. (2006). The response to intervention of English Language Learners at risk for reading problems. *Journal of Learning Disabilities, 39*, 390–398.

Linklater, D., O'Connor, R.E., & Palardy, G.P. (2009). Kindergarten literacy assessment of English only and English language learner students: Which measures are most predictive of reading skills? *Journal of School Psychology, 47*, 369–394.

Lovett, M.W., De Palma, M., Steinbach, K., Temple, M., Benson, N., & Lacerenza, L. (2008). Interventions for reading disabilities: A comparison of response to intervention by ELL and EFL struggling readers. *Journal of Learning Disabilities, 41*, 333–352.

McCutchen, D. & Berninger, V. (1999). Those who know, teach well: Helping teachers master literacy-related subject matter knowledge. *Learning Disabilities Research & Practice, 14*, 215–226.

McMaster, K.L., Fuchs, D., Fuchs, L.S., & Compton, D.L. (2005). Responding to nonresponders: An experimental field trial of identification and intervention methods. *Exceptional Children, 71*, 445–463.

Mehta, P.D., Foorman, B.R., Branum-Martin, L., & Taylor, W.P. (2005). Literacy as a unidimensional multilevel construct: Validation, sources of influence, and implications in a longitudinal study in grades 1–4. *Scientific Studies of Reading, 9*, 85–116.

O'Connor, R.E. (2000). Increasing the intensity of intervention in kindergarten and first grade. *Learning Disabilities Research and Practice, 15*, 43–54.

O'Connor, R.E., Bocian, K.M., Beach, K.D., & Sanchez, T. (in press). Access to a responsiveness to intervention model: Does beginning intervention in kindergarten matter? *Journal of Learning Disabilities*.

O'Connor, R.E., Bocian, K., Beebe-Frankenberger, M., & Linklater, D. (2010). Responsiveness of students with language difficulties to early intervention in reading. *Journal of Special Education, 43*, 220–235.

O'Connor, R.E., Fulmer, D., Harty, K., & Bell, K. (2005). Layers of reading intervention in kindergarten through third grade: Changes in teaching and child outcomes. *Journal of Learning Disabilities, 38*, 440–455.

O'Connor, R.E., Harty, K., & Fulmer, D. (2005). Tiers of intervention in kindergarten through third grade. *Journal of Learning Disabilities, 38*, 532–538.

O'Connor, R.E., White, A., & Swanson, H.L. (2007). Repeated reading versus continuous reading: Influences on reading fluency and comprehension. *Exceptional Children, 74*, 31–46.

Saenz, L., McMaster, K., Fuchs, D., & Fuchs, L.S. (2007). Peer-assisted learning strategies in reading for students with different learning needs. *Journal of Cognitive Education and Psychology, 6*(3), 395–410.

Schwanenflugel, P.J., Meisinger, E.B., Wisenbaker, J.M., Kuhn, M.R., Strauss, G.P., & Morris, R.D. (2006). Becoming a fluent and automatic reader in the early elementary school years. *Reading Research Quarterly, 41*, 496–522.

Simmons, D.C., Coyne, M.D., Kwok, O., McDonagh, S., Harn, B., & Kame'enui, E.J. (2008). Indexing response to intervention: A longitudinal study of reading risk from kindergarten through third grade. *Journal of Learning Disabilities, 41*, 158–173.

Smith, T.B., Cobb, P., Farran, D., Cordray, D., & Munster, C. (2011). *Evaluating Math Recovery: Assessing the causal impact of a diagnostic tutoring program on student achievement*. Manuscript submitted for publication.

Stecker, P.M., Fuchs, L.S., & Fuchs, D. (2005). Using curriculum-based measurement to improve student achievement: A review. *Psychology in the Schools, 42*, 795–819.

Vaughn, S. (2003, December). *How many tiers are needed for response to intervention to achieve acceptable prevention outcomes?* Paper presented at the National Research Center on Learning Disabilities "Responsiveness to Intervention" Symposium, Kansas City, MO.

An Overview of Programwide Positive Behavior Supports

Building a Comprehensive Continuum of Early Social Behavior Support for At-Risk Children

Timothy J. Lewis, Reesha Adamson, Barbara S. Mitchell, and Erica S. Lembke

The task of providing young children with the necessary social, emotional, and academic skills is essential for school and life success and a primary focus of all early childhood educational programs (Hemmeter, Fox, Jack, & Broyles, 2007). Early childhood educators are charged with guiding children's early development, including their social and emotional maturation, to set them up for success within the academic and social structures of the K–12 school system as well as lifelong learning. Through teacher-led instruction, play, peer interactions, parent supports, and naturally occurring learning opportunities, effective early childhood educators design their classrooms and programs to promote the development of socially and emotionally healthy children (Joseph & Strain, 2003; Katz & McClellan, 1997).

Unfortunately, many children served within publicly supported early childhood programs are already developmentally behind their peers due to disability, poor environmental conditions such as impoverished homes with limited access to good nutrition and health care, or exposure to violence and abuse, all placing the child at risk for later school and life challenges. One outcome of risk that poses significant challenges to early childhood educators is working with children who display high rates of problem behavior. Not only is it a challenge within the early childhood setting, but research has clearly documented links between early patterns of problem behavior and later more intense and chronic problem behavior, substance abuse, school dropout, unemployment, incarceration, and mental health issues well into adulthood (Campbell, 1998; Walker, Ramsey, & Gresham, 2004; Webster-Stratton & Reid, 2004). For example, Lavigne and colleagues report that if challenging behavior is not addressed within early childhood settings, 50% or more of young children who display difficulties at the age of 2 or 3 may continue to have problems well into their school years (Lavigne, Arend, Rosenbaum, Binns, Christoffel, & Gibbons, 1998).

The increasing number of children who demonstrate high rates of problem behavior at an early age is clearly a pressing concern. As many as 16% of 1- and 2-year-olds display difficulty with social and emotional competence, and an estimated 25% of 2- and 3-year-olds demonstrate challenging behavior (Briggs-Gowan,

Carter, & Skuban, 2001; Lavigne et al., 1998). It is estimated that between 30% and 40% of children enter kindergarten lacking necessary social and emotional skills that are essential for school success (Stage, 2005).

Although some instances of problem behavior may be developmentally typical during the early childhood years, children who do not develop adequate self-regulation and problem-solving skills are clearly at risk for future negative outcomes such as academic failure and difficulty developing and maintaining appropriate social relationships (Walker et al., 2004; Webster-Stratton & Reid, 2004). Alarmingly, expulsion rates are higher among preschool-age children in some early education programs than they are for students in elementary schools (Gilliam & Shabar, 2006). As a result of increasing numbers of children displaying problem behavior, early childhood educators describe working with students who demonstrate problem behavior as one of the most frustrating aspects of their job, often citing it as their reason for leaving the field (Hemmeter et al., 2007). Not only is the individual child who displays high rates of problem behavior at further risk, but those who engage in externalizing or acting out behavior also have a clear and unhealthy impact on the entire class. Fortunately, the call to better prepare and support early childhood educators to effectively address problem behaviors has been sounded among leaders in the field (e.g., Hemmeter et al., 2007).

Understanding the unique needs and challenges that face educators within early childhood settings is a crucial component of designing early childhood programs that support individual student needs. Supporting high-risk students' behavioral needs requires a system of behavior management that includes instruction for preacademic concepts and focuses on proactive strategies that foster the growth and development of needed skills for school success. Consider the following quote from Walker and colleagues underscoring the importance of early intervention among children at risk for antisocial behavior: "If antisocial behavior is not changed by the end of Grade 3, it should be treated as a chronic condition much like diabetes. That is, it cannot be cured but can be managed with appropriate supports and continuing intervention" (Walker, Colvin, & Ramsey, 1995, p. 6). In other words, there is a clear window of opportunity, starting in early childhood, to make significant impact on high-risk children. If the opportunity is missed, then clear, connected, and well-articulated systems of care will need to be in place for the remainder of the child's life in an attempt to minimize the early learned, and now ongoing, patterns of aberrant behavior.

The purpose of this chapter is to provide an overview of the essential features and the basic logic of schoolwide positive behavior support (SW-PBS) within the context of a response to intervention (RTI) framework, with an eye toward emerging early childhood application. Given the primary focus on addressing social behavior problems, the essential features of SW-PBS, research to date at the elementary and early childhood level, and future work will be discussed. An additional brief section on the importance of linking behavior support with academic and preacademic support through RTI is also included in this chapter.

SCHOOLWIDE / PROGRAMWIDE POSITIVE BEHAVIOR SUPPORT

Schoolwide positive behavior support (SW-PBS) is a problem-solving strategy that school-based teams follow to address challenging behavior noted within their school (Horner & Sugai, 2005; Lewis & Sugai, 1999; Sugai et al., 2000). Following the basic logic of 1) using data to guide all decision making with respect to identifying what student supports are needed as well as monitoring progress; 2) based on data, adopting evidence-based practices that will address the challenge; and 3) providing proactive, skill-based professional development and ongoing technical assistance for all educators within the school to ensure behavior supports are implemented with integrity. An additional hallmark of SW-PBS is building a continuum of supports based on whole school needs (universal supports, Tier 1) and small groups of students who may be at risk or require additional supports beyond universal (Tier 2), as well as supporting individual students who will require intensive supports (Tier 3) (see Figure 4.1). Universal supports consist of clearly identifying prosocial behaviors that serve to "replace" current problem behaviors and creating appropriate instructional and feedback strategies. Tier 2 are supports such as additional social skill instruction or a self-monitoring intervention. Tier 2 supports are not provided for all students (i.e., universals), and are not highly individualized. Tier 3 supports are individualized and intensive, such as conducting a functional behavior assessment that leads to an individualized behavior support plan. Key across each level of support is a clear connection to the larger schoolwide universal system. Further, each level or tier of support should be viewed as additional environmental supports to increase the likelihood of success. In other words, it isn't the case that schools have "Tier 2 and 3" kids; rather, schools carefully track data to see which students are not responding to universal supports—which could be due to risk, early learning patterns, or disability—and then put in place additional environmental supports to increase the likelihood that students experience social and academic success. Another critical feature of SW-PBS is its focus on appropriate social behaviors versus inappropriate behaviors and an instructional approach versus "punishment."

To date, SW-PBS randomized control trial research conducted at the elementary school level has documented significant decreases in overall rates of problem behavior (Bradshaw et al., 2008; Bradshaw, Mitchell, & Leaf, 2010; Horner et al., 2009). In addition, several quasi-experimental studies have also demonstrated a positive impact on the rate of problem behavior and increases in prosocial behavior (Barrett, Bradshaw, & Lewis-Palmer, 2008; Colvin & Fernandez, 2000; Lewis, Powers, Kelk, & Newcomer, 2002; Luiselli, Putnam, Handler, & Feinberg, 2005; Nelson, Martella, & Galand, 1998; Safran & Oswald, 2003; Taylor-Greene & Kartub, 2000).

Given that very few early childhood programs are organized similar to elementary schools, with multiple classrooms within a single building, administrative oversight provided by a principal and in some cases assistant principals, the focus of SW-PBS efforts to date at the preschool level have been referred to as programwide positive behavior support (PW-PBS; Lewis & Beckner, 2006). PW-PBS follows the same logic of using data to guide decision making, adopting evidence-based practices, and focusing on system supports for educators (Muscott, Pomerleau, & Szczesiul, 2009; Stormont, Lewis, & Beckner, 2005). In addition, an instructional focus on desired social behaviors is a key feature. However, there are some differences worth noting. The remainder of this section will provide an overview of additional critical features of the SW-PBS and the PW-PBS process, with implications for early childhood settings.

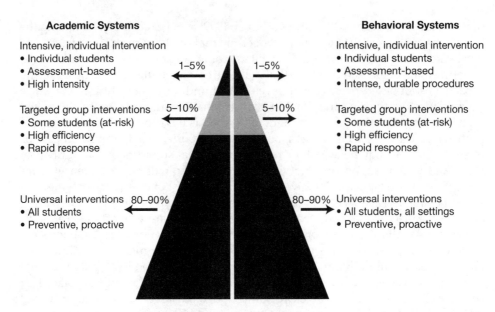

Academic Systems

Intensive, individual intervention
• Individual students
• Assessment-based
• High intensity

1–5%

Targeted group interventions
• Some students (at-risk)
• High efficiency
• Rapid response

5–10%

Universal interventions 80–90%
• All students
• Preventive, proactive

Behavioral Systems

Intensive, individual intervention
• Individual students
• Assessment-based
• Intense, durable procedures

1–5%

Targeted group interventions
• Some students (at-risk)
• High efficiency
• Rapid response

5–10%

80–90% Universal interventions
• All students, all settings
• Preventive, proactive

Figure 4.1. The continuum of schoolwide/programwide positive behavior support and response to intervention academic supports. Percentages indicate approximate numbers of students within a school expected to be successful with the given level of support. (From G. Sugai, Center on Positive Behavioral Interventions & Supports; reprinted by permission.)

School-Based Teams

Within the SW-PBS process, the focus of all professional development and technical assistance is to build expertise within the school-based team. Teams comprise an administrator, classroom teachers, and specialists. The idea is to develop a true multidisciplinary problem-solving team that can work through the SW-PBS process without relying on external behavior experts. In PW-PBS, teams typically comprise educators across classrooms, a program administrator, and any specialist that may be employed by the program. The PW-PBS team will engage in similar steps such as developing a data collection system, clearly defining common expectations across classrooms in response to problem behavior, and sharing instructional strategies to teach social behavior.

Data Decisions

An initial step in the SW-PBS process is to review current data and needs assessments to determine what challenges educators are facing, where most problem behavior is occurring, and what strategies are currently in place and the degree to which are effective. Tools such as the School Assessment Survey or the Benchmarks of Quality (see http://pbis.org) provide a school-wide needs assessment. Preschool versions of the School Assessment Survey, the School-wide Evaluation Tool, and similar programwide surveys have been developed (see Stormont, Lewis, Beckner, & Johnson, 2008; Horner & Sugai, 2005; pbis.org). Reviews of behavioral infractions, commonly referred to as "office discipline referrals" in the K–12 system, use electronic databases to provide the team with the who, where, when, and what of problem behaviors across the days, weeks, months, and school year. Because most early childhood programs do not have a central input point on behavioral infractions, data are typically collected and reviewed at the classroom level. The key is not to create multiple tools and steps for collecting data; rather, the PW-PBS team should identify what questions need answering and what is the simplest strategy to gather data to answer each question. For example, questions such as "What are the most common behavioral challenges teachers are experiencing?" "When do most problems occur?" and "What are the setting conditions that are linked to high rates of problem behavior?" should be posed by the team in an effort to create effective universal behavior supports. Likewise, once supports are put in place, data are continually monitored and reviewed to evaluate the impact of universal supports and identify those students who are not responding to universal supports alone and may be good candidates for Tier 2 or 3 supports.

Instruction and Feedback   Across each tier of support, an instructional focus is emphasized. As stated previously, data are used to determine what problems are commonly noted across the school or early childhood program. For example, high rates of physical and verbal aggression might be a noted concern. In this case, the team would identify a core expectation that will be taught across all classrooms such as "be kind" (typically 1–3 in most early childhood settings; Stormont et al., 2005). Specific examples of being kind, in response to noted problems, would be taught along with variations across settings, such as being kind during playtime means sharing with others, during circle time it means waiting your turn, and so forth. For each identified target behavior (e.g., sharing, taking turns) age-appropriate lessons are developed to provide multiple opportunities for children to practice appropriate behavior, versus being reprimanded for doing the wrong thing. Related to instruction and practice, an additional key step is to provide high rates of positive feedback, based on the expectations, to build student mastery and fluency. For example, when a child is observed sharing a toy the teacher can provide verbal feedback such as "Thank you so much, Rachel, for *sharing* your toy with Emilie. You are being a *kind* learner." Accompanying social behavioral expectations is the process of establishing, through instruction and feedback, clear routines that facilitate movement, transition, and how students get their needs met. In addition to teaching core social skills and routines children need to develop in order to be successful both in preschool and elementary school (e.g., being responsible, safe, cooperative, and respectful), early childhood educators also typically include instruction and feedback around healthy emotional development (e.g., what it means to be happy, sad, or angry) and strategies to manage emotions that may lead to conflict or peer difficulties (e.g., anger).

District, Region, Agency, and State Supports

Central to the success of SW-PBS within the K–12 system has been the careful attention paid to organizing multiple systems of support through leadership activities. School districts are encouraged to also develop an SW-PBS leadership team, similar to individual school buildings, to provide coordination of services and supports (Lewis, Beckner, & Stormont, 2009; Sugai et al., 2000). The leadership team performs several important functions, including securing funding and political support for SW-PBS efforts as well as coordinating training, technical assistance (coaching), and evaluation, while ensuring that sufficient behavioral expertise is available to school-based teams (see Figure 4.2). In addition, regional and state agencies, such as the state department of education, also form leadership teams to provide similar functions directed at supporting district work. Parallel leadership teams within and across early childhood agencies are also advocated (Lewis et al., 2009). For example, a regional Head Start agency can form a leadership team to support clusters of classrooms within the region. Likewise, a state or multistate Head Start leadership team can be formed to support regional clusters. As evidenced by the literature cited within the introduction of this chapter, as well as elsewhere throughout this text, the challenges high-risk preschool children present combined with the limited supports typically available within a single early childhood classroom will necessitate coordinated, comprehensive, and ongoing professional development and technical assistance to create meaningful change for all children.

Emerging Support for Programwide Positive Behavior Support

As noted previously, there is strong empirical and quasi-empirical support at the universal level on the overall impact of SW-PBS on reducing problem behavior and increasing appropriate social behavior. Work at the prekindergarten level is best characterized as emerging. Work to date has shown that critical features in elementary school applications can be adapted to meet the developmental needs and context of students in early childhood settings (e.g., Blair, Fox, & Lentini, 2010; Feil, Walker, Severson, Golly, Seeley, & Small, 2009; Fox & Little, 2001; Muscott et al., 2009), implemented with fidelity and sustained over time, and that the use of PW-PBS strategies is associated with reductions in challenging behavior and increases in student engagement among preschool-age children (Benedict, Horner,

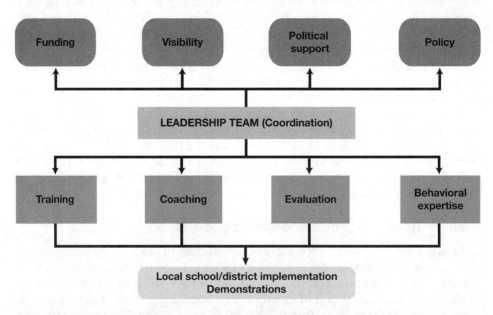

Figure 4.2. Essential functions of district, agency, or state schoolwide/programwide positive behavior support leadership team. (From Lewis, T.J., Adamson, R., Mitchell, B.S., & Lembke, E. [2012]. *Essential functions of district, agency, or state school-wide/program-wide positive behavior support leadership team*. Office of Special Education Programs Center on Positive Behavior Interventions and Supports. Retrieved from http://pbis.org)

& Squires, 2007; Blair, Fox, & Lentini, 2010; Muscott, Mann, & LeBrun, 2008; Muscott et al., 2009; Stormont, Covington-Smith, & Lewis, 2007). However, potential barriers for implementation unique to early childhood settings have also emerged, most of them related to the isolated nature of preschool classrooms (e.g., Fox & Little, 2001; Muscott et al., 2009).

Fox and Little (2001) provided one of the first descriptions of the application of SW-PBS in an early childhood setting. In this descriptive example, universal level schoolwide features were adapted and demonstrated in a private, community preschool serving approximately 50 students ages 1–4. Over a 3-year collaboration period, the school reported high teacher satisfaction, obtained positive parent evaluations, and documented individualized supports for eight students (Fox & Little, 2001). Stormont and colleagues (2007) examined the use of two universal level strategies, precorrection and specific praise statements, across three teachers and classrooms in a Head Start setting. Results indicated that teacher increases in use of these two simple strategies were effective in reducing overall problem behavior of students during a small-group instructional time. A case study by Muscott and colleagues (2009) using PW-PBS in a child care center that included 12 classrooms demonstrated high fidelity of implementation across multiple measures as well as increases in the percentages of children demonstrating appropriate behavior and decreases in the number of incidents of challenging behavior over time. Specifically, during the baseline year, 38% of students received two or more documented behavioral infractions, but by the end of the second year of implementation, only 8% of students had two or more infractions, and no children were suspended or expelled (Muscott et al., 2009). In addition to decreases in problem behavior, the staff also noted increases in appropriate behavior. In a recent study, Blair and colleagues (2010) demonstrated decreases in problem behavior and increases in appropriate behavior using PW-PBS strategies in preschool classrooms. Especially encouraging within the Blair study was the documented generalized use of effective strategies across nontargeted settings by the teaching staff.

At least three studies have also examined stakeholder opinions and perceptions regarding the use of PW-PBS for young children, indicating that participants viewed PW-PBS as important but questioned its overall feasibility given current early childhood program structures (Frey, Faith, Elliott, & Royer, 2006; Frey, Park, Browne-Ferrigno, & Korfhage, 2010; Stormont, Lewis, & Covington-Smith, 2005). Although few studies specifically address the effects of building accompanying system support, such as ongoing professional development and technical assistance to build programwide capacity and programwide evaluation efforts, there has been some research examining the value added by direct technical assistance, or coaching, related to the implementation of PW-PBS features. For example, Carter and Van Norman (2010) utilized a multiple baseline across four classrooms design to examine the effects of consultation on teacher implementation of PW-PBS practices and on student academic engagement. The *Preschool-wide Evaluation Tool* (Pre-SET; Horner & Sugai, 2005) was used to select classrooms that would participate in the intervention. Each of the four classrooms included in the study initially scored below 25%, indicating very few essential features were in place. Outcomes of the consultation intervention were assessed using direct observation of teacher implementation across the nine target skills. Results indicated that overall average implementation across the four classrooms increased by more than 42% (Carter &

Van Norman, 2010). In related work, Covington-Smith and colleagues (2011) demonstrated that through brief training and weekly technical assistance meetings, which included performance feedback on usage rates of targeted strategies, three Head Start teachers were able to dramatically increase overall rates of appropriate student behavior and decrease aggressive behavior.

Although the research base supporting the impact of PW-PBS on problem behavior within early childhood settings is promising, clearly more work is needed. In particular, there is a need for large-scale randomized control trials similar to those that have been conducted at the elementary level. In addition, no research could be found on the impact of Tier 2 PW-PBS strategies, or for that matter the feasibility of Tier 2 supports given the typical single early childhood classroom within a site, for students who require additional supports beyond universals within a continuum of PW-PBS. There are encouraging results from a handful of studies that have examined coaching among teachers who are not currently implementing universal features with fidelity (e.g., teaching with positive feedback), which in essence mirrors the purpose of Tier 2 or "targeted" supports. Likewise, although PBS research examining the impact on problem behavior at the individual level has shown behavior change is possible within the existing early childhood classroom structure, the "value-add" of connecting individual interventions with universal supports to promote maintenance and generalization of outcomes remains to be studied.

CONNECTIONS BETWEEN PROGRAMWIDE POSITIVE BEHAVIOR SUPPORT AND RESPONSE TO INTERVENTION IN EARLY CHILDHOOD SETTINGS

The focus of this chapter to this point has been on building effective PW-PBS systems to promote prosocial behavior and healthy social/emotional development among young children, particularly those at risk. However, an additional key feature of SW-PBS within K–12 education, and a frequent recommendation in the behavior support literature, is to pay equal attention to academic and preacademic skills and to use the same problem-solving logic for both (i.e., data – practices – systems). Simply stated, one of the most effective "behavior management" strategies remains effective academic and preacademic instruction; likewise, effective academic and preacademic instruction will have little impact within poorly managed classrooms. The remainder of this chapter will provide an overview on possible linkages between response to intervention and PW-PBS with an eye toward creating a true continuum of supports.

Given the strong and well-documented relationship that exists between behavior and academics (Hoge & Luce, 1979; McKinney, Mason, Perkerson, & Clifford, 1975) and how each can have positive or negative impacts on the other, RTI provides a parallel framework for school improvement that utilizes evidence-based *academic* practices within a problem-solving system to meet the needs of all students (National Association of State Directors of Special Education, 2005). Although originally documented in the Individuals with Disabilities Education Improvement Act (IDEA) of 2004 (PL 108-446) as an alternate method to identifying students with learning disabilities, essential elements of RTI have been researched and utilized in practice for some time (Burns, Appleton, & Stehouwer, 2005; Jimerson, Burns, &

VanDerHeyden, 2007). Essential elements that parallel SW/PW-PBS include 1) an effective problem-solving process for grade-level and schoolwide teams; 2) schoolwide screening and progress monitoring with accompanying data-decision rules; and 3) an evidence-based core instructional program and tiered interventions, supported by fidelity checks (Deno, 2003; Lembke, Garman, Deno, & Stecker, 2010). These essential elements mirror those in SW/PW-PBS, with slight variations in measures and structure due to the differences inherent in teaching and measuring academic and behavioral variables. Additional and more detailed information on RTI at the preschool level can be found throughout this text.

CONCLUSION

Increasing rates of problem behavior among young children within early childhood settings, coupled with the poor life prognosis of not altering these patterns, necessitates that early childhood educators address the challenge head-on. In addition, ensuring that the focus on building prosocial emotional and behavioral skills remains an essential feature of preschool education requires early childhood educators to become fluent in effective classroom social behavior strategies and supports. Unfortunately, features of current early childhood systems, including minimally supported teachers, isolated classrooms within programs, and overreliance on removing children, all create barriers to implementing best practice. Within this chapter we have provided an overview of the SW- and PW-PBS process and an evaluation of its effectiveness to date. Although certainly not a panacea, SW/PW-PBS does provide a proven problem-solving framework to provide early childhood educators, support personnel, and parents with a proactive, positive, instructional-based logic model that can be tailored to meet local need and capacity. Likewise, RTI is a process containing critical elements that can greatly enhance academic and preacademic instruction for all students by following the same problem-solving, data-driven process while building a continuum of environmental supports to increase the likelihood that children are successful (Lembke et al., 2010; Lembke, McMaster, & Stecker, 2010). As with PW-PBS, research to this point on the implementation of RTI in early childhood settings is providing emerging evidence that RTI elements can be effectively utilized to enhance student learning. As stated throughout this chapter, ongoing research on extending essential features of SW-PBS and RTI is clearly warranted within early childhood settings prior to any drastic program changes or enactment of policy pushing the field in this direction.

REFERENCES

Barrett, S., Bradshaw, C., & Lewis-Palmer, T. (2008). Maryland state-wide PBIS initiative. *Journal of Positive Behavior Interventions, 10*, 105–114.

Benedict, E.A., Horner, R.H., & Squires, J.K. (2007). Assessment and implementation of positive behavior support in preschools. *Topics in Early Childhood Special Education, 27*(3), 174–192.

Blair, K.S., Fox, L., & Lentini, R. (2010). Positive behavior support for young children with developmental and behavioral challenges: An evaluation of generalization. *Topics in Early Childhood Special Education, 30*(2), 68–79.

Bradshaw, C., Koth, C., Bevans, K., Ialongo, N., & Leaf, P. (2008). The impact of school-wide positive behavioral interventions and supports (PBIS) on the organizational health of elementary schools. *School Psychology Quarterly, 23*(4), 462–473.

Bradshaw, C.P., Mitchell, M.M., & Leaf, P.J. (2010). Examining the effects of school-wide positive behavior supports on student outcomes. *Journal of Positive Behavior Interventions, 12*(3), 133–148.

Briggs-Gowan, M.J., Carter, A.S., & Skuban, E.M. (2001). Prevalence of social-emotional and behavioral problems in a community sample of 1- and 2-year-old children. *Journal of American Academy of Child and Adolescent Psychiatry, 40*, 811–819.

Burns, M.K., Appleton, J.A., and Stehouwer, J.D. (2005). Meta-analytic review of responsiveness-to-intervention research: Examining field-based and research-implemented models. *Journal of Psychoeducational Assessment, 23*, 381–394.

Campbell, S.B. (1998). Developmental perspectives. In T.H. Ollendick & M. Hersen (Eds.), *Handbook of child psychopathology* (3rd ed., pp. 3–35). New York, NY: Plenum Press.

Carter, D.R. & Van Norman, R.K. (2010). Class-wide positive behavior support in preschool: Improving teacher implementation through consultation. *Early Childhood Education Journal, 38*, 270–288

Colvin, G., & Fernandez, E. (2000). Sustaining effective behavior support systems in an elementary school. *Journal of Positive Behavior Interventions 2*(4), 251–253.

Covington-Smith, S., Lewis, T.J., & Stormont, M. (2011). The effectiveness of two universal behavioral supports for children with externalizing behavior in Head Start classrooms. *Journal of Positive Behavior Interventions, 13*, 133–143.

Deno, S.L. (2003). Developments in curriculum-based measurement. *The Journal of Special Education, 37*(3), 184–192.

Feil, E.G., Walker, H.M., Severson, H., Golly, A., Seeley, J.R., & Small, J.W. (2009). Using positive behavior support procedures in Head Start classrooms to improve school readiness: A group training and behavioral coaching model. *National Head Start Association Dialog, 12*(2), 88–103.

Fox, L. & Little, N. (2001). Starting early: Developing school-wide behavior support in a community preschool. *Journal of Positive Behavior Interventions, 3*(4), 251–254.

Frey, A.J., Faith, T., Elliott, A., & Royer, B. (2006). A pilot study examining the social validity and effectiveness of a positive behavior support model in Head Start. *School Social Work Journal, 30*(2), 22–44.

Frey, A.J., Park, K.L., Browne-Ferrigno, T., & Korfhage, T.L. (2010). The social validity of program-wide positive behavior support. *Journal of Positive Behavior Interventions, 12*(4), 222–235.

Gilliam, W., & Shabar, G. (2006). Preschool and child care expulsion and suspension rates and predictors in one state. *Infants and Young Children, 19*, 228–245.

Hemmeter, M.L., Fox, L., Jack, S., & Broyles, L. (2007). A program-wide model of positive behavior support in early childhood settings. *Journal of Early Intervention, 29*(4), 337–355.

Hoge, R.D. & Luce, S. (1979). Predicting academic achievement from classroom behavior. *Review of Educational Research, 49*, 479–496.

Horner, R.H., & Sugai, G. (2005). School-wide positive behavior support: An alternative approach to discipline in schools. (pp. 359–390). In L. Bambara & L. Kern (Eds.) *Positive behavior support*. New York, NY: Guilford Press.

Horner, R., Sugai, G., Smolkowski, K., Todd, A., Nakasato, J., & Esperanza, J. (2009). A randomized control trial of school-wide positive behavior support in elementary schools. *Journal of Positive Behavior Interventions, 11*(3), 133–144.

Individuals with Disabilities Education Improvement Act (IDEA) of 2004, PL 108-446, 20 U.S.C. §§ 1400 *et seq.*

Jimerson, S., Burns, M., & VanDerHeyden, A.M. (Eds.). (2007). *Handbook of response to intervention: The science and practice of assessment and intervention* (pp. 3–9). New York, NY: Springer.

Joseph, G.E., & Strain, P.S. (2003). Comprehensive evidence-based social-emotional curricula for young children: An analysis of efficacious adoption potential. *Topics in Early Childhood Special Education, 23*(2), 65–76.

Katz, L.G., & McClellan, D.E. (1997). *Fostering children's social competence: The teacher's role.* Washington, DC: National Association for the Education of Young Children.

Lavigne, J.V., Arend, R., Rosenbaum, D., Binns, H.J., Christoffel, K.K., & Gibbons, R.D. (1998). Psychiatric disorders with onset in the preschool years: Stability and diagnosis. *Journal of American Academy of Child and Adolescent Psychiatry, 37*, 1246–1254.

Lembke, E., Garman, C., Deno, S.L., & Stecker, P.M. (2010). One elementary school's implementation of response to intervention (RTI). *Reading and Writing Quarterly, 26*, 361–373.

Lembke, E.S., McMaster, K.L., & Stecker, P.M. (2010). The prevention science of reading research within a response-to-intervention model. *Psychology in the School, 47*(1), 22–35.

Lewis, T.J., & Beckner, R. (2006, October). *Developing "program-wide" systems of PBS at the preschool level.* Invited presentation at the Third Annual School-wide PBS Implementation Forum, Chicago, IL.

Lewis, T.J., Beckner, R., & Stormont, M. (2009). Program-wide positive behavior supports: Essential features and implications for Head Start. *National Head Start Association Dialog, 12*(2), 75–84.

Lewis, T.J., Powers, L.J., Kelk, M.J., & Newcomer, L. (2002). Reducing problem behaviors on the playground: An investigation of the application of school-wide positive behavior supports. *Psychology in the Schools, 39*, 181–190.

Lewis, T.J. & Sugai, G. (1999). Effective behavior support: A systems approach to proactive school-wide management. *Focus on Exceptional Children, 31*(6), 1–24.

Luiselli, J.K, Putnam, R.F, Handler, M.W, & Feinberg, A.B. (2005). Whole-school positive behavior support: Effects on student discipline problems and academic performance. *Educational Psychology 25*(2–3), 183–198.

McKinney, J.D., Mason, J., Perkerson, K., & Clifford, M. (1975). Relationship between classroom behavior and academic achievement. *Journal of Educational Psychology, 67*, 198–203.

Muscott, H.S., Mann, E.L., & LeBrun, M.R. (2008). Positive behavioral interventions and supports in New Hampshire: Effects of large-scale implementation of school-wide positive behavior support on student discipline and academic achievement. *Journal of Positive Behavior Interventions, 10*(3), 190–205.

Muscott, H.S., Pomerleau, T., & Szczesiul, S. (2009). Large-scale implementation of program-wide positive behavioral interventions and supports in early childhood programs in New Hampshire. *National Head Start Association Dialog, 12*(2), 148–169.

National Association of State Directors of Special Education. (2005). *No Child Left Behind Act of 2001.* Washington, DC: Author.

Nelson, J.R., Martella, R., & Galand, B. (1998). The effects of teaching school expectations and establishing a consistent consequence on formal office disciplinary actions. *Journal of Emotional and Behavioral Disorders, 6*, 153–161.

Safran, S.P., & Oswald, K. (2003). Positive behavior supports: Can schools reshape disciplinary practices? *Exceptional Children, 69*, 361–373

Stage, E.K. (2005, Winter). Why do we need these assessments? *Natural Selection: Journal of the BSCS,* 11–13.

Stormont, M.A., Covington-Smith, S., & Lewis, T.J. (2007). Teacher implementation of precorrection and praise statements in Head Start classrooms as a component of a program-wide system of positive behavior support. *Journal of Behavior Education, 16*, 280–290.

Stormont, M., Lewis, T.J., & Beckner, R. (2005). Positive behavior support systems: Applying key features in preschool settings. *Teaching Exceptional Children, 37*(6), 42–49.

Stormont, M., Lewis, T.J., Beckner, R., & Johnson, N.W. (2008). *Implementing positive behavior support systems in early childhood and elementary settings.* Thousand Oaks, CA: Corwin Press.

Stormont, M., Lewis, T.J., & Covington-Smith, S. (2005). Behavior support strategies in early childhood settings: Teacher's importance and feasibility ratings. *Journal of Positive Behavior Interventions, 7*(3), 131–139.

Sugai, G., Horner, R.H., Algozzine, R., Barrett, S., Lewis, T., Anderson, C., . . . Simonsen, B. (2010). *School-wide positive behavior support: Implementers' blueprint and self-assessment.* Eugene, OR: University of Oregon.

Sugai, G., Horner, R.H., Dunlap, G. Hieneman, M., Lewis, T.J., Nelson, C.M., . . . Wilcox, B. (2000). Applying positive behavioral support and functional behavioral assessment in schools. *Journal of Positive Behavioral Interventions, 2*, 131–143.

Taylor-Greene, S.J. & Kartub, D.T. (2000). Durable implementation of school-wide behavior support: The High Five Program. *Journal of Positive Behavioral Interventions, 2*(4), 231–232.

U.S. Department of Education. (2004). *Twenty-fourth annual report to Congress on the implementation of the Individuals with Disabilities Education Act.* Washington, DC: Author.

Walker, H.M., Colvin, G., & Ramsey, E. (1995). *Antisocial behavior in school: Strategies and best practices*. Pacific Grove, CA: Brooks/Cole.

Walker, H.M., Ramsey, E., & Gresham, F.M. (2004). *Antisocial behavior in school: Evidence-based practices* (2nd ed.). Belmont, CA: Thomson/Wadsworth Learning.

Webster-Stratton, C., & Reid, J.M. (2004). Strengthening social and emotional competence in young children—The foundation for early school readiness and success: Incredible Years classroom social skills and problem-solving curriculum. *Infants and Young Children, 17,* 96–113.

5

Recognition & Response

A Model of Response to Intervention to Promote
Academic Learning in Early Education

Virginia Buysse, Ellen S. Peisner-Feinberg, Elena Soukakou,
Doré R. LaForett, Angel Fettig, and Jennifer M. Schaaf

Early educators face important questions every day about the best way to
respond to children with diverse learning needs enrolled in early care and
education programs. They must decide which children need additional supports to learn and what teaching strategies work best to help these children acquire
key readiness skills such as oral language, phonological awareness, print knowledge, and number concepts. Educators also must determine the nature and intensity of instruction—for example, whether it is better to work with these children
individually or in small groups, how often this instruction should occur, and what
information and curricular resources should be used as the basis of these instructional accommodations. Addressing the instructional needs of every learner is a
widely held value in the early childhood field, but early educators generally lack
guidance about the most effective way to respond to children who enter early
childhood programs with varying abilities and opportunities to learn.

Trends in early education such as greater access to public prekindergarten
(pre-K) and the increased emphasis on school readiness and early intervention
have focused national attention on the need to improve the quality of early education practices for an increasingly diverse population of young learners (Peisner-
Feinberg, Buysse, Benshoff, & Soukakou, 2011; Wesley & Buysse, 2010). As a part of a
high-quality program, early childhood teachers ideally are expected to implement
foundational instruction intended to meet the educational needs of all children
while also making adjustments for some children who need additional instructional supports—for example, those with disabilities or learning or behavioral difficulties, and those from diverse cultural and linguistic backgrounds (Buysse &
Wesley, 2010). School readiness skills addressing social-emotional development
and academic learning in language, literacy, and mathematics are widely reflected
in early learning and program standards at both the state and national levels and
serve as broad learning benchmarks for every child.

An intensified focus on supporting diverse learners has helped advance
an innovation known generically as tiered instruction, and more specifically as
response to intervention (RTI)—a set of related practices in which early educators
routinely gather information on children's progress in achieving school readiness

skills and use this information to make instructional adjustments to ensure that every child can succeed. There is now a strong body of evidence on the effectiveness of using RTI to improve reading and math skills with school-age children and emerging evidence for its effectiveness to improve language and literacy skills with pre-K children (Buysse, Peisner-Feinberg, & Burchinal, 2012; Gersten et al., 2009; Gersten et al., 2008). However, the field is at an early stage in understanding exactly how this approach will work in early childhood programs and determining whether these instructional accommodations can actually improve instruction and benefit the children who receive them.

In this chapter we present Recognition & Response (R&R), a model of response to intervention (RTI) specifically designed for use with pre-K children and focused on their academic learning. Developed by researchers at the Frank Porter Graham Child Development Institute at the University of North Carolina at Chapel Hill, R&R was designed to help early educators use children's formative assessment results to plan and evaluate specific instructional strategies addressing children's school readiness skills. We begin with an overview of the entire R&R system and then focus more specifically on the response (instructional) component (see Chapter 8 for more information about the recognition [assessment] component of R&R). Next, we describe several issues related to implementation of R&R in early childhood center-based programs. We end with a summary of the research underway to evaluate the R&R model and identify future directions in this regard.

RECOGNITION & RESPONSE: A FRAMEWORK FOR LINKING ASSESSMENT AND INSTRUCTION

Although additional research is needed to guide its use and determine its efficacy, R&R has generated widespread attention in the early childhood field as a promising RTI model for pre-K (see entire issue of NHSA Dialog; Smith, 2009; the CONNECT Module 7 on tiered approaches [Buysse, Epstein, Winton, & Rous, 2012]; and the U.S. Health and Human Services, Administration for Children and Families, web site at http://www.acf.hhs.gov/programs/ohs/). Greenwood et al. (2011) described two available models of RTI for pre-K: R&R, which is focused on academic learning (Buysse & Peisner-Feinberg, 2010; Peisner-Feinberg et al., 2011), and the Pyramid Model, which is focused on children's social-emotional development (Fox, Carta, Strain, Dunlap, & Hemmeter, 2010).

R&R is a model of RTI designed for 3- to 5-year-old children enrolled in center-based early childhood programs, including Head Start, child care, preschool, and public pre-K (Buysse & Peisner-Feinberg, 2010; Peisner-Feinberg et al., 2011). R&R has a dual focus: improving the quality of instructional practices for all children as well as providing additional supports for some children to ensure that every child succeeds in school. Consistent with the broader RTI literature addressing students in K–12, R&R essentially involves gathering information on children's skills to help teachers plan and organize instruction, providing research-based interventions and supports, and monitoring progress in learning.

Figure 5.1 shows the conceptual framework for R&R. R&R is a tiered model of instruction, meaning that instructional strategies are arranged from most to least intensive to show the level of adult involvement that corresponds to children's needs for instructional supports. In accordance with the broader RTI literature,

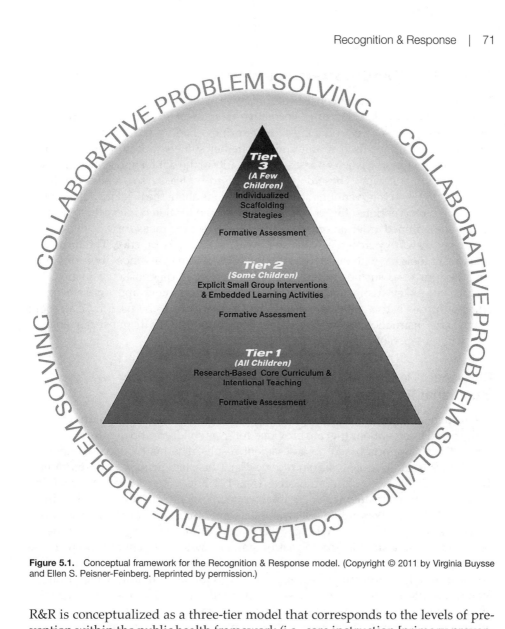

Figure 5.1. Conceptual framework for the Recognition & Response model. (Copyright © 2011 by Virginia Buysse and Ellen S. Peisner-Feinberg. Reprinted by permission.)

R&R is conceptualized as a three-tier model that corresponds to the levels of prevention within the public health framework (i.e., core instruction [primary prevention], strategic interventions [secondary prevention], and intensive interventions [tertiary prevention]; see Chapters 2 and 3). The R&R components also correspond closely to those on which RTI is based: 1) systematic assessment of students' performance on academic skills, 2) scientifically based core programs and interventions, and 3) criteria for instructional decision making. The specific components of R&R are 1) recognition, which involves gathering formative assessment information by screening all of the children and monitoring their progress; and 2) response, which includes providing an effective core curriculum, intentional teaching, and tiered interventions linked to formative assessment results. As part of both the recognition and response components, a process called collaborative problem solving is used to support data-based decision making, plan interventions within different tiers, and assess how well children respond to these interventions.

Recognition: Formative Assessment

The recognition component consists of formative assessment of key academic areas that are predictive of later learning. Formative assessment is conducted by classroom teachers three times a year on a fall-winter-spring schedule. Classwide assessment results in the fall are used to determine whether some children need additional instructional supports, whereas assessment results in the winter and spring are used for progress monitoring. These data also are used by teachers to assess children's responses to tiered interventions and make decisions about the need for adjustments to planned interventions. Target children are selected for tiered interventions based on a predetermined criterion or cut point on the screening measure (e.g., those scoring below the 25th percentile), consistent with typical RTI practice. The formative assessment tools have unique properties that differ from assessment tools designed for other purposes such as developmental screening or diagnostic evaluation (see Chapter 8). A key distinction between formative assessment and assessment for other purposes is that formative assessment is designed to be used by classroom teachers for instructional planning, rather than primarily for diagnostic evaluation and determination of eligibility for special education.

Response: Research-Based Core Curriculum, Intentional Teaching, and Targeted Interventions

The response component refers to the core instruction offered to *all* children as well as the tiered interventions that are provided for *some* children who require additional instructional supports based on assessment results. The instructional component across tiers is additive: *all* children receive Tier 1 instruction; *some* children receive Tiers 1 and 2; and a *few* children receive Tiers 1, 2, and 3. Tier 1 involves providing an effective core curriculum, along with intentional teaching of key school readiness skills. In Tier 2, teachers enhance learning for some children through explicit, small-group instruction (i.e., 15 minutes per day over 8–10 weeks) using a research-based curriculum similar to a lesson format or standardized treatment approach. These small-group lessons are augmented by embedded learning activities that extend opportunities for developing these skills through tailored environmental arrangements, additional learning activities, and curricular modifications. Tier 3 consists of more intensive, research-based scaffolding strategies (e.g., response prompting, modeling, peer support) for a few children who require additional supports to learn. In keeping with the additive nature of tiered instruction, Tier 3 supports are provided in the context of both Tier 1 instruction and Tier 2 interventions (small-group lessons and embedded learning activities), which these children continue to receive.

CLOSER LOOK AT THE RESPONSE COMPONENT

In this section we take a closer look at the response component of R&R. For each of the three tiers we describe how the response component is designed to be implemented in an early childhood classroom.

Tier 1: Core Curriculum and Intentional Teaching

An effective core curriculum and intentional teaching are the foundation of instructional practices within R&R. An effective core curriculum is one that has been evaluated through research (or based on a broader body of research), is developmentally appropriate, and covers all domains of learning, including academic learning and social-emotional development. Information about research findings for specific curricula in early childhood education can be obtained through the What Works Clearinghouse (U.S. Department of Education, 2007) and reports on research findings (e.g., Preschool Curriculum Evaluation Research Consortium, 2008). Intentional teaching means purposefully organizing the early learning environment and providing developmentally appropriate activities as part of a comprehensive curriculum to help children learn and develop key skills. It is critical that all children have ample opportunities to learn new skills throughout the curriculum and daily classroom activities and routines before teachers provide targeted interventions for some children. A key tenet of R&R and RTI is that an effective core curriculum along with intentional teaching should enable most children to make adequate progress in learning at Tier 1; however, it is important to note that both the composition of the classroom and nature of the early childhood program (e.g., a program in which the majority of children have disabilities) would affect the proportions of children who make adequate progress on the basis of foundational instruction and those who require tiered interventions to learn.

An early childhood program implementing R&R generally would continue using the core curriculum (e.g., *Creative Curriculum, HighScope, Opening the World of Learning [OWL]*) already in place in the district or program to serve as the foundation for the other components of the model. In our experience working with local programs across the country, adjustments to foundational instruction at Tier 1 often are needed prior to implementing R&R. For example, if a district or program prescribes a core curriculum but discovers that some of the teachers are not implementing it accurately or comprehensively, then the issue of how the curriculum is being implemented should be addressed prior to adding other components of tiered instruction such as formative assessment, tiered interventions, and collaborative problem solving. It may be necessary to make other adjustments to the early learning environment (e.g., materials, equipment, room arrangement), such as ensuring that interest centers provide sufficient and varied opportunities for children to interact with numbers and print, use writing materials, and develop oral language. Whole-group (e.g., circle time, music and movement activities, group read-alouds) and small-group activities (e.g., a writing activity designed for small groups of children, the addition of print materials to the dramatic play corner) and classroom routines (e.g., arrival, departure, transitions) represent additional contexts for teaching and learning key readiness skills that may require adjustments as part of the foundation for R&R and other tiered approaches. At Tier 1, it is critical that teachers offer many opportunities throughout the day for *all* children to participate in learning activities that are intentionally planned and linked to curriculum goals, as well as monitor, facilitate, and encourage *individual* children as needed to ensure active, full participation in these activities.

In addition to implementing an effective core curriculum and providing a high-quality learning environment, teachers should employ additional research-based practices such as dialogic reading. Because of its efficacy for improving oral language development for a broad group of children, dialogic reading should be implemented as a foundational early childhood practice and also considered an essential component of Tier 1 in conjunction with R&R. We have reviewed a number of commercially available early childhood core curricula and found that many provide some, but not all, of the components of a dialogic reading approach as defined by the What Works Clearinghouse. Consequently, it may be necessary to add dialogic reading as foundational practice for all children at Tier 1.

Dialogic reading is designed to guide adults in using the most effective methods for reading storybooks to young children to ensure that that these experiences are both enjoyable and beneficial for children (see U.S. Department of Education, 2007, for a research synthesis on dialogic reading). Dialogic reading is a specific type of interactive storybook reading that relies on 1) specific prompts (**C**ompletion, **R**ecall, **O**pen-ended, **W**h- questions, and **D**istancing) and 2) a standardized sequence for delivering these prompts (**P**rompt, **E**valuate, **E**xpand, **R**epeat). It was designed to create a conversation with children and help them take an increasingly active role in storytelling over repeated exposures to the book. Research on dialogic reading was reviewed and summarized by the What Works Clearinghouse. The approach was found to have positive effects on children's oral language development and vocabulary skills, but no discernible effects on their phonological processing skills (U.S. Department of Education, 2007). A web-based module on dialogic reading drawing on information from the What Works Clearinghouse and Doing What Works (focused on translating research findings from the What Works Clearinghouse) is available for use within professional development (Buysse, Winton, Rous, Epstein, & Cavanaugh, 2011).

Although most young children are expected to make adequate progress with foundational instruction at Tier 1, others will need instructional accommodations to ensure that they are able to make progress in developing oral language and other academic skills prior to kindergarten. R&R specifies how these instructional supports are designed to work at Tiers 2 and 3.

Tier 2: Small-Group Lessons and Embedded Learning Activities

Two recent efforts aimed at summarizing the research knowledge on academic learning in pre-K are useful in identifying both foundational content and differentiated instructional practices that are relevant to designing tiered interventions. The National Early Literacy Panel identified the following as the strongest and most consistent predictors of later literacy achievement: alphabet knowledge, phonological awareness and memory, rapid automatic naming of letters and objects, and writing letters (NELP, 2008). In a report published by the National Research Council (NRC; Cross, Woods, & Schweingruber, 2009), the Committee on Early Childhood Mathematics identified two areas of mathematics on which to focus with pre-K children: 1) number, including whole numbers, operations, and relations; and 2) geometry, spatial thinking, and measurement. The committee recommended that a greater proportion of time be devoted to number and operations than to the other topics. In addition to defining key content areas for academic learning, both reports emphasized the need to employ a variety of effective instructional methods at different levels of intensity to address children's diverse learning needs, including small-group instruction and individualized scaffolding—both of which are consistent with key principles of RTI and R&R.

At Tier 2, the secondary level of prevention within R&R, teachers provide additional instructional supports for some children who need them as determined through the universal screening. The instructional supports provided at Tier 2 consist of two approaches: 1) daily small-group lessons and 2) embedded learning activities that take place outside these lessons.

Small-Group Lessons With respect to the first of these approaches, teachers implement small-group lessons with three to six children who have similar learning goals (e.g., learning letter names, developing vocabulary, recognizing letter sounds) using a research-based curriculum designed to complement (not repeat) the core curriculum used at Tier 1. The goal of the small-group lessons at Tier 2 is to provide additional opportunities for children who are struggling to learn core concepts and skills introduced at Tier 1 by providing explicit, teacher-directed small-group lessons that reinforce these same skills using targeted teaching activities in a more optimal learning context (i.e., providing learners with more individualized attention and support). To ensure that early childhood teachers implement R&R consistently within a particular program or district, it is necessary to specify the parameters of Tier 2 small-group lessons in terms of the intervention frequency, duration, and intensity, as well as to specify the procedures for how the lessons will be implemented within a small-group format. Separate sets of lessons should be specified for the fall and spring intervention periods, each covering approximately two months. In our research and work with local programs, the approach that has worked most effectively involves adopting a research-based supplemental curriculum that complements the core curriculum as the basis of the Tier 2 small-group lessons. The approach of adopting a domain-specific curriculum for use at Tier 2 is advisable largely because these curricula are widely available, are clearly specified with respect to implementation procedures, and are easily adapted for use within small groups at Tier 2 (e.g., contain a sufficient number of lessons that can be delivered in 15–20 minutes). Further, a number of these curricula have been evaluated through research and were found to be effective for pre-K children, or are based on research findings on early childhood curricula more broadly. The Tier 2 curriculum should consist of sequenced, structured lessons that target specific skills in key academic areas such as language, literacy, and math that are most predictive of later learning and academic achievement (NELP, 2008; NRC, 2009). The small-group lessons take place for approximately 15 minutes a day over 8–10 weeks while the rest of the class is engaged in other activities such as participating in interest centers under the supervision of a teaching assistant or another adult.

As an example, if a school district or program was already using *OWL* as their core curriculum in pre-K classrooms, then they would continue using the *OWL* curriculum and other foundational practices such as dialogic reading at Tier 1, but add a different curriculum (e.g., *Imagine It!*) at Tier 2 for use in supplemental instruction for groups of three to six target children. The supplemental curriculum selected for the Tier 2 small-group lessons should offer a clearly defined scope and sequence of skills that is highly similar to the core curriculum, addressing areas such as oral language, phonological awareness, print awareness, and alphabet knowledge, and employing code-focused and book reading activities that are appropriate and engaging for young learners. To ensure that small-group lessons last no longer than 15–20 minutes, it is necessary to make adaptations by selecting only the most relevant parts of the lessons (those that directly reinforce key content skills) for use at Tier 2. Most important, the supplemental curriculum selected for use at Tier 2 in this example should complement *OWL*'s strong emphasis on these same language and literacy skills. We do *not* recommend employing a tutorial approach that consists of reteaching lessons or parts of lessons to small groups of children using the same core curriculum that constitutes foundational instruction at Tier 1, as this would not be a developmentally appropriate practice in pre-K.

It is important to distinguish the use of small-group instruction at Tiers 1 and 2, as we have observed this to be a growing source of confusion in the early childhood field. Most early educators and early childhood administrators are familiar with the concept of organizing instruction within small groups, but with the advent of RTI, traditional notions of small groups in early childhood classrooms as a way of promoting child-initiated learning have evolved and sometimes become enmeshed with newer concepts related to tiered interventions for children who require additional, explicit instructional supports. For example, some early childhood programs have replaced center time, an important foundational practice that provides children with the opportunity to make choices about the activities in which they participate, with "small-group time" in which children rotate through small groups involving explicit, teacher-directed instruction on academic skills, often relying on teacher-generated activities that do not follow a particular scope and sequence as part of a structured curriculum.

Within R&R, we distinguish the use of small groups at Tiers 1 and 2 along three dimensions: the way in which small groups are formed, the context and focus of instruction, and the teacher's role. At Tier 1, small groups take the form of flexible, child-initiated activities in interest centers (e.g., children choose activities in the book corner, the art center, dramatic play, or block area and are free to make a transition to a new center or activity as they desire) that are carefully planned to address broad curriculum goals across many domains to meet the learning needs of all children. In addition to organizing these activities within the early learning environment, the teacher's role is to observe and monitor children's participation in these learning activities, and to encourage and facilitate learning among individual children or small groups as needed. By contrast, the target children who participate in small-group instruction at Tier 2 are selected on the basis of individually administered formative assessment results, instruction focuses on specific skills within key content areas (e.g. language, literacy, mathematics), and the teacher's role is to teach academic skills explicitly using a structured lesson format that is developmentally appropriate. Table 5.1 summarizes these key distinctions in small groups at Tiers 1 and 2.

Embedded Learning Activities The second approach, which is specified within the R&R model at Tier 2, consists of embedded learning activities that are designed to complement and extend small-group instruction. Embedded learning activities offer children additional opportunities to practice, generalize, and maintain targeted skills that they acquire within the small-group lessons. Teachers intentionally plan and create embedded learning activities that are tailored to children's individual learning needs as part of the collaborative problem-solving process, rather than relying on a standardized set of activities. Teachers then embed these activities within various teaching and learning contexts such as whole-group activities, child-initiated activities, center time, and daily classroom routines (e.g., meal time, transitions). Although embedded learning activities are available and appropriate for all children in the classroom to use, teachers plan them specifically

Table 5.1. Differences between the use of small groups at Tiers 1 and 2 within Recognition & Response

	Tier 1	Tier 2
Way groups are formed	Child choice primarily determines how groups are formed. Small groups vary by size and composition with respect to children's interests and ability levels.	Selection of target children is informed by formative assessment and determined through collaborative problem solving. Small groups consist of a limited number of children (three to six) who have similar learning goals.
Context and focus of instruction	Various activities are planned by the teacher to address certain thematic concepts and/or broad curriculum goals that are designed to meet the needs of all children. Instruction is implemented primarily as child-initiated activities in interest centers such as the book center, the art area, a writing table, dramatic play, blocks and puzzles, and the science center.	Focus is on a set of specific skills within a certain content area (language, literacy, or math). Instruction consists of 15- to 20-minute daily lessons that are structured and sequenced and include developmentally appropriate activities and materials for prekindergarten children.
Teacher's role	Observe and monitor all children's participation in various learning activities; encourage and facilitate participation and learning as needed.	Explicitly teach lessons to target children using research-based curricula or instructional strategies. Systematically monitor progress of target children through formative assessment and make instructional adjustments as needed.

for children who receive the Tier 2 small-group lessons. The process we recommend teachers use in implementing embedded learning activities in early childhood classrooms consists of the following steps: 1) identify the specific skills within a particular domain being targeted as the content of the embedded learning activity (e.g., oral language, number concepts, rhyming, alliteration, alphabet knowledge); 2) determine the specific teaching and learning context (e.g., learning environment, whole group, child-initiated and interest centers, classroom routines); 3) select embedded activities to support the targeted skill areas (e.g., incorporating books that emphasize specific letter sounds, making alphabet games available during center time that include the letters introduced in a small-group lesson, adding a flannel board with story props for a book introduced during a small-group lesson); and 4) define the teacher's role in terms of monitoring, encouraging, or facilitating children's active engagement in these activities. In our work, we have provided teachers with planning forms to keep track of activities they plan to implement and to document children's exposure to these activities.

Tier 3: Individualized Scaffolding Strategies

At Tier 3 within R&R, teachers provide individualized scaffolding for a few children who require intensive supports as indicated by progress monitoring conducted at Tier 2. Scaffolding strategies are structured, targeted approaches that early educators can use with children who require more intensive supports across a wide range of teaching and learning contexts, and in combination with other approaches (e.g., as part of assistive technology or embedded interventions; Buysse, 2011). As mentioned earlier, children who receive Tier 3 individualized scaffolding also continue to receive both Tier 2 interventions (i.e., small-group instruction and embedded learning) and the foundational instruction that all children receive at Tier 1. The research literature is replete with information on the effectiveness of different types of scaffolding strategies and various combinations and hybrid approaches for use with young children with developmental delays (e.g., Chiara, Schuster, Bell, & Wolery, 1995; Craig-Unkefer & Kaiser, 2002; Gibson & Schuster, 1992; Girolametto, Weitzman, & Greenberg, 2004; Hancock & Kaiser, 2006; Hawkings & Schuster, 2007; Kaiser, Hester, & McDuffie, 2001; Kouri, 2005; Ostrosky & Kaiser, 1995; Ross & Greer, 2003; Walker, 2008; Wolery, 2000). However, the use of scaffolding strategies within tiered models of instruction in the context of general early education is relatively new. All of these individual scaffolding strategies have been organized under several broad categories to create a more practical framework for applying these approaches within R&R. These categories include modeling, response prompting, peer supports, and corrective feedback. Table 5.2 describes the primary scaffolding strategies used at Tier 3 within R&R. Table 5.3 describes additional behavioral supports that teachers can use in conjunction with the primary scaffolding strategies for children who exhibit problems with behavior regulation.

The process we recommend teachers use in implementing Tier 3 scaffolding strategies consists of the following steps: 1) use formative assessment results to

Table 5.2. Tier 3 individualized scaffolding strategies

Type of scaffolding	Definition	Example
Modeling	An instructional strategy in which a teacher demonstrates specific responses	During a rhyming matching game with a child, the teacher demonstrates finding two picture cards that show rhyming words for the child.
Response prompting	An instructional strategy in which a teacher uses verbal and nonverbal cues to elicit a response from a child	While retelling a story following a shared reading activity, the teacher intentionally sequences the story events incorrectly and asks, "Is that what happened in the story?" When the child does not respond to the incorrect sequence, she points to the picture in the book depicting the first event and asks the question again.
Variations of modeling and prompting	Variations include increasing or decreasing the level of assistance, adding wait time, and combining strategies	During an alphabet game, the teacher asks a child to identify the first letter on his or her name card. When the child gives an incorrect response, the teacher increases her assistance by modeling the sound of the letter. When the child still does not respond, she models the letter sound while pointing to the correct letter in an alphabet chart and then asks the child again to find the letter on the name card.
Peer supports	An instructional strategy in which peers support another child in learning	When prompted by the teacher, a peer demonstrates the use of a vocabulary word for another child.
Corrective feedback	Instructional strategies that reinforce correct responses and address incorrect responses and nonresponses	For a request to point to a picture showing a dog, a child responds incorrectly or does not respond. The teacher then points to the right picture and says, "Here is the dog."

Table 5.3. Tier 3 behavioral supports

Supplemental supports for Tier 2 small-group lessons	Example
Space/positioning arrangements	During the small-group activity, the teacher strategically positions a child who needs additional supports next to a peer who will help with some of the small group's activities.
Use of visual supports	At the beginning of a lesson, the teacher uses picture cues depicting behavior rules for participating in the activities (e.g., ear symbol reminds child to listen, stop symbol reminds child to wait for teacher to finish reading the story).
Communicating behavior expectations	In response to a child getting distracted during a lesson, the teacher verbally reminds him or her what will be happening next to redirect his or her attention to the group tasks.

determine which children need additional instructional supports (e.g., children who make little or no progress in acquiring key skills after one round of intervention at Tier 2), 2) determine which scaffolding strategies will be added to the small-group lessons and embedded learning activities (e.g., response prompting and peer supports with corrective feedback), 3) implement the scaffolding plan over a predetermined period (e.g., several weeks), and 4) use formative assessment results to adjust the scaffolding plan as needed.

IMPLEMENTATION ISSUES

Because R&R (and RTI more broadly) represents a set of related practices in the early childhood field, a number of decisions must be made to support its implementation in early care and education programs. A number of these decisions, such as selecting appropriate formative assessment tools and tiered interventions, will need to be made at the program or district level rather than by individual teachers, with input from key stakeholders such as administrators, practitioners, and families. In addition to making these key decisions, teachers will need professional development and ongoing supports through approaches such as coaching, consultation, and mentoring to ensure that they are equipped with sufficient knowledge and skill to implement assessment and intervention practices. Furthermore, early educators will need the full support of administrators, specialists, and families as members of collaborative problem-solving teams, an important mechanism that will need to be established to support data-based decision making within R&R. Drawing on recommendations from the concept paper on RTI in early childhood published by the National Professional Development Center on Inclusion (2012), issues that need to be addressed prior to implementation of R&R fall within three broad categories:

1. **Strategic planning process:** Programs that adopt R&R or another model of tiered instruction will need to engage in a planning process prior to implementation. Careful consideration should be given to who will be involved in the planning effort, how decisions will be made, and how logistics will be handled, such as obtaining administrative approvals and creating timelines for implementation.

2. **Decisions regarding the assessment and instructional components:** Key decisions will need to be made early in the planning process related to the context and scope of implementation. Will R&R be implemented with children from birth to age 5 or limited to pre-K children? Will R&R be implemented in a select number of demonstration sites initially versus implementing it more broadly across an entire system? What aspects of academic learning will be the focus of the R&R program, and will behavioral supports be incorporated within this approach? What formative assessment tools will be applied and what criteria will be used for determining children who need tiered interventions (e.g., selecting children for the first round of Tier 2 interventions based on those who score below the 25th percentile, selecting children who score in the bottom 50th percentile to receive two rounds of Tier 2 interventions)? What research-based curricula and tiered interventions will be used? How will practitioners collaborate with specialists and families to support data-based decision making?

3. **Infrastructure supports:** Planners should determine how practitioners will receive professional development and ongoing support for implementation of R&R. In addition, they should specify the collaborative problem-solving process, allocate time and resources to support these collaborative efforts, and determine how information will be shared about children's development with families and other professionals. Finally, planners should make provisions for evaluating the implementation and effectiveness of R&R.

RESEARCH EVIDENCE

Results from two small-scale, quasi-experimental studies offer evidence of the promise of the R&R model for improving children's language and literacy skills, with significant effects found across a variety of outcome measures in both studies (Buysse, Peisner-Feinberg, & Burchinal, 2012). The initial study (Study 1) included 24 pre-K classrooms and 320 4-year-old children in community-based early childhood programs. The second study (Study 2) included 24 public school pre-K classrooms and 354 4-year-old children. Seventy-five percent of the teachers in Study 1 and all of the teachers in Study 2 had a bachelor of arts degree or higher. About one half of the children in Study 1 and nearly all of the children in Study 2 were from low-income families. For both of these studies, teachers implemented the R&R model in the area of language and literacy development, including the assessment and tiered instruction components.

Results from these two studies provide evidence of the feasibility of implementation and usability of the R&R model. Observations of the tiered interventions showed that teachers could implement this component with high fidelity across the two studies. Mean scores on the implementation fidelity rating were 97% and 91% (Study 1 and 2), based on multiple (three to five) observations of each teacher conducting the Tier 2 interventions. In addition, teacher ratings indicate that they found the R&R system feasible and useful. In both Study 1 and 2, respectively, the vast majority of teachers rated the components as easy to use (assessment: 88%/90%; intervention: 96%/77%) and helpful (assessment: 96%/100%; intervention: 92%/90%), and indicated that they would recommend the R&R system to colleagues (92%/84%).

These studies also showed positive evidence of the promise of R&R for improving children's language and literacy skills, both in terms of formative assessments and norm-referenced measures. The amount of growth (pre- to post-intervention) exhibited by target children receiving the tiered interventions versus a comparison group of their classmates was examined. Target children made significantly greater gains than comparison children in language and literacy skills in both studies, with effect sizes predominantly in the low to moderate range for significant comparisons (range = .24 to .40). In Study 1, target children made greater gains in vocabulary and phonological awareness (based on formative assessments) and on print knowledge (based on a norm-referenced measure), and made similar gains in other areas. In Study 2, target children made greater gains in vocabulary and phonological awareness (based on formative assessment) and receptive and expressive language (based on norm-referenced measures), and made similar gains in other areas.

Across these two pilot studies, the results suggest that the R&R system offers evidence of promise for improving language and literacy outcomes for young children. Positive effects were found in the growth rates for target children compared with their peers on formative assessment and standardized measures in both studies. Although target children had substantially lower scores initially as well as after the intervention, their rates of growth were greater than or the same as those of comparison children. These results indicate that through the assessment and intervention components, teachers who used the R&R model were able to successfully identify target children for the interventions (i.e., those with significantly lower skill levels than their peers), and potentially to alter their developmental trajectory so that they began catching up to their peers in some areas while maintaining pace in others. Moreover, positive effects were found across different populations of children; although Study 2 included a relatively more disadvantaged population, as evidenced by their background characteristics and fall assessment scores, the model had positive effects for target children in both studies. Not surprisingly, stronger effects were found in critical areas of receptive and expressive language skills when R&R was implemented under more ideal conditions (i.e., a full year rather than one semester, with more highly educated teachers). Although these two pilot studies did not provide the opportunity for a true control group, the results clearly provide empirical evidence of the promise of R&R as an educational intervention for pre-K. Future studies are planned or underway to conduct a randomized control trial to evaluate the efficacy of R&R for improving pre-K children's language and literacy skills. Additional research also is needed to examine the differential effects of interventions at Tiers 2 and 3 and to develop and test other adaptions of the model for mathematics instruction and for use with dual language learners.

CONCLUSION

The use of RTI practices to support learning and development in children prior to kindergarten has generated widespread interest within the early childhood field. R&R is an emerging practice in early childhood based closely on the principles of RTI and adapted for younger children in early care and education programs. R&R holds promise for supporting learning and development prior to kindergarten, but additional research is needed to provide evidence of the effectiveness of this approach. This chapter focused on the response component of R&R—the core instruction and intentional teaching that all children receive as well as the targeted interventions and supports that some children require in order to learn. Early educators who plan to implement R&R will need to ensure that this approach complements effective practices and services already in place and adds value by providing additional supports for children who need them. Systemic supports such as ongoing, effective professional development are essential to ensure that R&R is implemented appropriately and is beneficial for young children and their families.

REFERENCES

Buysse, V. (2011). Access, participation, and supports: The defining features of high-quality inclusion. *Zero to Three Journal, 31*(4), 24–29.

Buysse, V., Epstein, D., Winton, P., & Rous, B. (2012). *CONNECT Module 7: Tiered Instruction* [Web-based professional development curriculum]. Chapel Hill: University of North Carolina, FPG Child Development Institute, CONNECT: The Center to Mobilize Early Childhood Knowledge. Retrieved from http://community.fpg.unc.edu/connect-modules/learners/module-7

Buysse, V., & Peisner-Feinberg, E. (2010). Recognition & response: Response to intervention for pre-K. *Young Exceptional Children, 13*(4), 2–13. doi:10.1177/1096250610373586

Buysse, V., Peisner-Feinberg, E., & Burchinal, M. (2012, March). *Recognition & response: Developing and evaluating a model of RTI for pre-K.* Poster presented at the Society on Research on Educational Effectiveness, Washington, DC.

Buysse, V., & Wesley, P.W. (2010). Program quality through the lens of disruptive innovation theory. In P.W. Wesley & V. Buysse (Eds.), *Quest for quality* (pp. 183–198). Baltimore, MD: Paul H. Brookes Publishing Co.

Buysse, V., Winton, P., Rous, B., Epstein, D., & Cavanaugh, C. (2011). *CONNECT Module 6: Dialogic reading practices* [Web-based professional development curriculum]. Chapel Hill: University of North Carolina, FPG Child Development Institute, CONNECT: The Center to Mobilize Early Childhood Knowledge. Retrieved from http://community.fpg.unc.edu/connect-modules/learners/module-6

Chiara, L., Schuster, J.W., Bell, J.K., & Wolery, M. (1995). Small-group massed-trial and individually distributed-trial instruction with preschoolers. *Journal of Early Intervention, 19,* 203–217. doi:10.1177/105381519501900305

Craig-Unkefer, L.A., & Kaiser, A.P. (2002). Improving the social communication skills of at-risk preschool children in play context. *Topics in Early Childhood Special Education, 22,* 3–13. doi:10.1177/027112140202200101

Cross, C.T., Woods, T.A., & Schweingruber, H. (2009). *Mathematics learning in early childhood: Paths toward excellence and equity.* National Research Council; Committee on Early Childhood Mathematics, Center for Education, Division of Behavioral and Social Sciences and Education (Eds.). Washington, DC: The National Academies Press.

Dickinson, D.K., Copley, J.V., Izquierdo, E., Schickedanz, J., & Wright, L. (2012), *Opening the world of learning: A comprehensive early literacy program.* Parsippany, NJ: Pearson Early Learning.

Dodge, D.T., Heroman, C., Colker, L., & Bickart, T.S. (2010). *The Creative Curriculum for preschool, Volume 1: The foundation and Volume 2: Interest areas* (5th ed.). Washington, DC: Teaching Strategies, LLC.

Epstein, A.S., & Hohmann, M. (2012). *The new HighScope preschool curriculum.* Ypsilanti, MI: HighScope Press.

Fox, L., Carta, J., Strain, P.S., Dunlap, G., & Hemmeter, M.L. (2010). Response to intervention and the pyramid model. *Infants and Young Children, 23,* 3–13. doi:10.1097/IYC.0b013e3181c816e2

Gersten, R., Beckmann, S., Clarke, B., Foegen, A., Marsh, L., Star, J.R., & Witzel, B. (2009). *Assisting students struggling with mathematics: Response to intervention (RTI) for elementary and middle schools* (NCEE 2009-4060). Washington, DC: National Center for Education Evaluation and Regional Assistance, Institute of Education Sciences, U.S. Department of Education. Retrieved from http://ies.ed.gov/ncee/wwc/publications/practiceguides/

Gersten, R., Compton, D.L., Connor, C.M., Dimino, J., Santoro, L., Linan-Thompson, S., & Tilly, W.D. (2008). *Assisting students struggling with reading: Response to intervention and multi-tier intervention for reading in the primary grades. A practice guide.* (NCEE 2009-4045). Washington, DC: National Center for Education Evaluation and Regional Assistance, Institute of Education Sciences, U.S. Department of Education. Retrieved from http://ies.ed.gov/ncee/wwc/publications/practiceguides/

Gibson, A.N., & Schuster, J.W. (1992). The use of simultaneous prompting for teaching expressive word recognition to preschool children. *Topics in Early Childhood Special Education, 12,* 247–267. doi:10.1177/027112149201200208

Girolametto, L., Weitzman, E., & Greenberg, J. (2004). The effects of verbal support strategies on small-group peer interactions. *Language, Speech, and Hearing Services in Schools, 35,* 254–268. doi:10.1044/0161-1461(2004/024)

Greenwood, C.R., Bradfield, R., Kaminski, R., Linas, M., Carta, J.J., & Nylander, D. (2011). The response to intervention (RTI) approach in early childhood. *Focus on Exceptional Children, 43*(9), 1–22.

Hancock, B., & Kaiser, A.P. (2006). Enhanced milieu teaching. In R. McCauley & M. Fey (Eds.), *Treatment of language disorders in children* (pp. 203–236). Baltimore, MD: Paul H. Brookes Publishing Co.

Hawkings, S.R., & Schuster, J.W. (2007). Using a mand-model procedure to teach preschool children initial speech sounds. *Journal of Developmental and Physical Disabilities, 19*(1), 65–80. doi:10.1007/s10882-006-9032-6

Kaiser, A.P., Hester, P.P., & McDuffie, A.S. (2001). Supporting communication in young children with developmental disabilities. *Mental Retardation and Developmental Disability Research Reviews, 7,* 143–150.

Kouri, T.A. (2005). Lexical training through modeling and elicitation procedures with late talkers who have specific language impairment and developmental delays. *Journal of Speech, Language, and Hearing Research, 48,* 157–171. doi:10.1044/1092-4388(2005/012)

National Early Literacy Panel. (2008). *Developing early literacy: Report of the National Early Literacy Panel.* Washington, DC: National Institute for Literacy.

National Professional Development Center on Inclusion. (2012). *Response to intervention (RTI) in early childhood: Building consensus on the defining features.* Chapel Hill: The University of North Carolina, FPG Child Development Institute, Author. Retrieved from http://npdci.fpg.unc.edu

National Research Council. (2009). *Mathematics learning in early childhood: Paths toward excellence and equity.* Committee on Early Childhood Mathematics, Christopher T. Cross, Taniesha A. Woods, and Heidi Schweingruber, Editors. Center for Education, Division of Behavioral and Social Sciences and Education. Washington, DC: The National Academies Press.

Ostrosky, M., & Kaiser, A.P. (1995). The effects of a peer-mediated intervention on the social communicative interactions between children with and without special needs. *Journal of Behavioral Education, 5*(2), 151–171. doi:10.1007/BF02110203

Peisner-Feinberg, E., Buysse, V., Benshoff, L., & Soukakou, E. (2011). Recognition & response: Response to intervention for pre-kindergarten. In C. Groark, S.M. Eidelman, L. Kaczmarek & S. Maude (Eds.), *Early childhood intervention: Shaping the future for children with special needs and their families, Vol. 3, Emerging trends in research and practice* (pp. 37–53). Santa Barbara, CA: Praeger.

Preschool Curriculum Evaluation Research Consortium. (2008). *Effects of preschool curriculum programs on school readiness* (NCER 2008–2009). Washington, DC: National Center for Education Research, Institute of Education Sciences, U.S. Department of Education.

Ross, D.E., & Greer, R.D. (2003). Generalized imitation and the mand: Inducing first instances of speech in young children with autism. *Research in Developmental Disabilities, 24,* 58–74.

Smith, S. (2009). Introduction: Supporting struggling learners in preschool: Emerging approaches and opportunities [Special section]. *NHSA Dialog, 12*(3), 185–191.

SRA/McGraw-Hill. (2008). *Imagine It!* Columbus, OH: McGraw-Hill.

U.S. Department of Education, Institute for Education Sciences, What Works Clearing-house. (2007). *Research summary on dialogic reading*. Retrieved from http://ies.ed.gov/ncee/wwc/resports/ece_ed/dialogic_reading/index.asp

Walker, H.M. (2008). Constant and progressive time delay procedures for teaching children with autism: A literature review. *Journal of Autism and Developmental Disorders, 38*, 261–275. doi:10.1007/s10803-007-0390-4

Wesley, P.W., & Buysse, V. (Eds.). (2010). *Quest for quality*. Baltimore, MD: Paul H. Brookes Publishing Co.

Wolery, M. (2000). Behavioral and educational approaches to early intervention. In J.P. Schonkoff & S.J. Meisels (Eds.), *Handbook of early childhood intervention* (2nd ed., pp. 179–203). Cambridge, United Kingdom: Cambridge University Press.

6

A Tiered Model for Promoting Social-Emotional Competence and Addressing Challenging Behavior

Mary Louise Hemmeter, Lise Fox, and Patricia Snyder

Social-emotional competence is widely recognized as foundational to children's readiness for school and early school adjustment (Bierman et al., 2008; Denham & Brown, 2010; High, 2008; LaParo & Pianta, 2000; Leerkes, Paradise, O'Brien, Calkins, & Lange, 2008). Social-emotional competence has been described by researchers as a multidimensional, complex construct that includes skills related to self-awareness, self-management, social awareness, responsible decision making, and relationship/social skills (Denham & Brown, 2010; Fantuzzo et al., 2007; Payton et al., 2000). A growing body of research is beginning to reveal the relationship between varying dimensions of social-emotional competence and cognitive and school readiness skills (e.g., Bierman et al. 2008; Graziano, Reavis, Keane, & Calkins, 2007; Howse, Calkins, Anastopoulos, Keane, & Shelton, 2003; Miller, Seifer, Stroud, Sheinkopf, & Dickstein, 2006). Denham and Brown (2010) present a compelling discussion of these findings by saying that social-emotional competence provides the child with the capacity to engage in academic tasks, benefit from interactions with teachers, work collaboratively with peers, imitate peers' learning, and dedicate sustained attention to learning.

There is also substantial research that confirms the critical relationship between children's challenging behavior and their social skill delays and deficits (Zins, Bloodworth, Weissberg, & Walberg, 2007; Campbell, 2002). Odom, McConnell, and Brown (2008) described a continuum of social competence with highly competent children who establish friendships easily and use strategies that are appropriate to the social context at one end and children who are aggressive, disruptive, or socially withdrawn and isolated at the other end. The prevalence of child behavior problems during the early childhood years is well documented, with estimates ranging from 10% (Campbell, 1995; West, Denton, & Germino-Hausken, 2000) to rates as high as 30% for children living in poverty (Qi & Kaiser, 2003). Of great concern is the stability of the condition, with more than half of toddlers and preschoolers with clinical levels of behavior disorders remaining in the clinical range in elementary school (Pierce, Ewing & Campbell, 1999; Shaw, Gilliom & Giovannelli, 2000).

The importance of ensuring that children are both academically and socially ready for school is well established. When behavior challenges are not resolved during the early years, children with persistent behavioral concerns experience problems in socialization, school adjustment, school success, and educational and vocational adaptation in adolescence and adulthood (e.g., Campbell & Ewing, 1990; Kazdin, 1995; Lane, Barton-Arwood, Nelson, & Wehby, 2008; Nelson, Benner, & Lane, 2004; Schwartz, McFayden-Ketchum, Dodge, Pettit, & Bates, 1998). Since the 1990s when prekindergarten programs became more common, there has been a focused emphasis on addressing problem behaviors in young children before their entry into kindergarten. The environments where intervention is most likely to occur are early education programs, including classrooms that enroll children with and without disabilities. However, many early childhood teachers feel unequipped to meet the needs of children who have social-emotional delays or exhibit challenging behavior (Kaufmann & Wischmann, 1999). Early educators report that disruptive behavior is one of the single greatest challenges they face in implementing effective practices, and that there seems to be an increasing number of children who have these problems (Arnold, McWilliams, & Arnold, 1998; Buscemi, Bennett, Thomas, & Deluca, 1996; Hemmeter, Corso, & Cheatham, 2006).

When early educators are not equipped to support young children with challenging behavior, children are more likely to be expelled from programs. A national survey on expulsion from state-funded preschool programs found that children were being expelled at a rate that was three times the expulsion rate for school-age children (Gilliam, 2005). In a study examining preschool expulsion in Massachusetts, the rate was 34 times the rate of students in K–12 programs (Gilliam & Shahar, 2006).

In an inclusive early education classroom, early educators are likely to encounter children who range widely in their social-emotional competence. The typical inclusive classroom is likely to enroll children with strengths in social competence, children who are beginning to show evidence of social-emotional skill deficits, and children who have behavioral issues that exceed what might be developmentally expected. A tiered model of evidence-based interventions for promoting all children's social-emotional competence and effectively addressing the significant behavior challenges of a few children offers the promise of meeting the needs of all children who might be enrolled in an early education program.

In this chapter, we describe the Pyramid Model for Promoting Social-Emotional Competence (Fox, Dunlap, Hemmeter, Joseph, & Strain, 2003; Hemmeter, Ostrosky, & Fox, 2006) and discuss how the Pyramid Model might be implemented in early care and education programs. As part of this discussion, we focus on issues related to fidelity of implementation and the supports that are needed to implement a comprehensive prevention framework within early childhood programs.

THE PYRAMID MODEL FOR
PROMOTING SOCIAL-EMOTIONAL COMPETENCE

The Pyramid Model (Fox et al., 2003; Hemmeter, Ostrosky, & Fox, 2006) was designed to address the social, emotional, and behavioral needs of all children, including children with disabilities or at risk for disabilities in preschool classrooms. The Pyramid Model provides a framework for implementing evidence-based practices to promote the social-emotional competence of all children, address the social-emotional and behavioral needs of children at risk for social-emotional or behavioral deficits, and develop supports for children with persistent social, emotional, or behavioral concerns. The Pyramid Model practices were identified through a review of the research on classroom promotion, prevention, and intervention practices that have been associated with positive social-emotional outcomes and decreases in challenging behavior in young children with and without disabilities (e.g., Dunlap et al., 2006; Howes & Hamilton, 1993; Walker et al., 1998; Webster-Stratton, Reid, & Hammond, 2004). An extensive review of the literature resulted in the identification of a set of practices that were aligned within and across the levels of the Pyramid Model to ensure that a comprehensive framework could be described and operationalized (Hemmeter et al., 2006).

The Pyramid Model provides guidance to early educators on using effective behavior support and instructional practices that are based upon research on effective instruction for young children (Burchinal, Vandergrift, Pianta, & Mashburn, 2010; National Research Council, 2001), using strategies that promote child engagement and appropriate behavior (Chien et al., 2010; Conroy, Brown, & Olive, 2008), promoting the development of children's social skills (Odom et al., 2008; Vaughn, Kim, Sloan, Hughes, Elbaum, & Sridhar, 2003), and implementing individualized assessment-based behavior support plans (i.e., functional assessment and individualized positive behavior interventions and supports) for children with the most severe behavior challenges (Blair, Fox, & Lentini, 2010; Conroy, Dunlap, Clarke, & Alter, 2005; McLaren & Nelson, 2009). The Pyramid Model is based on tiered promotion, prevention, and intervention frameworks described in prevention science (Gordon, 1983; Simeonsson, 1991) and provides an early childhood application of the core elements and science of schoolwide positive behavior supports (SW-PBS) (Horner, Sugai, Todd, & Lewis-Palmer, 2005; Walker et al., 1996).

We refer to the Pyramid Model as a framework of practices rather than a curriculum or treatment because it includes but is not limited to the use of curricula and/or evidence-based intervention strategies. Moreover, a framework allows for an adaptive intervention that is tailored to the characteristics of the context and individual needs of the children within that setting (Collins, Murphy, & Bierman, 2004). Adaptive intervention is a concept aligned with prevention models that accounts for the need to vary intervention across individuals or within individuals over time. Part of the appeal of adaptive prevention approaches is that they have greater alignment with real-world environments and the delivery of comprehensive systems of prevention supports (Weissberg & Greenberg, 1998).

The Pyramid Model offers a continuum of evidence-based practices related to promoting social-emotional competence and addressing challenging behavior in preschool children with and without disabilities, and programwide implementation of the model provides the processes and procedures that support implementation fidelity (Fox, Carta, Dunlap, Strain, & Hemmeter, 2010). In the remainder of the chapter, we describe the practices associated with the Pyramid Model, discuss implementation and outcomes, and explore issues and future directions related to the Pyramid Model and application of the model within early care and education programs.

Practices Associated with the Pyramid Model

The Pyramid Model includes four components to address the needs of all young children, including those with persistent, challenging behavior. The first two components (responsive relationships, high-quality environments) compose the universal level and include practices that would be implemented with all children in a classroom. The third component (targeted social-emotional supports) offers secondary prevention practices designed to address the needs of children at risk for problem behavior. The fourth component (intensive intervention) includes practices to support an individualized intervention approach for children with the most severe and persistent challenging behavior. Figure 6.1 provides an illustration of the Pyramid Model.

The universal promotion level of the Pyramid Model refers to practices related to building responsive and supportive interactions with children, including the following techniques: supporting children's play, responding to child conversations, supporting communication of children with special needs, providing positive feedback and encouragement of appropriate behavior, and building relationships with children (Birch & Ladd, 1998; Bodrova & Leong, 1998; Howes & Hamilton,

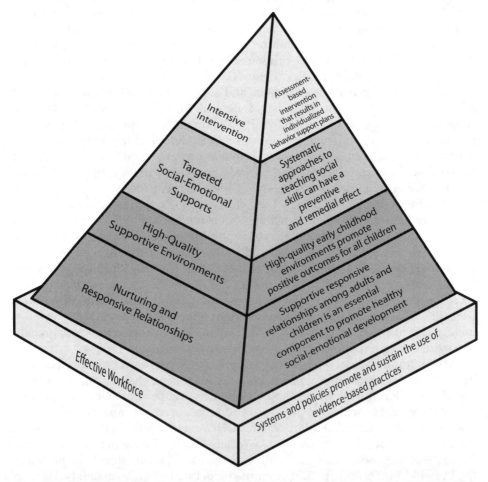

Figure 6.1. Pyramid Model. (From Fox, L., Carta, J., Strain, P.S., Dunlap, G., & Hemmeter, M.L. [2010]. Response to intervention and the pyramid model. *Infants and Young Children, 23,* 3–13; reprinted by permission from http://csefel.vanderbilt.edu/)

1993; Howes, Phillips, & Whitebook, 1992; Howes & Smith, 1995; Kontos, 1999; Mill & Romano-White, 1999; National Research Council, 2001; Peisner-Feinberg et al., 2000; Pianta, Steinberg, & Rollins, 1995). These practices are supported by studies that have identified responsive and nurturing relationships with adults and peers as critical for promoting children's social-emotional competence and developmentally appropriate behavior with peers and adults (National Research Council, 2000, 2001). At the nurturing and responsive relationship level, practices related to collaborative teaming, family engagement, communication with families, and family support are also included. These are foundational or core practices that are widely recognized as essential to the provision of high-quality early education and care for all young children (National Research Council, 2001; Sandall, Hemmeter, Smith, & McLean, 2005).

The universal promotion level also includes practices related to high-quality supportive environments that have been shown to promote children's developmentally appropriate engagement in learning activities. These practices include providing adequate materials in play centers; defining the boundaries of play centers; offering a balanced schedule of activities with length matched to developmental capacity of children (large- and small-group); structuring transitions; providing individualized directions to children who need support; teaching and promoting a small number of classroom rules; actively promoting the engagement of children; and providing clear directions (DeKlyen & Odom, 1989; Jolivette et al., 2001; National Research Council, 2001; Peisner-Feinberg et al., 2000). At the universal level, practices are designed to address the needs of all children but may also include modifications to support the engagement of children who have social, emotional, or behavioral needs. For example, structuring transitions might involve providing a class warning prior to the transition, acknowledging children who are engaging in the expectations of the transition, and having an activity for children who complete the transition more quickly than the other children. In addition, a visual schedule of the transition might be used to support a child who is having difficulty with the transition.

At the secondary prevention level, teaching practices include providing focused instruction on social skills to all children in the classroom and systematic instruction for small groups or individual children who are at risk of challenging behavior and emotional/behavioral disorders or who have social-emotional skill deficits. Within the Pyramid Model, we emphasize that social skills instruction often varies in form and intensity rather than function and purpose (Brown et al., 2001; Snyder, McLaughlin, & Denney, 2011). For example, although all children will need some assistance learning to identify and communicate their emotions in appropriate ways, some children may need more frequent or more explicit and systematic instruction to learn the same concepts. Secondary prevention practices include teaching children to identify and express emotions; teaching and supporting self-regulation; teaching and supporting children's use of strategies for handling anger and disappointment; teaching and supporting social problem solving; teaching and supporting friendship skills; teaching and supporting collaboration with peers; and providing individualized, systematic instruction for children who need additional support (Coie & Koeppel, 1990; Denham & Burton, 1996; National Research Council, 2001; Webster-Stratton, Reid, & Hammond, 2001).

For children with social-emotional delays or instructional support needs at the secondary level, specific social skills are targeted for acquisition and generalization, and a systematic instructional plan is designed to ensure increased learning opportunities that are embedded within meaningful activities (Snyder, McLaughlin, & Denney, 2011). For these children, instruction is more precise, learning opportunities are increased, and child progress is monitored more frequently (Fox, Hemmeter, & Jack, 2010).

In the individualized intervention (tertiary) level of the Pyramid Model, teachers are guided to collaborate with team members in developing and implementing assessment-based, individualized positive behavior interventions and supports. The practices involved in this level include convening a team to develop interventions, collecting data to determine the nature of problem behavior (i.e., conducting a functional assessment), developing individualized behavior support strategies; implementing behavior support plans with consistency, conducting ongoing monitoring of child progress; revising plans as needed, and partnering with families and colleagues to implement plans (Duda, Dunlap, Fox, Lentini, & Clarke, 2004; Kern, Ringdahl, Hilt, & Sterling-Turner, 2001; Strain & Timm, 2001). Individualized behavior support plans are designed to include each of the following critical elements: prevention strategies to ensure child engagement within activities and interactions, replacement skills that provide children with functionally equivalent skills to replace challenging behavior, and consequence strategies to ensure that challenging behavior is not reinforced or maintained (Fox, Carta et al., 2010). Children who have tertiary behavior support plans may be provided with the systematic instruction on individualized social-emotional targets described at the secondary level. Progress monitoring is frequent and tracks both reductions in challenging behavior and the use of replacement skills.

Evaluation of the Pyramid Model

Multiple investigations have been conducted to evaluate components or practices that are included in the Pyramid Model (e.g., Blair et al., 2010; Hemmeter, Snyder, Kinder, & Artman, 2011; Stormont, Smith, & Lewis, 2007). Descriptions of model implementation within early care and education programs have been published (Hemmeter & Fox, 2009; Hemmeter, Ostrosky et al., 2006; Hemmeter, Fox, Jack, & Broyles, 2007; Hunter & Hemmeter, 2009). In addition, a potential efficacy randomized controlled experimental evaluation has been completed to examine relationships between fidelity of model implementation and child social and behavioral outcomes (Hemmeter, Snyder, Fox, & Algina, 2011). In this study, a randomized two-group experimental design involving 40 preschool teachers (20 in intervention and 20 in wait-list control) and 484 children, including 97 target children identified as at risk for challenging behavior, was used to determine whether implementing practices associated with the Pyramid Model with fidelity was associated with changes in children's social skills and problem behavior.

Teachers in the intervention condition participated in professional development (PD) focused on the Pyramid Model. The professional development intervention had three primary components: 1) 18 hours of manualized workshop training, 2) an average of 13.4 sessions of in-classroom coaching by a project coach, and 3) materials and resources to support implementation of Pyramid Model practices in classrooms. Teachers in the control condition received training after the completion of an academic year of data collection.

Preliminary data analyses showed that following the PD intervention, teachers were able to implement significantly more Pyramid Model practices with fidelity than were teachers in the wait-list control condition. In addition, teachers' implementation of Pyramid Model practices was linked to promising outcomes for children (Hemmeter, Snyder, Fox et al., 2011). In intervention classrooms, children not identified as target children were rated by teachers as having better social skills than children in the control classrooms. These findings suggest that implementation of Pyramid Model practices provides all children with learning opportunities and instruction that promote improvement of social skills. Target children—children with identified behavior challenges—were rated by teachers as having significant decreases in problem behavior in comparison with target children in control classrooms. Target children were also observed to use positive social initiations more often during typical classroom activities and routines than were target children in control classrooms.

CONSIDERING FIDELITY OF IMPLEMENTATION AND EVALUATION OF OUTCOMES

To examine intervention efficacy or effectiveness, factors related to implementation should be considered. First, the practices associated with the intervention must be identified and defined. Second, there must be a process for measuring the fidelity with which the intervention is implemented. Finally, it is important to consider how educators are supported to implement the intervention. In the case of early childhood education interventions, this involves identifying the professional development strategies that support practitioners to implement an intervention with fidelity as well as the programwide or schoolwide strategies that are necessary for implementing the intervention with fidelity over time. These and other factors have been identified as implementation "drivers" (Fixsen, Blasé, Duda, Naoom, & Van Dyke, 2010; Snyder, McLaughlin, & Denney, 2011).

In the following section, we describe a tool that has been developed to quantify the extent to which Pyramid Model practices are implemented in preschool classrooms. In addition, we describe a professional development approach that has been used to support teachers to implement Pyramid Model practices with fidelity. We discuss work to date related to programwide implementation of the Pyramid Model. Each of these factors (measuring implementation fidelity, identifying promising strategies for supporting practitioners to implement practices with fidelity, programwide implementation) and other factors such as universal screening, progress monitoring, and data-based decision making are relevant for realizing the promise of response to intervention (RTI) frameworks in early childhood (Fox, Carta et al., 2010; VanDerHeyden & Snyder, 2006). We conclude this section with a discussion of the factors important for implementing tiered frameworks that have not yet been systematically examined to date in our work.

Measuring Fidelity of Implementation

Measuring the fidelity with which an intervention is implemented is critical for linking the intervention to observed child outcomes and for establishing the efficacy of interventions used in educational settings (Horner et al., 2005; O'Donnell, 2008; Sanetti, Dobney, & Gritter, 2012). In educational settings, fidelity of implementation is described as the extent to which components of a curriculum, intervention, or practice are implemented as prescribed by the curriculum or implementation protocol (O'Donnell, 2008).

In the Pyramid Model, fidelity of implementation is measured using the Teaching Pyramid Observation Tool (TPOT: Hemmeter, Fox, & Snyder, 2008). The TPOT is an observational, judgment-based rating scale designed to measure practitioners' implementation of Pyramid Model practices. The TPOT is a 38-item scale consisting of three sections. First, 7 items address environmental arrangements in the classroom and are scored as present or not present. Second, 15 items represent key instructional and behavior support practice categories associated with the Pyramid Model (e.g., transition, teaching children to express emotions, schedules, routines). Each item has 4 to 10 observable practice indicators, and each indicator is scored as present or not present. Third, the TPOT includes 16 "red-flag" items. Red flags are observable practices that either are counterproductive or not supportive of young children's social-emotional skills or are not appropriate prevention or intervention practices for addressing challenging behavior (e.g., teacher reprimands children for expressing their emotions). Red-flag items are rated as either present or not present. Items across these three sections are summarized to provide a composite score of implementation fidelity. The TPOT is completed based on a 2-hour observation of a preschool classroom and a brief interview with the teacher. In a recent study, we examined the psychometric integrity of TPOT scores and found promising results related to measurement dependability and convergent validity (Snyder, Hemmeter, Fox, Crowe, & Miller, 2011).

In the potential efficacy trial previously described, the TPOT was used in both intervention and control classrooms on four measurement occasions. Teachers who did not participate in the professional development intervention had, on average, implementation scores that were quite low and stable across time (implementing approximately 40% of TPOT practices). In contrast, TPOT scores for intervention teachers showed noteworthy changes in level and slope over time. These data and the data from the psychometric study suggest that the TPOT is a promising measure for examining implementation of Pyramid Model practices. Being able to dependably measure when practices are or are not being implemented as intended is important in RTI frameworks to help quantify the dose and type of intervention children are receiving and their responses to the intervention.

Professional Development to Support Implementation

Over the last 5 years, we have developed, validated, and evaluated a systematic professional development approach for supporting teachers to use multicomponent interventions (Hemmeter, Snyder, Fox et al., 2011; Snyder, Hemmeter, McLaughlin, et al., 2011). As noted previously, in our study on the Pyramid Model (Hemmeter et al., 2011), this approach included the provision of high-quality manualized workshops, implementation materials, and coaching with performance feedback.

Coaching included goal setting and action planning around priority areas of practice implementation, classroom observations, debriefing sessions, and e-mail messages summarizing the meeting and providing additional materials and feedback. Coaching was focused on the implementation of practices identified in an action plan developed by the teacher and coach. The action plan was informed by what the teacher wanted to address, as identified in the training workshops and with guidance from the coach using baseline observations of teacher implementation of the Pyramid Model practices. During observations, the coach would model strategies identified on the plan, give verbal or gestural feedback, and work one-on-one with an individual child. During debriefing sessions, the coach would use strategies such as general performance feedback on classroom practices that were targeted for implementation (e.g., "I saw you using the visual schedule for transition; the children were following your directions and changed activities more quickly today"), corrective feedback that included suggestions for improving implementation of practices (e.g., "I noticed that Jess didn't change activities with the other children; this would have been a good time to show him his individual schedule"), and action planning related to practices to be implemented during the next observation session. The coach would refer to implementation guides as a resource for materials or supports for the teacher and would offer to make materials (e.g., visual schedules, choice boards) for the teacher when needed. Debriefing sessions would offer the teacher an opportunity to ask questions and receive assistance with children who needed more individualized supports. Following each debriefing session, the coach would send the teacher an e-mail summarizing the meeting and offering additional support and/or resources.

As described previously, teachers who received this professional development intervention made significant gains in their use of Pyramid Model practices in comparison with teachers who did not receive the professional development intervention (Hemmeter, Snyder, Fox et al., 2011). We have also used this professional development model in our work on embedded instruction (Snyder, Hemmeter, McLaughlin, et al., 2011; see also Chapter 18 in this volume) and found similar results with respect to teachers' implementation of a multicomponent intervention.

Programwide Implementation of the Teaching Pyramid

Fixsen et al. (2010) have suggested that it is the combination of effective intervention practices and programs *and* effective implementation supports that results in positive outcomes for children and families. For teachers to implement interventions such as Pyramid Model practices with fidelity, programwide implementation supports (including professional development) will be needed. Although there is a substantial body of literature on schoolwide approaches to implementing RTI models in elementary, middle, and secondary schools, the literature on implementation of these models in early childhood settings is in its infancy (Fox & Hemmeter, 2009; Frey, Boyce, & Tarullo, 2009; Stormont, Lewis & Beckner, 2005; VanDerHeyden & Snyder, 2006; see also Chapter 1 in this volume).

Programwide implementation of the Pyramid Model is based on the essential components of SW-PBS and mirrors many of the same elements (Fox & Hemmeter, 2009). These elements include establishing a leadership team that guides programwide adoption and engages in data-based decision making, ensuring the buy-in of all staff to the model, using strategies for promoting family engagement, providing ongoing training and coaching for classroom staff, the use of universal screening and progress monitoring to ensure children's social-emotional intervention needs are addressed, developing a behavior support planning process for children whose challenging behavior is persistent, and implementing an ongoing process for monitoring implementation and outcomes of the approach.

Through our work on the Center on the Social Emotional Foundations for Early Learning (CSEFEL) and the Technical Assistance Center on Social Emotional Interventions (TACSEI), we have developed tools and processes for use when implementing the Pyramid Model programwide (Fox & Hemmeter, 2009; Hemmeter, Fox et al., 2006; Hemmeter et al., 2007). We have developed a tool that can be used to measure the extent to which programs are implementing the components of programwide implementation described previously. This tool, The Early Childhood Program-Wide PBS Benchmarks of Quality (Fox, Hemmeter, & Jack, 2010), is a measure of the fidelity of programwide implementation and is used as the basis for developing an implementation plan and tracking program implementation over time. In our work within states on CSEFEL and TACSEI, this tool has been effective for tracking programwide implementation over time. In addition, we have developed a system for measuring and analyzing behavior incidents that offers formative and summative analyses that programs use in determining the factors related to child behavior incidents, the support needs of children and teachers, and progress in resolving behavior incidents. We have also provided guidance to programs in the design and selection of progress monitoring tools to use in conjunction with the delivery of individualized teaching and behavior support plans. These data elements are used by programwide leadership teams for data-based decision making as they examine issues related to implementation fidelity, child and teacher support needs, and program outcomes.

ISSUES AND FUTURE DIRECTIONS

Although promising work has been conducted with the Pyramid Model to date, only in the past several years have we considered relationships between the model as originally conceptualized and response to intervention frameworks (Fox, Carta et al., 2010; Snyder, McLaughlin, & Denney, 2011). This had led us to identify the technical features of the model that are in place as well as those features that have yet to be specified or systematically examined.

With respect to measuring fidelity of implementation of Pyramid Model practices, we have what might be considered a universal measure of implementation fidelity—the TPOT. Although the TPOT measures teachers' implementation of the universal practices and teachers' capacity to implement targeted social skills curricula or individualized behavior support plans, it is likely not a comprehensive measure of fidelity of implementation of some secondary and tertiary practices. For example, because targeted secondary practices may involve implementation of scripted lessons or protocols and tertiary interventions involve individualized behavior support plans, different fidelity measures would be needed for these practices. These measures will need to map onto the targeted or individualized practices that are used.

The professional development approach we have used to provide practitioners with knowledge about the Pyramid Model practices and support their implementation is promising, but it is also "resource intensive." In both of our studies on this model (Hemmeter, Snyder, Fox et al., 2011; Snyder, Hemmeter, McLaughlin, et al., 2011), the professional development intervention was delivered to individual teachers and did not occur in the context of programwide implementation. It is possible that programwide supports for implementation might moderate the intensity of support that is needed for individual teachers. For example, if all teachers are implementing the model concurrently, peer coaching or group coaching might be used to supplement individual coaching.

Due to the design of the research studies in which this professional development intervention was tested (Hemmeter, Snyder, Fox et al., 2011; Snyder, Hemmeter, McLaughlin, et al., 2011), all teachers received approximately the same "dosage" of coaching. Based on the fidelity data, some teachers needed additional coaching, but it is also possible that some teachers would have made progress on implementation of practices with less support. In the context of programwide implementation, different levels of support could be provided based on implementation fidelity data for individual teachers (Fox, Hemmeter, Snyder, Binder, & Clarke, 2011).

Further, we have not conducted studies to compare whether different professional development approaches or different doses of the approach would be more or less efficacious implementation supports. Although we have data on the efficacy of the coaching model we describe previously, there is evidence that other models may be effective and perhaps more efficient. For example, in their work on My Teaching Partner, Pianta and his colleagues (Pianta, 2011; Pianta, Mashburn, Downer, Hamre, & Justice, 2008) have used a web-based model for delivering coaching to teachers from a distance. However, this approach to implementation support has not been tested with a tiered intervention framework. Much work is needed on how to maximize the effectiveness of coaching models while also addressing issues of efficiency. Further, resources will be needed for training and providing ongoing support to coaches.

Effective approaches for supporting teachers to implement practices with fidelity will require a commitment of resources. It is clear that episodic workshops or limited follow-up implementation support is not likely to improve the fidelity with which teachers implement multicomponent interventions like the Pyramid Model. A major challenge will be identifying resources to provide the level of implementation support (including professional development and administrative leadership) needed by practitioners.

There are several limitations to our work on programwide implementation, particularly as it applies to implementing the Pyramid Model within an RTI framework. First, our programwide work has been supported primarily by technical assistance grants that do not include funding for systematic evaluations. Thus, the evidence to support this type of programwide approach is based largely on similar approaches within elementary schools, and small case studies of programs with which we have worked. Second, we have done relatively little work on using progress monitoring to make decisions about the level of support individual children in a classroom or program need. This is due in part to limited tools for progress monitoring on social, emotional, and behavioral competence and in part to the need to specify, apply, and evaluate decision criteria using these progress monitoring tools. Our approaches to assessing social and behavioral competence for children receiving targeted or individualized interventions are primarily observational and resource-intensive. There is a need for progress monitoring tools that provide reliable estimates of children's social and behavioral competence while also being efficient, accurate, and valid. Third, most of our work has been done in the context of federally funded projects with adequate resources. We have not yet explored systematically the costs of implementing the Pyramid Model with fidelity without this type of support.

Although we have made significant progress in our work on the Pyramid Model and examining its use in preschool settings, we know far less about its application in other contexts and settings. Unlike K–12 education, preschool education takes place in a variety of settings, including Head Start, public school, center-based child care programs, family day care homes, and home visiting programs. These settings vary in a number of ways that may influence how implementation supports are provided, including different training and degree requirements for practitioners, different hours of operation, different administrative structures, different support systems (e.g., therapists, behavior support personnel), and different teacher–child ratios. The challenge in building a model of programwide supports for early childhood settings is how to design a model that is based on sound implementation principles yet is flexible enough to address the unique characteristics of these different early childhood settings (Fox & Hemmeter, 2009).

Further, our work on applying this model in settings serving infants and toddlers is just beginning. Although the Pyramid Model is conceptually relevant for programs serving infants and toddlers, the application and specific practices will be different. We are in the process of developing training materials and a fidelity tool that will articulate more specifically the practices that would be used in programs serving infants and toddlers. Our goal is to have a model that conceptually spans the birth to age 5 range but which articulates practices that are based on the unique developmental needs of children at different ages. Because many early childhood programs serve children across the birth to age 5 range, it will be important to have a cohesive model while at the same time communicating the need to design practices that are specific to the age of the children rather than appearing to "pull down" the preschool practices to infant-toddler programs.

To implement successfully a framework like the Pyramid Model, there will be a need for behavior support or mental health consultation for children with the most significant challenging behaviors in early childhood settings. Individualized positive behavior interventions and supports have been found to be effective with young children with ongoing, persistent challenging behavior (see review by Dunlap and Fox, 2011). However, it requires the availability of a person with behavior support expertise to support the process.

In Gilliam's work (2005; Gilliam & Shahar, 2006) on preschool expulsion, access to a behavior support or mental health consultant was associated with decreased rates of expulsion. The challenge for early childhood programs will be identifying the resources for ensuring that this type of support is available to teachers and other caregivers working directly with families and children. Even when resources are available, finding behavior support personnel who understand young children and early childhood settings may be difficult.

One final issue is how to integrate a tiered model focused on social competence with tiered models focused on early academic skills. We believe that the two fit together well conceptually, but the concurrent implementation of both has not been systematically examined using a response to intervention framework. Conceptually, the universal level of tiered frameworks that are focused on either behavior/social-emotional or preacademic competencies should have similar characteristics, including positive teacher–child interactions, well-designed class-room environments, differentiated instruction, and the promotion of positive relationships between children. Tier 2 and Tier 3 interventions focused on children's social skills and challenging behavior should be integrated with or at least supportive of Tier 2 and Tier 3 interventions around early literacy, early math, or other early academic skills. For example, the teacher might structure a small-group activity to promote positive peer interactions for a particular child, but also use this opportunity to teach other types of skills (e.g., early math or literacy). As a second example, challenging behavior often happens in the context of activities that are too difficult or too simple for an individual child. If Tier 2 and Tier 3 interventions are designed based on the individual needs of children, they are more likely to result in higher levels of child engagement, thus reducing challenging behavior. The emerging data on the importance of both early academic skills and social-emotional and behavioral competencies to school readiness, combined with the increasing demands on practitioner time related to documentation of child progress, suggests the need to develop, implement, and evaluate a tiered approach that integrates social-emotional competencies and early academic skills.

REFERENCES

Arnold, D.H., McWilliams, L., & Arnold, E.H. (1998). Teacher discipline and child misbehavior in day care: Untangling causality with correlational data. *Developmental Psychology, 34,* 276–287.

Bierman, K.L., Domitrovich, C.E., Nix, R.L., Gest, S.D., Welsh, J.A., Greenberg, M.T., . . . Gill, S. (2008). Promoting academic and social-emotional school readiness: The Head Start REDI program. *Child Development, 79,* 1802–1817.

Birch, S.H., & Ladd, G.W. (1998). Children's interpersonal behaviors and the teacher–child relationship. *Developmental Psychology, 34*(5), 934–946.

Blair, K.S.C., Fox, L., & Lentini, R. (2010). Use of positive behavior support to address the challenging behavior of young children within a community early childhood program. *Topics in Early Childhood Special Education, 30,* 68–79.

Bodrova, E., & Leong, D.J. (1998). Learning and development of preschool children from the Vygotskian perspective. In A. Kozulin, B. Gindis, V.S. Ageyev, & S.M. Miller (Eds.), *Vygotsky's educational theory in cultural context* (pp. 156–176). Cambridge, United Kingdom: Cambridge University Press.

Brown, W.H., Odom, S.L., & Conroy, M.A. (2001). An intervention hierarchy for promoting preschool children's peer interactions in natural environment. *Topics in Early Childhood Special Education, 21,* 162–175.

Burchinal, M., Vandergrift, N., Pianta, R., & Mashburn, A. (2010). Threshold analysis of association between child care quality and child outcomes for low income children in pre-kindergarten programs. *Early Childhood Research Quarterly, 25,* 166–176.

Buscemi, L., Bennett, T., Thomas, D., & Deluca, D.A. (1996). Head Start: Challenges and training needs. *Journal of Early Intervention, 20,* 1–13.

Campbell, S.B. (1995). Behavior problems in preschool children: A review of recent research. *Journal of Child Psychology and Psychiatry, 36,* 113–149.

Campbell, S.B. (2002). *Behavior problems in preschool children: Clinical and developmental issues.* New York, NY: Guilford Press.

Campbell, S.B., & Ewing, L.J. (1990). Follow-up of hard-to-manage preschoolers: Adjustment at age 9 and predictors of continuing symptoms. *Journal of Child Psychology and Psychiatry, 31,* 871–889.

Chien, N.C., Howes, C., Burchinal, M., Pianta, R.C., Ritchie, S., Bryant, D., . . . Barbarin, O.A. (2010). Children's classroom engagement and school readiness gains in pre-kindergarten. *Child Development, 81,* 1534–1549.

Coie, J.D., & Koeppel, G.K. (1990). Adapting intervention to the problems of aggressive and disruptive rejected children. In S.R. Asher & J.D. Coie (Eds.), *Peer rejection in childhood* (pp. 274–308). New York, NY: Cambridge University Press.

Collins, L.M., Murphy, S.A., & Bierman, K.L. (2004). A conceptual framework for adaptive preventive interventions. *Prevention Science, 5*(3), 185–196.

Conroy, M.A., Brown, W.H., & Olive, M.L. (2008). Social competence interventions for young children with challenging behaviors. In W.H. Brown, S.L. Odom, & S.R. McConnell (Eds.), *Social competence of young children: Risk, disability, and intervention* (pp. 205–231). Baltimore, MD: Paul H. Brookes Publishing Co.

Conroy, M.A., Dunlap, G., Clarke, S., & Alter, P.J. (2005). A descriptive analysis of behavioral intervention research with young children with challenging behavior. *Topics in Early Childhood Special Education, 25,* 157–166.

DeKlyen, M., & Odom, S.L. (1989). Activity structure and social interactions with peers in developmentally integrated play groups. *Journal of Early Intervention, 13,* 342–352.

Denham, S.A., & Brown, C. (2010). "Plays nice with others": Social-emotional learning and academic success. *Early Education and Development, 21*(5), 652–680.

Denham, S.A., & Burton, R. (1996). A social-emotional intervention for at-risk 4-year-olds. *Journal of School Psychology, 34,* 225–245.

Duda, M.A., Dunlap, G., Fox, L., Lentini, R., & Clarke, S. (2004). An experimental evaluation of positive behavior support in a community preschool program. *Topics in Early Childhood Special Education, 24,* 143–155.

Dunlap, G., & Fox, L. (2011). Function-based interventions for children with challenging behavior. *Journal of Early Intervention, 33,* 333–343.

Dunlap, G., Strain, P.S., Fox, L., Carta, J.J., Conroy, M.S., Kern, B.J., . . . Sowell, C. (2006). Prevention and intervention with young children's challenging behavior: Perspectives regarding current knowledge. *Behavioral Disorders, 23,* 29–45.

Fantuzzo, J., Bulotsky-Shearer, R., McDermott, P.A., McWayne, C.F., Frye, D., & Perlman, S. (2007). Investigation of dimensions of social-emotional classroom behavior and school readiness for low-income urban preschool children. *School Psychology Review, 36,* 44–62.

Fixsen, D.L., Blasé, K.A., Duda, M.A., Naoom, S.F., & Van Dyke, M. (2010). Implementation of evidence-based treatments for children and adolescents: Research findings and their implications for the future. In J.R. Weisz & A.E. Kazdin (Eds.), *Evidence-based psychotherapies for children and adolescents* (2nd ed., pp. 435–450). New York, NY: Guilford Press.

Fox, L., Carta, J., Dunlap, G., Strain, P., & Hemmeter, M.L. (2010). Response to intervention and the Pyramid Model. *Infants and Young Children, 23,* 3–14.

Fox, L., Dunlap, G., Hemmeter, M.L., Joseph, G.E., & Strain, P.S. (2003). The Teaching Pyramid: A model for supporting social competence and preventing challenging behavior in young children. *Young Children 58*(4), 48–52.

Fox, L., & Hemmeter, M.L. (2009). A program-wide model for supporting social emotional development and addressing challenging behavior in early childhood settings. In W. Sailor, G. Dunlap, G. Sugai, and R. Horner (Eds.), *Handbook of positive behavior support* (pp. 177–202). New York, NY: Springer.

Fox, L., Hemmeter, M.L., & Jack, S. (2010). *The Early Childhood Program-Wide PBS Benchmarks of Quality.* Unpublished assessment instrument. Tampa: University of South Florida.

Fox, L., Hemmeter, M.L., Snyder, P.S., Binder, D.P., & Clarke, S. (2011). Coaching early childhood special educators to implement a comprehensive model for the promotion of young children's social competence. *Topics in Early Childhood Special Education, 31,* 178–192.

Frey, A.J., Boyce, C.A., & Tarullo, L.B. (2009). Integrating a positive behavior support approach within Head Start. In W. Sailor, G. Dunlap, G. Sugai, & R. Horner (Eds.), *Handbook of positive behavior support* (pp. 125–148). New York, NY: Springer.

Gilliam, W.S. (2005). *Prekindergarteners left behind: Expulsion rates in state prekindergarten systems.* Unpublished manuscript, Yale University, New Haven, CT.

Gilliam, W.S, & Shahar, G. (2006). Preschool and child care expulsion and suspension: Rates and predictors in one state. *Infants and Young Children, 19*(3), 228–245.

Gordon, R.S. (1983). An operational classification of disease prevention. *Public Health Reports, 98,* 107–109.

Graziano, P.A., Reavis, R.D, Keane, S.P, & Calkins, S.D. (2007). The role of emotion regulation in children's early academic success. *Journal of School Psychology, 45*(1), 3–19.

Hemmeter, M.L., Corso, R., & Cheatham, G. (2006). *A national survey of early childhood educators: Training needs and strategies.* Paper presented at the Conference on Research Innovations in Early Intervention, San Diego, CA.

Hemmeter, M.L., & Fox, L. (2009). The Teaching Pyramid: A model for the implementation
of classroom practices within a program-wide approach to behavior support. *Head Start
Dialogue, 12*(2), 133–147.

Hemmeter, M.L., Fox, L., & Doubet, S. (2006). Together we can: An early childhood center's
program wide approach to addressing challenging behavior. *Young Exceptional Children
Monograph,* 1–14.

Hemmeter, M.L., Fox, L., Jack, S., & Broyles, L. (2007). A program wide model of positive
behavior support in early childhood settings. *Journal of Early Intervention, 29,* 337–355.

Hemmeter, M.L., Fox, L., & Snyder, P. (2008). *Teaching Pyramid Observation Tool—Research edition.* Unpublished assessment instrument. Nashville, TN: Vanderbilt University.

Hemmeter, M.L., Ostrosky, M.M., & Fox, L. (2006). Social and emotional foundations for
early learning: A conceptual model for intervention. *School Psychology Review, 35,* 583–601.

Hemmeter, M.L., Snyder, P., Fox, L., & Algina, J. (2011, April). *Efficacy of a classroom wide model for
promoting social-emotional development and preventing challenging behavior.* Paper presented at the
annual meeting of the American Educational Research Association, New Orleans, LA.

Hemmeter, M.L., Snyder, P., Kinder, K.A., & Artman, K.M. (2011). Impact of performance
feedback delivered via electronic mail on preschool teachers' use of descriptive praise.
Early Childhood Research Quarterly, 26, 96–109.

High, P.C., & The Committee on Early Childhood, Adoption, and Dependent Care and
Council on School Health. (2008). School readiness. *Pediatrics, 121,* 1008–1015.

Horner, R.H., Sugai, G., Todd, A.W., & Lewis-Palmer, T. (2005). School-wide positive behavior support. In L.M. Bambara & L. Kern (Eds.), *Individualized supports for students with problem behaviors: Designing positive behavior plans* (pp. 359–390). New York, NY: Guilford Press.

Howes, C., & Hamilton, C.E. (1993). The changing experience of child care: Changes in
teachers and in teacher–child relationships and children's social competence with peers.
Early Childhood Research Quarterly, 8, 15–32.

Howes, C., Phillips, D.A., & Whitebook, M. (1992). Thresholds of quality in child care centers and children's social and emotional development. *Child Development, 63,* 449–460.

Howes, C., & Smith, E.W. (1995). Relations among child care quality, teacher behavior, children's play activities, emotional security, and cognitive activity in child care. *Early Childhood Research Quarterly, 10,* 381–404.

Howse, R.B., Calkins, S.D., Anastopoulos, A.D., Keane, S.P., & Shelton, T.L. (2003). Regulatory contributors to children's kindergarten achievement. *Early Education and Development, 14,* 101–119.

Hunter, A., & Hemmeter, M.L. (2009). The Center on the Social and Emotional Foundations
for Early Learning: Addressing challenging behaviors in infants and toddlers. *Zero to
Three, 29*(3), 5–12.

Jolivette, K., Wehby, J.H., Canale, J., & Massey, G. (2001). Effects of choice-making opportunities on the behavior of students with emotional and behavioral disorders. *Behavioral
Disorders, 26,* 131–145.

Kaufmann, R., & Wischmann, A.L. (1999). Communities supporting the mental health of
young children and their families. In R.N. Roberts & R.R. Magrab (Eds.), *Where children
live: Solutions for serving young children and their families* (pp. 175–210) Stamford, CT: Ablex.

Kazdin, A.E. (1995). Conduct disorder in childhood and adolescence. Thousand Oaks, CA:
Sage.

Kern, L., Ringdahl, J.E., Hilt, A., & Sterling-Turner, H.E. (2001). Linking self-management
procedures to functional analysis results. *Behavioral Disorders, 26,* 214–226.

Kontos, S. (1999). Preschool teachers' talk, roles, and activity settings during free play. *Early
Childhood Research Quarterly, 14,* 363–382.

Lane, K.L., Barton-Arwood, S.M., Nelson, J., & Wehby, R.J. (2008). Academic performance
of students with emotional and behavioral disorders served in a self-contained setting.
Journal of Behavioral Education, 17, 43–62.

LaParo, K.M., & Pianta, R.C. (2000). Predicting children's competence in the early school years: A meta-analytic review. *Review of Educational Research, 70,* 443–484.

Leerkes, E.M., Paradise, M., O'Brien, M., Calkins, S., & Lange, G. (2008). Emotion and cognition processes in preschoolers. *Merrill Palmer Quarterly, 54,* 102–124.

McLaren, E.M., & Nelson, C.M. (2009). Using functional behavior assessment to develop behavior interventions for children in Head Start. *Journal of Positive Behavior Interventions, 11,* 13–21.

Mill, D., & Romano-White, D. (1999). Correlates of affectionate and angry behavior in child care educators of preschool-aged children. *Early Childhood Research Quarterly, 14,* 155–178.

Miller, A.L., Seifer, R., Stroud, L., Sheinkopf, S.J., & Dickstein, S. (2006). Biobehavioral indices of emotion regulation relate to school attitudes, motivation, and behavior problems in a low-income preschool sample. *Annals New York Academy of Sciences, 1094,* 325–329.

National Research Council. (2001). *Eager to learn: Educating our preschoolers.* [Full report and executive summary.] Washington, DC: National Academy Press.

National Research Council and Institute of Medicine. (2000). *From neurons to neighborhoods: The science of early childhood development.* Washington, DC: National Academy Press.

Nelson, J.R., Benner, G.J., & Lane, K. (2004). Academic achievement of K–12 students with emotional and behavioral disorders. *Exceptional Children, 71,* 59–73.

Odom, S.L., McConnell, S.R., & Brown, W.H. (2008). Social competence of young children: Conceptualization, assessment, and influences. In W.H. Brown, S.L. Odom, & S.R. McConnell (Eds.), *Social competence of young children: Risk, disability, and intervention* (pp. 31–59). Baltimore, MD: Paul H. Brookes Publishing Co.

O'Donnell, C.L. (2008). Defining, conceptualizing, and measuring fidelity of implementation and its relationship to outcomes in K–12 curriculum intervention research. *Review of Educational Research, 78,* 33–84.

Payton, J.W., Wardlaw, D.M., Graczyk, P.A., Bloodworth, M.R., Tompsett, C.J., & Weissberg, R.P. (2000). Social and emotional learning: A framework for promoting mental health and reducing risk behaviors in children and youth. *Journal of School Health, 70*(5), 179–185.

Peisner-Feinberg, E.S., Burchinal, M., Clifford, R., Culkin, M., Howes, C., Kagan, S., . . . Rustici, J. (2000). *The children of the cost, quality, and outcomes go to school: Technical report.* Chapel Hill: University of North Carolina at Chapel Hill, Frank Porter Graham Child Development Center.

Pianta, R.C. (2011). Individualized and effective professional development supports in early care and education settings. *Zero to Three, 32,* 4–10.

Pianta, R.C., Mashburn, A.J., Downer, J.T., Hamre, B.K., & Justice, L. (2008). Effects of web-mediated professional development resources on teacher–child interactions in prekindergarten classrooms. *Early Childhood Research Quarterly, 23*(4), 431–451.

Pianta, R.C., Steinberg, M.S., & Rollins, K.B. (1995). The first two years of school: Teacher–child relationships and deflections in children's classroom adjustment. *Development and Psychopathology, 7,* 295–312.

Pierce, E.W., Ewing, L.J., & Campbell, S.B. (1999). Diagnostic status and symptomatic behavior of hard-to-manage preschool children in middle childhood and early adolescence. *Journal of Clinical Child and Adolescent Psychology, 28,* 44–57.

Qi, C.H., & Kaiser, A.P. (2003). Behavior problems of preschool children from low-income families: Review of the literature. *Topics in Early Childhood Special Education, 23,* 188–216.

Sandall, S., Hemmeter, M.L., Smith, B., & McLean, M. (2005). *DEC recommended practices in early intervention/early childhood special education* (2nd ed.). Longmont, CO: Sopris West.

Sanetti, L.M.H., Dobney, L.M., & Gritter, K.L. (2012). Treatment integrity of interventions with children in the Journal of Positive Behavior Interventions from 1999 to 2009. *Journal of Positive Behavior Interventions, 14,* 29–46.

Schwartz, D., McFayden-Ketchum, S., Dodge, K.A., Pettit, G.S., & Bates, J.E. (1998). Early behavior problems as a predictor of later peer group victimization: Moderators and mediators in the pathways of social risk. *Journal of Abnormal Child Psychology, 27*(3), 191–201.

Shaw, D.S., Gilliom, M., & Giovannelli, J. (2000). Aggressive behavior disorders. In H. Zeanah (Ed.), *Handbook of infant mental health* (pp. 397–411). New York, NY: Guilford Press.

Simeonsson, R.J. (1991). Primary, secondary, and tertiary intervention in early intervention. *Journal of Early Intervention, 15,* 124–134.

Snyder, P., Hemmeter, M.L., Fox, L., Crowe, C., & Miller, D. (2011). *Evaluating implementation of evidence-based practices in preschool: Psychometric properties of the Teaching Pyramid Observation Tool*. Manuscript submitted for publication.

Snyder, P.A., Hemmeter, M.L., McLaughlin, T., Algina, J., Sandall, S., & McLean, M. (2011, April). Impact of professional development on preschool teachers' use of embedded instruction practices. Paper presented at the annual meeting of the American Educational Research Association, New Orleans, LA.

Snyder, P.A., McLaughlin, T., & Denney, M. (2011). Frameworks for guiding program focus and practices in early intervention. In J.M. Kauffman & D.P. Hallahan (Series Eds.) & M. Conroy (Section Ed.), *Handbook of special education: Section XII Early identification and intervention in exceptionality* (pp. 716–730). New York, NY: Routledge.

Stormont, M., Lewis, T.J., & Beckner, R. (2005). Positive behavior support systems: Applying key features in preschool settings. *Teaching Exceptional Children, 37* (July/August), 42–49.

Stormont, M.A., Smith, S.C., & Lewis, T.J. (2007). Teacher implementation of precorrection and praise statements in Head Start classrooms as a component of a program-wide system of positive behavior support. *Journal of Behavioral Education, 16*, 280–290.

Strain, P.S., & Timm, M.A. (2001). Remediation and prevention of aggression: A 25-year follow-up of RIP graduates. *Behavioral Disorders, 26*, 297–313.

VanDerHeyden, A.M., & Snyder, P. (2006). Integrating frameworks from early childhood intervention and school psychology to accelerate growth for all young children. *School Psychology Review, 35*, 519–534.

Vaughn, S., Kim, A., Sloan, C.V.M., Hughes, M.T., Elbaum, B., & Sridhar, D. (2003). Social skills interventions for young children with disabilities: A synthesis of group design studies. *Remedial and Special Education, 24*, 2–15.

Walker, H.M., Horner, R.H., Sugai, G., Bullis, M., Sprague, J., Bricker, D., & Kaufman, M.J. (1996). Integrated approaches to preventing antisocial behavior patterns among school-age children and youth. *Journal of Emotional and Behavioral Disorders, 4*, 194–209.

Walker, H.M., Kavanagh, K., Stiller, B., Golly, A., Severson, H.H., & Feil, E.G. (1998). First Step to Success: An early intervention approach for preventing school antisocial behavior. *Journal of Emotional and Behavioral Disorders, 6*(2), 66–80.

Webster-Stratton, C., Reid, M.J., & Hammond, M. (2001). Preventing conduct problems, promoting social competence: A parent and teacher training partnership in Head Start. *Journal of Clinical Child and Adolescent Psychology, 30*, 283–302.

Webster-Stratton, C., Reid, M.J., & Hammond, M. (2004). Treating children with early-onset conduct problems: Intervention outcomes for parent, child, and teacher training. *Journal of Clinical Child and Adolescent Psychology, 33*, 105–124.

Weissberg, R.P., & Greenberg, M.T. (1998). School and community competence enhancement and prevention programs. In I.E. Siegel & K.A. Renninger (Vol. Eds.), *Handbook of child psychology: Vol. 4. Child psychology in practice* (5th ed., pp. 877–954). New York, NY: Wiley.

West, J., Denton, K., & Germino-Hausken, E. (2000). America's kindergartener: Findings from the early childhood longitudinal study, kindergarten class of 1998–99: Fall 1998. *Education Statistics Quarterly, 2*(1), 7–13.

Zins, J.E., Bloodworth, M.R., Weissberg, R.P., & Walberg, H.J. (2007). The scientific base linking social and emotional learning to school success. *Journal of Educational and Psychological Consultation, 17*, 191–210.

Building Blocks

A Framework for Meeting the Needs of All Young Children

Susan R. Sandall and Ilene S. Schwartz

IT STARTS WITH INCLUSION

The Building Blocks framework (Sandall & Schwartz, 2002, 2008) provides a set of educational practices designed to help teachers be more effective at including, teaching, and meeting the specialized needs of young children with disabilities and other special needs in early childhood classrooms and other early learning settings. The Building Blocks framework grew out of our work with the Early Childhood Research Institute on Inclusion, as will be described later. It is this genesis in inclusion and collaboration that, perhaps, distinguishes Building Blocks from some of the other frameworks and models described in this book.

Many early childhood teachers welcome and include children with disabilities in their classrooms, but years of research have demonstrated repeatedly that the physical placement of children with disabilities into the same classroom with typically developing students does not guarantee that children will be socially and instructionally included (e.g., Bricker, 1995). Yet some teachers are able to achieve physical, social, and instructional inclusion. In our own careers as we taught, provided professional development, and conducted research in inclusive early childhood classrooms, we came to understand that successful inclusion is built on a foundation of quality early learning practices for all children. Within this quality early learning environment, teachers use a variety of methods—some obvious and some not so obvious—to help all children participate, interact, and learn from others, and form positive relationships with their peers.

A key lesson that we have learned both from our own professional practice and from the research is that inclusive practices such as the tiered instruction described in the Building Blocks framework cannot occur without successful collaboration. By definition, inclusion requires that professionals from different disciplines and approaches work together to create a learning environment and implement instruction that benefits all children (Buysse & Wesley, 2005).

Several factors are related to successful collaborative and inclusive practices. These are adequate time for team members to meet, respect for others' contributions, trust, effective communication, participation of all team members, and the ability to identify goals and develop strategies (Sandall & Schwartz, 2008). When these practices are implemented regularly, they create an environment in which adults can work together to ensure that a comprehensive and coordinated approach to planning, teaching, and evaluation is in place.

In the Building Blocks framework, we consider the team to be the educational team that makes regular and frequent instructional decisions. Members may be the teacher, assistant teacher, family member(s), therapists, and/or consulting teachers and therapists.

It is only when these collaborative practices exist that the Building Blocks framework (or any other tiered approach to instruction and evaluation) can be implemented with high fidelity and in a manner that results in quality outcomes for children.

THE CONTEXT FOR BUILDING BLOCKS

The construction of Building Blocks as a tiered framework grew out of our work with the Early Childhood Research Institute on Inclusion (Odom, 2002). The goal of this multistate study, funded by the U.S. Department of Education, was to investigate the barriers and facilitators of preschool inclusion. Starting in 1994, the researchers studied an assortment of inclusive programs and classrooms in five states dispersed across the country. As part of the investigation, we observed classroom practices; interviewed teachers, administrators, and parents; and reviewed policies and procedures that documented efforts to establish and sustain effective inclusive programs for young children.

One of the first challenges we faced was defining the characteristics of a successful inclusive classroom. Although our research group was made up of investigators from a number of universities who had been studying inclusion for many years, we did not have a standard definition of inclusion. We all agreed that parents and children should not be placed in the position of being asked to choose either inclusion or intensive instruction, but we did not have a uniform strategy to evaluate what practices were being implemented in the name of inclusion. In fact, we often fell back on the old adage that although we could not easily define the characteristics of inclusion, "we would know it when we saw it" (Schwartz, Sandall, Odom, Horn, & Beckman, 2002). Through systematic literature reviews, behavioral and ethnographic observations, interviews, and directed intervention studies we established parameters to define experiences and environments that were most likely to result in successful inclusive early care and education programs. These were a program philosophy committed to the celebration of diversity and implementation of inclusion, full participation of children with and without disabilities across all program activities, staff trained in and committed to high-quality early childhood education and effective instruction, systematic instruction on individual goals and objectives, and data-based decision making. Our particular interest was in the types of instructional strategies and supports that teachers used to promote the meaningful participation and learning of children with disabilities. Attention to participation and the methods to achieve participation is a defining feature of the Division for Early Childhood (DEC) and National Association for the Education of Young Children (NAEYC) position statement on early childhood inclusion (DEC/NAEYC, 2009).

We believed initially that we would be able to observe classroom teachers and see those practices that were used by teachers who successfully included all children and were not used by those teachers who struggled. As it turned out, we needed to interview successful teachers to truly uncover the careful planning that was necessary to meet the needs of all children. Through successive interviews, focus groups, and participant observation of planning time and class time, we learned more about the educational practices that teachers implement to make their classrooms effective learning environments for all children. Often, these practices were those that have been documented in the literature. Sometimes teachers knew the research that supported the practice, but frequently these effective teachers used their own observations, experimentation, and documented results as the evidence they needed to support their use of the practice. Whether they knew it or not, these teachers were data-based decision makers and intentional teachers.

What did these classrooms look and feel like? They had a positive social climate. The classrooms were, simply, pleasant places to be. There was an expectation that all children would participate and learn. There was also an expectation that adults were available to help by providing interesting activities and materials, by offering encouragement, and by sharing in the excitement of learning. We also observed what we called modifications and adaptations. Teachers provided additional assistance at just the right time, they adapted toys and materials, and they helped children understand directions and routines by using a variety of visual supports. And the classroom incorporated specialized instruction for some children when needed.

One characteristic of successful inclusive classrooms is that they engendered a sense of membership and community (Staub, Peck, Gallucci, & Schwartz, 2000). These classrooms offered activities and routines that supported full participation and hence, membership. Membership refers to how the child is accepted into and participates in groups, as well as the child's sense of belonging to the social fabric of the group. Membership can be achieved through participation in either formal (e.g., circle time) or informal (e.g., playing on the playground) activities. Membership can be informally assessed by looking for any accommodations that are made to facilitate a child's participation in classroom activities (e.g., changes in the rules of a classroom game to give a child with a disability extra time) and overt symbols of membership (e.g., a cubby or mailbox in the classroom). Membership can also be measured by observing teacher-designed groups in the classroom (e.g., literacy groups, snack groups), child-designed groups in and out of the classroom (e.g., play groups, child-initiated projects), activities in which the entire class participates as a whole group (e.g., class meetings), activities in which the entire school participates in one group (e.g., assemblies), and outside-of-school activities (e.g., dance classes, sports teams, activities at churches/synagogues).

We observed that programs that demonstrated higher rates of perceived membership were those that readily made accommodations for children to participate across the daily schedule and curricular activities. Often these accommodations were made spontaneously by the children, sometimes prompting the more observant adults to provide opportunities for children to take the lead in figuring out the most authentic ways to include their peers. Some examples of accommodations that we defined as markers of membership included playing with trains on a raised surface rather than the floor so that a child using a prone stander could participate, and using picture symbols to ask for turns with highly preferred toys so that children who were nonverbal could take part in the play activity.

As we watched classrooms and observed teachers and children, we realized that some of the modifications that teachers made were "behind the scenes." It seemed to us that children were grouped in particular ways, and that activities were sequenced intentionally, so we interviewed teachers to find out what was going on. Then we tested those notions by observing classrooms that were not as successful and by talking to struggling teachers to find out how they planned.

Teachers in successful inclusive classrooms knew a great deal about individual children. They could easily recall children's goals and objectives and also children's likes and dislikes. These teachers anticipated the school day and, whether they wrote elaborate lesson plans or jotted notes to themselves, they were purposeful in the learning experiences, the toys and materials, and the guidance they provided to the children. They weren't stymied if their plans did not quite work as intended. In these classrooms, the teachers were continually observing and listening, and willing to adjust their plans so that a child would get involved and try a little harder. Essentially, these teachers viewed themselves as responsible for children's learning and confident in their ability to figure out how to help children learn.

From our observations and conversations as well as from the literature, we also learned about the challenges and dilemmas that teachers face. Early childhood teachers told us that they lacked the specialized training in the skills needed to teach children with disabilities and special needs. Early childhood special education teachers related their struggles to meet the individualized needs of some students within the active, busy, and often noisy preschool classroom. Consulting and itinerant teachers reported that they lacked effective, easy-to-use, and easy-to-share methods that early childhood teachers could implement in their inclusive classrooms.

Based on our research and our work with teachers, the Building Blocks framework began to take shape.

OVERVIEW OF THE FRAMEWORK

Figure 7.1 depicts the Building Blocks framework. This framework is a set of educational practices for teachers and other members of the educational team to use in a variety of early learning settings. It is organized as a tower of blocks, with each block representing a level of support. There are four key components of the framework. The foundation—a high-quality early childhood program—is important for all children. The remaining blocks—curriculum modifications; embedded learning opportunities; and explicit, child-focused instructional strategies—represent educational practices that may be appropriate for some children to promote their participation in the classroom learning experiences and to acquire individualized learning objectives. The framework also indicates that the intensity and specificity of the practices increase as the blocks become smaller.

Consistent with response to intervention (RTI) principles, the Building Blocks framework begins with a strong foundation of providing an outstanding educational program for all children. In our framework, the universal intervention (i.e., Tier 1) is access to a quality program that implements the necessary modifications to support participation and learning. The secondary intervention (i.e., Tier 2) in the Building Blocks framework is embedded learning opportunities. This level of support is needed by some children to help them acquire individualized learning targets and is considered specially designed instruction. Embedded instruction is provided within the regular classroom during scheduled activities, routines, and

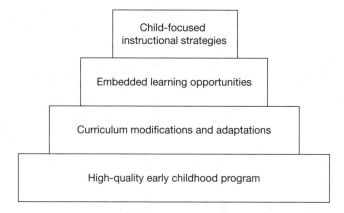

Figure 7.1. The Building Blocks framework. (From Sandall, S.R., & Schwartz, I.S. [2008]. *Building blocks for teaching preschoolers with special needs* [2nd ed., p. 12]. Baltimore, MD: Paul H. Brookes Publishing Co.; reprinted by permission.)

transitions. The tertiary intervention (i.e., Tier 3) in the Building Blocks framework is explicit, child-focused instructional strategies. These instructional strategies provide more intensive, individualized support to children who need more explicit instruction to make progress toward important educational outcomes. Although the aim is to provide as much of this instruction within the regular classroom as possible, this level of support may require quieter, less distracting settings for the initial stages of instruction. The following sections describe each of the Building Blocks components in more detail. These elements and assumptions provide the basis for the Building Blocks framework.

High-Quality Early Childhood Program

The foundational component of the Building Blocks framework is a high-quality early childhood program. Such a program meets principles of developmentally appropriate practice that are based on current knowledge of child development and learning (Copple & Bredekamp, 2006). A high-quality early childhood program is essential for all children and is fundamental to the success of inclusion (Bailey, McWilliam, Buysse, & Wesley, 1998).

High-quality early childhood programs are well-organized environments in which the teachers arrange the setting and prepare learning experiences with clear purposes in mind. Both teachers and children are actively involved in the teaching and learning enterprise. There is a balance of child-initiated and teacher-led activities. Reviews of the research highlight the critical importance of teacher behavior or instructional interactions on program quality and child outcomes (National Research Council, 2000; Pianta et al., 2005). Effective teachers have engaging interactions with children; they join with them, make suggestions and comments, ask thoughtful and thought-provoking questions, and give meaningful feedback.

Another feature of a high-quality early childhood program is attention to the curriculum content, the "knowledge and skills that teachers are expected to teach and children are expected to learn" (Epstein, 2007, p. 5). Child development science and community values inform curriculum content. The early learning guidelines or standards issued by the states represent efforts to articulate the content of the early childhood curriculum. The Head Start Child Development and Early Learning Framework (Administration of Children and Families, 2010) provides a description, based on a substantive review of the research, of the domains and domain elements that are important for a child's school progress and long-term success. The domains are physical development and health, social and emotional development, approaches to learning, logic and reasoning, language development, literacy knowledge and skills, mathematics knowledge and skills, science knowledge and skills, creative arts expression, and social studies knowledge and skills. From the beginning, Building Blocks has aimed to offer an organizing framework to help teachers think about and plan for the level of support a child needs to make meaningful progress across all curricular domains.

Curriculum Modifications and Adaptations

Changes to the ongoing activities, materials, and routines of the classroom are necessary to maximize children's participation and engagement. Early childhood teachers rely heavily on the environment to promote children's development and learning. This includes the physical, social, and temporal aspects of the learning environment—both indoors and outside. Despite the time and thought that teachers put into providing a safe and secure environment, organizing the interest areas, and supplying attractive toys and materials, some children do not take full advantage of the learning environment. Consequently, in the Building Blocks framework we propose modifications and adaptations to the environment as an important level or tier of support for children who are not making good progress. These curriculum modifications and adaptations help teachers make changes to their learning centers and interest areas—that is, the creative arts center, the dramatic play area, the library corner, the block area, and others—so that children engage with the materials and their peers, explore, and learn. Similarly, at this level of support, teachers who see that children are not participating as expected in daily routines are offered suggestions for changes to the schedule or to routine activities such as circle time or snack time. Curriculum modifications are relatively simple adjustments that do not require abundant resources but do require planning. The underlying rationale is that by increasing a child's participation, many more learning opportunities will become available and both teacher and child can take advantage of these opportunities.

Sandall and colleagues (2000) held focus groups consisting of teachers and therapists experienced in early childhood inclusion classrooms. Thirteen focus groups were convened in five states. Participants were given early childhood classroom scenarios featuring typical activities and routines and invited to share methods for including children with disabilities and other special needs. More than 500 unique modifications were shared. The modifications were grouped into eight categories. These categories (see Table 7.1) were confirmed by an expert group of researchers who studied early childhood inclusion.

Although the categories and examples of curriculum modifications surfaced from focus groups, it is not surprising that many of these modifications are supported by the research literature. Many of the modifications offered in the focus groups were environmental arrangements. Previous reviews of the literature (e.g., Kim et al., 2003; Schwartz, Garfinkle, & Davis, 2002) have documented the potential value of modifying features of the environment to enhance children's participation.

Table 7.1. Curriculum modifications

Modification category	Definition	Strategies
Environmental support	Altering the physical, social, and temporal environment to promote participation, engagement, and learning	• Change the physical environment. • Change the social environment. • Change the temporal environment.
Materials adaptation	Modifying materials so that the child can participate as independently as possible	• Have materials or equipment at the appropriate position. • Stabilize materials. • Modify the response. • Make the materials larger or brighter.
Activity simplification	Simplifying a complicated task or activity by breaking it down into smaller steps or by reducing the number of steps	• Break it down. • Change or reduce the number of steps. • Finish with success.
Child preference	If the child is not taking advantage of the available opportunities, identifying and integrating the child's preferences	• Hold a favorite toy. • Use a favorite activity. • Involve a favorite person.
Special equipment	Using special or adaptive devices that allow a child to participate or increase the child's level of participation	• Use special equipment to increase access. • Use special equipment to increase participation.
Adult support	Having an adult step in to support the child's participation and learning	• Model. • Join the child's play. • Use praise and encouragement.
Peer support	Having peers help the child participate and learn	• Model. • Pair the child with a helper or buddy. • Use praise and encouragement.
Invisible support	Purposefully arranging the events within an activity	• Sequence turns. • Sequence activities within a curriculum area.

From Sandall, S.R., & Schwartz, I.S. (2008). *Building blocks for teaching preschoolers with special needs* (2nd ed., p. 54). Baltimore, MD: Paul H. Brookes Publishing Co.; reprinted by permission.

Notably, we have found that by providing teachers with categories or groupings of modifications rather than supplying a "laundry list" of practices, we can better assist teachers in organizing their thinking and planning.

Embedded Learning Opportunities

Embedded learning opportunities (ELOs) are planned instructional interactions that are embedded or integrated within typically occurring activities, routines, and transitions to support children's learning. ELOs provide targeted intervention on individual learning objectives. Using the RTI vocabulary, these are secondary interventions.

Using the ELO strategy requires that teachers identify the learning objective (i.e., what to teach), select or create the opportunities most salient to the objective (i.e., when to teach), and design short, systematic instructional interactions (i.e., how to teach). The instructional interactions are essentially learning trials; they have planned antecedents designed to elicit the target behavior and planned consequences to provide feedback on the child's performance of the behavior. Because terms such as *antecedent* and *consequence* are likely to be unfamiliar to the lead teacher in a general early childhood classroom, our "ELO-at-a-Glance" planning form (Sandall & Schwartz, 2008) signals teachers to plan their instructional interactions by asking themselves the following questions: What are you going to do? What are you going to say? and How will you respond? In addition to planning the interaction, the effective use of ELO requires that teachers repeat the instructional interactions throughout the day to give the child sufficient opportunities to acquire and use the targeted skill or concept.

Embedding and distributing effective instructional practices within and across environments and people is a recommended practice in early childhood special education (Wolery, 2005). Recent research has examined the effectiveness of embedded learning opportunities. A number of terms are used to describe the practice, such as activity-based intervention, embedded instruction, and transition-based teaching. Much of this work builds on the research of Betty Hart and Todd Risley (Hart & Risley, 1975, 1980) on the use of incidental teaching to help children learn more complex language skills.

Embedded instruction is effective for teaching a variety of valued skills to young children. Children have learned preacademic skills, language skills, social skills, motor skills, and self-help skills through embedded instruction. The approach is effective across curricular domains (Daugherty, Grisham-Brown, & Hemmeter, 2001; Filla, Wolery, & Anthony, 1999; Fox & Hanline, 1993; Grisham-Brown, Schuster, Hemmeter, & Collins, 2000; Horn, Lieber, Li, Sandall, & Schwartz, 2000; Kohler, Anthony, Steighner, & Hoyson, 1998; Kohler, Strain, Hoyson, & Jamieson, 1997; Malmskog & McDonnell, 1999; Sewell, Collins, Hemmeter, & Schuster, 1998; VanDerHeyden, Snyder, Smith, Sevin, & Longwell, 2005; Venn et al., 1993; Wolery, Anthony, Caldwell, Snyder, & Morgante, 2002). A variety of instructional strategies have been used, with most employing prompt (i.e., assistance given to help the learner produce the target behavior) and prompt fading procedures (i.e., assistance is systematically removed to help the learner produce the target behavior independently) and reinforcement techniques (i.e., consequence that follows the target behavior and increases the probability that the behavior will occur more frequently) (Daugherty et al., 2001; Filla et al., 1999; Sewell et al., 1998; Venn et al., 1993; Wolery et al., 2002). Further, embedded instruction enhances generalization (Fox & Hanline, 1993; Losardo & Bricker, 1994; Wolery et al., 2002). Studies have also reported high teacher acceptability of the practice, a feature that increases the probability of the use of the practice in everyday classrooms (Horn et al., 2000). As with other specialized instructional practices, teachers differ in the extent to which they can apply embedded instruction in their activities and classrooms (Filla et al., 1999; Horn et al., 2000; Pretti-Frontczak & Bricker, 2001). However, reports from the professional development literature document effective methods for helping teachers learn the practice (Snyder et al., 2012). Reports from teacher preparation programs show that preservice teachers can learn and use embedded instruction in their field experience placements (Phillips & Halle, 2004; Sandall & Davis, 2004; Tate, Thompson & McKerchar, 2005). See Chapter 18 for more information on embedded instruction as a Tier 2 intervention.

Explicit, Child-Focused Instructional Strategies

Child-focused instructional strategies (CFIS) are the practices that teachers use to provide explicit instruction to a child on individual goals and objectives that either do not fit easily into ongoing classroom activities and routines, or on which the child requires more intensive instruction to make adequate progress. Instructional intensity may be achieved by providing more frequent repeated trials on the learning target, breaking down the learning target into smaller steps, and/or making greater use of external reinforcers. CFIS may be compared to tertiary intervention (i.e., Tier 3) in the traditional RTI model. Although CFIS may be used with only a few children in the inclusive classroom, teachers must be fluent in them and know when and how to implement these strategies when needed. As with other types of tertiary supports, CFIS are used after children have been given multiple opportunities to learn and practice targeted skills and concepts using less intensive strategies. If learning is not observed, CFIS are considered. CFIS are implemented when the educational team, after reviewing the data, sees that more intensive instruction or perhaps a different type of instruction is warranted.

The strategies used at this tier of support have a long history of success in education with people across the spectrum of developmental disabilities, including preschool children (Wolery, 2005). These strategies include systematic prompting and prompt fading (e.g., time delay), use of different schedules of positive reinforcement contingent on correct child responding (e.g., differential reinforcement), and explicit framing of instructional sequences (e.g., discrete trials—a systematic method of teaching involving breaking down behaviors into small steps and using planned discriminative stimuli and consequences; direct instruction). Teachers make their instruction explicit and direct enough to foster child success. As children demonstrate success and mastery of the skill and/or concept, the adult direction and support are faded so that correct responding is maintained by more typical levels of support.

Often, when teachers think of tertiary instructional supports, they assume that this level of instruction must be provided in different places, often using different materials, and usually in isolated or separated settings. CFIS are not conceptualized that way, nor should they be practiced that way. Although there may be some situations in which a child may benefit from receiving the initial stages of instruction in a quiet setting with fewer distractions, the Building Blocks framework is designed to help teachers add structure, intensity, and specificity to instruction within the inclusive classroom rather than removing the child from the classroom. For example, McBride and Schwartz (2003) demonstrated that CFIS could be used to improve child outcomes in inclusive classrooms. They systematically coached teachers to use more frequent discrete trial instruction within classroom routines and activities to provide instruction on individualized education program (IEP) objectives for children with disabilities. This explicit instruction increased the rate of acquisition of individual learning targets. An associated outcome was increased proximity of the target children with disabilities to typically developing children in the classroom, thereby enhancing the possibilities for social interactions.

CFIS are implemented most effectively when instruction is provided in the natural environment. The natural environment is defined as the setting in which the child will need to use that skill in the future, and it can include classroom, home, child care, playground, and community settings. When instruction is provided in settings other than those where the child will need to functionally demonstrate the target skill, issues of generalization must be addressed. If children are removed from the inclusive setting to receive intensive instruction, it is essential to remember that the skill is not achieved until it can be used independently in the natural environment. In this case, the instructional program includes a systematic plan to help the child generalize the newly acquired skill to the natural environment (Schwartz, Davis, McLaughlin, & Rosenberg, 2009; Stokes & Baer, 1977).

DATA-BASED DECISION MAKING

The use of evidence-based practices and data-based decision making has long been a cornerstones of early childhood special education practices and is now mandated for the education of all children through federal legislation (e.g., Individuals with Disabilities Education Improvement Act of 2004 [PL 108-446], No Child Left Behind Act of 2001 [PL 107-110], Improving Head Start for School Readiness Act of 2007 [PL 110-134]). The practice of observing child performance, collecting data, and reviewing data on both individual children and program effectiveness is part of what constitutes high-quality programming. There are many sources describing the use of evidence-based practices in early education (e.g., Buysse & Wesley, 2005; Joseph & Strain, 2003; Odom & Strain, 2002; Sandall, Hemmeter, Smith, & McLean, 2005). These documents are important for helping teachers understand the range of interventions that have an evidence base. In the context of the Building Blocks framework, we are interested in examining evidence that is related to the developmental and educational progress being made by a specific learner.

Ongoing child assessment is a key feature of the Building Blocks framework. Rather than designing a system specific to Building Blocks, we chose to use existing methods of child assessment that were compatible with the general early childhood context and could be incorporated into the continuous improvement initiatives of Head Start and state pre-K. For example, Head Start requires that programs collect, aggregate, and analyze child information two to three times per year using valid and reliable measures. This requirement can be aligned with the principle of formative assessment, a basic feature of RTI. As instructional intensity increases, more frequent progress monitoring is warranted. The Building Blocks framework accommodates different methods of collecting this information, including counting behaviors, taking regular notes based on observations, and collecting work samples.

Ensuring that accurate information on child progress is being collected on a regular basis is key. This information guides instructional decision making and helps the educational team evaluate whether an intervention that has a documented evidence base is actually effective in the way that it is being implemented with a specific child, to teach a specific skill in a specific context. This type of data-based decision making—looking at the evidence one child at a time—is central to the success of the Building Blocks framework or any type of tiered instructional system. There are three essential steps to data-based decision making: collecting the data, analyzing the data, and taking action based on the analysis. We will describe each of these steps and explain how they fit into the Building Blocks framework.

Collecting information about child progress is the first step. Although some teachers may get overwhelmed at the idea of frequent data collection, it is important to remember that many different types of artifacts and evidence can be used. We also know that although it may be difficult at first for some teachers to become fluent data collectors, children make more progress when they are in classrooms with teachers who collect and analyze child performance data (Hojnoski, Gischlar, & Missall, 2009). The purpose of collecting child performance data in this context is to gather information that will help the team answer important questions about the child's learning. Therefore, many types of evidence can be used, ranging from teachers' notes to children's artwork to systematic observations of child behavior by a trained observer to direct testing of a child's performance on a specific task. It is essential, however, when you are working with children who have significant instructional needs, to ensure that the data you collect match target behaviors and criteria listed in the individual goals and objectives.

Once the data are collected, they must be organized so that the educational team can analyze whether or not the child is progressing toward the desired goal. Traditionally, data have been displayed graphically to help teams analyze them, but any number of data displays, from summaries of children's work to carefully arranged teacher notes, can be used to track children's progress. The key to analyzing the data is that the information must be presented to all the team members in forms that are accessible and understandable so that the team can determine whether the child is learning the skills and behaviors that are being taught.

Next, the team formulates and implements an action plan based on their analysis. In the simplest terms, this may be "The child is making expected progress; continue the program as is." A more complicated analysis may be "The child is not progressing at the expected rate; we need to change something about the instructional programming (e.g., intensity, content, instructional strategies) to help the child be more successful." The underlying philosophy of data-based decision making is quite pragmatic—if the child is not making progress, the adults need to change something about the way the child is being taught. We assume that the problem lies with the instruction, not with the child, and that taking a wait-and-see approach is not the best option.

A tool to help teachers plan for effective instruction, including the data collection and analysis needed to implement data-based decision making, is an *activity matrix* (Sandall & Schwartz, 2008). The activity matrix described in the Building Blocks framework was originally conceptualized as a tool to help teachers plan for specially designed instruction within the context of an inclusive preschool environment. What we have found, however, is that many teams use their activity matrix as the blueprint for their planning, teaching, and evaluation. The flexibility of this approach allows every team to individualize the matrices to meet the needs of their students and the preferences of their staff. For example, some classrooms may use the activity matrix to organize teaching and learning opportunities (see Figure 7.2 for an example), updating the matrix as changes are made to individual goals and objectives, but collecting data on separate data sheets and creating graphs to display the data they collect. Other teams may use the activity matrix to help them keep track of the data that they are collecting. For example, if the aim is to collect data at least once a week for every active objective, teachers may indicate that data have been collected by marking specific objectives on the matrix with a yellow marker. Finally, some teams may choose to embed their data collection on the activity matrix, leaving room on that sheet of paper for staff to record

Classroom Activity Matrix

Date:	Rashan	Nadia	Teacher's name: Marco	Chloe			
Arrival				ELO—Follow two-step direction in context			
Morning meeting	ELO—Make comments/questions with picture book	ELO—Move from walker to chair and return	ELO—Sit and participate for 10 minutes.	CFIS—Use two-word utterance to comment			
Learning Centers	CFIS—Copy circular shape	ELO—Move from walker to chair and return	CFIS—Take turn in game with peer	CFIS—Use two-word utterance to comment			
Snack	ELO—Share/exchange objects with peers	ELO—Move from walker to chair and return	CFIS—Take turn in game with peer	CM—Group objects by color or shape			
Toileting	ELO—Pull up pants	ELO—Move from walker to chair and return					
Outside	ELO—Share/exchange objects with peers	CFIS—Walk with walker on uneven surface	ELO—Play near peers				
Small group time	CFIS—Copy circular shape ELO—Make comments/ask questions with picture book	ELO—Move from walker to chair and return		CM—Group objects by color or shape			
Departure				ELO—Follow two-step direction in context			

Figure 7.2. Classroom activity matrix. (Key: CM = curriculum modification; ELO = embedded learning opportunities; CFIS = child-focused instructional strategies.) (Source: Sandall & Schwartz, 2008.)

their observations. The important point is that an activity matrix is a tool that can be used to facilitate the implementation of assessment and intervention within a tiered framework in an inclusive early childhood classroom.

SUMMARY

Building Blocks was originally designed as a framework for planning and providing individualized support and instruction to preschoolers with disabilities and other special needs within inclusive preschool classrooms. Drawing on experience and research, we constructed a framework that rests on a firm foundation of a high-quality early childhood classroom. There are three additional levels of support—curriculum modifications, embedded learning opportunities, and explicit teaching. These levels of support are aimed at ensuring that children receive the attention and instruction they need. Ongoing child assessment is used to guide instructional decision making and monitor children's progress. Building Blocks grew out of our desire to achieve physical, social, and instructional inclusion for young children. The features of what became the Building Blocks framework are consistent with the components of an RTI approach in early childhood.

REFERENCES

Administration of Children and Families. (2010). *The Head Start child development and early learning framework: Promoting positive outcomes in early childhood programs serving children 3–5 years old*. Washington, DC: Health and Human Services/Adminstration for Children and Families/Office of Head Start.

Bailey, D.B., McWilliam, R.A., Buysse, V., & Wesley, P.W. (1998). Inclusion in the context of competing values in early childhood education. *Early Childhood Research Quarterly, 13*, 27–48.

Bricker, D. (1995). The challenge of inclusion. *Journal of Early Intervention, 19*, 179–194.

Buysse, V., & Wesley, P.W. (2005). *Consultation in early childhood settings*. Baltimore, MD: Paul H. Brookes Publishing Co.

Copple, C., & Bredekamp, S. (2006). *Basics of developmentally appropriate practice: An introduction for teachers of children 3 to 6*. Washington, DC: National Association for the Education of Young Children.

Daugherty, S., Grisham-Brown, J., & Hemmeter, M.L. (2001). The effects of embedded skill instruction on the acquisition of target and nontarget skills in preschoolers with developmental delays. *Topics in Early Childhood Special Education, 21*, 214–221.

Division of Early Childhood/National Association for the Education of Young Children. (2009). *Early childhood inclusion: A joint position statement of the Division for Early Childhood (DEC) and the National Association for the Education of Young Children (NAEYC)*. Chapel Hill: University of North Carolina, FPG Child Development Institute.

Epstein, A.S. (2007). *The intentional teacher: Choosing the best strategies for young children's learning*. Washington, DC: National Association for the Education of Young Children.

Filla, A., Wolery, M., & Anthony, L. (1999). Promoting children's conversations during play with adult prompts. *Journal of Early Intervention, 22*, 93–108.

Fox, L., & Hanline, M.F. (1993). A preliminary evaluation of learning within developmentally appropriate early childhood settings. *Topics in Early Childhood Special Education, 13*, 308–327.

Grisham-Brown, J.L., Schuster, J.W., Hemmeter, M.L., & Collins, B.C. (2000). Using an embedded strategy to teach preschoolers with significant disabilities. *Journal of Behavior Education, 10*, 139–162.

Hart, B., & Risley, T.R. (1975). Incidental teaching of language in the preschool. *Journal of Applied Behavior Analysis, 8*(4), 411–420.

Hart, B., & Risley, T.R. (1980). *In vivo* language intervention: Unanticipated general effects. *Journal of Applied Behavior Analysis, 13*(3), 407–432.

Hojnoski, R.L., Gischlar, K.L., & Missall, K.N. (2009). Improving child outcomes with data-based decision making: Collecting data. *Young Exceptional Children, 12*(3), 32–44.

Horn, E., Lieber, J., Li, S.M., Sandall, S.R., & Schwartz, I. (2000). Supporting young children's IEP goals in inclusive settings through embedded learning opportunities. *Topics in Early Childhood Special Education, 20*, 208–223.

Improving Head Start for School Readiness Act of 2007, PL 110-134, 42 U.S.C. §§ 9801 *et seq.*

Individuals with Disabilities Education Improvement Act (IDEA) of 2004, PL 108-446, 20 U.S.C. §§ 1400 *et seq.*

Joseph, G.E., & Strain, P.S. (2003). Comprehensive evidence-based social-emotional curricula for young children: An analysis of efficacious adoption potential. *Topics in Early Childhood Special Education, 23*, 65–76.

Kim, A., Vaughn, S., Elbaum, B., Hughes, M.T., Sloan, C.V.M., & Sridhar, D. (2003). Effects of toys or group composition for children with disabilities: A synthesis. *Journal of Early Intervention, 25*, 189–205.

Kohler, F.W., Anthony, L.J., Steighner, S.A., & Hoyson, M. (1998). Teaching social interaction skills in the integrated preschool: An examination of naturalistic tactics. *Topics in Early Childhood Special Education, 21*, 93–103.

Kohler, F.W., Strain, P.S., Hoyson, M., & Jamieson, B. (1997). Merging naturalistic teaching and peer-based strategies to address the IEP objectives of preschoolers with autism: An examination of structural and behavior outcomes. *Focus on Autism and Other Developmental Disabilities, 12*, 196–206.

Losardo, A., & Bricker, D.D. (1994). Activity-based intervention and direct instruction: A comparison study. *American Journal on Mental Retardation, 98*, 744–765.

Malmskog, S., & McDonnell, A.P. (1999). Teacher-mediated facilitation of engagement by children with developmental delays in inclusive preschools. *Topics in Early Childhood Special Education, 19*, 203–216.

McBride, B.J., & Schwartz, I.S. (2003). Effects of teaching early interventionists to use discrete trials during ongoing classroom activities. *Topics in Early Childhood Special Education, 23*(1), 5–18.

National Research Council. (2000). *Eager to learn: Educating our preschoolers.* Washington, DC: National Academy Press.

No Child Left Behind Act of 2001, PL 107-110, 115 Stat. 1425, 20 U.S.C. §§ 6301 *et seq.*

Odom, S.L. (Ed.) (2002). *Widening the circle: Including children with disabilities in preschool programs.* New York, NY: Teachers College Press.

Odom. S., & Strain, P.S. (2002). Early intervention practices supported by single case designs. *Journal of Early Intervention, 25*, 151–160.

Phillips, B., & Halle, J. (2004). The effects of a teacher-training intervention on student interns' use of naturalistic language teaching strategies. *Teacher Education and Special Education, 27*, 81–96.

Pianta, R.C., Howes, C., Burchinal, M., Bryant, D., Clifford, R., Early, D., & Barbarin, O. (2005). Features of pre-kindergarten programs classrooms, and teachers: Do they predict observed classroom quality and child–teacher interactions? *Applied Developmental Science, 9*, 144–159.

Pretti-Frontczak, K., & Bricker, D.D. (2001). Use of the embedding strategy by early childhood education and early childhood special education teachers. *Infant and Toddler Intervention: The Transdisciplinary Journal, 11*, 29–46.

Sandall, S.R., & Davis, C.A. (2004, November). *Learning to embed instruction: Effects of a field-based project for preservice teachers.* Paper presented at the Council for Exceptional Children Teacher Education Division Annual Conference, Albuquerque, NM.

Sandall, S.R., Hemmeter, M.L., Smith, B.J., & McLean, M.E. (2005). *DEC recommended practices: A comprehensive guide for practical application in early intervention/early childhood special education.* Longmont, CO: Sopris West.

Sandall, S.R., Joseph, G., Chou, H.-Y., Schwartz, I.S., Leiber, J., Horn, E., Wolery, R., & Odom, S.L. (2000). *Talking to practitioners: Focus group report on curriculum modifications in inclusive classrooms.* Unpublished manuscript.

Sandall, S.R., & Schwartz, I.S. (2002). *Building blocks for teaching preschoolers with special needs.* Baltimore, MD: Paul H. Brookes Publishing Co.

Sandall, S.R., & Schwartz, I.S. (2008). *Building blocks for teaching preschoolers with special needs* (2nd ed.). Baltimore, MD: Paul H. Brookes Publishing Co.

Schwartz, I.S., Davis, C.A., McLaughlin, A., & Rosenberg, N. (2009). Generalization in school setting: Strategies for planning and teaching. In C. Whalen (Ed.), *Real life: Real progress for children with autism spectrum disorders* (pp. 195–212). Baltimore, MD: Paul H. Brookes Publishing Co.

Schwartz, I.S., Garfinkle, A., & Davis, C. (2002). Arranging preschool environments to facilitate valued social and educational outcomes. In M. Shinn, H. Walker, & G. Stoner (Eds.), *Interventions for academic and behavior problems II: Preventive and remedial approaches.* Bethesda, MD: National Association of School Psychologists.

Schwartz, I.S., Sandall, S.R., Odom, S.L., Horn, E., & Beckman, P.J. (2002). "I know it when I see it": In search of a common definition of inclusion. In S.L. Odom (Ed.), *Widening the circle: Including children with disabilities in preschool programs* (pp. 10–24). New York, NY: Teachers College Press.

Sewell, T.J., Collins, B.C., Hemmeter, M.L., & Schuster, J.W. (1998). Using simultaneous prompting within an activity-based format to teach dressing skills to preschoolers with developmental delays. *Journal of Early Intervention, 21,* 132–145.

Snyder, P., Hemmeter, M.L., Artman Meeker, K., Kinder, K., Pasia, C., & McLaughlin, T. (2012). Characterizing key features of early childhood professional development intervention. Manuscript in submission.

Staub, D., Peck, C.A., Gallucci, C., & Schwartz, I.S. (2000) Peer relationships. In M. Snell & F. Brown (Eds.), *Instruction of students with severe disabilities* (pp. 381–408). Upper Saddle River, NJ: Merrill.

Stokes, T.F., & Baer, D.M. (1977). An implicit technology of generalization. *Journal of Applied Behavior Analysis, 10*(2), 349–367.

Tate, T.L., Thompson, R.H., & McKerchar, P.M. (2005). Training teachers in an infant classroom to use embedded teaching strategies. *Education and Treatment of Children, 28*(3), 206–221.

VanDerHeyden, A.M., Snyder, P., Smith, A., Sevin, B., & Longwell, J. (2005). Effects of complete learning trials on child engagement. *Topics in Early Childhood Special Education, 25*(2), 81–94.

Venn, M.L., Wolery, M., Werts, M.G., Morris, A., DeCesare, L.D., & Cuffs, M.S. (1993). Embedding instruction in art activities to teach preschoolers with disabilities to imitate their peers. *Early Childhood Research Quarterly, 8,* 277–294.

Wolery, M. (2005). DEC Recommended Practices: Child-focused practices. In S. Sandall, M.L. Hemmeter, B.J. Smith, & M.E. McLean, *DEC Recommended Practices: A comprehensive guide for practical application in early intervention/early childhood special education* (pp. 71–106). Longmont, CO: Sopris West.

Wolery, M., Anthony, L., Caldwell, N.K., Snyder, E.D., & Morgante, J.D. (2002). Embedding and distributing constant time delay in circle time and transitions. *Topics in Early Childhood Special Education, 22,* 14–25.

Assessment within
Response to Intervention

8

The Role of Assessment within Response to Intervention in Early Education

Ellen S. Peisner-Feinberg and Virginia Buysse

CURRENT CONTEXT OF EARLY CHILDHOOD ASSESSMENT

Assessment of children, especially young children, is a topic that has generated increasing attention, as well as some differences in perspectives about what is best practice. It has become a key focus in many current educational initiatives as policy makers, educators, and researchers grapple with issues around the best way to demonstrate program effects and promote children's development. As a prime example, the assessment of young children is a critical component of discussions around pre-K–3 alignment, the idea that teaching and learning should be coordinated from prekindergarten through third grade in order to optimize children's development. Assessment helps promote both horizontal and vertical alignment by offering a means for gathering the data necessary to find out whether children are learning the desired skills at each grade level. It also helps ensure that instruction is of high quality and aligned across grade levels by providing a means of measuring progress toward a set of expectations for skill development over time. A second example can be seen in the recent Race-to-the-Top Early Learning Challenge federal grant competition, in which one of the priorities focused on measuring outcomes and progress, including showing how kindergarten entry assessments were aligned with state early learning standards, covered all domains of learning, and were valid, reliable, and appropriate for the populations assessed. Some of the winning states added corresponding prekindergarten assessment to further promote alignment and school readiness. Another example derives from the increasing use of child assessment in state early childhood quality rating improvement systems (QRISs). The goal of a QRIS is to improve the overall quality of early care and education programs, ultimately leading to better outcomes for children, by creating a transparent and easily understood quality rating system that ideally involves feedback, technical assistance, and incentives (Zellman & Karoly, 2012). Accordingly, many QRISs incorporate some form of child assessment for measuring children's progress in developing key skills, although the use of these results is often limited (Zellman & Karoly, 2012). Finally, as state prekindergarten programs have become more widespread, their policies regarding child assessment offer another example of the growing emphasis, although not necessarily consensus, on this issue. A

121

recent analysis of these policies highlighted a great deal of variability across states in the types of measures mandated (direct assessments versus observational checklists and scales versus combinations versus no specification), practitioners' degree of choice in selecting particular measures (no choice versus a menu versus some local determination), and the frequency of assessment and reporting of results (ranging from one to five times per school year) (Ackerman & Coley, 2012).

With the large numbers of young children in early childhood programs in the United States and the increasing push toward accountability for educational programs, assessment is an important means of ensuring that children receive the appropriate level of instruction and intervention, of enabling access to necessary services, and of measuring program effects in regard to children's outcomes. Although all of these uses of assessment have a role, it is important to understand the differences among them when making assessment-related decisions. Because there are implications for children's education and well-being, it is important that both the assessment process and use of the results take into account the purpose for gathering this information, the appropriateness of the measurement instruments and procedures for the child, and the broader context within which this information is being used.

The National Research Council Report on early childhood assessment outlined two key principles regarding the use of assessment with young children: 1) the purpose of an assessment should be the guiding factor underlying assessment decisions, and 2) assessment should be conducted within a coherent system of educational, medical, and family support services to promote optimal development (National Research Council, 2009). Commensurate with the first principle, decisions about the types of measures, the particular instruments, and the assessment procedures should be guided by the validity of their use for the intended purpose. It is important to keep in mind that the evidence base supporting the use of an assessment for a given purpose may not support the use of that same assessment for a different purpose. Further, the characteristics of the particular child need to be taken into account as well in determining the appropriateness of the assessment tools and procedures.

Moreover, the context within which this information is being used needs to be considered. Assessment results in the early childhood field are used within policy, educational, and research contexts. Ideally, in accord with the second principle of the National Research Council Report, all of these different systems would be integrated and assessment results would be used across systems, with the common goal of optimizing children's development. In reality, however, these different applications can vary in the extent to which they are being used for low-stakes or high-stakes decision making. The greater the potential consequences of the results, the more critical it becomes that these decisions are based on reliable evidence that meets the highest standards.

Accordingly, consideration needs to be given to the context within which assessment information is being used, how the context itself may affect the meaning and use of that information, and whether the most appropriate information is being used to make decisions. Assessment results are used within a policy context to make decisions with regard to funding for programs or services, as an indicator of program accountability, and as a method of monitoring compliance with program standards. Many of these uses of assessment within policy contexts can have high-stakes consequences, resulting in decisions about whether programs continue to exist or not. If such decisions are made based on assessment results, it is critical that the information be appropriate with regard to the learning goals and population served by the program, be gathered using appropriate procedures, and be reviewed objectively and in accord with predetermined goals and objectives.

Within an educational context, assessment information has implications from both general and special education perspectives. From a general education perspective, assessment results can be used to inform instruction for early childhood programs, both at the level of the classroom and the individual child. The use of assessment to inform instruction has become recommended practice in early childhood education, as seen in the section on assessing children's development and learning in the most recent National Association for the Education of Young Children Position Statement on Developmentally Appropriate Practice in Early Childhood Programs (Copple & Bredekamp, 2009). However, for many early childhood programs, it is challenging to figure out how to determine the best assessment instruments to use for various purposes, how to integrate the variety of assessment information that they may be gathering for different purposes, and how to use that information to make instructional decisions. In many cases, there may be different assessment requirements related to various program guidelines and/or funding streams, further adding to this challenge. Moreover, teachers—the ones who are directly responsible for implementing instruction—do not always have the opportunity to see or use assessment results; many times these results are simply used for program-level reporting and accountability, not for classroom-level decision making. Accordingly, among the key issues for the use of assessment in educational practice is to determine how to make sure that only useful information is gathered, that it is relevant to the intended purposes, and that it is actually used to make appropriate decisions.

From a special education perspective, assessment information has a long history of use with regard to referral for evaluation and eligibility determination for special education services for individual children. This, of course, represents one of the classic high-stakes uses of assessment, and it is critical that both the measures and the decisions be based on valid, reliable, and appropriate information. There has been much concern within the field about this issue (e.g., Hosp & Madyun, 2007), and although it is beyond the scope of this chapter to delve into all of these issues, it is important to acknowledge them, as this history helps inform our current thinking about the use of assessment in early childhood education more broadly.

Within a research context, assessment typically plays a key role in many studies of early childhood education, both as outcome data and as part of the treatment in intervention studies. Assessment can be incorporated as part of the intervention itself, ideally linked to instruction, in research studies that seek to examine the impact of changing early childhood practices to improve teaching and learning. As outcome data from research, assessment results can inform decision making for early childhood programs by providing evidence for determining best practices.

In thinking about the use of assessment within a response to intervention (RTI) framework for early education, it is useful to consider all of these existing uses of assessment in order to understand what is similar and what is unique about this specific application and to make sure that it is being implemented appropriately. Because the use of assessment within RTI may be a new application for many early childhood programs, there will be many issues to address with regard to how this fits with current assessment practices and many decisions about what should stay the same and what should change. As a field, we currently have little guidance about these issues for early education, given that this is a relatively new practice for children in the preschool years. As programs work to create an integrated assessment plan that includes a focus on RTI, they need to consider the various purposes for which they are gathering assessment information; the types of assessment tools to use for those given purposes; how to interpret and use the information gathered for making instructional decisions; and whom to involve in the decision-making process, including the roles of educators and families. Accordingly, this chapter provides information about the definitions, purposes, and uses of assessment within RTI for early childhood; offers an illustration of the application of formative assessment within Recognition & Response (R&R), an RTI framework for early childhood education; and concludes with musings about future directions for the field.

DEFINITIONS AND PURPOSES OF CHILD ASSESSMENT

Child assessment can be defined as a systematic process for gathering and documenting information about a child's knowledge, skills, or abilities based on a sample of behavior. Although this definition may seem simple at first glance, it contains four important features: 1) it entails a defined process; 2) it involves the collection and documentation of information; 3) it focuses on a child's knowledge, skills, or abilities; and 4) it represents a sample of behavior. Each of these features is critical for distinguishing among different types of assessment approaches, as well as for distinguishing assessment from other activities that occur in educational settings, such as instruction or intervention. Although the latter distinction may seem obvious, it is reminiscent of the adage warning educators to beware of "teaching to the test," or in this case, of using the test as the medium for teaching. Especially in the early childhood field, where assessment items are often game-like and fun in order to appeal to young children, they may look similar to instructional activities designed to teach children new skills, as opposed to assessment activities that are designed to sample children's behavior in order to measure their level of skill acquisition.

Assessment Terminology

A variety of terms are used to refer to different types of educational assessment approaches, and their meanings are not always intuitive. In considering different types of assessment, one overarching term that applies to many of these forms is the idea of ongoing assessment. *Ongoing assessment* refers to information that is gathered periodically throughout the year to inform teachers about what children currently understand and how to proceed with subsequent teaching and learning. The key term used in early childhood education to refer to this idea is formative assessment (e.g., Copple & Bredekamp, 2009). *Formative assessment* refers to periodic gathering of information or data about children's knowledge and learning that is used to inform teachers about how to proceed with instruction. Formative assessment activities are usually low-stakes, and in the case of older children, do not contribute to the final evaluation or grade of the student. Formative assessment also is the general term used for assessment activities within RTI in early childhood, which comprise two specific types of activities: universal screening and progress monitoring. The first type of assessment activity used in RTI, *universal screening*, refers to brief standardized assessments of all children to determine which children are meeting benchmarks or learning goals and which children need additional instructional supports or interventions based on these results. Universal screening tools involve direct assessments of children's skills related to academic achievement or positive behavior change (Gresham, 2007), although the focus for assessment in RTI tends to be on academic learning. It is important to distinguish universal screening from other types of screening that are commonly used in early childhood settings, notably developmental screening. The purpose of *developmental screening* involves referral and evaluation for potential developmental delays or disabilities, in contrast with the purpose of universal screening, which is to inform instructional decision making. Developmental screening assessments are used to determine whether children are exhibiting basic developmental milestones as expected, and if they are not, children are referred for a diagnostic evaluation to determine whether there is evidence of a developmental delay or disability. Other types of screening assessments that routinely occur in early education, such as vision and hearing screenings, are similar in process to developmental screenings and can lead to follow-up diagnostic evaluations, depending on the results.

The second type of assessment activity used in RTI, *progress monitoring*, is designed to measure children's progress as a result of instructional adaptations (i.e., to measure their responsiveness to intervention), and to make adjustments to instruction based on these results. Thus, both progress monitoring and universal screening assessments should be tied to the broad educational goals of the program, should focus on skills that are consistent with those being taught through general instruction and targeted interventions, and should be used for ongoing instructional decision making. A specific approach to screening and progress monitoring commonly used in RTI contexts for school-age children is *curriculum-based measurement*, or *CBM*. This is sometimes referred to as *general outcome measurement*, or *GOM*, although this terminology applies to more generic procedures (Deno, 2003) and seems to be used less commonly with regard to RTI. CBM refers to a set of assessment methods designed to provide teachers with reliable and valid indicators of children's academic competence at a single point in time (for screening) and over time (for progress monitoring), based on standardized assessment tools and procedures (Deno, 2003; Fuchs & Fuchs, 2007). Despite its name, CBM is independent of any particular curriculum and focuses instead on generalizable academic skills in broad domains of learning, such as reading or math. CBM assessments are fluency based, using timed tests to measure the accuracy and ease with which children are able to perform component skills (Fuchs & Fuchs, 2007). Consistent with the basic principles of universal screening and progress monitoring in RTI, CBM was designed specifically to help teachers evaluate children's levels and rates of academic achievement, monitor their progress relative to peers or academic benchmarks, set short- and long-term instructional goals, and determine needs for instructional change, independent of a particular curriculum (Busch & Reschly, 2007; Fuchs & Fuchs, 2007). In contrast, *curriculum-based assessment*, or *CBA*, refers to assessments of children's performance in order to inform instruction and evaluate progress toward the specific learning goals that are unique to a given curriculum. Based on the results of performance on a CBA instrument, teachers can determine instructional goals and make adjustments to the curriculum as needed. Because CBAs are tied directly to a particular curriculum, they are not appropriate for use within RTI approaches.

One other approach that is often mentioned in conjunction with assessment in the early intervention field is that of *authentic assessment* (Bagnato, Neisworth, & Pretti-Frontczak, 2010; Stevenson, Grisham-Brown & Pretti-Frontczak, 2011). Although the idea of authentic assessment is commonly mentioned in early intervention, it is counter to the perspective of assessment within RTI in some ways. Authentic assessment has been defined as "the systematic recording of developmental observations over time about the naturally occurring behaviors and functional competencies of young children in daily routines by familiar and knowledgeable caregivers in the child's life" (Bagnato & Ye Ho, 2006). A related idea in early childhood education is that of *performance assessment*, most often associated with particular assessment techniques such as the *Work Sampling System*, where teachers observe and document children's performance using developmental guidelines and checklists, portfolios, and summary reports (Meisels, 1996; Meisels, 2005; Meisels, Fong-ruey, Dorfman, & Nelson, 1995). Although both RTI and these other perspectives share an emphasis on familiar caregivers (e.g., teachers) as an important feature, they differ in terms of the primary approach. Both authentic assessment and performance assessment focus on naturalistic observations of children's behaviors in their typical settings and routines (Bagnato, Neisworth, & Pretti-Frontczak, 2010; Meisels, 2005), in contrast to RTI approaches, which rely on direct assessments of children's skills and abilities using developmentally appropriate, standardized measures. In understanding the perspective of authentic assessment, it is important to recognize that this approach grew out of the early intervention field as a reaction to what was perceived as high-stakes testing of young children with disabilities that used limited approaches based on standardized assessment measures and procedures. In contrast, this approach emphasized functional behavior assessment for children with disabilities—that is, assessments that focus on basic functions such as self-help, adaptive, and social skills, as opposed to the academic or cognitive skills that are typically measured in standardized assessments and are the focus of RTI. The idea of performance assessment had a similar genesis but was largely a reaction to the impact of standardized testing on how teachers were teaching and children were learning (Meisels, 1993); as such, it shares the goal—if not the approach—of RTI, which focuses on linking assessment to instruction.

USE OF ASSESSMENT WITHIN A RESPONSE TO INTERVENTION CONTEXT IN EARLY EDUCATION

Within an RTI context in early education, as well as in school-age settings, formative assessment plays a key role in providing data for making instructional decisions. Based on formative assessment results, educators can determine whether children are meeting key benchmarks in terms of learning goals and monitor whether children are making adequate progress throughout the year. If it is determined that some children need additional instructional supports or interventions to help them learn, assessment results are used to monitor how well these are working and to make adjustments as needed. Formative assessment serves two purposes within RTI: universal screening and progress monitoring. For universal screening purposes, formative assessment information is used to determine whether some children might benefit from more intensive levels of instruction and intervention based on low performance on the assessment measures (e.g., scoring below the cut point). For progress monitoring purposes, formative assessment is used to determine children's responsiveness to the level of instruction and intervention provided and to make adjustments based on these results. This basic approach to assessment in RTI within early education settings is consistent with universal screening and progress monitoring in RTI that is commonly used with school-age children (e.g., Fuchs, Fuchs & Compton, 2012). In RTI within early education, most of the focus with regard to the use of assessment has been on academic learning as opposed to the social-emotional or behavioral domains. Most assessment used in RTI within school-age settings also has focused on academic learning, primarily reading and math, with assessments designed to measure specific skills within a content area, such as reading fluency (Kratochwill, Clements & Kalymon, 2007).

Because this is a new area for the early childhood field, there is little guidance from either the research or practice sides, although information is beginning to emerge (see, e.g., the concept paper on Response to Intervention in Early Childhood by the National Professional Development Center on Inclusion in Chapter 29 of this volume). However, a growing body of research on RTI in reading and math for the early primary grades has shown evidence of the reliability and validity of specific screening and progress monitoring measures as well as data regarding the average growth rates used to gauge the effectiveness of tiered interventions (Clarke, Gersten, & Newman-Gonchar, 2010; Foegen, Jiban, & Deno, 2007; Fuchs, Fuchs, & Compton, 2004; Fuchs et al., 2005). Two recent Institute of Education Sciences (IES) Practice Guides summarized empirical support in each of these areas, showing that universal screening can predict children's future performance and that progress monitoring can have a positive effect on teachers' instructional decision making (Gersten et al., 2009; Gersten et al., 2008). Recommendations for the practice of RTI related to assessment include providing universal screening for all children to focus on both prevention and early detection and using measurements of the response to intervention to determine whether adequate progress has been made and to make adjustments to instruction, if necessary.

In choosing assessment tools to use, consideration needs to be given to the representativeness and applicability of the information for the intended purpose, the appropriateness of the instruments and methods for the designated populations, and the particular characteristics of the assessment instruments themselves. Assessment information can be used for many different purposes, and it is important to fully recognize the intended purpose up front in order to guide the selection decision. How the assessment results will be used is a critical consideration for the type of information that is needed, the frequency with which it needs to be gathered, and the methods and source of the information. In RTI, the primary purpose of assessment is to inform instructional decision making. Assessment results are used from universal screening to determine whether children are meeting learning goals or need intervention, and results from progress monitoring are used to determine whether those children who are receiving intervention are responding adequately or whether adjustments are needed. This contrasts with other purposes of assessment, such as to provide information for program-level functions as related to program evaluation, accountability, program improvement, or reporting requirements. In the former case, the focus is on linking the results from individual children's performance to decisions about instruction and intervention, whereas in the latter case, the focus is on evaluating the program, with children's performance used as a gauge of program performance. Although assessment results are examined on an individual child basis in RTI, they are examined across all children as a whole group or compared among particular groups for purposes such as program evaluation.

Given the specific purpose of assessment in RTI in early education for instructional planning, instruments must incorporate particular characteristics in order to be appropriate and feasible for use in this context. First, the instruments used within RTI rely on formal or standardized assessment procedures using direct measurements of children's skills, as opposed to informal procedures using observations, ratings, checklists, or parent or teacher reports to measure children's skills. These measures may be either norm-referenced, where a child's performance is scored relative to a norming group, using either national or local norms (e.g., this child scored at the 75th percentile for letter knowledge based on the norms) or criterion-referenced, where a child's performance is scored relative to a predetermined set of criteria (e.g., this child met the criterion for letter knowledge). In both cases, the key for RTI applications is to determine appropriate thresholds for selecting children for additional instructional supports.

Second, these instruments measure key school readiness skills that are linked to later achievement within specific domains such as language and literacy or math. A consideration during assessment selection is whether the skills being measured and the results being used are focused on short-term prediction (How is this child doing on skills related to immediate curriculum goals?) versus long-term prediction (How is this child doing on skills that predict later academic success?). Assessment in RTI focuses on measuring skills that demonstrate long-term prediction, and the methods themselves are designed to enable consistency of measurement over time. Accordingly, such instruments need to measure specific skills in a particular content area that have been shown through research to be predictive of later academic abilities. For preschoolers, this would include assessments focusing on language and literacy skills such as alphabet knowledge, phonological awareness, and vocabulary that have been shown to be strong predictors of later reading ability (National Early Literacy Panel, 2008), or math skills such as counting, shape recognition, relations (more than, less than), and emerging understanding of operations (addition, subtraction) that are related to later math abilities (National Research Council, 2009).

Third, the tools used in RTI need to be sensitive to small increments of change, given that repeated assessments are used to measure growth over time. Such instruments are used multiple times throughout the year to determine whether children are making adequate progress with the instruction provided or whether adjustments to instruction are needed, and the results must reflect concurrent changes in children's skills and knowledge.

Fourth, on a related point, RTI tools must provide indicators of both the level of growth—that is, how well a child performs at a given point in time—and rate of growth, or how much a child learns over time. Measures of performance at a given point in time are used in universal screening to determine whether a child is meeting benchmarks or needs additional supports for learning. Data on growth over time are used in progress monitoring to indicate whether a child is making adequate gains with the level of instruction provided or whether adjustments are needed.

Fifth, given the frequency of administration of these assessments, particularly when teachers are involved, the instruments need to be quick and easy to administer. The instruments themselves belong to the category known as *screening measures*, which are brief assessments focused on target skills that are highly predictive of later outcomes (Jenkins, Hudson, & Johnson, 2007). Ideally, these instruments would utilize technology-based platforms for gathering, recording, scoring, and reporting information, in order to facilitate their use.

There are broader considerations that programs also may want to take into account in making selection decisions, such as the alignment of the tools with program goals and/or early learning standards. Other factors center around the resources needed, including the costs for materials; the level of training and skills required for assessors, including whether the tools are feasible for teachers to use; and the format for gathering the information, including whether a tool utilizes a technology-based platform for recording, scoring, and reporting information or is paper-and-pencil based, which is much more labor intensive.

The measures used in RTI also must demonstrate sound psychometric properties, including characteristics of reliability and validity. Given the key reliance on assessment within RTI for making decisions about the effectiveness of instruction and intervention, it is critical that these tools and procedures meet established standards for reliability and validity (Barnett et al., 2007; Christ & Hintze, 2007). *Reliability* refers to the idea that an assessment produces consistent results. Reliability is typically considered in terms of consistency over time, known as test–retest reliability (i.e., over a very short period of time, a child's performance should be similar across two separate assessment administrations); consistency across different assessors, or interrater reliability (i.e., a child's performance should not vary on the basis of who administers the assessment); consistency across forms, or form equivalence (i.e., performance should be similar on different forms of the assessment that test the same content); and internal consistency (i.e., correct/incorrect responses should be consistent across related items). *Validity* refers to the idea that an assessment is measuring what it is intended to measure. From a psychometric perspective, three types of validity are important for assessments used in RTI. *Construct* and *content validity* are related concepts that consider the extent to which an instrument is measuring the underlying theoretical constructs or content related to the given domain. For example, for a screening or progress monitoring measure of preschoolers' language and literacy skills to have construct or content validity, it would need to include appropriate items for measuring the key skills related to later reading achievement, such as letter knowledge, phonological awareness, and vocabulary. *Criterion validity* centers around the issue of whether the measure predicts outcomes, both in terms of concurrent validity (based on simultaneously assessed outcomes) and predictive validity (based on long-term associations with future outcomes). Given the focus of RTI on using assessment to determine which children need further supports based on current performance and measuring skills that predict later academic performance, criterion validity should be a key concern for selection of these measures. Finally, *face validity* refers to the issue of whether an instrument is measuring what it purports to be measuring based on face value. From a psychometric perspective, face validity is not considered as robust an indicator of an assessment's value as other types of validity, because it relies entirely on perceived judgments, but it is worth noting with regard to treatment acceptability issues.

Other characteristics of assessment tools that are relevant for RTI applications include the level of sensitivity and specificity, and correspondingly, the false positive and false negative rates. *Sensitivity* in this case concerns the extent to which an assessment correctly identifies children who need intervention (i.e., true positives), and correspondingly, the extent to which it minimizes the incorrect identification of children as needing intervention when they do not (i.e., false positive, or Type I error rate). With regard to specificity, the issue is the converse. In other words, *specificity* concerns the extent to which an assessment correctly identifies children who don't need intervention (i.e., true negatives), and correspondingly minimizes the extent to which it incorrectly identifies children as not needing intervention when they do (i.e., false negative, or Type II error rate).

Finally, as with any use of assessment, the representativeness and appropriateness of the information being gathered needs to be considered in relation to the populations being assessed and the specific assessment settings. Particular attention should be paid to issues involving children's ages, home language and language proficiency, and disability status when selecting instruments for use in RTI in early childhood. In addition to the factors discussed previously, the extent to which the sample used for development of the measure reflects similar characteristics to particular populations of interest and the extent to which information is available about the performance of the measure with regard to those populations should be examined. In interpreting the results, it is wise to be aware of the specific context for the assessment and consider other possible explanatory factors, such as language proficiency or situational factors (e.g., a stomachache, a distracting noise, extreme shyness), as part of the decision-making process. In making assessment decisions, it is important to keep in mind that the purpose of assessment in RTI is to provide data to help teachers so that they can ensure that every child receives the appropriate level of instruction and intervention needed to promote learning and development.

Given all of these considerations, there are at present quite limited options for appropriate assessment instruments for use in RTI in early education. There are more options available for school-age children, given the longer history of RTI with this age group, although these would not be appropriate for use with preschoolers. It is important to recognize that none of the suggested early education assessments were developed with an RTI application in mind, although they are adaptable for this purpose and some work is currently underway in the field in this regard. At present, there are two developed instruments that have been used within RTI applications for preschool-age children—the individual growth and development indicators, or IGDIs (McConnell & Missall, 2008; McConnell, Priest, Davis, & McEvoy, 2002), and the CIRCLE Phonological Awareness, Language, and Literacy System Plus, C-PALLS+ (Landry, Assel, Gunnewig, & Swank, 2007). Both are focused on academic learning; there are currently no corresponding assessments in the social-emotional domain because measures in this area tend to be based on methodologies such as observations, checklists, or ratings that are inconsistent with RTI assessment approaches.

The IGDIs, which examine children's oral language and phonological awareness skills, were designed using a CBM approach. These data currently are gathered using a paper-and-pencil format, although a web site is available where users can enter and manage the data. Work is underway by the Center for Response to Intervention in Early Childhood (CRTIEC) on a new version, IGDIs 2.0, which is being developed specifically for use in preschool RTI and will cover a wider range of language and literacy skills. There is also a set of infant and toddler IGDIs that have been developed using a CBM approach, although these are considered experimental at this point, with the exception of one scale examining communication. (See Chapter 9 for more information about all of these aspects of the IGDIs.)

The C-PALLS+ includes direct assessment of language and literacy skills (vocabulary, letter recognition, and phonological awareness) and math skills (counting, number naming/recognition, shape naming/recognition, and basic number operations), which are appropriate for use as formative assessment measures within RTI in early childhood. Some of the subscales are fluency tests, consistent with a CBM approach. The C-PALLS+ also includes observational assessments of other domains (emergent writing skills, print and book knowledge, social competence), as well as instructional groupings and activities that are not consistent with the design of formative assessment measures for RTI. The C-PALLS+ format is technology-based; the data are gathered using a handheld device and are uploaded to a web-based system for scoring and reports. (See Chapter 10 for more information about the C-PALLS+.)

There also are some efforts underway to develop new tools more directly designed for use in RTI within early education settings. Although these instruments may not be available for public use, they offer a glimpse of future possibilities. Examples include the School Readiness Indicators of Basic Language and Literacy Skills (SCRIBLLS), which focuses on language and literacy skills and is being developed by a team at the Children's Learning Institute at the University of Texas Health Science Center; the Preschool Early Literacy Indicators (PELI), which measures early literacy skills through a storybook reading task and is being developed by Dynamic Measurement Group, the creators of the Dynamic Indicators of Basic Early Literacy Skills (DIBELS), one of the most commonly used RTI instruments for school-age children; the Early Communication Indicator (ECI), which uses a CBM approach for measuring communication growth with infants and toddlers and is part of the IGDIs suite developed by the Juniper Gardens Children's Project at the University of Kansas (e.g., Greenwood, Buzhardt, Walker, Howard, & Anderson, 2011); and a tool focused on math skills, the Early Mathematics Assessment System (EMAS), which is being developed by a team at Teachers College at Columbia University.

FORMATIVE ASSESSMENT WITHIN THE RECOGNITION & RESPONSE MODEL

In considering applications of RTI within early education, Recognition & Response, or R&R (Buysse & Peisner-Feinberg, 2010; Peisner-Feinberg, Buysse, Benshoff, & Soukakou, 2011; http://randr.fpg.unc.edu/), has been acknowledged as one of the two available models and the only one focused on academic learning (Greenwood, Bradfield, et al., 2011). Although additional research is underway to examine its efficacy and applicability to a variety of content areas, R&R has generated widespread attention in the early childhood field as a promising RTI model for prekindergarten (see entire issue of NHSA Dialog, Smith, 2009; and the U.S. Health and Human Services, Administration for Children and Families, http://www.acf.hhs.gov/programs/ohs/).

Overview of Recognition & Response

Recognition & Response (R&R) is designed to help early educators in prekindergarten settings systematically use formative assessment results to plan and organize their general instruction and provide targeted interventions in a way that is matched to children's learning needs. R&R consists of two key components: 1) recognition, which consists of formative assessment used for both universal screening and progress monitoring purposes; and 2) response, which includes providing an effective core curriculum and intentional teaching for *all* children as well as targeted interventions for *some* children based on assessment results. As part of both the recognition and response components, a process called *collaborative problem solving* is used to support data-based decision making, plan interventions within different tiers, and assess how well children respond to instruction. R&R was developed for 3- to 5-year-old children enrolled in center-based early childhood programs, including Head Start, child care, preschool, and public prekindergarten, with a dual focus on improving the quality of instructional practices for *all* children and providing additional supports for *some* children to ensure that *every* child succeeds in school.

Figure 8.1 shows the conceptual framework for R&R. Consistent with the broader RTI literature, R&R is a three-tiered model of instruction, with more intensive instructional strategies (i.e., those that require greater adult involvement) at higher tiers, in accord with children's needs for learning supports. The R&R components also correspond closely to those of RTI: 1) systematic assessment of students' performance on academic skills, 2) scientifically based core programs and interventions, and 3) criteria for instructional decision making.

Within R&R, general instruction is provided for *all* children, with targeted interventions for *some* children who require additional instructional supports based on assessment results. The response component is additive across tiers: *all* children receive Tier 1 instruction; *some* children receive Tiers 1 and 2; and a *few* children receive Tiers 1, 2, and 3. Tier 1 involves providing an effective core curriculum, along with intentional teaching of key school readiness skills. At Tier 2, teachers provide additional supports for some children through explicit, small-group instruction (i.e., 15 minutes per day over 8–10 weeks) using a research-based curriculum, similar to a lesson format or standardized treatment approach. These small-group lessons are augmented by embedded learning activities that extend opportunities for developing these skills through tailored environmental arrangements, additional learning activities, and curricular modifications. Tier 3 consists of providing more intensive, research-based scaffolding strategies (e.g., response prompting, modeling, and peer supports, with corrective feedback) for a few children who require additional supports to learn within Tier 1 instruction and Tier 2 interventions. (See Chapter 5 for further information about the response component of R&R.)

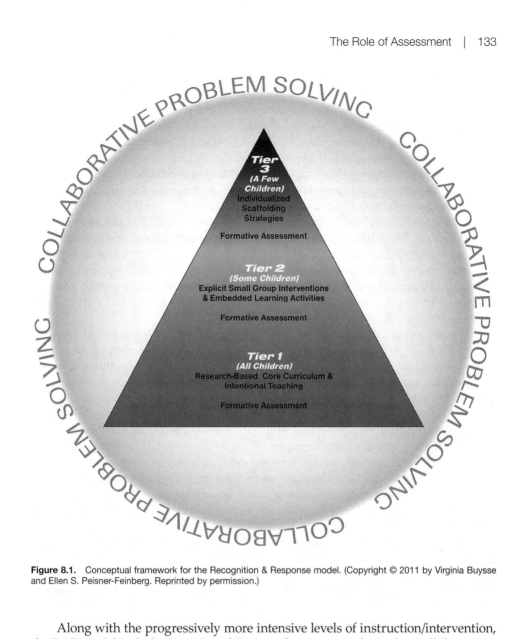

Figure 8.1. Conceptual framework for the Recognition & Response model. (Copyright © 2011 by Virginia Buysse and Ellen S. Peisner-Feinberg. Reprinted by permission.)

Along with the progressively more intensive levels of instruction/intervention, the R&R model includes corresponding use of assessment throughout all three tiers through the recognition component. Within this framework, assessment is integrally linked to instruction and intervention and is a fully integrated component of the educational system. The recognition component consists of formative assessment, which serves both universal screening and progress monitoring functions. Formative assessment in R&R involves teachers gathering assessment information on children's skill levels in particular content areas (e.g., language and literacy skills or math skills) related to the particular focus of instruction and intervention. For universal screening purposes, assessment information is gathered for *all* children in a classroom or program to determine whether individual children might require additional help to master certain skills. Teachers then use this screening information to recognize which children might need additional interventions. Consistent with an RTI approach, universal screening occurs three times a year, on a fall, winter, and spring schedule. Typically, the fall or baseline assessment occurs near the beginning of the school year, prior to the first intervention period; the winter assessment occurs midyear, following the first intervention period and prior to the second; and the spring assessment occurs near the end of the school year, following the second intervention period. We recommend gathering each round of assessment data within a 2-week window so that all children in a classroom or program are assessed within close proximity of one another and local norms can be established. Classroomwide screening results are used to establish an initial baseline in the fall and to determine at all three points whether most children are meeting key benchmarks in learning and development (Tier 1) and whether some children need additional instructional supports (Tiers 2 and 3). Based on these assessment results, if most children meet key learning benchmarks, it can be assumed that the general instruction is of sufficient quality. However, the universal screening data still may indicate that there are some children who are not making adequate progress, even with a high-quality core curriculum and intentional teaching activities. These children would be candidates for the targeted interventions offered within Tier 2 instruction.

The second element of the recognition component of R&R is progress monitoring. Progress monitoring is a systematic process in which teachers measure the progress of children's learning, with a particular focus on those children who are receiving targeted interventions (as determined by the universal screening results). In R&R, the results of the progress monitoring are used to assess children's responsiveness to interventions at Tiers 2 and 3 and make adjustments as needed. Teachers monitor progress using the same formative assessment tools over time to see how well individual children are responding to these added instructional interventions. Based on progress monitoring data, there still may be a few students who do not reach their goals and therefore need an even more intensive level of instructional support as offered within Tier 3. In this way, teachers use the results from their assessments to make decisions about the instructional approaches and interventions that best meet children's learning needs across all three tiers.

In our original conceptualization of R&R and our research to date, progress monitoring has entailed an additional assessment for children receiving targeted interventions between universal screenings, midway through each intervention period (i.e., in the fall between the first and second universal screenings and in the spring between the second and third universal screenings). However, we have found that for preschoolers, these additional progress monitoring assessments have contributed little to teachers' understanding of children's growth, given the variability in development at this age and the need to give the intervention time to have effects (if any). Instead, we have found that examining growth from one universal screening point to the next, which occurs just prior to and after the intervention period, served the progress monitoring function. On the basis of these data, it could be determined whether children were making adequate progress or whether adjustments to instruction were needed.

Application of Formative Assessment in Recognition & Response

A key characteristic of formative assessment used within R&R is that it is designed to be administered by classroom teachers, which is not always the case in models of RTI with older children. We believe that having teachers gather the data directly and use it for instructional planning is an approach that is both more informative for teachers and more consistent with general perspectives on assessment in early childhood education. As such, the instruments selected must be feasible and adequate for use within this approach. Namely, they need to be quick and easy for teachers to administer, generally requiring around 5 to 10 minutes per assessment, and they need to utilize technology-based formats to the extent possible to facilitate gathering, recording, scoring, and utilizing the data. The measures selected also must be feasible for teachers to learn to administer. In our work, we have provided professional development to teachers to ensure that they established proficiency on all model components, including formative assessment, through a process of demonstration, observation, guided practice, and corrective feedback, with performance-based standards used as a method of determining proficiency. We have found that virtually all teachers have been able to reach proficiency with this approach, even when this type of assessment was new to them, and they were able to use the formative assessment component of R&R successfully. In addition, of course, the assessment tools need to demonstrate the necessary properties of universal screening and progress monitoring measures used in RTI—they should involve direct assessments of children, measure key school readiness skills predictive of later academic achievement, measure both level and rate of growth, and be sensitive to small increments of change. Tools selected for formative assessment within R&R need to be appropriate both for universal screening with all children during the year and for monitoring the progress of some children receiving additional learning supports. We have typically used the same tool for both universal screening and progress monitoring and have found that this approach has worked well. In our research to date, we have used the C-PALLS+; the skills measured closely aligned with those targeted in our interventions, and of the two available measures for language and literacy, this was the only one that was technology-based and the only one that was also available for measuring math skills. However, we needed to modify the version we used by de-linking the instructional groupings and activities provided by the C-PALLS+ so that these did not interfere with the instruction and intervention related to R&R as determined by the assessment results. Further, we created a method for analyzing the data, since the measure does not offer a single summative score.

Given that none of the currently available assessment measures for preschoolers were designed specifically for RTI, we also have developed decision-making rules for determining which children need Tier 2 intervention and Tier 3 instructional supports based on the assessment results as part of our research. Using the data from Table 8.1, we illustrate an example of how these decision rules are applied within a hypothetical preschool classroom of 4-year-olds using assessment results from the first and second universal screenings for language and literacy, with data based on the C-PALLS+. For each universal screening assessment, results are presented for three scales—letter knowledge, vocabulary, and phonological awareness (PA)—along with the overall rank based on these scores (from 1 = highest scoring in class to 18 = lowest scoring in class). Because this measure does not provide an overall score, we created a method for analyzing the data in order to determine which children need the language and literacy interventions based on an RTI approach. Children's rank order was calculated on each scale and the overall rank was calculated based on the average across the three rank orders. Using

Table 8.1. Sample classroom universal screening results

Child	First universal screening/first intervention period					Second universal screening/second intervention period				
	Letters	Vocab	PA	Overall rank	Tiers	Letters	Vocab	PA	Overall rank	Tiers
Jacob	3	4	2	18	T1, T2	11	15	3	18	T1, T2, T3
Sophia	6	10	1	17	T1, T2	10	17	9	17	T1, T2
Adrian	3	8	3	16	T1, T2	14	22	12	15	T1, T2
Olivia	8	12	2	15	T1, T2	28	26	17	9	T1
Caleb	11	17	8	14	T1	14	20	8	16	T1, T2
Martin	10	20	9	13	T1	18	24	14	14	T1
Jasmine	12	18	11	12	T1	18	26	16	12	T1
Nicholas	15	16	13	11	T1	24	21	19	12	T1
Mason	13	21	12	8	T1	22	27	17	11	T1
Juan	12	23	11	8	T1	25	28	23	8	T1
Makayla	14	19	16	8	T1	27	26	21	9	T1
Chloe	16	20	16	6	T1	28	27	23	7	T1
Jayden	17	18	18	6	T1	34	29	22	6	T1
Isabella	18	21	15	5	T1	35	29	30	2	T1
Bobby	20	21	19	4	T1	31	30	32	4	T1
Kate	22	25	18	3	T1	30	32	33	2	T1
Mia	24	22	21	2	T1	32	28	34	4	T1
Aaron	26	27	22	1	T1	33	31	37	1	T1

Key: T1, Tier 1; T2, Tier 2; T3, Tier 3; Vocab, vocabulary; PA, phonological awareness.

the results from each universal screening, decisions were made about the level of instruction and intervention each child needs, indicated by the tiers of instruction/intervention for each child. Results from the first universal screening assessment are used to determine which children would benefit most from Tier 2 intervention for the first intervention period, based on those children scoring in the bottom 20th to 25th percentiles of the classroom (typically about 3 to 6 children). Alternatively, recent research has been underway to establish cut points for making such decisions based on normative data (see Chapter 10 for more information). As seen in the table, four children in this classroom (Jacob, Sophia, Adrian, and Olivia) were identified as needing Tier 2 interventions during the first period based on low scores in all three areas, as evidenced by their overall rankings. Following the first intervention period, results from the second universal screening are used to determine whether any adjustments to instruction are needed during the subsequent period. Specifically, these results are used to determine whether children who received Tier 2 interventions during the first round would benefit from continued intervention during the second round, whether any of these children need additional Tier 3 instructional supports, and whether additional children need Tier 2 interventions at this point. Similar to the first round, the decision rules for Tier 2 interventions during the second round also are based on children's relative rankings in the classroom at the second universal screening, although the thresholds are different. Children who participated in the first round of Tier 2 intervention and are ranked in the bottom 50th percentile of the classroom continue in the second round of intervention. In our example, three children would fall into this category (Jacob, Sophia, Adrian). The idea underlying this decision rule is that in order to maintain the progress these children have made with this additional level of support and to continue to meet learning goals, given the limitations of this single intervention period, the intervention exposure may need to be sustained. In contrast, children who participated in the first round of Tier 2 intervention and are ranked in the upper 50th percentile of the classroom would not continue in the second round of intervention. One child in our example falls into this category (Olivia). The idea underlying this decision rule is that children who score in the upper half of the classroom at this point have demonstrated adequate progress, indicating that they have benefited from the boost offered by this first round of intervention and no longer need this additional level of instructional support in order to meet learning goals. In addition, one child (Jacob) is identified as also needing Tier 3 instructional supports in one area, phonological awareness, based on evidence of little to no growth from the first to the second universal screening. Finally, one child (Caleb) is identified as needing Tier 2 intervention during the second round based on his low ranking at the second universal screening as well as his relatively limited growth from the first to second assessments.

In accord with the idea of an integrated assessment plan, a collaborative problem-solving process is used within R&R to make such data-based decisions about instruction and intervention. Collaborative problem solving relies on assessment results to define the problem and make decisions related to implementing and evaluating instructional adjustments (Bergan, 1977; Bergan & Kratochwill, 1990; Buysse & Wesley, 2005). Ideally, programs establish collaborative problem-solving teams that may include teachers, specialists, other relevant staff, and parents. These teams review the formative assessment results, in conjunction with other relevant sources of information (e.g., parent reports, teacher observations, and other assessment results), to determine who would benefit most from additional instructional supports and whether adjustments are needed to the level of intensity of intervention or to instruction for an individual child. This process involves developing a plan for modifying instruction for children as needed, based on the tiered instructional approach of the R&R model, along with a plan for supporting teachers in their implementation. Finally, the team needs to evaluate these modifications, implement a plan for monitoring children's progress, and continue to make needed instructional adjustments based on data. The problem-solving team also determines the times and ways for documenting and sharing information with others, including parents, professionals, and specialists.

In our research to date, we have used a more limited approach to collaborative problem solving, focused on supporting teachers as they implemented R&R within their classrooms. We have conducted collaborative problem solving through a community of practice or professional learning community model, whereby groups of teachers and administrators, facilitated by the researchers, meet on a regular basis to reflect on practice and problem-solve around implementation issues, as well as to review assessment results and make instructional decisions. We have found that it was particularly helpful if administrators took part in these meetings, as teachers often were implementing new practices and needed their guidance and support regarding how these practices fit with program guidelines and prior practice. During these collaborative problem-solving meetings, we provided teachers with summaries of the results of the assessment data they had gathered, similar to those described earlier (because there was no summative score for the measure), in order to inform the selection decisions regarding which children would receive the Tier 2 and 3 interventions. Teachers contributed additional relevant information to the decision-making process based on their knowledge of each child and other sources of data (e.g., identifying which children had significant behavioral challenges or cognitive delays that would interfere with participating in or benefitting from the small-group lessons) and finalized the selection decisions. Further development work is still needed in this area to figure out the most effective ways to establish core problem-solving teams in early education programs, as well as how to include other individuals such as specialists and families across the variety of different types of private and public settings that exist (see Chapter 20 for more discussion about the potential roles of families within RTI in early childhood).

CONCLUSIONS

As program administrators consider adopting RTI approaches and incorporating related assessment strategies, it is useful to think about these in the context of an integrated assessment plan, which considers all of the existing needs for assessment on behalf of the program, teachers, children, and families, and creates the most efficient plan for collecting and sharing data to optimize teaching and learning. In moving toward an integrated assessment plan, early education programs need to consider the purposes of the various types of assessment information that they are gathering. Conducting formative assessment for use in instructional decision making related to RTI is one purpose, but it may not be the only purpose. There are other types of assessment information and other sources of data that offer useful information about children as well. In addition to formative assessment, there is a need for basic screenings for vision, hearing, and other health-related issues; for developmental screenings related to determining whether children need further evaluation for developmental delays or disabilities; for information from families about the home environment and about their child; and for observations from teachers about children in their daily routines. The key challenges to creating an integrated assessment plan are to figure out how to provide complementary information that is not redundant, how to ensure that the time and resource demands across the various assessment components do not become unmanageable; how to ensure that there is adequate training, knowledge, and support for using the various assessment measures; and how to facilitate the exchange of information so that the data both are gathered and used efficiently, with the important corollary that the data that *are* gathered *are* used. Further, in order to best integrate the various components of assessment information and gain the most complete picture of children's functioning, it is important to understand the context, source, method, and measure used in each case, both to ensure that the results are being interpreted correctly and to recognize potential explanations for discrepancies in results across different assessments. In examining the needs for information and the types of data collected, it is worth considering whether some measures may be used for more than one purpose, although simultaneous attention must be paid to ensuring that they are being used appropriately. Assessment measures used within RTI, for example, have certain properties that allow them to be used for universal screening and progress monitoring functions. Although it may be tempting to use other measures already in place for these functions that do not have all of these properties, they will not provide the needed information for instructional decision making within this framework.

The ideas about formative assessment within RTI for early childhood proposed in this chapter offer what may be a new way of thinking about assessment for many early education programs. This is an emerging idea for the early childhood field, and as such, there are still many unanswered questions and many directions for future research. Clearly, we need more research on the efficacy and acceptability of RTI models in early education, including the assessment component. There also is a great need for more development work with regard to formative assessment for early childhood RTI. There is a paucity of instruments available, with few in the language and literacy domain, fewer in math, and no analogous tools in any other domain of which we are aware. In conjunction with this development, research is needed on the long-term predictive associations between performance on screening measures and later academic performance. In addition, research is needed to provide information about normative development with regard to universal screening measures for early childhood in order to address issues around appropriate cut points or criteria for selecting children for Tier 2, as well as to provide an evidence base for making determinations of inadequate progress indicating the need for Tier 3. This latter issue mirrors debates in the school-age literature about the definition of adequate progress (Gresham 2007; Kratochwill, Clements, & Kalymon, 2007). This concept is not always clearly defined even for school-age children, where there is a much longer history of RTI. In some cases it is based on normative standards (e.g., > 25th percentile) and in others on benchmarks from criterion-referenced measures, depending on the learning goals and assessment strategies involved.

In thinking about the future, there is some research on innovative approaches to the assessment process taking place with school-age children that eventually could offer alternative ways of structuring formative assessment for young children as well. These include two-stage screening and dynamic assessment, both of which are approaches to what is deemed "Smart RTI," based on the idea of providing more effective and efficient next-generation RTI models (Fuchs, Fuchs, & Compton, 2012). Two-stage screening entails a two-stage screening assessment process in which the first broad screening level rules out those clearly not at risk and the second more intensive screening level identifies those who are more likely to be at risk among those remaining. Two-stage screening was designed to address the high false positive rates that are typically obtained with the current one-stage universal screening processes used with school-age children. Dynamic assessment, a particular type of second-stage screening, measures the amount of assistance a child requires to learn novel content as an indicator of learning potential, in contrast to traditional assessments that present the same task in a standardized way to all children. As early education programs adopt RTI, there will be many issues to address with regard to how RTI will affect assessment practices. Although as a field we currently have little guidance about these issues for early education, there is much to be learned from the school-age literature and there is emerging literature in the early childhood arena as well. As the practice of RTI in early childhood becomes more widespread and as the research evidence continues to grow, it presents the opportunity to achieve the dual goals of improving the quality of instructional practices and ensuring that every child succeeds in school.

REFERENCES

Ackerman, D.J., & Coley, R.J. (2012). *State pre-K assessment policies: Issues and status.* Princeton, NJ: Educational Testing Service. Retrieved from http://www.ets.org/Media/Research/pdf/PIC-PRE-K.pdf

Bagnato, S.J., Neisworth, J.T., & Pretti-Frontczak, K. (2010). *LINKing authentic assessment and early childhood intervention: Best measures for best practices* (2nd ed.). Baltimore, MD: Paul H. Brookes Publishing Co.

Bagnato, S., & Ye Ho, H. (2006). High stakes testing with preschool children: Violation of professional standards for evidence-based practice in early childhood intervention. *KEDI Journal of Educational Policy, 3*(1), 23–43.

Barnett, D.W., Hawkins, R., Prasse, D., Graden, J., Nantais, M., & Pan, W. (2007). Decision-making validity in response to intervention. In S.R. Jimerson, M.K. Burns, & A.M. VanDerHeyden (Eds.), *Response to intervention: The science and practice of assessment and intervention* (pp. 106–116). New York, NY: Springer.

Bergan, J.R. (1977). *Behavioral consultation.* Columbus, OH: Merrill.

Bergan, J.R., & Kratochwill, T.R. (1990). *Behavioral consultation and therapy.* New York, NY: Plenum.

Busch, T.W., & Reschly, A.L. (2007). Progress monitoring in reading: Using curriculum-based measurement in a response-to-intervention model. *Assessment for Effective Intervention, 32*(4), 223–230.

Buysse, V., & Peisner-Feinberg, E.S. (2010). Recognition & Response: Response to intervention (RTI) for pre-K. *Young Exceptional Children, 13*(4), 2–13.

Buysse, V., & Wesley, P.W. (2005). *Consultation in early childhood settings.* Baltimore, MD: Paul H. Brookes Publishing Co.

Christ, T.J., & Hintze, J.M. (2007). Psychometric considerations when evaluating response to intervention. In S.R. Jimerson, M.K. Burns, & A.M. VanDerHeyden (Eds.), *Response to intervention: The science and practice of assessment and intervention* (pp. 93–105). New York, NY: Springer.

Clarke, B., Gersten, R., & Newman-Gonchar, R. (2010). RTI in mathematics: Beginnings of a knowledge base. In T. Glover & S. Vaughn (Eds.), *The promise of response to intervention: Evaluating current science and practice* (pp. 187–203). New York, NY: Guilford Press.

Copple, C., & Bredekamp, S. (2009). *Developmentally appropriate practice in early childhood programs.* Washington, DC: National Association for the Education of Young Children.

Deno, S.L. (2003). Developments in curriculum-based measurement. *The Journal of Special Education, 37*(3), 184–192.

Foegen, A., Jiban, C., & Deno, S. (2007). Progress monitoring measures in mathematics: A review of the literature. *Journal of Special Education, 41*, 121–139.

Fuchs, D., Fuchs, L.S., & Compton, D.L. (2004). Identifying reading disabilities by responsiveness-to-instruction: Specifying measures and criteria. *Learning Disabilities Quarterly, 27*, 216–227.

Fuchs, D., Fuchs, L.S., & Compton, D.L. (2012). Smart RTI: A next-generation approach to multilevel prevention. *Exceptional Children, 78*(3), 263–279.

Fuchs, L.S., Compton, D.L., Fuchs, D., Paulsen, K., Bryant, J.D., & Hamlett, C.L. (2005). The prevention, identification, and cognitive determinants of math difficulty. *Journal of Educational Psychology, 97*, 493–513.

Fuchs, L.S., & Fuchs, D. (2007). The role of assessment in the three-tier approach to reading instruction. In D. Haager, J. Klingner, & S. Vaughn (Eds.), *Evidence-based reading practices for Response to Intervention* (pp. 29–42). Baltimore, MD: Paul H. Brookes Publishing Co.

Gersten, R., Beckmann, S., Clarke, B., Foegen, A., Marsh, L., Star, J.R., et al. (2009). *Assisting students struggling with mathematics: Response to intervention (RTI) for elementary and middle schools* (NCEE 2009-4060). Washington, DC: National Center for Education Evaluation and Regional Assistance, Institute of Education Sciences, U.S. Department of Education. Retrieved from http://ies.ed.gov/ncee/wwc/publications/PracticeGuide.aspx?sid=2/

Gersten, R., Compton, D.L., Connor, C.M., Dimino, J., Santoro, L., Linan-Thompson, S., & Tilly, W.D. (2008). *Assisting students struggling with reading: Response to intervention and multi-tier intervention for reading in the primary grades. A practice guide* (NCEE 2009-4045). Washington, DC: National Center for Education Evaluation and Regional Assistance, Institute of Education Sciences, U.S. Department of Education. Retrieved from http://ies .ed.gov/ncee/wwc/publications/practiceguide.aspx?sid=3/

Greenwood, C.R., Bradfield, R., Kaminski, R., Linas, M., Carta, J.J., & Nylander, D. (2011). The response to intervention (RTI) approach in early childhood. *Focus on Exceptional Children, 43*(9), 1–22.

Greenwood, C.R., Buzhardt, J., Walker, D., Howard, W.J., & Anderson, R. (2011). Program-level influences on the measurement of early communication for infants and toddlers in Early Head Start. *Journal of Early Intervention, 33*(2), 110–134.

Gresham, F.M. (2007). Evolution of the response-to-intervention concept: Empirical foundations and recent developments. In S.R. Jimerson, M.K. Burns, & A.M. VanDerHeyden (Eds.), *Handbook of response to intervention: The science and practice of assessment and intervention* (pp. 10–24). New York, NY: Springer.

Hosp, J.L., & Madyun, N.H. (2007). Addressing disproportionality with response to intervention. In S.R. Jimerson, M.K. Burns, & A.M. VanDerHeyden (Eds.), *Handbook of response to intervention: The science and practice of assessment and intervention* (pp. 172–181). New York, NY: Springer.

Jenkins, J.R., Hudson, R.F., & Johnson, E.S. (2007). Screening for at-risk readers in a response to intervention framework. *School Psychology Review, 36*(4), 582–600.

Kratochwill, T.R., Clements, M.A., & Kalymon, K.M. (2007). Response to intervention: conceptual and methodological issues in implementation. In S.R. Jimerson, M.K. Burns, & A.M. VanDerHeyden (Eds.), *Handbook of response to intervention: The science and practice of assessment and intervention* (pp. 25–52). New York, NY: Springer.

Landry, S. H., Assel, M., Gunnewig, S., & Swank, P.R. (2007). *CIRCLE Phonological Awareness, Language, & Literacy System Plus*. Houston, TX: Ridgway.

McConnell, S.R., & Missall, K.N. (2008). Best practices in monitoring progress for preschool children. In A. Thomas & J. Grimes (Eds.), *Best practices in school psychology* (5th ed., pp. 561–573). Washington, DC: National Association of School Psychologists.

McConnell, S.R., Priest, J.S., Davis, S.D., & McEvoy, M.A. (2002). Best practices in measuring growth and development for preschool children. In A. Thomas & J. Grimes (Eds.), *Best practices in school psychology IV* (4th ed., pp. 1231–1246). Washington, DC: National Association of School Psychologists.

Meisels, S.J. (1993). Remaking classroom assessment with the Work Sampling System. *Young Children, 48*(5), 34–40.

Meisels, S. (1996). Charting the continuum of assessment and intervention. In S.J. Meisels & E. Fenichel, *New visions for the developmental assessment of infants and young children* (pp. 27–52). Washington, DC: ZERO TO THREE.

Meisels, S.J. (2005). Early childhood performance assessment. In C.B. Fisher & R.M. Lerner (Eds.). *Encyclopedia of applied developmental science* (Vol. 1, pp. 101–105). Thousand Oaks, CA: Sage Publishing.

Meisels, S., Fong-ruey, L., Dorfman, A., & Nelson, R.F. (1995). The Work Sampling System: Reliability and validity of a performance assessment for young children. *Early Childhood Research Quarterly, 10*, 277–296.

National Early Literacy Panel. (2008). *Developing early literacy: Report of the National Early Literacy Panel*. Washington, DC: National Institute for Literacy. Retrieved from http://lincs .ed.gov/publications/pdf/NELPReport09.pdf

National Research Council. (2008). *Early childhood assessment: Why, what, and how.* Committee on Developmental Outcomes and Assessments for Young Children, C.E. Snow & S.B. Van Hemel (Eds.). Washington, DC: The National Academies Press.

National Research Council. (2009). *Mathematics learning in early childhood: Paths toward excellence and equity.* Committee on Early Childhood Mathematics, C.T. Cross, T.A. Woods, & H. Schweingruber (Eds.). Center for Education, Division of Behavioral and Social Sciences and Education. Washington, DC: The National Academies Press.

Peisner-Feinberg, E., Buysse, V., Benshoff, L., & Soukakou, E. (2011). Recognition & Response: Response to intervention for pre-kindergarten. In C. Groark, S.M. Eidelman, L. Kaczmarek, & S. Maude (Eds.), *Early childhood intervention: Shaping the future for children with special needs and their families. Vol. 3, Emerging trends in research and practice* (pp. 37–53). Santa Barbara, CA: Praeger.

Smith, S. (2009). Introduction: Supporting struggling learners in preschool: Emerging approaches and opportunities [Special section]. *NHSA Dialog, 12*(3), 185–191.

Stevenson, W.A., Grisham-Brown, J., & Pretti-Frontczak, K. (2011). Authentic assessment. In J. Grisham-Brown & K. Pretti-Frontczak (Eds.), *Assessing young children in inclusive settings: The blended practices approach.* Baltimore, MD: Paul H. Brookes Publishing Co.

Zellman, G.L., & Karoly, L.A. (2012). *Moving to outcomes: Approaches to incorporating child assessments into state early childhood quality rating and improvement systems.* Santa Monica, CA: Rand Corporation. Retrieved from http://www.rand.org/pubs/occasional_papers/OP364.html

9

General Outcome Measures in Early Childhood and Individual Growth and Development Indicators

Scott McConnell and Charles R. Greenwood

The landscape of early childhood education has been changing to embrace the concept of response to intervention (RTI) specifically and intentional teaching more broadly as a means of improving all children's outcomes. As this occurs, the need for measurement capable of informing instructional and care decisions has increased. Several trends have contributed. First, we have more evidence about the skills children need to learn prior to kindergarten if they are to be successful learning to read in school (Shanahan & Lonigan, 2008). Second, general outcome measurement (GOM), an approach common in K–12 education (Wayman, Wallace, Wiley, Tichá, & Espin, 2007), provides a model for measures that early childhood practitioners will need to produce formative data on children's growth over time and how such measures might be developed and effectively used in early childhood. Third, adherents of the RTI approach in early childhood are using this information to achieve a greater level of effectiveness by increasing the intensity of instruction for students who need it (Greenwood, Carta, McConnell, Goldstein, & Kaminski, 2008).

These three developments—greater knowledge of essential preschool competencies, development and evaluation of GOMs for preschool children, and growing interest in and implementation of RTI models in early childhood programs—have brought new attention to the role of formative assessment, both at levels of screening and progress monitoring, from researchers and teachers interested in improving school readiness outcomes. Our purpose in this chapter is to describe what we have learned about this new kind of measurement and its role in early childhood education.

ROLE OF ASSESSMENT IN EARLY CHILDHOOD RESPONSE TO INTERVENTION

In the broadest of terms, the role of assessment in early childhood response to intervention (EC-RTI) is to provide a basis for intervention decision making and program planning for individuals and groups of children. Two big ideas focus our attention on issues of assessment in RTI. First, knowledge of a student's measurable success or failure in learning what is taught should drive the design and adjustment of instructional programs (Fuchs & Deno, 1991). Rich sources of objective data are needed for decision making in EC-RTI, given that our reason for doing so is to achieve comparatively greater effectiveness improving child outcomes than has been achieved with traditional approaches.

Second, assessment in EC-RTI should be part of a larger commitment to evidence-based practices, multiple tiers of support, decision making to direct service provision, attention to fidelity of implementation, and program/center-based teams assisting teachers and parents in the operation of the RTI system (Greenwood, Bradfield, et al., 2011). *Evidence-based practices* are those supported by research demonstrating that children learn significantly more when exposed to a practice compared with its alternatives. *Multiple tiers of support*, typically three, are used to increase the intensity of instruction for children who are not making progress in the general education or most basic and universal program level (see Chapters 3, 6, 7, and 8). *RTI decision making* is the process of evaluating children's performance by applying benchmarking criteria as a basis for making decisions about which tier of service is most likely needed by a student at that point in time. *Fidelity of implementation* is the principle that evidence-based practices must be implemented by practitioners in ways that closely match those used by developers if similar results are to be achieved. *Program-level teams* often work as consultants and evaluators to support teachers' implementation of the RTI approach, helping teachers acquire or use the skills and resources needed for effective intervention.

EC-RTI assessment with GOMs is similar to that of other RTI assessments that rely on different measures (see Chapters 1 and 3). As in most other assessment models, EC-RTI models using GOMs will conduct seasonal universal assessments, apply systematic decision-making criteria employing multiple sources of information to identify children who might benefit from more intensive intervention, and then use GOMs or complementary measures to assess children's progress, and confirm the appropriateness of intervention, for children receiving Tier 2 and Tier 3 levels of support.

At least three factors *differentiate* GOMs in EC-RTI assessment. First, by design, GOMs are time-, cost-, and personnel-efficient, making universal seasonal screening likely less burdensome than other assessment approaches. Second, also by design, GOMs represent close functional and empirical relations to measures of long-term desired outcome (e.g., second- and third-grade reading), and thus increase practitioners' and program managers' confidence that children in need of supplementary and more intensive service are indeed identified and served. Third, because of their direct assessment of change over time, GOMs provide a second dimension—that of *growth*—to the assessment of child progress. With growth estimates, parents and practitioners can make more direct forecasts of the likelihood of individual children meeting long-term goals given current levels of intervention.

GOM assessment in EC-RTI characteristically employs the same or highly related measures used for both identification and progress monitoring. If children fall below a benchmark standard at an age or point in time, they are moved to a more intensive tier of service; if not, they continue in the same tier. Thus, the principle that RTI measurement systems should be used to support educational decision making and to adapt instruction has a legacy in the general outcome measurement approach.

GENERAL OUTCOME MEASUREMENT

GOM is designed to inform teachers and other caregivers when and when not to change instructional intervention (Fuchs & Deno, 1991). This approach to assessment began with efforts to describe children's reading achievement in ways that supported ongoing monitoring and intervention (Deno, Mirkin, & Chiang, 1982); GOMs have grown in sophistication and domain coverage over the last 30 years (Wayman et al., 2007). GOMs are distinguished by several core features: They are brief and easy to use, can be repeated often, provide measures of child behavior on a constant metric over time (thus yielding growth estimates), demonstrate strong psychometric characteristics, and are sensitive to changes in child performance due to development or intervention (Early Childhood Research Institute on Measuring Growth and Development, 1998a).

A practical example of a GOM is the physician's use of the thermometer as a brief, standardized, repeatable indicator of one's general health status. Scores above or below body temperature benchmarks are used by the physician and the patient to guide their decision making and next steps in treatment selection and implementation (Carta, Greenwood, Walker, & Buzhardt, 2010).

What makes GOMs different from most testing in early childhood education is frequency of measurement using the same test (or an equivalent form) each time. Because GOMs are designed to sample content skills that are representative of a future outcome, such as the expected performance in phonological awareness at entry to kindergarten, GOMs measure children's growth in their partial attainment of the general outcome expected at a distant point in time.

The thought process behind decision making using GOMs is illustrated by Tilly's iterative strategy (Tilly, 2008). The strategy consists of completing ordered steps in a cycle that structures the practitioner's inquiry and reflection. The cycle is repeated a second time or more, if data indicate a failure to accelerate child outcomes after the first five-step iteration. This leads to subsequent decisions to modify or replace the current intervention. Briefly, the steps outlined by Tilly (2008) are as follows:

1. Is there a problem? (universal screening)

2. What is causing the problem? (clinical review of likely causes)

3. What intervention should be used? (intervention selection)

4. Is the intervention being implemented? (fidelity of implementation)

5. Is the intervention working? (progress monitoring)

These steps, supported by GOMs and use of evidence-based intervention practices, enable the practitioner to manage the RTI programs of individual children in a more systematic, timely, and dynamic way than most traditional approaches to providing services.

It is obvious GOMs are uniquely different from other assessment methods. To be repeatable, they must be brief, efficient, and easy to administer by the teacher. GOMs can be administered to all children as frequently as quarterly in a school year for screening. For children receiving Tier 2 or 3 services, they can be administered monthly (or weekly in some cases) to monitor progress, to estimate short-term growth, and to track individual response to intervention. Because the GOMs are repeated frequently to measure progress, the teacher uses equivalent, alternate forms of the test to prevent children from "learning the test."

GOMs describe a child's growing proficiency, often as the result of mastering selected key skills and/or growing in mastery over time. As such, GOMs are representative of the larger and more complex array of skills that a child knows and needs to learn to achieve a later desired level of competence (the general outcome). Thus, children's performance on GOMs at any point in time reflect their partial, but growing, attainment of component skills and their overall, and growing, status on the general outcome. Linear growth scores can be calculated from at least three individual measurement occasions to help teachers and parents understand how well interventions are moving the child to the general outcome; this index of growth, and reference to important long-term expectations, standards, or goals, further distinguishes GOMs from other progress measures.

GOMs also provide point-in-time performance-level scores of child performance, as do most traditional measures of development and achievement. Growth and status scores in GOMs provide two important and complementary indicators of a child's response to intervention and predict whether or not he or she will reach desired, future levels of performance (Missall et al., 2007). In some cases, *one-time performance measures* will indicate that a child may benefit from more intensive intervention; imagine a case where, in October of the year before kindergarten, performance indicates a child falls well below levels associated with later reading success. At other times, *growth* estimates will be more important; imagine that same child, two months later, still scoring below performance-level expectations but also demonstrating strong and consistent growth (at above expected rates) in the current tier of intervention. Whereas the first instance might lead to increasing the intensity of intervention, the second instance might indicate that intervention is producing the desired effects and should be continued. Both scores can be linked to norms and benchmarks to aid this kind of reflection and instructional decision making. In this way, GOMs help teachers understand when changes in their teaching will be needed.

These features provide important improvements to instructionally relevant measurement. A significant limitation with some traditional measures is the amount of time needed to measure each child's performance and the impracticality of using the measure with all children in a program frequently enough to screen and/or monitor progress. Because of length and normative standards, some traditional measures may only be administered as frequently as every 6 months. The utility of data collected at intervals this far apart in the school year to teacher planning and changing interventions for individual children is obviously low. And, some traditional norm-referenced measures are too cumbersome, specialized, and not interpretable by the teacher or parents.

As we have noted, GOMs emerged from efforts to improve assessment of reading performance in ways that allowed more tailored, effective intervention (Deno et al., 1982), and this assessment method has expanded significantly over time (Wallace, Espin, McMaster, Deno, & Foegen, 2007). These measures, collectively called curriculum-based measurement (CBM), are recognized as an evidence-based practice in special education (National Center on Response to Intervention, 2011). Prior to 2002, however, CBM that could be used for universal screening and progress monitoring did not exist in early childhood programs.

INDIVIDUAL GROWTH AND DEVELOPMENT INDICATORS

Individual growth and development indicators (IGDIs) were some of the earliest GOMs for preschool and early elementary school children (McConnell et al., 1996); these measures were intended for use by preschool and primary-grade teachers, child care practitioners, home visitors, and parents to inform their practice (Priest et al., 2001). Because of their novelty in early childhood, many wondered if IGDIs would work and if they did, whether they would be embraced by programs (Brown, 2001; Fewell, 2001; Odom, 2001).

Early acceptance and use may have been affected by the lack of well-defined curriculum targets in early childhood, unlike those in K–12 education. This fact was reflected in the name selected for the tools—"individual growth and development indicators" rather than "curriculum-based measures"—intended to embrace a range of early childhood outcomes, some of which were attributed to developmental experiences at home and others to preschool instruction. Eventually a set of IGDIs has emerged that are supported by a range of evidence, and these measures are increasingly understood and used in early childhood research and practice (e.g., VanDerHeyden & Snyder, 2006).

IGDIs exist for infants and toddlers (Greenwood, Carta, Baggett, et al., 2008; Greenwood, Luze, & Carta, 2002) and preschool-age children (McConnell & Missall, 2008; McConnell, Priest, Davis & McEvoy, 2002) across a variety of academic and developmental outcomes as well as populations (Cadigan & Missall, 2007; Floyd, Hojnoski, & Key, 2006; Hojnoski, Silberglitt, & Floyd, 2009), and have served as a basis for the ongoing development of other GOMs and similar measures of kindergarten and early elementary grade children (Good, Gruba, & Kaminski, 2002).

The original suite of IGDIs was developed as part of a cross-age, coordinated effort to develop program performance measures that monitored children's partial attainment of important developmental achievements (Early Childhood Research Institute on Measuring Growth and Development, 1998a, 1998b). During the period of initial development (1996–2001), IGDIs for infants and toddlers and for preschool-age children were developed and tested. Collectively, we now describe these as IGDIs 1.0. IGDI 1.0 measures are supported by web sites (http://www.igdi.ku.edu; http://ggg.umn.edu) where practitioners may access information about the measures, learn to use them, and utilize data management services. Assessors may enter scores using online data system tools at the web sites that automatically compute and graph scores. When the scores are plotted against benchmarks (normed values), one can quickly see how a child's performance and growth over time compares with expectations at specific age points.

Individual Growth and Development Indicators 1.0 for Infants and Toddlers

The field has at least four IGDIs for infants and toddlers based on GOMs with supporting evidence available for use (Carta et al., 2010). They are the *Early Communication* Indicator (ECI), the *Early Social* Indicator (ESI), the *Early Movement* Indicator

(EMI), and the *Early Problem Solving (Cognitive)* Indicator (EPSI). These IGDIs use direct observational measurement to record the frequency of responding during a 6-minute semistructured play situation with a familiar adult.

Administration of the ECI requires the use of two toys—a house and a barn— used on alternate occasions as equivalent forms. During administration, an adult play partner interacts with a child using toys in a nondirective way to evoke child communications. The partner is taught to follow the child's lead by commenting and playing with objects that are of interest to the child. Occurrences of targeted communicative skills or behaviors (e.g., single-word or multiple-word utterances) are recorded either in vivo or from a videotape. The totals of these target skills are converted to a rate-per-minute score and aggregated to provide a total communication score, an index of expressive communication. The scores are graphed (Carta et al., 2010).

Although fully developed, the social, problem-solving, and movement indicators are based on small samples, and in this sense they remain experimental. They have yet to be used widely by anyone beyond the original developers. The ECI has been used with large sample populations with data collected by other users around the country in local and state programs, accompanied by research and evaluation studies in the United States and other countries (Greenwood, Buzhardt, Walker, Howard, & Anderson, 2011; Greenwood, Walker, & Buzhardt, 2010).

Individual Growth and Development Indicators 1.0 for Preschoolers

Three measures—one for oral language and two for phonological awareness— emerged from our first round of research and development of outcome measures for preschool children. *Picture Naming* is an individually administered, 1-minute measure of expressive language for children 3–6 years of age. Using a stimulus set of approximately 120 randomly ordered individual photos and line drawings of everyday objects with labels in the lexicon of typical 5-year-olds, the administrator 1) describes and demonstrates the task to the child, 2) instructs the child to "name the pictures as quickly as you can," and 3) presents the cards sequentially for 1 minute (more information is available at http://ggg.umn.edu). Early-stage research indicated that Picture Naming scores were stable over 1 month (McConnell, Priest, Davis, & McEvoy, 2002), correlated at moderate to high-moderate levels with results on the Peabody Picture Vocabulary Test–Third Edition (Dunn & Dunn, 1997) and the Preschool Language Scale 3 (Early Childhood Research Institute on Measuring Growth and Development, 1998a; Priest, Davis, McConnell, McEvoy, & Shinn, 1999; Zimmerman, Steiner, & Pond, 1992), and were sensitive to growth over time and related to classroom practices (Missall, McConnell, & Cadigan, 2006).

Rhyming and Alliteration are individually administered 2-minute measures of phonological awareness developed for children ages 3–6. For each of these measures, the examiner uses a standard set of six cards to teach the task and test for basic understanding of the response demand with each child, then presents items randomly and sequentially from a set of approximately 75 items. For Rhyming, the child is presented with a target picture (e.g., cat) and a row of three possible responses— one of which rhymes with *cat* (e.g., table, hat, and fork). Alliteration is somewhat similar, again with a target image (e.g., mouse) and an adjacent row of three possible responses (e.g., bird, fish, and monkey). For both measures, the child's score is the number of correct alliteratives identified in 2 minutes.

Evidence supporting these two measures is fairly robust at the group level, with moderate to high consistency in scores over 1 month, moderate to high-moderate correlations with criterion standardized measures, and evidence of growth over time. As McConnell and Missall (2008) suggested, however, younger or lower-performing children often fail to complete a single item correctly on these two measures, producing a significant floor effect and limited utility in RTI models intended to identify children who might benefit from additional intervention.

A fourth measure, *Sound Blending*, showed promise in research applications but fared less well when implemented by classroom teachers. Sound Blending is an individually administered, 1-minute measure in which the examiner orally presents words segmented at the compound word (bath/tub), syllable (ta/ble) and phoneme (m/o/m) and asks the child to telescope the sounds to "say the word the right way." The child's score is the number of blended words in 1 minute.

Individual Growth and Development Indicators 2.0 for Preschoolers

In 2008, researchers at the University of Minnesota began a focused effort to expand and improve IGDIs available for assessing language and early literacy development of preschool children. This work, dubbed IGDIs 2.0 and carried out by the Center for Response to Intervention in Early Childhood (Greenwood, Carta, McConnell, et al., 2008), is intended to produce an assessment system for use in preschool RTI models. This work is also intended to address several problems, shortcomings, and as-yet-undeveloped features of IGDIs (McConnell & Missall, 2008).

Research and development of IGDIs 2.0 was prompted by several observations. First, application of IGDIs 1.0 among programs serving high-risk children often produced high proportions of zero-correct responses from individual children, particularly on Rhyming and Alliteration. Second, child performance over time demonstrated considerable variation around a linear trend (McConnell & Missall, 2008). This variability was attributed to variations in difficulty of assessment stimuli across assessment occasions. Third, IGDIs 1.0 covered a rather restricted range of domains or skill clusters associated with early literacy development (National Early Literacy Panel, 2009), and utility for effective prevention and intervention efforts was thus limited.

To address these limitations and to bring the measures to a higher level of development and rigor, two related efforts were initiated. First, four domains of early literacy were identified and defined operationally, reflecting advances and current perspectives in the academic literature. These domains—oral language, phonological awareness and analysis, alphabet knowledge, and comprehension—served as foci of research and development for IGDIs 2.0 and for the Tier 2 and Tier 3 intervention programs developed as part of the larger Center.

Second, researchers adopted a set of contemporary approaches to measurement in this more recent round of research. Specifically, given the fact that IGDIs are generally based on children's responses to individual, discrete elements (e.g., photos of objects in Picture Naming or selection of a rhyme for a presented target word in Rhyming), measure development here was well-suited to Item Response Theory and Rasch Modeling (Rodriguez, 2010). This methodological approach gave developers the opportunity to achieve greater precision in the design, evaluation, and revision of individual items, the development and evaluation of sets of items (or scales) for different purposes (e.g., seasonal screening for RTI assessment), and the design of cut scores and procedures to produce these scores in classroom settings. Although this work is ongoing, some provisional information about five different IGDIs 2.0 is available.

Picture Naming 2.0 is a revision of the original Picture Naming. Researchers reviewed words/items included in the original measure, added words that interventionists suggested were key to young children's development, and modified stimulus materials to increase clarity and reduce ambiguity. Preliminary results indicate that Picture Naming continues to perform as a measure of oral language.

Rhyming 2.0 and *Alliteration 2.0* are also revisions of original IGDI phonological awareness measures, although both measures have been changed considerably. Rhyming 2.0 and Alliteration 2.0, like other second-generation IGDIs, are not timed; in addition, rather than a target stimulus and three possible responses, stimulus materials now provide a target stimulus (e.g., map) and two possible responses (e.g., bed, cap). Children respond to a preselected set of 15–25 items (selected for a particular function of assessment), with scores calculated from the sum of Rasch values for each correct item. Extensive effort was directed to 1) selecting item content that represented earlier development in the domain of interest, 2) creating clearer and more standardized task introduction and administration procedures, and 3) paring down information presented in each item to carefully isolate response dimensions of interest. To date, research results for Rhyming 2.0 and Alliteration 2.0 indicate that revisions have improved both measures (Wackerle-Hollman, Schmitt, Bradfield, Rodriguez, & McConnell, 2011). Perhaps most important for the redesign of these measures, however, is the observation that in a diverse sample that included high proportions of children at risk for language and literacy delays, the number of zero-correct scores declined to very low levels.

Sound Identification provides assessment of alphabet knowledge and print concepts. Children view a card with two or three letters, the examiner presents the phoneme for one of the letters, and the child responds by pointing to or naming the target letter. Correlations with subtests of the Test of Preschool Early Literacy and the Clinical Evaluation of Language Fundamentals (CELF-Preschool 2; Lonigan, Wagner, & Torgeson, 2007; Wiig, Secord, & Semel, 2004) indicate that it is sensitive to children's acquisition of letter–sound correspondence.

Minnesota researchers have also worked to select and improve a workable measure of comprehension for nonreading preschool children. Although this domain is challenged by little theoretical agreement or empirical guidance about definitive features to be assessed, a number of possible measures were explored. Currently, a conceptual category task, *Which One Doesn't Belong*, is being developed. In this measure, the child is presented (and the examiner names) pictures of three objects (e.g., rabbit, dog, chair) and the child is asked to identify the object that does not belong to a common class (i.e., chair). Preliminary results suggest this measure does share common variance with both language development and early comprehension measures.

THE ARCHITECTURE OF PRESCHOOL RESPONSE TO INTERVENTION ASSESSMENT

GOMs have become the assessment backbone of formal RTI models in K–12 education (Fuchs & Fuchs, 2006) and, more recently, in early childhood education

(Buysse & Peisner-Feinberg, 2009, 2010; Buzhardt et al., 2011; Greenwood, Carta, Baggett, et al., 2008). In part, this uptake of IGDIs and other GOMs in early childhood RTI has been serendipitous: IGDIs and related measures were developed relatively recently, reflected contemporary developmental and preacademic standards and desired outcomes, and were logistically efficient and readily available. However, IGDIs and related measures have also been picked for substantive reasons related to their conceptual coherence with the assessment needs of many RTI models.

The Center for Response to Intervention in Early Childhood (CRTIEC) has proposed a broad assessment and decision-making model that incorporates IGDIs as the backbone of assessment. As in most RTI assessment systems, we foresee the identification phase encompassing several key features, including 1) *universal screening*, or assessment of all children enrolled in participating classrooms and programs; 2) *seasonal screening*, three or four times in the year before kindergarten, to identify children who are not making expected progress and for whom more intensive intervention might be indicated; and 3) a *multiple-gating decision model*, where IGDIs and other information (e.g., teacher evaluation of child performance) contribute to decisions about the most appropriate intervention tier.

IGDIs will be central to identification phase assessment in this model. All five IGDIs will be administered every quarter (by classroom teachers, support staff, and/or others) to all children in a particular classroom or program. Each child's score on each measure will be compared to empirically derived, seasonally adjusted cut scores that classify current performance as *at or above expectations* (indicating that the child's developmental growth is on track to achieve long-term language and literacy goals), or *below expectations* (indicating that the child is likely a candidate for more intensive intervention), or that *more information is needed* (suggesting that although the child's performance was somewhat below expectations, more information is needed to determine whether more intensive intervention is warranted). These determinations will be followed by more focused data gathering and interpretation; teachers will gather information about child status, performance, and behavior (as well as other factors) and will compare these data with other criteria to help determine the most appropriate tier of intervention for each child.

Once selected for Tier 2 or Tier 3 intervention, the CRTIEC model (like many other RTI approaches) calls for frequent and repeated assessment of child progress, accompanied by evaluation of this assessed progress against medium-term objectives that indicate intervention success. At the time of this writing, CRTIEC progress monitoring procedures are still under development and may include IGDIs from the targeted domain (e.g., Picture Naming for a vocabulary and comprehension intervention, Alliteration or Sound Identification for phonological awareness and alphabet knowledge intervention) and/or mastery monitoring measures derived directly from content of intervention. In either case, child performance on a weekly or biweekly basis will be compared with a priori standards; children whose progress meets these standards will likely stay in current intervention, whereas children whose progress is below these standards will be considered for more intensive levels of service. We expect this model to be fully specified and implemented for initial evaluation in the 2012–2013 school year. More details about its implementation, and early evidence of its effects, will be available after that point.

CONCLUSION

Assessment in early childhood education—its acceptance and role in professional practice, and its sophistication, rigor, and scope—has expanded dramatically in recent years. From early professional recommendations that discouraged child-specific assessment in preschool, we have evolved to approaches that *require* assessment that adds value and improves outcomes in many intervention systems, and to tools that are better suited to these tasks, and to the unique features of infants, toddlers, and preschool-age children and the programs that serve them.

In many ways, however, this work—in assessment generally, and in specific areas like GOM—is still in early stages of development. Deliberate attention by researchers, practitioners, policy makers, and funders is still needed to sharpen our thinking about the roles and functions of assessment, the different ways to achieve these roles and functions, and ways to bring these practices to scale in efficient, rigorous, value-adding ways.

Research and practice on general outcome measurement in EC-RTI will be one part of this ongoing development. We expect future work to expand the scope and types of measures, to refine the use of these measures in RTI (and other) assessment and intervention models, and to successively refine and improve the use of these tools to support earlier, and more effective, intervention for all children.

REFERENCES

Brown, W.H. (2001). General growth outcomes or developmental and readiness domains? Naming is not knowing! *Journal of Early Intervention, 24*(3), 181–184.

Buysse, V., & Peisner-Feinberg, E. (2009). Recognition & Response. *Early Childhood RTI Roadmap, 7–8.*

Buysse, V., & Peisner-Feinberg, E. (2010). Recognition & Response: Response to intervention for pre-K. *Young Exceptional Children, 13*(4), 2–13.

Buzhardt, J., Greenwood, C.R., Walker, D., Anderson, R., Howard, W.J., & Carta, J.J. (2011). Effects of web-based support on Early Head Start home visitors' use of evidence-based intervention decision making and growth in children's expressive communication. *NHSA Dialog: A Research-to-Practice Journal for the Early Childhood Field, 13*(3), 121–146.

Cadigan, K.C., & Missall, K.N. (2007). Measuring expressive language growth in young children with autism spectrum disorders. *Topics in Early Childhood Special Education, 27*(2), 110–118.

Carta, J.J., Greenwood, C.R., Walker, D., & Buzhardt, J. (2010). *Using IGDIs: Monitoring progress and improving intervention results for infants and young children.* Baltimore, MD: Paul H. Brookes Publishing Co.

Deno, S.L., Mirkin, P.K., & Chiang, B. (1982). Identifying valid measures of reading. *Exceptional Children, 49*(1), 36–45.

Dunn, L.M., & Dunn, L.M. (1997). *Peabody Picture Vocabulary Test–Third Edition (PPVT-III).* New York, NY: Pearson.

Early Childhood Research Institute on Measuring Growth and Development. (1998a). Research and development of individual growth and development indicators for children between birth and age eight (Technical Report 4). *Technical Reports of the Early Childhood Research Institute on Measuring Growth and Development.* Minneapolis: Center for Early Education and Development, University of Minnesota.

Early Childhood Research Institute on Measuring Growth and Development. (1998b). Theoretical foundations of the Early Childhood Research Institute on Measuring Growth and Development: An early childhood problem-solving model (Technical Report 6). Minneapolis: Center for Early Education and Development, University of Minnesota.

Fewell, R. (2001). A continuous measure of growth outcomes: Will it do what it proposes to do? *Journal of Early Intervention, 24*(3), 185–187.

Floyd, R.G., Hojnoski, R.L., & Key, J. (2006). Preliminary evidence of technical adequacy of the Preschool Numeracy Indicators. *School Psychology Review, 35,* 627–644.

Fuchs, L.S., & Deno, S.L. (1991). Paradigmatic distinctions between instructionally relevant measurement models. *Exceptional Children, 57,* 488–500.

Fuchs, L.S., & Fuchs, D. (2006). The role of assessment in the three-tier approach to reading instruction. In D. Haager, J. Klingner, & S. Vaugh (Eds.), *Evidence-based reading practices for response to intervention* (pp. 29–44). Baltimore, MD: Paul H. Brookes Publishing Co.

Good, R.H., Gruba, J., & Kaminski, R.A. (2002). Best practices in using dynamic indicators of basic early literacy skills (Dibels) in an outcomes-driven model. In A. Thomas & J. Grimes (Eds.), *Best practices in school psychology* (4th ed., Vol. 1, pp. 699–720). Washington, DC: National Association of School Psychologists.

Greenwood, C.R., Bradfield, T., Kaminski, R., Linas, M., Carta, J.J., & Nylander, D. (2011). The response to intervention (RTI) approach in early childhood. *Focus on Exceptional Children, 43*(9), 1–22.

Greenwood, C.R., Buzhardt, J., Walker, D., Howard, W.J., & Anderson, R. (2011). Program-level influences on the measurement of early communication for infants and toddlers in Early Head Start. *Journal of Early Intervention, 33*(2), 110–134.

Greenwood, C.R., Carta, J.J., Baggett, K., Buzhardt, J., Walker, D., & Terry, B. (2008). Best practices in integrating progress monitoring and response-to-intervention concepts into early childhood systems. In A. Thomas & J. Grimes (Eds.), *Best practices in school psychology* (5th ed., pp. 535–548). Washington, DC: National Association of School Psychology.

Greenwood, C.R., Carta, J.J., McConnell, S.R., Goldstein, H., & Kaminski, R.A. (2008). Center for Response to Intervention in Early Childhood. Retrieved from http://www.crtiec.org

Greenwood, C.R., Luze, G.J., & Carta, J.J. (2002). Best practices in assessment and intervention results with infants and toddlers. In A. Thomas & J. Grimes (Eds.), *Best practices in school psychology* (4th ed., Vol. 2). Washington, DC: National Association of School Psychologists.

Greenwood, C.R., Walker, D., & Buzhardt, J. (2010). The early communication indicator (ECI) for infants and toddlers: Early Head Start growth norms from two states. *Journal of Early Intervention, 32*(5), 310–334.

Hojnoski, R.L., Silberglitt, B., & Floyd, R.G. (2009). Sensitivity to growth over time of the preschool numeracy indicators with a sample of preschoolers in Head Start. *School Psychology Review, 38,* 402–418.

Lonigan, C.J., Wagner, D.A., & Torgesen, J.K. (2007). *Test of preschool early literacy (TOPEL).* Austin, TX: Pro-Ed.

McConnell, S.R., McEvoy, M.A., Carta, J.J., Greenwood, C.R., Kaminski, R., Good, R.I., & Shinn, M. (1996). *Early childhood research institute on program performance measures: A growth and development approach.* Minneapolis: University of Minnesota.

McConnell, S.R., & Missall, K.N. (2008). Best practices in monitoring progress for preschool children. In A. Thomas & J. Grimes (Eds.), *Best practices in school psychology* (5th ed., pp. 561–573). Washington, DC: National Association of School Psychologists.

McConnell, S.R., Priest, J.S., Davis, S.D., & McEvoy, M.A. (2002). Best practices in measuring growth and development for preschool children. In A. Thomas & J. Grimes (Eds.), *Best practices in school psychology* (4th ed., pp. 1231–1246). Washington, DC: National Association of School Psychologists.

Missall, K.N., McConnell, S.R., & Cadigan, K. (2006). Early literacy development in preschool: Skill growth and relations between classroom variables for preschool children. *Journal of Early Intervention, 29,* 1–21.

Missall, K.N., Reschly, A., Betts, J., McConnell, S.R., Heistad, D., Pickart, M., . . . Marston, D. (2007). Examination of the predictive validity of preschool early literacy skills. *School Psychology Review, 36*(3), 433–452.

National Center on Response to Intervention. (2011). *Progress monitoring tools standards.* Washington, DC: National Center on Response to Intervention. Retrieved from http://rti4success.org/progressMonitoringTools

National Early Literacy Panel. (2009). *Developing early literacy: Report of the National Early Literacy Panel—A scientific synthesis of early literacy development and implications for intervention.* Jessup, MD: National Institute for Literacy.

Odom, S.L. (2001). A worthy challenge: Assessing child developmental growth in a systematic manner. *Journal of Early Intervention, 24*(3), 188–190.

Priest, J.S., Davis, K.M., McConnell, S.R., McEvoy, M.A., & Shin, J. (1999). *Early Childhood Research Institute on Measuring Growth and Development: Update on preschool measures.* Paper presented at the Division for Early Childhood, Council for Exceptional Children.

Priest, J.S., McConnell, S.R., Walker, D., Carta, J.J., Kaminski, R.A., McEvoy, M.A., . . . Shinn, M.R. (2001). General growth outcomes for young children: Developing a foundation for continuous progress measurement. *Journal of Early Intervention, 24*(3), 163–180.

Rodriguez, M.C. (2010). *Building a validity framework for second-generation IGDIs.* Minneapolis: University of Minnesota.

Shanahan, T., & Lonigan, C.J. (2008). *Developing early literacy.* Washington, DC: National Early Literacy Panel. Retrieved from http://www.nifl.gov/publications/pdf/NELPReport09.pdf

Tilly, W.D. (2008). The evolution of school psychology to a science-based practice: Problem solving and the three-tiered model. In A. Thomas & J. Grimes (Eds.), *Best practices in school psychology* (5th ed., Vol. 1, pp. 17–36). Washington, DC: National Association of School Psychologists.

VanDerHeyden, A.M., & Snyder, P. (2006). Integrating frameworks from early childhood intervention and school psychology to accelerate growth for all young children. *School Psychology Review, 35*(4), 519–534.

Wackerle-Hollman, A., Schmitt, B., Bradfield, T.A., Rodriguez, M., & McConnell, S.R. (2011). *Redefining individual growth and development measures: Phonological awareness.* Technical Reports of the Center for Response to Intervention in Early Childhood. Minneapolis: University of Minnesota.

Wallace, T.A., Espin, C., McMaster, K.L., Deno, S.L., & Foegen, A. (2007). CBM progress monitoring within a standards-based system: Introduction to the special series. *Journal of Special Education, 41*(2), 66–67. doi: 10.1177/00224669070410020201

Wayman, M.M., Wallace, T.A., Wiley, H.I., Tichá, R., & Espin, C.A. (2007). Literature synthesis on curriculum-based measurement in reading. *Journal of Special Education, 41*, 85–120.

Wiig, E., Secord, W., & Semel, E. (2004). *Clinical evaluation of language fundamentals—preschool second edition.* San Antonio, TX: Harcourt Assessment.

Zimmerman, I.L., Steiner, V.G., & Pond, R.E. (1992). *Preschool Language Scale–Third Edition.* San Antonio, TX: The Psychological Corporation.

10

Development of a Universal Screening and Progress Monitoring Tool and Its Applicability for Use in Response to Intervention

Susan H. Landry, Michael A. Assel, Jason L. Anthony, and Paul R. Swank

Many states estimate that half of their students start kindergarten lacking the set of early academic skills that will allow them to be successful in school (National Assessment for Educational Progress, 2003; Zill & West, 2001). The achievement gap is also associated with high dropout rates (Juel, Griffith, & Gough, 1986), and children from low socioeconomic status, ethnic, and language minority backgrounds are particularly at risk for academic failure (NAEP, 2003). Evidence for the critical nature of this continued problem is that the achievement gap between white students and black or Hispanic children has not narrowed. Over the last decade, states have grappled with issues surrounding how to provide children from low-income households with experiences that they need to be successful once they enter kindergarten (Bowman, Donovan, & Burns, 2001; Kagan & Kauerz, 2007). This has become a priority, given an expanding body of research that documents the critical importance of high-quality prekindergarten (pre-K) programs for supporting young children's learning and evidence that there are effective instructional strategies to help them become better prepared for school (National Early Literacy Panel, 2008).

In light of this priority, identification of effective early childhood instructional approaches has received a great deal of attention. In addition to professional development for teachers, one aspect of effective pre-K instructional practices that has proven to be helpful is the use of valid and reliable universal screening and progress monitoring measures to inform instruction (Landry, Anthony, Swank, & Monsegue-Bailey, 2009). This chapter provides an overview of the development of a progress monitoring tool used in a statewide program. The CIRCLE-Phonological Awareness, Language, and Literacy System (C-PALLS; Landry, Assel, Gunnewig, & Swank, 2004a, 2004b) is a progress monitoring tool that was developed prior to the use of response to intervention frameworks in pre-K classrooms. It was developed originally to support teachers in Head Start programs, public school pre-K classes, and child care centers as part of an integrated, comprehensive set of instructional

155

supports. C-PALLS evaluates vocabulary development, letter recognition skills, and phonological awareness abilities in children enrolled in preschool programs, and teachers are trained to assess these skills using this measurement approach three times during the school year. In addition to evaluation of literacy skills via direct assessment, C-PALLS also includes observational assessments of children's emergent writing skills, print and book knowledge, and social competence. The literacy skills assessed by classroom teachers using C-PALLS are generally recognized to be strong predictors of academic success in kindergarten (e.g., National Early Literacy Panel, 2008). Although the initial progress monitoring system was limited to evaluating early literacy skills, a subtest evaluating early mathematical skills was added in 2008.

A RESPONSE TO INTERVENTION FRAMEWORK

Monitoring of children's academic progress has been used for some time in the elementary grades to identify children who are struggling to master academic content and to help teachers target their instruction on weak areas within a child's learning profile. Response to intervention (RTI) is described as a comprehensive early detection and prevention strategy for identifying students who are struggling academically so that teachers can provide these students with assistance to avoid academic deficits (Gersten et al., 2008). RTI is often used in the elementary grades for linking assessment to instruction through data-based problem solving. RTI includes 1) an effective core curriculum for all children; 2) tiered instruction for students who need additional support; 3) integrated assessment, including universal screening and progress monitoring; and 4) use of assessment results to guide instruction (Greenwood et al., 2011; Gersten et al., 2008).

Assessment in RTI supports individualized instruction through a number of means. First, all children are screened to determine their level of risk for difficulty in a given area of achievement (e.g., universal screening for risk of reading failure). Children identified as being at risk may then receive more frequent, more intensive, and/ or different kinds of instructional programming. For example, small-group reading instruction for 60 minutes per week over and above core classroom reading instruction may comprise Tier 2. Second, frequent assessment (i.e., progress monitoring) is used to evaluate children's responsiveness to the instructional changes. If a child is not responding positively to the changes, then additional modifications to the frequency, intensity, and/or nature of instruction are made. For example, individual reading instruction for 90 minutes per week may comprise Tier 3. A tiered service delivery model guided by assessment (a.k.a. RTI) can be implemented by teachers to improve student achievement (Fuchs, Deno, & Mirkin, 1984; Fuchs, Fuchs, & Hamlett, 1989; Graney & Shinn, 2005; VanDerHeyden, Witt, & Gilbertson, 2007). A recent meta-analysis of 24 studies reported impressive average effect sizes of 1.02 for field-based efforts and 1.54 for university-based efforts (Burns, Appleton, & Stehouwer, 2005). Recent Institute of Educational Sciences (IES) practice guides likewise conclude there is strong evidence for the effectiveness of RTI (Gersten et al., 2008; Gersten et al., 2009).

PROGRESS MONITORING AND APPLICATION OF RESPONSE TO INTERVENTION IN EARLY CHILDHOOD SETTINGS

Measures used for progress monitoring have a number of noteworthy strengths that make them particularly amenable for use by teachers to monitor children's progress and to determine children's specific instructional needs. These measures are referred to in the literature under a number of names, including curriculum-based measures, formative assessments, and general outcome measures. Regardless of one's preferred name, measures used for progress monitoring are brief, easy to administer, and typically include alternate forms. Ideally, they should be sensitive to small increments in learning, and the results should readily translate to instructional recommendations. These assets make progress monitoring measures easy for teachers to administer, and they help teachers evaluate students' levels and rates of academic achievement, determine needs for instructional change, set appropriate short- and long-term goals, and monitor students' progress relative to peers or academic benchmarks (Busch & Reschly, 2007; Shapiro, Angello, & Eckert, 2004; VanDerHeyden, 2005). As such, progress monitoring measures have come to the forefront of educational assessment with the emergence of RTI frameworks for service provision and identification of children with learning difficulties.

The use of progress monitoring measures and the application of RTI in early childhood education settings are rather recent developments. There is growing interest in implementing RTI approaches in pre-K settings (e.g., Recognition & Response [R&R] developed by Buysse & Peisner-Feinberg, 2010, and the Pyramid Model developed by Fox, Carta, Strain, Dunlap, & Hemmeter, 2010). However, there is a need for further empirical evidence to support the efficacy of RTI approaches for pre-K (Greenwood et al., 2011). Nonetheless, their use is supported by a growing body of evidence (see Coleman, Roth, & West, 2009). As part of a multisite evaluation of professional development and approaches for monitoring children's learning (Landry et al., 2009), we developed an online professional development course (eCIRCLE) and a progress monitoring tool called C-PALLS (mentioned at the beginning of this chapter). The version of C-PALLS on a technology platform provides instructionally relevant feedback and groups children by skill profiles. A 2x2 research design crossed mentoring and C-PALLS conditions to compare impacts of these program components. Some teachers received mentoring; others did not. Some teachers received detailed, instructionally relevant feedback from C-PALLS on a technology platform; others received only raw scores from the paper-and-pencil version of C-PALLS. The four professional development groups participated in a yearlong online course and were compared to each other and a "business as usual" group. Across Texas, Florida, Maryland, and Ohio, 158 schools (N = 262 classrooms) were randomly assigned to one of the five conditions. Observations of teachers and standardized testing of 1,786 children took place at the beginning and end of the school year. Teachers using either version of C-PALLS were observed to make greater gains in instructional practices and to provide better quality teaching than control teachers (effect sizes [ES] = .79 to 1.49). Teachers who received technology-based support from C-PALLS engaged in more instruction targeting language and literacy skills and better quality teaching than teachers who were provided with only raw scores from the paper-and-pencil version of C-PALLS (ES = .52 to .78). Most important, relative to teachers who received only raw scores, teachers who received technology-based feedback relevant for guiding instruction had students who demonstrated greater achievement on standardized tests of vocabulary and letter knowledge (ES = .15 to .44).

Although much of the development of C-PALLS pre-dates the application of RTI in pre-K classrooms, C-PALLS has been used to inform instruction in early childhood classrooms that use an RTI or R&R Approach (Buysse & Peisner-Feinberg, 2010). For example, preliminary findings concerning the impact of RTI in early childhood are available from Buysse, Peisner-Feinberg, and Burchinal (2012). Achievement of 337 children from 24 classrooms in two states was monitored using C-PALLS. In this research, C-PALLS was adapted to allow for more frequent assessments to assess responsiveness to Tier 2 instruction, and results were used initially to group children and thereafter to guide Tier 2 intervention. Children in Tier 2 demonstrated faster learning of vocabulary, greater print awareness, and higher phonological awareness than their typically developing peers (ES = .34 to .50), demonstrating closing of the achievement gap.

Also, as multitiered instructional frameworks have become a recommended approach for providing instruction that targets the individual learning needs of children in pre-K settings, C-PALLS recently has been used in the Texas School Ready program to assist teachers in making decisions about which children need Tier 2 small-group targeted language instruction. In classrooms in Texas that have been using C-PALLS to guide what might now be referred to as high-quality Tier 1 instruction, the program recently implemented a vocabulary and language comprehension curriculum, Developing Talkers, in English and Spanish using a two-tiered vocabulary instruction framework. Findings from a brief intervention using this approach showed a significant and large effect size on receptive vocabulary for the randomly assigned children who received the small-group instruction in comparison with those who did not (Zucker, Solari, Landry, & Swank, 2012).

PRINCIPLES GUIDING DEVELOPMENT OF C-PALLS

Primary considerations driving the development of C-PALLS were that teachers would need to receive immediate access to results and that the results would be organized in a way that could guide instruction. C-PALLS was originally conceptualized as a tool to help educators link child assessment with instruction, and therefore it broadly served a progress monitoring purpose in pre-K classrooms. One reason that early childhood educators have found the measures to be helpful is that computerized applications organize children into ability-level groupings and suggest appropriate classroom activities. Activities were developed as part of our prior professional development studies (Landry et al., 2006). Activities to bolster student knowledge in vocabulary, letter recognition, and phonological awareness skills were gathered from a range of sources (e.g., curricula, web sites), evaluated for the appropriateness of content, and rank ordered for difficulty level by content experts. Therefore, children who are deemed to be at risk are provided with easier activities so that they have a reasonable chance to be successful. As children begin to improve in their ability to demonstrate early literacy skills, the difficulty level of selected activities can be increased. C-PALLS has the potential to seamlessly inform instruction for at-risk students (i.e., Tier 2) and also helps ensure that the classroom teacher can provide quality instructional supports to all children in the classroom (i.e., Tier 1).

EVOLUTION OF C-PALLS PLATFORMS

The original version of C-PALLS was administered with an easel board book (i.e., flipbook) and paper protocols on which teachers recorded children's responses.

Over time, administration has become easier as C-PALLS has been adapted to computer-assisted assessments. In the first computer-assisted version, teachers used an easel board book to administer test items and recorded child responses on a personal digital assistant (PDA). More recent versions of C-PALLS, developed by Tango, Teachscape, and Wireless Generation, include electronic administration of test items in which picture stimuli are presented on the screen of a desktop, laptop, or notebook computer. Prompts and timing assistance are also provided. During the development of C-PALLS, it became clear that teachers wanted to maintain the final authority for determining how the test should proceed. Therefore, even though the product is technologically sophisticated, teachers still maintain control of scoring and progressing through the assessment.

DESCRIPTION OF C-PALLS SUBTESTS

The content included within C-PALLS was determined via a careful review of the literature regarding early literacy. The C-PALLS system originally included three subtests for direct assessment of children's letter knowledge, vocabulary, and phonological awareness. These three subtests can be administered in approximately 10 to 15 minutes. C-PALLS also includes observational assessments of children's writing, social skills, and print concepts. Each subtest will be described in turn.

Rapid Letter Naming

This subtest assesses the number of letters a child is able to name in 60 seconds. Alphabet knowledge at school entry is a strong predictor of early reading skills (Adams, 1990; Stevenson & Newman, 1986). Letter knowledge skills have also been shown to relate to phonological sensitivity in preschool (Burgess & Lonigan, 1998). In addition, the links between letter naming fluency and reading skills have been demonstrated in the literature (Wolf & Bowers, 1999). Therefore, the Rapid Letter Naming tasks could best be thought of as a measure of alphabet knowledge that includes a fluency component.

Rapid Vocabulary Naming

This subtest assesses the number of pictures a child is able to label in 60 seconds. Pictures illustrate words selected from a review of national lists of appropriate vocabulary words and preschool curricula on Texas' state-adopted list. Vocabulary and oral language skills in general have been shown to be highly correlated with reading ability. For instance, the National Research Council (Snow et al., 1998) reported that most reading problems could be prevented by increasing children's language-based abilities, and the National Reading Panel (2000) reiterated the need to include vocabulary as one of the components of oral reading instruction.

Phonological Awareness

The link between phonological awareness abilities and early reading is well documented in the research literature. Phonological processing refers to the ability to use the sounds in words to process spoken language (Adams, 1990; Wagner & Torgesen, 1987). Phonological sensitivity in young children typically involves skills such as identifying rhyming words, blending, and deleting syllables or phonemes from words to form a new word, and it is thought to develop without exposure to print (Adams, 1990; Anthony et al., 2002, Lonigan et al., 2000). Our Phonological Awareness screener contains seven tasks that comprise 43 items. Tasks include 1) Listening (i.e., discriminating between like-sounding words), 2) Rhyme Recognition (e.g., do these words rhyme? *frog . . . dog*), 3) Rhyme Production (e.g., what word rhymes with *fan*?), 4) Alliteration (e.g., *silly . . . sun*, tell me if these words start with the same sound), 5) Sentence Segmentation (e.g., move a block for each different word you hear in "My books are new"), 6) Syllabication (e.g., How many parts do you hear in "/cow/ /boy/?"), and 7) blending of Onset-Rime (e.g., Repeat these parts and then say the word I am making . . . . /m/ /om/). A single phonological awareness score is totaled across the seven tasks.

Observational Assessment of Social Skills, Writing, and Print Concepts

Although the assessment of language and early literacy skills is an important function, C-PALLS was also designed to evaluate children's social skills, knowledge about books, and emergent writing abilities. Assessment of these skills occurs via an unstructured classroom observation. The Book and Print Awareness Checklist contains 10 items (e.g., how to hold the book, where to start reading, moving from one page to the next). Teachers sit with children and ask them to demonstrate their print and book knowledge skills in a format that is less structured than with direct assessment. The Social Assessment contains seven items and teachers rate positive aspects of children's social skills on a five-point scale (from "seldom" to "often"). Examples of items on the social scale include evaluation of whether children are able to regulate their emotions, engage in conversation with peers, and interact positively with peers. The Early Writing Checklist contains 11 items that evaluate whether children are writing letter-like forms or real letters, whether they understand that writing typically moves from left to right, whether they tend to engage in writing activities within centers, and whether they are able to write in response to literature. In conjunction with maintaining student portfolios, the C-PALLS system allows teachers to provide parents of enrolled students with detailed information about their child's literacy, language, math, social, writing, and print knowledge skills in an easy-to-understand format.

PSYCHOMETRICS OF C-PALLS

Because C-PALLS was developed as one part of a multifaceted professional development program, stand-alone evaluations of the reliability and validity of C-PALLS have not been conducted. Instead, data from several state and federally funded pre-K intervention projects have been pooled to examine the psychometric properties of C-PALLS. As such, the psychometric evaluations are limited to the confines of the larger studies. In addition, although a large number of children informs the psychometric analyses, the vast majority of these children were enrolled in Head Start agencies or state-funded pre-K programs that serve low-income children. Therefore, findings may not generalize to children from a broader socioeconomic range.

Samples

Data used to evaluate reliability and validity of C-PALLS came from numerous research studies conducted by the Children's Learning Institute over the course of several years. Data were gathered as part of our Interagency Education Research Initiative (IERI) study of professional development (Landry et al., 2009), Texas Education Agency (TEA) evaluation contracts (Landry et al., 2006), and the Texas Early Education Model (TEEM) demonstration project (Landry et al., 2011). Some piloting of C-PALLS occurred during our Preschool Curriculum Evaluation Research (PCER) grant as well. These studies were conducted in preschools, Head Start centers, and child care centers in low-income areas of Texas, Maryland, Ohio, and Florida. Children ranged from 3.5–5.5 years of age, although some of the variance in age is due to the longitudinal nature of all of the studies. The samples represent a diverse set of racial and ethnic groups and include an approximately equal number of males and females. Table 10.1 reports the number of children enrolled in each project by school year. Table 10.2 shows the breakdown of the sample's age at each of the three waves of assessment, collapsed across years.

Reliability

Reliability refers to the stability or consistency of the score obtained on a test when different items, examiners, or measurement time points are used to obtain the scores. We examined two types of reliability of C-PALLS subtests. First, we examined internal consistency, which measures how consistently individuals respond to different items that measure the same construct. Measures of internal consistency are not appropriate for speeded tests, so we only calculated internal consistency values for the Phonological Awareness screener. Internal consistency values for the Phonological Awareness screener for each 1-year age group and for all age groups combined were all greater than .90. These values indicate a strong degree of agreement among the items used to measure phonological awareness.

Second, because all C-PALLS subtests are typically administered to the same children three times during the school year, we were able to evaluate test–retest reliability. The test–retest correlation quantifies the stability of a test score across a period of time. Three-month test–retest correlations for Rapid Letter Naming were quite impressive, rs = .76 to .83 for various age groups, in light of the fact that the time interval was arguably long enough to permit instructional influences. Three-month test–retest correlations for Rapid Vocabulary Naming and Phonological

Table 10.1.   Number of assessments by study and year

Project name	Project year 2003–2004	Project year 2004–2005	Project year 2005–2006
Interagency Education Research Initiative (IERI; Landry et al., 2009)		2,412	434
Texas Education Agency–Project C (TEA-C; Landry et al., 2007)		10,856	4,337
Texas Education Agency–Project D (TEA-D; Landry et al., 2007)		5,335	1,589
Texas Early Education Model (TEEM; Landry et al., 2011)	2,697	8,992	1,079

Table 10.2. Number of assessments by age and time of year

Age	Beginning of year	Middle of year	End of year
3-year-olds	3,505	1,190	750
4-year-olds	10,627	5,987	4,689
5-year-olds	2,140	3,567	5,273
Total	16,272	10,744	10,712

Awareness were also acceptable, rs = .60 to .68 and .56 to .75 respectively for the various age groups. Scores on all subtests were generally more stable in older children. Finally, it was not surprising that higher test–retest correlations were found among measurement time points that were closer together.

Validity

Validity refers to the extent that a test measures the construct it is intended to measure. Demonstration of the validity of C-PALLS subtests was especially important because they are brief measures, some of which employ speeded tasks, and teachers were using an unfamiliar technology. To examine validity, we compared C-PALLS scores with scores obtained from standardized, norm-referenced measures of like constructs that were also administered during our program evaluation studies.

The standardized, norm-referenced tests had been administered at the beginning and end of the school year by trained research assistants. Therefore, validity analyses included only C-PALLS data that were likewise gathered at the beginning or end of the year, albeit by teachers. Correlations among C-PALLS scores and those derived from the norm-referenced measures that were administered during the same time period were tested to examine concurrent and discriminant validity. Concurrent validity assesses the degree of convergence between tests that measure the same thing. In contrast, discriminant validity assesses the degree that a test measures theoretically different constructs. Both types of validity are assessed with correlation coefficients. Tests with strong validity demonstrate both high correlations with measures of the same construct (i.e., concurrent validity) and lower correlations with measures of dissimilar constructs (i.e., discriminant validity).

As expected, convergent validity was supported by moderate to high correlations among measures of the same construct (see C-PALLS manual for validity coefficients). Discriminant validity was evidenced in that the standardized, norm-referenced tests had their highest correlation with subtests from C-PALLS that measured the same construct. More specifically, correlations among tests that measured dissimilar constructs were only small to moderate in size. Convergent and discriminant validity were similarly demonstrated with data collected at the beginning of the school year and with data gathered at the end of the school year.

MAKING C-PALLS WORK FOR TEACHERS: CUT SCORES

Given demonstration that the measures had adequate reliability and validity characteristics, guidelines were developed to help teachers determine which children within the classroom were most at risk for struggling on early academic tasks during kindergarten. Over time, the risk categories have been identified using different terminology (e.g., cut scores, cut points, thresholds) and have utilized nomenclature familiar to teachers (e.g., red, yellow, and green lights to determine the child's level of proficiency at different C-PALLS tasks). Cut scores were developed using logistical regressions that were based upon standard scores of the measures used within the validity studies. In this approach, children were considered to be at risk when their scores on outcome measures were outside of the Low Average range, generally less than the 10th percentile. Over time, these criteria for determining which children were at risk were broadened to take into account children who scored less than one standard deviation below the mean on the published outcome measures used in our validity studies. Outcome measures for our validity studies included the Expressive One Word Picture Vocabulary Test (Brownell, 2000), the Developing Skills Checklist: Auditory subscale (CTB, McGraw-Hill, 1990), and the Print Knowledge subtest from the Preschool-Comprehensive Test of Phonological and Print Processing (Lonigan, Wagner, Torgeson, & Rashotte, 2003). In the logistic regression model, a child's C-PALLS score was used to predict the score on the outcome measures to determine cut scores. Similar procedures were used to develop cut scores for children who were 3.5, 4, or 4.5 years of age at the beginning of the school year.

Prior to the 2008 school year, children were classified as being "not at risk/green," "slight risk/yellow," or "at risk/red." As our predictions about the children in the "slight risk/yellow" category were not very accurate, a new approach has been adopted. Specifically, predictions about whether children in the top tier (green) or bottom tier (red) were fairly accurate. However, predictions of whether children in the yellow group (i.e., slight risk) would move up or down in their early literacy skills were only slightly better than chance. Therefore, the current system provides teachers with two categories (i.e., "not at risk" and "at risk").

A strength of the C-PALLS system is that it provides teachers with suggested activities to improve the skills of children who have been determined to be at risk. In addition to suggesting activities for children who score low on a C-PALLS subtest, the system also provides teachers with extension activities for children who score higher than the cut scores within a particular area. For instance, teachers are provided with a range of activities in the Teacher's Activity (CIRCLE) manual to use with children who score below the cut score on the Rapid Vocabulary Naming subtest during the fall assessment. Activities to promote language/vocabulary development include story retells, labeling classroom objects (e.g., desk, door, window), Simon Says, Identification of Feelings, and What's in the Bag. The activities are described in detail in teacher manuals. However, abbreviated instructions are provided on the assessment device (e.g., laptop, desktop, notebook computer). Teachers have commented that once they have read the manual instructions for activities a few times, they are generally comfortable completing the activity using the abbreviated instructions that are provided electronically.

The cut scores and educational recommendations developed for the Phonological Awareness screener deserve further explanation. Specifically, the Phonological Awareness subtest includes seven tasks, and the total number of correct items across all seven tasks is used to determine whether a child is struggling within the area of phonological awareness. This is based upon the fact that the overall score on the Phonological Awareness screener is a much better indicator of a child's ability than are scores obtained on any individual task. However, as children often score better in certain areas within the Phonological Awareness screener, suggestion of appropriate activities is based upon a child's score on individual subtests. Therefore, even though a child's overall score on the Phonological Awareness subtest might indicate that he or she is not at risk, there is a chance that the classroom teacher would be encouraged to practice certain activities with the child in order to improve areas of weakness.

It is important to note that although the specific pairing of certain instructional activities to particular at-risk classifications has not been scientifically evaluated, the instructional strategies were developed and sequenced according to scientifically based research (Center for Improving the Readiness of Children for Learning and Education, 2008). Moreover, use of the technology-based C-PALLS system, which does provide instructional recommendations, has been shown in a large-scale randomized controlled trial to lead to significantly greater achievement among children than use of the paper-and-pencil-based C-PALLS test, which does not provide instructional recommendations (Landry et al., 2009).

RESPONDING TO THE FIELD: ADDITION OF A MATH SUBTEST AND BIRTH OF C-PALLS+

The literacy subtests of C-PALLS have been used in large-scale program evaluations and general preschool settings since 2003. However, as the system became more widely used in Texas, school district personnel and program directors asked that math content be included. Therefore, we developed and piloted mathematics items in 2007, and the Math screener was added to C-PALLS in 2008. This marked the first formal revision and renaming as C-PALLS+. The Math screener evaluates skills across multiple math domains considered to be important by the National Council of Teachers of Mathematics, including counting (i.e., rote counting and counting sets), shape naming, operations, number identification, and shape discrimination.

Two formats were explored as ways to assess children's patterning skills. One format involved highly scripted and detailed administration procedures along with the use of manipulatives. However, some teachers had difficulty administering these items according to the directions, and including manipulatives raised many practical challenges. We also piloted a multiple-choice format of assessing patterning skills. However, multiple-choice pattern recognition and multiple-choice pattern extension proved inappropriate for pre-K children. Specifically, nearly 60% of children's responses were to the multiple-choice item that was presented first in an array.

To date, initial efforts to evaluate the validity of the Math screener support its convergent validity. Specifically, the Math screener was found to correlate strongly ($r = .77$) with the Child Math Assessment (see Starkey, Klein, & Wakeley, 2004, for a description), and it was found to be moderately correlated ($r = .55$) with the Applied Problems subtest of the WJ-III.

The Math screener was piloted and validated in separate studies in 2008 and 2009. These studies were limited to working with children who were at least 4 years of age at the beginning of the school year. Therefore, the Math screener has the same cut score for all ages at all times of the year. The cut score for the Math screener is based upon the total raw score obtained by children. However, teachers are directed toward appropriate activities based upon a child's score on subsections within the screener (e.g., counting, operations). Table 10.3 provides examples of the cut scores for children who are 3.5, 4, or 4.5 years of age at the beginning of the school year.

Table 10.3. Cut scores demonstration risk levels for CIRCLE-Phonological Awareness, Language, and Literacy System (C-PALLS) subtests across age groups and administration time points

C-PALLS Subtest	3.5 at BOY	4.0 at BOY	4.5 at BOY
Rapid Vocabulary Naming BOY	≤10	≤16	≤20
Rapid Vocabulary Naming MOY	≤11	≤19	≤22
Rapid Vocabulary Naming EOY	≤12	≤22	≤24
Rapid Letter Naming BOY	≤7	≤8	≤10
Rapid Letter Naming MOY	≤7	≤11	≤12
Rapid Letter Naming EOY	≤8	≤14	≤15
Phonological Awareness BOY	≤2	≤8	≤9
Phonological Awareness MOY	≤4	≤9	≤10
Phonological Awareness EOY	≤7	≤10	≤12
MATH ALL TIME POINTS (all ages)	≤12	≤12	≤12

BOY, MOY, and EOY = beginning of school year, middle of school year, and end of school year

CONCLUSIONS

The C-PALLS system was developed as a universal screening/progress monitoring measure that could be one part of a comprehensive professional development program for early childhood education teachers. The professional development system also includes providing teachers with research-based curricula, ongoing professional development, and regular mentoring; monitoring children's learning; and integrating early childhood education service delivery systems. A strength of the C-PALLS system is that although it was developed as part of a broader professional development program (i.e., Tier 1), it has also been used to intervene in Tier 2 approaches with children who are struggling to make early academic progress. Regardless of how researchers define these systems (i.e., R&R or RTI), C-PALLS fills a need in the early childhood community for approaches that can identify children who are at risk and provide teachers with the tools they need to intervene in meaningful ways. The system is useful in pre-K multitiered approaches because it efficiently identifies students who are at risk within the first few weeks of school entry, provides teachers with suggestions to ameliorate early language and literacy weaknesses, and evaluates progress over the course of the academic year. At the time of its development (2002–2003), there were no assessments available that offered the benefits of teacher administration, immediate tabulation of scores leading to ability-level groupings, and suggestions for appropriate activities for struggling pre-K students. Although there were commercially available measures evaluating similar constructs (i.e., children's letter knowledge, vocabulary, and phonological awareness skills), most of these assessments were too lengthy, too expensive, and too complicated for teachers to administer, and their results were not readily usable for teachers, thereby making them unsuitable for directing Tier 2 interventions. The Children's Learning Institute has tried to address the need for a universal screening/progress monitoring assessment to be seamlessly integrated into curricula and professional development. Our approach has been validated across several large program evaluation studies (e.g., Landry et al., 2006;

Landry et al., 2009; Landry et al., 2011) and successfully integrated into more formalized R&R activities (i.e., Buysse et al., 2010).

Although C-PALLS seems to represent a significant advancement in the efficiency with which teachers are able to evaluate the early language, literacy, and mathematics skills of children, our goal is to develop a truly computer adaptive testing platform that will span the preschool years and extend through kindergarten. This would allow us to shorten the length of the evaluation without having to use fluency measures (e.g., Rapid Letter and Rapid Vocabulary subtests). For example, item response theory can be used to determine which items are the most predictive and thereby significantly decrease the overall length of the assessment. To date, more than 400,000 children have completed C-PALLS. Teachers have benefited from the classroom activities that are suggested by the system, the system's capacity to develop ability-level groupings, and the fact that the system allows classroom teachers to do what they were trained to do. That is, teachers are allowed to spend time providing assistance to those children who are at greatest risk for struggling in kindergarten.

REFERENCES

Adams, M.J. (1990). *Learning to read: Thinking and learning about print*. Cambridge, MA: MIT Press.

Anthony, J.L., Lonigan, C.J., Burgess, S.R., Driscoll, K., Phillips, B.M., & Bloomfield, B.G. (2002). Structure of preschool phonological sensitivity: Overlapping sensitivity to rhyme, words, syllables, and phonemes. *Journal of Experimental Child Psychology, 82*, 65–92.

Bowman, B.T., Donovan, M.S., & Burns, M.S. (Eds.) (2001). *Eager to learn: Educating our preschoolers*. Washington, DC: National Academy Press.

Brownell, R. (2000). *Expressive one-word picture vocabulary test*. Novato, CA: Academic Therapy.

Burgess, S.R., & Lonigan, C.J. (1998). Bidirectional relations of phonological sensitivity and prereading abilities: Evidence from a preschool sample. *Journal of Experimental Child Psychology, 70*, 117–141.

Burns, M., Appleton, J., & Stehouwer, J. (2005). Meta-analytic review of responsiveness-to-intervention research: Examining field-based and research-implemented models. *Journal of Psychoeducational Assessment, 23*, 381–394.

Busch, T.W., & Reschly, A.L. (2007). Progress monitoring in reading: Using curriculum-based measurement in a response-to-intervention model. *Assessment for Effective Intervention, 32*, 223–230.

Buysse, V., & Peisner-Feinberg, E. (2010). Recognition & response: Response to intervention for pre-K. *Young Exceptional Children, 13*(2), 2–13.

Buysse, V., Peisner-Feinberg, E., & Burchinal, M. (2012, March). *Recognition & response: Developing and evaluating a model of RTI for pre-K*. Poster session presented at the annual meeting of the Society for Research on Educational Effectiveness, Washington, DC.

Center for Improving the Readiness of Children for Learning and Education (CIRCLE). (2008). *Preschool early language and literacy teacher manual*. Houston: Ridgway.

Coleman, M.R., Roth, F.P., & West, T. (2009). *Roadmap to pre-K RTI: Applying response to intervention in preschool settings*. New York, NY: National Center for Learning Disabilities.

CTB/McGraw-Hill. (1990). *Developing skills checklist*. Monterey, CA: CTB/McGraw-Hill.

Fox, L., Carta, J., Strain, P., Dunlap, G., & Hemmeter, M.L. (2010). Response to intervention and the pyramid model. *Infants & Young Children, 23*(1), 3–13.

Fuchs, L., Deno, S.L., & Mirkin, P.K. (1984). The effects of frequent curriculum-based measurement and evaluation of pedagogy, student achievement, and student awareness of learning. *American Educational Research Journal, 21*, 449–460.

Fuchs, L.S., Fuchs, D., & Hamlett, C.L. (1989). Effects of alternative goal structures within curriculum-based measurement. *Exceptional Children, 55*, 429–438.

Gersten, R., Beckman, S., Clarke, B., Foegen, A., Marsh, L., Star, J.R., . . . Witzel, B. (2009). *Assisting students struggling with mathematics: Response to intervention (RTI) for elementary and middle schools* (NCEE200-4060). Washington, DC: National Center for Education and Evaluation and Regional Assistance, Institute of Education Sciences, U.S. Department of Education. Retrieved from http://ies.ed.gov/ncee/wwc/pdf/practice_guides/rti_math _pg_042109.pdf

Gersten, R., Compton, D., Connor, C.M., Dimino, J., Santoro, L., Linan-Thompson, S., . . . Tilly, W.D. (2008). *Assisting students struggling with reading: Response to intervention and multi-tier intervention for reading in the primary grades: A practice guide* (NCEE 2009-4045). Washington, DC: National Center for Education Evaluation and Regional Assistance, Institute of Education Sciences, U.S. Department of Education. Retrieved from http://ies .ed.gov/ncee/wwc/pdf/practice_guides/rti_reading_pg_021809.pdf

Graney, S.B., & Shinn, M.R. (2005). Effects of reading curriculum-based measurement (R-CBM) teacher feedback in general education classroom. *School Psychology Review, 34,* 184–201.

Greenwood, C.R., Bradfield, R., Kaminski, R., Linas, M., Carta, J.J., & Nylander, D. (2011). The response to intervention (RTI) approach in early childhood. *Focus on Exceptional Children, 43*(9), 1–22.

Juel, C., Griffith, P.L., & Gough, P.B. (1986). Acquisition of literacy: A longitudinal study of children in first and second grade. *Journal of Educational Psychology, 78,* 243–255.

Kagan, S.L., & Kauerz, K. (2007). Reaching for the whole: Integration and alignment in early education policy. In R.C. Pianta, M.J. Cox, & K. Snow (Eds.), *School readiness and the transition to kindergarten in the era of accountability* (pp. 11–30). Baltimore, MD: Paul H. Brookes Publishing Co.

Landry, S., Anthony, J.L., Swank, P., & Monsegue-Bailey, P. (2009). Effectiveness of comprehensive professional development for teachers of at-risk preschoolers. *Journal of Educational Psychology, 101,* 345–358.

Landry, S.H., Assel, M.A., Gunnewig, S., & Swank, P.R. (2004a). *CIRCLE-Phonological Awareness, Language & Literacy System* (paper and pencil version). Houston, TX: Ridgway.

Landry, S.H., Assel, M.A., Gunnewig, S., & Swank, P.R. (2004b). *MCLASS: CIRCLE-Phonological Awareness, Language & Literacy System* (PDA Version). New York, NY: Wireless Generation.

Landry, S., Swank, P., Anthony, J.L., & Assel, M. (2011). An experimental study evaluating professional development activities within a state-funded pre-kindergarten program. *Reading and Writing: An Interdisciplinary Journal, 24,* 971–1010.

Landry, S.H., Swank, P.R., Smith, K.E., Assel, M.A., & Gunnewig, S. (2006). Enhancing early literacy skills for pre-school children: Bringing a professional development model to scale. *Journal of Learning Disabilities, 39,* 306–324.

Lonigan, C.J., Burgess, S.R., & Anthony, J.L. (2000). Development of emergent literacy and early reading skills in preschool children: Evidence from a latent variable longitudinal study. *Developmental Psychology, 36,* 596–613.

Lonigan, C.J., Wagner, R.K., Torgesen, J.K., & Rashotte, C.A. (2003). *Preschool comprehensive test of phonological and print processing.* Austin, TX: Pro-Ed.

National Assessment for Educational Progress. (2003). *Highlighting NAEP 2003.* National Assessment for Educational Progress. Retrieved from http://www.ode.state.or.us/initiatives/ naep/naepnews_vol01num01.pdf

National Early Literacy Panel. (2008). *Report of the National Early Literacy Panel.* Washington, DC: National Institute for Literacy.

National Reading Panel. (2000). *Report of the National Reading Panel: Teaching children to read.* Washington, DC: U.S. Department of Health and Human Services.

Shapiro, E., Angello, L., & Eckert, T. (2004). Has curriculum-based assessment become a staple of school psychology practice? An update and extension of knowledge, use, and attitudes from 1990 to 2000. *School Psychology Review, 33,* 249–257.

Snow, C.E., Burns, M.S., & Griffin, P. (Eds.) (1998). *Preventing reading difficulties in young children.* Washington, DC: National Academy Press.

Starkey, P., Klein, A., & Wakeley, A. (2004). Enhancing young children's mathematical knowledge through a pre-kindergarten mathematics intervention. *Early Childhood Research Quarterly, 19,* 99–120.

Stevenson, H.W., & Newman, R.S. (1986). Long-term prediction of achievement and attitudes in mathematics and reading. *Child Development, 57*, 646–659.

VanDerHeyden, A.M. (2005). Intervention-driven assessment practices in early childhood/early intervention: Measuring what is possible rather than what is present. *Journal of Early Intervention, 28*, 28–33.

VanDerHeyden, A., Witt, J.G., & Gilbertson, D. (2007). A multi-year evaluation of the effects of a response to intervention (RTI) model on identification of children for special education. *Journal of School Psychology, 45*, 225–256.

Wagner, R.K., & Torgesen, J.K. (1987). The natural of phonological processing and its causal role in the acquisition of reading skills. *Psychological Bulletin, 101*, 192–212.

Wolf, M., & Bowers, P. (1999). The "Double-Deficit Hypothesis" for the developmental dyslexias. *Journal of Educational Psychology, 91*(3), 1–24.

Zill, N., & West, J. (2001). *Entering kindergarten: A portrait of American children when they begin school*. Washington, DC: U.S. Department of Education, Office of Educational Research and Improvement, National Center for Education Statistics.

Zucker, T.A., Solari, E.J., Landry, S.H., & Swank, P.R. (2012, in press). Effects of a brief, tiered language intervention for pre-kindergartners at risk. *Early Education and Development*.

Response to Intervention for Early Mathematics

Scott Methe and Amanda M. VanDerHeyden

Response to intervention (RTI) is a system of decision making that uses child performance data to allocate instructional supports and resources to advance child learning and growth toward important outcomes (VanDerHeyden & Snyder, 2006). The use of RTI is particularly well suited to early intervening systems because RTI emphasizes prevention through provision of high-quality instruction to all children, active universal screening to detect children who may need additional support, and data-driven progress monitoring to evaluate instruction and system improvement over time. Through the use of progress monitoring, RTI avoids the high error rate associated with single-point-in-time decisions that are particularly problematic for young children whose skills are rapidly emerging in response to both intervention and development.

Applying principles of RTI to early mathematics can be straightforward, despite the novelty of this topic in the research literature. A new paradigm is taking shape, which is evident in the work of professional organizations and policy making bodies that are striving to reduce the complexity and breadth of the early mathematics curriculum and thus focusing number sense on fewer and important skills. As a result, research into formative assessment has advanced considerably and many useful instruments are available to support the types of data-based decisions necessary to build and sustain an RTI model.

This chapter is intended to assist implementers of an RTI model in early mathematics in two primary ways. First, we will describe skills and professional standards that define early mathematics to best align instruction and assessment with these skills and standards. Second, we will detail how the structures and steps of RTI (including screening, progress monitoring, and monitoring intervention effectiveness) can facilitate learning of early mathematical skills.

EARLY MATHEMATICS AS THE DEVELOPMENT OF NUMBER SENSE

The most focused set of recommendations for young children to date emerged from the National Research Council's Committee on Early Childhood Mathematics (National Research Council, 2009). These recommendations informed the Common Core State Standards (CCSS, 2010), which are rapidly being adopted as the de facto set of learning standards that will drive the courses of study in districts across the country. In early childhood, the CCSS initiative helped to focus what the National

Council of Teachers of Mathematics (Fennell, 2006) identified as five separate strands of knowledge (number and operations; algebra; geometry; measurement; and data analysis and probability) and emphasize learning and teaching of number sense.

Number sense can be thought of as the key that opens the door to deeper understanding of mathematical reasoning and problem solving. Griffin (2004) defined number sense as a child knowing that numbers represent quantity and therefore have magnitude, that one number may be bigger or more than another number (or quantity), and that numbers occupy fixed positions in a counting sequence and therefore have a fixed order, with numbers appearing later in the sequence representing more (greater quantities) than numbers appearing earlier in the sequence. With regard to specific skills necessitating focus, number sense provides the core for counting in sequence, counting objects, ordering, classifying, and adding and subtracting numbers (Sarama & Clements, 2009). Number sense has been seen as the foundation for the entirety of the mathematics curriculum because it establishes the basis for understanding the properties of number such as the associative property, the commutative property, and the distributive property (Harniss, Stein, & Carnine, 2002). Very young children who use a sum strategy for counting to five, for example, may sometimes use two fingers on the left hand and three on the right hand but at other times use two fingers on the right hand and three on the left hand, thus demonstrating rudimentary knowledge of commutativity.

Developing number sense through early experience is critical to support a preschooler's transition to kindergarten, which is characterized by an introduction to increasingly abstract depictions of number. The preschool years are a critical developmental period for mathematics learning because knowledge and curricular content change as children move toward kindergarten. Experts in mathematical cognition and curriculum design have identified the completion of preschool and the transition into kindergarten as the interface of informal and formal mathematical knowledge and curricular content (Clements, Sarama, & DiBiase, 2004; Ginsburg, 1997; Ginsburg & Seo, 1999; National Research Council, 2009). The terms "informal" and "formal" specifically refer to the content of knowledge and curriculum rather than instructional rigor. In addition, these terms were coined to both 1) indicate the presence of abstract numerals in learning standards and 2) depict the contrast between learning that does and does not involve numerals as abstract entities (Ginsburg, 1997). Development from informal to formal mathematics learning takes children from a language- and object-based understanding of number to an understanding of number that can be represented through the use of numerals, the latter of which is notable in kindergarten curriculum standards (Common Core State Standards Initiative, 2010; Ginsburg, Lee, & Boyd, 2008; National Research Council, 2009).

Without robust early learning experiences that focus on building informal knowledge prior to kindergarten, problems may arise in kindergarten because the ability to understand and use numerals is predicated upon experience with language and number concepts like quantities and magnitude. In research and policy documents, preschool learning standards emphasize "connecting and communicating" (National Research Council, 2009, p. 43), suggesting that developing a language for mathematics (e.g., less, more, fewer, seven, three) is of critical importance. Additionally, research into preschool learning standards recommends rich representational environments where mathematical talk, pictures, and objects can be frequently used to represent number and numerals (Clements, Sarama, & DiBiase,

2004; National Research Council, 2009). Overall, flexibility in representing number using words, objects, and then more abstract means (i.e., numerals) should be emphasized as children ready themselves for the challenges of the more numeral-heavy kindergarten curriculum.

A facile number sense is achieved when a child learns to use concrete, representational (i.e., pictorial), and abstract (i.e., numerals) depictions of number (Griffin & Clements, 2007), and replaces less efficient and lower-order knowledge with more efficient higher-order skill (e.g., replacing counting on fingers to solve addition to quickly retrieving the fact when presented with a written problem such as 5 + 7). Instruction that changes in form from concrete to representational to abstract is popularly known as the concrete-representational-abstract (CRA) sequence. Indeed, this relatively linear CRA sequence not only is an effective organizer for the development of basic to advanced number sense but also characterizes the overall system of prompts to be used as a child gains knowledge and experiences success. A critical step in development occurs when young children no longer need to depict a number with their fingers, for example, and instead use a word, drawings, or a numeral to characterize the number. From the perspective of RTI, interventionists must use content-valid assessments to detect these transitions (Baroody, 2004) as they provide interventions to support movement toward higher levels of abstraction, especially for students who do not respond to core classroom instruction provided to all learners.

Much like the CRA sequence, but more rigorous in terms of its bases in neuropsychology, the *number sense access view* indicates that success is predicated upon a seamless transition from and interconnections among 1) perceptual knowledge of magnitudes, 2) language or verbal knowledge, and 3) visual knowledge in the form of a numeral (Dehaene, Piazza, Pinel, & Cohen, 2005). Young children who are beginning to count and represent numerals must rely on a concrete representation of number, and manipulatives are useful for this purpose. At this stage, a wide array of concrete representations can be used to build knowledge of the base-ten system, such as counters or base-ten blocks. During the process of counting and representing number with concrete objects, young children learn to associate number words (e.g., *seven, three, twenty-two*) with these quantities. Educational psychologists who are examining and building early mathematics intervention curricula, such as *Number Worlds* (Griffin & Clements, 2007), use the CRA sequence (Griffin, Case, & Siegler, 1994; Griffin, 2004; Griffin & Clements, 2007) to build number sense access. When intervention is sequenced correctly, concrete representations of number are faded as children become accurate and fluent with identifying and combining number symbols. Effective interventions teach children that concrete representations are essentially impractical when children are faced with and given opportunities to use representations like pictures and eventually number symbols. Over time, numerals become the primary vehicle for learning more advanced mathematics content.

NUMBER SENSE LEARNING STANDARDS

The CCSS represent the most recent effort to articulate and sequence expected learning outcomes across grade levels. This effort is notable because it attempts to ensure that all states build their instructional programs to accomplish the same end goals (i.e., mastery of the learning standards). Although the CCSS were influenced heavily by the many research committees and policy guidelines that preceded them, they are distinguished from past recommendations because they are streamlined rather than exhaustive of every possible learning task that a child might encounter during the school year. Although the CCSS may be considered the best organized set of recommendations for learning standards to date, it should be noted that prekindergarten standards are not included in the CCSS. However, a logical extrapolation to preschool expectations can be made by emphasizing the kindergarten domain of counting and cardinality and the development of mathematical language (National Research Council, 2009; Sarama & Clements, 2009). Many comprehensive resources have been developed to refine and clarify skills within the number sense and operations strand for preschool and beyond. Clements (2004) arranged the broad number sense and operations strand into six areas: counting, comparing and ordering, equal partitioning, composing and decomposing, and adding to and taking away. This work was subsequently refined into a learning trajectories approach that emphasized five areas (Sarama & Clements, 2009). The five-faceted learning trajectories approach informed much of the work of the Committee on Early Childhood Mathematics that focused on number (as opposed to geometry): 1) quantity, number, and subitizing; 2) verbal and object counting; 3) comparing, ordering, and estimating; 4) early addition, subtraction, and counting strategies; and 5) composition of number, place value, and multidigit addition and subtraction (Sarama & Clements, 2009).

Although many references for prekindergarten and kindergarten mathematics include counting, the CCSS emphasizes both counting and cardinality as major curriculum topics for kindergarten. Cardinality is a fundamentally important early transition in knowledge because it follows one-to-one correspondence and indicates that the last number counted is the number that makes up a set (Baroody, 2004; National Research Council, 2009). With cardinality comes an advance in logic; for example, children learn to see a counted set of six items as equal to one group.

In early mathematics, three critically important interrelated ideas that follow cardinality are ordinality, composition, and decomposition. These ideas make up the core of the NCTM Focal Points for prekindergarten and kindergarten that focus on "representing, comparing, and ordering whole numbers and joining and separating sets" (Clements & Sarama, 2009, p. 12). Ordinality introduces the idea of movement along a number line, thus facilitating the knowledge that number can be compared in terms of magnitude *and* position. Contrasting cardinality with ordinality, the cardinal language of "one, two, three" becomes first (relative to nothing and second), second (relative to first and third), and third (relative to second and fourth). Knowing that a counted set equals one complete unit is important because sets are frequently composed to make up another set. However, inflexibility can develop if a cardinal number is not understood as a number that can be decomposed. Therefore, understanding decomposition (Clements, 2004; Ma, 1999) can assist children in moving beyond cardinality and toward partitioning and rationing. Not only is a counted set one group of that number (e.g., six), but it is also two groups of three, for example, or one group of four and one group of two.

The CCSS also includes number and operations in *base ten*. In kindergarten, knowledge of base ten facilitates skill in place value and grouping (Clements, 2004). Place value and grouping are treated as higher-order concepts that are informed by counting, comparing and ordering, composing and decomposing, and partitioning.

Harniss, Stein, and Carnine (2002) emphasized the importance of decomposition in the transition from number sense to operating with numerals for addition and subtraction. Furthermore, their work supports the recommendations of the National Mathematics Advisory Panel (2008), which emphasized algebraic thinking across all levels of the curriculum. Because a fundamental task in algebra is solving for an unknown quantity, it becomes important to emphasize how basic number sense can facilitate algebraic thinking. Related to identifying a missing quantity, Baroody (2004) discussed part–whole relations where, for example, knowledge of three and "how many more" might result in five, and the "how many more" (two) comprises the unknown quantity. Additionally, children learning to recompose around a base-ten unit can benefit from knowledge of part–whole relations. Knowing that the number 5 is made of 2 and 3 can help a child when adding 8 and 5 because this problem can be treated as $(8 + 2) + 3$. Therefore, part–whole knowledge can support understanding of the associative property (Harniss, Stein, & Carnine, 2002), place value, and proportions.

Standards as Instructional Goals

Specifying the skills that are most essential for mastery in prekindergarten and kindergarten provides teachers with meaningful instructional targets (Slentz & Hyatt, 2008). However, specifying a sequence of skills that represent critical outcomes of instruction can be a point of confusion for some teachers. Some teachers may view such a list as representing the full range of all instruction and may also assume that skills can best be taught through rote memorization methods. Consistent with policy and research recommendations, we recommend balanced mathematics instruction that is sequenced logically, paced to permit children to reach mastery for essential skills, matched to student instructional level, and connected to real-world problem solving (Ginsburg et al., 2008). We have argued that before teachers can decide *how* to teach, they must decide *what* to teach. In the next section, we will describe a framework for ensuring child mastery of essential early learning skills.

IMPORTANT FEATURES OF CORE INSTRUCTION IN EARLY MATHEMATICS

The goal of early mathematics instruction is to connect children's informal knowledge to number representations and operations in base-ten language. Children have a natural curiosity and deep understanding of pivotal math concepts (Ginsburg et al., 2008) that can and should be met by the teacher and facilitated with intentional instructional techniques. The first step toward promoting early mathematical understanding is to focus content and specify which skills should be targeted for instruction. The second step is to provide well-sequenced instruction that facilitates conceptual understanding and facility using numbers and numerals to solve problems. Teachers and interventionists must understand the instructional hierarchy (IH), and use this model to facilitate mastery of learning standards. The IH is a fundamental and progressive set of four levels, or benchmarks, related to learning: acquiring skill and knowledge, developing fluency with the skill, generalizing the skill to other skills and settings, and adapting the skill to solve real-world problems (Haring, Lovitt, Eaton, & Hansen, 1978). Each day, children should participate in mathematics learning opportunities that provide acquisition-level support for new or emerging skills. New skills are skills that a child cannot yet perform accurately. During acquisition instruction, teachers should emphasize strategies like modeling correct and incorrect responding, providing immediate corrective feedback that is more detailed and concludes by asking a child or the whole class to give or show the correct response, and guided practice completing the task accurately.

Once children can respond accurately when presented with a task, and have attained the next step above acquisition in the IH, fluency-building strategies can be used to facilitate growth toward skill mastery. Fluency-building strategies include using short intervals of timed practice (sometimes referred to as timed trials), embedding multiple opportunities to respond into a math game or applied activity, setting goals for more fluent performance, and rewarding fluent performance. At this stage of instruction, the teacher can vary the task presentation as long as support is available to ensure that correct responding continues. Once children have become accurate and fluent, the teacher can and should introduce opportunities to move further up the instructional hierarchy and use the mastered skill to solve applied or more complex problems. For example, a task of counting coins can be used to teach counting object correspondence and counting by fives and tens. As children become fluent in counting coins, concepts related to conservation of number, equivalence, place value, and associative and distributive property can be introduced. Teachers should guide discussion around these concepts and provide opportunities for students to construct hypotheses, estimate solutions, test solutions, and discuss findings related to math concepts.

Although core instruction should be guided by standards and assessment of how children are learning these standards, the curriculum and its related assessment do not prescribe teaching. Rather, a sequence of skills based upon early mathematics standards provides teachers with a series of measurable outcomes that can be tracked to ensure that children are mastering essential skills over time. Using instructional standards in number sense as essential outcomes allows teachers to avoid blind adherence to a specific set of curriculum materials that may include suboptimal content. When teachers use research-based criteria for selecting skills, they are free to select the instructional tools and resources that will best advance students to mastery on these essential skills. In addition to focusing on content, teachers must have a system for knowing the children's development on a given skill. A common mistake in mathematics instruction is to advance content or task difficulty when prerequisite skills have not actually been mastered. This mistake is costly because children will be prone to errors and misunderstanding as learning tasks become more complex. Using the steps described next, we have identified a number of techniques and models (i.e., the instructional hierarchy) to ensure that instruction is sensitive to the developmental levels and learning needs of students.

THE PROCESS OF RESPONSE TO INTERVENTION

The purpose of RTI is to ensure that the core instructional environment is adequate for most children and equipped with resources to provide systematic support to children who do not readily respond to instruction. Core classroom instruction (also referred to as Tier 1) in early mathematics is the most fundamental structure of an RTI model and should be guided by a sequence of instructional standards, include formative assessments, and be carefully balanced to provide the type of instruction that is needed by children at various stages of the learning or instructional hierarchy (acquisition, fluency-building, and generalization). Rigorous scientific standards for all materials adopted in core classroom instruction should be used to choose materials that are most likely to result in student learning. When children struggle to learn expected skills, supplemental small-group (referred to as Tier 2) and/or individualized (referred to as Tier 3) intervention is provided. To accomplish RTI, student data must be collected and used by decision makers. These data can be obtained from universal screening and allow decision makers to reach conclusions about the adequacy of Tier 1 instruction and further pinpoint instructional needs for students.

Step 1: Conduct Universal Screening

Teachers should select a skill for screening that 1) has been taught within the current curriculum, and 2) most children are expected to be able to do to benefit from the instruction. With the knowledge of key early mathematics content discussed in the first part of this chapter, readers are urged to use the screening measures identified in Table 11.1. Users of these measures should briefly assess the extent to which a learning standard is exemplified by the measure, and choose the correct screener based on this assessment. If a selected measure such as identifying which object set has more or less (i.e., quantity discrimination; Floyd, Hojnoski, & Key, 2006)

Table 11.1. Curriculum-based measures for screening and progress monitoring in preschool

Quantity, number, and subitizing	• Number Selection (VanDerHeyden et al., 2004; http://www.isteep.com)
	• Number Naming (Floyd, Hojnoski, & Key, 2006; Methe, Hintze, & Floyd, 2008; VanDerHeyden et al., 2004; http://www.isteep.com)
	• Count Objects, Say Number (VanDerHeyden et al., 2004; http://www.isteep.com)
	• Count Objects, Select Number (Methe, Hintze, & Floyd, 2008; VanDerHeyden, Witt, Naquin, & Noell, 2001; http://www.isteep.com)
	• Count Objects, Write Number (VanDerHeyden et al., 2001; www.isteep.com).
	• Quantity Array (Lembke & Foegen, 2009)
Verbal and object counting	• Oral Counting (Clarke & Shinn, 2004; www.aimsweb.com; VanDerHeyden et al., 2004; www.isteep.com)
Comparing, ordering, and estimating	• Quantity Discrimination (Floyd, Hojnoski, & Key, 2006; VanDerHeyden et al., 2011)
	• Relative Size (Methe, Begeny, & Leary, 2011)
	• Ordinal Position Fluency to Five (Methe, Hintze, & Floyd, 2008; Methe, Begeny, & Leary, 2011)
	• Identify/Discriminate the Object that Is Different (VanDerHeyden et al., 2001, VanDerHeyden et al., 2004; http:// www.isteep.com)
	• Equal Partitioning Fluency (Methe, Begeny, & Leary, 2011)
Composition and place value	• Math Numbers and Operations and Algebra (http://www.easycbm.com)
	• Group Five (Methe, Begeny, & Leary, 2011)
	• Math Concepts and Operations (http://www.aimsweb.com)

For more detailed reports of these and other screening and progress monitoring measures, see http://www.rti4success.org

indicates low performance for a given student, teachers can target one or more of the prioritized skills that are prerequisite to quantity discrimination and use this measure to monitor progress. Once a screening measure has been selected, teachers should follow standard or scripted instructions to administer the screening measures to all children in the classroom. Following scripted instructions allows the teacher to compare students and to track individual student progress over time.

Figure 11.1 depicts 11 separate classrooms that used the Count and Circle Number measure (VanDerHeyden, Witt, Naquin, & Noell, 2001). Student performance on this measure was aggregated by classroom to look at the percentage of students who had attained an important instructional benchmark. Ideally, all classes within a program at the same grade or level will administer the same measure so that the progress of all children across classes can be compared and tracked over time. All children should participate in screening in the fall, winter, and spring, and progress monitoring should occur more frequently for classes and students when a learning problem is detected. Adequate screening measures are well aligned with learning expectations in the classroom, yield sufficiently reliable scores that correlate well with more comprehensive measures of mathematics proficiency, forecast mathematics proficiency over time, and require minimal time to administer and score. All of the early numeracy measures listed in Table 11.1 meet these criteria.

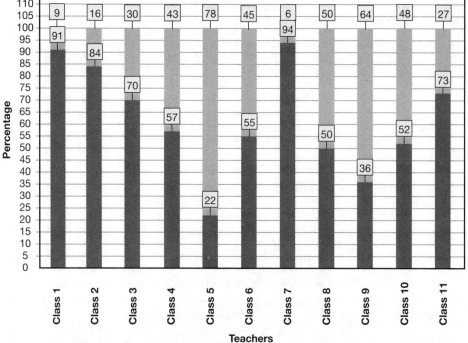

Instructional Effects
Grade: K, Date Range: 7/1/2010–10/30/2010
Assessment: KEHALA, Numeracy, Count and Circle Number

Figure 11.1.   Classroom performance on the Count and Circle Number probe. (Copyright © 2012 by Amanda M. VanDerHeyden; used by permission.)

Step 2: Identify and Address
Class, Grade, and Schoolwide Problems

Once screening data are collected, they can be examined to identify the extent to which problems in student learning can be differentiated from problems in classroom, grade-level, or schoolwide instruction. Common problems in the instructional ecology include poor teacher agreement on instructional goals, failure to use research-based curricula and intervention programs, poor professional development, lack of common planning time, and other related issues (Woodward & Kaufman, 1998). Using an assessment instrument that broadly represents a set of curriculum-relevant skills for the grade and age level (see Table 11.1), the aggregate score obtained for any classroom can be compared to a benchmark criterion or goal that the instructional leadership deems ambitious. Examining Figure 11.1 closely, it is notable that some classrooms (i.e., Classrooms 4, 5, 6, 8, 9, and 10) are not attaining the same level of skill development as the others, indicating a grade-level problem. Comparing the obtained performance with a more desirable goal state (e.g., average classroom performance exceeds 80%–90% accuracy, as in Classrooms 1 and 2 from Figure 11.1) helps determine whether most of the children in the class are learning effectively and also helps to uncover effective classroom strategies. Where a classroom aggregated score is well below the criterion, a problem that should be addressed through classwide intervention is indicated (VanDerHeyden, Witt, & Naquin, 2003). This same procedure can be used to identify grade- and school-level problems. Where more than half of the classes at any given age or grade-level exhibit scores below the benchmark, a larger systems-based intervention may be necessary. When this pattern is detected, the first step taken by the intervention team must be to evaluate the instructional "basics" in the classroom, including consensus for a sequence of learning outcomes for early mathematics linked to a calendar of instruction, availability of and correct use of curriculum materials to facilitate child learning of essential skills, use of routine child assessment to guide instruction, sufficient instructional time allocated to early mathematics instruction, and more frequent progress monitoring to track whether or not corrective actions reduce the numbers of students scoring in the risk range on subsequent screenings. Where classwide learning problems are detected, classwide intervention can be planned and delivered using a research-supported program like Peer Assisted Learning Strategies (PALS; http://kc.vanderbilt.edu/pals/).

Step 3: Identify Individual Child Learning
Problems for Tier 2 or Tier 3 Intervention

If a classwide problem has been addressed through intervention, the scores of all children in the class can be evaluated to identify individual children in need of additional intervention. Figure 11.2 depicts the different levels of skill demonstrated by students within a classroom when they are assessed with the Count and Circle Number probe. After depicting student scores in this type of graphical array, the next step is to differentiate among two types of skill deficits in a classroom. This differentiation (or diagnosis) is critical because homogenous grouping is still frequently deployed in schools and it cannot be assumed that every child shares the same root cause of poor performance. To further differentiate within an instructional grouping, one decision rule that can be applied is to use the bottom

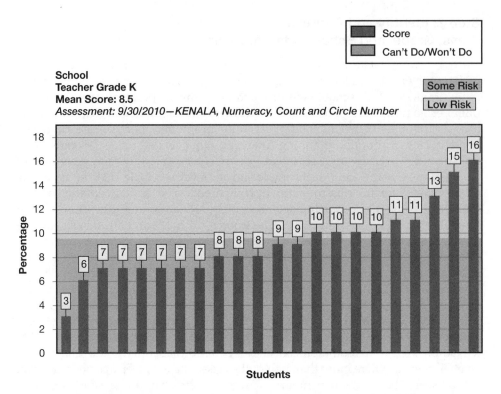

Figure 11.2. Ranked performance by classroom on the Count and Circle Number probe. (Copyright © 2012 by Amanda M. VanDerHeyden; used by permission.)

16th percentile of children in a classroom as a cutoff point to indicate the need for further assessment (VanDerHeyden et al., 2003). After these children are identified, interventions should be judiciously selected as a means to pinpoint the cause of poor performance. The intervention provider is therefore linking assessment and intervention by examining which intervention, implemented in brief trials, leads to the most robust student response. Therefore, this step requires a follow-up assessment and/or progress monitoring. The functional assessment literature (Martens & Gertz, 2009) provides an empirical basis for the idea that this procedure will indeed differentiate students and identify the intervention that will best indicate the root cause of poor performance. Also, the indicated intervention can be selected and adapted for more extended use.

Common interventions to use at this step include maximizing motivation (tested by offering incentives for improved performance), reducing task difficulty (tested by administering successively easier tasks at skill level and at the prerequisite skill level), and providing guided support to correctly respond (tested by conducting a brief instructional session followed by a timed trial; see the appendix following this chapter). The cause has been identified when students respond more readily to one or more interventions than to others. In addition to a functional assessment, the student's screening data should be used to differentiate between accuracy and fluency deficits. This type of problem analysis uses the instructional hierarchy to aid in intervention selection. For example, if a student's scores on a number naming assessment indicate that he or she incorrectly named 10 numbers out of 30 attempted in 1 minute, this low (66%) accuracy indicates a need for acquisition-level support. Acquisition-level support would not be used for a student who, for example, says 15 of 15 numeral names in 1 minute. Instead, intervention for the "accurate but not fluent" student would be targeted at fluency-building strategies. Figure 11.3 indicates how two students, Danae and Katelyn, responded to the chosen intervention and in turn demonstrated two very different types of skill deficits. Katelyn's response to the intervention indicated that she is in great need of acquisition-level support, as she has not likely attained the skill of counting a set and circling the number that corresponded to the set. Therefore, a fluency-level intervention strategy like the one detailed in the appendix is not likely to be appropriate for Katelyn. Danae's response to the intervention indicates that she has learned this skill but is either not motivated to perform the skill or has not practiced the skill enough to have attained fluency. The intervention in the appendix may be more useful for Danae. The cases depicted in Figure 11.3 have been chosen to exemplify Step 3 in an RTI model but also to warn educators that placing children with similar screening scores in homogenous groups *without a problem analysis* may be inappropriate.

Step 4: Effectively Deploy Interventions

One of the most prevalent causes of intervention failure is poor intervention implementation (McIntyre, Gresham, DiGennaro, & Reed, 2007). Research suggests that intervention failures should be rare events (Torgesen et al., 2001; VanDerHeyden, Witt, & Gilbertson, 2007; Vaughn, Linan-Thompson, & Hickman, 2003), and that intervention failure should be examined prior to concluding that the student has not learned the skill. When interventions fail to produce the desired change in learning, the first step should be to verify correct intervention use. A variety of excellent resources is available at www.interventioncentral.org that can help implementers identify the critical components of an intervention and observe the intervention as it is implemented. Witt, VanDerHeyden, and Gilbertson (2004) indicate that using data to evaluate intervention integrity is a critical aspect of ensuring intervention success and that these data should be used in concert with progress monitoring data. By identifying the specific aspects of the intervention tasks and using checklists to evaluate the extent to which they have been accomplished, schools not only

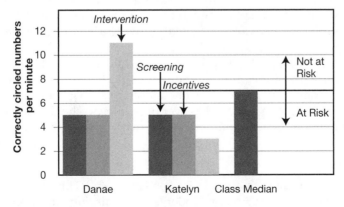

Figure 11.3. Response to a fluency-building intervention for two students. (Copyright © 2012 by Amanda M. VanDerHeyden; used by permission.)

facilitate exemplary intervention adherence, but also help teachers, students, and staff to collaborate and maximize learning outcomes. After implementers have decided which intervention is needed and ensured the effective deployment of the intervention, they must decide how and when to monitor progress of those interventions, and how to train and support high-quality intervention implementation.

Step 5: Monitor Intervention Effects and Evaluate Outcomes

Critical components of this step include 1) establishing schedules for monitoring all students, 2) selecting a progress monitoring measure or measures that are sensitive to growth, 3) ensuring that data are displayed visually (Riley-Tillman & Burns, 2009), and 4) ensuring that implementers agree on rules that allow ineffective interventions to be modified as needed. With regard to monitoring schedules, screening results can be used to indicate the frequency of monitoring. Using a three-tiered model of risk (i.e., risk for not meeting the end-of-year learning standards), schools can use criteria, normative data, or teacher nominations of risk level to prescribe monitoring schedules. Students at low risk (Tier 1) are likely to respond to classroom instruction and can be monitored infrequently in the fall, winter, and spring. Students at some risk (Tier 2) should be monitored every two weeks, and students who are at high risk (Tier 3) should be monitored weekly.

With regard to the choice of a progress monitoring measure, in some cases the adopted measure may be too difficult for a student. Although it is important to continue monitoring in this skill, implementers should feel free to select an easier skill to monitor concurrently. A visual display of data allows implementers to focus on one key goal, which is to reduce the discrepancy between actual and expected child performance (i.e., the aimline). When growth is not demonstrated over a period of 2–3 weeks, assuming that a student whose screening data indicated the need for weekly monitoring and intensive intervention, implementers should verify intervention integrity and then make systematic changes to the intervention and reevaluate after another 2–3 weeks. The most difficult part of monitoring intervention effects is ensuring that there is enough time for the intervention to work, but not waiting too long and concluding that the student is not responding to the intervention. If the intervention implementation has been monitored, however, and measures have been selected that are sensitive to growth, implementers can be more confident that the graphed data reflect reality. Because similar data are collected across all classrooms and evaluated relative to a benchmark criterion, effects of intervention efforts should also be evaluated over time (Shapiro & Clemens, 2009) to evaluate the extent to which groups of children experiencing unexpected rates of failure at baseline close the performance gap between themselves and not-at-risk peers. Examining proportions of children in each group at the beginning, middle, and end of the year, as well as over time, allows school personnel to evaluate the effectiveness of the overall program of instruction in early mathematics.

SUMMARY

This chapter was written to assist in implementing an RTI model for early mathematics. We focused content on prekindergarten skills with an emphasis on effective transition into kindergarten. Furthermore, we gave attention to both informal and formal skills that can be used as assessment and intervention targets. It is critical for teachers choosing assessment and intervention methods in an RTI model to understand that number is a code-based system and that many children experiencing problems with combining numerals, an earmark of mathematics disability (Gersten & Jordan, 2005), need instruction that helps them understand number language and concepts as well as numerals and basic numeral combinations. Thankfully, broad-based recommendations from policy-making bodies indicate that substantial momentum is building in the area of early mathematics.

The process of RTI discussed in this chapter allows teachers to understand how the content of early mathematics can be effectively combined with the process of screening, progress monitoring, intervention integrity, and ongoing program evaluation. Although this chapter represents an updated collection of research in the foundations of effective RTI models in early mathematics, such as early learning standards, assessment, and intervention, it is likely that more advances will be made in the short term. Readers are urged to stay updated on research and policy changes and to advocate for a more focused curriculum that can be evaluated with innovative and precise instructional tools designed to maximize learning for all students.

REFERENCES

Baroody, A.J. (2004). The developmental bases for early childhood operations and number standards. In D.H. Clements & J. Sarama (Eds.), *Engaging young children in mathematics: Standards for early childhood mathematics education*. Mahwah, NJ: Lawrence Erlbaum Associates.

Clarke, B., & Shinn, M.R. (2004). A preliminary investigation into the identification and development of early mathematics curriculum based measurement. *School Psychology Review, 33*, 234–248.

Clements, D.H. (2004). Major themes and recommendations. In D.H. Clements, J. Sarama, & M. DiBiase (Eds.), *Engaging young children in mathematics: Standards for early childhood mathematics education*. Mahwah, NJ: Lawrence Erlbaum Associates.

Clements, D.H., & Sarama, J. (2009). *Learning and teaching early math: The learning trajectories approach*. New York, NY: Routledge.

Clements, D.H., Sarama, J., & DiBiase, M. (Eds.). (2004). *Engaging young children in mathematics: Standards for early childhood mathematics education*. Mahwah, NJ: Lawrence Erlbaum Associates.

Common Core State Standards Initiative. (2010). *Common core state standards for mathematics*. Retrieved from http://www.corestandards.org/assets/CCSSI_Math%20Standards.pdf

Dehaene, S., Piazza, M., Pinel, P., & Cohen, L. (2005). Three parietal circuits for number processing. In J.I.D. Campbell (Ed.), *Handbook of mathematical cognition* (pp. 433–453). New York, NY: Psychology Press.

Fennell, F. (2006). Curriculum focal points for pre-K–grade 8 mathematics: A quest for coherence. *Teaching Children Mathematics, 13*, 159.

Floyd, R.G., Hojnoski, R., & Key, J. (2006). Preliminary evidence of the technical adequacy of the preschool numeracy indicators. *School Psychology Review, 35*, 627–644.

Gersten, R., & Jordan, N.C. (2005). Early screening and intervention for mathematics difficulties: The need for action. *Journal of Learning Disabilities, 38*, 291–292.

Ginsburg, H.P. (1997). Mathematics learning disabilities: A view from developmental psychology. *Journal of Learning Disabilities, 30*, 20–33.

Ginsburg, H.P., Lee, J.S., & Boyd, J.S. (2008). Mathematics education for young children: What it is and how to promote it. *Social Policy Report: Giving Child and Youth Development Knowledge Away, 22*, 3–22.

Ginsburg, H.P., & Seo, K.H. (1999). Mathematics in children's thinking. *Mathematical Thinking and Learning, 1*(2), 113–129.

Griffin, S.A. (2004). Building number sense with Number Worlds: A mathematics program for young children. *Early Childhood Research Quarterly, 19*, 173–180.

Griffin, S.A., Case, R., & Siegler, R.S. (1994). Rightstart: Providing the central conceptual prerequisites for first formal learning of arithmetic to students at risk for school failure. In K. McGilly (Ed.), *Classroom lessons: Integrating cognitive theory and classroom practice* (pp. 25–49). Cambridge, MA: The MIT Press.

Griffin, S.A., & Clements, D. (2007). *Number worlds: A prevention / intervention curriculum.* Columbus, OH: Science Research Associates.

Haring, N.G., Lovitt, T.C., Eaton, M.D., & Hansen, C.L. (1978). *The fourth R: Research in the classroom.* Columbus, OH: Merrill.

Harniss, M.K., Stein, M., & Carnine, D. (2002). Promoting mathematics achievement. In M.R. Shinn, H.M. Walker, & G. Stoner (Eds.), *Interventions for academic and behavior problems II: Preventive and remedial approaches* (pp. 571–587). Washington, DC: National Association of School Psychologists.

Lembke, E., & Foegen, A. (2009). Identifying early numeracy indicators for kindergarten and first-grade students. *Learning Disabilities Research & Practice, 24*, 12–20.

Ma, L. (1999). *Knowing and teaching elementary mathematics.* Mahwah, NJ: Lawrence Erlbaum Associates.

Martens, B., & Gertz, L. (2009). Brief experimental analysis: A decision tool for bridging the gap between research and practice. *Journal of Behavioral Education, 18*, 92–99.

McIntyre, L.L., Gresham, F.M., DiGennaro, F.D., & Reed, D.D. (2007). Treatment integrity of school-based interventions with children, 1991–2005. *Journal of Applied Behavior Analysis, 40*, 659–672.

Methe, S.A., Begeny, J.C., & Leary, L.L. (2011). Development of conceptually focused early numeracy skill indicators. *Assessment for Effective Intervention, 36*, 230–242.

Methe, S.A., Hintze, J.M., & Floyd, R.G. (2008). Validation and decision accuracy of early numeracy skill indicators. *School Psychology Review, 37*, 359–373.

National Mathematics Advisory Panel. (2008). *Final report of the national mathematics advisory panel: Reports of the subgroups.* Retrieved from http://www.ed.gov/about/bdscomm/list/mathpanel/reports.html

National Research Council. (2009). *Mathematics learning in early childhood: Paths toward excellence and equity.* Washington, DC: The National Academies Press.

Riley-Tillman, T.C., & Burns, M.K. (2009). *Evaluating educational interventions: Single-case design for measuring response to intervention.* New York, NY: Guilford Press.

Sarama, J., & Clements, D. (2009). *Early child mathematics education research: Learning trajectories for young children.* New York, NY: Routledge.

Shapiro, E.S., & Clemens, N.H. (2009). A conceptual model for evaluating system effects of response to intervention. *Assessment for Effective Intervention, 35*, 3–16.

Slentz, K.L., & Hyatt, K.J. (2008). Best practices in applying curriculum-based assessment in early childhood. In A. Thomas & J. Grimes (Eds.), *Best practices in school psychology* (Vol. IV, pp. 519–534). Bethesda, MD: National Association of School Psychologists.

Torgesen, J., Alexander, A., Wagner, R., Rashotte, C., Voeller, K., & Conway, T. (2001). Intensive remedial instruction for children with severe reading disabilities: Immediate and long-term outcomes from two instructional approaches. *Journal of Learning Disabilities, 34*, 33–58. doi:10.1177/002221940103400104

VanDerHeyden, A.M., Broussard, C., Fabre, M., Stanley, J., Legendre, J., & Creppell, R. (2004). Development and validation of curriculum-based measures of math performance for preschool children. *Journal of Early Intervention, 27*, 27–41.

VanDerHeyden, A.M., Broussard, C., Snyder, P., George, J., Lafleur, S.M., & Williams, C. (2011). Measurement of kindergartners' understanding of early mathematical concepts. *School Psychology Review, 40*, 296–306.

VanDerHeyden, A.M., & Snyder, P. (2006). Integrating frameworks from early childhood intervention and school psychology to accelerate growth for all young children. *School Psychology Review, 35*, 519–534.

VanDerHeyden, A.M., Witt, J.C., & Gilbertson, D.A. (2007). Multi-year evaluation of the effects of a response to intervention (RTI) model on identification of children for special education. *Journal of School Psychology, 45*, 225–256.

VanDerHeyden, A.M., Witt, J.C., & Naquin, G. (2003). Development and validation of a process for screening referrals to special education. *School Psychology Review, 32,* 204–227.

VanDerHeyden, A.M., Witt, J.C., Naquin, G., & Noell, G. (2001). The reliability and validity of curriculum-based measurement readiness probes for kindergarten students. *School Psychology Review, 30,* 363–382.

Vaughn, S., Linan-Thompson, S., & Hickman, P. (2003). Response to instruction as a means of identifying students with reading/learning disabilities. *Exceptional Children, 69,* 391–409.

Witt, J.C., VanDerHeyden, A.M., & Gilbertson, D. (2004). Troubleshooting behavioral interventions: A systematic process for finding and eliminating problems. *School Psychology Review, 33,* 363–383.

Woodward, J.P., & Kaufman, M.J. (1998). Contextual issues and their influence on curricular change. In E.J. Kameenui & D.W. Carnine (Eds.), *Effective teaching strategies that accommodate diverse learners.* Upper Saddle River, NJ: Prentice Hall.

Student: _____   Teacher: _____

Build Fluency Counting Objects to 20—Response Cards

This intervention is designed to **build fluency with one-to-one correspondence in counting objects**. Requires approximately 10 minutes each day.

Materials Needed: digital count-down timer, this intervention protocol, 20 counters per child, number cards 11–20

Teacher Coach Card: (complete these steps every day)

_____ Sit with child in a quiet corner of the classroom.

_____ Set timer for 5 minutes.

_____ Arrange number cards face up in front of the student. Put the number cards in order from lowest to highest, left to right.

_____ Shake counters in a cup and pour some or all onto the floor or desk.

_____ Ask child to quickly count the objects and hold up the matching card as quickly as possible.

_____ If the child makes an error counting, say, "Count again." If the child counts incorrectly again, say, "Count with me" and count the objects aloud with the child.

_____ If the child holds up the incorrect card, say, "Is that a _____ [name the number]? Try again." If the child does not respond correctly, say, "Let's find the _____ [name the number] together" and find the card together.

_____ If the child requires assistance to correctly count the objects and/or find the correct number card more than once during the 5-minute session, then this intervention is probably too difficult and should be adjusted (either target number naming, or reduce counting difficulty to smaller set sizes until the child can respond correctly before using this intervention).

_____ If there is not a match (the child's response was incorrect), guide the student to count again and assist as needed to ensure correct counting.

_____ When the timer rings, tell the student to stop working.

_____ Count the number of correctly completed problems. Write this number on the Progress Monitoring Chart.

_____ Allow the child to select a small reward from the treasure chest for beating his or her last best score.

12

Assessment of Social-Emotional and Behavioral Skills for Preschoolers within a Response to Intervention Model

Edward G. Feil and Andy J. Frey

The social costs of behavior problems are well documented (Bower, 1960; Patterson, Reid, & Dishion, 1992; Shinn, Ramsey, Walker, O'Neill, & Steiber, 1987; Whitehead, Stockdale, & Razzu, 2003), and preschool children who exhibit them are at particularly high risk for these social complications. National survey results indicate that preschool-age children are expelled at three times the rate of K–12 students (Gilliam, 2005). Consequently, preschool children with challenging behaviors may be at greater risk of being excluded from important early education opportunities, thereby limiting the availability of early education services to those children who stand to benefit the most from the socializing impact of preschool programs.

As is the case in K–12 education, assessment in early childhood has seen a major transition in the use of assessment data. Although the transition began over two decades ago, it has been spurred by evidence of positive effects of the response to intervention (RTI) framework (Bradley, Danielson, & Doolittle, 2005; Horner et al., 2005; Horner et al., 2009), which are likely to continue influencing what type of information is collected, how it is collected, and the processes for entering and interpreting it in a practical fashion. The goal of social-emotional assessment procedures within the RTI framework is early identification of students who are at risk for school failure in order to provide them with an appropriate level of intervention (Batsche et al., 2005). Experts in the field of positive behavior interventions and supports (PBIS) recommend a three-tiered model of behavior support to prevent and intervene with severe problem behavior, similar to that promoted by RTI (Sugai & Horner, 2002; Walker et al., 1996). In addition, models based on the logic of RTI and PBIS have been developed specifically for early childhood settings (Buysse & Peisner-Feinberg, 2010; Fox, Dunlap, Hemmeter, Joseph, & Strain, 2003; Hemmeter, Fox, Jack, & Broyles, 2007; Sandall & Schwartz, 2008; Sutherland, Conroy, Abrams, & Vo, 2010). Models and resources are now available so that early childhood personnel can implement practices consistent with the RTI model; however, access to feasible, socially valid assessment tools and systems capable of monitoring progress of all children at multiple points during a school year currently is limited because such tools and systems are still under development. This chapter provides practitioners with resources to assess preschool children who exhibit social competency deficits or challenging behavior in the classroom to a degree that impedes their academic achievement and increases their risk for school failure. Herein, we provide an overview of the prevalence, stability, and long-term outcomes of preschoolers with challenging behavior; we discuss the importance of intervening prior to school entry; and we describe available resources for screening and progress monitoring. Next, we highlight three systems: 1) the Early Screening Project (ESP); 2) the Behavior Incident Reporting System-NH; and 3) the Data-Based Decision Making process. The chapter concludes with a discussion of future research, practice, and policy implications regarding assessment in early childhood settings.

PRESCHOOLERS WITH CHALLENGING BEHAVIORS: PREVALENCE, STABILITY, AND LONG-TERM OUTCOMES

Although not all children who exhibit challenging behaviors progress from trivial to more serious behavior problems, approximately 75% do (Reid, 1993). It has been shown that the further the children move into the progression, the greater their risk for later delinquency (Patterson et al., 1992). Patterson and Reid's research suggests that the extreme antisocial scores are actually more stable than scores in the middle of the distribution. It has been estimated that youth with early childhood onset of antisocial behavior comprise 3%–5% of the population, but they account for half of all crimes committed by children (Hinshaw, Lahey, & Hart, 1993). About 8% of all preschoolers (children ages 3–5 years) exhibit challenging behavior severe enough to warrant a psychiatric diagnosis (Keenan & Wakschlag, 2004); these children are at more serious risk than any other subgroup (with the possible exception of children with autism or schizophrenia) for a wide spectrum of adult adjustment problems such as substance abuse, institutionalization for crimes and mental disorders, disrupted marriages, and marginal employment records (Patterson et al., 1992).

Increasingly, many children do not enter school equipped with the foundational social-emotional and academic readiness skills to experience early educational success (DiPerna & Elliott, 2002; Gresham, Cook, Crews, & Kern, 2004; Rimm-Kaufman, Pianta, & Cox, 2000; Squires & Bricker, 2007). Of equal and perhaps greater concern is the presence of younger children in preschool settings who display challenging behavior patterns that severely stress the management skills of teachers. In a study by Rimm-Kaufman et al. (2000), teachers reported that about half the children in their classes entered kindergarten with problems in one or more areas related to school success (i.e., difficulty following directions, working independently, or working as part of a group; problems with social skills; immaturity; and difficulties with language and/or communication). Prevalence estimates suggest that the number of children with serious behavior problems ranges from 21.4% in pediatric settings (Lavigne et al., 1996) to over 25% in preschool settings (Feil et al., 2005; Keenan, Shaw, Walsh, Delliquadri, & Giovannelli, 1997; Qi & Kaiser, 2003).

Research has demonstrated that children who present with challenging behavior at a young age are at significantly higher risk for ongoing problem behavior and long-term detrimental outcomes. Moffitt and colleagues (Caspi & Moffitt, 1995;

Odgers et al., 2008; Moffitt, 1993; Moffitt, 1994; Moffitt, 1997) distinguished between *life-course-persistent* and *adolescence-limited* behavior patterns. Life-course-persistent behavior originates early in life with aggressiveness, impulsivity, difficult temperament, and poor relations with peers and teachers. Conversely, adolescence-limited behavior emerges during puberty when it is more normative to demonstrate autonomy from parents, attend to peers, and rebel. Moffitt and Caspi found that most young people who become adolescence-limited delinquents are able to desist from crime when they age into real maturity because their early childhood development was healthy.

Many teachers and parents believe that problem behavior will be "outgrown," but in many cases children do not outgrow their problem behaviors (Dougherty, Saxe, Corss, & Silverman, 1987; Rolf & Haazi, 1977). In spite of developmental changes, the core of the behavior pattern changes very little over time (Patterson et al., 1992). For many children, behavior problems follow a progression from 1) disobedience in the home, to 2) temper tantrums, and 3) teacher reports of fighting and stealing (Patterson et al., 1992). These acts, often frequent yet relatively trivial, lead to acts that are infrequent and more serious (Patterson et al., 1992). Each step in this process puts the child at ever-increasing levels of risk for long-term social maladjustment, which underscores the importance of intervening as early as possible (Patterson et al., 1992).

THE IMPORTANCE OF INTERVENTION PRIOR TO SCHOOL ENTRY

Research has shown the effects of poor social behavior on academic outcomes. The term *academic enablers* has been coined to describe social behaviors that are fundamental to the development of social competence and effective learning (Gresham et al., 2004). Academic enablers include cooperating, sharing, listening to others, and focusing attention (DiPerna, 2006; DiPerna & Elliott, 1999; Malecki & Elliot, 2002). Children who begin their school careers with serious limitations in these competencies fail to derive maximal benefits from the process of schooling, thus taking their first steps on a path that spirals downward over time.

All students are required to make two essential adjustments in the schooling process (Feil, Walker, & Severson, 1995). First, they must satisfactorily negotiate the demands of teachers, who control instructional settings; second, they must also learn to cope with the peer-group dynamics that play out primarily within free-play settings. Teacher-related adjustment mediates the student's academic development and achievement; peer-related adjustment, on the other hand, governs peer relations and social development. Failure in either of these adjustment domains can severely impair a student's school success; failure in both can be catastrophic. Students with established behavior disorders are severely at risk for failure in the peer-related adjustment area (Eddy, Reid, & Fetrow, 2000). Students who come to school not ready to learn are especially vulnerable to failing the teacher-related adjustment test. Some of these same students are equally at risk for failure in the peer-relations domain, especially if they come from impoverished backgrounds.

The preschool-age period, from 3–5 years old, represents a unique opportunity to dramatically affect children's lives in positive ways. This period of time is different from later childhood. It furnishes a window of opportunity for enriching input and a window of vulnerability to the development of behavior problems. Thus, the preschool period can be viewed as providing *developmental leverage* for preventing potential problems. Leverage is defined as the increased power or advantage gained from using a lever and fulcrum (Funk, 1956). Developmental leverage is the increased effectiveness or impact of an intervention used at an advantageous time during a certain developmental stage or period. The preschool age affords an opportunity to avert the future development of antisocial behavior that would lead to behaviors such as violence, substance abuse, educational failure, and criminal involvement. That is, during the preschool period there is an increased opportunity to remediate behavior problems before they become chronic and intractable (Kazdin, 1987). Early intervention is the best hope for diverting children from this path, and such intervention depends on effective screening and progress monitoring for identifying children who require additional support.

RESPONSE TO INTERVENTION FRAMEWORK

The RTI framework provides a system for conducting early intervention screening and providing services of varying intensity. The goal of the three-tiered RTI model is to identify students early in their school career who are at risk for school failure and to provide an appropriate level of intervention (Batsche et al., 2005). As mentioned previously, experts in the field of PBIS recommend a similar three-tiered model of behavior support to prevent and intervene with severe problem behavior in school-age populations (Sugai & Horner, 2002; Walker et al., 1996). Although the three-tiered RTI logic seems to apply to academic supports as well as behavioral prevention and intervention, RTI is most commonly mentioned in the context of academic supports and the prevention of learning disabilities for school-age children. This chapter argues that the RTI model for preschool-age children should include assessment to provide a foundation for targeted interventions as well as ongoing monitoring of student behaviors to increase the likelihood of maintaining gains.

In 1996, Walker and his colleagues adapted the U.S. Public Health classification system governing prevention outcomes for use as a scaffold in coordinating the integrated delivery of behavioral interventions within school settings (Walker et al., 1996). The goal of this adaptation was to enable the coordination and integration of differing intervention approaches (i.e., primary, secondary, tertiary) and to maximize the resources needed to respond to the needs and problems of the three groups of students found within any school or preschool setting: 1) those who are not at risk and are progressing typically, 2) those who have mild to moderate risk status as a result of prior risk exposure, and 3) those who are severely at risk due to chronic and longer term exposure to destructive influences. This classification schema allows schools to 1) address primary, secondary, and tertiary prevention goals and outcomes in a coordinated fashion, 2) deliver PBIS and other services in a cost-effective manner, and 3) create and sustain a positive school climate and social ecology that provides a supportive context for teaching and strengthening school expectations governing student conduct (e.g., be safe, be respectful, be responsible). Figure 12.1 illustrates this classification schema and the primary, secondary, and tertiary interventions that are used to achieve academic and behavioral outcomes.

This model of service delivery defines prevention as a goal or outcome of intervention rather than as an approach. Differing intervention types are used to

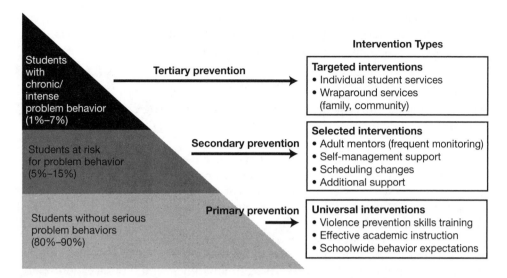

Figure 12.1. Preventing destructive behavior in schools: primary, secondary, and tertiary systems of intervention. (From Severson, H.H., Walker, H.M., & Feil, E.G. [1997]. *Project PROACT: Preventing recurrence of antisocial children's troubles.* Oregon Research Institute grant application; reprinted by permission.)

achieve specific prevention goals and outcomes. For example, primary interventions are intended to keep problems from emerging. Secondary interventions are used to reduce or eliminate the emergent problems of students who are behaviorally at risk. Finally, tertiary interventions are designed to reduce problem behaviors for student populations that have severe risk status. This delivery model allows for cost-effective use of available, school-based resources. The schema in Figure 12.1, sometimes referred to as the teaching pyramid, was adapted for use in coordinating interventions for very young preschool children by Fox, Dunlap, Hemmeter, Joseph, and Strain (2003).

Family Involvement in Response to Intervention

McCart et al. (2010) assert that RTI should be implemented within the context of family support in the early childhood service delivery system. A clear mechanism of family involvement and collaboration should be included at each tier of assessment, prevention, and intervention. The role of families in the RTI process is a bit complex and unique in that parents are both contributors and recipients of RTI. Families contribute support to each step of the RTI process while also serving in the roles of provider and recipient of support at the corresponding tier. In the RTI model, four components provide opportunities for family involvement: 1) early universal screening, 2) evidence-based interventions, 3) progress monitoring, and 4) data-based decision making.

SCREENING AND PROGRESS MONITORING

Although the RTI movement is altering *what* is assessed and *how* assessments are conducted in early childhood settings, the issues surrounding high-quality assessment data are largely unchanged. In this section, we discuss methodological issues related to assessment generally, then provide examples of resources used for screening and early identification as well as progress monitoring.

Methodological Issues in Assessment

Irrespective of the purpose of assessment, three methodological issues are critical to sound assessment practices: validity, triangulation, and cultural sensitivity.

Validity   Assessment instruments should have characteristics that lead to an accurate and valid description of the child's behavior. That is, the assessment device's results should reflect the objective features of behavior (Gresham & Carey, 1988). The question of validity of both rating scales and direct observations is frequently a topic in assessment research. Skiba (1989) states that neither rating scales nor observations have shown themselves to have construct validity. That is, there are weak relationships between raters and across methods when compared to (poorly defined) diagnostic criteria. Also, although behavioral observations have been regarded as the final measure of construct validity because observations are the most direct type of assessment, psychometric results have been mixed.

Triangulation   A second methodological issue in assessment, as described by Schaughency and Rothlind (1991), is *multimethod assessment*, or triangulation of multiple methods. Agreement among more than one person important in the child's life also contributes unique information about the child's behavior. If there is agreement across measures and/or people, then the results have a high amount of credibility. In eligibility decisions, for example, if a child was rated as exhibiting severely challenging behavior in both home and school, and the behavior's severity was independently confirmed with observations, the child would be eligible for services. Similarly, during treatment, agreement among measures and/or across people important in a child's life showing a decrease in antisocial behavior would confirm the intervention's effectiveness. In their review of the literature, Gresham and Elliot (1984) found that a multimethod approach yielded the most accurate assessment results. Unfortunately, few assessment systems have been created to utilize convergent validity across methods, settings, and raters to make important decisions about the child.

Cultural Sensitivity   Finally, culturally sensitive measurement is a critical methodological assessment issue. Overrepresentation of ethnic minority students within special education has been a persistent finding (Artiles & Trent, 1994; Sugai & Maheady, 1988). Especially within intellectual assessments, nondiscriminatory testing has been at the center of several court decisions (e.g., *Larry P. v. Riles*, 1979). In the area of social-emotional assessment, there is nothing as pivotal as a court ruling that drives the field, although it could be argued that social behavior more directly reflects cultural variation than do the results of IQ testing (Carlson & Stephens, 1986). Cultural factors help shape the environments in which children develop. However, complex interplays of these cultural factors with other aspects of children's environments and with biological factors may contribute as much to individual differences within cultural groups as to differences between groups

(Achenbach et al., 2008). The measurement of child behavior problems is very complex because the phenomena to be measured cannot be defined in terms of physical units. Instead, measurement of child psychopathology involves judgments by multiple people that certain behavioral, emotional, cognitive, and/or social characteristics are sufficiently detrimental to warrant intervention. At this stage in our knowledge, it is not realistic to expect universal agreement on a single definition of behavior problems. In lieu of a single definition, we focus on behavioral, emotional, and social problems that 1) can be reported by parents, teachers, and children; and 2) are found to be associated with referral for mental health services and for similar kinds of help in multiple societies (Achenbach et al., 2008).

EARLY SCREENING AND IDENTIFICATION

In this section, we review measures used for early screening and identification of preschool children exhibiting social competency deficits and/or challenging behaviors. We also examine many of the strengths and weaknesses of each system, and we discuss their likely cost-effectiveness and practicality. The screening and identification strategies reviewed next include rating scales and direct behavioral observations.

Rating Scales

Teacher and parent ratings of children's behavior, based on Likert scales, have been a popular, albeit unsystematic, approach in the evaluation of students referred for social, emotional, and behavioral problems (see Merrell, 1999, 2001). Such Likert scales typically ask the rater to assess students' behavior along 3-, 5-, or 7-point dimensions of problem frequency or severity. Merrell (2001) has pointed out that Likert behavioral ratings have a number of additional advantages. They 1) are relatively inexpensive; 2) provide essential information on low-frequency behavioral events of potential importance; 3) are generally objective and reliable, especially in comparison with interview and projective assessment methods; 4) can assess individuals who are unable to contribute self-reports; 5) take into account the many observations and judgments of child behavior made by social agents within natural settings over the long term; and 6) reflect the judgments of expert social informants who are familiar with the student's behavioral characteristics (i.e., parents, teachers, peers).

Several rating systems are appropriate for early childhood settings. The *Child Behavior Checklist* (Achenbach, 1991) has become the rating scale standard for measuring child and youth psychopathology and is, by far, the most widely used instrument for this purpose. The *Ages and Stages Questionnaires®: Social-Emotional* (ASQ:SE) (Squires, Bricker, & Twombly, 2002) is an example of a widely used parent questionnaire. The ASQ:SE was designed specifically as a low-cost screening instrument for assessing social-emotional functioning, requiring 10–15 minutes of time. Internal consistency was found to be high, with an overall alpha of .82. Test–retest reliability across 1- to 3-week intervals was 94%. The *Social Skills Improvement System* (SSIS; Gresham & Elliot, 2008) is a series of parent and teacher rating scales that includes two domains of social skills and problem behaviors. In older age groups, an academic subscale is added. Merrell (1999) has contributed a comprehensive analysis of assessment instruments for use in social, emotional, and behavioral domains. These ratings have the advantage of defining and pinpointing the behavioral content of a student's perceived adjustment problems and can be standardized to allow valid social comparisons that are referenced to normative age and gender scores. The *Preschool and Kindergarten Behavior Scales* (Merrell, 1996) include subscales for social cooperation, social interaction, social independence, and externalizing and internalizing problem behaviors. These measures have been found to be reliable and valid standardized, norm-referenced measures for early childhood populations; their utility for progress monitoring has yet to be evaluated.

Direct Observations

The goal of direct observation is to record all relevant behavioral events of the child and those with whom the child interacts within a specific setting, including enduring characteristics of the child, temporary states of the child, interpersonal acts, interaction between settings, and institutional norms. Rating scales attempt to measure more stable characteristics, whereas observations can be the key for identifying how actual behaviors are elicited, maintained, and displayed. The procedures occupy different places on the continuum of assessment information. For those who describe consistencies in individual differences in behavioral styles or interactions over time, rating can be more useful. For those who are interested in understanding how behavior is maintained and changed by environmental events, observations are more useful (Cairns & Green, 1979). Both methods can be used in planning intervention strategies as well as screening and early identification. The utility of direct observation for progress monitoring has not yet been investigated.

PROGRESS MONITORING

As previously mentioned, assessment in early childhood education is changing rapidly. Specifically, the use of standardized, norm-referenced tests and procedures, which have traditionally been used for early screening and identification for service eligibility, have been criticized since the 1980s as being inadequate and flawed for informing instruction (Bagnato, McLean, Macy, & Neisworth, 2011). The need for data to inform instructional decision making has been amplified by the RTI movement, which has reinforced the importance of identifying children who would benefit from additional services, and has expanded the purpose of assessment to include making decisions about whether children have responded to increasingly intensive services along the three-tiered continuum (i.e., progress monitoring). In describing the changing landscape of assessment in early childhood education, Greenwood, Carta, and McConnell (2011) suggested that the major limitations of standardized assessment tools are that they 1) require too much time to administer to every child often enough to monitor progress, 2) are not sensitive to short-term growth, and 3) lack benchmarks categorizing children along a continuum of risk. In response to these limitations, researchers have developed individual growth and development indicators (IGDIs). An in-depth description, analysis, and discussion of IGDIs can be found in Chapter 9. The developments in IGDIs will undoubtedly improve the ability of early childhood personnel to use data-based decision making to conduct universal screening, determine appropriate levels of intervention intensity, evaluate whether the intervention is being implemented with fidelity, and monitor progress. Currently, however, only a few exemplars show promise for responding to these new assessment challenges.

In a related line of research, Gresham and colleagues (2010) propose a model based on best practice in the progress monitoring of academic behavior, curriculum-based measurement (CBM). CBM has a well-established empirical history and close connection to assessment practices based on problem solving (Deno, 2005). Although several tools have been proposed, currently there is no "CBM analogue" for dependably measuring students' response to short-term interventions in the area of social skills and problem behaviors (Gresham, Cook, Collins, & Rasethwane, 2010).

PROMISING INNOVATIONS IN EARLY CHILDHOOD ASSESSMENT

In this section, three promising innovations in early childhood assessment are presented. These include the ESP (Feil et al., 1995; Walker, Severson, & Feil, 1995), the Behavior Incident Reporting System-NH (BIRS-NH) (New Hampshire Center for Effective Behavioral Interventions and Supports at Southeastern Regional Education Service Center, 2008), and the Data-Based Navigation process (Muscott et al., 2012). These assessment systems provide support for decision making using various methodologies developed over different points in time. The methods all take a universal-based RTI approach and range from individual screening to program-wide evaluation.

A Multimethod Assessment Tool: The Early Screening Project

The ESP is a three-stage, multiple-gating screening system for identifying at-risk children in the preschool age range. The first two screening stages rely upon teacher judgment and can be completed in approximately 1 hour. Stage III screening requires completion of two 10-minute observations recorded in free play or unstructured settings. Observations are conducted by someone other than the classroom teacher (e.g., counselor, psychologist, special consultant). Application of the ESP provides for the screening of all children enrolled in a preschool classroom. The ESP system also gives each child the opportunity to be screened and identified for possibly having either an externalizing or internalizing behavior disorder. Figure 12.2 illustrates the three interrelated screening stages of the ESP.

Stage I is based on teachers' rankings of their students on externalizing and internalizing behavior dimensions. Teachers are asked to list the three children who best exemplify a description of externalizing characteristics and the three children who best exemplify a description of internalizing characteristics. Next, the teachers rank the children on each list from most characteristic to least characteristic of the externalizing or internalizing dimension. In Stage II, the teacher is asked to complete the Critical Events Index and the Combined Frequency Indices (Adaptive and Maladaptive Behavior Indices) on the three highest-ranked externalizing and internalizing children in the class. Also, teachers complete an Aggressive Behavior Scale for Externalizers and a Social Interaction Scale for Internalizers.

The parent questionnaire has 12 items divided into three scales: 1) Playing with other children, 2) Getting along with caregivers, and 3) Playing with materials and self-care. All items are adapted from the ESP Stage II teacher questionnaires. The first two scales, "Playing with other children" and "Getting along with caregivers," are stated in positive prosocial behavioral language, and the third scale,

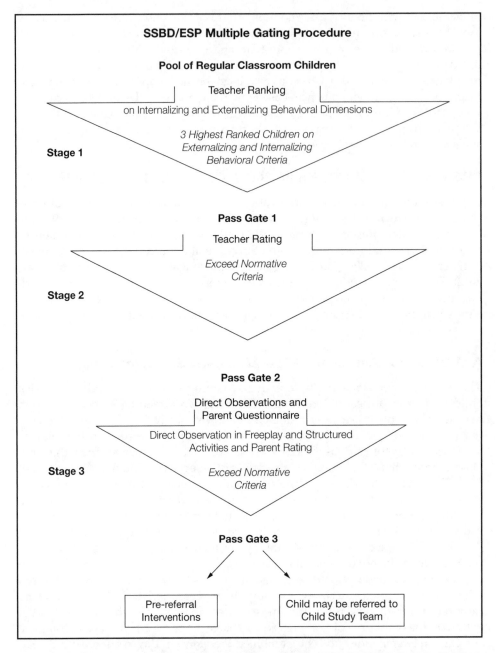

Figure 12.2. Multiple gating procedure for the Early Screening Project. (*Key:* SSBD, Systematic Screening for Behavioral Disorders.) (From Feil, E., Walker, H., & Severson, H. [1993]. Multiple gating procedure. In Validation and field testing of a multiple gating approach to preschool screening for behavior problems. Oregon Research Institute grant application; reprinted by permission.)

"Playing with materials and self-care," is oriented to more problematic critical behaviors, such as biting or cutting oneself.

The observation codes used in ESP Stage III were derived from codes developed by Walker, Hops, and Greenwood (1984) for recording children's behavior within instructional and playground settings. The observation code used for the ESP has been revised and refined over time to simplify the observation process while maintaining accuracy and specificity. Observer training times on these coding procedures are relatively brief (3–4 hours), and a training video is included in the ESP materials to allow easy self-instruction. During normative data collection, the interobserver agreement between two observers was consistently above .80, with most interobserver agreement ratios above .85 (Feil & Becker, 1993; Walker & Severson, 1990).

In order to streamline ESP for screening purposes and to provide assessment information that creates a comprehensive picture of a child's behavior, the authors have developed two types of measures: 1) normative comparison measures and 2) clinical measures. The normative comparison measures (Critical Events Index, Aggressive Behavior Scale, and Social Interaction Scale) are used to decide whether a child should be referred for further assessment and/or prereferral intervention. The clinical measures (Adaptive Behavior Scale, Maladaptive Behavior Scale, and Parent Questionnaire) are used to supplement other assessment activities (e.g., a structured interview).

Beginning in 1991, a series of studies was conducted on the ESP to assess its reliability and validity. These findings have been very promising to date (Feil & Becker, 1993; Feil, Severson, & Walker, 1998; Feil et al., 1995). The ESP procedure was field-tested in eight states (including more than 20 preschool and Head Start programs) across the country. The ESP reliability and validity data show strong results. The interrater reliability coefficients of most ESP measures are at least .80, which meets guidelines laid out by Salvia and Ysseldyke (1988) for a screening instrument. Validity studies show consistently high relationships to criterion measures: Conners Teacher Rating Scales (Conners, 1989), Preschool Behavior Questionnaire (Behar & Stringfield, 1974), and Child Behavior Checklist—Teacher Report (Achenbach & Edelbrock, 1979). Correlations with these criterion measures were highly significant, ranging from .34 to .87, with most above .70. Further, a discriminant analysis provided a measure of the accuracy of the ESP with both specificity and sensitivity coefficients. Additionally, two studies (Feil, Walker, Severson, & Ball, 2000; Hix-Small, Small, Feil, & Yovanoff, 2005) evaluated the ESP's cultural sensitivity with a variety of children representing Hispanic, African American, Native American, and Asian American backgrounds. Each ESP measure was analyzed to test for differences among ethnic groups. These test results were very encouraging, with no significant differences among ethnic groups, even among teacher ratings and observations. Overall, we were encouraged by the results obtained with respect to the cross-cultural nature of the ESP, but it is possible that the number of subjects was not great enough for sufficient statistical power to detect differences. Finally, the ESP has been found to be user-friendly, and reports from staff users and reviewers have been positive regarding both its length and simplicity (Yoshikawa & Knitzer, 1997).

It is possible that the ESP could be used for progress monitoring since the ESP Adaptive and Maladaptive scales are more global in nature and therefore are designed to reflect prevalent changes in the child's behavior. Since the scales have only nine or fewer items, both scales can be given without an excessive use of teacher time. In addition to teacher judgments, an objective observation measure of progress is a brief (15- to 30-minute) duration recording of the percentage of time that a child is engaged in on-task and prosocial behaviors.

Behavior Incident Reporting System–NH

The Behavior Incident Reporting System–NH (BIRS-NH) is a web-based software system designed to identify challenging behavior in early childhood programs (New Hampshire Center for Effective Behavioral Interventions and Supports [NH CEBIS], 2008). This system, developed by the NH CEBIS and Lise Fox from the Louis De La Parte Florida Mental Health Institute at the University of South Florida, provides preschool programs with an early-childhood-friendly data management system for collecting, aggregating, and summarizing incidents of challenging behavior.

The BIRS-NH is flexible and can be used for screening, internal decision making regarding programwide systems and practices, and progress monitoring. The BIRS-NH database is managed by the NH CEBIS, a project of the Southeastern Regional Education Service Center (SERESC) in Bedford, New Hampshire, and is accessible to licensed users via a secure login at the NH CEBIS web site at www.nhcebis.seresc.net.

Data-Based Decision Making in Early Childhood Programs

In early education, there have been few models for early educators who want to incorporate child outcome data into decision making. The Data-Based Navigation process was developed by Muscott and colleagues to help early childhood educators who wanted to employ effective and efficient strategies for using data to inform programmatic decision making (Muscott et al., 2012). These authors note the process of using data to adopt evidence-based practices, monitor the implementation fidelity of those practices, and monitor progress requires a fundamental shift for many programs, and—particularly in large programs—the shift may take years to complete.

Data-Based Navigation is an early childhood adaptation of the Data-Based Decision Making model originally conceived by Bransford and Stein (1984) and infused in the PBIS framework previously described. Data-Based Navigation comprises five steps organized in a nautical theme: 1) Determine Your Destination; 2) Establish Your Current Position and Plan for Stormy Weather; 3) Chart Your Course and Prepare to Sail; 4) Stay on Course, Check Compass, and Make Course Corrections; and 5) Evaluate and Plan for the Next Voyage. Each step is discussed in turn.

The first step in the process, "Determine Your Destination," requires early childhood administrators (or ideally, programwide leadership teams comprising administration, teaching staff, support staff, and parents) to note the general program outcome area(s) they wish to prioritize and the designated time period for the focused effort (usually yearly). "Determine Your Destination" can be enhanced by asking key questions such as "What do we want to focus on this year?" or "What outcomes do we want to achieve?" This step concludes when the team identifies a focus area for improvement, such as social skill development, listening comprehension, parenting skills, or reducing instances of challenging behavior, and then delineates goals for success.

The second step in the process, "Establish Your Current Position and Plan for Stormy Weather," requires early childhood administrators and teams to determine their current position in relation to the desired destination. In this step, early childhood education programs identify their current status as well as potential obstacles that might prevent success by systematically collecting data and using it for decision making. The process can be enhanced by asking key questions about where the program is in relation to the desired outcomes. For example, if the yearly goal is to reduce the number of incidents of challenging behavior exhibited by students in the program by 10%, the following questions might be appropriate: "How many students are currently exhibiting challenging behaviors and how often?" "Which challenging behaviors are most prevalent?" and "What do we want to know about the context (e.g., location, routine, day of week) in which challenging behavior occurs?" Once teams determine their current position, they should plan for challenges ("stormy weather") that may threaten their goals. Planning for potential barriers is important in keeping the plan on target. Some guiding questions to isolate potential obstacles to implementation of high-quality practices include "What issues might affect progress toward achieving the desired outcome?" or "What professional development activities, resources, or coaching support do we need to accomplish our goals?" Barriers that affect the staff should also be identified, such as lack of expertise in critical content areas or insufficient planning time for teachers.

The third step, "Chart Your Course and Prepare to Sail," requires early childhood administrators and teams to determine precisely what objectives and methods they will use to reach their goals. "Chart Your Course" begins by translating broad outcomes into specific objectives with criteria for success based on the data delineated in an action plan. During this step, the team answers questions like "How much of a reduction in aggression on the playground by the 4-year-olds do we want to achieve by the end of June?" "What skills do the children need to achieve the outcome?" "How will the teachers and team teach and reinforce the critical expected behaviors?" and "Who needs to do what and by when?" "Prepare to Sail" involves making strategic preparations that will increase the likelihood of reaching each milestone. The action plan creates an organizational and accountability structure that increases the likelihood that activities will be implemented with fidelity. This is particularly important as the team embarks on the fourth step.

In the fourth step, "Stay on Course, Check Compass, and Make Course Corrections," it is important for the team to reliably follow the action plan and regularly monitor progress toward the goals. "Stay on Course" requires the administrator and team to set a schedule to review the plan to see if implementation is occurring as designed. It also requires a simple system of progress monitoring against benchmarks at least three or four times a year. During this step, the team addresses questions such as "How will we know if we are doing what we set out to do?" and "How will we know if the tasks are being completed on time?" Establishing a process to oversee and monitor progress toward the objectives in the action plan will facilitate staying on the plan, thereby increasingly the likelihood of reaching the desired goals on time. In early childhood settings, there are predictable challenges to meeting goals, such as staff turnover, differences in beliefs, consistency of implementation across classrooms, and sustainability of recommended practices with a high degree of fidelity. During "Check Compass and Make Course Corrections," effective early childhood administrators and teams regularly monitor adherence to the plan and, if necessary, make modifications. This is accomplished by instituting processes and strategies to regularly review the action plan (e.g., monthly, quarterly) to assess fidelity of implementation and review the data collected in order to monitor and evaluate progress. The analysis of the action plan and outcome data is also used to identify impediments to success and provide support, encouragement, and resources as necessary to maintain clear sailing. During this part of the step, the team addresses questions like "Are we doing what we set out to do in a timely manner?" and "What else do we need to do to make sure that the teachers and staff are following the recognition plan on the playground?" New actions are added based on priorities and data. Staff are regularly provided with summary data and updates throughout the year.

In the fifth and final step, early childhood administrators and teams "Evaluate and Plan for the Next Voyage" to determine how close they came to arriving at the desired goals and to begin the planning process for (typically) the next school year. Key questions to consider in this phase include "Was the plan implemented correctly?" and "Did it work?" If the program achieves its goals and objectives, the team shares and celebrates those successes with staff, children, families, and the community. When it does not, the team should determine whether re-implementation during the next program year is desirable and if so, what changes would be necessary to ensure future success.

Data-based decision making has the potential to help early childhood programs proactively address barriers related to 1) differences in philosophy (e.g., approaches to early childhood assessment, evaluation, and program management); 2) adequacy of resources, such as inequities in funding, materials, infrastructure, and staffing; and 3) readiness in terms of how implementation can proceed with current staff knowledge and comfort, particularly with assessment and technology tools used to meet the needs of increasingly diverse populations of preschoolers.

DIRECTIONS FOR FUTURE RESEARCH, PRACTICE, AND POLICY

The origins of behavior patterns that frequently lead to school failure are in evidence at a very early age, and these behavioral signs can be prevented from escalating into more serious and intractable problems. Efficient and effective assessment practices have historically been used for screening and identification. More recently, research, practice, and policy advancements have led to an increased emphasis on universal screening and early identification, as well as progress monitoring to determine the type and intensity of interventions required, fidelity of implementation, and whether or not children have responded favorably to the interventions.

Many of the children who are currently entering school have already been exposed to numerous severe risks in their first years of life. The damaging effects of such exposure can easily be seen in the behavioral, emotional, and social characteristics of such children as they try to cope with the unfamiliar demands of the schooling process. In many cases, these children come from such dysfunctional backgrounds that the normalizing and protective influences of the schooling process are insufficient to undo their background's negative impact. These children often struggle in school and in many other sectors of their lives. They are candidates for secondary and tertiary prevention strategies from the moment they begin their school careers (Eddy, Reid, & Curry, 2002). Other children also are at risk, but at far less severity, and they are much more likely to have successful school experiences. These children are more likely to demonstrate the social resiliency necessary to lead productive, fulfilling lives (Katz, 1997).

It can be argued that the current way of identifying students with behavioral needs is failing. From the available data on current practices, it appears that systematic identification procedures, effectively applied interventions, and consistent outcomes are in short supply. As a result, children with emotional and behavioral disorders are identified too late in their school careers, at a stage when interventions are not only less successful but also come at increasing cost. Albers, Glover, and Kratochwill (2007) characterized prevailing practices to identify, prevent, and treat children at risk of school failure as "too little, too late." Early proactive assessment and subsequent intervention with an RTI model can help mitigate deleterious factors for children at risk for the development of behavior disorders.

The movement toward using an RTI approach to address both academic and behavioral concerns needs to begin with increased awareness. Teachers, administrators, policy makers and trainers, and researchers need to become aware of the integral relationship between academic and social performance. Continuing to address the two domains separately may lead to stunted progress for children and continued frustration for teachers. Recent developments in general outcome measurements and IGDIs are promising, but these measures—and the technology systems to use them—are in their formative stages. As these systems are developed, it will be critical not only to consider validity, cultural sensitivity, and triangulation issues, but also to study the *social validity* of these systems. Social validity refers to the evaluation of interventions by early childhood staff and administrators, and involves examining the social significance of goals, appropriateness of procedures, and importance of outcomes (Schwartz & Baer, 1991; Wolf, 1978). Consistent with the Treatment Acceptability Model (Witt & Elliott, 1985), understanding social validity is important because consumers' satisfaction with the purpose, process, and outcome of an intervention or approach influences its acceptability, use, compliance, and effectiveness (Papalia-Berardi & Hall, 2007). Assessment measures and systems must not only be conceptually sound but must also be feasible given the levels of expertise and resources typically available in early childhood settings. Assessing social validity is particularly important in the early stages of implementation because consumer satisfaction may influence a model's conceptualization and improve technical assistance efforts (Odom et al., 2005), which are likely to be critical given the lack of training, skill, and experience in data analysis and interpretation within early childhood settings (Frey, Boyce, & Tarullo, 2009; Frey, Young, Gold, & Trevor, 2008; Muscott, Pomerleau, & Dupuis, 2009; Stormont, Covington, & Lewis, 2006). Ultimately, these systems must not only be valid and reliable but must also be efficient and easy to use.

REFERENCES

Achenbach, T. (1991). *The Child Behavior Checklist: Manual for the teacher's report form.* Burlington, VT: Department of Psychiatry, University of Vermont.

Achenbach, T.M., Becker, A., Döpfner, M., Heiervang, E., Roessner, V., Steinhausen, H., . . . Rothenberger, A. (2008). Multicultural assessment of child and adolescent psychopathology with ASEBA and SDQ instruments: Research findings, applications, and future directions. *Journal of Child Psychology & Psychiatry, 49*(3), 251–275.

Achenbach, T.M., & Edelbrock, C.S. (1979). The Child Behavior Profile: II. Boys aged 12–16 and girls aged 6–11 and 12–16. *Journal of Consulting and Clinical Psychology, 47*(2), 223–233.

Albers, C., Glover, T., & Kratochwill, T. (2007). Where are we, and where do we go now? Universal screening for enhanced educational and mental health outcomes. *Journal of School Psychology, 45*, 257–263.

Artiles, A.J., & Trent, S.C. (1994). Overrepresentation of minority students in special education: A continuing debate. *The Journal of Special Education, 27*, 410–437.

Bagnato, S.J., McLean, M., Macy, M., & Neisworth, J.T. (2011) Identifying instructional targets for early childhood via authentic assessment: Alignment of professional standards and practice-based evidence. *Journal of Early Intervention, 33*, 243–253.

Batsche, G., Elliot, J., Graden, J.L., Kovaleski, J.F., Prasse, D., Reschly, D.J., . . . Tilly III, W.D. (2005). *Response to intervention: Policy considerations and implementation*. Alexandria, VA: National Association of State Directors of Special Education.

Behar, L., & Stringfield, S. (1974). *Manual for the preschool behavior questionnaire*. Durham, NC: Behar.

Bower, E.M. (1960). *Early identification of emotionally handicapped children in school*. Springfield, IL: Charles C. Thomas.

Bradley, R., Danielson, L., & Doolittle, J. (2005) Response to intervention. *Journal of Learning Disabilities, 38*(6), 485–486.

Bransford, J.D., & Stein, B.S. (1984). *The IDEAL problem solver: A guide for improving thinking, learning, and creativity*. New York, NY: W. H. Freeman and Company.

Buysse, V., & Peisner-Feinberg, E. (2010). Recognition & Response: Response to intervention for pre-K. *Young Exceptional Children, 11*(4), 18–30.

Cairns, R.A., & Green, J.A. (1979). How to assess personality and social patterns: Observations or rating. In R.B. Cairns (Ed.) *The analysis of social interaction: Methods, issues, and illustrations*. Hillsdale, NJ: Lawrence Erlbaum Associates.

Carlson, P.E., & Stephens, T.M. (1986). Cultural bias and identification of behaviorally disordered and learning disabled students. *Behavioral Disorders, 3*, 191–199.

Caspi, A., & Moffitt, T.E. (1995). The continuity of maladaptive behavior: From description to explanation in the study of antisocial behavior. In D. Cicchetti & D. Cohen (Eds.), *Developmental psychopathology* (Vol. 2, pp. 472–511). New York, NY: Wiley.

Conners, C.K. (1989). *Manual for the Conners' Rating Scales*. North Tonawanda, NY: Multi-Health Systems.

Deno, S.L. (2005). Curriculum-based measurement: Development and extensions. In B.G. Cook & B.R. Schirmer (Eds.), *What is special about special education: Examining the role of evidence-based practices*. Austin, TX: PRO-ED.

DiPerna, J.C. (2006) Academic enablers and student achievement: Implications for assessment and intervention services in the schools. *Psychology in the Schools, 43*(1), 7–17.

DiPerna, J.C., & Elliott, S.N. (1999). The development and validation of the Academic Competence Evaluation Scales. *Journal of Psychoeducational Assessment, 17*, 207–225.

DiPerna, J.C., & Elliott, S.N. (2002). Promoting academic enablers to improve student achievement: An introduction to the miniseries. *School Psychology Review, 31*, 293–297.

Dougherty, D.M., Saxe, L.M., Corss, T., & Silverman, N. (1987). *Children's mental health problems and services, December 1986*. Washington, DC: U.S. Government Printing Office.

Eddy, J.M., Reid, J.B., & Curry, V. (2002). The etiology of youth antisocial behavior, delinquency, and violence: A public health approach to prevention. In M.R. Shinn, H.M. Walker, & G. Stoner (Eds.), *Interventions for academic and behavior problems, II: Preventive and remedial approaches* (pp. 27–51). Washington, DC: National Association of School Psychologists.

Eddy, J.M., Reid, J.B., & Fetrow, R.A. (2000). An elementary school-based prevention program targeting modifiable antecedents of youth delinquency and violence: Linking the Interests of Families and Teachers (LIFT). *Journal of Emotional & Behavioral Disorders, 8*(3), 165–176.

Feil, E.G., & Becker, W.C. (1993). Investigation of a multiple-gated screening system for preschool behavior problems. *Behavioral Disorders, 19*(1), 44–53.

Feil, E.G., Severson, H.H., & Walker, H.M. (1998). Screening for emotional and behavioral delays: Early screening project. *Journal of Early Intervention, 21*(3), 252–266.

Feil, E.G., Small, J.W., Forness, S.R., Serna, L.A., Kaiser, A.P., Hancock, T.B., . . . Lopez, M.L. (2005). Using different measures, information, and clinical cut-off points to estimate prevalence of emotional or behavioral disorders in preschoolers: Effects on age, gender, and ethnicity. *Behavioral Disorders, 30*(4), 375–391.

Feil, E., Walker, H., & Severson, H. (1993). Multiple gating procedure. In *Validation and field testing of a multiple gating approach to preschool screening for behavior problems*. Oregon Research Institute grant application.

Feil, E.G., Walker, H.M., & Severson, H.H. (1995). Young children with behavior problems: Research and development of the Early Screening Project. *Journal of Emotional and Behavioral Disorders, 3*(4), 194–202.

Feil, E.G., Walker, H.M., Severson, H.H., & Ball, A. (2000). Proactive screening for emotional/behavioral concerns in Head Start preschools: Promising practices and challenges in applied research. *Behavior Disorders, 26*(1), 13–25.

Fox, L., Dunlap, G., Hemmeter, M.L., Joseph, G.E., and Strain, P.S. (2003). The teaching pyramid: A model for supporting social competence and preventing challenging behavior in young children. *Young Children, 58*(4), 48–52.

Frey, A.J., Boyce, C.A., & Tarullo, L.B. (2009). Implementing a positive behavior support approach within Head Start. In W. Sailor, G. Dunlap, G. Sugai, & H.F. Horner (Eds.), *Handbook of positive behavior support: Issues in clinical child psychology* (pp. 125–148). New York, NY: Springer.

Frey, A., Young, S., Gold, A., & Trevor, E. (2008). Utilizing a positive behavior support approach to achieve integrated mental health services. *NHSA Dialog: A Research-to-Practice Journal for the Early Intervention Field, 11,* 135–156.

Funk, C.A. (Ed.). (1956). *New practical standard dictionary of the English language.* New York, NY: Funk & Wagnalls Company.

Gilliam, W.S. (2005). *Prekindergarteners left behind: Expulsion rates in state prekindergarten systems.* Retrieved from http://info.med.yale.edu/chldstdy

Greenwood, C.R., Carta, J.J., & McConnell, S. (2011). Advances in measurement for universal screening and individual progress monitoring of young children. *Journal of Early Intervention, 33,* 254–267.

Gresham, F.M., & Carey, M.P. (1988) Research methodology and measurement. In J. Witt, S.N. Elliott, & F.M. Gresham (Eds.), *Handbook of behavior therapy in education* (pp. 37–65), New York, NY: Plenum.

Gresham, F.M., Cook, C.R., Collins, T., & Rasethwane, K. (2010). Developing a change-sensitive brief behavior rating scale as a progress monitoring tool for social behavior: An example using the Social Skills Rating System—Teacher Form. *School Psychology Review, 39*(3), 364–379.

Gresham, F.M., Cook, C.R., Crews, S.D., & Kern, L. (2004). Social skills training for children and youth with emotional and behavioral disorders: Validity considerations and future directions. *Behavioral Disorders, 30*(1), 32–46.

Gresham, F.M., & Elliot, D.S. (2008). *Social Skills Improvement System (SSIS)—Performance Screening Guide.* Upper Saddle River, NJ: Pearson.

Gresham, F.M., & Elliott, S.N. (1984) Assessment and classification of children's social skills: A review of methods and issues. *School Psychology Review, 13,* 292–301.

Hemmeter, M.L., Fox, L., Jack S., & Broyles, L. (2007) A program-wide model of positive behavior support in early childhood settings. *Journal of Early Intervention, 29*(4), 337–355.

Hinshaw, S.P., Lahey, E.B., & Hart, E.L. (1993) Issues of taxonomy and comorbidity in the development of conduct disorders. *Development & Psychopathology, 5,* 31–49.

Hix-Small, H., Small, J.W., Feil, E.G., & Yovanoff, P. (2005, April). *Cultural equivalence of the ESP: An examination of differential item functioning with American Indian children.* Poster session presented at the meeting of the Society for Research on Child Development, Atlanta, GA.

Horner, R.H, Carr, E.G., Halle, J., McGee, G., Odom, S., & Wollery, M. (2005). The use of single-subject research to identify evidence-based practice in special education. *Exceptional Children, 71*(2), 165–179.

Horner, R.H., Sugai, G., Smolkowski, K., Eber, L., Nakasato, J., Todd, A.W., & Esperanza, J. (2009). A randomized, wait-list controlled effectiveness trial assessing school-wide positive behavior support in elementary schools, *Journal of Positive Behavior Interventions, 11*(3), 133–144.

Katz, M. (1997). *On playing a poor hand well.* New York, NY: Norton.

Kazdin, A. (1987). Treatment of antisocial behavior in children: Current status and future directions. *Psychological Bulletin, 102,* 187–203.

Keenan, K., Shaw, D.S., Walsh, B., Delliquadri, E., & Giovannelli, J. (1997). DSM-III-R disorders in preschoolers from low-income families. *Journal of the American Academy of Child and Adolescent Psychiatry, 36,* 620–627.

Keenan, K., & Wakschlag, L.S. (2004). Are oppositional defiant and conduct disorder symptoms normative behaviors in preschoolers? A comparison of referred and nonreferred children. *American Journal of Psychiatry, 161,* 356–358.

Larry P. v. Riles, 495 F. Supp. 926 (N.D. Cal. 1979).

Lavigne, J.V., Gibbons, R.D., Christoffel, K.K., Arend, R., Rosenblaum, D., Binns, H., . . . Isaacs, C. (1996). Prevalence rates and correlates of psychiatric disorders among preschool children. *Journal of the American Academy of Child and Adolescent Psychiatry, 35,* 889–897.

Malecki, C.M., & Elliott, S.N. (2002). Children's social behaviors as predictors of academic achievement. A longitudinal analysis. *School Psychology Quarterly, 17,* 1–23.

McCart, A., Lee, J., Frey, A.J., Wolf, N., Choi, J.H., & Haynes, H. (2010). Response to Intervention in early childhood centers: A multitiered approach promoting family engagement. *Early Childhood Services, 4*(2), 87–104.

Merrell, K.W. (1996). Social-emotional assessment in early childhood: The Preschool and Kindergarten Behavior Scales. *Journal of Early Intervention, 20*(2), 132–145.

Merrell, K.W. (1999). *Behavioral, social, and emotional assessment of children and adolescents.* Mahwah, NJ: Lawrence Erlbaum Associates.

Merrell, K.W. (2001). Assessment of children's social skills: Recent developments, best practices, and new directions. *Exceptionality, 9*(1–2), 3–18.

Moffitt, T.E. (1993). "Life-course-persistent" and "adolescence-limited" antisocial behavior: A developmental taxonomy. *Psychological Review, 100,* 674–701.

Moffitt, T.E. (1994). Natural histories of delinquency. In E. Weitekamp & H.J. Kerner (Eds.), *Cross-national longitudinal research on human development and criminal behavior* (pp. 3–61). Dordrecht, Netherlands: Kluwer Academic Press.

Moffitt, T.E. (1997). Adolescence-limited and life-course-persistent offending: A complementary pair of developmental theories. In T. Thornberry (Ed.), *Advances in criminological theory: Developmental theories of crime and delinquency* (pp. 11–54). London, UK: Transaction Press.

Muscott, H., Pomerleau, T., & Dupuis, S. (2009). Anchors Away! Implementing program-wide positive behavior supports at the Visiting Nurses Association Child Care and Family Resource Center. *National Head Start Association dialog: A research to practice journal for the early intervention field, 12*(2), 104–121.

Muscott, H.S., Pomerleau, T.M., Park, K.L., Steed, E.A., Frey, A.J., & Korfhage, T.L. (2012). Setting sail for early learning success: Using a data-based decision making process to measure and monitor student outcomes in early childhood programs. *Kentucky Teacher Educator Journal, 1,* 23–41.

New Hampshire Center for Effective Behavioral Interventions and Supports at the Southeastern Regional Education Service Center. (2008). *The behavior incident reporting system–New Hampshire.* Bedford, NH: Author.

Odgers, C.L., Moffitt, T., Broadbent, J.M., Dickson, N., Hancox, R.J., Harrington, H., . . . Caspi, A. (2008) Female and male antisocial trajectories: From childhood origins to adult outcomes. *Development and Psychopathology, 20,* 673–716. doi: 10.1017/S0954579408000333

Odom, S.L., Brantinger, E., Gersten, R., Horner, R.H., Thompson, B., & Harris, K.R. (2005). Research in special education: Scientific methods and evidence-based practices. *Exceptional Children, 71,* 137–148.

Papalia-Berardi, A., & Hall, T.E. (2007). Teacher assistance team social validity: A perspective from general education teachers. *Education and Treatment of Children, 30*(2), 89–110.

Patterson, G.R., Reid, J.B., & Dishion, T.J. (1992) *Antisocial boys.* Eugene, OR: Castalia.

Qi, C.H., & Kaiser, A.P. (2003) Behavior problems of preschool children from low-income families: Review of the literature. *Topics in Early Childhood Special Education, 23,* 188–216.

Reid, J.B. (1993). Prevention of conduct disorder before and after school entry: Relating interventions to developmental findings. *Development & Psychopathology, 5,* 311–319.

Rimm-Kaufman, S.E., Pianta, R.C., & Cox, M.J. (2000) Teachers' judgments of problems in the transition to kindergarten. *Early Childhood Research Quarterly, 15*(2), 147–166.

Rolf, J.E., & Haazi, J.E. (1977). Identification of preschool children at risk and some guidelines for primary prevention. In G.W. Albee & J.M. Joffe (Eds.), *Primary prevention of psychopathology.* Hanover, NH: University Press of New England.

Salvia, J., & Ysseldyke, J.E. (1988). *Assessment in special and remedial education.* Boston: Houghton Mifflin.

Sandall, S.R., & Schwartz, I.S. (2008). *Building blocks for teaching preschoolers with special needs* (2nd ed.). Baltimore, MD: Paul H. Brookes Publishing Co.

Schaughency, L.A., & Rothlind, J. (1991) Assessment and classification of attention deficit hyperactive disorders. *School Psychology Review, 2*(20), 187–202.

Schwartz, I.S., & Baer, D.M. (1991). Social validity assessments: Is current practice state of the art? *Journal of Applied Behavior Analysis, 24,* 89–204.

Shinn, M.R., Ramsey, E., Walker, H.M., O'Neill, R.E., & Steiber, S. (1987). Antisocial behavior in school settings: Initial differences in an at-risk and normal population. *Journal of Special Education, 21,* 69–84.

Skiba, R.J. (1989). The importance of construct validity: Alternative models for the assessment of behavior disorders. *Behavioral Disorders, 14*(3), 175–185.

Squires, J., & Bricker, D. (2007). *An activity-based approach to developing young children's social emotional competence.* Baltimore, MD: Paul H. Brookes Publishing Co.

Squires, J., Bricker, D., & Twombly, E. (2002). *The ASQ:SE user's guide for the Ages & Stages Questionnaires®: Social-Emotional.* Baltimore, MD: Paul H. Brookes Publishing Co.

Stormont, M., Covington, S., & Lewis, T.J. (2006). Using data to inform systems: Assessing teacher implementation of key features of program-wide positive behavior support in Head Start classrooms. *Beyond Behavior, 15*(3), 10–14.

Sugai, G., & Horner, R.H. (2002). The evolution of discipline practices: School-wide positive behavior supports. *Child & Family Behavior Therapy, 24,* 23–50.

Sugai, G., & Maheady, L. (1988). Cultural diversity and individual assessment for behavior disorders. *Teaching Exceptional Children, 21*(1), 28–31.

Sutherland, K.S., Conroy, M., Abrams, L., & Vo, A. (2010). Improving interactions between teachers and young children with problem behavior: A strengths-based approach. *Exceptionality, 18,* 70–81.

Walker, H.M., Hops, H., & Greenwood, C.R. (1984). The CORBEH research and development model: Programmatic issues and strategies. In S. Paine, T. Bellamy, & B. Wilcox (Eds.), *Human services that work.* Baltimore, MD: Paul H. Brookes Publishing Co.

Walker, H.M., Horner, R.H., Sugai, G., Bullis, M., Sprague, J.R., Bricker, D., & Kaufman, M.J. (1996). Integrated approaches to preventing antisocial behavior patterns among school-age children and youth. *Journal of Emotional Behavioral Disorders, 4,* 194–209.

Walker, H.M. & Severson, H.H. (1990). *Systematic screening for behavior disorders user's guide and administration manual.* Longmont, CO: Sopris West.

Walker, H.M., Severson, H.H., & Feil, E.G. (1995). *Early Screening Project: A proven child-find process.* Longmont, CO: Sopris West.

Whitehead, C., Stockdale, J., & Razzu, G. (2003). *The economic and social costs of antisocial behavior: A review.* London, UK: London School of Economics.

Witt, J.C., & Elliott, S.N. (1985). Acceptability of classroom intervention strategies. In T.R. Kratochwill (Ed.), *Advances in school psychology* (Vol. 4, pp. 251–288). Mahwah, NJ: Lawrence Erlbaum Associates.

Wolf, M.M. (1978). Social validity: The case for subjective measurement or how applied behavior analysis is finding its heart. *Journal of Applied Behavior Analysis, 11,* 203–214.

Yoshikawa, H., & Knitzer, J. (1997). *Lessons from the field: Head Start mental health strategies to meet changing needs.* New York, NY: National Center for Children in Poverty and the American Orthopsychiatric Association.

Curriculum and Instruction within Response to Intervention

13

Use of a Comprehensive Core Curriculum as the Foundation of a Tiered Model

Diane Trister Dodge

The rich diversity of early childhood classrooms offers teachers great opportunities but also great challenges. Visit a preschool classroom and you may hear a variety of languages, see children of many different ethnic backgrounds, and notice children who are developing as expected and those with identified disabilities. You will meet children who have had nurturing experiences at home, and you will observe children whose families are struggling to cope with life and unable to provide the emotional and experiential support their children need. Some children can follow directions, relate positively to others, and choose and stay involved in a task. Others have poor self-regulation skills and are not able to fully participate in and benefit from learning experiences. How can we prepare teachers to meet children's diverse needs, interests, and abilities? How can we help teachers discover each child's strengths and areas of need so they can plan experiences that support each child's development and learning?

A comprehensive core early childhood curriculum recognizes and addresses this diversity. It helps teachers build the knowledge and skills they need to create inclusive classrooms and to be responsive and intentional in their practices. A comprehensive, developmentally appropriate curriculum is an essential resource for helping teachers meet the needs and support the development and learning of *all* children in *all* settings (Hyson, 2008). It includes ongoing assessment for the purpose of individualizing instruction and following children's progress. The assessment and instructional strategies presented in the curriculum rest on the principles of developmentally appropriate practice. This means being responsive to the ways children develop and learn; to the individual needs, abilities, and circumstances of each child; and to the influences of a child's culture on development and learning (Copple & Bredekamp, 2009). Universally designed practices, which take the diverse characteristics of learners into account, must be in place so that teachers can plan learning opportunities for all young children. A comprehensive curriculum is the foundation for *all* early childhood programs, and it has an essential role in a tiered model.

This chapter defines a comprehensive core curriculum and then discusses three central aspects that make it the foundation for a tiered model and for all effective teaching. These aspects are

- A high-quality learning environment

- Positive relationships and interactions

- Intentional teaching linked to ongoing assessment

DEFINING CURRICULUM

There is general agreement in the field of early childhood education today that high-quality programs require the adoption and implementation of a comprehensive written curriculum linked to ongoing assessment and program evaluation (Copple & Bredekamp, 2009). Several professional organizations have used the implications of research to develop position statements to guide policy and practice. These documents identify the necessary elements of a high-quality early childhood curriculum and have been widely used by early childhood professionals (Copple & Bredekamp, 2009; Division for Early Childhood [DEC]/National Association for the Education of Young Children [NAEYC], 2009; Division for Early Childhood, 2007; NAEYC & National Association of Early Childhood Specialists in State Departments of Education [NAECS/SDE], 2003). The curriculum should

- Clearly define objectives that address all developmental domains as well as content areas, and that are aligned to early learning guidelines and standards

- Focus on relationships and teacher–child interactions

- Engage children in learning important content through active investigations, play, and intentional teaching

- Guide evidence-based instruction that takes into account the diverse characteristics of the children in the group, including ability, culture, ethnicity, family makeup, life experiences, and dual-language learning

- Describe a range of intentional teaching approaches, including teacher-guided instruction, child-initiated learning, and integrated learning experiences

- Support partnerships with families

A comprehensive curriculum must be applicable to and respectful of teachers with years of experience as well as those who are new to the profession. An important goal for curriculum developers is to provide the information and resources that will help all teachers to be intentional in their practices and responsive to the children they teach (Daniels & Shumow, 2003; Fox, Carta, Strain, Dunlap, & Hemmeter, 2009). The curriculum must offer choices and flexibility so teachers can apply their own experiences and build on what they learn about the children in their classrooms.

In *The Creative Curriculum* (Dodge, Heroman, Colker, & Bickart, 2010), for example, we first provide the background knowledge teachers need: research findings and theories about child development; clear objectives for children's development and learning; strategies for setting up the classroom and planning the daily program; an overview of the essential components of literacy, mathematics, science, social studies, and the arts; guidance for using a range of teaching strategies; and ways to involve families as partners in children's learning. In addition to this general knowledge and guidance on best practices, *The Creative Curriculum* offers detailed information about what to teach, when to teach it, and how to adapt instruction to include all children (Teaching Strategies, 2010). New teachers may follow this guidance closely; those with more experience may use the guidance as a starting point and incorporate their own ideas; "master" teachers may refer to the curriculum for new ideas to expand on what they teach and how they teach it.

All aspects of a comprehensive curriculum are essential for effective teaching. The three discussed here define a high-quality program and are particularly important as the foundation for a tiered model.

A HIGH-QUALITY LEARNING ENVIRONMENT

The learning environment of a high-quality early childhood program provides a setting and structure that support effective teaching and successful learning. This environment helps children develop skills for relating positively to others, functioning as part of a group, initiating ideas, regulating their own emotions and behavior, and engaging fully in learning opportunities. A high-quality learning environment includes a well-organized physical setting, a consistent structure for each day, and a classroom community that promotes children's social skills and engages them in meaningful learning experiences (Dodge, Heroman, Colker, & Bickart, 2010).

Organization of the Physical Space

In settings for effective teaching and learning, the classroom furniture and materials and the outdoor environment are organized carefully. The way space is allocated, the selection of materials, and the ways materials are displayed can support children's self-regulation by helping them feel secure, develop independence, select and take care of materials, use them constructively, and focus and attend to tasks (Hyson, 2008). Well-designed learning environments maintain children's attention, foster meaningful connections with prior understanding, and guide learning behavior through multiple opportunities for active problem solving (Rushton & Larkin, 2001).

Effective preschool classrooms are organized into well-defined interest areas that offer children a range of choices. Interest areas are ideal settings for child-initiated play, a primary way that preschool children develop cognitive and language skills and acquire foundational learning of content (Fantuzzo & McWayne, 2002; Montie, Xiang, & Schweinhart, 2006). Children's learning in the content areas is enhanced by the addition of new materials and teacher guidance and support (Wayne, DiCarlo, Burts, & Benedict, 2007). Interest areas enable children to decide where they want to work and how they will use the materials. Children may work independently or with a few other children. There are distinct areas for block building, dramatic play, art, a library with a rich selection of books, toys and games, sand and water play, making discoveries, cooking, music and movement, and computers. The materials in each area are attractively displayed, with picture and word labels to indicate that everything has a place. Such arrangements convey important messages to children about the value of materials, how they should be used, and the need to share responsibility for their care (Curtis & Carter, 2003;

Riley, San Juan, Klinkner, & Ramminger, 2008). The size of each area makes it an ideal setting for just a few children at a time. When they are part of a small group, children are better able to concentrate, be more engaged, and work constructively with others (Howes et al., 2011; Rimm-Kaufman, La Paro, Downer, & Pianta, 2005). Classroom environments that are overstimulating and cluttered make it difficult for children to focus and stay on task (Inan, 2009).

A Consistent Structure for Each Day

The second aspect of a high-quality learning environment involves establishing a consistent structure for each day's activities. This includes an appropriate daily schedule, routines, and well-planned transitions. With a predictable structure in place, children know what is expected. They feel more secure and calm, are more self-directed, and can benefit from learning experiences (Hyson, 2008). Posting an illustrated schedule and talking with children about the sequence of the day or what will happen tomorrow helps them learn to plan ahead and wait for an event (Riley et al., 2008).

The schedule identifies the order and time allocated for daily events: arrival and attendance, large-group meetings, small-group activities, choice time (indoors and outside), story reading, mealtimes, rest time in full-day programs, and departure. To ensure that the schedule and routines address the needs of all children and support self-regulation, a comprehensive curriculum offers a balance of active and quiet times, child-initiated and adult-guided learning, and appropriate amounts of time for specific routines and activities. Curricular guidance includes explanations of how to make the schedule explicit and meaningful for children; clarify choices for children; and modify the learning environment, instruction, and interactions to provide extra support as needed.

Transitions are the in-between times of the day when children are regrouping or moving from one routine or activity to the next. When children do not know what is expected or they are asked to wait with nothing to do, their behavior can become disruptive. These times of the day should be planned carefully so children feel safe and in control.

A comprehensive core curriculum treats transitional times as opportunities for learning. It offers specific guidance about conveying clear directions to children so they know what to do and how to make the most of these times of the day. To help teachers approach transitions intentionally, the curriculum might provide a repertoire of songs and fingerplays that teach skills and concepts, suggest the kinds of directions that reinforce literacy or math skills, and offer strategies for preparing children for transitions. Short games like "Simon Says" or "Freeze" encourage children to inhibit behavior, thereby promoting self-regulation skills (Riley et al., 2008).

The Classroom as a Community

A comprehensive curriculum guides teachers in creating a caring classroom community in which children feel safe, experience a sense of belonging, learn to participate in a group, and share responsibility for making the classroom a good place for everyone (Copple & Bredekamp, 2009; Hannikainen, 2007; Jones, 2005; Whitin, 2001). During the first month or more of a new program year, the curriculum outlines classroom experiences that help children get to know and appreciate each other, learn how to participate in group experiences, follow classroom rules, and share responsibility for taking care of the classroom.

A comprehensive curriculum provides specific strategies for creating a classroom community. These include

- Getting to know what is unique and special about each child and family and using that knowledge to build positive relationships

- Creating an environment that respects the different cultural and familial backgrounds of the children in the classroom

- Involving children in creating classroom rules, stating the rules in positive terms, posting them, and helping children follow them

- Fostering a sense of belonging to a group by having discussions about what the class is doing together (e.g., "*We* have been studying trees, so today *we're* going to have a special visitor who may be able to answer some of *our* questions.")

- Taking note and expressing concern about any children who are missing each day

- Having conversations with children during meals

- Planning large- and small-group experiences in which children can participate actively and learn to listen to each other

- Establishing classroom jobs so that everyone has a responsibility each day

A high-quality learning environment provides a structure and setting where teaching and learning can take place. It helps children form positive relationships and work collaboratively with others.

POSITIVE RELATIONSHIPS AND INTERACTIONS

Young children learn in the context of relationships. A comprehensive curriculum focuses on teacher–child relationships and the kinds of interactions that help children develop positive relationships. The curriculum should offer specific guidance on how to build a supportive relationship with each child, interact positively with children, promote children's social competence, and build partnerships with families.

Teacher–Child Relationships and Interactions

How adults form relationships and interact with children is the primary influence on positive outcomes for development and learning (Shonkoff & Phillips, 2000). Substantial research findings indicate that the quality of teacher–child relationships affects children's short- and long-term social competence, academic success, and the ways they approach learning. Children who have positive relationships with their teachers are likely to be more socially competent (Copple & Bredekamp, 2009; Palermo, Hanish, Martin, Fabes, & Reiser, 2007; Howes, 2000), exhibit positive approaches to learning (Hyson, 2008), and experience greater academic success (Downer, Lopez, Grimm, Hamagami, Pianta, & Howes, 2012). Caring and teaching cannot be separated. Although each child is unique and has individual strengths, needs, and interests, every child needs to feel accepted, cared for, and appreciated.

How can a core curriculum support positive relationships and teacher–child interactions? Knowledge of child development—what children are like in terms of their social-emotional, cognitive, physical, and language development—gives teachers a starting point for building positive relationships with children. Knowledgeable teachers are more likely to have reasonable expectations, to be sensitive to what children need from adults in order to thrive, and to plan experiences that are appropriate and sufficiently challenging. A comprehensive curriculum begins with this knowledge base and then describes the many ways that children may differ in terms of their temperament, interests, culture, abilities, life experiences, gender, and primary language. To build a positive relationship with each child, teachers must become good observers and learn about children's unique qualities (e.g., how they react to new experiences, what they enjoy doing, how they relate to peers, what they are concerned about). Teachers must use what they learn about each child to build a relationship and interact in supportive ways (Jablon, Dombro, & Dichtelmiller, 2007).

A comprehensive curriculum can help teachers learn to interact positively with children in these ways:

- Explaining the research on the types of teacher–child interactions that support positive relationships and promote children's development and learning

- Raising awareness of the many ways that children are unique so teachers know what to look for as they observe children

- Providing guidance on creating a positive social environment

- Giving multiple examples of how to respond to children in respectful and supportive ways

The positive relationships that teachers build with each child enable children to feel secure and safe in the classroom and nurture children's social-emotional competence.

Supporting Children's Social-Emotional Competence

Social-emotional competence plays a key role in academic achievement (Espinosa, 2010) and is vital if children are to have successful relationships with others in school and in life (Bulotsky-Shearer, Dominguez, Bell, Rouse, & Fantuzzo, 2010). Social-emotional competence includes understanding one's own feelings and the feelings of others, regulating and expressing emotions in a constructive way, building positive relationships with others, and developing the social skills to participate in a group and make friends (Howes et al., 2011). In addition to creating a classroom community and developing a positive relationship with every child, teachers must promote children's social-emotional skills systematically and explicitly. A comprehensive curriculum offers guidance for

- Acknowledging children's feelings and helping children express their feelings verbally

- Helping children interpret the facial expressions, gestures, and other emotional cues of others

- Providing techniques children can use and quiet places where they can go to calm down and regain control

- Reading stories with social-emotional themes and discussing them with children

- Intervening when a child is being excluded to ensure that no child is rejected from group play experiences

- Coaching children on how to approach and interact with others in constructive ways

- Planning activities and games during which children have to control their impulses and otherwise strengthen self-regulation

- Providing opportunities for children to work together to accomplish appropriately challenging tasks

Systematic teaching of social-emotional skills, along with the structured, high-quality learning environment described earlier, enable most children to function productively and positively in the classroom (Epstein, 2007).

Building Partnerships with Families

Early childhood educators have always valued involving families in the program. Research on the short- and long-term benefits of strong partnerships with families is substantial. When families are involved in the program and have positive experiences with their children's teachers, children feel more secure and do better academically, teachers gain valuable support and insights, and families are better able to guide their child's development and learning (Graue, Clements, Reynolds, & Niles, 2004; Hemmeter, Ostrosky, & Fox, 2006). For these reasons, a comprehensive early childhood curriculum includes guidance on building partnerships with families.

A true partnership rests on mutual respect and appreciation for what each party brings to the relationship. Teachers must recognize that culture and personal experiences affect the way family members view the role of a teacher and whether or not a partnership is valued and considered appropriate (Huntsinger & Jose, 2009). Understanding a family's life circumstances and the stresses they may be experiencing also helps teachers have realistic expectations and value whatever support and involvement the family can manage (Koralek, 2007).

All families bring knowledge of their children that is invaluable to teachers. Sharing information about a child, both informally and formally, gives both the teacher and family insights into ways of supporting the child's development and learning.

A comprehensive curriculum views family involvement as a critical component that builds a bridge between home and school. Strategies offered for ongoing and positive communication promote relationships based on trust. This groundwork is essential for addressing any challenging problems a child may have that require targeted and consistent support at home and school.

INTENTIONAL TEACHING LINKED TO ONGOING ASSESSMENT

A goal of early childhood programs is to help children become confident and enthusiastic learners, ready to continue learning in school and throughout life. The field of early childhood education clearly defines what preschool children should know and be able to do in all areas of development and learning related to their success in school. Teachers and programs are increasingly being held accountable for achieving positive outcomes for children. States have developed early learning standards, and Head Start programs are expected to ensure that preschool children make progress in all areas outlined in the *Head Start Early Child Development and Learning Framework* (U.S. Department of Health & Human Services, 2010). Teachers need to know how to actively support children's engagement, embed instruction in daily routines and play experiences, engage children in conversations, promote communication skills in additional ways, and encourage the learning of skills and concepts (Hemmeter et al., 2006). A comprehensive core curriculum should explain *what, how,* and *when* to teach and also explain *why* particular practices are most effective. The curriculum should empower teachers to respond intentionally to children by showing them how to base classroom decisions on what they learn about the children they teach.

The two components of a comprehensive curriculum previously discussed—a high-quality learning environment and positive relationships and interactions— set the stage for intentional teaching and successful learning for all children. For teachers to be intentional in their teaching practices and actively engage all children in meaningful learning experiences, the core curriculum must include objectives for children's development and learning, and it must describe the content to be taught in language and literacy, mathematics, science, social studies, and the arts. The curriculum must also be linked to ongoing assessment enabling teachers to identify what each child knows and can do in order to provide instruction that will help every child progress. It should offer strategies for embedding intentional instruction throughout the day, show teachers how to individualize instruction, and help teachers offer meaningful investigations through which children integrate learning.

Objectives for Development and Learning

Imagine having a road map but no destination in mind. That is what it would be like to have a curriculum without clear objectives. A comprehensive curriculum includes clearly defined objectives for all areas of children's development: social-emotional, physical, communication, and cognition/approaches to learning. The objectives also define the essential content and skills to be learned in language and literacy, mathematics, science and technology, social studies, and the arts. Curriculum objectives should be based on research that has identified the skills and knowledge most predictive of school success, and they should align closely with state and Head Start early learning standards (Heroman, Burts, Berke, & Bickart, 2010).

To plan instruction effectively, teachers need to be able to see the sequence and expected pace of learning for each of the development and learning objectives. A progression gives a picture of child development—the predictable sequence children typically go through in all areas of development. It shows the widely held expectations for children at particular ages and classes/grades so teachers and families will have realistic expectations of children. A progression for content learning shows teachers the recommended sequence and pace so they can "introduce children to the concepts and skills in a coherent way and scaffold children's progress from each idea and ability to the next" (Copple & Bredekamp, 2009, p. 160).

Understanding the Content to Be Taught

Early childhood teachers have always taught content in their work with children. When they ask two children to compare the quantities of their bottle cap collections, they teach number concepts. When they ask children whose names begin with the sound /t/ to get their coats to go outside, they are promoting phonological awareness. Involving children in planting and caring for a garden is science. Experiences like these take place in many early childhood programs, but to varying degrees of intensity and intentionality. The challenge is to ensure that teachers know the important skills and knowledge of each content area and understand how to address them throughout each day in an intentional way.

Fortunately, we have a growing body of research on the essential components of all content areas and the best approaches for teaching skills and knowledge in a planned and meaningful way. Some early childhood teachers lack the knowledge or skills they need to teach content intentionally and appropriately (Hsieh, Hemmeter, McCollum, & Ostrosky, 2009; Neuman & Wright, 2010). A comprehensive curriculum describes the research behind each of the components so that teachers can appreciate their importance and draw upon a repertoire of strategies for engaging children in meaningful learning experiences every day. For example, consider the content area of language and literacy. Strong language and literacy skills are essential to a child's success in school and in life (National Early Literacy Panel, 2009). There are vast differences in children's experiences, such as differences in their familiarity with stories and books and differences in the number of words they have heard, understood, and learned to use before attending a preschool program (Hart & Risley, 1995). Early childhood programs can help make up for children's lack of experience if the programs are of high quality and teachers know how to teach intentionally.

Researchers and practitioners have identified the early language and literacy concepts and skills that children need to become successful readers and writers (National Institute of Child Health and Human Development, 2000; Snow, Burns, & Griffin, 1998). The components of literacy learning include oral language skills, phonological awareness, knowledge and appreciation of books, alphabet knowledge, print concepts, and writing.

A comprehensive curriculum helps teachers understand the importance of each component of language and literacy learning and shows teachers how to intentionally teach these concepts and skills throughout the day (Heroman & Jones, 2010). For example, to support oral language skills, the curriculum would include strategies such as these:

- Speaking clearly, modeling standard language, and elaborating on what children say

- Engaging children in frequent conversations that involve five or more exchanges

- Asking open-ended questions to encourage children to express their ideas

- Providing interesting materials and objects and using descriptive words as children play

- Introducing and defining unfamiliar words in the contexts of songs, poems, stories, and informational texts

- Ensuring that children who are English- and dual-language learners are included and understand what is happening

- Involving children in interactive story reading

To help children develop phonological awareness, the curriculum would present the following intentional practices:

- Using songs, poems, nursery rhymes, stories, and chants that feature rhyme and alliteration

- Talking about words that begin with the same sounds and playing word games

- Reading books with language that plays with sounds

- Calling children's attention to letter sounds

- Clapping the syllables in children's names

Such strategies would be infused into the curriculum so teachers use them intentionally throughout the day. With a comprehensive curriculum, teachers learn about the components of mathematics, science and technology, social studies, and the arts, and they are given a range of teaching strategies for supporting children's development and learning.

Ongoing Assessment to Plan Instruction

Ongoing assessment plays a central role in all early childhood programs. Without a system of ongoing assessment, teachers cannot teach intentionally in ways that support each child's learning and development. Ongoing observation-based assessment and collections of children's work give teachers invaluable knowledge of each child's individual strengths, interests, and areas that need strengthening. Technology makes it possible for teachers to capture evidence of children's learning and use new ways of looking at the data collected. A system of ongoing assessment linked with curriculum enables teachers to determine what each child knows and can do, supports them in using the information to plan and tailor experiences for each child, and enables them to track each child's progress. The assessment system is most useful when it is based on the curriculum's objectives for children's development and learning and linked to early learning standards.

Embedding Teaching and Learning in Everyday Experiences

Every period of the day offers opportunities for teachers to create an environment and interact with children in meaningful ways that support children's successful learning. Morning arrival can involve a literacy experience if the teacher provides an attendance chart on which children find and move their names from the side that says "Home" to the side that says "School" or if the teacher provides a sheet on which children sign their names. The teacher can also prominently post a "Question of the Day" related to a topic the children are studying. Talking about the question encourages children to express their ideas and reflect on important content.

Daily routines such as washing hands and brushing teeth, mealtimes, transitions, and rest can all be learning times. For example, the steps for hand-washing or toothbrushing can be illustrated on a chart to remind children of the procedures to follow and support literacy skills. Mealtimes offer opportunities for children to take responsibility for serving themselves, setting the tables, and cleaning up. They are also times for conversations about classroom events, experiences children want to share, and the food being served. The period of the day for rest should allow flexibility, because not all children will need or want to sleep. Teachers can offer quiet activities for children to do on their cots, such as looking at books or drawing.

Choice time is an especially important part of the day. Children can choose where they want to play, what they will do, and with whom they will interact. As described earlier, high-quality classrooms are arranged for a variety of different play experiences, and teachers include materials in each interest area that will encourage children to use skills in literacy, mathematics, and the arts as they explore concepts in science and social studies. For example, informational books may be made available in the block and the discovery areas, cookbooks and storybooks can be placed in the dramatic play area, and various types of books will be included in the library area. Paper and writing tools are also available in several areas of the room so children can record their observations of a classroom pet, practice writing, make signs for their buildings, and write prescriptions for a sick baby or shopping lists. A waiting list for a popular activity or a new toy helps children not only develop literacy skills but also learn to delay gratification and wait, knowing they will have a turn. Tools for scientific investigations should be available, such as magnifying glasses, scales, magnets, containers for sorting, eyedroppers, and tweezers. It is often insufficient to simply provide these materials; teachers must take an active role in encouraging and helping children learn to use tools appropriately as part of their play.

During choice time children are encouraged to come up with their own ideas about how to use the materials they choose. Although this is a time for child-initiated play, it is not a time for teachers to be uninvolved and simply "let children play." In addition to interacting in ways that extend purposeful play, teachers can learn a great deal about each child by carefully observing what a child does and says during this period. They can take note of what skills a child needs to develop to fully participate. For example, research supports the value of complex sociodramatic play in helping children develop self-regulation skills and learning (Bodrova & Leong, 2005; Elias, Eisenberg, & Berk, 2002; Riley et al., 2008; Smilansky & Shefatya, 1990). If a child does not have the skills needed, teachers can take an active role in children's pretend play to teach these skills (Copple & Bredekamp, 2009; Trawick-Smith & Dziurgot, 2011).

In *The Creative Curriculum*, for example, we present a range of strategies for teaching concepts and skills and for scaffolding each child's learning (Dodge, Heroman, Colker, & Bickart, 2010).

- **Acknowledge and describe what children are doing.** "I didn't put out green paint, but you made it yourself. Tell me how you did it." "That puzzle had a lot of pieces, and it was hard. You didn't give up, and you finished it."

- **Coach and make suggestions**. "I see you made a road for your cars. What happens when they run out of gas?" "Try using a magnifying glass so you can see the spider's legs more clearly. Then they will be easier to count."

- **Extend children's thinking with open-ended questions.** "What happened when you added more water to the play dough?" "What would happen if you tried it another way?" "How did you decide to put these objects together? How are they alike?" "What worked last time when you made the sand stick together?"

- **Give information.** "When you count, slow down and put your finger on each object for each number." "Notice that when I write your name, I start with an uppercase letter M. Then I write the rest of your name in lowercase letters."

These are just a few among many possible examples of the kinds of thoughtful, individualized, instructional responses teachers can provide during choice time, daily routines, and throughout the day.

Planned Group Instruction

Teachers also plan small- and large-group activities for children every day. These activities target one or more curricular objectives for children's development and learning. Intentional teachers use what they have learned from ongoing observation and documentation to identify the strengths and needs of the group and individual children. They think about what materials they need to collect, how they will introduce the activity, how to make the activity more and less challenging so all children can participate successfully, and ways to carry out any other adaptations that might be needed to include a child with a disability, a child whose competencies exceed developmental expectations, or a child who is just beginning to learn English.

Individualizing instruction requires thoughtful planning by the teacher. As an example, suppose a teacher of 4-year-olds reviews the assessment data she has been collecting and notices that a number of children are not able to copy, extend, and create simple repeating patterns, an important mathematical skill that is a widely held expectation for this age (Heroman et al., 2010; National Council of Teachers of Mathematics, 2000). If the curriculum and/or assessment system show the sequence for developing patterning skills, teachers can see how to adapt a patterning activity on the basis of what individual children are able to do.

Engaging Children in Active Investigations

Young children are curious about the world around them and have been attempting to make sense of their world since birth. They wonder how things work, what things do, what will happen if they try something, and where things come from. A comprehensive curriculum supports teachers in engaging children in active investigations of topics that children want to learn more about. As they investigate, children apply their skills in literacy, mathematics, the arts, and technology as they observe, investigate, record, and share what they are learning. This type of active investigation is what Lilian Katz and her colleagues call the *project approach* (Helm & Katz, 2011; Katz & Chard, 2000). Another name for this approach is *studies*.

The key to a good project or study is finding an appropriate topic—something that children are curious about and one for which they can think of questions, investigate answers to their questions, and gain deeper understanding. Ideas for a study can come from many sources. The curriculum may include suggested studies and guide teachers in planning and implementing them over a period of weeks. The topic might originate from children's interests, such as the worms that emerge on the playground after the rain and intrigue children to find out how they move, what they eat, and more. The topic might emerge from an event in the community such as a building going up in the neighborhood or a recycling initiative. Good study topics are those about which children have some knowledge as well as a desire to learn more. Teachers help children generate questions related to what they wonder about a topic, and these questions form the basis for investigations. A study can go on for many weeks—even months—as children become more and more involved and excited about their discoveries. Children apply many skills: they may count, weigh, and compare objects (math); draw and write down what they observe (the arts and literacy); find information in books (literacy); and use a computer and other tools (technology). Their investigations often involve working with others, which promotes social skills and friendships.

When teachers can lead children successfully in actively investigating topics of interest, children are engaged and excited about what they are doing. Families have a better idea of what their children are learning and can often contribute to and participate in some of the investigations. Studies are an effective way to integrate content learning and skills. Children develop confidence in their abilities as learners and are much more likely to participate positively in classroom experiences.

CONCLUSION

A comprehensive curriculum is the foundation for effective teaching, but only if it is implemented as intended (Bowman, Donovan, & Burns, 2000; Copple & Bredekamp, 2009). As described here, implementing a curriculum requires hard work on the part of the teacher. Teachers who are expected to provide meaningful, planned, and engaging curriculum for all children need not only the guidance of a comprehensive core curriculum and a usable, valid, and reliable system of assessment, they also need ongoing, individualized support. Teachers need time to assess children, to reflect on assessment results with colleagues and families, and to plan and make needed improvements in the environment and experiences they offer children. Targeted, individualized support for teachers is just as important as it is for children. It is essential to ensuring that the curriculum is being implemented with strong fidelity. Only then will early childhood teachers be able to create high-quality programs that support the development and learning of every child and serve as a solid foundation for a tiered system.

REFERENCES

Bodrova, E., & Leong, D.J. (2005). Self-regulation as a key to school readiness: How can early childhood teachers promote this critical competency? In M. Zaslow & I. Martinez-Beck (Eds.), *Critical issues in early childhood professional development* (pp. 223–270). Baltimore, MD: Paul H. Brookes Publishing Co.

Bowman, B.T., Donovan, S., & Burns, M.S. (2000). *Eager to learn: Educating our preschoolers.* Washington, DC: National Academies Press.

Bulotsky-Shearer, R.J., Dominguez, X., Bell, E.R., Rouse, H.L., & Fantuzzo, J.W. (2010). Relations between behavior problems in classroom social and learning situations and peer social competence in Head Start and kindergarten. *Journal of Emotional and Behavioral Disorders, 18,* 195–210.

Copple, C., & Bredekamp, S. (Eds.). (2009). *Developmentally appropriate practice in early child-hood programs serving children from birth through age 8* (3rd ed.). Washington, DC: National Association for the Education of Young Children.

Curtis, D., & Carter, M. (2003). *Designs for living and learning: Transforming early childhood environments.* St. Paul, MN: Redleaf Press.

Daniels, D.H., & Shumow, L. (2003). Child development and classroom teaching: A review of the literature and implications for educating teachers. *Applied Developmental Psychology, 23,* 495–526.

Division for Early Childhood. (2007). *Promoting positive outcomes for children with disabilities: Recommendations for curriculum, assessment, and program evaluation.* Missoula, MT: Author.

Division for Early Childhood & National Association for the Education of Young Children. (2009). *Early childhood inclusion: A joint position statement of the Division for Early Childhood (DEC) and the National Association for the Education of Young Children (NAEYC).* Chapel Hill: The University of North Carolina, Frank Porter Graham Child Development Institute.

Dodge, D.T., Heroman, C., Colker, L., & Bickart, T.S. (2010). *The Creative Curriculum for preschool, Volume 1: The foundation* and *Volume 2: Interest areas* (5th ed.). Washington, DC: Teaching Strategies, LLC.

Downer, J.T., Lopez, M.L., Grimm, K., Hamagami, A., Pianta, R.C., & Howes, C. (2012). Observations of teacher–child interactions in classrooms serving Latinos and dual language learners: Applicability of the Classroom Assessment Scoring System in diverse settings. *Early Childhood Research Quarterly, 27*(1), 21–32. doi:10.1016/j.ecresq.2011.07.005

Elias, C.L., Eisenberg, N., & Berk, L.E. (2002). Self-regulation in young children: Is there a role for socio-dramatic play? *Early Childhood Research Quarterly, 17,* 216–238.

Epstein, A.S. (2007). *The intentional teacher: Choosing the best strategies for young children's learning.* Washington, DC: National Association for the Education of Young Children.

Espinosa, L. (2010). *Getting it right for young children with diverse backgrounds: Applying research to improve practice.* Washington, DC: National Association for the Education of Young Children.

Fantuzzo, J., & McWayne, C. (2002). The relationship between peer-play interactions in the family context and dimensions of school readiness for low-income preschool children. *Journal of Educational Psychology, 94*(1), 79–87.

Fox, L., Carta, J., Strain, P., Dunlap, G., & Hemmeter, M.L. (2009). *Response to intervention and the pyramid model.* Tampa: University of South Florida, Technical Assistance Center on Social Emotional Intervention for Young Children.

Graue, E., Clements, M.A., Reynolds, A.J., & Niles, M.D. (2004). More than teacher directed or child initiated: Preschool curriculum type, parent involvement, and children's outcomes in the child–parent centers. *Education Policy Analysis Archives,* North America, 12 Dec. 2004. Retrieved from http://epaa.asu.edu/ojs/article/view/227

Hannikainen, M. (2007). Creating togetherness and building a preschool community of learners: The role of play and games. In T. Jambor & J. Van Gils (Eds.), *Several perspectives in children's play: Scientific reflections for practitioners* (pp. 147–160). Antwerpen and Apeldoorn: Garant.

Hart, B., & Risley, T. (1995). *Meaningful differences in the everyday experience of young American children.* Baltimore, MD: Paul H. Brookes Publishing Co.

Helm, J.H., & Katz, L.G. (2011). *Young investigators: The project approach in the early years.* New York, NY: Teachers College Press and Washington, DC: National Association for the Education of Young Children.

Hemmeter, M.L., Ostrosky, M.M., & Fox, L. (2006). Social and emotional foundations for early learning: A conceptual model for intervention. *School Psychology Review, 35*(4), 583–601.

Heroman, C., Burts, D., Berke, K., & Bickart, T.S. (2010*). The Creative Curriculum for preschool, Volume 5: Objectives for development and learning: Birth through kindergarten.* Washington, DC: Teaching Strategies, LLC.

Heroman, C., & Jones, C. (2010). *The Creative Curriculum for preschool, Volume 3: Literacy* (5th ed.). Washington, DC: Teaching Strategies, LLC.

Howes, C. (2000). Social-emotional classroom climate in child care. Child–teacher relationships and children's second grade peer relations. *Social Development, 9*(2), 191–204.

Howes, C., Guerra, A.W., Fuligni, A., Zucker, E., Lee, L., Obregon, N.B., . . . Spivak, A.L. (2011). Classroom dimensions predict early peer interaction when children are diverse in ethnicity, race, and home language. *Early Childhood Research Quarterly, 26*(4), 399–408. doi:10.1016/j.ecresq.2011.02.004

Hsieh, W.-Y., Hemmeter, M.L., McCollum, J.A., & Ostrosky, M.M. (2009). Using coaching to increase preschool teachers' use of emergent literacy teaching strategies. *Early Childhood Research Quarterly, 24,* 229–247.

Huntsinger, C.S., & Jose, P.E. (2009). Parental involvement in children's schooling: Different meanings in different cultures. *Early Childhood Research Quarterly, 24,* 398–410.

Hyson, M. (2008). *Enthusiastic and engaged learners: Approaches to learning in the early childhood classroom.* New York, NY: Teachers College Press.

Inan, H.Z. (2009). The third dimension in preschools: Preschool environments and classroom design. *European Journal of Educational Studies, 1*(1), 55–66.

Jablon, J.R., Dombro, A.L., & Dichtelmiller, M.L. (2007). *The power of observation for birth through eight* (2nd ed.). Washington, DC: Teaching Strategies, LLC & National Association for the Education of Young Children.

Jones, N.P. (2005). Big jobs: Planning for competence. *Young Children, 60*(2), 86–93.

Katz, L.G., & Chard, S.C. (2000). *Engaging children's minds: The project approach* (2nd ed.). Norwood, NJ: Ablex Publishing Co.

Koralek, D. (Ed.). (2007). *Spotlight on young children and families.* Washington, DC: National Association for the Education of Young Children.

Montie, J.E., Xiang, Z., & Schweinhart, L.J. (2006). Preschool experience in 10 countries: Cognitive and language performance at age 7. *Early Childhood Research Quarterly, 21,* 313–331.

National Association for the Education of Young Children & National Association of Early Childhood Specialists in State Departments of Education. (2003). *Early childhood curriculum, assessment, and program evaluation: Building an effective, accountable system in programs for children birth through age 8.* Joint position statement.

National Council of Teachers of Mathematics. (2000). *Principles and standards for school mathematics.* Reston, VA: Author.

National Early Literacy Panel. (2009). *Developing early literacy: Report of the National Early Literacy Panel: A scientific synthesis of early literacy and implications for intervention.* Washington, DC: National Institute for Literacy.

National Institute of Child Health and Human Development. (2000). *Report of the National Reading Panel: Teaching children to read: An evidence-based assessment of the scientific research literature on reading and its implications for reading instruction* [NIH Publication No. 00-4754]. Washington, DC: U.S. Government Printing Office.

Neuman, S.B., & Wright, T.S. (2010). Promoting language and literacy development for early childhood educators: A mixed-methods study of coursework and coaching. *Elementary School Journal, 111*(1), 63–86.

Palermo, F., Hanish, L.D., Martin, C.L., Fabes, R.A., & Reiser, M. (2007). Preschoolers' academic readiness: What role does the teacher–child relationship play? *Early Childhood Research Quarterly, 22,* 407–422.

Riley, D., San Juan, R.R., Klinkner, J., & Ramminger, A. (2008). *Social and emotional development: Connecting science and practice in early childhood settings.* St. Paul, MN: Redleaf Press and Washington, DC: National Association for the Education of Young Children.

Rimm-Kaufman, S.E., La Paro, K.M., Downer, J.T., & Pianta, R.C. (2005). The contribution of classroom setting and quality of instruction to children's behavior in kindergarten classrooms. *Elementary School Journal, 105*(4), 377–394.

Rushton, S., & Larkin, E. (2001). Shaping the learning environment: Connecting developmentally appropriate practices to brain research. *Early Childhood Education Journal, 29*(1), 25–33.

Shonkoff, J.P., & Phillips, D.A. (Eds.). (2000). *From neurons to neighborhoods: The science of early child development.* A report of the National Research Council. Washington, DC: National Academies Press.

Smilansky, S., & Shefatya, L. (1990). *Facilitating play: A medium for promoting cognitive, socioemotional, and academic development in young children.* Gaithersburg, MD: Psychosocial and Educational Publications.

Snow, C.E., Burns, M.S., & Griffin, P. (Eds.). (1998). *Preventing reading difficulties in young children.* Washington, DC: National Academies Press.

Teaching Strategies, LLC. (2010). *The Creative Curriculum system for preschool.* Washington, DC: Author.

Trawick-Smith, J., & Dziurgot, T. (2011). 'Good-fit' teacher–child play interactions and the subsequent autonomous play of preschool children. *Early Childhood Research Quarterly, 26,* 110–123.

U.S. Department of Health and Human Services, Administration for Children and Families, Office of Head Start. (2010). *The Head Start child development and learning framework: Promoting positive outcomes in early childhood programs serving children 3–5 years old.* Washington, DC: Author.

Wayne, A., DiCarlo, C.F., Burts, D.C., & Benedict, J. (2007). Increasing the literacy behaviors of preschool children through environmental modifications and mediation. *Journal of Research in Childhood Education, 22*(1), 5–16.

Whitin, P. (2001). Kindness in a jar. *Young Children, 65*(5), 18–22.

14

A Curriculum Framework for Supporting Young Children Served in Blended Programs

Jennifer Grisham-Brown and Kristie Pretti-Frontczak

Despite sharing common missions, many early childhood intervention programs are operated by personnel with widely divergent training and experiential backgrounds. Programs also vary in their philosophical perspectives, maintain different eligibility or admission criteria, employ differing assessment practices, offer a wide variety of intervention approaches, and engage in differing levels of evaluation efforts (Pretti-Frontczak, Jackson, McKeen, & Bricker, 2008). Such variability has resulted in an array of programs and services that may have little in common either conceptually or practically. Although variability can often have a positive influence, it can also pose challenges for the growing numbers of children with disabilities who are placed in community-based/blended programs.[1] Early childhood providers are increasingly expected to serve diverse groups of children even if they lack training or experience in how to effectively manage and educate children with unique learning needs. Of further concern is the increased need for teachers[2] to deliver high-quality instruction grounded in an evidence base that is appropriate for all children and to use ongoing assessment and progress monitoring to determine when to augment or intensify interventions and support (Coleman, Buysse, & Neitzel, 2006; Division of Early Childhood, 2007; Duhon, Mesmer, Atkins, Greguson, & Olinger, 2009; Grisham-Brown, Hemmeter, & Pretti-Frontczak, 2005; Jackson, Pretti-Frontczak, Harjusola-Webb, Grisham-Brown, & Romani, 2009; Levitt & Merrell, 2009; Pretti-Frontczak et al., 2008; Spectrum K12 School Solutions, AASA, CASE, NASDSE, & RTI Action Network/NALD, 2011). Essentially, blended early childhood programs need a foundation upon

---

[1]The term *blended* is used to describe programs that serve children with diverse cultural, linguistic, and ability needs, using theories and practices from early childhood education and early childhood special education, in programs that rely on resources from a variety of entities including Head Start, child care, and publicly funded preschool (Grisham-Brown, Hemmeter, & Pretti-Frontczak, 2005).

[2]A variety of terms such as *early childhood educator, interventionist, direct service provider, child care provider,* and *practitioner* are used to describe the adults who work with young children. Regardless of the setting in which the adult works or the type of children with whom the adult works, one common role these adults have is that of teacher. Therefore, we use the term *teacher* throughout this chapter to refer to the adults who work to develop positive and trusting relationships with children, attend to individual needs, and support development, regardless of the setting or context in which they work.

which complex and high-quality services can be systematically designed, implemented, and evaluated.

HISTORY AND OVERVIEW OF A CURRICULUM FRAMEWORK

The need for a strong foundation for the delivery of quality instruction in blended early childhood intervention programs, paired with the complexity of linking ongoing assessment with instructional efforts, has led to efforts to better define and conceptualize early childhood curricula. In early childhood, the term *curriculum* has many different definitions (Dodge, 2004; Kessler, 1991; Ornstein & Hunkins, 2004) but refers to a comprehensive guide for instruction and day-to-day interactions with young children (Division of Early Childhood, 2007; Pretti-Frontczak et al., 2008). Therefore, conceptually, a curriculum framework is a "complex idea containing multiple components including goals, content, pedagogy, and instructional practices" (National Association for the Education of Young Children & National Association of Early Childhood Specialists in State Education [NAEYC/SDE], 2003, p. 6). Practically, a curriculum framework is composed of four linked or related elements: 1) assessment, 2) scope and sequence, 3) activities and instruction, and 4) progress monitoring. In essence, a curriculum framework can serve as an underlying support to allow complex information to be classified and organized. Specifically, the curriculum framework exists to 1) link early childhood assessment processes with what is taught for all children, 2) align early childhood practices with early education content standards, and 3) provide a clear guide for decision making that leads to improved consistency across program practices and improves the likelihood that children will achieve intended outcomes.

With the help of members of a Division of Early Childhood work group (Division of Early Childhood, 2007), the curriculum framework was conceptualized and illustrated using the analogy of an umbrella. As depicted in Figure 14.1, the panels of the umbrella symbolize the four elements of the curriculum framework. Further, just as the fabric of an umbrella is connected, the panels of the curriculum framework are linked together to create a foundation for all program practices. The functional use of an umbrella depends on the panels being intact and without gaps. Further, a functional umbrella has strong support and is well constructed, as illustrated in Figure 14.1 with collaborative planning as the structure that holds the umbrella together along with professional development and support, a representative leadership team, and data-driven decision making. Three of the panels are tiered (represented by horizontal lines to divide broader portions of the panel at the bottom and narrower portions at the top), illustrating that there are practices appropriate for all children (bottom), practices appropriate for some children (middle), and practices designed for individual children (top).

Our purpose in this chapter is to describe the four elements of the curriculum framework and to provide teachers with a means of supporting high-quality services. Each element represents a critical practice in serving children with diverse abilities. First, all children's current abilities, interests/preferences, needs, and family resources, priorities, and concerns are determined and used to plan instruction. Second, child outcomes are identified from assessment information and used to promote efficient instructional sequences. Third, evidence-based instructional strategies are used to differentiate learning environments and activities to ensure needed

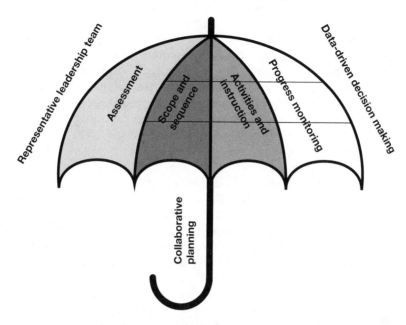

Figure 14.1. Conceptualization of a curriculum framework. (From Pretti-Frontczak, K., Jackson, S., Gross, S., Grisham-Brown, J., Horn, E., Harjusola-Webb, S., Lieber, J., & Matthews, D. [2007]. A curriculum framework that supports quality early childhood education for all young children. *Young exceptional children monograph series 9: Linking curriculum to child and family outcomes, Table 1: Illustration of a curriculum framework including four recommended elements supported by collaborative partnership*, p. 19; reprinted by permission.)

access and supports. Fourth, procedures for evaluating children's development and learning are used to revise instructional efforts. Each element is described next.

ASSESSMENT ELEMENT

Assessment information is gathered for many purposes in early childhood intervention (Division of Early Childhood, 2007; Grisham-Brown & Pretti-Frontczak, 2011; Grisham-Brown, Pretti-Frontczak, Hawkins, & Winchell, 2009; NAEYC & NAECS/SDE, 2003). Perhaps the most important purpose is to guide instruction. In practice, the curriculum framework highlights two types of assessment: program planning and progress monitoring (discussed later in the chapter). For the assessment element of the curriculum framework, teachers need to select and administer a high-quality curriculum-based assessment (CBA) that 1) is aligned with program standards/outcomes, 2) provides opportunities for family input, and 3) can be administered in the child's natural environment (see Bagnato, Neisworth, & Pretti-Frontczak, 2010, for detailed information about how to select a CBA). The purpose of administering a CBA is to collect baseline information on every child in a program to determine 1) *what* to teach individual children, as well as groups of children; 2) *how* to provide instruction and support to young children; and 3) *where* to provide instruction, with an emphasis on children's interests and preferences.

The process teachers engage in to make program planning assessment decisions is referred to as *data-driven decision making* (DDDM; Grisham-Brown

& Pretti-Frontczak, 2011) and involves observing children in their natural environments and documenting their behaviors. Once observations are conducted, teachers summarize, analyze, and interpret the data for the purpose of making programming decisions. Results of the baseline assessment generate three important pieces of information that are essential for program planning. First, information on children's preferences is generated. Through naturalistic observation and speaking with the child's family, the teacher will gain knowledge of how best to teach the child (e.g., grouping arrangement, prompting strategies), what activities are most motivating to the child (e.g., outdoor play, art activities, dramatic play), and what materials the child prefers (e.g., blocks, books, vehicles). Data gathered from interviews with children's families should yield information about concerns and priorities they have regarding their child's development. While families may not identify specific skills they want their child to learn (e.g., write first name), they will likely share their concerns about areas of development in which they believe their child needs additional support (e.g., getting along with other children, being more independent during self-care routines, paying attention to adult directions). Finally, the baseline assessment will yield information about the developmental and content areas in which children need universal, targeted, or intensive instruction. Collecting information on the skills children need to learn, their individual preferences, and the concerns and priorities of their families provides teachers with the information needed to select appropriate outcomes and design high-quality instruction.

SCOPE AND SEQUENCE ELEMENT

As teachers interpret assessment information, they begin to engage in practices involving scope and sequence to ensure strong connections between assessment and instructional efforts. Specifically, teachers determine which children need to learn which outcomes and how best to organize and deliver learning opportunities to groups and individual children. In other words, they sort and prioritize children's needs, identifying the "best" instructional sequence to meet the desired outcome.

Scope

Generally speaking, *scope* refers to concepts and skills from developmental areas (e.g., motor, communication, social) and content areas (e.g., reading, mathematics) for which learning opportunities will be created. *Sequence* refers to the order in which learning opportunities are embedded into daily activities. The scope for young children is increasingly influenced by state and federal early learning standards (National Governors Association [NGA], 2010; Scott-Little, Kagan, Frelow, & Reid, 2008; Scott-Little, Lesko, Martella, & Milburn, 2007; White House, 2002). Regardless of definition, however, the scope of an early childhood curriculum should not come from a single source and should not be seen as a single book, approach, or even theory, but rather a complex guide designed to ensure high-quality learning opportunities in the context of everyday routines and events. Further, early development and learning are highly variable and subject to environmental and social influences such as stressors, risk factors, and transactions between the child and the environment. Therefore, the *sequence* aspects of the curriculum framework should be viewed less as a strict or predictable order in which teaching should occur than as a guide for prioritizing needs and identifying the most effective and efficient instruction.

Within the curriculum framework, *scope* is tiered to acknowledge that as one moves up the tiers, the skills, needs, and concepts being taught or addressed will change. In other words, unlike other tiered models, in the curriculum framework the size of the group or the instructional strategy used is not the only variable that changes as one moves between tiers. For example, if a teacher identifies participation (defined as watching, listening, remaining with the group, and following directions) as a Tier 1 outcome for *all* children, she may determine from assessment information that *some* children are having trouble with a particular component of the outcome (e.g., remaining with the group) and will need different or additional learning opportunities directed specifically at a component of participation. Further, an *individual* child may be missing a foundational or prerequisite skill needed to participate (e.g., joint attention). Thus, the focus of instruction—or rather, the scope of what is taught—varies across tiers.

Tier 1 Scope Generally speaking, Tier 1 scope is composed of broad-based concepts and skills that *all* children are expected to learn and perform. In other words, Tier 1 represents expectations or standards that are held for all children. As mentioned previously, Tier 1 scope is increasingly influenced by state early learning standards, federal standards (e.g., Office of Special Education child outcomes), and even agency standards (e.g., domain elements of The Head Start Child Development and Learning Framework: Promoting Positive Outcomes in Early Childhood Programs Serving Children 3–5 Years Old). Tier 1 scope is also generated by generally agreed-upon developmental milestones for a given population of children, which are often reflected in the items contained in early childhood CBAs.

Tier 2 Scope Within Tier 2, the content represents children's needs that are emerging toward the acquisition and use of common concepts and skills, indicating that a child may require additional practice and/or support to gain independence with *components* or *parts* of a broader expectation or standard. At times, the content of Tier 2 can focus on a means of expression (verbal or nonverbal). Means of expression include the ways in which children navigate their environment and demonstrate what they know. At Tier 2, teachers would address children's need to improve or broaden their ability to express and demonstrate what they know and can do. Lastly, at Tier 2, content is identified by understanding the interrelatedness of development. In other words, a teacher may identify a Tier 1 outcome of counting for a class of preschoolers and find that after 3 months of instruction, several children are not counting any higher, faster, or better—their growth has stalled. A natural inclination would be to provide more instruction or even different instruction on the outcome of counting instead of considering the impact of delayed achievement of developmental milestones that should be emerging concurrently (e.g., sequencing, one-to-one correspondence) to support the child's progress toward the original outcome.

Tier 3 Scope Within Tier 3, the content focuses on foundational skills and/or prerequisite skills that are tied to a common expectation or standard (i.e., tied to Tier 1 scope). Tier 3 content is designed to ensure full access, participation, and progress toward common outcomes (for example, a child may rely on the use of pictures to answer questions as a foundation for later using words). Tier 3 needs often translate into individualized education program/individualized family service plan goals given the intensity, intentionality, and individualization often required to ensure acquisition and use. Within our conceptualization of a curriculum framework, however, we do not differentiate between children who do and do not qualify for early intervention/early childhood special education (EI/ECSE) services. In other words, based upon assessment information, a teacher may find that any child has any combination of needs, given a whole host of variables and factors. For example, a child who is learning English as a second language may demonstrate a Tier 3 matched need for intensive intervention but may not qualify for EI/ECSE. Further, a child who does qualify for special services in the area of motor skills may be performing as expected across a variety of other Tier 1 outcomes/standards (e.g., reading, comparing and contrasting, participating, counting), and therefore the matched instruction will be far less intensive and correlated with more universal or classwide learning opportunities.

Sequence

As mentioned previously, early development and learning are highly variable and affected by environmental and social influences. Thus, no single sequence of learning can be predicted for all children, and teachers need to use the information from their comprehensive assessment in prioritizing children's needs and selecting appropriate instructional strategies and "dosages." Three sequences have been identified to help link assessment information to instructional efforts, based on what is known about human development, effective and efficient instruction, and the diversity of learning preferences and learning rates among young children.

Developmental Sequences Developmental sequences follow an agreed-upon order in which children generally learn various concepts and skills. Although children will learn skills at different rates, there is sufficient evidence that many skills, across areas of development, are typically acquired in some general order. It is important to realize that developmental sequences may be influenced by culture and/or various impairments. Still, planning instruction according to developmental sequences continues to be a common way to focus curriculum planning.

Pedagogical Sequences Some skills have been found to lay the foundation for later learning, although the skills are not necessarily acquired in an orderly developmental sequence. Such sequences have been identified from repeated instruction and research in content areas. An example involves the development of *rhyming*. Research has shown that when children learn to rhyme words, it increases other early literacy skills (Bryant, MacLean, Bradley, & Crossland, 1990; Lonigan & Whitehurst, 2001; Wagner, Torgesen, & Rashotte, 1994). When skill sequences are well documented, it is safe for teachers to rely on pedagogical sequences to guide curriculum planning.

Logical Sequences   Children's development and growth are affected by a number of factors, including culture (Darling-Hammond & Snyder, 2000; Quintana et al., 2006) and the degree to which they are exposed to developmentally appropriate experiences (Greenough, Black, & Wallace, 1987; Ramey & Ramey, 2000). Thus, it is critical that teachers think logically as they prioritize and match instructional efforts. Sometimes "what is next" on a developmental checklist is *not* the most important skill to teach a particular child. For example, it is more important to teach a child to "move around his environment" than to teach him the developmental sequences of walking. Similarly, it may be more important for a child to communicate many messages (e.g., gaining attention, expressing wants/needs, making comments) than to use grammatically correct verbal speech. Teachers working with children who have diverse abilities need to consider the most logical sequence in which to teach each child.

ACTIVITIES AND INSTRUCTION ELEMENT

Multiple tiers characterize the activities and instruction element of the curriculum framework. Tiered models are usually organized on a hierarchy of intervention intensity (Denton et al., 2010; Duhon et al., 2009). Regardless of tier, however, all activities and instructional efforts should be grounded in evidence-based practice, which is not the same as research-based practice. Coleman and Shah-Coltrane (2001) have identified three considerations for determining the evidence base for any given practice including "the research base, the wisdom of respected practitioners, and the values held by the [family and] community that will be implementing the practice" (p. 37).

In the curriculum framework, the primary evidence-based practice that is implemented across tiers is embedded learning opportunities (ELO; Division of Early Childhood, 2007; Horn & Banerjee, 2009). Pretti-Frontczak & Bricker (2004) defined embedding as a

> Process that occurs across daily activities (child directed, routine, and planned), offering multiple and varied learning opportunities that in turn elicit desired responses from children (i.e., demonstrating functional and generative skills) that are supported by timely and integral feedback or consequences that are directly related to or contingent on children's behaviors. (p. 31)

In other words, teachers identify activities throughout the day to provide instruction on important learning targets. The remainder of this section outlines the application of embedded learning opportunities to each tier of the activities and instruction element of the curriculum framework.

Tier 1: Universal Instruction

Universal instruction serves as the foundation for all that occurs in early childhood classrooms. The principles underlying universal instruction are rooted in practices promoted by early childhood professional organizations including the National Association for the Education of Young Children (Copple & Bredekamp, 2009) and the National Association of Early Childhood Specialists in State Departments of Education (NAEYC & NAECS/SDE, 2003) as well as the Division of Early Childhood

(2007). Central to these practices is the philosophy that children learn best 1) in developmentally responsive environments; 2) when they are actively involved in activities, with materials in which they are interested; and 3) when their families are actively involved in their education. In addition, high-quality Tier 1 instruction employs the principle of universal design for learning (UDL) in an effort to differentiate instruction to meet the unique learning needs of *all* children. UDL is an approach to "planning and developing curricula in ways that promote access, participation, and progress in the general education curriculum for all students" (U.S. Department of Education, n.d.). Activities designed using the principles of UDL 1) represent information using multiple methods (e.g., auditory, visual, tactile) and multiple layers of complexity (e.g., familiar to novel, easy to difficult, single to many) to assist children in growing and developing; 2) allow children to demonstrate what they know and can do in a variety of ways using multiple means of expression (e.g., verbal, sign language, picture exchange); and 3) engage children by building upon their interests, supporting their sustained efforts, and motivating them to engage and participate.

In addition to developmentally appropriate and universally designed instruction at Tier 1, teachers tend to rely less on teacher-mediated strategies (Wolery, 2004) than on nondirective instructional strategies (Bredekamp & Rosegrant, 1995) that include such actions as modeling and describing. Nondirective strategies are used to "ensure the continuation of learning and that the social environment in the classroom reflects appropriate behaviors from which the child can learn" (Grisham-Brown et al., 2005, p. 225).

Tier 2: Targeted Instruction

Targeted instruction is designed to increase opportunities to embed learning opportunities regarding the fluency of emerging skills and/or support a child's stalled growth and development. Tier 2 instruction is often characterized by additional embedded learning opportunities across *smaller instructional groups* and through the *use of adaptations*. Tier 2 is also characterized by the increased *use of teacher-mediated instructional strategies* geared toward *targeted* versus universal outcomes.

Grouping children with similar goals together allows for more targeted instruction and promotes interactions between children (Grisham-Brown et al., 2005). Small-group activities may center on a particular content area such as math (e.g., number Bingo) or they may be integrated activities (e.g., making a snack) that promote learning across multiple developmental (e.g., fine motor—stirring; cognitive—problem solving; social—cooperating) and/or content areas (e.g., literacy—"reading a recipe"; math—measuring ingredients). In addition to increasing ELOs and using small-group instruction, teachers use adaptations for targeted instruction at Tier 2. Three types of adaptations can be used to support children's acquisition of emerging or stalled skills (Grisham-Brown et al., 2005). First, homemade adaptations such as a name card, contrasting color, and tilted writing surface may be useful. In addition, a variety of commercially available materials may be of use in promoting skill acquisition, including adapted seating equipment, feeding devices, and mobility equipment. Second, technological adaptations may be useful for some children who cannot verbally communicate or have limited fine motor skills. For example, there are a variety of communication applications for the iPad that may be useful in promoting children's acquisition of emerging skills. Last, at Tier 2, teachers may use more mediating instructional strategies, including peer mediation and the use of shared activities. Mediating teaching strategies are applied on an as-needed basis and include the use of more specific prompts and cues (Grisham-Brown et al., 2005).

Tier 3: Intensive, Individualized, Intentional (III) Instruction

Intensive, individualized, intentional—"triple I" or "III" instruction—is used primarily at Tier 3. The best way to define III instruction is to define each descriptor. *Intensive* implies that children receive a sufficient number of ELOs to address the identified Tier 3 need. Intensive should *not* imply massed or repeated trials of instruction. As was previously described, effective ELOs are embedded into developmentally appropriate activities and routines. That fact does not change just because the type of instruction or need changes; what changes is the *amount* of ELOs children receive and the type of skill that is identified at Tier 3. Second, III instruction is highly *individualized*. In other words, III instruction is specifically planned around the learning and behavioral characteristics of specific children. Individualized instruction *does not* imply one-to-one instruction. Although the teacher will deliver planned prompts and cues when delivering III instruction, the ELOs should be embedded in activities that are of interest to the child and do not separate him from his peers. Finally, III instruction is *intentional*. Intentional instruction implies that the teacher has identified a specific way to deliver support to the child, often as part of a specific instructional strategy to meet the identified Tier 3 need. There is a wide base of evidence supporting many instructional strategies that can be used to create intentional ELOs at Tier 3, and these are often more teacher mediated or directed. For example, correspondence training is used to teach engagement (Bevill, Gast, Maguire, & Vail, 2001); constant time delay to teach object counting (Daugherty, Grisham-Brown, & Hemmeter, 2001) and prewriting skills (Grisham-Brown, Pretti-Frontczak, Hawkins, & Winchell, 2009); high probability request sequences to teach social interactions (Jung, Sainato, & Davis, 2008); and model to teach requesting (Mobayed, Collins, Strangis, Schuster, & Hemmeter, 2000); and simultaneous prompting to teach dressing skills (Sewell, Collins, Hemmeter, & Schuster, 1998). See Collins (2012) for complete descriptions of these procedures.

Two important features related to implementing III instruction are worthy of discussion. First, it is important to understand that children receiving III instruction will continue to receive universal instruction. In other words, children receiving III instruction will receive universal instruction in the form of access to developmentally appropriate activities and through the principles of universal design for learning.

A second important feature is that III instruction is *not* designed only for children with disabilities. Instead, III is used when the identified need cannot be met solely through universal and targeted instruction. For example, Ms. Jessica planned instruction for a group of children in her blended program that included children with disabilities, children who were dual language learners, children who were at risk, and children who were considered to be developing typically. The common outcomes included math skills (e.g., counting, one-to-one correspondence, cardinality, and spatial relations). Ms. Jessica embedded instructional learning opportunities for all children related to the common math outcomes during daily activities and by using universal instruction (i.e., Tier 1). For many children, Tier 1 instruction was sufficient to enhance their math skills over time. Ms. Jessica learned, through ongoing progress monitoring, that for some children targeted instruction was needed, particularly related to components of the common math outcomes (e.g., instruction on correct number names for items counted, instruction on counting in correct order, or instruction on counting without assigning the same number name to more than one object). Ms. Jessica increased the number of daily ELOs and created small-group activities to teach more targeted math skills (i.e., Tier 2 needs). Unfortunately, for select children, even the targeted instruction did not produce the desired results. Ms. Jessica determined that III instruction was needed to address key foundational or prerequisite skills related to the math curriculum for a few children. Thus, highly intensive, individualized, and intentional instruction was delivered through ELOs on Tier 3 needs such as imitation and very early/foundational math constructs such as subitizing and demonstrating an awareness of place in space.

PROGRESS MONITORING ELEMENT

The progress monitoring element of the curriculum framework refers to a recursive feedback loop where, over time, changes in performance of individual children or groups of children are observed, documented, summarized, analyzed, and interpreted (Division of Early Childhood, 2007; Grisham-Brown et al., 2005; Grisham-Brown & Pretti-Frontczak, 2011). Information gained by monitoring children's performance is used for different purposes, including 1) to identify when a child needs additional or more intensive support or instruction; 2) as the foundation of a DDDM model designed to inform, modify, and revise instruction; and 3) to evaluate the degree to which targeted outcomes are being met (e.g., whether children are acquiring critical concepts and skills as expected). The primary focus of the progress monitoring element is on revising instruction. In other words, teachers observe children demonstrating curricular goals, document those observations, summarize their findings, and analyze and interpret results.

Sufficient data are needed to interpret and draw conclusions regarding children's growth and development following instruction. That said, how much data is enough? There is no easy answer to such questions; however, a tiered model of progress monitoring provides a process for making revisions to instruction that not only differentiates the amount of data collected but matches instructional efforts (i.e., matches in frequency, intensity, and intent). Within Tier 1, all children's performance toward common outcomes is monitored in a less frequent and less intensive way than efforts at subsequent tiers. For example, a teacher might re-administer a CBA three or four times a year on *all* children's performance related to Tier 1 outcomes. Since most states have aligned CBAs with state and/or federal outcomes/standards, when children make progress on the CBA, they demonstrate progress on outcomes/standards, or the common curriculum. At Tier 2, teachers may need to engage in more frequent data collection and interpretation. Teachers may find that they need to collect weekly or monthly data to better track how children are responding to instructional efforts and whether they were correct in identifying whether the focus of efforts should be on a component of a Tier 1 outcome, a means of expression, or a related outcome. At Tier 3, data are collected with the most intensity, with increased frequency, and with the intention of monitoring on a daily basis a child's performance on foundational or prerequisite skills. Closely monitoring performance at Tier 3 is time intensive; however, it allows teachers to revise instruction in a highly responsive fashion to ensure that children are reaching their maximum potential.

When interpreting data and revising instruction, teachers should consider whether enough data were collected and whether the data were unbiased and accurate. For example, teachers should determine whether a given performance monitoring practice (e.g., rating rubric, checklist, CBA, standardized assessment, interview, survey, individual growth and development indicators) has been validated for the purpose and population for which it is being used (Bagnato, Macy, Salaway, & Lehman, 2007; Bagnato et al., 2010; Brown, Hubbell, & Winchell, 2010). Teachers should also consider the influence of related factors such as the sociocultural context and past rates of learning, and compare children's progress with typical sequences and timetables of development. For example, research has shown that children learning a second language (i.e., sequential language learners) acquire the second language at rates that differ from language acquisition rates of children developing their first language. Knowing that such factors will influence a child's performance helps teachers accurately interpret data and revise instruction accordingly.

SUMMARY

The curriculum framework was designed to support blended early childhood programs serving children from a variety of cultural, ethnic, and socioeconomic backgrounds. Today there is an increased need for models such as the curriculum framework to support an ever-growing number of programs with the demographics described previously. We recognize the complexity of implementing the curriculum framework as described here; thus, programs attempting to implement the curriculum framework must foster collaborative relationships among families, community members, related service personnel, and teaching staff. In addition, the curriculum framework requires strong leadership to provide necessary supports for its implementation, including time for teachers to plan instruction, collaborate with others, and reflect on how to use data collected. Finally, and perhaps most important, there is a need for planned, intentional professional development that utilizes up-to-date practices including spaced training, coaching, and mentoring to ensure its success.

REFERENCES

Bagnato, S.J., Macy, M., Salaway, J., & Lehman, C. (2007). *Research foundations for conventional tests and testing to ensure accurate and representative early intervention eligibility.* Pittsburgh, PA: TRACE Center for Excellence in Early Childhood Assessment.

Bagnato, S.J., Neisworth, J., & Pretti-Frontczak, K. (2010). *LINKing authentic assessment and early childhood intervention: Best measures for best practices* (2nd ed.) Baltimore, MD: Paul H. Brookes Publishing Co.

Bevill, A., Gast, D., Maguire, A., & Vail, C. (2001). Increasing engagement of preschoolers with disabilities through correspondence training and picture cues. *Journal of Early Intervention, 24,* 129–145.

Bredekamp, S., & Rosegrant, T. (1995). *Reaching potentials: Transforming early childhood curriculum and assessment* (Vol. 2). Washington, DC: National Association for the Education of Young Children.

Brown, T., Hubbell, S.P., & Winchell, B. (2010). *Understanding the evidence behind commonly used assessments in early childhood.* Presentation at the Division for Early Childhood Annual Conference, Kansas City, MO, October 2010.

Bryant, P.E., MacLean, M., Bradley, L.L., & Crossland, J. (1990). Rhyme and alliteration, phoneme detection, and learning to read. *Developmental Psychology, 26,* 429–438.

Coleman, M.R., Buysse, V., & Neitzel, J. (2006). *Recognition and response: An early intervening system for young children at risk for learning disabilities.* Chapel Hill, NC: The University of North Carolina, FPG Child Development Institute.

Coleman, M.R., & Shah-Coltrane, S. (2011). *U-STARS~PLUS: Professional development kit manual.* Arlington, VA: Council for Exceptional Children.

Collins, B. (2012). *Systematic instruction for students with moderate and severe disabilities.* Baltimore, MD: Paul H. Brookes Publishing Co.

Copple, C., & Bredekamp, S. (Eds.). (2009). *Developmentally appropriate practices in early childhood programs servicing children birth to age 8.* Washington, DC: National Association for the Education of Young Children.

Darling-Hammond, L., & Snyder, J. (2000). Authentic assessment of teaching in context. *Teaching and Teacher Education, 16*(5), 523–545.

Daugherty, S., Grisham-Brown, J., & Hemmeter, M.L. (2001). The effects of embedded skill instruction on the acquisition of target and nontarget skills in preschoolers with developmental delays. *Topics in Early Childhood Special Education, 21,* 213–222.

Denton, C., Kethley, C., Nimon, K., Kurz, T., Mathes, P., Minyi, S., . . . Swanson, E.A. (2010). Effectiveness of a supplemental early reading intervention scaled up in multiple schools. *Exceptional Children, 76,* 394–416.

Division of Early Childhood. (2007). *Promoting positive outcomes for children with disabilities: Recommendations for curriculum, assessment, and program evaluation.* Missoula, MT: Author.

Dodge, D.T. (2004). Early childhood curriculum models: Why, what, and how programs use them. *Child Care Informational Exchange,* 72–75.

Duhon, G., Mesmer, E., Atkins, M., Greguson, L., & Olinger, E. (2009). Quantifying intervention intensity: A systematic approach to evaluating student response to increasing intervention frequency. *Journal of Behavioral Education, 18*(2), 101–118. doi:10.1007/s10864-009-9086-5

Greenough, W.T., Black, J.E., & Wallace, C.S. (1987). Experience and brain development. *Child Development, 58,* 539–559.

Grisham-Brown, J., Hemmeter, M.L., & Pretti-Frontczak, K. (2005). *Blended practices for teaching young children in inclusive settings.* Baltimore, MD: Paul H. Brookes Publishing Co.

Grisham-Brown, J., & Pretti-Frontczak, K. (Eds.). (2011). *Assessment practices for working with young children in blended classrooms.* Baltimore, MD: Paul H. Brookes Publishing Co.

Grisham-Brown, J., Pretti-Frontczak, K., Hawkins, S., & Winchell, B. (2009). Early learning standards: An examination of how to teach in blended preschool classrooms. *Topics in Early Childhood Special Education, 29*(3), 131–142.

Horn, E., & Banerjee, R. (2009). Understanding curriculum modifications and embedded learning opportunities in the context of supporting all children's success. *Language, Speech, and Hearing Services in Schools, 40,* 406–415.

Jackson, S., Pretti-Frontczak, K., Harjusola-Webb, S., Grisham-Brown, J., & Romani, J. (2009). Response to intervention: Implications for early childhood professionals. *Language, Speech, and Hearing Services in Schools, 40,* 424–434.

Jung, S., Sainato, D.M., & Davis, C.A. (2008). Using high-probability request sequences to increase social interactions in young children with autism. *Journal of Early Intervention, 30*(3), 163–187.

Kessler, S.A. (1991). Alternative perspectives on early childhood education. *Early Childhood Research Quarterly, 6,* 183–197.

Levitt, V.H., & Merrell, K.W. (2009). Linking assessment to intervention for internalizing problems of children and adolescents. *School Psychology Forum: Research in Practice, 3*(1), 13–26.

Lonigan, C.J., & Whitehurst, G.J. (2001). Getting ready to read: Emergent literacy and family literacy. In B.H. Wasik (Ed.), *Synthesis of research on family literacy programs* (pp. 2–23). Chapel Hill: University of North Carolina.

Mobayed, K.L., Collins, B.C., Strangis, D., Schuster, J.W., & Hemmeter, M.L. (2000). Teaching parents to employ mand-model procedures to teach their children to make requests. *Journal of Early Intervention, 23,* 165–179.

National Association for the Education of Young Children & National Association of Early Childhood Specialists in State Departments of Education. (2003). *Early childhood curriculum, assessment, and program evaluation: Building an effective, accountable system in programs for children birth through age 8.* Retrieved from http://www.naeyc.org/files/naeyc/file/positions/CAPEexpand.pdf

National Governors Association. (2010). *ECW-04 early education and care: A vision for the federal–state partnership for students birth to age 5.* Retrieved from http://www.nga.org/cms/home/federal-relations/nga-policy-positions/page-ecw-policies/col2-content/main-content-list/title_early-education-and-care-a-vision-for-the-federal-state-partnership-for-students-birth-to-age-5.html

Ornstein, A., & Hunkins, F. (2004). *Curriculum: Foundation, principles, and issues.* Boston, MA: Pearson.

Pretti-Frontczak, K.L., & Bricker, D.D. (2004). *An activity-based approach to early intervention* (3rd ed.). Baltimore, MD: Paul H. Brookes Publishing Co.

Pretti-Frontczak, K., Jackson, S., McKeen, L., & Bricker, D. (2008). Supporting quality curriculum frameworks in early childhood programs. In A. Thomas & J. Grimes (Eds.), *Best practices in school psychology* (Vol. V, pp. 1249–1259). Bethesda, MD: NASP Publications.

Quintana, S.M., Aboud, F.E., Chao, R.K., Contreras-Grau, J., Cross, W.E., Jr., Hudley, C., . . . Vietze, D.L. (2006). Race, ethnicity, and culture in child development: Contemporary research and future directions. *Child Development, 77,* 1129–1141. doi:10.1111/j.1467-8624.2006.00951.x

Ramey, C., & Ramey, S. (2000). Early childhood experiences and developmental competence. In S. Danziger & J. Waldfogel (Eds.), *Securing the future: Investing in children from birth to college* (pp. 122–152). New York: Russell Sage Foundation.

Scott-Little, C., Kagan, S.L., Frelow, V.S., & Reid, J. (2008). *Inside the content of infant–toddler early learning guidelines: Results from analyses, issues to consider, and recommendations.* Greensboro: University of North Carolina at Greensboro.

Scott-Little, C., Lesko, J., Martella, J., & Milburn, P. (2007). Early learning standards: Results from a national survey to document trends in state-level policies and practices. *Early Childhood Research & Practice, 9*(1). Retrieved from http://ecrp.uiuc.edu/v9n1/little.html

Sewell, T.J., Collins, B.C., Hemmeter, M.L., & Schuster, J.W. (1998). Using simultaneous prompting to teach dressing skills to preschoolers with developmental delays/disabilities. *Journal of Early Intervention, 21,* 132–145.

Spectrum K12 School Solutions, American Association of School Administrators, Council of Administrators of Special Education, National Association of State Directors of Special Education, & RTI Action Network/National Association of Learning Disabilities. (2011). *Response to intervention (RTI): Adoption survey 2011.* Bellevue, WA: Global Scholar. Retrieved from http://www.spectrumk12.com//uploads/file/RTI%20Report%202011%20FINAL.pdf

U.S. Department of Education. (n.d.) *Toolkit on universal design for learning.* Retrieved from http://osepideasthatwork.org/udl/instrpract.asp

Wagner, R.K., Torgesen, J.K., & Rashotte, C.A. (1994). The development of reading-related phonological processing abilities: New evidence of bi-directional causality from a latent variable longitudinal study. *Developmental Psychology, 30,* 73–87.

White House. (2002). *Good start, grow smart: The Bush administration's early childhood initiative.* Washington, DC: Executive Office of the President

Wolery, M. (2004). Monitoring child progress. In M. McLean, M. Wolery, & D.B. Bailey (Eds.), *Assessing infants and preschoolers with special needs* (3rd ed., pp. 545–584). Upper Saddle River, NJ: Prentice Hall.

15

Language and Literacy Curriculum and Instruction

Stephanie M. Curenton, Laura M. Justice, Tricia A. Zucker, and Anita S. McGinty

There is strong and consistent longitudinal evidence demonstrating an association between children's language and literacy skills during the preschool years and future success at reading in the primary grades (e.g., National Early Literacy Panel, 2008). In fact, many children who exhibit reading difficulties in elementary school had previously exhibited observable lags in their language and literacy development during preschool (e.g., Justice, Bowles, & Skibbe, 2006). It stands to reason that if young children who are at risk for reading problems could be identified early (i.e., prior to formal school entry) and given timely and responsive interventions during preschool, then the prevalence rate for reading difficulties could be reduced drastically. In this chapter we describe instructional targets, classroom contexts, and curricular and instructional approaches that serve as the foundation for a response to intervention (RTI) approach in prekindergarten (pre-K).

RTI is a tiered educational model that provides teachers with a system that links student assessment with specific instructional approaches (Buysse & Peisner-Feinberg, 2010). Perhaps the most welcome component of RTI in preschool settings is that it invites the opportunity to deliver intensive language and literacy interventions to children much earlier, rather than waiting for them to demonstrate reading problems in elementary school. Like elementary school models of RTI (see Fuchs & Fuchs, 2006), preschool RTI models must include 1) a high-quality, research-based core curriculum delivered at Tier 1 that meets all domains of school readiness; 2) targeted instruction delivered in small groups at Tier 2 for children who have been identified as needing focused instruction; and 3) intensive, individualized interventions at Tier 3 for children who still need additional differentiated instruction (Peisner-Feinberg, Buysse, Benshoff, & Soukakou, 2011).

In this chapter, we primarily emphasize language and literacy instruction and intervention at Tier 1 and Tier 2. Typically, Tier 3 services during elementary school are delivered by specialized personnel (e.g., speech-language pathologists), but pre-K Tier 3 services might also be delivered by teachers. For both Tier 1 and Tier 2, preschool educators and allied professionals (e.g., classroom aides, literacy coaches) are encouraged to adopt RTI instructional approaches that include 1) the appropriate scope and sequence of language and literacy instructional targets within the core classroom instruction (Tier 1), 2) regular monitoring of children's progress in relation to this scope and sequence, and 3) timely intervention in the form of additional Tier 2 instructional supports to children whose skills continue to lag behind normative expectations.

INSTRUCTIONAL TARGETS IN LANGUAGE AND LITERACY

Mastering the art of reading relies on merging meaning-based (described here as *language targets*) and code-based (*literacy targets*) aspects of oral and written language (see National Early Literacy Panel, 2008). Meaning-based targets refer to language skills that are foundational to later reading comprehension, such as vocabulary, morphosyntax skills, and listening comprehension. Code-based targets allow children to "crack the symbolic code" of reading, and these targets include such skills as print awareness and phonological awareness. Code-based targets are foundational to such later skills as word recognition, decoding, and spelling. Young children may demonstrate relative lags in their development of *either* meaning-related or code-related skills during the early childhood years, or they may show risk in *both* sets of skills (Cabell, Justice, Konold, & McGinty, 2010). Since both sets of targets provide the precursors for reading, both need to be included in high-quality preschool language and literacy instruction at Tier 1 and Tier 2. We will briefly describe each of these instructional targets.

Vocabulary

Vocabulary generally refers to children's expressive and receptive knowledge of words. Children's knowledge about a word grows in "bits and pieces" over time (see Adams, 2010–2011) and relies on repeated exposures across multiple contexts (e.g., during play, during shared reading). Some words are difficult for children to learn because they represent abstract concepts (e.g., *freedom, know, logical;* see Gleitman et al., 2005) or because they are words children encounter infrequently. By contrast, words that are easy to learn refer to concrete concepts and occur frequently in children's environments (e.g., *yellow, cheek, run*).

As a rule, early childhood educators want to ensure that they are systematically promoting both the *breadth* and *depth* of children's vocabulary knowledge. Breadth of vocabulary knowledge refers to the sheer volume of words that an individual has some understanding of, whereas depth of vocabulary knowledge refers to how detailed a person's understanding of a word is. Breadth is increased simply through exposure to a variety of words, whereas depth is increased with multiple, varied interactions with words across several contexts (Beck, McKeown, & Kucan, 2002). Depth has multiple levels and moves from a shallow knowledge of a word's meaning (e.g., *predator* is an animal) to a nuanced understandings of synonyms, contexts in which the word is used, and multiple meanings of the word (e.g., a predator is a type of animal that pursues other animals as food) (Christ & Wang, 2011). Both breadth and depth of vocabulary knowledge are related to reading comprehension (Tannenbaum, Torgesen, & Wagner, 2006).

Children who are considered to be at risk for future reading problems commonly have problems with both breadth and depth of vocabulary knowledge. In the early elementary grades, the difference in vocabulary breadth between typically developing children and those considered at risk for reading difficulties can be in the neighborhood of 7,000 words (Nagy & Herman, 1985). Because of the potential for the gap in vocabulary knowledge to grow so large and so rapidly, teachers must take a strong role in shaping children's word knowledge by including systematic and explicit instruction promoting vocabulary breadth and depth.

Morphosyntax

Morphosyntactic skills refer to children's tacit knowledge of the rules that govern the internal organization of words (morphology) and the internal organization of sentences (syntax), which together represent children's grammar skills. Children's growth in this area blossoms naturally if they are rooted in a rich oral language environment in which they are exposed to numerous, and varied, examples of morphosyntactic forms. With respect to morphology, children's skills advance rapidly prior to school entry as they learn words can be "morphed" (manipulated) to change their meaning. Children begin to inflect words by using grammatical suffixes (also called grammatical morphemes) to signify grammatical information such as the plural -s (*cat–cats*), the possessive -'s (*Mom–Mom's*), the past tense -ed (*walk–walked*), and the present progressive -ing (*do–doing*). At 12 months, most children are producing only single simple words (*walk*), but by age 5, children are highly skilled at inflecting words to be grammatically precise (e.g., producing such variations of *walk* as *walked*, *walking*, *walker*). Children's morphology advances help them express themselves more precisely (e.g., "I want those dolls," where the plural noun clarifies that the child wants not one, but two or more items). Morphology gains also support vocabulary growth because they allow a small core of root words to be expanded into a much larger pool of word families.

With respect to syntax, children's ability to produce and comprehend complex sentences also advances dramatically prior to school. Sentences are complex when they contain multiple phrases and embedded clauses, as in "Boys and girls, I want you to come and sit in a circle because it's time for morning meeting." This sentence contains one infinitive phrase (*to come*) and two prepositional phrases (*in a circle*, *for morning meeting*); it also contains three clauses, making it a compound-complex sentence. Not only do children become quite adept at an early age in comprehending such complex sentences, they also become skilled at producing them (e.g., "A frog was in there, and the dog was looking in there, and the little boy was looking," a 4-year-old's sentence from Curenton & Justice, 2004). It is important for teachers to recognize the variability among children in their syntactic skills, namely the ability to comprehend and produce grammatically complex utterances, because children who show lags in this area are at a heightened risk for future reading difficulties (Catts et al., 2002). Instruction for this target should be intentional. At this stage in children's development such instruction should be contained within rich classroom conversations in which teachers are modeling complex grammar.

Listening (Reading) Comprehension

The ability to read for meaning—representing the construct of *reading comprehension*—is a multidimensional ability that draws upon an individual's background knowledge, vocabulary knowledge, morphosyntactic skills, literal and inferential verbal reasoning skills, and knowledge of text structures (Scarborough, 2001). Research with elementary school children shows that 20% of children who are struggling readers are good at decoding and reading common words but are poor at understanding what they read (Buly & Valencia, 2002). In other words, a number of children who have reading difficulties have problems specific to comprehension. Consequently, to prevent such future problems, some experts argue that building young children's listening comprehension, which draws upon largely the same set of skills as reading comprehension except within spoken contexts (e.g., listening to stories), is an important aspect of early language and literacy instruction (e.g., van Kleeck, Vander Woude, & Hammett, 2006). Listening comprehension, like reading comprehension, is a multidimensional ability that draws upon such skills as vocabulary knowledge, morphosyntactic skills, literal and inferential reasoning, and text-structure knowledge. We have previously described the first two skill sets; next we will describe the others: literal and inferential reasoning and text structure knowledge.

Literal and inferential reasoning refers to children's ability to "fill in the blanks" based on information that is present or that they must infer. For instance, when children listen to a story, they can reason that a child is sad because the text and illustrations make it transparent (e.g., a boy who is crying in front of a broken window leads one to infer he is crying because he broke the window) or because they can make a connection to their own life experiences (e.g., a child uses his own experience and knowledge base to infer why someone is sad). *Text structure knowledge* refers to the schema that organizes various texts, such as the distinction between how text is structured to make a cause–effect argument versus a description of a bicycle. Even young children can learn to be sensitive to various text structures used to organize printed information. For example, they might organize lists to serve one purpose (e.g., to make a list of friends to invite to a party) and write a story to serve a different purpose.

Listening comprehension skills should be taught in global activities that require children to integrate skills (e.g., vocabulary knowledge, inferential reasoning) in a focused and functional manner. Classroom instruction must employ children in rich conversations about texts that require them to deploy the multiple dimensions of listening comprehension and to engage in comprehension as deeply as possible. For instance, teachers can engage children in conversations during shared reading that require them to draw inferences within the text (e.g., to predict what might happen after a particular problem surfaces) and to comprehend at deeper levels (Zucker, Justice, Piasta, & Kaderavek, 2010). One way to do this is by asking children to demonstrate their understanding of texts, including the ability to integrate the dimensions of listening comprehension, by acting out stories, story retellings, or emergent readings. Allowing children to spend some time engaging in emergent writing that is linked to the theme or the content of the text is also important.

Discussions before, during, and after reading are also powerful tools to further children's listening comprehension. Research has shown that asking questions about stories during and after reading improves preschoolers' vocabulary comprehension (Reese & Cox, 1999). Work with older populations shows that discussion-based learning improves elementary school children's comprehension (Applebee, Langer, Nystrand, & Gamoran, 2003), and this effect was shown for children across achievement and ethnic groups. Unfortunately, it is also the case that lower-track classes had shorter (4 minutes on average) discussions than higher-track classes (15 minutes on average). Class discussion is important for comprehension because it provides students with a different perspective: It helps them understand that not everyone understands a story in the same way. It also might help them see that there were other students who also had a problem understanding the story. The value of asking children to focus on comprehension while they are reading has been confirmed with studies of older readers (see Mastropieri et al., 1998). Mastropieri and colleagues' meta-analysis indicated that teaching readers to pose questions to themselves while reading—or even after reading—substantially increased children's comprehension.

It is imperative that instruction regarding comprehension be focused on expanding children's metacognitive skills, as these are critical to helping children actually monitor their own understanding. Metacognitive skills entail the ability to think about, monitor, and/or evaluate what one is doing (or reading or saying) as he or she is doing it. Examples of metacognitive skills include knowing a number of different ways to figure out how to decode a word, knowing how to draw on one's personal background knowledge to understand an event, knowing how to present a summary in a way that others will understand, and knowing how to construct mental images about what one is planning to do. Enhancing children's metacognitive skills helps them develop the skills they will need for becoming successful readers. The following list provides additional suggestions for fostering comprehension.

1. Ask children to summarize what they have read or what they have done, using emergent writing (like drawings), guided conversations, story retellings, or story acting.

   a. Help them articulate what they have learned, such as new vocabulary or moral lessons.

   b. Help children articulate what they did not understand about a story.

2. Teach children how to understand the theme and plot of narrative texts.

   a. Ask them to talk about, draw, or act out what has happened in a story.

   b. Engage them in guided conversation about the motives and intentions of characters within the story.

3. Model the use of private speech by mapping your own language while engaging in an activity and encourage children to do the same.

4. Encourage children to predict what will happen next or brainstorm about what might have happened differently.

5. Help children to "visualize" story characters or "act out" story plots in order to make the story come to life.

Print Awareness

Print awareness refers to children's knowledge of the *forms* and *functions* of print. *Forms of print* refers to children's knowledge of the various forms that are relevant to written language, such as alphabet letters, words, and punctuation devices. With early and frequent exposure to print, most children will know that a word comprises letters—and not the other way around—prior to entering kindergarten. (However, this should not be taken for granted, as discovery of the "concept of word" in print—that words are the basic chunks of written language—is one that can elude many children [Justice & Ezell, 2001]). Prior to kindergarten entry, many children will know several alphabet letters, particularly those in their own names. Although children show a strong bias toward learning the letters in their own name first, there are some letters that seem to be acquired earlier than other letters (i.e., *A, B, O,* and *X*) (Justice, Pence, Bowles, & Wiggins, 2006). Knowing a letter typically means that children can map a visual symbolic representation (the grapheme) to its label. Within the United States, letter-sound instruction typically follows letter-name instruction, meaning students learn the sound a letter makes after they learn to name the letter (Treiman, Tincoff, & Richmond-Welty, 1996).

Print function refers to understanding the *purpose* of print or a text. Print serves many, if not all, of the same functions of spoken language (e.g., to explain, inform, entertain). However, the purpose of print can vary depending on the structure of the text. For instance, a list has a different text structure and purpose from a love letter, and a love letter has a different text structure and purpose from a recipe. Preschool children begin to explore the functions of print when they engage in activities that use print for different purposes. For example, teachers might have children scribble a note to a friend, make a sign for the wall, or draw a map to a secret treasure. This early knowledge of the functions of print may help children later navigate the numerous text structures that they will confront in elementary school, such as compare/contrast charts, dictionaries, magazines, storybooks, and textbooks.

Phonological Awareness

Phonological awareness is an individual's sensitivity to the sound structure of language. At its most refined level, it refers to an individual's sensitivity to phonemes, often referred to as phonemic awareness. Phonemes are the individual sounds in a language that signify changes in meaning. In alphabetic languages, like English, reading is based on the alphabetic code in which phonemes (e.g., /l/ and /r/) are mapped to letters (*L* and *R*). The consonant sounds /r/ and /l/ are phonemes, and changing these sounds in the context of other sounds produces changes in meaning (*rip* versus *lip* or *rot* versus *lot*). To achieve success in reading, children must learn this alphabetic code and automate its application. Phonological awareness is an important accomplishment that emerges during the preschool years because it helps children become sensitive to the sound structure of language, which facilitates their ability to learn and automatize children's developing abilities.

Typically, children's acquisition of phonological awareness follows a pathway such that they first become sensitive to large segments of the spoken sound system, such as syllables and rime units, and then later become sensitive to the smaller units, like the individual phonemes (Anthony, Lonigan, Driscoll, Phillips, & Burgess, 2003). Thus, young children will typically be able to complete a phonological awareness task requiring them to display sensitivity to rhyme patterns (e.g., "Tell me a word that rhymes with *fog*") prior to being able to complete a task requiring them to identify or manipulate individual sounds in a word (e.g., "Tell me the first sound you hear in the word *fog*"). Teachers need to be aware of this developmental sequence and design instruction that is coordinated with children's developing abilities.

LANGUAGE AND LITERACY INSTRUCTION AT TIER 1 AND TIER 2

At Tier 1 (core curriculum), instruction should be designed to facilitate children's development of meaning-related and code-related language and literacy targets that are predictive of later reading success. Such instruction should be integrated into daily classroom activities that are delivered in a developmentally appropriate group learning context (e.g., small groups or free play), and it should strive to meet the following instructional aims: 1) consistently engage children in thought-provoking conversations; 2) scaffold their ability to verbally express themselves, particularly as it relates to what they think, feel, remember, or plan for the future; 3) help students construct meaning from text by providing systematic opportunities to discuss what is read; and 4) offer regular and explicit instruction related to print and phonological awareness.

At Tier 2 (targeted instruction), these same four instructional aims must be met, but they should be delivered in small groups that are focused explicitly on the language and literacy targets (vocabulary, morphosyntax, listening comprehension, print awareness, and phonological awareness) for which individual students need additional support. Although there is not a definitive research base on the appropriate dosage for each tier of instruction, current practice is that Tier 2 instruction should be conducted in small groups two to three times a week for approximately 20 minutes (see Justice, 2006). This Tier 2 small-group instruction is *in addition to* the regular Tier 1 core curriculum instruction. For children who still do not respond, further individualized and more intensive Tier 3 instruction is required, which may lead to additional assessments and/or a special education referral to determine how to modify intervention to meet the child's individual needs. This Tier 3 instruction may be delivered by the teacher, a reading specialist, speech-language pathologist, or other trained interventionist.

In this chapter we describe three daily classroom routines within the core curriculum that can address the language and literacy targets, as well as two specific curricular supplements that were designed to make teaching more intentional and that are suitable for targeted Tier 2 instruction.

DAILY CLASSROOM CONTEXTS FOR LANGUAGE AND LITERACY

Shared Book Reading

Preschool teachers frequently use shared book reading to expose children to language and literacy targets. For instance, research has shown that educators can use cognitively challenging questions during shared reading to improve children's language skills (Gest et al., 2006). Discussions before, during, and after reading encourage children to draw inferences, apply their reasoning skills, and draw upon their listening comprehension skills to summarize the story (e.g., van Kleeck et al., 2006). Teachers' use of inferential (or decontextualized) conversations during shared reading predicts children's vocabulary and comprehension growth both during preschool and into elementary school (Dickinson & Porche, 2011). Several studies indicate that children can learn vocabulary words from repeatedly listening to the same story (Penno, Wilkinson, & Moore, 2002), but their vocabulary improves even more substantially when teachers intentionally coach children on vocabulary within the book by defining words during shared reading (Johnson & Yeates, 2006; Justice, Meier, & Walpole, 2005). Shared book reading has also demonstrated significant effects on code-related skills such as print awareness (for reviews, see Mol, Bus, & de Jong, 2009). However, shared-reading activities only account for 1% to 4% of the total preschool day (Dickinson, 2001). Therefore, suggestions about how teachers can enhance these skills using other instructional activities are needed, and we describe some of these other learning contexts next.

Classroom Conversations

Another classroom context that is particularly salient for improving children's language and literacy is conversation. As Dickinson (2006) pointed out, the most powerful preschool classroom predictor accounting for children's later literacy skills is teacher instruction strategies that support extended and sophisticated conversations. Mealtimes, in particular, are natural opportunities for rich conversations as they provide a unique opportunity for back-and-forth exchanges where children can use decontextualized language to talk about past or future events (Gest et al., 2006; Snow & Beals, 2006). One intentional strategy for stimulating rich classroom conversations is to create a designated space for extended discourse in the classroom. Bond and Wasik (2009) provided some evidence that preschool teachers can sit down with small groups of children at the "conversation station" and use open-ended, intentional questions to scaffold children's conversational skills. Another strategy is the *Conversation Compass* (CC; Curenton, 2012). The CC is a conversation-based instructional support strategy designed to increase the quality of language modeling and concept development within classrooms. It is based on a body of interdisciplinary research demonstrating the effectiveness of engaging children in decontextualized discourse and/or inferential reasoning via responsive conversation strategies (de Rivera et al., 2005; Dickinson, 2001, 2006; Girolametto & Weitzman, 2002; van Kleeck et al., 2006; Wasik et al., 2006). For the CC, teachers use specific lesson planning tools to systematically and explicitly incorporate culturally sensitive, higher-level, thought-provoking discussion into daily routine classroom activities.

Play Activities

Classroom activities that focus on hands-on play can also be effective for promoting language and literacy targets. Connor and her colleagues (2006) found a positive relationship between time spent in play within the preschool classroom and children's vocabulary growth, and they noted that this relationship was even stronger for children who had weaker language skills at the start of the school year. Other researchers have also found that when children play in literacy-enriched dramatic play settings, such as a post office, kitchen, office, library, or other centers with thematic activities that include literacy objects (e.g., writing tools, phone books, grocery lists), they learn to read environmental print and improve their alphabet knowledge (Neuman & Roskos, 1993; Vukelich, 1994). From an instructional standpoint, research indicating that play provides an important context for the development of language and literacy skills is important because preschoolers in Head Start and child care spend about 20% of their instructional time in free play (Dickinson, 2001). During these free-play sessions teachers appear to talk less and encourage the children to talk among themselves (Dickinson, 2001), and teachers also use more inferential language than in other activities (Gest et al., 2006; O'Brien & Bi, 1995).

CURRICULAR AND INSTRUCTIONAL
APPROACHES FOR LANGUAGE AND LITERACY

Because there are several rigorous and reliable comprehensive core curricula that provide the overall foundation and philosophy for core instruction in the early childhood classroom (e.g., see Buysse & Peisner-Feinberg, 2010), we concern ourselves with describing two curricular supplements that may be useful for organizing the second tier of instruction for students requiring additional supports in meaning- and/or code-based targets. The curricular supplements we describe are *Read It Again Pre-K!* (Justice et al., 2010) and *Developing Talkers: Pre-K* (Children's Learning Institute, 2010).

Read It Again Pre-K!

Read It Again Pre-K! (*RIA*) is a semiscripted language and literacy supplemental curriculum that requires the use of 15 commercial storybooks to organize 60 lessons. RIA is available online for free download at http://www.myreaditagain.com. RIA was developed to meet the needs of preschool programs and school districts that may not have the financial resources for high-cost language and literacy curricula or ongoing intensive professional development. The authors designed it for use as a whole-group instructional tool to embed explicit language and literacy instruction within the core curriculum or as a Tier 2 supplement for one-on-one or small-group interventions.

Results of a quasi-experimental study in which RIA was embedded in 11 classrooms (as compared with 11 control classrooms; Justice et al., 2010) show that RIA can successfully be delivered with high fidelity by educators with relatively little background knowledge or prior training. When teachers used RIA twice a week for 20 to 30 minutes across 30 weeks, there were positive benefits for at-risk children's language and literacy skills. Children improved across several language measures (e.g., vocabulary, morphology, syntax) and early literacy measures such as rhyme, alliteration, alphabet knowledge, and print concepts. Effect-size estimates were medium to large, indicating that such a curricular supplement could have meaningful influence on improving skills within the preschool population. Additional research investigating impacts of RIA for children with language disorders who received it in one-on-one sessions provides additional evidence of its potential as a Tier 2 tool (McNamara, Vervaeke, & Van Lankveld, 2008).

RIA offers educators a useful Tier 2 instructional approach for facilitating children's language and literacy skills, particularly because it is responsive to children's individual learning needs through a heavy emphasis on individualized scaffolding. Although the actual targets to be addressed during lessons are static (i.e., they are systematically and explicitly organized to address a specific scope and sequence), specific guidelines are included in each lesson on how to provide scaffolding to promote children's skill development over time. The lessons provide a guide for addressing certain objectives with children who require high support (e.g., modeling the answer, reducing choices) versus those who require low support (e.g., generalizing responses, predicting). As we noted previously, a child can have well-developed skills in one area of language/literacy (e.g., phonological awareness) but more limited skills in another area (e.g., vocabulary). Therefore, within Tier 2 supplements scaffolding is a key component in light of such individual differences. The use of such strategies can be informed through ongoing use of an RIA Pupil Progress Checklist, which provides a way to examine children's progress across all skill areas targeted within RIA. More specific details about how RIA can be implemented in an RTI framework can be found in Justice, McGinty, Guo, and Moore (2009).

Developing Talkers: Pre-K

Developing Talkers was designed as a curriculum supplement for improving preschooler's language skills using a multitiered instructional framework that can be implemented by classroom teachers; it can be downloaded at no cost at http://www.ChildrensLearningInstitute.org. Developing Talkers employs interactive shared book reading, classroom conversations, and small-group activities to build children's vocabulary and listening comprehension skills. To increase vocabulary, procedures are used to increase both breadth and depth of word knowledge; the goal of comprehension is emphasized through questioning and activities that require reasoning and other types of inferential thinking and language skills.

Developing Talkers uses brief vocabulary explanations during large-group Tier 1 shared reading to build all students' vocabulary skills, while more extended vocabulary instruction is delivered to at-risk children in Tier 2 small groups. After the shared reading experience, children transition to learning centers. Transition activities are provided that support teachers in using vocabulary words in playful ways and through science center activities that involve hands-on exploration of the topics addressed in the shared reading.

An essential component of Developing Talkers is the provision of tiered assessment tools that allow classroom teachers to 1) make decisions about which students require more intensive Tier 2 instruction and 2) monitor students' response to the more intensive Tier 2 instruction. To identify students who are not responding adequately with Tier 1 alone, teachers administer a language screening measure such as the technology-based CIRCLE Phonological Awareness, Language, and Literacy System (C-PALLS) assessment (Landry, Swank, Assel, & King, 2009) to all students three times a year (fall, winter, spring). In addition, they administer two formative assessments to evaluate Tier 2 students' responsiveness, such as a weekly check of target vocabulary learning for the six words explicitly taught in the lesson.

Evidence suggests Developing Talkers is a promising approach for at-risk preschoolers' vocabulary knowledge; furthermore, researchers found that students who were unresponsive at Tier 1 were successful at Tier 2 (Zucker, Solari, Landry, & Swank, in press). Developing Talkers was extended to include 16 weeks of activities, and a Spanish version called *Hablemos Juntos: Pre-K* was developed for students in bilingual programs.

CONCLUSION

In this chapter we discussed how high-quality, empirically sound language and literacy curriculum and instruction is an important foundation for pre-K RTI models. The promise of preschool RTI models is that children facing risk factors such as poverty, language impairment, or being a dual language learner can receive timely and responsive services well before they start to exhibit reading problems in elementary school. In fact, it is the hope among researchers, policy makers, and practitioners in the early education field that the prevalence of later reading difficulties can be substantially reduced if at-risk children are provided with responsive Tier 1 (core instruction) and Tier 2 (small-group instruction tailored to remediate specific literacy targets) instructional opportunities.

REFERENCES

Adams, M.J. (2010–2011, Winter). Advancing our students' language and literacy. *American Educator,* 3–12.

Anthony, J.L., Lonigan, C.J., Driscoll, K., Phillips, B.M., & Burgess, S.R. (2003) Phonological sensitivity: A quasi-parallel progression of word structure units and cognitive operations. *Reading Research Quarterly, 389*(4), 470–487. doi: 10.1598/RRQ.38.4.3

Applebee, A.N., Langer, J.A., Nystrand, M., & Gamoran, A. (2003). Discussion-based approaches to developing understanding: Classroom instruction and student performance in middle and high school English. *American Education Research Journal, 40,* 685–730.

Beck, I.L., McKeown, M.G., & Kucan, L. (2002). *Bringing words to life: Robust vocabulary instruction. Solving problems in the teaching of literacy.* New York, NY: Guilford Press.

Bond, M.A., & Wasik, B.A. (2009). Conversation stations: Promoting language development in young children. *Early Childhood Education Journal, 36*(6), 467–473. doi: 10.1007/s10643-009-0310-7

Buly, M.R., & Valencia, S.W. (2002). Below the bar: Profiles of students who fail state reading assessments. *Educational Evaluation and Policy Analysis, 24,* 219–239.

Buysse, V., & Peisner-Feinberg, E. (2010). Recognition & Response: Response to intervention for pre-K. *Young Exceptional Children, 13*(4), 1–13.

Cabell, S.Q., Justice, L.M., Konold, T.R., & McGinty, A.S. (2010). Profiles of emergent literacy skills among preschool children who are at risk for academic difficulties. *Early Childhood Research Quarterly, 26*(1), 1–14. doi:10.1016/j.ecresq.2010.05.003

Catts, H.W., Fey, M.E., Tomblin, J.B., & Zhang, X. (2002). A longitudinal investigation of reading outcomes in children with language impairments. *Journal of Speech, Language, and Hearing Research, 45,* 1142–1157. doi:10.1044/1092-4388(2002/093)

Children's Learning Institute. (2010). *Developing talkers: Pre-K curricular supplement to promote oral language.* Houston: University of Texas Health Science Center.

Christ, T., & Wang, X. C. (2011). Closing the vocabulary gap? A review of research on early childhood vocabulary practices. *Reading Psychology, 32*(5), 426–458. doi:10.1080/02702711.2010.495638.

Connor, C.M., Morrison, F.J., & Slominski, L. (2006). Preschool instruction and children's emergent literacy growth. *Journal of Educational Psychology, 98,* 665–689.

Curenton, S.M. (2012, June). *"Chatty children who tell stories": Using classroom conversations and oral stories for Tier 1 and Tier 2 language instruction.* Presented to trainers for the Iowa Department of Education. New Brunswick, NJ: Author.

Curenton, S.M., & Justice, L. (2004). African American and Caucasian preschoolers' use of decontextualized language: Use of literate language features in oral narratives. *Language, Speech, and Hearing Services in the Schools, 35,* 240–253.

de Rivera, C., Girolametto, L., Greenberg, J., & Weitzman, E. (2005). Children's responses to educators' questions in day care play groups. *American Journal of Speech-Language Pathology, 14,* 14–26.

Dickinson, D.K. (2001). Large-group and free-play times: Conversational settings supporting language and literacy development. In D.K. Dickinson & P.O. Tabors (Eds.), *Beginning literacy with language* (pp. 223–255). Baltimore, MD: Paul H. Brookes Publishing Co.

Dickinson, D.K. (2006). Toward a toolkit approach to describing classroom quality. *Early Education and Development, 17,* 177–202.

Dickinson, D.K., & Porche, M.V. (2011). Relation between language experiences in preschool classrooms and children's kindergarten and fourth-grade language and reading abilities. *Child Development, 82*(3), 870–886. doi: 10.1111/j.1467-8624.2011.01576.x

Fuchs, D., & Fuchs, L.S. (2006). Introduction to response to intervention: What, why, and how valid is it? *Reading Research Quarterly, 41,* 93–99. doi:10.1598/RRQ.41.1.4

Gest, S.D., Holland-Coviello, R., Welsh, J.A., Eicher-Catt, D.L., & Gill, S. (2006). Language development subcontexts in Head Start classrooms: Distinctive patterns of teacher talk during free play, mealtime, and book reading. *Early Education and Development, 17,* 293–315.

Girolametto, L., & Weitzman, E. (2002). Responsiveness of child care providers in interactions with toddlers and preschoolers. *Language, Speech, and Hearing Services in Schools, 33,* 268–281.

Gleitman, L.R., Cassidy, K., Nappa, R., Papafragou, A., & Trueswell, J.C. (2005). Hard words. *Language Learning and Development, 1,* 23–64. doi: 10.1207/s15473341lld0101_4

Johnson, C., & Yeates, E. (2006). Evidence-based vocabulary instruction for elementary students via storybook reading. *EBP Briefs, 1*(3), 1–24.

Justice, L.M. (2006). Evidence-based practice, response to intervention, and the prevention of reading difficulties. *Language, Speech, and Hearing Services in Schools, 37,* 284–297.

Justice, L.M., Bowles, R.P., & Skibbe, L.E. (2006). Measuring preschool attainment of print-concept knowledge: A study of typical and at-risk 3- to 5-year-old children using item response theory. *Language, Speech, and Hearing Services in Schools, 37,* 224–235.

Justice, L.M., & Ezell, H.K. (2001). Written language awareness in preschool children from low-income households: A descriptive analysis. *Communication Disorders Quarterly, 22*(3), 123–134. doi: 10.1177/152574010102200302

Justice, L.M., McGinty, A., Cabell, S.Q., Kilday, C.R., Knighton, K., & Huffman, G. (2010). Language and literacy curriculum supplement for preschoolers who are academically at risk: A feasibility study. *Language, Speech, and Hearing Services in Schools, 41,* 161–178.

Justice, L.M., McGinty, A., Guo, Y., & Moore, D. (2009). Implementation of responsiveness to intervention in early education settings. *Seminars in Speech and Language Pathology, 30,* 59–73.

Justice, L., Meier, J., & Walpole, S. (2005). Learning new words from storybooks: An efficacy study with at-risk kindergartners. *Language, Speech, and Hearing Services in Schools, 36*(1), 17. doi: 10.1044/0161-1461(2005/003)

Justice, L.M., Pence, K.L., Bowles, R.P., & Wiggins, A. (2006). An investigation of four hypotheses concerning the order by which children learn the letters of the alphabet. *Early Childhood Research Quarterly, 21*(3), 374–389. doi:10.1016/j.ecresq.2006.07.010

Landry, S.H., Swank, P.R., Assel, M.A., & King, T. (2009). *The CIRCLE phonological awareness, language, and literacy system (C-PALLS): Technical manual.* Children's Learning Institute, Houston, TX. Unpublished research.

Mastropieri, M.A., Scruggs, T.E., Bakken, J.P., & Whedon, C. (1998). Reading comprehension: A synthesis of research on learning disabilities. In T.E. Scruggs & M.A. Mastropieri (Eds.), *Advances in learning and behavioral difficulties* (Vol. 10, Part B, pp. 201–227). Greenwich, CT: JAI Press.

McNamara, J., Vervaeke, S., & Van Lankveld, J. (2008). An exploratory study of emergent literacy intervention for preschool children with language impairments. *Exceptionality Education Canada, 18,* 9–32.

Mol, S.E., Bus, A.G., & de Jong, M.T. (2009). Interactive book reading in early education: A tool to stimulate print knowledge as well as oral language. *Review of Educational Research, 79,* 979–1007.

Nagy, W.E., & Herman, P.A. (1985). Incidental vs. instructional approaches to increasing reading vocabulary. *Educational Perspectives, 23*(1), 16–21.

National Early Literacy Panel. (2008). *Developing early literacy: Report of the National Early Literacy Panel.* Washington, DC: National Institute for Literacy.

Neuman, S., & Roskos, K. (1993). Access to print for children of poverty: Differential effects of adult mediation and literacy-enriched play settings on environmental and functional print tasks. *American Educational Research Journal, 30,* 95–122.

O'Brien, M., & Bi, X. (1995). Language learning in context: Teacher and toddler speech in three classroom play areas. *Topics in Early Childhood Special Education, 15,* 148–163.

Peisner-Feinberg, E., Buysse, V., Benshoff, L., & Soukakou, E. (2011). Recognition & Response: Response to intervention for pre-kindergarten. In C. Groark, S.M. Eidelman, L. Kaczmarek, & S. Maude (Eds.), *Early childhood intervention: Shaping the future for children with special needs and their families, Vol. 3, Emerging trends in research and practice* (pp. 37–53). Santa Barbara, CA: Praeger.

Penno, J., Wilkinson, I., & Moore, D. (2002). Vocabulary acquisition from teacher explanation and repeated listening to stories: Do they overcome the Matthew effect? *Journal of Educational Psychology, 94*(1), 23–33. doi: 10.1037/0022-0663.94.1.23

Reese, E., & Cox, A. (1999). Quality of adult book reading affects children's emergent literacy. *Developmental Psychology, 35,* 20–28.

Scarborough, H.S. (2001). Connecting early language and literacy to later reading (dis)abilities: Evidence, theory, and practice. In S.B. Neuman & D.K. Dickinson (Eds.), *Handbook of early literacy research* (pp. 97–110). New York, NY: Guilford Press.

Snow, C.E., & Beals, D.E. (2006). Mealtime talk that supports literacy development. *New Directions for Child and Adolescent Development, 111,* 51–66. doi:10.1002/cd.155

Tannenbaum, K.R., Torgesen, J.K., & Wagner, R.K. (2006). Relationships between word knowledge and reading comprehension in third-grade children. *Scientific Studies of Reading, 10*(4), 381–398. doi:10.1207/s1532799xssr1004_3

Treiman, R., Tincoff, R., & Richmond-Welty, E.D. (1996). Letter names help children to connect print and speech. *Developmental Psychology, 32,* 505–514. doi:10.1037/0012-1649.32.3.505

van Kleeck, A., Vander Woude, J., & Hammett, L. (2006). Fostering literal and inferential language skills in Head Start preschoolers with language impairment using scripted book-sharing discussion. *American Journal of Speech-Language Pathology, 15,* 85–96.

Vukelich, C. (1994). Effects of play interventions on young children's reading of environmental print. *Early Childhood Research Quarterly, 9,* 153–170.

Wasik, B.A., Bond, M.A., & Hindman, A. (2006). The effects of a language and literacy intervention on Head Start children and teachers. *Journal of Educational Psychology, 98,* 63–74.

Zucker, T., Justice, L.M., Piasta, S.B., & Kaderavek, J.N. (2010). Preschool teachers' literal and inferential questions and children's responses during whole-class shared reading. *Early Childhood Research Quarterly, 25,* 65–83. doi:10.1016/j.ecresq.2009.07.001

Zucker, T.A., Solari, E.J., Landry, S.H., & Swank, P.R. (in press). Effects of a brief, tiered language intervention for pre-kindergarteners at risk. *Early Education and Development.*

16

Math Curriculum and Instruction for Young Children

Herbert P. Ginsburg, Barbrina Ertle, and Ashley Lewis Presser

Recent research and development efforts have 1) provided insight into the remarkable development of children's mathematical thinking and learning, 2) identified the need for quality early childhood mathematics education (ECME), 3) led to a sound formulation of the nature and goals of ECME, and 4) resulted in the development of innovative and effective math curricula for young children. This chapter provides an introduction to this body of work, from which response to intervention (RTI) efforts can benefit, and discusses the kinds of efforts and research needed to promote effective future development of RTI.

CHILDREN'S MATHEMATICAL THINKING AND LEARNING

Since the mid 1980s or so, researchers have accumulated a wealth of evidence (Baroody, Lai, & Mix, 2006; Clements & Sarama, 2007b; Ginsburg, Cannon, Eisenband, & Pappas, 2006) showing that nearly from birth to age 5, young children develop an *everyday mathematics*—including informal ideas of more and less, taking away, shape, size, location, pattern, and position—that is surprisingly broad, complex, and sometimes sophisticated. Everyday mathematics is an essential and even inevitable feature of the child's cognitive development, and like other aspects of the child's cognition, such as theory of mind or critical thinking, develops in the ordinary environment, usually without direct instruction.

Origins in Infancy

Even infants display core mathematical abilities. They can, for example, discriminate between two collections varying in number (Lipton & Spelke, 2003) and develop elementary systems for locating objects in space (Newcombe & Huttenlocher, 2000). Geary (1996) argued that all children, regardless of background and culture, are endowed with "biologically primary" abilities including not only number, but also basic geometry. These kinds of abilities are virtually universal to the species and require only a minimum of environmental support to develop.

Everyday Mathematics

In the ordinary environment, the development of young children's comprehensive everyday mathematics comprises several important features.

Spontaneous Interest   Young children have a spontaneous and some-times explicit interest in mathematical ideas. Naturalistic observation has shown, for example, that in their ordinary environments, young children spontaneously count (Saxe, Guberman, & Gearhart, 1987), even up to relatively large numbers, like 100 (Irwin & Burgham, 1992), and may want to know what is the "largest number" (Gelman, 1980). Also, mathematical ideas permeate children's play: in the block area, for example, young children spend a good deal of time determining which tower is higher than another, creating and extending interesting patterns with blocks, exploring shapes, creating symmetries, and the like (Seo & Ginsburg, 2004). Everyday mathematics is not an imposition from adults; indeed adults, including teachers, are often blissfully ignorant of it.

Competence and Incompetence   Children's minds are not simple. From an early age, they seem to understand basic ideas of addition and subtraction (Brush, 1978) and spatial relations (Clements, 1999). They can spontaneously develop (Groen & Resnick, 1977) various methods of calculation, like counting on from the larger number (asked to determine the sum of 9 and 2, the child counts, "nine. . . ten, eleven") (Baroody & Wilkins, 1999). At the same time, children display certain kinds of mathematical incompetence, such as having difficulty understanding that the number of objects remains the same even when they are merely shifted around (Piaget, 1952) or failing to realize that an odd-looking triangle (for example, a scalene triangle) is as legitimate as one with three sides of the same length (Clements, 1999).

Concrete and Abstract   In some ways, young children's thinking is rela-tively concrete. They see that this set of objects is more numerous than that one, and they can add three blocks to four blocks to get the sum. Yet in other ways, young children's thinking is very abstract. They know that adding always makes more and subtracting less. They can easily create symmetries in three dimensions (Seo & Ginsburg, 2004). They have abstract ideas about counting objects, includ-ing the one-to-one principle (one and only one number word should be assigned to each object) and the abstraction principle (any discrete objects can be counted, from stones to unicorns) (Gelman & Gallistel, 1986).

Language and Metacognition   Learning mathematics requires learning several kinds of language. From the age of 2 or so, children learn the language and grammar of counting. They memorize the first ten or so counting words (which are essentially nonsense syllables, with no underlying structure or meaning), and then learn a set of rules to generate the higher numbers (Ginsburg, 1989).

Young children also learn other kinds of mathematical language, like the names of shapes ("square") and words for quantity ("bigger," "less"). Indeed, some of these words (like "more") are among the first ones spoken by many babies (Bloom, 1970). Mathematical words are so pervasive that they are not usually thought of as belonging to "mathematics" and are instead considered aspects of general cognitive development or intelligence.

Language is also required to express and justify mathematical thinking. With development, children become increasingly aware of their own thinking and begin to express it in words (Kuhn, 2000).

The hardest form of language for children to learn is the special written symbolism of mathematics (e.g., 5, +, −, =). For example, when asked to represent a quantity like five blocks, young children exhibit idiosyncratic (e.g., scribble) and pictographic (e.g., drawing blocks) responses and only much later can employ iconic (e.g., tallies) and symbolic (e.g., numerals such as 5) responses (Hughes, 1986).

Finally, the importance of mathematical language is underscored by the fact that the amount of teachers' math-related talk is significantly related to the growth of preschoolers' conventional mathematical knowledge over the school year (Klibanoff, Levine, Huttenlocher, Vasilyeva, & Hedges, 2006). Language is clearly deeply imbedded in mathematics learning and teaching.

Motivation for Learning Before the early school years, young children often exhibit play that entails mathematical concepts and explorations (Ginsburg, 2006); they can engage in meaningful mathematics activities and are motivated to do so. These young children generally begin schooling with positive motivation, self-confidence, and positive attitudes toward school. Yet in many cases students' motivation decreases within the first few years of school, most likely because of educational factors such as boring and inappropriate teaching (Arnold & Doctoroff, 2003, p. 521).

Mathematical Thinking and Socioeconomic Status

The literature reveals complex and interesting differences in mathematical thinking and learning related to socioeconomic status (SES). First, although lower-SES children's performance on informal addition and subtraction problems often lags behind that of middle-SES children, the two groups often employ similar strategies to solve problems (Ginsburg & Pappas, 2004). Second, although lower-SES children exhibit difficulty with *verbal* addition and subtraction problems, they perform as well as middle-SES children on *nonverbal* forms of these tasks (Jordan, Huttenlocher, & Levine, 1994). They do not lack the basic skills or concepts of addition and subtraction. Third, lower- and middle-SES children exhibit few, if any, differences in the everyday mathematics they spontaneously employ in free play (Ginsburg, Pappas, & Seo, 2001). In brief, although their cognitive skills are sometimes weak, low-SES children exhibit a good deal of competence on which ECME can build. Of particular concern should be the enhancement of language and metacognition.

Conclusions

In the ordinary environment, young children develop an everyday mathematics entailing a variety of topics, including space, shape and pattern, number, and operations on number. Their understanding is both concrete and abstract, involves both skills and concepts, and may be learned spontaneously as well as with adult assistance. Low-SES children show less proficient mathematical performance than do their middle-SES peers. Young children are motivated to learn and, even without much direct adult assistance, acquire some real mathematical skills and ideas. Learning mathematics is a "natural" and developmentally appropriate activity for young children—one that needs to be fostered formally in early education settings.

THE NEED FOR EARLY CHILDHOOD MATHEMATICS EDUCATION

The need for ECME is clear: American children's mathematics performance is below standard. On the *National Assessment of Educational Progress* (National Center for Education Statistics, 2007), 19% of fourth-grade children score "below basic," 43% are in the "basic" category, only 33% are "proficient," and only 6% are "advanced." Children from East Asia outperform their American counterparts in mathematics achievement, perhaps as early as preschool (Miller & Parades, 1996) or kindergarten (Stevenson, Lee, & Stigler, 1986), but certainly by the third or fourth grade, according to the *Trends in International Mathematics and Science Study* (TIMSS) (Lemke & Gonzales, 2006).

Given the findings of cognitive differences for low-SES children, it is not surprising to learn that the picture is especially bleak for disadvantaged children, namely those from poor and poorly educated families often living in unsafe neighborhoods and disproportionally composed of African Americans and Latinos (National Center for Children in Poverty, 2006). Unfortunately, the number of such children is disturbingly large: 6.1 million children, about 22% of the entire U.S. child population under 6, are from poor families (those falling below the official U.S. poverty line, which is extremely low) (Chau, Thampi, & Wight, 2010).

These findings are particularly concerning given that early math achievement differences are related to later performance. Examination of several large data sets (including the Early Childhood Longitudinal Study, Kindergarten [ECLS-K]) shows that early math test scores (at entry to school) predict later performance with considerable accuracy (Duncan et al., 2007).

Yet, regardless of SES, early education teachers often provide little math teaching at the preschool and kindergarten levels (Ginsburg, Lee, & Boyd, 2008) and the teaching that does take place frequently is of poor quality. "We can characterize these early education environments as socially positive but instructionally passive" (Pianta & La Paro, 2003, p. 28).

The bottom line is that early mathematics achievement sets the stage for overall achievement, but current teaching practices do not focus on mathematics sufficiently or provide quality mathematical experiences. These inadequacies place all children at a disadvantage, particularly low-SES students.

Several professional organizations (National Association for the Education of Young Children and National Council of Teachers of Mathematics, 2002) and the National Research Council (Cross, Woods, & Schweingruber, 2009) concur in recommending strong efforts to develop, evaluate, and implement strong programs of ECME. Early education has been shown to provide a foundation for later academic success (Bowman, Donovan, & Burns, 2001; Campbell, Pungello, Miller-Johnson, Burchinal, & Ramey, 2001; Reynolds & Ou, 2003), especially in the short term (Gormley, 2007) and arguably in the years thereafter (Ludwig & Phillips, 2007).

RTI has a special role to play in efforts to improve mathematics achievement. Current recommendations (Cross et al., 2009) stress Tier 1 innovative curriculum and intentional teaching. But ECME can benefit from further efforts to develop Tier 2 activities involving small groups and Tier 3 activities focusing on individual children experiencing severe math learning difficulties. Also, RTI needs to make a special effort to focus on low-SES children from preschool and beyond because they are at high risk of school failure.

THE GOALS OF EARLY CHILDHOOD MATHEMATICS EDUCATION

From the RTI perspective, the main and quite worthy goals of ECME should be to prepare young children, particularly those at risk of school failure, to perform well in school, and to help those children who are already failing to get on track for success. Achieving these goals is feasible: as we have seen, young children are ready to learn math; they have considerable mathematical understanding and interest on which RTI efforts can build.

But consider other goals. One is to help children, particularly those at risk of school failure, to look "smart." Unfortunately, teachers generally "have lower expectations and more negative perceptions of low-SES students than their higher-SES peers" (Arnold & Doctoroff, 2003, p. 522). If this is so, then one of the goals of RTI should be not only to improve students' work but to raise teachers' expectations about what children can do. Teachers need to realize that children can learn much more math than is typically assumed, and that given effective teaching, even children who are at risk of school failure can make substantial progress.

Although a focus on future performance is essential, another goal is to have students benefit from and enjoy current experience. Focusing too much on preparation for the future may introduce unnecessary pressure and anxiety on the part of both teacher and child, rob children of the joys of learning, and in the end produce only superficial success in the form of high achievement test scores.

THE NATURE OF EARLY CHILDHOOD MATHEMATICS EDUCATION

Fortunately, the cognitive and motivational research findings discussed previously point the way to the development of innovative Tier 1 programs of ECME that can set the stage for intensive Tier 2 and 3 interventions. These programs share several key features.

Broad and Deep Content

The mathematics young children need to learn is both broad and deep. True mathematics involves *broad* strands of "big ideas," such as number, geometry, measurement, and pattern. Each of these, in turn, entails interesting subtopics. For example, *number* covers such matters as the counting words ("one, two, three. . ."), the ordinal positions ("first, second, third. . ."), the idea of cardinal value ("How many are there?"), and the various operations on number such as addition and subtraction. *Shape* includes not only simple figures like circles and triangles, but also hexagons and octagons as well as solids (like cubes and cylinders), and symmetries in two and three dimensions. The topic of *spatial relations* includes ideas like position (in front of, behind), navigation ("first go three steps to the left") and mapping (for example, creating a schematic representing the location of objects in the classroom). *Pattern* includes interesting topics like repetition (ABB, ABB, ABB. . .) and different kinds of growth (e.g., a staircase increasing in height, one step at a time). Mathematics is broad in scope.

Early mathematics is also *deep*. For example, if you show a child a set of three objects—a red block, a toy dog, and a penny—you may ask the apparently simple question: "How many things are here?" To answer, the child obviously needs to know the counting words, "One, two, three. . ." But that's only the beginning. To be successful at "enumeration" (determining a set's numerical value), the child needs to understand several basic mathematical ideas.

One is that elements of any kind in a set can be counted. The set doesn't have to be composed of like objects. Counting is an enormously powerful tool that can be applied to any discrete real or imagined object.

A second idea is that each number word, such as "one, two, three. . . ," must be associated once and only once with each of the objects in the set. You point at the red block and say "one," the dog and say "two," and the penny and say "three." You cannot skip an object in the set. Each counting word must be in one-to-one correspondence with each element of the set.

A third idea is that the final number in the sequence, "three," does not refer to the penny alone. When you say "three" while pointing to the penny, the number word describes not that individual object but instead the whole group of objects— how many there are altogether, or the cardinal value.

Enumeration entails a very strange and distinctive use of language. In ordinary speech, we call an object a block or a dog or a penny because that is its name. But when we enumerate, the number name we assign to the objects does not refer to the individual object but to a very abstract property of the set as a whole. And that is just the beginning of the depth of the idea of cardinality.

Math Is Thinking

As the preceding example shows, early mathematics does not involve simply memorizing some number words. It must include *abstract thought*. Children need to learn to *reason* about number (if 2 and 3 is 5, then 3 and 2 must also be 5), making *inferences* (if we add something other than 0 to 3, the sum must be bigger than 3), and developing a *mental number line* (100 is much farther away from 2 than is 20). Understanding shape involves more than knowing a figure's name, although knowledge of correct mathematical vocabulary is certainly necessary. Children need to learn to analyze and construct shapes and to understand their defining features (Clements, 2004).

Metacognition and Mathematizing

Various *metacognitive* functions also play a key role in mathematics learning. Children need to learn to be aware of and verbalize their mathematical strategies. They need to be able to put their thinking into words so that they can communicate it to others and thus take their first steps toward joining a community that values (or should value) discussion, argument, and proof. Learning mathematics is in part learning expressive language.

Children also need eventually to *mathematize*—to conceive of problems in explicitly mathematical terms. For example, they will need to explicitly learn that when you want to determine the combined number of two sets, you should "add," and that the symbol + refers to adding. Young children should certainly not receive rote drill on memorizing symbols. They can learn to mathematize when they experience interesting problems in a rich context.

Positive Disposition

Learning math also involves feelings and motives. Unfortunately, many adults dislike math and avoid learning or teaching it. Indeed, some of our early child-hood education students—at Teachers College Columbia University and Adelphi University—say that they chose the profession *because* they would not have to teach mathematics, do not like mathematics, or feel they are not very good at it. To counter attitudes like these, ECME needs to teach not just the math, but also positive dispositions toward it. ECME needs to focus on promoting motivation, interest, initiative, persistence, and focused engagement in mathematical activities.

Curriculum and Teaching

Preschools often rely on play as the major and often only approach to ECME. The rationale is that play has many benefits for young and old alike (Singer, Golinkoff, & Hirsh-Pasek, 2006). Children have a good time when they play, it can help them to learn to interact with others and to develop self-regulation, it stimulates cognitive development, and it is true that children do indeed learn a good deal of everyday mathematics on their own in the course of free play (Seo & Ginsburg, 2004). This rationale further assumes that offering direct instruction in math concepts, especially within an organized curriculum, is inappropriate for young children.

But play is not enough. It does not by itself prepare children for school and usually does not help children to mathematize—to interpret their experiences in explicitly mathematical form and understand the relations between the two. Children will not learn many important aspects of mathematics unless teachers engage in intentional teaching. Deliberate instruction is a key part of ECME. "In high-quality mathematics education for 3- to 6-year-old children, teachers and other key professionals should. . .actively introduce mathematical concepts, methods, and language through a range of appropriate experiences and teaching strategies" (National Association for the Education of Young Children and National Council of Teachers of Mathematics, 2002, p. 4). Preschool teachers need to *teach* a math *curriculum*, which can be developmentally appropriate and even enjoyable.

What does early math teaching entail? Very little is known about it, partly because it is so seldom done. But like all teaching, it must involve at least under-standing the mathematics to be taught (Ball & Bass, 2000), understanding how children think about mathematics and learn it (Ginsburg, 2009), and understanding appropriate pedagogies (Ball, 1993; Lampert, 2001). Indeed, teaching mathematics at this level (and all others) is very complicated (Ginsburg & Amit, 2008).

What do we mean by a curriculum? It can be characterized as "a written instructional blueprint and set of materials for guiding students' acquisition of certain culturally valued concepts, procedures, intellectual dispositions, and ways of reasoning" (Clements, 2007, p. 36). A curriculum offers a carefully planned sequence of activities for the teaching of mathematics. The sequence should be based on knowledge of children's "learning trajectories" (Clements, Sarama, & DiBiase, 2004)—that is, the progression in which they normally learn mathematical concepts. And the sequence should provide young children with opportunities to engage in active, meaningful learning. Note that like anything else, the quality of curricula may vary: they may be good or bad or in between. But an early math curriculum is not necessarily developmentally inappropriate, rigid, or vapid.

An Example: Big Math for Little Kids

To get a "feel" for an ECME program, consider an example. *Big Math for Little Kids (BMLK)* is a prekindergarten (pre-K) and kindergarten curriculum developed with funding from the National Science Foundation (Ginsburg, Greenes, & Balfanz, 2003). The program incorporates several basic principles deriving from research, including the following:

- Young children are already engaged in learning (informal) mathematics. They do not need to be made ready to learn.

- Young children already possess many basic informal mathematical ideas upon which instruction can be built.

- Sensitive adult guidance and teaching—*not* a pushdown curriculum—can help children engage in complex forms of mathematics learning and realize their learning potential.

- Play is not enough. It is crucial to provide stimulating ECME for children—particularly low-income children—to build upon their everyday mathematical experiences and help them achieve their potential.

- The mathematics curriculum should stress not only basic ideas and procedures, but also the verbal expression of mathematical thinking. Low-income children in particular need help describing their mathematical thinking and making explicit their mathematical competence.

BMLK offers separate curricula for pre-K (roughly age 4) and kindergarten (age 5) children. At each age level, the curriculum is a systematic approach to teaching mathematics. *BMLK* offers a structured sequence of activities designed to promote challenging mathematical learning and related verbal expression. *BMLK* is designed for use at least 20–30 minutes each day of the week, for a total of approximately 32 weeks, the length of the typical academic year at these age levels (not counting holidays and the like). A teachers' guide describes the *BMLK* "lessons" in detail and helps teachers implement them in large groups, small groups, and with individual children. The lessons take the form of games, activities with manipulatives, explorations, stories, a very small amount of work with writing and reading mathematics, and various other activities.

The curriculum covers six units: number, shape, patterns and logic, measurement, number operations, and space. Each of these math concepts is first introduced in the pre-K curriculum and then further developed in the kindergarten curriculum. In addition to activities, each unit includes explicit learning goals and outcomes as well as formative assessments and follow-up. The program also provides activities and letters to be sent home to inform family members of the mathematical goals and ideas that are introduced and to involve family members in the learning process.

Each unit also addresses mathematical learning through literacy. Lessons include a list of mathematical terms that teachers should use, introduce to children, and encourage children to use. Also, each unit includes a storybook that engages the children in the mathematical ideas and utilizes the relevant vocabulary. Additionally, a black-and-white take-home version of the storybook is given to each child to share with their families.

EARLY CHILDHOOD MATHEMATICS
EDUCATION PROGRAMS AND THEIR EVALUATION

Several successful mathematics curricula and approaches drawing on contemporary research have been shown to produce learning gains in young children, although much more needs to be learned, particularly if the goal is to provide Tier 2 and 3 interventions.

BMLK has been described previously. Its evaluation (Lewis Presser, Ginsburg, Clements, & Ertle, under review) involved a 2-year longitudinal cluster-randomized control trial involving two groups, *BMLK* and a Business-as-Usual group that for the most part used *Creative Curriculum* (Dodge, Colker, & Heroman, 2002). The results showed that the *BMLK* group performed better than the comparison group, although the significant difference between the two groups did not emerge until the kindergarten year. The study also offered modest support for the proposition that *BMLK* children were more adept than the comparison children in employing both mathematical words and justifications.

Building Blocks (Clements & Sarama, 2007a) draws upon an extensive body of research on developmental trajectories to create materials "designed to help children extend and mathematize their daily activities, from building blocks . . . to art and stories" (Clements & Sarama, 2007c, p. 138). *Building Blocks* is probably the most extensively examined ECME program: several evaluations using cluster-randomized design and curriculum-based assessments attest to the effectiveness of the program (Clements & Sarama, 2008; Clements & Sarama, 2007c; Clements, Sarama, Spitler, Lange, & Wolfe, 2011).

The *Measurement-based Approach* (Sophian, 2004) was developed for teaching mathematics in the Head Start program. A small-scale evaluation "showed significant, albeit modest, positive effects of the intervention" (Sophian, 2004, p. 59). Sophian also noted that an indirect outcome of the program was to elevate teacher and parent expectations about preschool children's potential for learning mathematics.

The *Number Worlds* curriculum (Griffin, 2007) covers basic number concepts from preschool through sixth grade. The program, aimed primarily at low-SES children struggling in school, has shown promising results (pp. 390–392) in a small-scale evaluation.

The *Pre-K Mathematics Curriculum* (Klein, Starkey, & Ramirez, 2002) includes 29 small-group preschool classroom activities employing manipulatives and 18 home activities for parents to use with their children. Evaluation research employing cluster-randomized design and curriculum-based assessments showed impressive gains for low-SES children in the treatment group.

Storytelling Sagas (Casey, 2004) is a series of specially created supplementary mathematics storybooks for preschool through Grade 2. Each of the six books focuses on a different content area (such as space, pattern, or measurement) and combines oral storytelling with hands-on activities. Evaluations of the program are underway.

WHERE DO WE GO FROM HERE?

The evaluation research has shown that the various ECME programs are effective in varying degrees in achieving their goals. Yet there is still a great deal more to learn about the programs and about ECME generally. The evaluation research is not informative with respect to the relative power of different pedagogical techniques, activities, and materials, and to the ways in which they work. Sometimes the ECME curricula use small groups, and sometimes they use large ones. Sometimes the approach is relatively didactic and sometimes it is more open-ended. Sometimes the programs use games, and sometimes stories. Some programs use computers; most do not. Sometimes they do math as a stand-alone activity, and sometimes it is integrated into other activities.

There are many questions to ask about these practices. How effective are the various methods—games, manipulatives, stories, and the like—under various circumstances? How well do they work with different groups of children? How should different pedagogies (for example, directive versus open-ended or games versus lessons) be used in presenting the material? Questions about *why* and *how* various pedagogical techniques, activities, and materials work are of course central to the design of ECME in general and to RTI in particular. Yet the evaluation research is not designed to answer basic questions like these.

So where does that leave those of us who want to develop a sound RTI approach to early mathematics? Unlike curricula for Grade 1 and above, preschool ECME programs are not tied to a rigid system of textbook instruction. Because preschool education must deal with young children who vary in all kinds of abilities, and should take into account different ideas for appropriate instruction of these children, ECME programs typically offer a variety of activities and methods of teaching, ranging from large-group lessons to small-group activities, and often include games and manipulatives. The general approach of *BMLK*, for example, is to begin most topics with a large-group activity or even a story, and then to follow up with small-group activities. Furthermore, within each topic, activities are carefully arranged in order of increasing difficulty. In a sense, the program already offers both Tiers 1 and 2, albeit in an unsystematic way. Given this arrangement, the RTI developer can use or modify existing *BMLK* small-group (Tier 2) activities, and from them create Tier 3 activities. Then, much of the program development work can focus on when and how to introduce the different activities to students identified by screening instruments or other assessments as needing special help. Recent curriculum efforts provide a rich body of material from which developers can draw to create useful RTI materials. The new ECME curricula are grist for the RTI mill.

Support for this proposal is provided by Recognition & Response (R&R), an example of an RTI program adapted specifically for early childhood. R&R has shown promising results with literacy development in young children, and outlines a system that could be used broadly for all academic areas (Buysse & Peisner-Feinberg, 2010; Peisner-Feinberg, Buysse, Benshoff, & Soukakou, 2011). The R&R system is consistent with the features of RTI, including assessment, intervention, and progress monitoring. Most importantly, R&R emphasizes the use of high quality, research-based, developmentally appropriate curriculum and intentional teaching to provide instruction and develop targeted intervention. The previously described ECME curricula fit these criteria. In addition, R&R includes the beneficial practice of involving families in a collaborative problem-solving process with teachers and other professionals.

Finally, implementation of RTI materials can lead to fruitful research on targeted math instruction. Unlike most evaluation efforts, research on ECME through an RTI approach can help answer questions about the relative effectiveness of different activities for teaching specific topics, about which activities and approaches are effective for particular groups of children at different tiers, about how the activities work, and about the relative effectiveness of different approaches to teaching for different groups of students.

CONCLUSION

Researchers have produced an explosion of knowledge concerning the development of young children's math learning and thinking. Drawing on this knowledge, developers have created effective ECME programs that can relatively easily be modified for use at all three tiers of the RTI model. Development of and research on RTI programs in ECME could then lead to deeper understanding concerning the effects of specific activities and pedagogical techniques designed to target specific mathematical difficulties. These are efforts from which children at all tiers of RTI could benefit.

REFERENCES

Arnold, D.H., & Doctoroff, G.L. (2003). The early education of socioeconomically disadvantaged children. *Annual Review of Psychology, 54,* 517–545.

Ball, D.L. (1993). With an eye on the mathematical horizon: Dilemmas of teaching elementary school mathematics. *The Elementary School Journal, 93*(4), 373–397.

Ball, D.L., & Bass, H. (2000). Interweaving content and pedagogy in teaching and learning to teach: Knowing and using mathematics. In J. Boaler (Ed.), *Multiple perspectives on the teaching and learning of mathematics* (pp. 83–104). Westport, CT: Ablex.

Baroody, A.J., Lai, M., & Mix, K.S. (2006). The development of young children's early number and operation sense and its implications for early childhood education. In B. Spodek & O. Saracho (Eds.), *Handbook of research on the education of young children* (Vol. 2, pp. 187–221). Mahwah, NJ: Lawrence Erlbaum Associates.

Baroody, A.J., & Wilkins, J.L.M. (1999). The development of informal counting, number, and arithmetic skills and concepts. In J.V. Copley (Ed.), *Mathematics in the early years* (pp. 48–65). Reston, VA: National Council of Teachers of Mathematics.

Bloom, L. (1970). *Language development: form and function in emerging grammars.* Cambridge, MA: MIT Press.

Bowman, B.T., Donovan, M.S., & Burns, M.S. (Eds.). (2001). *Eager to learn: Educating our preschoolers.* Washington, DC: National Academy Press.

Brush, L.R. (1978). Preschool children's knowledge of addition and subtraction. *Journal for Research in Mathematics Education, 9,* 44–54.

Buysse, V., & Peisner-Feinberg, E. (2010). Recognition & Response: Response to intervention for pre–K. *Young Exceptional Children, 13*(4), 2–13.

Campbell, F.A., Pungello, E.P., Miller-Johnson, S., Burchinal, M.R., & Ramey, C.T. (2001). The development of cognitive and academic abilities: Growth curves from an early childhood education experiment. *Developmental Psychology, 37,* 231–242.

Casey, B. (2004). Mathematics problem-solving adventures: A language-arts–based supplementary series for early childhood that focuses on spatial sense. In D.H. Clements, J. Sarama, & A.-M. DiBiase (Eds.), *Engaging young children in mathematics: Standards for early childhood mathematics education* (pp. 377–389). Mahwah, NJ: Lawrence Erlbaum Associates.

Chau, M., Thampi, K., & Wight, V.R. (2010). *Basic facts about low-income children, 2009: Children under age 6.* New York, NY: National Center for Children in Poverty.

Clements, D.H. (1999). Geometric and spatial thinking in young children. In J.V. Copley (Ed.), *Mathematics in the early years* (pp. 66–79). Reston, VA: National Council of Teachers of Mathematics.

Clements, D.H. (2004). Geometric and spatial thinking in early childhood education. In D.H. Clements, J. Serama, & A.-M. DiBiase (Eds.), *Engaging young children in mathematics: Standards for early childhood mathematics education* (pp. 267–297). Mahwah, NJ: Lawrence Erlbaum Associates.

Clements, D.H. (2007). Curriculum research: Toward a framework for "research-based curricula." *Journal for Research in Mathematics Education, 38*(1), 35–70.

Clements, D.H., & Sarama, J. (2007a). *Building blocks—SRA real math, Grade PreK.* Columbus, OH: SRA/McGraw-Hill.

Clements, D.H., & Sarama, J. (2007b). Early childhood mathematics learning. In F.K. Lester (Ed.), *Second handbook of research on mathematics teaching and learning* (pp. 461–555). Charlotte, NC: Information Age Publishing.

Clements, D.H., & Sarama, J. (2007c). Effects of a preschool mathematics curriculum: Summative research on the Building Blocks project. *Journal for Research in Mathematics Education, 38*(2), 136–163.

Clements, D.H., & Sarama, J. (2008). Experimental evaluation of the effects of a research-based preschool mathematics curriculum. *American Educational Research Journal, 45,* 443–494.

Clements, D.H., Sarama, J., & DiBiase, A.-M. (Eds.). (2004). *Engaging young children in mathematics: Standards for early childhood mathematics education.* Mahwah, NJ: Lawrence Erlbaum Associates.

Clements, D.H., Sarama, J., Spitler, M.E., Lange, A.A., & Wolfe, C.B. (2011). Mathematics learned by young children in an intervention based on learning trajectories: A large-scale cluster randomized trial. *Journal for Research in Mathematics Education, 42*(2), 127–166.

Cross, C.T., Woods, T.A., & Schweingruber, H. (Eds.). (2009). *Mathematics learning in early childhood: Paths toward excellence and equity.* Washington, DC: National Academy Press.

Dodge, D.T., Colker, L., & Heroman, C. (2002). *The Creative Curriculum for preschool* (4th ed.). Washington, DC: Teaching Strategies, Inc.

Duncan, G.J., Dowsett, C.J., Claessens, A., Magnuson, K., Huston, A.C., & Klebanov, P. (2007). School readiness and later achievement. *Developmental Psychology, 43*(6), 1428–1446.

Geary, D.C. (1996). Biology, culture, and cross-national differences in mathematical ability. In R.J. Sternberg & T. Ben-Zeev (Eds.), *The nature of mathematical thinking* (pp. 145–171). Mahwah, NJ: Lawrence Erlbaum Associates.

Gelman, R. (1980). What young children know about numbers. *Educational Psychologist, 15,* 54–68.

Gelman, R., & Gallistel, C.R. (1986). *The child's understanding of number.* Cambridge, MA: Harvard University Press.

Ginsburg, H.P. (1989). *Children's arithmetic: How they learn it and how you teach it* (2nd ed.). Austin, TX: Pro Ed.

Ginsburg, H.P. (2006). Mathematical play and playful mathematics: A guide for early education. In D. Singer, R.M. Golinkoff, & K. Hirsh-Pasek (Eds.), *Play = Learning: How play motivates and enhances children's cognitive and social-emotional growth* (pp. 145–165). New York, NY: Oxford University Press.

Ginsburg, H.P. (2009). The challenge of formative assessment in mathematics education: Children's minds, teachers' minds. *Human Development, 52,* 109–128.

Ginsburg, H.P., & Amit, M. (2008). What is teaching mathematics to young children? A theoretical perspective and case study. *Journal of Applied Developmental Psychology, 29*(4), 274–285.

Ginsburg, H.P., Cannon, J., Eisenband, J.G., & Pappas, S. (2006). Mathematical thinking and learning. In K. McCartney & D. Phillips (Eds.), *Handbook of early child development* (pp. 208–229). Oxford, UK: Blackwell.

Ginsburg, H.P., Greenes, C., & Balfanz, R. (2003). *Big Math for Little Kids.* Parsippany, NJ: Dale Seymour Publications.

Ginsburg, H.P., Lee, J.S., & Boyd, J.S. (2008). Mathematics education for young children: What it is and how to promote it. *Social Policy Report—Giving Child and Youth Development Knowledge Away, 22*(1), 1–24.

Ginsburg, H.P., & Pappas, S. (2004). SES, ethnic, and gender differences in young children's informal addition and subtraction: A clinical interview investigation. *Journal of Applied Developmental Psychology, 25,* 171–192.

Ginsburg, H.P., Pappas, S., & Seo, K.-H. (2001). Everyday mathematical knowledge: Asking young children what is developmentally appropriate. In S.L. Golbeck (Ed.), *Psychological perspectives on early childhood education: Reframing dilemmas in research and practice* (pp. 181–219). Mahwah, NJ: Lawrence Erlbaum Associates.

Gormley, W.T. (2007). Early childhood care and education: Lessons and puzzles. *Journal of Policy Analysis & Management, 26*(3), 633–671.

Griffin, S. (2007). *Number Worlds: A mathematics intervention program for grades preK–6.* Columbus, OH: SRA/McGraw-Hill.

Groen, G., & Resnick, L.B. (1977). Can preschool children invent addition algorithms? *Journal of Educational Psychology, 69,* 645–652.

Hughes, M. (1986). *Children and number: Difficulties in learning mathematics.* Oxford, United Kingdom: Basil Blackwell.

Irwin, K., & Burgham, D. (1992). Big numbers and small children. *The New Zealand Mathematics Magazine, 29*(1), 9–19.

Jordan, N.C., Huttenlocher, L., & Levine, S.C. (1994). Assessing early arithmetic abilities: Effects of verbal and nonverbal response types on the calculation performance of middle- and low-income children. *Learning and Individual Differences, 6,* 413–432.

Klein, A., Starkey, P., & Ramirez, A. (2002). *Pre–K mathematics curriculum.* Glenview, IL: Scott Foresman.

Klibanoff, R.S., Levine, S.C., Huttenlocher, J., Vasilyeva, M., & Hedges, L.V. (2006). Preschool children's mathematical knowledge: The effect of teacher "math talk." *Developmental Psychology, 42*(1), 59–69.

Kuhn, D. (2000). Metacognitive development. *Current Directions in Psychological Science, 9*(5), 178–181.

Lampert, M. (2001). *Teaching problems and the problems of teaching.* New Haven, CT: Yale University Press.

Lemke, M., & Gonzales, P. (2006). *U.S. student and adult performance on international assessments of educational achievement: Findings from The Condition of Education 2006, U.S. Department of Education.* Washington DC: National Center for Educational Statistics.

Lewis Presser, A., Ginsburg, H.P., Clements, P., & Ertle, B. (under review). *Effects of a preschool and kindergarten mathematics curriculum: Big Math for Little Kids.*

Lipton, J.S., & Spelke, E.S. (2003). Origins of number sense: Large-number discrimination in human infants. *Psychological Science, 14*(5), 396–401.

Ludwig, J., & Phillips, D. (2007). The benefits and costs of Head Start. *Social Policy Report, 21*(3), 3–18.

Miller, K.F., & Parades, D.R. (1996). On the shoulders of giants: Cultural tools and mathematical development. In R.J. Sternberg & T. Ben-Zeev (Eds.), *The nature of mathematical thinking* (pp. 83–117). Mahwah, NJ: Lawrence Erlbaum Associates.

National Association for the Education of Young Children and National Council of Teachers of Mathematics. (2002). *Position statement. Early childhood mathematics: Promoting good beginnings.* Retrieved from http://www.naeyc.org/about/positions/psmath.asp

National Center for Children in Poverty. (2006). *Basic facts about low-income children: Birth to age 18.* New York, NY: Author.

National Center for Education Statistics. (2007). *National Assessment of Educational Progress.* Washington, DC. Retrieved from http://nces.ed.gov/pubsearch/pubsinfo.asp?pubid =2007494

Newcombe, N.S., & Huttenlocher, J. (2000). *Making space: The development of spatial representation and reasoning.* Cambridge, MA: MIT Press.

Peisner-Feinberg, E., Buysse, V., Benshoff, L., & Soukakou, E. (2011). Recognition & Response: Response to intervention for pre-kindergarten. In C. Groark, S.M. Eidelman, L. Kaczmarek, & S. Maude (Eds.), *Early childhood intervention: Shaping the future for children with special needs and their families, Vol. 3, Emerging trends in research and practice* (pp. 37–53). Santa Barbara, CA: Praeger.

Piaget, J. (1952). *The child's conception of number* (Trans. C. Gattegno & F.M. Hodgson). London, United Kingdom: Routledge & Kegan Paul Ltd.

Pianta, R.C., & La Paro, K. (2003). Improving early school success. *Educational Leadership, 60*(7), 24–29.

Reynolds, A.J., & Ou, S.-R. (2003). Promoting resilience through early childhood intervention. In S.S. Luthar (Ed.), *Resilience and vulnerability: Adaptation in the context of childhood adversities* (pp. 436–459). New York, NY: Cambridge University Press.

Saxe, G.B., Guberman, S.R., & Gearhart, M. (1987). Social processes in early number development. *Monographs of the Society for Research in Child Development, 52*(2, Serial No. 216).

Seo, K.-H., & Ginsburg, H.P. (2004). What is developmentally appropriate in early childhood mathematics education? Lessons from new research. In D.H. Clements, J. Sarama, & A.-M. DiBiase (Eds.), *Engaging young children in mathematics: Standards for early childhood mathematics education* (pp. 91–104). Hillsdale, NJ: Lawrence Erlbaum Associates.

Singer, D., Golinkoff, R.M., & Hirsh-Pasek, K. (Eds.). (2006). *Play = Learning: How play motivates and enhances children's cognitive and social-emotional growth.* New York, NY: Oxford University Press.

Sophian, C. (2004). Mathematics for the future: Developing a Head Start curriculum to support mathematics learning. *Early Childhood Research Quarterly, 19*(1), 59–81.

Stevenson, H., Lee, S.S., & Stigler, J. (1986). The mathematics achievement of Chinese, Japanese, and American children. *Science, 56,* 693–699.

Supporting Social and Emotional Development in Preschool Children

Carolyn Webster-Stratton and M. Jamila Reid

A school's ability to strengthen preschool children's emotional literacy and self-regulation, to problem-solve, to teach social behavior and encourage meaningful friendships, and to form positive partnerships with parents is crucial in providing the structural foundation and protective scaffolding necessary for children's eventual academic and school success (Webster-Stratton, 1999; Webster-Stratton & Herman, 2010). Research has indicated that children's emotional, social, and behavioral development is as important for promoting better school performance and academic learning as is their cognitive and academic preparedness (Raver et al., 2008; Reinke, Stormont, Herman, Puri, & Goel, 2010; Zins & Elias, 2006). Children who lack foundational social and emotion regulation skills are at high risk for impeded learning and academic difficulties in the classroom (Guerra & Bradshaw, 2008).

This chapter will address the development of emotional and social competence in the preschool years with the goals of 1) defining the components of emotional and social competence, 2) identifying core Tier 1 teaching practices that scaffold social-emotional development in a classroom setting, and 3) providing an overview of two evidence-based Incredible Years teacher training programs that have been shown to promote emotional and social learning and school readiness in young children.

DEFINING THE COMPONENTS OF EMOTIONAL AND SOCIAL COMPETENCE

From infancy onward, children participate in emotional and social interactions with caregivers that teach them how they are perceived by others as well as how to navigate social relationships and regulate their emotional responses. For most young children, the emotions, thoughts, and behaviors that will eventually result in emotional and social competence are learned through parent and teacher support, positive relationships, coaching strategies, trial-and-error experiences, proactive discipline, and repeated learning trials with new opportunities to be successful. For some children this learning comes relatively easily, as long as a supportive environment is provided. In other cases, a variety of child biological, developmental, and environmental risk factors impede, disrupt, or delay this learning and have been shown to be associated with increased social and behavioral problems (e.g., Coie & Dodge, 1998). However, skilled teachers can use numerous techniques to help students learn the myriad of discrete skills that make up social-emotional competence (Reinke & Herman, 2002). We begin by outlining the specific milestones that preschool children achieve in their emotional and social development.

Emotional Development

Just like walking, talking, and toilet training, regulating emotional responses is a developmental achievement that requires maturation of the immature brain. This ability is not present in the early years, and it must be learned. For babies, parents and child care providers play an integral role in helping the infant modulate her physiological state and reduce internal tension. For toddlers, the emotional regulatory system begins to shift from the caregivers to the child in conjunction with the development of language skills.

Emotional Literacy   One key developmental milestone for young children is the development of *emotional literacy,* which is defined as the ability to recognize and label emotions in oneself and others. By the age of 4, the average child in Head Start can label about three feelings: mad, sad, and happy (Webster-Stratton & Reid, 2005). The task of children over the next few years is to expand feeling recognition to include a much broader range of feelings—for example, proud, frustrated, excited, surprised, anxious, calm, brave, patient, and pleased. With each new feeling that children learn, the range of their possible responses expands. The task is twofold: first recognizing and labeling the feeling in oneself and then recognizing and naming it in others, and finally learning ways to think about and respond to these feelings. Becoming aware of one's feelings and beginning to verbalize them to others is the beginning of emotion regulation, for it is not until children recognize how they feel and can label the feeling that they can begin to learn strategies for talking about and regulating these emotions rather than acting them out physically. Understanding the feelings of others occurs as children learn to use facial cues, body language, verbal cues, and environmental cues to read others' emotions and to name them. This is the beginning of empathy development, for it is not until children can read and identify feelings in others that they can begin to respond appropriately to others' feelings (Decety & Meyer, 2008). For all children, emotional literacy, like other language development, is a developmental task that develops gradually throughout the toddler and preschool years and proceeds at its own individual pace.

For some children, developing emotional literacy is much more difficult and progresses at a much slower rate. Children at risk for behavior problems often have language delays and limited vocabulary to express their feelings, thus contributing to their difficulties regulating emotional responses (Frick et al., 1991; Kaiser, Hancock, Cai, Foster, & Hester, 2000). These children will need repeated practice recognizing and defining their own emotions as a beginning step. They will need to be taught specific cues to look for and feel in their own bodies and cues to look and listen for in others. They will need to have their own feelings and those of others validated and constantly labeled and coached as they experience or witness these feelings. They will need to talk about and role-play situations that commonly lead to particular feelings (Webster-Stratton & Reid, 2008a).

Because these children usually have received considerable attention for their negative emotions, teachers will need to emphasize and label regulated and positive emotions with greater frequency, noticing and providing attention when children are calm, patient, courageous, curious, persistent, proud, caring, and forgiving. When teachers notice dysregulated emotions in these children, they are advised to validate the feeling and then pair it with a coping strategy; for example, "You look frustrated, but your body is staying calm" or "I can see that you are angry, but I bet you will be able to use your words to tell me what is wrong."

Emotion Regulation As children develop emotional literacy, they can begin to learn how to regulate their emotional responses. Both positive and negative emotional states are gradually modulated so that the unrestrained exuberance or violent and aggressive temper tantrums typical of the toddler years are replaced by positive and negative affect and verbal responses that are more often appropriate to the situation and are paired with coping thoughts and prosocial behavioral responses that help the child receive the positive attention he or she needs. For example, a preschooler may jump up and down with a peer to show excitement, or may be able to say, "That's mine. I had it first," instead of exploding into a temper tantrum or hitting to get what he wants. Again, this is a developmental journey that progresses unevenly. Even a well-regulated child will occasionally lose control, and it is developmentally normal for some children to learn these emotion regulation skills more quickly than others, just as some children learn to walk or talk earlier than others.

Self-Management An important result of emotion regulation is the ability of children to eventually self-manage or self-regulate their own emotions and behavior. As children develop this skill, they are able to integrate their emotional responses into the expected behavior for different situations and to respond in ways that allow them to work effectively in a variety of different situations. Children who are good self-managers can work independently, with less need for constant supervision from teachers, and can adapt their behaviors to fit the needs of different situations. They eventually learn to self-evaluate and to provide themselves with feedback for their own performance, as well as to self-correct or self-congratulate. Although development of self-management takes many years and will vary with the age, developmental ability, and temperament of the child, teachers can begin to foster and teach some of the beginning skills of self-regulation even to preschool children.

One of the central features of children with behavior problems is the absence of self-management skills. They are easily frustrated, impulsive, find it hard to persist with something that requires concentration, and become easily discouraged. Children with emotion regulation difficulties need to be targeted for learning a series of sequentially mastered small steps leading to eventual self-management skills (e.g., emotional language, deep breathing, positive self-talk, positive imagery methods, waiting skills, positive social behaviors). Teachers must also realize that these children will need more external teacher scaffolding and supports than will their more regulated peers.

Social Skills

Specific teaching of social skills builds on the scaffolding provided by the teacher's emotion coaching as well as the child's development of language skills. Emotional literacy and self-regulation develop gradually as children proceed at their own pace.

Friendship Skills   Few teachers need to be convinced that friendships are important for young children. Through the successful formation of friendships, children learn social skills such as cooperation, sharing, helping, waiting, and taking turns; friendly communication skills such as suggesting, asking, and complimenting; and conflict management strategies (Howes, 2000). Friendships also foster a child's sense of group belonging and connectedness and begin to facilitate children's empathy skills—that is, their ability to understand another's perspective. The formation (or absence) of friendships has been shown to have an enduring impact on the child's emotional, social, and academic adjustment in later life (Burgess, Wojslawowicz, Rubin, Rose-Krasnor, & Booth-LaForce, 2006; Roza, Hofstra, Van der Ende, & Verhulst, 2003).

For some young children, making friends is not easy. Researchers have found that children who have a more difficult temperament—including hyperactivity, impulsivity, and inattention—have particular difficulty forming and maintaining friendships (Brown, Odom, & McConnell, 2008; Campbell, 1994; Pope, Bierman, & Mumma, 1989). These children have significantly delayed play skills that include difficulties waiting their turn, accepting their peers' suggestions, offering an idea rather than demanding something, or collaborating in play with peers (Webster-Stratton & Lindsay, 1999). Consequently, these children need explicit teaching of a repertoire of friendly behaviors such as ability to agree with others, being a team player, giving compliments, and apologizing.

Problem-Solving Skills   The first step to problem solving involves the ability to recognize when one has a problem. This awareness is linked with feeling identification; that is, a negative or uncomfortable feeling usually indicates that there is a problem. Good problem solvers eventually are able to articulate, define, and understand the problem; look at it from other points of view; generate possible prosocial solutions to the problem; think ahead to evaluate the consequences of different solutions; select the best solution; put a solution into action; and then reflect on the outcome of that solution for possible use in the future. There is evidence that children who employ appropriate problem-solving strategies play more constructively, are better liked by their peers, and are more cooperative at home and school. This complex problem-solving sequence requires a high degree of cognitive self-awareness, emotional control, forward thinking, and self-reflection that will likely take many years to develop. In the preschool years, children will begin to learn to identify and verbalize a feeling and a problem and to think about a possible prosocial solution. Some preschoolers will be able to independently use simple solutions (e.g., ask for a toy, wait for a turn), but many will need teacher assistance and coaching with problem-solving interactions, especially when their first solution does not work (e.g., when their request for a toy is refused). Children who are temperamentally more difficult—that is, hyperactive, impulsive, or inattentive—have been shown to have cognitive impairments in key aspects of social problem solving

(Beauchaine, Neuhaus, Brenner, & Gatzke-Kopp, 2008; Dodge & Crick, 1990). Consequently, these students need more teacher guidance and additional supportive scaffolding to generate and practice prosocial solutions to their problems and to evaluate which solutions are more likely to lead to positive consequences.

Importance of Emotional and Social Teaching in Tier 1

All children are helped to learn and achieve emotional and social maturity through the guidance and teaching of others, and all children can benefit from focused teacher attention, social and emotional coaching, and curricula to strengthen these skills. For children with a more difficult temperament and developmental delays (e.g., hyperactivity, impulsivity, and inattention; language and learning delays) or for those children whose home environment has not supported emotional and social development, an intense school and teacher focus on the development of these skills will be crucial for assuring the healthy development of social skills, emotion regulation, conflict management, and making friends (e.g., Coie & Dodge, 1998; Dodge & Price, 1994).

Teaching emotional and social skills, particularly to children who are at risk because of biological and temperament factors or because of family or environmental risk factors, is likely to be most effective when offered as early as possible in children's development and school learning experience. The goal is to target intervention *before* children have developed secondary risk factors such as social rejection, loneliness, formation of deviant peer groups, school absences, and a history of negative teacher and parental responses to their disruptive behaviors (Johnston & Mash, 2001). Because development of these emotional and social skills is not automatic, particularly for higher risk children, more explicit and intentional teaching in the preschool and early school-age period (2–6 years) is strategic (Bredekamp & Copple, 1997). Moreover, some research has shown that involving parents in this teaching adds to the impact of the outcomes (Kumpfer, Alvarado, Tait, & Turner, 2002; Reid, Webster-Stratton, & Hammond, 2007; Webster-Stratton, Reid, & Hammond, 2004).

Core Tier 1 Teaching Practices
Associated with Social-Emotional Development

Although specific emotional and social curricula enhance children's development in this area, general teaching classroom management strategies and practices as well as the overall classroom environment and teacher–student–family relationships also support children's optimal emotional, social, and academic development. Research points to key teacher risk factors related to the development of academic underachievement, social-emotional difficulties, and conduct problems (Brophy, 1996; Conroy & Sutherland, 2008; Walker, 1995). Poor classroom management skills such as low rates of praise and harsh discipline, negative teacher–student–parent relationships, failure to focus on teaching curricula that build emotional and social competence, and poor efforts to promote home–school collaboration are all linked to escalating aggression, peer rejection, and poor academic performance (Brophy, 1996; Conroy & Sutherland, 2008; Simonsen & Fairbanks, 2008; Walker, 1995). Considerable research has demonstrated that teachers' use of effective classroom management strategies can reduce disruptive behavior and enhance emotional, social, and academic achievement and school readiness skills (Conroy & Sutherland, 2008; Webster-Stratton, Reid, & Stoolmiller, 2008). Unfortunately, many teachers simply are not adequately supported to manage the escalating number of behavior problems in the classroom; some even enter the workforce without having taken a single course on behavior management or cognitive social learning theory (Barrett & Davis, 1995; Evertson & Weinstein, 2006; Houston & Williamson, 1992). Very few teachers have been trained to deliver evidence-based emotional literacy, social skills, and problem-solving curricula or to collaborate successfully with parents. Surveys indicate that many schools do not use evidence-based emotional and social curricula or use them with poor fidelity (Gottfredson & Gottfredson, 2002).

OPTIMAL TEACHING STRATEGIES AND PRACTICES TO SUPPORT SOCIAL-EMOTIONAL DEVELOPMENT

The next section outlines key teaching elements that are necessary to support children's emotional, social, and academic success. The model, which is derived from cognitive social learning theory (Bandura, 1986), is pulled from the *Incredible Years (IY) Series Teacher Classroom Management Program,* an empirically validated teacher training program (Webster-Stratton, 1994; Webster-Stratton & Reid, 2008b). For detailed descriptions of these classroom management strategies, see *Incredible Teachers: Nurturing Children's Social, Emotional and Academic Competence* (Webster-Stratton, 2012).

Using the Incredible Years Teaching Pyramid as the Road Map for Content

The Incredible Years Teaching Pyramid serves as the road map for effective teacher strategies content (see Figure 17.1). The teaching pyramid describes the program's components and helps teachers conceptualize effective and supportive classroom environments. The bottom of the pyramid depicts teacher behaviors and activities that should be liberally applied because they provide the foundation needed for children to learn other skills and behaviors. The base of the pyramid encompasses building positive relationships with students; providing positive attention; adhering to specific academic, persistence, social, and emotional coaching methods; and maintaining warm and friendly communication with students and families. Other skills further up the pyramid include offering specific praise, providing incentive programs, and celebrating successes. A basic premise of the model is that a positive relationship foundation precedes discipline strategies, and attention to positive opposite behaviors should occur far more frequently in effective classroom environments than attention to negative behaviors. Only when this positive foundation is in place do higher aspects on the pyramid function successfully. The discipline part of the model includes starting with the least intrusive methods such as the use of distraction, redirection, and clear limit setting; ignoring inappropriate behaviors; using time-out to help students calm down from aggressive behaviors; and administering logical consequences (a method that is used sparingly). The left side of the pyramid focuses on teaching students problem-solving and conflict management strategies, as well as helping them develop emotional literacy, self-regulation, and self-management

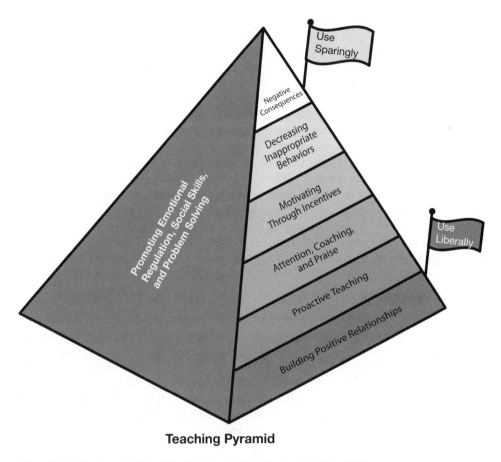

Teaching Pyramid

Figure 17.1. The Incredible Years® Teaching Pyramid™. © The Incredible Years 2009.

skills. Teachers are encouraged to use their professional judgment, including their knowledge of their classroom and their students, to make decisions on a moment-to-moment basis about how the principles on the pyramid will be enacted in their class. The pyramid also provides a foundation for flexible adherence to program principles. However, only when the positive foundation is in place do strategies higher on the pyramid work well.

Building Positive Relationships with Parents

The foundation of the Teaching Pyramid is based on the premise that teachers ought to work with the parents of their students in a collaborative, nonblaming, and nonhierarchical model that involves forming a partnership to support students in learning classroom and school readiness skills at home, to address children's developmental issues, and to develop behavior plans. This home–school partnership is crucial in helping support students across environments to enhance their emotional, social, academic, and language learning (Battistich, Schaps, & Wilson, 2004; Chavkin & Williams, 1988).

Building Positive Relationships with Students

The importance of building trusting, sensitive, responsive, and nurturing teacher–student relationships should not be underestimated. Perhaps the most obvious reason for teachers to develop meaningful relationships with preschool children is that a positive teacher–student relationship built on trust, caring, and understanding of the child's developmental stage, temperament style, and particular family situation will foster students' cooperation, motivation, and school readiness skills, thereby increasing their eventual learning and achievement at school (O'Connor, Dearing, & Collins, 2011). Relationship-building is especially vital for students who come from stressful home environments or from situations where they have been neglected or abused. These children often do not feel secure or confident and may react by being aggressive, noncompliant, shy, withdrawn, or depressed. In other words, the preschoolers who are hardest to reach are those who will benefit most from a nurturing relationship with their teachers that begins as early as possible.

Proactive Teaching

When students are disruptive it is easy for teachers to automatically react emotionally. This understandable impatience and frustration in response to negative behavior undermines a teacher's ability to think strategically about the most effective response to the child's behavior. Instead of reacting in this way, teachers can learn to anticipate the kinds of classroom conditions that are likely to produce disruptive or disengaged behaviors and take *proactive* steps to prevent them. Research has shown that proactive teachers structure the classroom environment and the school day in ways that make children feel connected, safe, and joyful so that problem behaviors are less likely to occur (Battistich et al., 2004; Doll, Zucker, & Brehm, 2004; Good & Brophy, 1994). Fun, playful school activities utilizing imaginative play and promoting curious discovery as well as clear rules and schedules, predictable routines, job responsibilities, consistent limit setting, and norms of behavior help students know the expectations for the classroom and create an environment conducive to learning (Jones & Jones, 2004).

Promoting Social Competence: Coaching, Praise, and Teacher Attention

The quality of the teacher's attention, coaching, and praise emerges as one of the most important factors in helping young children become motivated and successful learners. Consistent and meaningful encouragement, coaching, and praise from a teacher nurtures and increases children's emotional and social competence and academic readiness (Reinke & Lewis-Palmer, 2008). Children who are coached are self-confident, have high self-esteem, and seem to internalize these early messages so as not to need them in the future (Cameron & Pierce, 1994). Child-directed descriptive commenting (Hanf & Kling, 1973) during children's play and work experiences is associated with better emotional social adjustment and academic outcomes for students. Descriptive commenting is a running commentary used to describe the children's behaviors, thoughts, feelings, interests, and activities. It includes describing actions as well as the appearance and positions of the objects they are playing with. Descriptive commenting bathes the child in language, providing important verbal information about behavior and the objects being played with. It also directs positive attention (and reinforcement) to whatever aspect of the play that the commenting focuses on. Thus, descriptive commenting can be delivered strategically and tailored to meet a number of academic, social, emotional, and other behavioral goals according to children's needs and developmental levels. Teachers can adjust the focus of their descriptive commenting to cover *academic and persistence coaching*, which fosters children's language development and sustained attention so that they can continue to work hard even if a task is frustrating to learn, or *social and emotional coaching*, which fosters friendship skills, self-regulation, and emotional literacy (Webster-Stratton & Reid, 2009). More details regarding these four coaching methods can be found in the book *Incredible Teachers* (Webster-Stratton, 2012).

Using Incentives

One way to make learning tangible is to use incentives such as stickers, special rewards, and celebrations to give students concrete evidence of their progress. Incentives also provide extra motivation for children to tackle a difficult learning area, and can sustain a child's motivation until a positive relationship has been developed with the teacher that will make praise and attention more motivating. Positive results from using such incentive programs have ranged from increasing classroom participation, on-task work, and attention (Jones & Jones, 2007), to promoting cooperative behaviors and improving academic outcomes (Nevin & Johnson, 1982), to decreasing transition time (Yarbrough & Skinner, 2004), reducing talk-outs and out-of-seat behavior (Barrish & Saunders, 1969; Embry, 2002), as well as decreasing more serious behavior problems (see, e.g., Rhode, Jenson, & Reavis, 1992). For preschool children, spontaneous and immediate rewards such as hand stamps, stickers, getting to line up first, choosing a story to be read to the class, or performing a special job are preferred to the more complex reward systems used with older children.

Managing Misbehavior

Even when the best teacher-proactive classroom management is in place, misbehavior will still occur. A discipline plan that clearly spells out rules, expectations, and consequences if the rules are broken is fundamental to successful management of disruptive behaviors. These plans should be organized in a hierarchy from the *least* disruptive intervention to the most disruptive. The consistency of the teachers' follow-through with this discipline plan increases children's sense of security and trust. A classroom discipline plan will address the needs of most children. However, for children who exhibit higher than normal levels of disruptive or withdrawn classroom behavior, individual behavior plans must tailor strategies to meet each student's developmental needs. Behavior plans should be designed collaboratively with parents and begin by drawing from strategies at the bottom of the teaching pyramid (coaching and building relationships) and progressing to appropriate, proactive discipline strategies as the foundation is well developed (Gable, Hester, Rock, & Hughes, 2009).

Ignoring Misbehavior and Using Redirection

Research has shown planned ignoring to be extremely effective in reducing inappropriate behavior in young children (Hall & Lund, 1968; Madsen & Becker, 1968). Planned ignoring occurs when the teacher systematically withholds attention or ignores the targeted negative behavior until it stops and then immediately returns her attention to the positive opposite behaviors. In one sense ignoring misbehavior is unnatural, for there is a natural tendency for teachers to attend to students who are out of their seat or being disruptive or argumentative. However, teacher attention only reinforces such behavior. Ignoring can be a powerful tool for modifying behavior because it deprives the child of the attention all children want.

Natural and Logical Consequences

No matter how consistently teachers use ignoring, redirecting, warnings, and reminders to deal with inappropriate classroom behavior, and no matter how consistently they coach and reinforce appropriate behavior, preschool children will continue to misbehave. This is a necessary part of their developmental drive for independence and curious exploration of the limits of their environment. In these cases, their misbehavior needs to be dealt with by imposing a brief, immediate, and consistent discipline response so that children can learn the connection between their own behaviors and positive and negative consequences.

A negative (logical or natural) consequence is something the child does not want, such as being last in line, losing a few minutes of recess, missing free time, or being denied a special activity or a privilege. Consequences do not have to be severe to be effective. In fact, the key is brevity and immediacy, not severity. Consequences are most effective when they are applied immediately, consistently, and uniformly when misbehavior occurs. This ensures that students understand and can predict the consequences for their actions, and that they perceive that the teacher uses them fairly. Consequences will only be effective when they are followed immediately by a new learning trial to be successful accompanied by teacher coaching and praise.

Managing Misbehavior: Time-Out

The top of the discipline hierarchy involves consequences for students who display behavior that is aggressive, out of control, or hurtful to someone else. These behaviors cannot be ignored and often occur when a preschooler is too dysregulated to respond to another consequence or to be amenable to problem-solving approaches. Time-out or the calm-down strategy is reserved specifically for these high-intensity problems. It is also useful for highly noncompliant, oppositional, or defiant children, because compliance is the cornerstone of a parent's or teacher's ability to socialize a child. Time-out to calm down is probably the most intrusive short-term consequence a teacher will employ for disruptive behavior, as sending a child home or to the principal's office is counterproductive to the child's learning. A teacher's effective use of time-out models a nonviolent and calm response to conflict, stops the conflict and frustration and attention for misbehavior, provides a "cooling off" or calming-down period for students and teachers, and maintains a respectful, trusting relationship in which children feel they can be honest with their teachers about their problems and mistakes. Time-out also allows children to practice the calm-down strategies they have been taught, such as deep breathing, positive imagery, and self-talk, and it encourages them to reflect on other solutions that are safer and lead to better feelings. If time-out steps are practiced in advance as part of the school classroom rules and delivered with respect, this approach enhances children's development of self-regulation skills, promotes a sense of safety, and builds an internal sense of responsibility. Effective time outs are brief—no longer than 3–4 minutes for preschoolers—and end when the student is calm and ready to rejoin the group.

Moving Beyond Discipline: Repair and Rebuild

Young children who are impulsive, oppositional, inattentive, and aggressive will need constant teacher scaffolding and targeted coaching. This also means providing redirections, warnings, reminders, and consistent follow-through and monitoring. However, one of the hardest and most important things for a teacher to do when teaching a disruptive child is to move beyond discipline to repair and rebuild positive teacher–student, student–student, and teacher–parent relationships. Teachers need strategies to help move past an unpleasant encounter with a child and to let go of grudges and resentments after consequences have been implemented.

Moving to Self-Management and Social-Emotional Maturity

Difficult and aggressive preschoolers will initially need tight external management, coaching, incentives, and consistent proactive discipline in order to keep their behavior under control. Indeed, research has indicated that evidence-based classroom management strategies result in decreased negative classroom behaviors and increased positive social skills. However, as children develop their emotional and social skills, teachers must work toward the eventual goal of shifting from exclusive teacher external management to increasing student self-management. This is necessary so that students can become less dependent on teachers to provide direction and incentives for their behavior. Such an approach produces more durable and generalizable behavior gains in situations outside the classroom, but for some children, particularly those who are at high risk for problems, it may take many years to achieve competence in emotion regulation and social skills and an ability to self-evaluate.

Summary of Teaching Strategies

Teachers who are skilled in positive classroom management and patient with varying rates of developmental progress will be able to provide a classroom environment that is most conducive to students' learning. Students will feel confident and secure in their relationships with the teacher and their peers, their familiarity with classroom expectations and rules, and their awareness of the consequences if those rules are broken. When teachers provide an environment that supports each student's emotional and social development, they are also setting the stage for effective and optimal academic learning.

OVERVIEW OF TWO EVIDENCE-BASED INCREDIBLE YEARS TEACHER TRAINING PROGRAMS THAT PROMOTE EMOTIONAL AND SOCIAL LEARNING IN YOUNG CHILDREN

Supporting teachers and students in learning and applying the skills outlined in this chapter must be part of a strategic and thoughtful plan, using curricula with proven efficacy. Webster-Stratton and colleagues have developed and researched a set of empirically validated programs designed to assist teachers to support young children's social-emotional development and reduce early-onset conduct problems (Webster-Stratton & Reid, 2010; Webster-Stratton, Reid, & Hammond, 2001, 2004). One such program, *The Incredible Years Teacher Classroom Management Program* (*IY TCM*) (Webster-Stratton, 1994), is designed to provide teachers with the necessary classroom management strategies (outlined previously) to effectively manage challenging behaviors while supporting optimal emotional, social, and academic learning for all students. Information about the training and the delivery of the program can be found elsewhere (Reinke, Stormont, Webster-Stratton, Newcomer, & Herman, in press; Webster-Stratton & Herman, 2010; Webster-Stratton, Reinke, Herman, & Newcomer, 2011). A second program, the *IY Dinosaur School*, is a classroom curriculum for preschool to second-grade students that is targeted toward building children's emotional literacy, empathy or perspective taking, friendship and communication skills, anger management, interpersonal problem solving, and strategies needed for academic success (Webster-Stratton & Reid, 2008a, 2008b). These elements are widely acknowledged foundational response to intervention (RTI) instructional principles and provide a social-emotional curriculum that is believed to be a core component of transformational teaching in the early years of children's development. The remainder of this chapter will provide a brief research summary and description of these two programs as examples of specific school-based interventions. Both programs have been researched as selective prevention interventions for entire classrooms (in schools where 60% or more of the student population belongs to families living in poverty) as well as targeted interventions for students who display higher levels of behavior problems.

Research on the Incredible Years Teacher Classroom Management and Dinosaur School Programs

The teacher training program is a 6-day (or 42-hour) group format program delivered monthly throughout the year for teachers, school counselors, and psychologists. The IY TCM program has been evaluated in treatment studies training involving teachers whose classes include preschool and early school-age students with diagnosed oppositional defiant disorder (Webster-Stratton et al., 2004) as well as schoolwide selective prevention training of Head Start and early primary grade classroom teachers (Webster-Stratton, Reid, & Hammond, 2001). The TCM training model adheres to the teaching pyramid described in this chapter, focusing first on strategies for enhancing relationships with students, setting up a proactive learning environment, and increasing students' emotional and social competencies. When this foundation is in place, teachers discuss strategies for reducing negative behaviors using the least intrusive discipline possible. These strategies are applied within a problem-solving framework in which teachers are teaching and reinforcing students for using specific prosocial and emotion regulation skills. Results indicated that trained teachers were rated by independent classroom observers as less critical, harsh, and inconsistent, as well as more nurturing than teachers in a control group. Observations also indicated significant reductions in children's aggressive behaviors with peers and teachers and improvements in school readiness behaviors and prosocial skills compared with controls. Independent replications have supported these results in the United States (Carlson, Tiret, Bender, & Benson, 2011; Raver et al., 2008; Shernoff & Kratochwill, 2007; Williford & Shelton, 2008), Wales (Hutchings et al., 2007), and Jamaica (Baker-Henningham & Walker, 2009). IY TCM has also been investigated as a standalone self-administered training program with preschool teachers (Shernoff & Kratochwill, 2007) that produces positive effects.

The classroom Dinosaur School program is designed for children in preschool through second grade (with different lesson plans for each age group). The curriculum lessons are delivered two to three times per week throughout the school year (60 lessons per year) in the format of a large-group circle time lesson followed by a small-group activity designed to give students a chance to practice the skills taught during the circle time. The curriculum specifically targets the key components of social-emotional development outlined previously in this chapter (emotional development, self-management, and social/problem-solving skills). Teachers coach, praise, and reinforce curriculum skills taught at other times throughout the day. Research evaluating the classroom Dinosaur program in Head Start and early elementary classrooms found improvements in children's conduct problems, self-regulation, social competence, and school readiness skills among students who received the intervention in comparison with control-group students who were not involved in the program. Effect size comparing treatment versus control groups post assessment showed the intervention had small to moderate effects on children whose baseline behavior was in the average range but had large effects on children with high initial levels of conduct problems (Webster-Stratton et al., 2008).

For children who need more intensive treatment intervention, there is a separate small-group, pullout Dinosaur treatment curriculum that is offered once or twice a week for a total of 30–40 hours (Webster-Stratton & Reid, 2005). This Dinosaur child intervention has been validated by itself and in combination with the Incredible Years parent and teacher interventions in three randomized research trials for children with diagnoses of oppositional defiant disorder (ODD) or attention deficit hyperactivity disorder (ADHD) or with high levels of internalizing problems (Borden, Herman, Reinke, & Webster-Stratton, in press; Drugli & Larsson, 2006; Webster-Stratton & Hammond, 1997; Webster-Stratton, Reid, & Beauchaine, 2011; Webster-Stratton et al., 2004). Results have shown reductions in externalizing and internalizing behavior problems and increases in emotion regulation, social competence, and problem-solving skills, according to teacher and parent reports and independent observations in the classrooms. Nonetheless, the largest effect sizes in children's behavior change are brought about when the Incredible Years parent program is offered in combination with child and teacher interventions (Reid et al., 2007; Webster-Stratton et al., 2004).

SUMMARY

In this chapter we have defined core elements of emotional and social development in preschool children and described foundational Tier 1 teaching practices that support the development of these important skills. The two teacher and child evidence-based curricula reviewed are designed to specifically target each of these important teaching practices and promote the development of children's emotional and social skills. The IY TCM program provides teachers with the essential skills to set up successful, nurturing relationships; create a positive classroom environment; and decrease levels of behavior problems while fostering positive prosocial replacement behaviors. The Dinosaur School curriculum also works to eliminate disruptive child behaviors and to explicitly teach children emotion self-regulation skills, prosocial friendship behaviors, and problem-solving strategies. The programs can be used at Tier 1 on a schoolwide basis to enhance the emotional, social, and academic development of young children (Webster-Stratton & Herman, 2010) and to prevent behavior problems from developing in the classroom. For children who need more intensive (Tier 2) intervention, the small-group Dinosaur treatment curriculum can be offered as a pullout program twice a week and, if combined with the Incredible Years parenting intervention, would promote teacher–parent partnerships and cross-setting consistency in strategies used to address the child's goals. Teacher partnerships with parents provide coordinated scaffolding and together offer incredible potential for providing all children with the opportunity to attain an education that addresses their social and emotional trajectories as well as their academic achievement.

REFERENCES

Baker-Henningham, H., & Walker, S. (2009). A qualitative study of teachers' perceptions of an intervention to prevent conduct problems in Jamaican pre-schools. *Child: Care, Health, and Development, 35,* 632–642.

Bandura, A. (1986). *Social foundations of thought and action.* Englewood Cliffs, NJ: Prentice-Hall.

Barrett, E.R., & Davis, S. (1995). Perceptions of beginning teachers' needs in classroom management. *Teacher Education and Practice, 11,* 22–27.

Barrish, H.H., & Saunders, M. (1969). Good behavior game: Effects of individual contingencies for group consequences on disruptive behavior in a classroom. *Journal of Applied Behavior Analysis, 2*(2), 119–124.

Battistich, V., Schaps, E., & Wilson, N. (2004). Effects of an elementary school intervention in students "connectiveness" to school and social adjustment during middle school. *The Journal of Primary Prevention, 24,* 243–262.

Beauchaine, T.P., Neuhaus, E., Brenner, S.L., & Gatzke-Kopp, L. (2008). Ten good reasons to consider biological processes in prevention and intervention research. *Development and Psychopathology, 20,* 745–774.

Borden, L.A., Herman, K.C., Reinke, W.M., & Webster-Stratton, C. (in press). The impact of the Incredible Years Parent, Child and Teacher Training Programs on children's co-occurring internalizing symptoms. *School Psychology Quarterly.*

Bredekamp, S., & Copple, C. (1997). *Developmentally appropriate practice in early childhood programs.* Washington, DC: NAEYC.

Brophy, J.E. (1996). *Teaching problem students.* New York, NY: Guilford Press.

Brown, W.H., Odom, S.L., & McConnell, S.R. (2008). *Social competence of young children: Risk, disability, and intervention.* Baltimore, MD: Paul H. Brookes Publishing Co.

Burgess, K.B., Wojslawowicz, J.C., Rubin, K.H., Rose-Krasnor, L., & Booth-LaForce, C. (2006). Social information processing and coping strategies of shy/withdrawn and aggressive children: Does friendship matter? *Child Development, 77,* 371–383.

Cameron, J., & Pierce, W.D. (1994). Reinforcement, reward, and intrinsic motivation: A meta-analysis. *Review of Educational Research, 64,* 363–423.

Campbell, S.B. (1994). Hard-to-manage preschool boys: Externalizing behavior, social competence, and family context at two-year followup. *Journal of Abnormal Child Psychology, 22*(2), 147–166.

Carlson, J.S., Tiret, H.B., Bender, S.L., & Benson, L. (2011). The influence of group training in the Incredible Years teacher classroom management program on preschool teachers' classroom management strategies. *Journal of Applied School Psychology, 27*(2), 134–154.

Chavkin, N.F., & Williams, D.L. (1988). Critical issues in teacher training for parent involvement. *Educational Horizons, 66*, 87–89.

Coie, J.D., & Dodge, K.A. (1998). Aggression and antisocial behavior. In W. Damon & N. Eisenberg (Eds.), *Handbook of child psychology: Social, emotional and personality development* (5th ed., Vol. 3, pp. 779–862). New York, NY: Wiley.

Conroy, M., & Sutherland, K. (2008). Preventing and ameliorating young children's chronic problem behaviors: An ecological classroom-based approach. *Psychology in the Schools, 46*(1), 3–17.

Decety, J., & Meyer, M. (2008). From emotion resonance to empathic understanding: A social developmental neuroscience account. *Development and Psychopathology, 20*, 1053–1080.

Dodge, K.A., & Crick, N.R. (1990). Social information processing bases of aggressive behavior in children. *Personality and Social Psychology Bulletin, 16*, 8–22.

Dodge, K.A., & Price, J.M. (1994). On the relation between social information processing and socially competent behavior in early school-aged children. *Child Development, 65*, 1385–1397.

Doll, B., Zucker, S., & Brehm, K. (2004). *Resilient classrooms: Creating healthy environments for learning.* New York, NY: Guilford Press.

Drugli, M.B., & Larsson, B. (2006). Children aged 4–8 years treated with parent training and child therapy because of conduct problems: Generalisation effects to day-care and school settings. *European Child and Adolescent Psychiatry, 15*, 392–399.

Embry, D.D. (2002). The Good Behavior Game: A best practice candidate as a universal behvioral vaccine. *Clinical Child and Family Psychology Review, 5*(4), 273–297.

Evertson, C.M., & Weinstein, C.S. (2006). Classroom management as a field of inquiry. In C.M. Evertson & C.S. Weinstein (Eds.), *Handbook of classroom management: Research, practice, and contemporary issues* (pp. 3–15). Mahwah, NJ: Lawrence Erlbaum Associates.

Frick, P., Kamphaus, R.W., Lahey, B.B., Loeber, R., Christ, M.G., Hart, E., . . . Tannenbaum, L.E. (1991). Academic underachievement and the disruptive behavior disorders. *Journal of Consulting and Clinical Psychology, 59*, 289–294.

Gable, R.A., Hester, P.H., Rock, M.L., & Hughes, K.G. (2009). Back to basics: Rules, praise, ignoring and reprimands revisited. *Intervention in School and Clinic, 44*, 195–205.

Good, T.L., & Brophy, J.E. (1994). *Looking in classrooms.* New York, NY: Harper Collins.

Gottfredson, D.C., & Gottfredson, G.D. (2002). Quality of school-based prevention programs: Results from a national survey. *Journal of Research in Crime and Delinquency, 39*, 3–35.

Guerra, N.G., & Bradshaw, C.P. (2008). Linking the prevention of problem behaviors and positive youth development: Core competencies for positive youth development and risk prevention. *New Directions for Child and Adolescent Development, 122*, 1–17.

Hall, R., & Lund, D. (1968). Effects of teacher on study behavior. *Journal of Applied Behavior Analysis, 1*(1), 1–12.

Hanf, E., & Kling, J. (1973). *Facilitating parent–child interactions: A two-stage training model.* Portland: University of Oregon Medical School.

Houston, W.R., & Williamson, J.L. (1992). Perceptions of their preparation by 42 Texas elementary school teachers compared with their responses as student teachers. *Teacher Education and Practice, 8*, 27–42.

Howes, C. (2000). Social-emotional classroom climate in child care, child–teacher relationships and children's second grade peer relations. *Social Development, 9*(2), 291–204.

Hutchings, J., Daley, D., Jones, E.E., Martin, P., Bywater, T., & Gwyn, R. (2007). Early results from developing and researching the Webster-Stratton Incredible Years teacher classroom management training programme in North West Wales. *Journal of Children's Services, 2*(3), 15–26.

Johnston, C., & Mash, E.J. (2001). Families of children with attention-deficit/hyperactivity disorder: Review and recommendations for future research. *Clinical Child and Family Psychology Review, 4*, 183–207.

Jones, V.F., & Jones, L.S. (2004). *Comprehensive classroom management: Creating positive learning environments.* Boston, MA: Allyn & Bacon.

Jones, V.F., & Jones, L.S. (2007). *Comprehensive classroom management: Creating positive learning environments.* Boston, MA: Allyn & Bacon.

Kaiser, A.P., Hancock, T.B., Cai, X., Foster, E.M., & Hester, P. (2000). Parent-reported behavior problems and language delays in boys and girls enrolled in Head Start classrooms. *Behavior Disorders, 26,* 26–41.

Kumpfer, K.L., Alvarado, R., Tait, C., & Turner, C. (2002). Effectiveness of school-based family and children's skills training for substance prevention among 6- to 8-year-old rural children. *Psychology of Addictive Behaviors, 16,* S65–S71.

Madsen, C.H., & Becker, W.C. (1968). Rules, praise and ignoring: Elements of elementary classroom control. *Journal of Applied Behavior Analysis, 1*(2), 139–150.

Nevin, A., & Johnson, D.W. (1982). Effects of group and individual contingencies on academic performance and social relations of special needs students. *The Journal of Social Psychology, 116*(1), 41–59.

O'Connor, E., Dearing, E., & Collins, B.A. (2011). Teacher–child relationship and behavior problem trajectories in elementary school. *American Educational Research Journal, 48*(1), 120–162.

Pope, A.W., Bierman, K.L., & Mumma, G.H. (1989). Relations between hyperactive and aggressive behavior and peer relations at three elementary grade levels. *Journal of Abnormal Child Psychology, 17*(3), 253–267.

Raver, C.C., Jones, S.M., Li-Grining, C.P., Metzger, M., Champion, K.M., & Sardin, L. (2008). Improving preschool classroom processes: Preliminary findings from a randomized trial implemented in Head Start settings. *Early Childhood Research Quarterly, 23,* 10–26.

Reid, M.J., Webster-Stratton, C., & Hammond, M. (2007). Enhancing a classroom social competence and problem-solving curriculum by offering parent training to families of moderate-to-high-risk elementary school children. *Journal of Clinical Child and Adolescent Psychology, 36*(5), 605–620.

Reinke, W.M., & Herman, K.C. (2002). Creating school environments that deter antisocial behaviors in youth. *Psychology in the Schools, 39,* 549–559.

Reinke, W.M., & Lewis-Palmer, T. (2008). The classsroom check-up: A class wide teacher consultation model for increasing praise and decreasing disruptive behavior. *School Psychology Review, 37*(3), 315–332.

Reinke, W.M., Stormont, M., Herman, K.C., Puri, R., & Goel, N. (2010). Supporting children's mental health in schools: Teacher perceptions of needs, roles and barriers. *School Psychology Quarterly.*

Reinke, W.M., Stormont, M., Webster-Stratton, C., Newcomer, L., & Herman, K. (in press). The Incredible Years Classroom Management Program: Using coaching to support generalization to real world settings. *Psychology in Schools, 49*(2), 416–428.

Rhode, G., Jenson, W.R., & Reavis, H.K. (1992). *The tough kid book.* Longmont, CO: Sopris West.

Roza, S.J., Hofstra, M.B., Van der Ende, J., & Verhulst, F.C. (2003). Stable prediction of mood and anxiety disorders based on behavioral and emotional problems in childhood: A 14-year follow-up during childhood, adolescence, and young adulthood. *American Journal of Psychiatry, 160*(12), 2116–2121.

Shernoff, E.S., & Kratochwill, T.R. (2007). Transporting an evidence-based classroom management program for preschoolers with disruptive behavior problems to a school: An analysis of implementation, outcomes, and contextual variables. *School Psychology Quarterly, 22,* 449–472.

Simonsen, B., & Fairbanks, S. (2008). Evidence-based practices in classroom management: Considerations for research to practice. *Education & Treatment of Children, 31*(3), 351–380.

Walker, H.M. (1995). *The acting-out child: Coping with classroom disruption.* Longmont, CO: Sopris West.

Webster-Stratton, C. (1994). *The Incredible Years (IY) Series Teacher Classroom Management Program.* Seattle, WA: Incredible Years.

Webster-Stratton, C. (1999). *How to promote children's social and emotional competence.* London, United Kingdom: Sage Publications.

Webster-Stratton, C. (2012). *Incredible teachers.* Seattle: Incredible Years.

Webster-Stratton, C., & Hammond, M. (1997). Treating children with early-onset conduct problems: A comparison of child and parent training interventions. *Journal of Consulting and Clinical Psychology, 65*(1), 93–109.

Webster-Stratton, C., & Herman, K.C. (2010). Disseminating Incredible Years Series early intervention programs: Integrating and sustaining services between school and home. *Psychology in the Schools, 47*(1), 36–54.

Webster-Stratton, C., & Lindsay, D.W. (1999). Social competence and early-onset conduct problems: Issues in assessment. *Journal of Child Clinical Psychology, 28*, 25–93.

Webster-Stratton, C., & Reid, M.J. (2005). Treating conduct problems and strengthening social and emotional competence in young children: The Dina Dinosaur Treatment Program. In M. Epstein, K. Kutash, & A.J. Duchowski (Eds.), *Outcomes for children and youth with emotional and behavioral disorders and their families: Programs and evaluation best practices* (2nd ed., pp. 597–623). Austin, TX: PRO-ED, Inc.

Webster-Stratton, C., & Reid, M.J. (2008a). Adapting the Incredible Years Child Dinosaur Social, Emotional and Problem Solving intervention to address co-morbid diagnoses. *Journal of Children's Services, 3*(3), 17–30.

Webster-Stratton, C., & Reid, M.J. (2008b). Strengthening social and emotional competence in socioeconomically disadvantaged young children: Preschool and kindergarten school-based curricula. In W.H. Brown, S.L. Odom, & S.R. McConnell (Eds.), *Social competence of young children: Risk, disability, and intervention* (pp. 185–203). Baltimore, MD: Paul H. Brookes Publishing Co.

Webster-Stratton, C., & Reid, M.J. (2009). Parents, teachers and therapists using the child-directed play therapy and coaching skills to promote children's social and emotional competence and to build positive relationships. In C.E. Schaefer (Ed.), *Play therapy for preschool children* (pp. 245–273). Washington, DC: American Psychological Association.

Webster-Stratton, C., & Reid, M.J. (2010). A school-family partnership: Addressing multiple risk factors to improve school readiness and prevent conduct problems in young children. In S.L. Christenson & A.L. Reschly (Eds.), *Handbook on school-family partnerships for promoting student competence* (pp. 204–227). Seattle, WA: Routledge/Taylor and Francis.

Webster-Stratton, C., Reid, M.J., & Beauchaine, T.P. (2011). Combining parent and child training for young children with ADHD. *Journal of Clinical Child and Adolescent Psychology, 40*(2), 1–13.

Webster-Stratton, C., Reid, M.J., & Hammond, M. (2001). Preventing conduct problems, promoting social competence: A parent and teacher training partnership in Head Start. *Journal of Clinical Child Psychology, 30*(3), 283–302.

Webster-Stratton, C., Reid, M.J., & Hammond, M. (2004). Treating children with early-onset conduct problems: Intervention outcomes for parent, child, and teacher training. *Journal of Clinical Child and Adolescent Psychology, 33*(1), 105–124.

Webster-Stratton, C., Reid, M.J., & Stoolmiller, M. (2008). Preventing conduct problems and improving school readiness: Evaluation of the Incredible Years teacher and child training programs in high–risk schools. *Journal of Child Psychology and Psychiatry, 49*(5), 471–488.

Webster-Stratton, C., Reinke, W.M., Herman, K.C., & Newcomer, L. (2011). The Incredible Years Teacher Classroom Management Training: The methods and principles that support fidelity of training delivery. *School Psychology Review, 40*, 509–529.

Williford, A.P., & Shelton, T.L. (2008). Using mental health consultation to decrease disruptive behaviors in preschoolers: Adapting an empirically supported intervention. *Journal of Child Psychology and Psychiatry, 49*(2), 191–200.

Yarbrough, J.L., & Skinner, C.H. (2004). Decreasing transition times in a second grade classroom: Scientific support for the Timely Transitions game. *Journal of Applied School Psychology, 20*(2), 85–107.

Zins, J.E., & Elias, M.J. (2006). Social and emotional learning. In G.G. Bear & K.M. Minke (Eds.), *Children's needs III: Development, prevention, and intervention* (pp. 1–13). Bethesda, MD: National Association of School Psychologists.

18

Embedded Instruction to Support Early Learning in Response to Intervention Frameworks

Patricia Snyder, Mary Louise Hemmeter, Mary E. McLean, Susan R. Sandall, and Tara McLaughlin

A major purpose of instruction in early childhood education is to provide sufficient experiences and opportunities for preschool children to learn skills that facilitate their access to and participation in a preschool curriculum, their attainment of desired developmental and learning outcomes, and their readiness for school. Two sources have had significant influence on practices used in early childhood education programs: 1) developmentally appropriate practices (DAP) disseminated by the National Association for the Education of Young Children (NAEYC; 2009), and 2) the Division for Early Childhood's (DEC) recommended practices for early intervention/early childhood special education (Sandall, Hemmeter, Smith, & McLean, 2005). Both sources are intended to serve as guidelines for the application of recommended practices, including practices related to teaching and instruction.

When DAP guidelines were first disseminated in 1986, questions were raised about whether the practitioner's identified role as a guide or facilitator for child-initiated and child-directed learning experiences was sufficient for addressing the instructional needs of children with learning challenges or those with disabilities (e.g., Carta, Schwartz, Atwater, & McConnell, 1991; Wolery, Strain, & Bailey, 1992). For early learning experiences and opportunities to be maximally beneficial, some asserted, a central role for practitioners was to influence the interactions children have with activities, peers, adults, toys, and materials in preschool environments. Systematic efforts to influence child–environment interactions were characterized as *interventions*, particularly when interventions involved intentional teaching strategies carried out in the context of activities in the preschool classroom and as part of practitioners' ongoing interactions with children (Wolery & Wilbers, 1994).

Successive updates to the DAP guidelines in 1996 and 2009 have emphasized the importance of both child-initiated and teacher-guided learning experiences and opportunities (NAEYC, 1996, 2009). The 2009 DAP position statement emphasizes the importance of *intentionality* in teaching. As stated in the DAP position statement,

> A hallmark of developmentally appropriate teaching is intentionality. Good teachers are intentional in everything they do—setting up the classroom, planning curriculum,

making use of various teaching strategies, assessing children, interacting with them, and working with their families. (2009, p. 10)

The 2009 DAP guidelines emphasize instructional quality and effectiveness. *Intentional* teachers are defined as those who are purposeful and reflective about actions they take in their teaching in support of the instructional or learning goals that the early childhood education program is trying to help all children, and each child, reach.

With respect to recommended practices of the DEC, the 27 child-focused practices are particularly relevant for the present chapter. These practices provide guidance about how children should be taught, when and where instructional practices and arrangements should be implemented, and how children's learning and development should be monitored to inform data-based decision making (Wolery, 2005). The DEC child-focused recommended practices reflect accumulated empirical evidence emphasizing that children at risk for learning challenges or those with identified disabilities benefit from intentional, differentiated, and systematic teaching and instruction. Consistent with tenets expressed in the 2009 DAP position statement, DEC child-focused practices emphasize the importance of intentional interactions and instruction by adults who interact with young children to support their development and accelerate their learning toward desired outcomes.

In addition to DAP guidelines and DEC recommended practices, preschool curricula, state early learning guidelines and standards, and accountability practices have informed practitioners' decisions about what children should know and be able to do as well as how instruction should be implemented. Across these sources is recognition that teaching and instruction should be intentional and differentiated using a variety of strategies.

Response to intervention (RTI) frameworks are useful for organizing and integrating practices related to what will be taught and how it will be taught. Achieving desired results or learning outcomes for young children in the context of RTI frameworks should be inextricably linked to the application of evidence-informed and differentiated teaching and instructional practices that have been shown to support early development and accelerate learning (Snyder, McLaughlin, & Denney, 2011).

Within RTI frameworks, decisions about the types and intensities of instructional strategies are informed by analyses of child-environment "fit" to support learning and development. Where there is a lack of fit, intentional and systematic instructional strategies are implemented to alter the learning environment or the child's capacity to interact with the environment. Responses to child–environment fit involve instruction being delivered along a continuum from less structured to highly structured. The type and intensity of instruction is informed by data related to children's capacities for meeting environmental or learning task expectations and by examining children's responses to the learning opportunities they are provided.

Embedded instruction is an evidence-informed approach to intentional and systematic instruction that aligns well with early childhood RTI instructional principles and practices. Embedded instruction focuses on 1) specifying the instructional content to be taught, 2) identifying when this content should be taught, 3) using intentional and systematic instructional procedures to teach specified content, and 4) evaluating whether instruction is implemented as planned and results in child learning as part of data-informed decision making. Initially developed as an approach for teaching young children with identified disabilities, embedded instruction can be used to support the learning and development of young children within RTI frameworks (VanDerHeyden & Snyder, 2009).

The purpose of this chapter is to consider how embedded instruction would be used within RTI frameworks. We begin the chapter by defining embedded instruction. The empirical evidence related to embedded instruction is reviewed briefly to set the context for descriptions of each component of embedded instruction and the practices associated with each component. We illustrate how these components and associated practices could be applied in RTI frameworks, with particular emphasis on the component related to using intentional and systematic instructional procedures. We discuss treatment intensity as a way to consider the dose of embedded instruction provided to young children within RTI frameworks. The chapter concludes by identifying future directions for embedded instruction research and practice.

DEFINING EMBEDDED INSTRUCTION

Embedded instruction is a multicomponent approach for planning, implementing, and evaluating instruction. It is one variant of several naturalistic instructional approaches that have been described in the early intervention/early childhood special education literature (Snyder et al., 2012). It involves providing instruction on children's priority learning goals (referred to as learning targets) during typically occurring activities, routines, and transitions. This approach to intentional instruction is distinguished by an emphasis on providing learning opportunities to young children that are embedded rather than decontextualized. The instructional strategies used vary on a continuum from less to more structured but are intentional and systematic.

Embedded instruction is related to naturalistic instructional approaches that have been described in the early intervention/early childhood special education literature since at least the late 1960s. Beginning with the seminal work of Hart and Risley (1968, 1974, 1975), which focused on incidental teaching, several naturalistic instructional approaches have subsequently been described and examined (e.g., milieu teaching, enhanced milieu teaching, activity-based intervention, embedded instruction, naturalistic teaching; Snyder et al., 2012). Despite different labels, each of these instructional approaches involves the use of teaching and instructional strategies that provide learning opportunities in typically occurring activities and routines.

Several common features have been identified across the various naturalistic instructional approaches, including embedded instruction (Horn & Banerjee, 2009; Rule, Losardo, Dinnebeil, Kaiser, & Rowland, 1998; Snyder et al., 2012). First, the contexts for instruction are children's typically occurring activities, routines, or everyday learning experiences. Second, the content of instruction focuses on learning targets or skills needed by the child to meet activity expectations or characteristics, participate in typically occurring activities and routines, demonstrate competence with respect to early learning curricular standards or guidelines, or achieve desired child developmental or learning outcomes. Third, each instructional episode is child-initiated or initiated by an adult based on the child's focus of attention or interest, and a natural or logically planned consequence follows the child's response. Fourth, the adults who implement the instruction are those who interact regularly with the child.

EMPIRICAL EVIDENCE FOR EMBEDDED INSTRUCTION

Naturalistic instructional approaches, including embedded instruction, have empirical support. Findings from 44 studies reported in 38 articles published from 1981 through 2009 have shown that these approaches are effective for teaching young children at risk or those with disabilities a variety of functional, developmental, and school readiness skills, including language, adaptive, literacy, and social skills. In addition, systematic instructional procedures (e.g., naturalistic time delay, least-to-most prompting) have been implemented with fidelity as part of these approaches (Snyder et al., 2012). Use of naturalistic instructional approaches, including embedded instruction, has been demonstrated to support children's participation in the general preschool curriculum while addressing individualized learning and instructional needs.

Embedded instruction would be considered a "practice" as defined by the What Works Clearinghouse (2010, p. 4) because it is "a named *approach* [emphasis added] to promoting children's development that staff implement in interacting with children and materials in their classroom." In the Snyder et al. (2012) review, 15 studies either explicitly identified the naturalistic instructional approach examined as embedded instruction or included intervention features that were consistent with the definition of embedded instruction used in the review. Across the embedded instruction studies, the instruction focused on learning targets related to a range of content areas for child learning (i.e., preacademic, communication, social, motor, cognitive, and adaptive skills) and the embedded instruction involved a range of instructional strategies to facilitate child learning (e.g., environmental arrangements, curricular modification, mand/model, antecedent-based strategies, feedback strategies, time delay, response prompting). All studies examined children's acquisition of skills, whereas about one third examined skill generalization and one third examined skill maintenance.

IDENTIFYING KEY COMPONENTS OF EMBEDDED INSTRUCTION

The studies identified as part of the Snyder et al. (2012) review were analyzed to identify practices included as part of the naturalistic instruction intervention. Fourteen practices were identified from the reviewed studies. The practices identified were subsequently organized under four key components: 1) what is taught, 2) when it is taught, 3) how it is taught, and 4) how embedded instruction is evaluated in relation to instructional quality and effectiveness for children.

A validation panel composed of researchers, curriculum specialists, professional development experts, practitioners, and family members verified and made recommendations about both the components and practices (Snyder, Hemmeter, Sandall, & McLean, 2008). The validation panel made suggestions about how to describe and clarify the key components and practices for practitioners. Based on panel recommendations, Snyder et al. (2008) subsequently used four heuristic labels under which the 14 practices were organized: 1) what to teach, 2) when to teach, 3) how to teach, and 4) how to evaluate. Table 18.1 shows each of these components and associated practices. Each component of embedded instruction and the associated practices will be described further. We discuss how these components and practices might be implemented in the context of RTI frameworks, with particular emphasis on the *how to teach* component.

What to Teach

Four key practices are shown in Table 18.1 related to what to teach: 1) develop high-quality activities, 2) use activity-focused assessment, 3) break instructional goals down into teachable learning targets, and 4) develop high-quality learning targets. What to teach involves identifying instructional content and specifying learning targets for all children, a group of children, or an individual child. Descriptions of what young children should know or be able to do as specified in early learning standards or guidelines often influence the content focus of instruction as well as teaching and instructional practices used in early education and care settings. Cultural, historical, institutional, and political forces influence views about what skills, knowledge, and abilities are considered important instructional content in early learning standards or guidelines (Scott-Little, Kagan, & Frelow, 2006).

The *what to teach* component of embedded instruction is based on a premise similar to a core premise of RTI, which is that the core curriculum provides children with opportunities to be engaged and to learn during activities that are motivating, developmentally appropriate, and challenging for a range of diverse learners (Greenwood, Bradfield, Kaminski, Linas, Carta, & Nylander, 2011). High-quality activities provide opportunities to address priority learning targets in logical and appropriate contexts.

When determining what to teach, assessment during ongoing activities can be used to analyze child–environment "fit" and identify activities where there is a lack of fit. In an activity-focused assessment, children are observed during ongoing activities and routines. Behaviors and skills used by the majority of children

Table 18.1. Intervention components and practices identified in embedded instruction literature

Component	Practice
What to teach	Develop high-quality activities.
	Use activity-focused assessment.
	Break instructional goals down into teachable learning targets.
	Develop high-quality learning targets.
When to teach	Develop an activity matrix based on a balanced classroom schedule.
	Select activities that are a good fit for embedded learning opportunities given the specified learning target.
	Distribute embedded instruction learning trials within and across activities.
How to teach	Use intentional and systematic instructional procedures.
	Implement complete learning trials.
	Use massed, spaced, or distributed learning trials.
	Align instructional procedures with the learning target behavior.
How to evaluate	Evaluate fidelity of implementation. (*Am I doing it?*)
	Evaluate child outcomes. (*Is it working?*)
	Use data-informed decision making. (*Do I need to make changes?*)

Practices listed were examined in Snyder, Hemmeter, Sandall, and McLean (2007) and were recommended by a validation panel (Snyder, Hemmeter, Sandall, & McLean, 2008).

to participate in the activities and routines are noted. If one or more children have difficulty participating, their level of participation and present skill level within or across activities or routines are noted. Information gathered during an activity-focused assessment can be used to inform the development of learning targets. Activity-focused assessment is similar to activity-based or curriculum-based assessment (Cook, 2004; Macy, Bricker, & Squires, 2005). It is an appropriate complement to universal screening or progress-monitoring procedures used as part of RTI frameworks (VanDerHeyden, 2005).

Once an activity-focused assessment has been conducted, instructional goals and associated learning targets can be identified. Often, instructional goals are broad statements of skills or behaviors that the activity-focused assessment suggests are important to improve child–environment fit. For example, an activity-focused assessment might reveal that a child rarely initiates interactions with peers even though the characteristics or expectations of many activities in the preschool classroom involve peer-to-peer interactions. If almost all children engage in peer-to-peer interactions during classroom activities and the activity-focused assessment suggests that child–environment fit would be improved for a small number of children or an individual child if peer-to-peer interaction skills were improved, then peer-to-peer interaction skills might be identified as an appropriate embedded instructional goal. The instructional goal is broken down further into a learning target.

Learning targets are written as part of the *what to teach* component of embedded instruction. A learning target is a behavioral objective. It specifies the skill, the conditions under which the skill will be used, and the criteria for determining when the skill is acquired, mastered, or generalized. Skills specified in learning targets should be observable, age-appropriate, functional, and generative (Grisham-Brown, Hemmeter, Pretti-Frontczak, 2005; Notari-Syverson & Schuster, 1995; Snyder, McLaughlin, et al., 2009). The quality of written learning targets has been linked to the quality of embedded instruction learning opportunities practitioners provide to young children (Pretti-Frontczak & Bricker, 2000; Snyder et al., 2011).

The skill specified in a learning target is a proximal instructional priority to improve child–environment fit and to support engagement and learning in ongoing activities, routines, or transitions. In the context of an RTI framework, the skill specified as part of a learning target aligns with skills specified in early learning content standards or guidelines and the preschool curriculum. For children with identified disabilities, the learning target skill also would align with the child's individualized education program (IEP) goals, benchmarks, or short-term objectives.

When to Teach

Embedded instruction involves intentional and systematic instruction implemented during activities, routines, and transitions. Contextualized learning opportunities have been linked to increases in children's motivation (Dunst, 2000; Dunst & Bruder, 1999) and generalization and maintenance of learned skills or behaviors (Horn, Lieber, Li, Sandall, & Schwartz, 2000; Losardo & Bricker, 1994; Venn, Wolery, Werts, Morris, DeCesare, & Cuffs, 1993). Three key practices shown in Table 18.1 are related to when to teach: 1) develop an activity matrix based on a balanced classroom schedule, 2) select activities that are a good fit for embedded learning opportunities given the specified learning target, and 3) distribute embedded instruction learning trials within and across activities.

An activity matrix is developed that reflects a balanced classroom schedule. A balanced classroom schedule includes a mix of teacher-directed and child-initiated activities and opportunities for children to experience large-group, small-group, and individualized instruction, if needed. In addition, a balanced schedule provides opportunities for children to alternate between activities or routines that primarily involve attending or group participation with those that involve active child participation or movement. A balanced classroom schedule extends the importance of developmentally appropriate activities and core curriculum emphasized as part of the *what to teach* component.

An activity matrix shows the balanced classroom schedule and is used to plan when instruction on learning targets will occur for all children, for targeted groups of children, or for an individual child. On an activity matrix, planning teams identify activities that are a good fit for embedded learning opportunities, based on the learning target skill(s). The matrix specifies the number of learning trials for each learning target within and across each activity.

To select activities that are logical and appropriate for embedded instruction, the "fit" between the activity expectations and the learning target skill are considered in relation to key information about the child, including current abilities, preferences, and support needs. For example, a teacher might select art activities and writing activities as logical and appropriate opportunities for children to practice writing their names. Moreover, a teacher might create a computer sign-in system or plan for sidewalk chalk to be available during outdoor play to provide additional opportunities for children to practice writing their names. The activities the teacher has selected or created provide logical and appropriate opportunities for children to write their names. In contrast, asking children to write their names during routines such as hand washing generally would not be considered logical or appropriate. In the previous example, the teacher identified two existing logical and appropriate opportunities for children to write their names. To ensure sufficient and varied learning opportunities, the teacher *created* two additional activities during which it would be logical and appropriate for children to write their names. Identifying logical and appropriate opportunities to teach learning target skills helps specify the planned dose of embedded instruction for all children, some children, or individual children. To quantify dose, the activity matrix shows when embedded instruction learning trials will be provided; how many learning trials are planned for each activity, routine, or transition; and the children for whom the trials will be provided.

How to Teach

Practices related to how to teach reflect instructional strategies ranging from universal design for teaching and learning to the use of specific and precise instructional procedures. As part of embedded instruction, the instructional strategies are implemented within and across activities, routines, and transitions. The strategies use or build upon existing environmental or discriminative stimuli that are part of an activity, routine, or transition and set the occasion for learning target skill responses to be followed by naturally occurring or logically planned consequences. Four key practices are shown in Table 18.1 related to how to teach: 1) use intentional and systematic instructional procedures; 2) implement complete learning trials; 3) use massed, spaced, or distributed learning trials; and 4) align instructional procedures with the learning target behavior.

Instructional procedures are used to characterize the interactions among teachers, children, and the environment during a teaching or learning episode. A variety of "named" instructional procedures have been described in the embedded instruction literature (e.g., environmental arrangements, mands, models, response prompting, response shaping). The extent to which these instructional procedures exert influence over a child's interactions during the teaching or learning episode varies (Wolery & Schuster, 1997). For example, constant time delay (Doyle, Wolery, Gast, Ault, & Wiley, 1990; Schuster, Griffen, & Wolery, 1992) outlines a highly structured interaction to ensure "errorless" learning, and a series of decision rules are used to guide interactions during the teaching or learning episode. In contrast, environmental arrangements are a less structured instructional strategy that might involve the use of within-stimulus or extra-stimulus cues that set the occasion for responding (VanDerHeyden, Snyder, DiCarlo, Stricklin, & Vagianos, 2002).

In their embedded instruction approach, Snyder et al. (2007) have emphasized complete learning trials rather than specific instructional procedures such as time delay or most-to-least prompting. This emphasis does not suggest that specific instructional procedures such as time delay are not used as part of embedded instruction; rather, it emphasizes that all instructional trials involve three or four primary features. A complete embedded instruction learning trial includes a sequence of 1) antecedent, 2) learning target behavior (skill), and 3) consequence. In addition, a prompt or correction might occur as part of the complete learning trial when the target skill is not emitted or is incorrect. By focusing on complete learning trials as part of an embedded instruction approach, the occurrence of trials and the components of these trials can be reliably observed and documented. Counting and analyzing the components of complete learning trials helps practitioners and researchers quantify the dose of embedded instruction learning trials children are receiving on priority learning targets (Snyder, Hemmeter, et al., 2011).

Instructional learning trials can be massed or spaced within an activity or distributed within or across activities. Decisions about whether to mass, space, or distribute learning trials are based on the child's phase of learning in relation to the target behavior, the type of learning target specified, and the need to adjust intervention intensity.

Massed trials refer to instructional learning trials in which the same target behavior is elicited repeatedly with very little time between trials. Massed trials are appropriate for learning target behaviors that emphasize repetition, or they might be used when the child is acquiring or becoming fluent with a skill. For example, massed trials might occur when a child is identifying objects, naming pictures, or stacking one object on top of another.

Spaced trials involve longer intervals between trials (e.g., more than 3 seconds) and provide opportunities for the learner to pause or engage in a different behavior before the next targeted learning trial occurs. Spaced trials typically are used when learning target behaviors occur frequently during an activity, routine, or transition and when the child is acquiring or becoming fluent with a skill. Examples of learning target behaviors for which spaced trials might be appropriate are scooping food from a bowl using a spoon, taking successive drinks from a cup, and placing objects in defined spaces (e.g., puzzles).

Distributed trials are learning trials in which instruction focused on a learning target is interspersed with one or more other skills within or across an activity, routine, or transition. In distributed trial instruction, there is a longer time between instructional trials during which the child can engage in other behaviors. For example, during snack time, it would be logical to distribute trials for a learning target focused on using two-word utterances to request "more." Distributed trials generally are appropriate when a child has acquired or is fluent with a skill, and maintenance as well as generalization of the learning target behavior across people, settings, or materials is desired. In addition, distributed trials often are used when it is logical or appropriate for the learning target behavior to occur only once or twice within an activity or across activities. For example, it might only be logical and appropriate for a child to practice skills related to putting on a coat when going outside to play or leaving school at the end of the day.

How to Evaluate

Practices associated with what to teach, when to teach, and how to teach involve planning and implementing instruction. *How to evaluate* focuses on examining whether embedded instruction is implemented as planned and whether it results in child learning, and this information is used to inform data-based decision making. As shown in Table 18.1, three key practices are associated with how to evaluate: 1) evaluate fidelity of implementation, 2) evaluate child outcomes, and 3) use data-informed decision making. These three key practices have been framed as questions to help practitioners answer three questions: 1) Am I doing it? 2) Is it working? and 3) Do I need to make changes? These three questions are used as part of *how to evaluate* to provide a framework for data-informed decision making (Snyder et al., 2007).

The first practice (*Am I doing it?*) focuses on fidelity of embedded instruction implementation. This includes evaluating whether 1) the planned number of embedded instructional learning trials within and across activities were implemented, and 2) the learning trials implemented were complete instructional learning trials. Implementation fidelity data might include how many learning trials occurred for a learning target, when learning trials occurred for a learning target, and whether implementation resulted in complete learning trials. The second practice (*Is it working?*) focuses on monitoring child progress and learning in relation to the learning target skill. Monitoring of child progress occurs during ongoing activities, routines, and transitions in the classroom or during activity-focused assessments, not in decontextualized "testing" situations. The third practice (*Do I need to make changes?*) focuses on examining both implementation fidelity and child progress or learning data to determine whether changes are needed either in embedded instruction implementation or in the learning target(s) being addressed.

APPLYING EMBEDDED INSTRUCTION IN THE CONTEXT OF RESPONSE TO INTERVENTION FRAMEWORKS

Embedded instruction can be used in RTI frameworks by differentiating or "tiering" instruction. Decisions about the types and intensities of instruction to be used are based on analyses of child–environment fit to support learning and development. When there is a lack of fit, instruction occurs to alter the learning environment or the child's capacity to interact within the environment. Instructional decisions are made through direct measurement of learning opportunities and child responses to these opportunities in order to identify the type, specificity, and intensity of instruction needed to optimize child–environment fit. Operationalized decision criteria are used to evaluate whether instruction is associated with desired learning outcomes or if more intensive instruction is needed for some children or individual children. Emphasis is placed on conducting activity-focused assessment to identify priority learning targets, using progress monitoring measures to quantify child learning, and measuring fidelity of implementation of instructional strategies. In a child–environment fit approach to embedded instruction, instructional learning targets are defined based on the gap between what the child can do and what is expected of the child in a particular task or activity in a certain setting (VanDerHeyden & Snyder, 2009). Instruction is designed to build skills or modify the task or environment.

Embedded instruction components and associated practices, which we have described as what to teach, when to teach, how to teach, and how to evaluate, can be used across RTI tiers and can support other RTI activities. Embedded instruction, when used as part of Tier 1 interventions, occurs in the context of core instruction being provided to all children. With respect to what to teach, instructional content would be aligned with early learning content standards and curricular frameworks. Developmentally appropriate activities and a balanced schedule would be the context for embedded learning opportunities. Universal design, curricular modifications, environmental arrangements, and naturalistic instructional procedures would often be used to support the implementation of embedded learning trials. The dose of embedded instruction provided for some children or for individual children would vary based on several contextual features (e.g., the structure of the "core curriculum" activity or routine, the number of staff available to provide intentional or systematic instruction during ongoing activities and routines, or the learning targets specified for some children or for an individual child). When embedded instruction practices are used as part of Tier 1 instruction, children generally need to be able to respond to less precise instruction and to natural cues and consequences. Embedded instruction implemented at Tier 1 would likely require fewer instructional trials for children to reach the desired criteria on their learning targets, and child responses to logically occurring antecedents and consequences would more often be correct or approximations to the target behavior rather than absent or incorrect.

Within targeted or Tier 2 interventions, embedded instruction would often include more and more precisely implemented learning trials in the context of ongoing activities, routines, and transitions. This would include more systematic instructional procedures, increases in the number of learning opportunities provided, and planned increases and decreases in task or activity difficulty. Skill acquisition and building fluency through practice and through increasing motivation to practice in relation to a learning target behavior would be emphasized. Opportunities to respond would occur in the context of activities or routines that often are more structured or adult-directed or involve smaller numbers of children to ensure instructional pacing and available contingencies. More frequent monitoring of embedded instruction implementation fidelity and child learning would occur.

For individualized or Tier 3 interventions, embedded instruction typically would focus on direct, discrete, and precise instruction in the context of ongoing activities, routines, and transitions, often following a "scripted" instructional plan. Learning targets would be taught with systematic response prompting or shaping procedures, and available contingencies would be those identified as reinforcing for the learner. Skill acquisition and building fluency through repeated practice and through increasing motivation to practice in relation to a learning target skill is emphasized, similar to Tier 2. In Tier 3, however, instructional content as reflected in the learning target skill often is focused on "critical skills." Critical skills are behaviors that when acquired set the occasion for new learning or more rapid learning of other skills (Wolery & Hemmeter, 2011). Examples of skills that have been identified as critical for preschool children to learn in classroom contexts include imitation, initiating interactions, joint attention, and object manipulation. Adherence to an instructional protocol or script would be evaluated, and frequent monitoring of child learning would occur.

Figure 18.1 illustrates criteria that might be used to inform decisions about embedded instruction learning trials within Tier 1, 2, or 3 interventions. As this figure illustrates, often the specificity and dose of embedded instruction learning trials differ across tiers. In addition, this figure shows relationships between screening, progress monitoring, activity-focused assessment, and measurement of implementation fidelity and embedded instruction implementation.

TREATMENT INTENSITY AND EMBEDDED INSTRUCTION

As noted by Wolery and Hemmeter (2011), additional empirical data are needed with respect to when embedded instruction learning trials should occur, how frequently trials should be inserted, how much spacing should occur between trials, how many trials should be provided per activity or day, and the number of activities in which instruction should occur to promote child learning. These issues involve treatment intensity. Warren, Fey, and Yoder (2007) suggested the need for systematic lines of research focused on this topic. As Warren et al. noted, very limited empirical literature exists on differential treatment intensity for any practice in

	Tier 1	• Responds to less precise instruction • Responds to more natural cues • Responses are more often correct • Requires fewer trials to criterion	Screening	Progress monitoring and activity-focused assessment	Measurement of implementation fidelity
Embedded instruction	Tier 2	• Requires more systematic prompt hierarchies • Requires more gradual increases and decreases in task difficulty • Requires more trials to criterion			
	Tier 3	• Requires acquisition-level instruction for prerequisite skills • Requires explicit support to generalize • May require very well controlled instructional trials to establish skills			

Figure 18.1. Criteria to help inform decisions about embedded instruction learning trials within a response to intervention framework. (Adapted from VanDerHeyden, A. [2009, October]. *Technically adequate RTI implementation*. Presentation at the first annual RTI early childhood summit, Albuquerque, NM, and Snyder, P., & Wilcox, J. [2009, October]. *The promise and challenge of RTI in early childhood*. Presentation at the first annual RTI early childhood summit. Albuquerque, NM. Copyright 2010 by Patricia Snyder and Amanda VanDerHeyden.)

early childhood education, including embedded instruction. To advance research related to treatment intensity, Warren et al. proposed terminology for the measurement of intervention intensity by defining and describing five terms: 1) dose, 2) dose form, 3) dose frequency, 4) total intervention duration, and 5) cumulative intervention intensity. We consider how these terms might be useful for advancing conceptualizations and specification of embedded instruction treatment intensity and future research to inform instruction-focused decision criteria within RTI frameworks.

Warren et al. (2007) defined *dose* as "the number of properly administered teaching episodes during a single intervention session" (p. 71). This involves measuring fidelity of implementation and three subcomponents: 1) length of intervention session, 2) average rate of teaching episodes (frequency of episodes per unit of time), and 3) distribution of episodes over the session. For example, as part of a 20-minute mealtime routine for all children, if a teacher provided five embedded instruction learning trials approximately every 4 minutes focused on using two-word phrases to request "more," the rate is one episode every 4 minutes and episodes are distributed approximately equally across the session.

Turning to dose form, Warren et al. (2007) suggested this term be used to describe the task or activity in which the teaching episodes are delivered. For example, teaching episodes focused on generalized imitation skills might be delivered in a highly structured one-to-one format in the context of an adult-directed activity. Alternatively, the dose form for the mealtime learning target focused on using two-word phrases to request "more" might be delivered in core preschool activities and routines.

Dose frequency was defined by Warren et al. (2007) as the number of times a dose of intervention is provided per day or per week. This might be one of the more difficult dimensions of treatment intensity to quantify, particularly in inclusive classroom settings when doses of systematic instruction are likely to be distributed throughout the day. Nevertheless, strategies for planning when instruction occurs using forms such as activity matrixes or embedded instruction plans (e.g., Sandall & Schwartz, 2002, 2008; Snyder, Sandall et al., 2009) might be useful for planning and documenting dose frequency.

Warren et al. (2007) defined total intervention duration as the time over which a specified intervention is presented. They noted that cumulative intervention intensity is the product of dose × dose frequency × dose duration. These authors suggested several research studies that might be conducted to examine systematically these various dimensions of treatment intensity. To conduct these studies, it would be important to specify an instructional episode for a given content-focused intervention "in a way that allows an episode to be observed and counted" (p. 72). Although acknowledged as challenging work, the approaches Warren et al. suggested for measuring treatment intensity might hold particular promise for quantifying treatment intensity when embedded instruction is used within RTI frameworks.

In the context of embedded instruction, Snyder, Crowe, et al. (2009) have quantified the intensity of embedded instruction learning trials provided to young children with disabilities in inclusive preschool classrooms using a measure known as the Embedded Instruction Observation System (EIOS). Given that RTI levels or tiers are distinguished by the intensity or specificity of the intervention, it seems reasonable to suggest that a future trend in embedded instruction research might focus on intensity and specificity of instructional trials using the differential treatment intensity framework suggested by Warren et al. (2007).

FUTURE DIRECTIONS IN EMBEDDED INSTRUCTION RESEARCH AND PRACTICE

In addition to treatment intensity, several other directions in embedded instruction research and practice need to be addressed to realize fully the promise of this approach within tiered frameworks. Contemporary perspectives from prevention science related to adaptive prevention–intervention frameworks hold particular promise for future developments in the application of embedded instruction. In contrast with frameworks in which the composition and dose of intervention components associated with each tier is fixed, adaptive frameworks assign different doses of intervention across different groups or individuals based on decision rules that link characteristics of the learner with specific levels and types of intervention components (Collins, Murphy, & Bierman, 2004). Adaptive frameworks appear to hold particular promise with respect to considering different doses of instruction on priority learning targets.

Use of an adaptive perspective would ensure instruction is not categorized solely by a tier and instruction does not move in a linear fashion from one tier to the next in either an ascending (increasing intensity) or descending (decreasing intensity) sequence. Rather, adaptive frameworks promote decision making about how much support or instruction a young child needs with a specific skill at a specific time given a specific context with consideration for the child's phase of learning (Sandall, Schwartz, & Joseph, 2001; VanDerHeyden & Snyder, 2009). Particularly for young children at risk for or with disabilities, decisions about dose or differential instructional intensity often are based on individual characteristics, needs, and values using an evidence-based practice framework (Buysse & Wesley, 2006; Snyder, 2006; Winton, 2006).

Additional research is needed to provide clearer guidance and decision rules about which embedded instruction components and associated practices should be implemented for which children, under what circumstances, and for which learning targets. Promising work related to specifying the key components and associated practices for embedded instruction has been conducted (Snyder, Hemmeter, et al., 2011). Preliminary data exist to support the premise that when preschool teachers are provided with professional development comprised of workshops, coaching, and resources to support implementation, they are able to implement the practices associated with key components of embedded instruction with fidelity, particularly the components related to what to teach and how to teach. In addition, the average number and procedural accuracy of instructional learning trials provided to preschool children with disabilities during ongoing classroom activities, routines, and transitions increases (Snyder, Hemmeter, et al., 2011). Nevertheless, important questions remain to be addressed, such as 1) whether embedded instruction is more or less effective for certain types of learning target behaviors (e.g., dispositions, response classes, behavior chains, discrete responses; Wolery & Hemmeter, 2011); 2) whether generalization of learning target behaviors occurs when embedded instruction procedures involve systematic attention to motivating operations across people, activities, or materials; and 3) when to increase or decrease embedded instruction treatment intensity. Each of these questions and others that might be addressed in future research necessitate addressing challenges related to measuring fidelity of implementation, quantifying intensity, and monitoring child learning.

SUMMARY

Embedded instruction is a multicomponent approach that includes a continuum of instructional strategies to support active participation and meaningful learning in the context of activities, routines, and transitions that occur regularly in the preschool classroom. Within RTI frameworks, embedded instruction is viewed as multitiered and differentiated instruction on learning targets that might not otherwise be addressed with sufficient intensity or specificity for all children, some children, or individual children to support or accelerate their progress toward desired learning outcomes. Embedded instruction components and associated practices can be used across RTI tiers using an adaptive perspective and data-based decision making to inform instructional intensity. For the promise of embedded instruction to be realized within tiered intervention frameworks, evidence available to date suggests practitioners must be supported to implement embedded instruction practices with fidelity and to apply appropriate decision-making criteria to their evaluations of intervention fidelity and instructional effectiveness.

REFERENCES

Buysse, V., & Wesley, P.W. (2006). Making sense of evidence-based practice: Reflections and recommendations. In V. Buysse & P.W. Wesley (Eds.), *Evidence-based practice in the early childhood field* (pp. 227–246). Washington, DC: ZERO TO THREE.

Carta, J.J., Schwartz, I.S., Atwater, J.B., & McConnell, S.R. (1991). Developmentally appropriate practice: Appraising its usefulness for young children with disabilities. *Topics in Early Childhood Special Education, 11,* 1–20.

Collins, L.M., Murphy, S.A., & Bierman, K. (2004). A conceptual framework for adaptive preventive interventions. *Prevention Science, 5,* 185–196.

Cook, R.J. (2004). Embedding assessment of young children into routines of inclusive settings. *Young Exceptional Children, 7,* 3–11.

Doyle, P.M., Wolery, M., Gast, D.L., Ault, M., & Wiley, K. (1990). Comparison of constant time delay and the system of least prompts in teaching preschoolers with developmental delays. *Research in Developmental Disabilities, 1,* 1–22.

Dunst, C.J. (2000). Everyday children's learning opportunities: Characteristics and consequences. *Children's Learning Opportunities Report, 2*(1).

Dunst, C.J., & Bruder, M.B. (1999). Family and community activity settings, natural learning environments, and children's learning opportunities. *Children's Learning Opportunities Report, 1*(2).

Greenwood, C.R., Bradfield, T., Kaminski, R., Linas, M., Carta, J., & Nylander, D. (2011). The response to intervention (RTI) approach in early childhood. *Focus on Exceptional Children, 43,* 1–24.

Grisham-Brown, J., Hemmeter, M.L., & Pretti-Frontczak, K. (2005). *Blended practices for teaching young children in inclusive settings.* Baltimore, MD: Paul H. Brookes Publishing Co.

Hart, B.M., & Risley, T.R. (1968). Establishing the use of descriptive adjectives in the spontaneous speech of disadvantaged children. *Journal of Applied Behavior Analysis, 1,* 109–120.

Hart, B.M., & Risley, T.R. (1974). Using preschool materials to modify the language of disadvantaged children. *Journal of Applied Behavior Analysis, 7,* 243–256.

Hart, B.M., & Risley, T.R. (1975). Incidental teaching of language in the preschool. *Journal of Applied Behavior Analysis, 8,* 411–420.

Horn, E., & Banerjee, R. (2009). Understanding curriculum modifications and embedded learning opportunities in the context of supporting all children's success. *Language, Speech, and Hearing Services in Schools, 40,* 406–415.

Horn, E., Lieber, J., Li, S., Sandall, S., & Schwartz, I. (2000). Supporting young children's IEP goals in inclusive settings through embedded learning opportunities. *Topics in Early Childhood and Special Education, 20,* 208–223.

Losardo, A., & Bricker, D. (1994). Activity-based intervention and direct instruction: A comparison study. *American Journal on Mental Retardation, 98,* 744–765.

Macy, M.G., Bricker, D.D., & Squires, J. (2005). Validity and reliability of a curriculum-based assessment approach to determine eligibility for Part C services. *Journal of Early Intervention, 28,* 1–16.

National Association for the Education of Young Children. (1996). *Developmentally appropriate practice in early childhood programs serving children from birth through age 8* (Position statement). Washington, DC: Author.

National Association for the Education of Young Children. (2009). *Developmentally appropriate practice in early childhood programs serving children from birth through age 8* (Position statement). Retrieved from http://www.naeyc.org/files/naeyc/file/positions/position%20 statement%20Web.pdf

Notari-Syverson, A., & Schuster, S. (1995). Putting real life skills into IEPs/IFSPs for infants and young children. *Teaching Exceptional Children, 27,* 29–32.

Pretti-Frontczak, K., & Bricker, D. (2000). Enhancing the quality of individualized education plan goals and objectives. *Journal of Early Intervention, 23,* 92–105.

Rule, S., Losardo, A., Dinnebeil, L.A., Kaiser, A., & Rowland, C. (1998). Research challenges in naturalistic intervention. *Journal of Early Intervention, 21,* 283–293.

Sandall, S., Hemmeter, M.L., Smith, B.J., & McLean, M.E. (2005). *DEC recommended practices: A comprehensive guide for practical application in early intervention/early childhood special education.* Longmont, CO: Sopris West.

Sandall, S.R., & Schwartz I.S. (2002). *Building blocks for teaching preschoolers with special needs.* Baltimore, MD: Paul H. Brookes Publishing Co.

Sandall, S.R., & Schwartz I.S. (2008). *Building blocks for teaching preschoolers with special needs* (2nd ed.). Baltimore, MD: Paul H. Brookes Publishing Co.

Sandall, S.R., Schwartz, I., & Joseph, G. (2001). A building blocks model for effective instruction in inclusive early childhood settings. *Young Exceptional Children, 4,* 3–9.

Schuster, J.W., Griffen, A.K., & Wolery, M. (1992). Comparison of simultaneous prompting and constant time delay procedures in teaching sight words to elementary students with moderate mental retardation. *Journal of Behavioral Education, 2,* 305–325.

Scott-Little, C., Kagan, S.L., & Frelow, V.S. (2006). Conceptualizations of readiness and the content of early learning standards: The intersection of policy and research? *Early Childhood Research Quarterly, 21,* 153–173.

Snyder, P. (2006). *Best available research evidence: Impact on research in early childhood.* In V. Buysse & P.W. Wesley (Eds.), Evidence-based practice in the early childhood field (pp. 35–70). Washington, DC: ZERO TO THREE.

Snyder, P., Crowe, C., Hemmeter, M.L., Sandall, S., McLean, M., Crow, R., & Embedded Instruction for Early Learning Project. (2009). *EIOS: Embedded instruction for early learning observation system.* [Manual and training videos]. Unpublished instrument. Gainesville: University of Florida.

Snyder, P., Hemmeter, M.L., McLaughlin, T., Algina, J., Sandall, S., & McLean, M. (2011, April). *Impact of professional development on preschool teachers' use of embedded-instruction practices.* Paper presented for the American Educational Research Association Annual Conference, New Orleans, LA.

Snyder, P., Hemmeter, M.L., Sandall, S., & McLean, M. (2007). *Impact of professional development on preschool teachers' use of embedded-instruction practices* (Grant R324A070008). Abstract available from the Institute of Education Sciences, U.S. Department of Education.

Snyder, P., Hemmeter, M.L., Sandall, S., & McLean, M. (2008). *Impact of professional development on preschool teachers' use of embedded instruction practices: 2007–2008 annual report* (R324A070008). Gainesville, FL: Authors.

Snyder, P., McLaughlin, T., & Denney, M. (2011). Frameworks for guiding program focus and practices in early intervention. In J.M. Kauffman & D.P. Hallahan (Series Eds.) & M. Conroy (Section Ed.), *Handbook of special education, Section XII: Early identification and intervention in exceptionality* (pp. 716–730). New York, NY: Routledge.

Snyder, P., McLaughlin, T., Sandall, S., McLean, M.E., Hemmeter, M.L., Crow, R., Scott, C., & Embedded Instruction for Early Learning Project. (2009). *LTRS: Learning target rating scale*. [Manual]. Unpublished instrument. Gainesville: University of Florida, College of Education.

Snyder, P., Rakap, S., Hemmeter, M.L., McLaughlin, T., Sandall, S., & McLean, M. (2012). *Naturalistic instructional approaches in early learning: A systematic review of the empirical literature*. Manuscript submitted for publication.

Snyder, P., Sandall, S., McLean, M.E., Hemmeter, M.L., McLaughlin, T., Edelman, L., & Embedded Instruction for Early Learning Project. (2009). *Tools for teachers*. [CD workshop series]. Center for Excellence in Early Childhood Studies, University of Florida, Gainesville.

VanDerHeyden, A.M. (2005). Intervention-driven assessment practices in early childhood/early intervention: Measuring what is possible rather than what is present. *Journal of Early Intervention, 28,* 28–33.

VanDerHeyden, A.M., & Snyder, P. (2009). Training adaptive skills within the context of multi-tiered intervention systems: Application of the instructional hierarchy. *Early Childhood Services, 3,* 143–155.

VanDerHeyden, A.M., Snyder, P., DiCarlo, C.F., Stricklin, S.B., & Vagianos, L.A. (2002). Comparison of within-stimulus and extra-stimulus prompts to establish desired play behaviors in an inclusive early intervention program. *Behavior Analyst Today, 3,* 189–198.

Venn, M.L., Wolery, M., Werts, M.G., Morris, A., DeCesare, L.D., & Cuffs, M.S. (1993). Embedding instruction in art activities to teach preschoolers with disabilities to imitate their peers. *Early Childhood Research Quarterly, 8,* 277–294.

Warren, S.F., Fey, M.E., & Yoder, P.J. (2007). Differential treatment intensity research: A missing link to creating optimally effective communication interventions. *Mental Retardation and Developmental Disabilities Research Reviews, 13,* 70–77.

What Works Clearinghouse. (2010). *WWC evidence review protocol for early childhood education interventions for children with disabilities* (Version 2.0). Available from http://ies.ed.gov/ncee/wwc/references/idocviewer/doc.aspx?docid=30

Winton, P.J. (2006). The evidence-based practice movement and its effect on knowledge utilization. In V. Buysse & P.W. Wesley (Eds.), *Evidence-based practice in the early childhood field* (pp. 71–115). Washington, DC: ZERO TO THREE.

Wolery, M. (2005). DEC recommended practices: Child-focused practices. In S. Sandall, M.L. Hemmeter, B.J. Smith, & M.E. McLean (Eds.), *DEC recommended practices: A comprehensive guide for practical application in early intervention/early childhood special education* (pp. 71–106). Longmont, CO: Sopris West.

Wolery, M., & Hemmeter, M.L. (2011). Classroom instruction: Background, assumptions, and challenges. *Journal of Early Intervention, 33,* 371–380.

Wolery, M., & Schuster, J.W. (1997). Instructional methods with students who have significant disabilities. *The Journal of Special Education, 31,* 61–79.

Wolery, M., Strain, P.S., & Bailey, D.B. (1992). Reaching the potentials of children with special needs. In S. Bredekamp & T. Rosegrant (Eds.), *Reaching potentials: Appropriate curriculum and assessment for young children* (pp. 92–101). Washington, DC: National Association for the Education of Young Children.

Wolery, M., & Wilbers, J.S. (1994). Introduction to the inclusion of young children with special needs in early childhood programs. In M. Wolery & J.S. Wilbers (Eds.), *Including children with special needs in early childhood programs* (pp. 1–22). Washington, DC: National Association for the Education of Young Children.

Program-Level Supports for Implementing Response to Intervention in Early Childhood

19

Using Consultation to Support the Implementation of Response to Intervention in Early Childhood Settings

Steven E. Knotek, Carly Hoffend, and Kristina S. Ten Haagen

The general emphasis in response to intervention (RTI) models is on using screening measures, multilevel problem solving, and early intervention and prevention practices to support children's educational success rather than waiting to provide corrective measures after children begin to fail (Barnett, Van-DerHeyden, & Witt, 2007). This approach requires substantial changes in how teachers and early interventionists individually and collectively conduct their professional duties (Hoagwood & Johnson, 2002). For example, how will teachers choose between a standard treatment protocol and a problem-solving approach? How will early childhood educators adopt "evidence-based interventions" that may work well under ideal conditions in a university-based preschool but must be implemented within the ecological complexity of their underfunded individual setting? Program implementation and accompanying professional development does not happen in a vacuum. What processes can be used to support early childhood practitioners' development of skills needed to implement RTI, such as screening and progress monitoring?

This chapter begins with a brief overview of the elements and aims of RTI and then considers challenges that get in the way of its implementation. Next, consultation is defined and a rationale presented for using consultation to facilitate the development of skills that will be needed by consultees to implement and sustain the RTI model in individual sites. Finally, the chapter ends with a discussion of how consultation can facilitate consultees' acquisition of RTI-related skills and why specific aspects of early childhood settings should be considered when implementing consultation.

In order for RTI to successfully be embedded in early education settings and become a fixture in a preschool's prevention and problem-solving procedures, consultants need to create a development plan to implement and sustain RTI (Kratochwill, Volpiansky, Clements, & Ball, 2007). At a minimum, RTI requires that staff adopt a prevention and early intervention conceptual framework while applying a host of potentially new skills and procedures.

Guskey (2002) highlighted three major issues that must be attended to as professionals acquire new skills. First, it is important to understand that change is a gradual process that can be challenging. Preschool and child care staff have acquired preferred methods and extensive funds of knowledge (Hiatt-Michael, 2007) that they access to achieve their professional aims. In some ways, innovation implementation is audacious in that it asks staff to move out of their comfort zone and/or to confront the idea that some aspect of their professional practice could and should be improved, while trusting that the newest thing will not have a negative impact on their students or themselves. Being asked to invest precious time to acquire and implement a new skill that may or may not help students may seem overwhelming and even foolish. A program's structure and process must include a mechanism (i.e., consultation) to support staff so that they can successfully address the challenges presented throughout the change process and consider how the intervention (i.e., RTI) offers a positive alternative to current practice. Second, teachers will need consistent feedback on how RTI is supporting their children in the desired dimensions of prevention and early intervention. Third, professionals must be provided with a supportive experience that will foster their acquisition of the scientific tools (Vygotsky, 1986) offered by RTI that will further enhance their practice. In combination, these three principles all highlight the need for a teacher (i.e., preschool teacher as consultee) to receive competent, respectful, thoughtful, data-driven support from an engaged supporter (i.e., itinerant specialist as consultant).

BREADTH AND DEPTH OF RESPONSE TO INTERVENTION MODELS

RTI models are striking in their large-scale reach across the whole population of children in a preschool and in their multidimensional array of interventions. The philosophy of RTI incorporates a prevention perspective and reframes students' performance from a deficit approach to one of potential; this theoretical change in turn redefines how preschool teachers, staff, and itinerant specialists should carry out their professional practice. RTI will require that sites use an intervention hierarchy; utilize screening, assessment, and progress monitoring; successfully implement a research-based curriculum; and embed a collaborative problem-solving approach throughout the process (Buysse & Peisner-Feinberg, 2010). These training challenges are daunting, and the complex RTI process will not be successfully embedded through a series of disconnected workshops. As Guskey (2002) suggests, a sustained interactive process will be needed to help staff acquire and master the RTI process. This need is especially relevant in early childhood settings that tend to serve high-risk children and also experience exceedingly high teacher turnover (Ball & Trammell, 2011). Consultation is an interpersonal problem-solving process that can be used to manage and sustain the implementation of RTI in a preschool.

RESPONSE TO INTERVENTION FOCUSED CONSULTATION

The National Association for the Education of Young Children (NAEYC) and the National Association of Child Care Resource & Referral Agencies (NACCRRA) have outlined components of technical assistance that should be part of ongoing professional development (NAEYC & NACCRR, 2011). NAEYC and NACCRRA (2011, p. 9) defined *technical assistance* as the "provision of targeted and customized supports by a professional(s) with subject matter and adult learning knowledge and skills to strengthen processes, knowledge application, or implementation of services by recipients." Five types of technical assistance are presented, and two—coaching and consultation—have particular salience for supporting early childhood practitioners' implementation of RTI.

Consultation

Consultation may be generally defined as an indirect service through which a consultee (e.g., a preschool teacher) gains support for a client (e.g., a student) by engaging in a problem-solving process with a consultant (itinerant consultant) (Bergan & Kratochwill, 1990; Caplan, 1970). The goal of consultation is to use systematic problem solving to enhance the consultee's ability to solve a pressing work-related problem while simultaneously improving his or her capacity to successfully meet similar challenges in the future. In this sense, consultation has a here-and-now focus in the service of a future-oriented prevention approach.

The consultation process centers on the joint development of new approaches to improve service delivery. Consultation may focus on resolving a specific issue with a specific client or it may involve addressing challenges to providing services to many students in a classroom or an even higher level of organization such as an entire school or school district. For instance, in a preschool setting a teacher may initiate consultation with an itinerant consultant in order to problem-solve about ways to provide classroom support for a child with developmental delays who is experiencing peer rejection. In this case the teacher has primary responsibility for the child and the itinerant consultant has primary responsibility to facilitate the teacher's acquisition of new perspectives and possible solutions to the work problem (i.e., interventions to support the other children's welcoming of the student into class).

Coaching

Coaching is a process in which a coach uses knowledge about adult learning to support professional development (Sugai & Horner, 2006). The coach is considered to be an expert who helps a "learner" to acquire new skills or dispositions to address child-related problems. The relationship between coach and peer is the focus of the coaching process and includes elements such as rapport building and reflection (Cheliotes & Reilly, 2010). In early childhood education, coaching has been used traditionally in home-based settings and more recently as a component of professional development in quality improvement and other initiatives. Like consultation (Knotek, 2011), coaching has been cited as an important means to facilitate the implementation and continued fidelity of interventions newly applied in educational settings (George, Kincaid, & Pollard-Sage, 2009).

In their traditional definitions, consultation and coaching are described as differing in their foci (capacity building/prevention versus specific skill development), relationships (collaborator versus learner), process (joint problem solving versus reflection), and impact level (individual to system versus individual to individual) (Killion & Harrison, 2006; Gutkin & Curtis, 2008; NAEYC & NACCRR, 2011). However, the distinctions between consultation and coaching are blurring as each practice evolves to utilize best practice and to address current needs in the field. Both models focus on using effective communication skills, a collaborative relationship, and focused problem solving to enhance teachers' service delivery. For example, the movement toward implementing evidence-based interventions has highlighted the need to provide a mechanism to support implementation and the ongoing fidelity of innovations. Practitioners who call themselves consultants or coaches must utilize focused problem solving along with focused professional development to meet the needs of current practice.

Consultation, coaching, and RTI share the core aims of prevention and early intervention along with a focus on enhancing service delivery through professional development at the individual and system levels. This chapter refers to the use of RTI-focused consultation in its discussion of consultation, coaching, and change. However, the RTI-focused consultation described here can be considered to be a blend of consultation and coaching approaches. It is defined as an indirect service in which the consultant/coach enhances the capacity of the consultee/peer to support his or her clients/students. The process emphasizes nonhierarchical collaboration, effective communication, joint problem solving, and professional development in the service of prevention, early intervention, and competency building in children.

RTI-focused consultation is well suited to support the implementation of RTI because 1) it is also prevention focused, 2) it is designed to foster consultees' adaptation to novel work problems such as deciding how to implement new Tier 2 group interventions, 3) it is content neutral and can be used to discuss implementation issues ranging from individual cases to systemwide sustainability, and 4) it incorporates knowledge about adult learning to foster the embedded professional development that will be needed to help teachers and other care providers implement the array of new skills and dispositions that will be needed for RTI to be successful (Knotek, 2007).

CONSULTATION TO PROMOTE SKILL ACQUISITION

The skills and procedures that are needed to operate RTI with fidelity will have to be learned on the job by many of the staff. Peske and Haycock (2006) noted that teachers in high-risk preschool settings tend to have lower levels of education and competency. Few teachers or teachers' aides will be fully trained in, for example, progress monitoring or data-based decision making. Consultation can be used to support the staff's sustained acquisition of skills and their subsequent application to the R&R process; however, the consultant will have to consider a consultee's level of skill development when engaging in problem solving around implementation of RTI. An understanding of Showers and Joyce's (1996) levels of professional development will help consultants target and refine their consultation.

As preschools attempt to provide ongoing professional training, it has become clear that this training should be targeted to a consultee's current level of skill development (Baldwin & Ford, 1988; Showers & Joyce, 1996). The model presented by Showers and Joyce (1996) suggests that staff will progress through four developmental levels as they learn to implement new skills. A consultant can target his or her consultation to fit the developmental demands the staff/consultees may be experiencing as they progress through these four levels: awareness, conceptual understanding, skill acquisition, and application of skills.

Level One: An awareness of the problem is heightened through didactic presentations that result in a person's ability to cite the general ideas and principles associated with the intervention. In RTI, staff would be able to cite the essential components of the model.

Level Two: An individual's deepening conceptual understanding of an intervention is facilitated through modeling and demonstration. For example, within RTI an individual who had acquired conceptual understanding of the importance of prevention and early intervention would be able to conceptually articulate the difference between RTI and the preschool's previous stance.

Level Three: Skill acquisition occurs when a person engages in simulated practices that are observed and commented on by a facilitator. A staff member would learn how to use a new screener and then problem-solve which students might benefit from Tier 2 group interventions.

Level Four: This level of professional development is reached when a person is able to demonstrate a successful application of the new intervention within the actual context of his or her school site. A teacher who is able to implement RTI would be able to adjust her teaching role to support identified students in small-group activities.

It is likely that the implementation of RTI will have varying levels of success across sites. In an era of tight funding, professional development may be limited to the more traditional didactic approaches and the essential longer-term supports may be restricted. Consultation is not a substitute for a deep and extensive professional development program; however, it can be targeted to support staff/consultees' acquisition of the concepts, skills, and procedures that will be required to implement RTI with a high degree of fidelity.

Awareness

RTI has attained a high level of visibility in elementary and secondary schools as districts and states have moved to require it as the core prevention and early intervention problem-solving process. Stakeholders in school districts, from parents to teachers, are being made aware of the changes to school policies and procedures that will accompany RTI's implementation. However, in early childhood education settings RTI is currently emerging as a potential prevention and early intervention process. Administrators may face a tough sell as they ask busy staff to disrupt their current practice to implement an emerging innovation that will require them to acquire new skills and apply new procedures, no matter how beneficial the innovation may be to students.

Given the fact that early childhood RTI models are just being developed, staff and parents may not know about the specifics or even the generalities of RTI. Lack of knowledge has been cited as an ongoing challenge to implementing RTI in preschools (Carta & Greenwood, 2009). Confusion may surround even the rationale for it as stakeholders may not be aware of the theoretical prevention/early intervention underpinnings of RTI. Administrators will need to make staff and families aware of not only what RTI is, but why it is necessary.

A consultant can help the administrator think through the message and means to use to present the case for RTI to the preschool community. The consultant can help the administrator/consultee anticipate initial objections and challenges to RTI that may be put forward. A goal will be to have the consultee think through the most propitious means to present the idea of RTI to the staff and the preschool community and then to have advantages of RTI's implementation ready to share.

At a more basic level, the consultation may need to focus on how to address gaps in some staff members' prior knowledge about key domains in development and instruction. In preschool settings the range of education and accreditation of staff can vary widely, and professional development may need to be individualized so as to properly engage individual personnel. The consultation can focus on ways to provide some staff with prerequisite knowledge that will be needed to successfully engage in the RTI training.

Conceptual Understanding

Consultation can be used to facilitate change in the conceptual understandings of the consultee(s), and that application is important because RTI embodies a conceptual shift in how instruction and assessment are utilized to support the success of all children in a preschool setting. This perspective assumes that we can take prevention and early intervention to new levels of efficacy by careful applying the RTI process. We are asking staff to expand their conception of their professional role to encompass working as proponents of public health as well. The ideas of prevention and early intervention are most likely not foreign to most preschool teachers, yet for many they may simply be ideas. Successful implementation of RTI will likely result in at least a modest change in procedures and even a shift in professional identity for many preschool teachers.

As an example of such changes, consider the fact that many teachers already practice some form of naturalistic instruction to support students with autism spectrum disorder (ASD). However, the RTI process offers a systematic tiered approach to help teachers plan and evaluate their instruction of students with ASD in the least restrictive environment. It does so via a comprehensive process that utilizes screening, a range of instructional options, and progress monitoring to achieve what teachers may believe they are already doing in a far more simple and parsimonious manner. Therefore, some teachers may ask, "Where is the gain for my students and myself if I use RTI?" or "Why can't I just use the same structured teaching methods with all of my students?"

Consultation provides an avenue to help a teacher/consultee address this work problem of conceptual mismatch. Initially, the consultant will endeavor to understand the teacher's beliefs about the role and benefits of naturalistic instruction and other relevant issues. To gain insight into the teacher's perspective, the consultant will pose questions such as "In your opinion, what is the purpose of naturalistic instruction?" "How is the RTI process different from your usual instructional decision-making process?" "What do you see as the challenges to using RTI?" and "What are the similarities between RTI and your current practice?" After this joint exploration of alternative ways to understand the fit of naturalistic instruction in the teacher's classroom, the consultee and consultant will then consider alternative ways to address the challenges involved in meeting the instructional needs of children with ASD.

Skill Acquisition

RTI is a powerful integration of many skills and processes, some of which will be new to preschool teachers and staff. Personnel will undoubtedly experience challenges and setbacks as they try to link and coordinate the discrete components of the model. The one-size-fits-all professional development paradigm that accompanies many training platforms and packages will not be sufficient in many preschool settings. Given the variability in education, experience, and certification that is found within and between preschools, it is likely that differentiation of development will be advantageous to support RTI's consistent implementation. Ball and Trammell noted that there will be training differences in "the necessary level of structure and explicit instruction in the supplemental activities, both for the teachers implementing them and for the students receiving them" (2011, p. 508). Consultation can be used as a means to individually support staff as they learn the intricacies of the complex RTI process on the job. Reflection, status checking, question posing, and problem solving during consultation can help staff integrate different pieces of the RTI puzzle.

Application of Skills

The goal of the whole professional development process is to bring staff to the point where they can apply, with fidelity, the RTI process in their classrooms. However, fidelity and effectiveness may be difficult to achieve given the developmental and readiness levels of students in settings that focus on serving children from high-risk backgrounds. If an RTI model assumes that 80% of a classroom's students will be able to thrive with basic core instruction, but it is being implemented in a high-risk context where only 40% of the children will benefit, then the Tier 1 application of the model may be in jeopardy. Teachers will need to modify and supplement the standard core instruction; however, given the potential variability of the teachers' own education, some staff may need support to be able to enhance the prescribed curriculum. At this level, consultation can be used to provide feedback and promote discussion of how to best implement and sustain RTI with individual teachers as they work with individual students.

A classic tenet of consultation is that helping a consultee resolve a particular type of problem empowers the consultee to adequately address the situation when it arises again in the future. For example, if a teacher is having trouble embedding small-group activities in the classroom because of the extreme range of his or her students' abilities, and if the consultation successfully leads to a solution (increased teacher monitoring of the groups), then the teacher may use this approach in the future. Consultation can offer the consultee perspective on challenges, roadblocks, and successes.

USE OF CONSULTATION TO SUPPORT IMPLEMENTATION OF RESPONSE TO INTERVENTION IN EARLY CHILDHOOD SETTINGS

The RTI paradigm has the potential to transform how preschool children's academic and social functioning are assessed and supported. Its implementation may require change in many systems of care at the district, site, class, and individual levels. Challenges will need to be met to alter the programmatic and professional infrastructure of preschools to allow them to achieve the basic RTI aims of systematic provision of high-quality instruction for all children (Tier 1) while also providing secondary (Tier 2, group) and tertiary (Tier 3, individual) prevention interventions to children who are not making expected developmental progress. The precise challenges are many and include nurturing parent collaboration, initiating screening procedures, changing instructional and assessment practices to align with delivery of service within a tiered framework, and providing professional development. However, implementation is rarely a straightforward process, as we must adapt evidence-based interventions to fit within usual systems of care in a manner that is ecologically valid yet also stays within an acceptable range of treatment fidelity.

Context

The RTI model was initially developed to intervene with students before they were in later stages of academic failure and to provide a systematic, data-based means to identify children for special education based upon their responsiveness to high-quality instruction in elementary and secondary regular education settings (Ball & Trammell, 2011). Coleman, Buysse, and Neitzel (2006a) recognized that given the differing contexts and aims of preschool education in comparison with elementary education and beyond, in order for RTI to be useful and ecologically valid it would need to be modified for use in early education settings. They stress that the context of early childhood schooling includes an emphasis on high-quality care and education, is focused on promoting school readiness, occurs in a variety of settings (e.g., private preschools, Head Start), and through the Individuals with Disabilities Education Improvement Act of 2004 (PL 108-446) Parts B and C maintains an emphasis on prevention and early intervention.

What to Look For

To be an effective RTI consultant, an individual will need to understand the unique early childhood instantiation of the process. As with RTI in elementary and secondary settings, RTI in early childhood settings will need to offer a framework to explicitly and systematically prevent academic delays where possible and also provide an intervention path for children who may be at risk for or already experiencing developmental delays. The consultant will need to be cognizant of developmental issues with an eye toward helping the teacher manage the RTI process so that it will lead to children's successful transition to kindergarten and then elementary school.

Early childhood RTI will likely have a tiered intervention hierarchy that utilizes screening, assessment, and progress monitoring to guide the focused use of research-based interventions while the process is facilitated through collaborative problem solving. However, the interventions will need to be modified to take into account the context of early childhood education and care settings (Peisner-Feinberg, Buysse, Benshoff, & Soukakou, 2011). For example, very young children are not focused so much on learning to use text as they are on mastering skills related to verbal communication and fine and gross motor development. Screeners and interventions currently available for the RTI process in older students do not focus as much on these domains.

The intervention and assessment protocols that will be used in early childhood RTI will likely not have the benefit of the nationally available training and research infrastructure that is in place for RTI in elementary and secondary settings. Consultants will need to help teachers/consultees think through how to interpret and adapt measures to fit their unique settings. In addition, early childhood care and education occurs in a much wider range of environments than primary and secondary education. For successful implementation, RTI will need a great deal of flexibility and responsiveness so as to meet the needs of young children who are being served by teachers and teachers' aides who vary widely in terms of training, education, experience, and licensing—all within sites that range from profit to non-profit and from basic care to school readiness. Consequently, consultants will need to broaden their scope of practice to include and embrace consultees with a wide range of education and experience. They will need to understand the commitment and competence that all care providers, regardless of their level of certification and degrees, bring to their work.

Specific Issues in Early Childhood Settings

RTI consultants will work with consultees who present a myriad of challenges related to implementing RTI in their early childhood settings. Not all of the potential challenges a consultant will be presented with are knowable given the range of contexts and the evolving nature of RTI in preschool settings. However, the consultant can reasonably expect that certain issues found in RTI consultation in elementary and secondary settings will have their own expression at the early childhood level. Consultants may have consultees who require support for the following challenges related to the implementation of RTI in early childhood settings: 1) how to manage professional development, 2) how to apply RTI within the idiosyncrasies of their school site, 3) how to reconcile "how things have always been done" with the need for fidelity of implementation, 4) how to undertake formative evaluation of the process and its outcomes, and 5) how to ensure the sustainability of RTI after the initial training and implementation have been completed.

Professional Development

RTI consultants may be presented with the challenge of how to support early childhood care and preschool providers' acquisition or enhancement of their professional skill set (Buysse & Peisner-Feinberg, 2009). For example, in Tier 1 educators may need to become proficient with the use of progress monitoring that has a formative as opposed to a strictly diagnostic focus. Small-group interventions in Tier 2 may require teachers to adjust their teaching roles by scaffolding through monitoring, encouraging, and facilitating. Other new areas of knowledge that teachers may need to acquire include mastering a defined problem-solving process (e.g., hypothesis formulation, defining concerns in observable terms, charting and graphing data, selecting evidence-based interventions), conducting a broader range of authentic assessments of critical skills (e.g., phonological and print awareness), and developing active/reflective listening skills to facilitate enhanced collaboration between parents and teachers.

RTI-focused consultation can be especially useful to the professional development process during the skill acquisition and application of skills levels of professional development (Knotek, 2007; Russo, 2004; Showers & Joyce, 1996). Consultees may believe that they have mastered a new skill in the structured and constrained environment of a formal training session, only to find that they do not remember much of the material from the session and cannot begin to make sense of how to apply it within the walls of their own classroom. Consultation can offer problem solving and reflection on how to utilize the new skills between formal training sessions and after the sessions have terminated.

Unique Settings

The care and education of young children takes place in complex environments whose functioning is impinged upon by macrosystem issues (e.g., state of the economy, current legislative mandates), mesosystem issues (e.g., interactions between neighborhoods and schools), and microsystem issues (e.g., current class size). RTI will need to be implemented so that it is congruent with the dimensions extant in individual sites. Consultants must be mindful of the qualities of these dimensions as they help to facilitate RTI into a particular setting. For example, if it is found that far less than 80% of the children in a class are making expected progress, then the consultant may want to help the teacher consider how he or she is providing service delivery (instruction) to the whole class before working on implementing more intensive services in the hypothetical Tiers 2 and 3. When the consultant helps the consultee consider multiple aspects of the problem, encompassing instructional as well as individual issues, the consultee may be able to reconceptualize the problem into a more powerful model of the circumstances.

Fidelity

The issue of fidelity (George, Kincaid, & Pollard-Sage, 2009; Gresham, 1989; Walker, 2004) will be very important once implementation has begun. A consultant who is facilitating RTI might wonder: Is delivery consistent? Do personnel choose which components to utilize? Do personnel at a preschool have the skills necessary to implement all of the components of RTI in each classroom? For example, if the screening tool includes assessing receptive language for English as a Second Language (ESL) students and the preschool's teachers do not have ample background in second language acquisition, will they simply ignore this piece of the screener? Teachers and/or intervention specialists who are accustomed to a more laissez-faire approach to implementing new prevention programs may not feel the need to acquire the understanding and skills necessary to make use of the ESL portion of the instrument. A consultant could use clarifying questions and perception checking to gauge the consultee's understanding of the importance of fidelity and then match the consultee's need for improved outcomes for her students with higher degrees of adherence to the RTI protocols.

Evaluation

The following questions speak to some of the most important issues related to integrity: Who at the site has training in evaluation? Who could be responsible for carrying out evaluation? Is it even possible to implement RTI as it was conceived and tested at a site where evaluation is not currently practiced (Hoagwood, 2003–2004; Schoenwald & Hoagwood, 2001)? Consultants supporting the implementation of RTI models that are designed for pre-K populations may need to begin by conducting a simple survey of staff skills and professional responsibility before proceeding to plan professional development to support the transfer of knowledge and skills to appropriate personnel.

Sustainability

Innovations like RTI are considered to be successful when they are sustained in a site after the original period of implementation has passed (Burns & Hoagwood, 2002; Rones & Hoagwood, 2000). A consultant might need to help the site administrator think through and develop a plan of action for sustainability. The consultee would be encouraged to reflect on the following types of questions (Schoenwald & Hoagwood, 2001): What are the congruencies/incongruencies between the goals of RTI and of the preschool itself? How can RTI become embedded in the school's goals? What processes will be used to facilitate training, buy-in, and organizational support? Who will conduct the intervention in question, under what circumstances, and to what effect?

CONCLUSION

The RTI model can be conceptualized as having many moving elements, structures, and processes. It is comprehensive in its approach to the big challenges of prevention and early intervention with young children. Given its complexity, there will be a need for a mechanism to provide support for personnel development during both the initial implementation and ultimate sustaining of RTI in a preschool. RTI-focused consultation is an interpersonal problem-solving process that can be used to help early childhood practitioners develop the skills and dispositions necessary to meet the challenges they will face as they move to embed RTI in their professional practice.

REFERENCES

Baldwin, T.T., & Ford, J.K. (1988). Transfer of training: A review and directions for future research. *Personnel Psychology, 41,* 63–105.

Ball, C.R., & Trammell, B.A. (2011). Response to intervention in high-risk preschools: Critical issues for implementation. *Psychology in the Schools, 48,* 502–512.

Barnett, D.W., VanDerHeyden, A.M., & Witt, J.C. (2007). Achieving science-based practice through response to intervention: What it might look like in preschools. *Journal of Educational and Psychological Consultation, 17,* 31–54.

Bergan, J.R., & Kratochwill, T.R. (1990). Behavioral consultation and therapy. New York, NY: Plenum Press.

Burns, B., & Hoagwood, K. (2002). *Community treatment for youth: Evidence-based interventions for severe emotional and behavioral disorders.* New York, NY: Oxford University Press.

Buysse, V., & Peisner-Feinberg, E. (2009). *Recognition & Response: Findings from the first implementation study.* Retrieved from http://randr.fpg.unc.edu/sites/randr.fpg.unc.edu/files/KeyFindingsHandout.pdf

Buysse, V., & Peisner-Feinberg, E. (2010). Recognition & Response: Response to intervention for pre-K. *Young Exceptional Children, 13*(4), 2–13.

Caplan, G. (1970). *The theory and practice of mental health consultation.* New York, NY: Plenum.

Carta, J.J., & Greenwood, C.R. (2009, March 16). *RTI in pre-kindergarten.* Conference call presentation to the USDE OSEP National Center on Response to Intervention Community of Practice, University of Kansas, Lawrence.

Cheliotes, L.M., & Reilly, M.A. (2010). *Coaching conversations: Transforming your school one conversation at a time.* Thousand Oaks, CA: Sage Publishing.

Coleman, M.R., Buysse, V., & Neitzel, J. (2006). Establishing the evidence base for an emerging early childhood practice: Recognition and Response. In V. Buysse & P.W. Wesley (Eds.),

Evidence-based practice in the early childhood field (pp. 195–225). Washington, DC: ZERO TO THREE Press.

George, H.P., Kincaid, D., & Pollard-Sage, J. (2009). Primary-tier interventions and supports. In W. Sailor, G. Dunlap, G. Sugai, & R. Horner (Eds.), *Handbook of positive behavior support* (pp. 307–326). New York, NY: Springer.

Gresham, F.M. (1989). Assessment of treatment integrity in school consultation and prereferral intervention. *School Psychology Review, 17,* 211–226.

Guskey, T. (2002, March). Does it make a difference? Evaluation of professional development. *Educational Leadership,* 45–51.

Gutkin, T.B., & Curtis, M.J. (2008). School-based consultation: The science and practice of indirect service delivery. In T.B. Gutkin & C.R. Reynolds (Eds.), *The handbook of school psychology* (4th ed., pp. 591–635). New York, NY: Wiley.

Hiatt-Michael, D.B. (2007). Engaging English language learner families as partners. In D. Hiatt-Michael (Ed.), *Promising practices for teachers to engage families of English language learners* (pp. 1–10). Charlotte, NC: Information Age Publishing.

Hoagwood, K. (2003–2004). Evidence-based practice in child and adolescent mental health: Its meaning, application and limitations. *Emotional & Behavioral Disorders in Youth, 4,* 7–8.

Hoagwood, K., & Johnson, J. (2002). School psychology: A public health framework, I. From evidence-based practices to evidence-based policies. *Journal of School Psychology, 41,* 3–21.

Individuals with Disabilities Education Improvement Act (IDEA) of 2004, PL 108-446, 20 U.S.C. § § 1400 *et seq.*

Killion, J., & Harrison, C. (2006). *Taking the lead: New roles for teachers and school-based coaches.* Oxford, OH: National Staff Development Council.

Knotek, S.E. (2007). Consultation within response to intervention models. In S. Jimerson, M. Burns, & A. VanDerHeyden (Eds.) *The handbook of response to intervention: The science and practice of assessment and intervention* (pp. 53–64). New York, NY: Springer.

Knotek, S.E. (2011). Utilizing culturally responsive consultation to support innovation implementation in a rural school. *Consulting Psychology Journal: Practice and Research, 64,* 46–62.

Kratochwill, T.R., Volpiansky, P., Clements, M., & Ball, C. (2007). The role of professional development in implementing and sustaining multi-tier prevention and intervention models: Implications for response to intervention. *School Psychology Review 36,* 618–631.

National Association for the Education of Young Children & National Association of Child Care Resource & Referral Agencies. (2011). *Early childhood education professional development: Training and assistance glossary.* Washington, DC: NAEYC.

Peisner-Feinberg, E., Buysse, V., Benshoff, L., & Soukakou, E. (2011). Recognition & Response: Response to intervention for pre-kindergarten. In C. Groark, S.M. Eidelman, L. Kaczmarek, & S. Maude (Eds.), *Early childhood intervention: Shaping the future for children with special needs and their families, Vol. 3: Emerging trends in research and practice* (pp. 37–53). Santa Barbara, CA: Praeger.

Peske, H.G., & Haycock, K. (2006). *Teaching inequality: How poor and minority students are shortchanged on teacher quality.* Washington, DC: The Education Trust.

Rones, M., & Hoagwood, K. (2000). School-based mental health services: A research review. *Clinical Child and Family Psychology Review, 3,* 223–241.

Russo, A. (2004, July/August). School-based coaching: A revolution in professional development or just the latest fad? *Harvard Education Letter, 20*(4), 1–3.

Schoenwald, S., & Hoagwood, K. (2001). Effectiveness, transportability, and dissemination of interventions: What matters when? *Psychiatric Services, 52,* 45–50.

Showers, B., & Joyce, B. (1996). The evolution of peer coaching. *Educational Leadership, 53,* 12–16.

Sugai, G., & Horner, R.R. (2006). A promising approach for expanding and sustaining school-wide positive behavior support. *School Psychology Review, 25*(2), 245–259.

Vygotsky, L.S. (1986). *Thought and language.* Cambridge, MA: MIT Press.

Walker, H.M. (2004). Commentary: Use of evidence-based interventions in schools: Where we've been, where we are, and where we need to go. *School Psychology Review, 33,* 398–410.

20

Family Engagement within Early Childhood Response to Intervention

Shana J. Haines, Amy McCart, and Ann Turnbull

Increasingly, innovative early childhood educators are successfully implementing a response to intervention (RTI) framework (Linas, Carta, & Greenwood, 2010). Through the use of multitiered intervention systems, progress-monitoring tools, evidence-based practices (including fidelity of implementation), and a problem-solving process, these programs are paving the way for universal high-quality curriculum and instruction that matches each child's needs. RTI brings to early childhood education a systematic approach for providing comprehensive supports for all children.

Despite the emergence of RTI, the field of early childhood education currently lacks a universally accepted approach to engaging families in partnering with practitioners to meet children's educational needs. Philosophies embraced by early childhood educators underscore the benefits of family engagement in their children's education. Family engagement enables practitioners and families to partner to carry out authentic assessment; gain a holistic view of the child; and design instruction that is responsive to each family's values, beliefs, and priorities (McCart, Wolf, Sweeney, & Choi, 2009). Educators who actively foster family engagement affirm to families that they are valued and integral to the success of their children. In turn, families are more likely to understand their importance to their children's education and learn how to best advocate for and educate their children (Christenson, 2010). In other words, fostering family engagement enables educators to help families develop their capacities to partner with educators so that educators and families can work together to meet children's needs in a comprehensive and responsive fashion. Developing these capacities can equip families to be effective educational decision makers in the present and throughout their children's academic journeys. In their review of the state of early childhood RTI, Greenwood and colleagues emphasized the important roles of families as follows: "Early childhood as reflected in its professional organizations and published literature is supported by knowledge that learning begins before birth and that after birth the child's family members are its most important teachers" (2011, p. 5). As RTI becomes more widespread in early childhood, the time is ripe for embedding family engagement into core RTI elements to ensure that families are engaged in all aspects of their children's education.

313

In this chapter, we outline a model of embedded family engagement in early childhood RTI for the purpose of meeting children's needs. First, we provide a definition for family engagement in early childhood RTI and review its foundations in early childhood education and early childhood special education. Second, we briefly highlight literature on family roles in the RTI approach. Third, we describe the embedded family engagement model and provide sample programmatic options that educators can offer families to further their engagement. Fourth, we offer caution about potential pitfalls and describe corresponding proactive practices of family engagement in early childhood RTI. Last, we identify implications for teacher education, policy, and research.

FOUNDATIONS AND DEFINITIONS

We draw from the fields of both early childhood education and early childhood special education to define family engagement in RTI. In this section, we begin by highlighting foundations of family engagement related to policy, research, and ethical guidelines. We then review definitions of *family engagement* from the early childhood education field and family–professional partnerships from the early childhood special education field. From these two definitions, we create a merged definition on which we base our recommendations.

The two most prominent education laws relating to family engagement in education are the Elementary and Secondary Education Act (ESEA) of 1965 (PL 89-10), and the Individuals with Disabilities Education Improvement Act (IDEA) of 2004 (PL 108-446). The primary theme of ESEA requirements is that schools provide comprehensive information to families, such as the results of their children's academic assessments, data on the whole school's performance on standardized assessments, and transfer options if their child's school does not make adequate yearly progress for 2 years. The primary theme of IDEA for parents whose child is diagnosed with a disability is that parents should be decision makers in ensuring that their child receives an appropriate education through participation in the development of individualized family service plans (IFSPs) and individualized education programs (IEPs) as well as in providing consent for evaluations and placement.

Research, especially in the general early childhood field, provides empirical evidence on the benefits that accrue to children when their parents engage in education-related roles. Reynolds and Shlafer (2010) found that comprehensive parent involvement activities improved children's performance on basic skills at school entry, reduced special education placement and grade retention, and increased postsecondary attendance. Webster-Stratton and Reid (2010) found that focusing on strengthening parental competency and parents' involvement with their child's school improved behavior at home for children with conduct problems. In fact, Marcon (1999) found that higher levels of parent involvement in school and more active types of parent involvement were related to increases in children's adaptive behavior and basic school skills. Fantuzzo, McWayne, Perry, and Childs' (2004) findings concurred: parents' home-based involvement improved children's classroom behavior, receptive language skills, attention, and motivation. Arnold, Zeljo, Doctoroff, and Ortiz (2008) also found that parental involvement enhanced children's preliteracy skills.

Research in the field of early childhood special education has primarily focused on IDEA requirements and family-centered practice (Bailey, 2001; Dunst & Bruder,

2002; Epley, Summers, & Turnbull, 2010; McWilliam, Snyder, Harbin, Porter, & Munn, 2000; Turnbull, Turnbull, Erwin, Soodak, & Shogren, 2011) and has usually emphasized parent outcomes (e.g., satisfaction, stress). Calderon (2000) reported the child outcome of having readiness skills was predicted by parents' participation in IEP meetings, classroom volunteering, and attendance at school activities. Similarly, Epley (2009) found that home-based parent involvement significantly predicted academic and social-behavioral performance of kindergarten children with disabilities. The interventions used in these research studies primarily focused on tasks carried out by parents that increased their involvement with their child's school activities and/or their time and attention allocations to learning at home.

Both the National Association for the Education of Young Children (NAEYC) and the Council for Exceptional Children's Division of Early Childhood (DEC) have codes of ethics that include strong sections on family roles. In the NAEYC Code of Ethics (2005), Section II addresses ethical responsibilities to families and includes nine ideals and 15 principles. Ideals include "To develop relationships of mutual trust and create partnerships with the families we serve" (p. 3) and "To respect the dignity and preferences of each family and to make an effort to learn about its structure, culture, language, customs, and beliefs" (p. 4).

DEC's Code of Ethics (2009) includes four guidelines for enhancing children's and families' quality of life and seven guidelines focusing on responsive family-centered practices. Examples of these guidelines include "We shall demonstrate our respect and concern for children, families, colleagues, and others with whom we work, honoring their beliefs, values, customs, languages, and culture" (p. 3) and "We shall recognize and respect the dignity, diversity, and autonomy of the families and children we serve" (p. 3).

These two leading early childhood organizations have ethical guidelines that are largely aligned. The examples highlighted here focus on the quality of the relationship between parents and educators in terms of elements such as respect and dignity. Although relationship quality is not the exclusive focus of the NAEYC and DEC ethical guidelines, it clearly is the primary emphasis.

In sum, a relationship focus derived from ethical guidelines contrasts with the task-oriented focus in research and the educational decision-making focus in policy. Merging these three foci provides a comprehensive foundation for family engagement.

Leaders within the field of general early childhood education have conceptualized the new construct of family engagement as follows: "Family engagement occurs when there is an ongoing, reciprocal, strengths-based partnership between families and their children's early childhood program" (Halgunseth, Peterson, Stark, & Moodie, 2009, p. 3). The distinguishing concept in this definition is forming a relationship based on partnership. Although the authors do not explicitly define partnership, they implicitly define how to create it through their explication of family engagement factors. These factors include parents and teachers engaging in reciprocal communication, extending learning into the home and community, parents participating as active educational decision makers to advocate for their child, and parents volunteering for school activities. One way to characterize these factors is that partnerships are created through jointly carrying out *tasks* for the purpose of improving children's educational outcomes. This is consistent with the policy and research foundation.

This approach of conceptualizing partnerships primarily around tasks contrasts with the approach of the early childhood special education field, where partnerships focus on the *quality of the relationships* and how families and educators interact with each other. Turnbull and colleagues define *partnership* as follows:

> Partnership refers to a relationship in which families (not just parents) and professionals agree to build on each other's expertise and resources, as appropriate, for the purpose of making and implementing decisions that will directly benefit students and indirectly benefit other family members and professionals. (2011, p. 137)

Based on mixed-methods research with families and professionals (Blue-Banning, Summers, Frankland, Nelson, & Beegle, 2004; Summers, Hoffman, Marquis, Turnbull, & Poston, 2005), Turnbull and colleagues (2011) identified the following principles of partnership: 1) *enhanced communication:* building on basic communication skills to dignify each child and family by honoring their uniqueness in terms of their family history, present circumstances, and future possibilities; 2) *professional competence:* being highly qualified and having confidence in one's own competence in actualizing positive outcomes for children; 3) *respect:* regarding families with dignity and demonstrating that dignity through actions and words; 4) *commitment:* providing a sense of assurance that the relationship with the family and child represents devotion and loyalty to the child and family and a shared belief in the importance of goals being pursued; 5) *equality:* ensuring that families have equal power as practitioners in all interactions; and 6) *advocacy:* speaking out and taking action in pursuit of finding just solutions to problems.

Another general difference between early childhood education and early childhood special education in defining partnerships is the emphasis on the family as the ultimate decision makers about their role. Through the factors of family engagement, NAEYC (2005) implied what the family "should" do; they did not offer a discussion regarding the family as the ultimate decision makers regarding their involvement. Alternatively, a cornerstone of disability policy (i.e., legislation and judicial decisions) in the United States is that families have autonomy in terms of experiencing freedom from outside interference related to family decision making (Turnbull & Stowe, 2001). Family autonomy is actualized in the early childhood special education field through the concept of family-centered practice (Epley et al., 2010). Family choice is a core element of family-centered practice that encompasses determining the nature of family–professional relationships; identifying concerns, priorities, and resources; and making decisions regarding service delivery for the family and child.

Building on the contributions of family engagement within the early childhood field as well as family–professional partnerships and family-centered practice within the early childhood special education field, we use the following blended definition of family engagement.

Family engagement occurs when there is a trusting partnership between families and educators and when educators offer families options for ways to be engaged in their children's education. Trusting partnerships are relationships that are engendered through enhanced communication, professional competence in actualizing outcomes, respect, commitment, equality, and advocacy on the part of educators. Family engagement options include engaging in reciprocal communication, exchanging knowledge, participating in decision making, and creating with educators mutual goals to be promoted in program and home environments. From a range of options for family engagement, families are supported through trusting partnerships with educators to make choices that align with considerations for what they perceive to be in the best interest of their families.

Throughout this chapter, we use this definition as a foundation for our recommendations for effective family engagement within an RTI approach.

HIGHLIGHTS OF LITERATURE CONCERNING FAMILY ROLES IN RESPONSE TO INTERVENTION

In this section, we briefly highlight current literature on the role of families in RTI. We use the term *family roles* in a broad sense rather than *family engagement* in particular because authors in the field use a variety of terms and definitions. We located six articles from the fields of early childhood education, early childhood special education, special education, and school psychology that specifically address family roles in RTI (Byrd, 2011; Christenson, 2010; Fox, Carta, Strain, Dunlap, & Hemmeter, 2010; McCart et al., 2009; McCart et al., 2010; McIntyre & Phaneuf, 2007). Indicative of the early stages of implementing family roles in RTI, all of the articles are descriptive. Space limitations preclude reviewing the specific details of these articles, but themes across them include 1) the potential of strong parent roles across tiers to improve child outcomes, 2) the necessity for developing sound principles and practices for family roles, 3) the importance of providing information to families about RTI, and 4) implications of research for the roles of family members and educators.

OVERVIEW OF AN EMBEDDED FAMILY ENGAGEMENT MODEL

At this propitious time of RTI's growth throughout the country, we propose embedding family engagement in RTI models to foster the educational progress of all children. The ultimate purpose of embedding family engagement in RTI models is to strengthen partnerships with families in order to augment child progress. Simultaneous to fostering child progress, embedded family engagement can empower families to be educational advocates for their children starting in early childhood and continuing throughout their lives.

The responsibility of nurturing family engagement belongs to both educators and families. Educators are responsible for providing a full array of options for engagement and for supporting families through trusting partnerships to engage in the options they select for themselves. Families are responsible for considering the full array of options and making decisions about the role that is appropriate for them in light of their preferences, resources, and concerns. Families' decisions of how they engage in their children's education need to be based on a full understanding of the potential benefits to their child, family, and the educators working with their child, as well as the potential drawbacks of lack of engagement. There may also be drawbacks to engagement, including additional stress for families, lack of time and attention for other family priorities because of putting more time and attention into a child's education, and other related considerations. As discussed previously, family autonomy is a core concept of disability policy (Turnbull & Stowe, 2001), and families are the ultimate decision makers about their roles in their children's education. Through partnership, educators and families can recip-rocally augment their own and each other's motivation and capacity for shared roles in educating children (Turnbull, Turbiville, & Turnbull, 2000).

The model we propose in the following sections identifies educators' respon-sibilities for providing options for family engagement. Families are more likely to fully engage in their children's education when they have a trusting partnership with educators (Turnbull et al., 2011). In addition, we suggest that early childhood programs involve stakeholders, including families, in planning and decisions. For example, an organized council can facilitate communication between educa-tors and families in order to ensure that all groups of stakeholders understand the needs and opinions of their fellow stakeholders (Byrd, 2011).

The core elements of RTI in which family engagement options can be embedded include multiple tiers of intervention, use of progress-monitoring tools, evidence-based practice (including fidelity of implementation), and use of a problem-solving model (Buysse & Peisner-Feinberg, 2010; Greenwood et al., 2011).

Multiple Tiers of Intervention

The first core element of RTI is multiple tiers of intervention. A way to envision family engagement options is to pair them with intensity of child need, so the options differ when children receive supports in each of the three tiers. When con-ceptualizing family engagement in this way, we stress that families also vary at each tier in terms of the intensity of their own needs and their personal preferences for being engaged in their children's education. Thus, we recommend that educa-tors offer a continuum of support intensity and multiple options for family engage-ment aligned with child need.

Since all children receive Tier 1 intervention, we encourage educators to pro-vide information about RTI to all families. This information could be provided in a variety of ways and include RTI's purpose, a description of the RTI process, and a list of pertinent dates and times of assessment. In addition to this basic information that enables families to understand a little about the RTI process at school, edu-cators might consider scheduling educational sessions during which families can learn ways to work with their children and talk about school with their children at home. Certain attitudes and practices are implicit in Tier 1. For example, educa-tors could encourage and seek families' input and involvement, view meeting chil-dren's needs as a top professional goal, and provide a safe environment for families to openly and honestly share relevant information about their child and family.

When children receive Tier 2 supports, educators might boost the level of sup-port offered to families. Educators should consider discussing with families their children's assessment data and making decisions together with families using the problem-solving model. Also, when possible, educators might offer to teach fami-lies how to implement home components of evidence-based practices.

When children receive Tier 3 supports, educators may consider offering more intense support and outreach to families so they can optimally help their children at home and in the community. In this case, meetings with families will likely be more frequent and ongoing. In addition, as the complexity of need increases, so does the need for service coordination in terms of involving representatives from multiple disciplines and agencies.

Use of Progress-Monitoring Tools

Family engagement in using progress-monitoring tools (i.e., when educators and families use timely data to guide the educational process for each child) is multifaceted. Reciprocal communication promotes the increased competency of the family–educator dyad because the combined information creates a much more accurate assessment of the child while solidifying parent understanding and facilitating the use of data to guide educational planning for the child. Knowledge sharing underscores the need to think about the child comprehensively across settings, validates information from families and educators, and offers in-depth understanding of the child for effective progress monitoring. Family participation in decision making incorporates family ideas about progress monitoring tools and the resulting educational goals. Shared goals for the center and home promote a transparent process of progress monitoring that results in a mutual understanding of the importance of working toward common goals.

Because all children receive Tier 1 supports, we recommend that educators inform all families about the purposes and goals of progress monitoring tools. Children benefit when their families know when their children are being evaluated, so educators could communicate assessment dates and let parents know when the data will be available for discussion. Because families are not usually professionally trained to make sense of the data for their children, educators might consider offering information sessions about progress monitoring. In addition, since progress monitoring is confusing to many people, educators may find ways to praise families for their involvement and let them know that they truly welcome their input.

When children receive supports in Tiers 2 and 3, we encourage educators to offer families an increasing level of support in progress monitoring. To do this, educators could invite families to conferences as needed to review progress-monitoring data together. In addition, educators could communicate as needed with families about child progress on goals at school and home while also promoting ongoing family development to build skills to meet child need.

Use of Evidence-Based Practices

The use of evidence-based practice requires that educators and families use interventions with fidelity that represent an integration of the best available research, policy, and experience-based knowledge of seasoned families and practitioners (Turnbull et al., 2010) and is optimized by incorporating family engagement options. Reciprocal communication enables families to understand the importance of evidence-based practice, including fidelity of implementation. Knowledge sharing encourages families to provide information about the child's reactions to the evidence-based practices they implement at home, the fidelity with which they are able to implement interventions at home, and the evidence-based practices that educators implement at school. Family participation in decision making incorporates family ideas about the efficacy, fidelity, and contextualization of specific evidence-based practices as well as the child's interests in these practices. Shared goals for school and home promote comprehensive implementation of evidence-based practices across settings.

In order to put into practice these options for family engagement, we encourage educators to provide information about evidence-based practice to all families. In Tier 1, educators should consider providing general information sessions to teach all families about aspects of the evidence-based curriculum that occurs in school and ways that families can extend it at home. These general information sessions could also stress the importance of fidelity of implementation. Educators might use these sessions to solicit questions from families and invite feedback about their children's responses to the curriculum at school and home.

When a child receives supports in Tier 2, we recommend that educators clearly communicate to the family that, since their child has been identified as requiring increased exposure to instruction, their child will participate in evidence-based interventions at greater frequency and intensity. To foster a trusting partnership, educators should emphasize that the tiers are fluid and intervention for the child is aimed at proactively providing instruction that will help the child succeed. Educators might inform families about the scheduling of the interventions so they can try to minimize disrupting the schedule. Educators could also provide information and training about home-based components of the evidence-based curriculum, encourage families to implement what they are able to do, and ask how they can support them. Educators could find ways to encourage and praise families for providing support at home with interventions. Along the same lines, a strategy for encouraging and helping families is for educators to first inquire about specific components of the evidence-based interventions that are positive, negative, and/or confusing for families or their children and then do their best to solve identified problems and increase clarity.

When a child receives supports in Tier 3, we encourage educators to communicate more frequently by establishing ongoing meetings to discuss the child's response to intervention. Depending upon the complexity of the intervention, some families may not be able to effectively implement interventions with fidelity. We encourage educators to gauge families' interest, time availability, and comprehension of the nuances of intervention and make individualized decisions about how to best implement programs in the home and in other community settings. Educators can encourage each family to implement interventions in light of their preferences, strengths, and needs with recognition that any amount of support at home can foster overall progress.

Use of Problem-Solving Model

Families play an integral part in the problem-solving model when educators and families use a clearly defined approach to problem resolution (i.e., asking the following questions: What is the problem? Why is it happening? What should be done about it? Did it work? How could it work better?) and employ decision rules (e.g., weighing short- and long-term implications, weighing pros and cons for family impact, considering the impact on the child's self-esteem) for selecting interventions matched to each child's needs, strengths, and preferences. Family engagement in the problem-solving model improves its comprehensiveness and applicability across contexts. Reciprocal communication expands the knowledge of families and educators by promoting the use of the problem-solving model as a systematic method of evaluating and solving issues that arise in the center, home, and community. Knowledge sharing offers increased comprehensive understanding of the child and family for effective problem solving across settings. Participation in decision making incorporates family input about the problem as well as discussion of the viability of a menu of possible solutions. Shared goals for school and home promote input from families and educators in order to create joint goals across settings.

For many people, the problem-solving model represents a new, systematic method for approaching dilemmas. It is nearly impossible to fully explain that the problem-solving model is a cyclical process that seeks to identify problems, select interventions based on comprehensive data and team reflection, and constantly evaluate each intervention's efficacy through continued cycling. Therefore, a strategy to consider is for educators to go beyond simple explanation and, instead, practice the problem-solving model when meeting with families and also when working with children. In addition, we recommend that educators provide all families with information about the process and consider including a guiding worksheet and illustrated diagram of the process (asking the following questions: What is the problem? Why is it happening? What should be done about it? Did it work? How could it work better?). Educators might also consider using videos of the process at work with children and families in order to explain it fully to families. In addition to using this model with children, we recommend that educators use this model at their meetings with each other and with families. As always, educators should solicit and listen to families' input about their children's needs.

Although we encourage educators and all families to participate in the problem-solving model during everyday occurrences, educators should take particular care to emphasize the importance of this process to families whose children receive supports in Tier 2 intervention because their participation in problem-solving teams is vital to intervention success. Educators should schedule problem-solving team meetings at convenient times for families and consider how to structure meetings to encourage family participation. To solicit input from families at each step of the problem-solving process, educators could ask families what they perceive to be the child's main needs, techniques they use at home to work on specific problems, their rationale for choosing specific strategies, and ideas for how these strategies could be adapted for use in the classroom. In addition, educators implicitly model how to use data to interpret children's responses to intervention and might consider explicitly teaching family members how to interpret their child's data.

When a child receives supports in Tier 3, educators should establish a schedule of regular problem-solving team meetings that is convenient for the family. At these meetings, educators might continue to seek information regarding how the child learns and responds behaviorally in a variety of contexts, including the home and community. Modeling the problem-solving model and teaching families how to use it in everyday circumstances as well as at the problem-solving team meetings is extremely important in Tier 3 because families will remain on their child's education team across the life span. Their children will benefit from these effective skills for years to come.

POTENTIAL PITFALLS AND PROACTIVE PRACTICES

Early childhood RTI creates an opportunity to systematically increase family engagement, but this opportunity must be purposeful because, as with any comprehensive change, implementation of RTI in early childhood settings brings with it the possibility of misapplication of its strategies and systems. Failing to put forth the necessary effort toward family engagement could inadvertently alienate families. In the following paragraphs, we highlight a few potential pitfalls and pair them with proactive practices we recommend in order to avoid unintentionally alienating families while embarking on implementing RTI in early childhood settings.

A first potential pitfall is that educators might inadvertently create a new system for labeling children and families when implementing RTI (e.g., "That's a Tier 3 family"). One proactive practice is for educators to recognize that child and family needs are fluid and tiers reflect specific current needs, not permanent characteristics. As discussed previously, we recommend that this fluidity be communicated to families as well. Of course, it is inappropriate for educators to refer to or judge children or families by the tier in which they receive supports. Another proactive practice is for educators to establish and maintain high expectations for children and families regardless of the tiers in which the children currently receive support (e.g., use progress-monitoring data to establish goals in partnership with families that energize the family and the team).

A second potential pitfall is that educators might alienate families by using scientific vocabulary that families might not understand. A proactive practice for educators to employ is to scaffold the explanation of terms and processes to families and only use complicated language when necessary. The language of RTI is foreign to most noneducators (and to many educators as well!).

A third potential pitfall happens when educators adhere rigidly to a stagnant list of supports without considering the needs and desires of the family. A proactive practice we recommend is for educators to recognize the family as the expert on the child and facilitate shared responsibility for identifying family and child needs. Part of this recognition involves discussing possible interventions with families and continually seeking their input while remembering that evidence-based practice does not mean that "one size fits all"; just because an intervention has an evidence base does not mean that it will work for all children all the time. Another part of this proactive practice is to encourage family autonomy by offering decision-making power and respecting the family's decisions.

IMPLICATIONS FOR FUTURE DEVELOPMENT

Although the growth of early childhood RTI programs presents an opportunity to implement embedded family engagement, many barriers currently block its widespread implementation. Surmounting these barriers requires significant progress, including a need for teacher education to adapt, for policy to change, and for more research to be conducted on effective family engagement. Teacher educators must increase their emphasis on family engagement in teacher preparation programs, which includes diminishing the traditional teacher-as-expert model and expanding culturally responsive teaching and partnership skills. Policy can expand the role of families in the RTI process, just as IDEA now requires that parents participate as decision makers in IFSP/IEP development and in the provision of consent for services. It will be timely to develop this policy option in the next reauthorization of ESEA and IDEA.

Research on RTI models to address children's needs should incorporate embedded family engagement. Given the strong ethical, policy, and research foundation for family engagement (discussed at the beginning of this chapter), research should focus on how to systematically embed family engagement into all elements of RTI. Current research on RTI has had such a strong focus on child need that it has not simultaneously addressed family engagement. In order to ensure that family engagement is an integral part of RTI, future research is needed to strengthen the evidence base on family engagement across all RTI elements.

Early childhood RTI is an opportunity to improve child outcomes through the implementation of the four core elements of RTI (i.e., multiple tiers of intervention, use of progress-monitoring tools, evidence-based practice, and use of a problem-solving model), with family engagement practices embedded in each element. The bedrock of successful family engagement is the development and implementation of trusting partnerships that enable practitioners and families to establish mutual goals and reciprocally contribute to the actualization of those goals.

REFERENCES

Arnold, D.H., Zeljo, A., Doctoroff, G.L., & Ortiz, C. (2008). Parent involvement in preschool: Predictors and the relation of involvement to preliteracy development. *School Psychology Review, 37*(1), 74–90.

Bailey, D.B. (2001). Evaluating parent involvement and family support in early intervention and preschool programs. *Journal of Early Intervention, 24*(1), 1–14.

Blue-Banning, M.J., Summers, J.A., Frankland, H.C., Nelson, L.L., & Beegle, G. (2004). Dimensions of family and professional partnerships: Constructive guidelines for collaboration. *Exceptional Children, 70*(2), 167–184.

Buysse, V., & Peisner-Feinberg, E. (2010). Recognition & Response: Response to intervention for pre-K. *Young Exceptional Children, 13,* 12.

Byrd, E.S. (2011). Educating and involving parents in the response to intervention process: The school's important role. *Teaching Exceptional Children, 43*(3), 32–39.

Calderon, R. (2000). Parental involvement in deaf children's education programs as a predictor of child's language, early reading, and social-emotional development. *Journal of Deaf Studies and Deaf Education, 5*(2), 140–155.

Christenson, S.L. (2010). Engaging with parents: The power of information, responsiveness to parental need, and ongoing support for the enhanced competence of all students. *National Association of School Psychologists, 39*(1), 20–24.

Division of Early Childhood (DEC). (2009). *Code of ethics.* Retrieved from http://www.dec-sped.org/uploads/docs/about_dec/position_concept_papers/Code%20of%20Ethics_updated_Aug2009.pdf

Dunst, C.J., & Bruder, M.B. (2002). Valued outcomes of service coordination, early intervention, and natural environments. *Exceptional Children, 68*(3), 361–375.

Elementary and Secondary Education Act (ESEA) of 1965, PL 89-10, 20 U.S.C. §§ 241 *et seq.*

Epley, P.H. (2009). *Early school performance for students with disabilities: Examining the impact of early childhood special education, parental involvement, and family quality of life.* Unpublished doctoral dissertation. Lawrence: University of Kansas.

Epley, P., Summers, J.A., & Turnbull, A. (2010). Characteristics and trends in family-centered conceptualizations. *Journal of Family Social Work, 13,* 269–285.

Fantuzzo, J., McWayne, C., Perry, M.A., & Childs, S. (2004). Multiple dimensions of family involvement and their relations to behavioral and learning competencies for urban, low-income children. *School Psychology Review, 33*(4), 467–480.

Fox, L., Carta, J., Strain, P.S., Dunlap, G., & Hemmeter, M.L. (2010). Response to intervention and the pyramid model. *Infants & Young Children, 23*(1), 3–13.

Greenwood, C.R., Bradfield, T., Kaminski, R., Linas, M., Carta, J.J., & Nylander, D. (2011). The response to intervention (RTI) approach in early childhood. *Focus on Exceptional Children, 43,* 1–22.

Halgunseth, L.C., Peterson, A., Stark, D., & Moodie, S. (2009). *Family engagement, diverse families, and early childhood education programs: An integrated review of the literature.* Retrieved from http://www.naeyc.org/files/naeyc/file/research/FamEngage.pdf

Individuals with Disabilities Education Improvement Act (IDEA) of 2004, PL 108-446, 20 U.S.C. §§ 1400 *et seq.*

Linas, M., Carta, J.J., & Greenwood, C.R. (2010, June). *Taking a snapshot of early childhood response to intervention across the United States: 2009 and 2010.* Poster displayed at the annual Head Start Research Conference, Washington, DC.

Marcon, R.A. (1999). Positive relationships between parent school involvement and public school inner-city preschoolers' development and academic performance. *School Psychology Review, 28*(3), 395–412.

McCart, A., Lee, J., Frey, A.J., Wolf, N., Choi, J.H., & Haynes, H. (2010). Response to intervention in early childhood centers: A multitiered approach promoting family engagement. *Early Childhood Services, 4*(2), 87–104.

McCart, A., Wolf, N., Sweeney, H.M., & Choi, J.H. (2009). The application of a family-based multi-tiered system of support. *NHSA Dialog, 12*(2), 122–132.

McIntyre, L.L., & Phaneuf, L.K. (2007). A three-tier model of parent education in early childhood. *Topics in Early Childhood Special Education, 27*(4), 214–222.

McWilliam, R.A., Snyder, P., Harbin, G.L., Porter, P., & Munn, D. (2000). Professionals' and families' perceptions of family-centered practices in infant–toddler services. *Early Education and Development, 11*(4), 519–538.

NAEYC. (2005). *NAEYC code of ethical conduct and statement of commitment.* Retrieved from http://www.naeyc.org/files/naeyc/file/positions/PSETH05.pdf

Reynolds, A.J., & Shlafer, R.J. (2010). Parent involvement in early education. In S.L. Christenson & A.L. Reschly (Eds.), *Handbook of school–family partnerships* (pp. 158–174). New York, NY: Routledge.

Summers, J.A., Hoffman, L., Marquis, J., Turnbull, A.P., & Poston, D. (2005). Parent satisfaction with their partnerships with professionals across different ages of their children. *Topics in Early Childhood Special Education, 25*(1), 48–58.

Turnbull, A., Stowe, M., Zuna, N., Hong, J.Y., Hu, X., Kyzar, K., Obremski, S., . . . Turnbull, R. (2010). Knowledge-to-action guides for preparing families to be partners in making educational decisions. *Teaching Exceptional Children, 42*(3), 42–53.

Turnbull, A.P., Turbiville, V., & Turnbull, H.R. (2000). Evolution of family–professional partnership models: Collective empowerment as the model for the early 21st century. In S.J. Meisels & J.P. Shonkoff (Eds.), *Handbook of early intervention* (pp. 630–650). New York, NY: Cambridge University Press.

Turnbull, A.P., Turnbull, H.R., Erwin, E., Soodak, L., & Shogren, K. (2011). *Families, professionals, and exceptionality: Positive outcomes through partnerships and trust* (6th ed.). Upper Saddle River, NJ: Merrill/Prentice Hall.

Turnbull, H.R., & Stowe, M.J. (2001). Five models for thinking about disability: Implications for policy. *Journal of Disability Policy Studies, 12*(3), 198–205.

Webster-Stratton, C., & Reid, M.J. (2010). A school–family partnership: Addressing multiple risk factors to improve school readiness and prevent conduct problems in young children. In S.L. Christenson & A.L. Reschly (Eds.), *Handbook of school–family partnerships* (pp. 204–227). New York, NY: Routledge.

Professional Development

Supporting the Evidence-Based Early Childhood Practitioner

Pamela J. Winton

Many factors affect the extent to which new approaches to improving early childhood educational practice, such as response to intervention (RTI), become embedded and sustained into the culture and practices of service settings (Fixsen, Naoom, Blase, & Wallace, 2007; Kitson, Harvey, & McCormack, 1998; Kreuter & Bernhardt, 2009). These include the strength of the evidence supporting the innovation; the presence or absence of an organizational culture, climate, and resources that could support and sustain change; and the competence and confidence of staff in implementing the approach. During this current period when the field is in the early stages of exploring the meaning and application of RTI in early childhood, it is an optimal time to think systemically and strategically about work-force support and professional development (PD) to implement the new approach. A complicating factor in doing this type of planning is the slim body of research on what constitutes effective PD in early childhood and almost nonexistent literature on PD related to early childhood RTI.

The purpose of this chapter is to apply what is known about effective PD in early childhood to early childhood RTI. In the first part of this chapter, a definition of PD and a framework from the National Professional Development Center on Inclusion (NPDCI, 2008) are used to characterize key components that must be addressed in designing PD on RTI in early childhood education. In the second part of this chapter, an innovative, clinical teaching approach to designing PD curricula—the CONNECT 5-Step Learning Cycle—is introduced.

DEFINITION AND CONCEPTUAL FRAMEWORK

Until recently something as basic as an agreed-upon definition of PD within early childhood education has not been available, and this absence has been an obstacle in the quest to develop a highly qualified early childhood work force (Maxwell, Feild, & Clifford, 2005). To address this challenge, the National Professional Development Center on Inclusion (NPDCI) put forth the following definition: "Professional development (PD) is defined as facilitated teaching and learning experiences that are transactional and designed to support the acquisition of professional knowledge, skills, and dispositions as well as the application of this knowledge in practice" (NPDCI, 2008, p. 3). The NPDCI definition includes a framework in which the interconnected elements of learners (the "who"), key content (the "what"), and PD approaches (the "how") are considered within a broader set of contextual and infrastructure factors (e.g., organizational support, resources, leadership) as depicted in Figure 21.1. Snyder, Hemmeter, and McLaughlin (2011) noted that the NPDCI definition provides a basis for advancing to the next generation of early childhood PD in which more systematic attention is paid to the who, what, and how of PD.

In the next section of this chapter, we apply the NPDCI framework to RTI. Because RTI is a multifaceted framework used broadly at a programwide or schoolwide level, key groups (e.g., teachers, administrators, specialists) must have a basic understanding of the components of RTI and be supported in making decisions about a number of issues, such as which assessment tools and intervention strategies to use and what roles different groups will play in implementing RTI (NPDCI, 2012). These decisions will guide a more detailed plan for PD using the NPDCI framework. The current discussion delineates the who, what, and how at a basic level.

Who Needs Professional Development on Response to Intervention in Early Childhood?

The practitioners (i.e., teachers and specialists) who directly serve children play the most direct role in the implementation of RTI and as such are a prime target for PD.

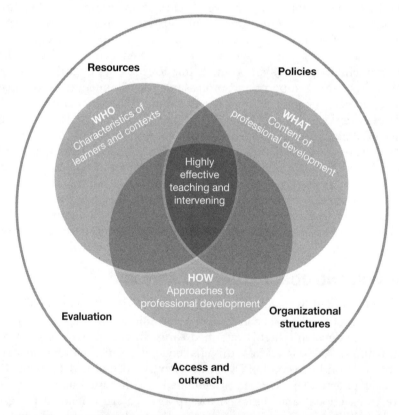

Figure 21.1. National Professional Development Center on Inclusion conceptual framework for professional development in early childhood, 2008. (From National Professional Development Center on Inclusion. [2008]. *What do we mean by professional development in the early childhood field?* Chapel Hill: University of North Carolina, Frank Porter Graham Child Development Institute; reprinted by permission.)

Teachers need PD on methods for integrating the multiple components that comprise the RTI framework, in addition to support in implementing the individual practices within each RTI tier. Specialists may play a role in implementing the practices associated with small-group and more intensive, individualized instruction in collaboration with teachers and families.

Collaboration among administrators, teachers, families, specialists, and other professionals who play supporting roles (e.g., school psychologists) is an important component of planning for and implementing RTI. Issues for consideration include understanding the characteristics (e.g., needs, interests, experiences, existing knowledge, readiness to change related to RTI) of the many RTI partners and then designing opportunities to help these partners explore their unique roles within an RTI approach and develop the skills to implement practices that may be associated with their roles. For instance, families are central to their children's development and may need support in implementing practices at home that complement the classroom practices within the RTI components. School psychologists have expertise in child assessment but may need additional support to conduct screenings and formative assessments linked to instructional planning and monitoring within a tiered approach. Administrators at state, district, and local program levels need an understanding of the policies, research, and practices associated with RTI so they can build infrastructure support for professionals who are directly implementing the approach, thus ensuring an "effective host environment" (Hemmeter, Fox, Jack, & Broyles, 2007, p. 339), a critical implementation feature emphasized in the K–12 literature on RTI (Sugai, Sprague, Horner, & Walker, 2000; Sugai & Horner, 2002).

The individuals with responsibility for PD on RTI are an additional prime target because of their role in preparing and supporting staff. PD providers can be grouped into three types: 1) faculty who develop knowledge and skills of preservice students, 2) consultants or coaches who provide direct support to practitioners in implementing RTI, and 3) trainers who provide information and skill development to the work force through workshops and other in-service activities. These individuals need knowledge and skills in implementing RTI as well as knowledge and skills for planning, delivering, and evaluating effective PD on RTI. This is a daunting task for PD providers, especially because RTI is an emerging concept within early childhood and therefore PD providers are unlikely to have had direct experience implementing the approach in practice settings. Typically, PD providers, including faculty, are not the target for PD designed specifically for them (Hyson, Horm, & Winton, 2012), in spite of their critical role in supporting the work force, suggesting that they may be left out when PD planners consider who needs PD on RTI.

What Is the Content of Professional Development on Response to Intervention?

As has been already stated in other chapters in this book, RTI is a comprehensive model or framework for organizing classroom management and instruction that has been applied to both social-emotional and academic learning. Regardless of whether the focus is on behavior or academics, certain content components are universal within an RTI framework: 1) formative assessment, 2) core curriculum and instructional and behavioral interventions at multiple levels that vary in intensity or level of support to children, 3) collaboration among professionals and families, and 4) data-based decision making tailored to children's performance or growth (NPDCI, 2012). Knowledge of the components of the framework is essential content for PD. In addition, within each of these four components are multiple sets of practices that will vary, based on decisions made at local program or district levels that frontline staff must know about and implement on a daily basis. Some of the content related to assessment and instructional practices may be part of 2- and 4-year college curricula (Early & Winton, 2001; Maxwell, Lim, & Early, 2006). However, it is unlikely that the practices are presented within an RTI framework. In addition, the extent to which teacher education focuses on building skills to implement assessment and instructional strategies is subject to scrutiny (Hyson et al., 2012; National Council on Accreditation of Teacher Education [NCATE], 2010). A recent NCATE report called for a transformation of teacher education with the strong admonition to move away from the traditional focus on general content knowledge to an increased emphasis on research-based clinical practices.

The emphasis on clinical teaching is in keeping with the evidence-based practice (EBP) movement that is affecting how teachers teach (Buysse & Wesley, 2006) and how PD providers organize and focus PD (Winton, 2006). The definition of EBP put forth by Buysse, Wesley, and colleagues (Buysse & Wesley, 2006; Buysse, Wesley, Snyder, & Winton, 2006) that EBP is a decision-making process that integrates the best available research evidence with family and professional wisdom and values suggests that, above and beyond knowing and using certain research-based practices, practitioners must also have skills related to decision making. The new set of competencies required for practitioners by the emergence of EBP and an approach such as RTI is the ability to integrate multiple sources of evidence, including data, using certain decision rules to determine appropriate instruction strategies for each child. In addition, practitioners must implement those practices and use outcome information to determine the effectiveness of their intervention efforts. Then they must make necessary adjustments in a continuous cycle. This involves competencies related to integrating multiple sources of evidence and information to make and implement decisions—competencies that are not part of most traditional courses or PD curricula.

The expectations for content expertise for PD providers are even greater than those for practitioners. As already mentioned, they must have mastery of the knowledge and practices associated with RTI components and how to integrate those components, as well as knowledge and skills related to organizing and delivering PD on RTI. PD providers must be able to measure whether teachers have mastered and implemented RTI practices with fidelity. This information is important so that PD providers can use this evidence to determine the effectiveness of their PD and make necessary adjustments based on learner outcome data—a process that parallels what teachers are doing when implementing RTI in classrooms. This requires conducting formative assessment of PD learners and linking that to PD instruction using data-based decision making (Snyder & Wolfe, 2008). The concept of linking assessment of learner needs and baseline competencies with the level and type of PD and then evaluating the impact of the PD on teacher practices and child outcomes is not necessarily a new idea (Snyder & Wolfe, 2008); however, the scarcity of examples of PD interventions characterized by this sequence (Pianta

& Hamre, 2012; Snyder et al., 2011; Winton, 2010) is indicative of the complexities of implementing high-quality PD.

Considering the wide array of content associated with RTI that PD providers must master, some of which may be part of traditional PD courses and curricula and some of which is emerging content, PD providers face a large task in preparing themselves to deliver PD on RTI content. The challenge is heightened by the fact that there are few PD interventions or PD curricula available on this topic to support those providing PD.

How Can Professional Development on Response to Intervention Be Delivered Effectively?

Policy makers increasingly want evidence that the PD they fund has been delivered in a way that has made a difference in the lives of children and families. Unfortunately, the body of rigorous empirical research on the key ingredients of effective early childhood PD is limited (Pianta & Hamre, 2012: Snyder et al., 2011; Winton, 2010; Zaslow, Tout, Halle, Whittaker, & Lavelle, 2010). Given the slim evidence base for PD in general, coupled with the fact that RTI in early childhood is an emerging practice, it is not surprising that information on PD delivery approaches on RTI is scarce. Developers and early adopters of RTI in early childhood have provided few details about the development, implementation, and evaluation of PD approaches or curricular resources associated with these approaches. Hemmeter et al. (2007) provided descriptive information on a PD sequence for positive behavior support implemented in a rural Head Start program. Hawkins and colleagues (2008) described an interdisciplinary preservice field placement experience focused on RTI and identified some of the challenges of addressing RTI at the preservice level. These included finding field sites that reflect effective RTI practices, locating field supervisors who have expertise in RTI, and designing placements that model the interdisciplinary collaboration between teachers and specialists that undergirds the RTI model. Kratochwill and colleagues (2007) summarized PD activities on RTI developed by six research centers funded by the Office of Special Education Programs (OSEP) K–3 Reading and Behavioral Models Project in terms of some common core elements that appeared to be effective. The common elements included the following characteristics: 1) built upon and worked in conjunction with existing programs at school sites; 2) used activities that promoted active learning, such as role plays, discussions, and case studies; 3) featured collaborative problem solving; 4) used co-teaching, mentoring, and coaching as part of early implementation; 5) provided ongoing support for staff, including mentoring; and 6) utilized self-report and observations of treatment integrity and data on student outcomes as part of PD.

These common elements summarized by Kratochwill et al. (2007) reflect some of the themes from the literature on effective PD in general. What we can conclude from a variety of research summaries (Snow-Renner & Lauer, 2005; Wei, Darling-Hammond, Andree, Richardson, & Orphanos, 2009; Zaslow et al., 2010) is that PD is more likely to affect learner outcomes if it has the following characteristics:

- Focuses on specific instructional strategies rather than general content

- Is sustained over time

- Is infused with active learning opportunities

- Includes collective participation (e.g., team-based)

- Is aligned with standards, curriculum, and assessments

As pointed out by Winton (2010), these themes are not unlike the key principles of adult learning identified over a decade ago by Knowles, Holton, and Swanson (1998). They are important but not sufficient for developing a plan for PD on a new concept such as RTI in early childhood.

Applying the National Professional Development Center on Inclusion Framework to Professional Development on Response to Intervention in Early Childhood

Using the NPDCI framework to identify and align the characteristics of the individuals needing PD with the content they require, delivered through PD methods that build the desired knowledge and skills, is a starting point for developing an intentional sequence of PD on RTI.

As already stated, a number of different groups (e.g., administrators, teachers, specialists, family members, PD providers) comprise the "who" that need PD on RTI. Social marketing literature suggests that how messages are crafted for particular audiences makes a difference in the degree to which individuals are willing to change their behavior. For example, policy makers may want information on the effectiveness and efficiency of RTI; teachers' concerns may focus on how well RTI fits with their existing practices and how easy it is to use; families may be more concerned about the impact of RTI on children, especially their own. These considerations need to shape individualized messages directed to these different population segments.

PD providers must also consider individual cognitive processes, apart from roles, that influence the adoption of new practices. Public health literature suggests that individuals are more likely to adopt new ideas if they have a sense of control and ownership of them (Dearing & Kreuter, 2010). However, honoring the concept of ownership can create tension around fidelity issues unless the critical components of an innovation, such as RTI and the research-based practices associated with it, are clearly identified and held constant, and areas where customization is permissible and even desirable are communicated to adopters. Individuals are also motivated to change by social influencers; that is, organizations or people with credibility (Dearing & Kreuter, 2010). These internal characteristics related to the "who" should guide the organization of the "what" and "how" of PD.

External factors such as resources, access, and organizational structures also play a critical role in planning PD for RTI. Pianta and Hamre (2012) pointed out the fundamental mismatch between what we know constitutes effective PD and the resources available to support it. Data from national surveys of state administrators indicate that the workshop is the PD format most frequently used by in-service contexts (Center to Inform Personnel Preparation Policy and Practice in Early Intervention and Preschool Education, 2007a, 2007b), a fact that has been decried in the literature (Zaslow et al., 2010; Pianta & Hamre, 2012) but reflects the financial reality that the cost of the more intensive forms of PD far outstrips PD budgets. Access to PD is another external factor to consider. If there are no financial or career incentives for participating in PD, as is the case for many early childhood teachers (Institute of Medicine & National Research Council, 2012), the likelihood of participating is slim. It is also important to realize that simply creating opportunities to learn a new skill does not guarantee that the skills will be used in a practice context. Administrative support, classroom resources, and factors such as teacher turnover and staff–child ratios determine the extent to which a teacher is able to implement a set of new practices.

Considering the multiple factors that shape whether PD on an innovative model such as RTI is effective, PD planners are well advised to develop systemic plans that include careful thought about which segments of a population should be targeted by PD and how this can be done to create a system of PD for RTI. The NPDCI framework provides guidance for considering a spectrum of PD options, from low to high cost and intensity, depending upon the needs of the target audience. For example, for those needing certain information at an awareness level, such as an overview of RTI, a low-intensity form of PD such as a webinar or workshop series might be sufficient. For those needing to develop skills on a discrete practice such as dialogic reading, a medium level of PD intensity (workshops with short-term follow-up coaching) might suffice. For those needing to learn and apply a new comprehensive set of practices, more intensive and costly PD options are warranted.

The information in this chapter provides a catalyst for beginning discussions about the design of a PD plan for RTI. Discussions are likely to include quandaries such as the following: If collective participation of teachers, specialists, families, and administrators in PD is the desired mode of some aspects of PD delivery, how does one orchestrate that across roles, disciplines, and sectors? For instance, teachers might be employed by public schools and specialists employed by contract agencies. If some of the RTI-related competencies, such as assessment, methods, and curriculum, are addressed in existing personnel standards and coursework/in-service while other competencies, such as those related to data-based decision making, are rarely addressed in traditional coursework/in-service, how does integration of content take place? What structures can shape PD in ways that take advantage of existing efforts? Whose job is that? Unlike K–12 school settings where RTI first emerged as a model, early childhood settings are tremendously diverse, ranging from private child care programs to public pre-K programs housed in K–12 school settings. Factors that vary from setting to setting include education and compensation levels of teachers; staff turnover; availability of specialists and consultants; professional standards and training requirements for staff; and availability of high-quality, accessible PD opportunities. The diversity of sectors and PD networks at both national and state levels, including early childhood's ambivalent and evolving relationship with K–12, means that changes to the PD system must be done with intentionality and must include multiple sectors.

AN INNOVATIVE APPROACH TO A PROFESSIONAL DEVELOPMENT CURRICULUM ON RESPONSE TO INTERVENTION

An integral part of an overall plan for PD on RTI is a core PD curriculum for faculty and PD providers (an essential "who") focused on the RTI framework (the "what"). As already mentioned, such a curriculum has not yet been developed, implemented, and evaluated. However, an approach to PD curriculum development from the Frank Porter Graham Child Development Institute, University of North Carolina at Chapel Hill, has promise for providing PD providers and faculty (the "who") with essential RTI content (the "what"), designed using a clinical teaching approach that builds evidence-based decision-making skills (the "how"). This PD curriculum model is the focus of this section.

Through funding from the U.S. Department of Education, OSEP, the Center to Mobilize Early Childhood Knowledge (the CONNECT project[1]) developed an innovative approach for developing PD curricula on research-based practices. The PD curriculum consists of a series[2] of free, web-based, multimedia modules (http://community.fpg.unc.edu), each focused on a discrete set of practices. Each module is organized around a 5-Step Learning Cycle (see Figure 21.2), drawn from evidence-based medicine (EBM) and designed to build learners' skills in integrating multiple sources of evidence to make the kinds of decisions that must be made every day in clinical settings.

The modules are targeted for early childhood faculty and PD providers to enhance their teaching in face-to-face, hybrid, or distance education formats. A more detailed description of the modules is provided next, along with an explanation of how the CONNECT approach integrates principles from EBM (Sackett, Straus, Richardson, Rosenberg, & Haynes, 2000), a precursor of EBP in early childhood, social marketing (Heath & Heath, 2008), and public health (Dearing & Kreuter, 2010; Hinyard & Kreuter, 2007; Steiner, 2007), and a summary of what is known about effective approaches to PD (Snyder et al., 2011; Winton, 2010; Zaslow et al., 2010). Examples from *CONNECT Module 7: Tiered Instruction* (Buysse, Epstein, Winton, & Rous, 2012) are provided to illustrate the information.

In Step 1, learners are introduced to the practice focus by viewing a video clip of a real-life dilemma told from the perspective of a practitioner. The dilemma

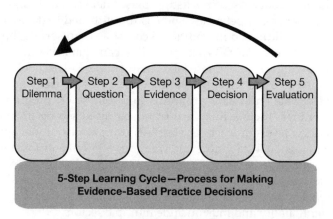

Figure 21.2. CONNECT 5-Step Learning Cycle. (From CONNECT: The Center to Mobilize Early Childhood Knowledge. [2012]. *5-step learning Cycle*™. Retrieved from http://community.fpg.unc.edu/connect-modules/5-step-learning-cycle; reprinted by permission.)

---

[1]The CONNECT Project is a partnership between the Frank Porter Graham Child Development Institute at the University of North Carolina and the Institute on Human Development at the University of Kentucky.

[2]The content focus of the seven CONNECT modules encompasses embedded interventions, transitions, communication for collaboration, family–professional partnerships, assistive technology, dialogic reading, and RTI in early childhood.

reflects what is known from marketing research about the value of using stories to persuade individuals to change behavior, especially those who are likely to resist didactic information (Hinyard & Kreuter, 2007; Steiner, 2007). That is, each dilemma is authentic and told compellingly. It encourages learners to identify with story characters and context, and it expresses the themes of the practice-focused module while acknowledging uncertainty about the research and whether a particular intervention will work (Steiner, 2007). In *CONNECT Module 7: Tiered Instruction* (Buysse et al., 2012), the dilemma focuses on two preschool teachers, one of whom is being encouraged to use a tiered approach to instruction on academic practices and the other of whom is contemplating a tiered approach to practices that support social-emotional development.

In Step 2, the learners are prompted to identify a specific research question based on the dilemma. In doing this, they use PICO, an EBM process designed to assist learners in developing a question that leads to a literature search. Each letter of PICO represents a term for a descriptor that could be entered into a scholarly database or search engine to locate relevant research. The letter P stands for *persons,* meaning the characteristics of the children or families who are the targets for the intervention; I stands for *intervention,* meaning the intervention or practice being considered; C stands for *comparison,* if there is a dilemma in which a comparison of two or more interventions is being considered; and O stands for *outcome*—that is, the desired outcomes for the child or family in the dilemma. For example, a PICO question from *CONNECT Module 7: Tiered Instruction* (Buysse et al., 2012) is expressed as follows: For preschool children enrolled in early care and education programs (P), is tiered instruction (also known as RTI and positive behavioral interventions and supports) (I) effective in promoting children's development and learning (O)? (Buysse et al., 2012). Note that there is no comparison (C) descriptor in this PICO question on RTI. Asking learners to pose a researchable question leads them to the research evidence, an element in Step 3.

Step 3 is the largest section of each module. This step moves the learner away from the dilemma into the larger body of information on the module practice. It includes multiple sources of evidence as well as opportunities to learn and develop skills related to the practice. The three key sources of evidence (research, policies, and experience-based knowledge) are presented in clear, succinct, credible, and concrete ways—characteristics recommended by literature on social media for ensuring that messages will make an impact (Heath & Heath, 2008). The importance of winnowing information down to manageable and evidence-based chunks is especially important given the burgeoning amount of information available online, some of which is credible and some of which is not. More about each of the three sources of evidence and the teaching content and strategies in Step 3 follows.

The first source of evidence is a short summary of the best available research on the practice, based on either a research synthesis if one is available or a research summary from other sources. The research summary for *CONNECT Module 7: Tiered Instruction* (Buysse et al., 2012) is based on the best available research in the K–12 literature, using syntheses and practice guides from the What Works Clearinghouse as well as a meta-analysis of 24 studies of RTI. This feature of Step 3 helps faculty and PD providers who want to expose learners to high-quality, easily digestible research but do not have time in their curricula for learners to conduct literature reviews and/or do not have time to keep abreast of current research themselves. The skills of research appraisal are addressed in an activity in which learners address questions about the research summary, such as identifying the characteristics of the sample and context in which the research studies in the summary were conducted, as a precursor in a later step (Step 4) to considering the relevance of the research to the practice dilemma in Step 1. A second source of evidence in Step 3 is a short CONNECT Policy Advisory, which summarizes laws, regulations, position statements, and other consensus documents related to the practice. The Policy Advisory for *CONNECT Module 7: Tiered Instruction* (Buysse et al., 2012) is based on specific policies and a consensus statement that address the use of tiered instructional approaches for school-age students in kindergarten through Grade 12. This information can be found within eight provisions of the Individuals with Disabilities Education Act (IDEA) of 2004 (PL 108-446) and a position paper published by the Council for Exceptional Children (CEC). A third source of evidence in each module is called "experienced-based knowledge." This consists of short audio clips from practitioners, families, and recognized leaders in the field (i.e., social influencers) whose experiences with the particular practice add a valued perspective for learners' consideration. In *CONNECT Module 7: Tiered Instruction* (Buysse et al., 2012), the perspectives of a state administrator, a preschool director, and a researcher who has adopted the RTI approach for dual language learners are shared through audio clips.

The second component of Step 3 focuses on defining and demonstrating the practice and describing activities that provide opportunities for performance feedback, an important element of a clinical teaching approach. Each module has a succinct definition of the practice. For example, tiered approaches in early childhood are defined as follows in the *CONNECT Tiered Instruction* module:

> A tiered instructional approach is a framework for linking assessment with instructional and behavioral supports that are matched to children's learning needs. Tiered instruction also is called response to intervention (RTI) and positive behavioral interventions and supports (PBIS). The key components of tiered instruction are: formative assessment, instruction, and targeted interventions and supports, and supports for data-based decision making. (NPDCI, 2012)

Step 3 also includes multiple, short (2- to 3-minute) video exemplars of the foundational and targeted practices within an RTI framework being used in a variety of real-life settings (family or center-based child care, pre-K classroom, Head Start, home). The video exemplars in the CONNECT modules serve a variety of purposes. They provide a clear video example of a practice being implemented by a practitioner in a realistic setting, thus addressing the concern from faculty (Hawkins et al., 2008; Rosenkoetter & Stayton, 1997) that there are few high-quality practica sites where students can see live demonstrations of effective practices being implemented. The videos can be viewed multiple times by learners who are first being exposed to a new practice. When used in conjunction with an observational rubric, as is done in most CONNECT modules, the videos can hone observation skills and the ability to recognize nuanced aspects of a discrete set of practices. Step 3 also includes activities designed to have learners implement the practices in real life or simulated circumstances, with the observational rubrics being available for self-assessment or constructive expert feedback from faculty and PD providers. The reusable nature of video clips makes it easy for faculty to download them into different formats such as PowerPoint files, DVDs, or Web pages, or project them in classrooms for face-to-face discussions about the practice. *CONNECT Module 7: Tiered Instruction* (Buysse et al., 2012) includes video demonstrations of practices that promote both academic learning and social-emotional development.

In Step 4, the learner is brought back to the original dilemma in Step 1 for the purpose of integrating the evidence and information from Step 3 with the unique perspectives and context of the dilemma. The learners consider the relevance of the research and policies related to the practice, given the characteristics of the child, family, and context in the dilemma. They integrate that with the experiences of social influencers, and attitudes of their own about the practice in question, and then make a decision about whether they will implement the practice; and if so, how they will develop a plan for doing that. Learners are provided with sample implementation plans and checklists to aid them in developing a plan of their own.

In Step 5, learners are prompted to consider ways that they can evaluate the impact of the practice being implemented on children and families. In the case of *CONNECT Module 7: Tiered Instruction* (Buysse et al., 2012), the evaluation of the RTI practices is the progress monitoring component of the RTI model and therefore is a natural fit with Step 5.

Each module includes a number of supports to faculty and PD providers. These include facilitation tips for conducting activities, assessment rubrics for key assignments, and a list of the relevant personnel preparation standards of the National Association for the Education of Young Children (NAEYC), Council for Exceptional Children/Division of Early Childhood (CEC/DEC), and the U.S. Department of Education, along with OSEP indicators and outcomes for IDEA, which is an important aspect of maintaining a strong connection with early childhood accreditation and monitoring systems. In addition, there is an online discussion area where faculty and PD providers can share ideas, syllabi, and challenges, and pose questions to one another and to CONNECT staff about using the modules. The discussion area has yielded other instructional aids, such as a list of courses and textbooks used in conjunction with the modules, provided by faculty across the country who are users of the modules. The discussion area reinforces the underlying CONNECT tenet that the modules can be customized by faculty and PD providers depending upon their unique settings and learners within the framework of the essential CONNECT 5-Step Learning Cycle. The modules are designed to strengthen the clinical component of existing coursework or PD. They are not viewed as wholesale replacements of PD practices that are already in place, which is in keeping with the literature on how adoption of innovations, including new PD curricula, is best promoted. That is, innovations must build on and be compatible with existing practices at the same time that the relative advantages of the new approach over other approaches are made clear (Rogers, 1995).

Formative evaluation data collected during the course of development indicate that the modules are being increasingly used across the nation and internationally, and suggest positive reactions from faculty and PD providers who have used the modules and preservice students who have learned from the modules as part of their teacher education programs. Feedback from faculty and PD users has been used to develop and refine the modules, which has contributed to the social validity and growing use of the modules. However, more rigorous evaluation is needed now that CONNECT module use has been established in accordance with the goals of the funding agency. A summative evaluation of the 5-Step Learning Cycle in CONNECT modules, focused on a targeted population of learners and faculty, is being planned for the future.

CONCLUSION

As stated at the beginning of the chapter, many factors affect the extent to which new approaches to service delivery, such as RTI, become embedded and sustained into the culture and practices of service settings (Fixsen et al., 2007; Kitson et al., 1998; Kreuter & Bernhardt, 2009). These include the strength of the evidence supporting the innovation; the presence or absence of an organizational culture, climate, and resources that support change; and the competence and confidence of staff in implementing the approach. This book presents evidence that the field is moving forward with the adoption of RTI in early childhood settings and that a number of infrastructure pieces are falling into place to ensure that the movement in this direction will continue. In light of these developments it is important to think systematically and strategically about designing professional development to support RTI in early childhood. A conceptual framework for designing a PD plan for addressing RTI was shared as well as an innovative approach—CONNECT's 5-Step Learning Cycle—for developing PD curricula associated with RTI. The CONNECT approach is a multimedia, clinical teaching model for PD that is practice-centered, research-based, anchored in measures of performance and feedback, and designed to build evidence-based decision-making skills, holding promise for helping to ensure that the early childhood work force has the confidence and competence to implement RTI.

REFERENCES

Buysse, V., Epstein, D., Winton, P., & Rous, B. (2012). *CONNECT Module 7: Tiered Instruction* [Web-based professional development curriculum]. Chapel Hill: University of North Carolina, Frank Porter Graham Child Development Institute, CONNECT: The Center to Mobilize Early Childhood Knowledge. Available at http://community.fpg.unc.edu/connect-modules/learner/module-7

Buysse, V., & Wesley, P.W. (2006). Making sense of evidence-based practice: Reflections and recommendations. In V. Buysse & P.W. Wesley (Eds.), *Evidence-based practice in the early childhood field* (pp. 227–246). Washington, DC: ZERO TO THREE.

Buysse, V., Wesley, P.W., Snyder, P., & Winton, P. (2006). Evidence-based practice: What does it really mean for the early childhood field? *Young Exceptional Children, 9*(4), 2–11.

Center to Inform Personnel Preparation Policy and Practice in Early Intervention and Preschool Education. (2007a, October). *Study VI data report: Training and technical assistance survey of state Part C coordinators.* Farmington: University of Connecticut, A.J. Pappanikou Center for Excellence in Developmental Disabilities, Education, Research, and Service.

Center to Inform Personnel Preparation Policy and Practice in Early Intervention and Preschool Education. (2007b, October). *Study VI data report: Training and technical assistance survey of state Part 619 coordinators.* Farmington: University of Connecticut, A.J. Pappanikou Center for Excellence in Developmental Disabilities, Education, Research, and Service.

Dearing, J.W., & Kreuter, M.W. (2010). Designing for diffusion: How can we increase uptake of cancer communication innovations? *Patient Education and Counseling, 81S*, S100–S110. doi: 10.1016/j.pec.2010.10.013

Early, D., & Winton, P. (2001). Preparing the workforce: Early childhood teacher preparation at 2- and 4-year institutes of higher education. *Early Childhood Research Quarterly, 16*, 285–306.

Fixsen, D.L., Naoom, S.F., Blase, K.A., & Wallace, F. (2007). Implementation: The missing link between research and practice. *APSAC Advisor, 19*(1 & 2), 4–11.

Hawkins, R.O., Kroeger, S.D., Musti-Rao, S., Barnett, D.W., & Ward, J.E. (2008). Preservice training in response to intervention: Learning by doing an interdisciplinary field experience. *Psychology in the Schools, 45*, 745–762.

Heath, C., & Heath, D. (2008). *Made to stick: Why some ideas survive and others die.* New York, NY: Random House.

Hemmeter, M.L., Fox, L., Jack, S., & Broyles, L. (2007). A program-wide model of positive behavior support in early childhood settings. *Journal of Early Intervention, 29,* 337–355.

Hinyard, L.J., & Kreuter, M.W. (2007). Using narrative communication as a tool for health behavior change: A conceptual, theoretical, and empirical overview. *Health Education & Behavior, 34,* 777–792.

Hyson, M., Horm, D.M., & Winton, P.J. (2012). Higher education for early childhood educators and outcomes for young children: Pathways toward greater effectiveness. In R. Pianta, L. Justice, S. Barnett, & S. Sheridan (Eds.), *Handbook of early education* (pp. 553–583). New York, NY: Guilford Press.

Individuals with Disabilities Education Improvement Act (IDEA) of 2004, PL 108-446, 20 U.S.C. 1400 *et seq.*

Institute of Medicine & National Research Council. (2012). The early childhood care and education workforce: Challenges and opportunities: A workshop report. Washington, DC: National Academies Press.

Kitson, A., Harvey, G., & McCormack, B. (1998). Enabling the implementation of evidence-based practice: A conceptual framework. *Quality in Health Care, 7,* 149–158.

Knowles, M.S., Holton, E.F., III, & Swanson, R.A. (1998). *The adult learner: The definitive classic in adult education and human resource development* (5th ed.). Houston, TX: Gulf.

Kratochwill, T.R., Volpiansky, P., Clements, M., & Ball, C. (2007). Professional development in implementing and sustaining multitier prevention models: Implications for response to intervention. *School Psychology Review, 36,* 618–631.

Kreuter, M.W., & Bernhardt, J.M. (2009). Reframing the dissemination challenge: A marketing and distribution perspective. *American Journal of Public Health, 99,* 2123–2127. doi: 10.2105/AJPH.2008.155218

Maxwell, K.L., Feild, C.C., & Clifford, R.M. (2005). Defining and measuring professional development in early childhood research. In M. Zaslow & I. Martinez-Beck (Eds.), *Critical issues in early childhood professional development.* Baltimore, MD: Paul H. Brookes Publishing Co.

Maxwell, K.L., Lim, C.-I., & Early, D.M. (2006). *Early childhood teacher preparation programs in the United States: National report.* Chapel Hill: University of North Carolina, Frank Porter Graham Child Development Institute.

National Council on Accreditation of Teacher Education. (2010). *Transforming teacher education through clinical practice: A national strategy to prepare effective teachers.* Washington, DC: Author.

National Professional Development Center on Inclusion (NPDCI). (2008). *What do we mean by professional development in the early childhood field?* Retrieved from http://npdci.fpg .unc.edu/sites/npdci.fpg.unc.edu/files/resources/NPDCI_ProfessionalDevelopmentInEC _03-04-08_0.pdf

National Professional Development Center on Inclusion (NPDCI). (2012). *Response to intervention (RTI) in early childhood: Building consensus on the defining features.* Chapel Hill: University of North Carolina at Chapel Hill, Frank Porter Graham Child Development Institute. http://npdci.pg.unc.edu/sites/npdci/fpg.unc.edu/files/resources/NPDCI-RTI-Concept -Paper-FINAL-2-2012.pdf

Pianta, R.C., & Hamre, B.K. (2012). Scaling-up a program of research, development, and implementation for professional development to improve teacher–student interactions. In C. Howes, B.K. Hamre, & R.C. Pianta (Eds.), *Effective early childhood professional development: Improving teacher practice and child outcomes* (pp. 193–230). Baltimore, MD: Paul H. Brookes Publishing Co.

Rogers, E.M. (1995). *Diffusion of innovations.* New York, NY: Free Press.

Rosenkoetter, S.E., & Stayton, V.D. (1997). Designing and implementing innovative, interdisciplinary practica. In P.J. Winton, J.A. McCollum, & C. Catlett (Eds.), *Reforming personnel preparation in early intervention* (pp. 453–474). Baltimore, MD: Paul H. Brookes Publishing Co.

Sackett, D.L., Straus, S.E., Richardson, W.S., Rosenberg, W., & Haynes, R.B. (2000). *Evidence-based medicine: How to practice and teach EBM* (2nd ed.). Edinburgh, Scotland: Churchill Livingstone.

Snow-Renner, R., & Lauer, P.A. (2005). Professional development analysis. *McREL Insights.* Denver, CO: Mid-continent Research for Education and Learning. Retrieved from http://www.mcrel.org/topics/ProfessionalDevelopment/products/234/

Snyder, P., Hemmeter, M.L., & McLaughlin, T. (2011). Professional development in early childhood intervention: Where we stand on the silver anniversary of PL 99-457. *Journal of Early Intervention, 33,* 357–370.

Snyder, P., & Wolfe, B. (2008). The big three process components of effective professional development: Needs assessment, evaluation, and follow-up. In P.J. Winton, J. McCollum, & C. Catlett (Eds.), *Practical approaches to early childhood professional development: Evidence, strategies, and resources* (pp. 13–51). Washington, DC: ZERO TO THREE.

Steiner, J.F. (2007). Using stories to disseminate research: The attributes of representative stories. *Journal of General Internal Medicine, 22,* 1603–1607.

Sugai, G., & Horner, R.H. (2002). The evolution of discipline practices: School-wide positive behavior supports. *Child & Family Behavior Therapy, 24*(1 & 2), 23–50.

Sugai, G., Sprague, J.R., Horner, R.H., & Walker, H.M. (2000). Preventing school violence: The use of office discipline referrals to assess and monitor school-wide discipline interventions. *Journal of Emotional and Behavioral Disorders, 8,* 94–101.

Wei, R.C., Darling-Hammond, L., Andree, A., Richardson, N., & Orphanos, S. (2009). *Professional learning in the learning profession: A status report on teacher development in the United States and abroad.* Dallas, TX: National Staff Development Council.

Winton, P. (2006). The evidence-based practice movement and its effect on knowledge utilization. In V. Buysse & P.W. Wesley (Eds.), *Evidence-based practice in the early childhood field* (pp. 71–115). Washington, DC: ZERO TO THREE.

Winton, P. (2010). Professional development and quality initiatives: Two essential components of an early childhood system. In P.W. Wesley & V. Buysse (Eds.), *The quest for quality: Promising innovations for early childhood programs.* Baltimore, MD: Paul H. Brookes Publishing Co.

Zaslow, M., Tout, K., Halle, T., Whittaker, J.E.V., & Lavelle, B. (2010). Emerging research on early childhood professional development. In S.B. Neuman & M.L. Kamil (Eds.), *Preparing teachers for the early childhood classroom: Proven models and key principles* (pp. 17–47). Baltimore, MD: Paul H. Brookes Publishing Co.

Preschool Inclusion and Response to Intervention for Children with Disabilities

William H. Brown, Herman T. Knopf, Maureen A. Conroy, Heather Smith Googe, and Fred Greer

Preschool inclusion and response to intervention (RTI) have been two contemporary educational movements related to emerging societal values and evidence-informed practices in early childhood education and early childhood special education (cf. Kauffman, Nelson, Simpson, & Mock, 2011). These two underlying approaches, which are preventive in nature (cf. Conroy & Brown, 2004; Dunlap et al., 2006), may constitute a reliable foundation for high-quality and effective preschool education (cf. Carta & Kong, 2007; Fox & Hemmeter, 2009; Greenwood et al., 2008; Greenwood et al., 2011; Marshall, Brown, Conroy, & Knopf, 2011). Although both preschool inclusion and RTI have advanced over the years and are addressed in the literature, we believe that further progress on promoting preschool inclusion with an integration of RTI principles in early childhood programs is sorely needed in the "age of accountability" (No Child Left Behind Act of 2001, PL 107-110; President's Commission on Excellence in Special Education, 2002). Our purposes in this chapter are to 1) provide an overview of preschool inclusion and basic practices related to the individualized education program (IEP) process, 2) discuss the common conceptual core and essential elements of IEP and RTI processes and how they might strengthen preschool inclusive services, and 3) present the primary contemporary challenge related to a better integration of preschool inclusion and RTI principles.

A BRIEF HISTORY OF PRESCHOOL SERVICES

Historically, the lives of many young children have been marked by harsh conditions at worst and benign neglect at best (Safford & Safford, 1996), especially for children with disabilities (Scheerenberger, 1983). Indeed, widespread societal attention to and provision of educational services before first grade have been circumscribed for most of the twentieth century (Meisels & Shonkoff, 2000; Safford & Safford, 1996). During the 1970s, Caldwell (1973) outlined three distinct epochs in educational services for young children. She noted that prior to the 1950s, societal perspectives were characterized by "forgetting and hiding" many children, especially those living in poverty and with developmental delays. A subsequent period during the 1950s and 1960s was marked by initial societal efforts in "screening and segregating" some children who needed educational and social services, and this era established a foundation for later early intervening services (e.g., Klaus & Gray, 1968; see Consortium for Longitudinal Studies, 1983, for review). In her 1970s article, Caldwell reported a *zeitgeist* for "identifying and helping" children and their families with expansion of early childhood programs for young children with special needs. Nevertheless, many of the early preschool services continued to be segregated programs for children with disabilities. Hence, Brown and Conroy (1997) argued for a fourth epoch based on "including and supporting" young children with developmental delays in inclusive preschools (see also Meisels & Shonkoff, 2000, who later also noted an additional period, "educate and include," p. 10).

Since the 1970s, preschool services in the United States have expanded greatly (for reviews, see Barnett et al., 2010, for prekindergarten and Trohanis, 2008, for special needs preschool services). Today, millions of 3-, 4-, and 5-year-old children not in kindergarten are served in preschool settings. Specifically, more than 2.1 million children are provided state-funded prekindergarten services or Head Start Programs (Barnett et al., 2010), more than 708,000 are served in Part B 619 services (Individuals with Disabilities Education Act Data, 2009), and several million additional children attend child care or other preschool programs (National Center for Education Statistics, 2010). Indeed, since 2005, a majority of the 3-, 4-, and 5-year-old children not in kindergarten have been enrolled in either part-time or full-time community-based preschool settings (Federal Interagency Forum on Child and Family Statistics, 2012). Coleman, Buysse, and Neitzel (2006) noted national trends that may result in even more children being served in community-based preschools in the future: 1) societal attention to high-quality early childhood education, 2) the contemporary "school readiness" movement, 3) interest in expanding and enhancing prekindergarten services, and 4) awareness of a need for prevention and early intervening services.

PRESCHOOL INCLUSION

Preschool inclusion is not a novel idea in the field of early childhood education. Indeed, in Kirk and Johnson's (1951) early description of preschools for children with intellectual disabilities, they noted that most children with developmental delays should be served in early childhood classrooms with typical early childhood education methods along with any needed adaptations for the preschoolers' varying abilities. Moreover, a number of demonstration programs (e.g., Allen, Benning, & Drummond, 1972; Bricker & Bricker, 1976; Brown, Horn, Heiser, & Odom, 1996; Rule et al., 1987) and interventions have shown the benefits of preschool inclusion.

Preschool Inclusion Definitions

Because terminology used with respect to preschool inclusion has changed across time (i.e., *mainstreaming, integration, inclusion*), two definitions of inclusion might be helpful. Brown and Conroy (1997) defined *inclusion* as "the degree to which children with developmental delays are playing, learning, working, and living with family and friends in their communities." (p. 7). More recently, the Division of Early Childhood and the National Association for the Education of Young Children defined early childhood inclusion more broadly as

> the values, policies, and practices that support the right of every infant and young child and his or her family, regardless of ability, to participate in a broad range of activities and contexts as full members of families, communities, and society. The desired results of inclusive experiences for children with and without disabilities and their families include a sense of belonging and membership, positive social relationships and friendships, and development and learning to reach their full potential. *The defining features of inclusion that can be used to identify high quality early childhood programs and services are access, participation, and support.* (Division for Early Childhood, 2009, p. 2, emphasis added)

Clearly, participating in and belonging to one's community is an essential component of inclusion; however, a common element of inclusion is the emphasis on children's "development" and "learning" in inclusive environments. Not only is it important for children to be a part of their community, but inclusion must go beyond being a "place" where children with developmental delays are served and include effective "practices" that foster children's learning and development in community settings alongside their typically developing peers.

Present Knowledge Base of Preschool Inclusion

The purpose of this chapter is not to review the extensive conceptual and empirical literature on preschool inclusion. Others have published comprehensive and coherent reviews (see Buysse & Bailey, 1993; Odom et al., 2004, for comprehensive examinations). Indeed, Odom and colleagues' (2004) evaluation of preschool inclusion continues to be instructive and applicable to the field. In their systematic review they reached the following conclusions: 1) practitioners have reported various teaching procedures and curricula with children with and without developmental delays that led to positive behavioral and attitudinal outcomes; 2) preschools have been most likely to enroll children with mild disabilities and have used a number of forms of inclusion (e.g., itinerant models, team teaching, reverse mainstreaming) and types of programs (e.g., public schools, Head Start programs, child care centers) to serve children with developmental delays, including preschoolers with severe disabilities; 3) the quality of inclusive preschools has been similar to that of noninclusive early childhood programs; 4) although many children with developmental delays interact less frequently with their typically developing peers and may at times be at risk for social rejection, a number of interventions have been developed to address preschoolers' social competence needs; 5) in general, both practitioners and parents have expressed positive dispositions about preschool inclusion; and 6) contemporary policy, administrative, and cultural and linguistic challenges have existed and may affect the success and sustainability of preschool inclusion (see "What we know about preschool inclusion?" subsection of Odom et al., 2004, p. 40, for additional details). Moreover, several researchers have delineated common synthesis points from the preschool inclusion literature (Buysse & Hollingsworth, 2009; National Professional Development Center on Inclusion, 2009; Odom, Schwartz, & ECRII Investigators, 2002). As Odom, Buysse, and Soukakou

(2011) noted, these synthesis points focus on 1) important outcomes for inclusion (e.g., child engagement, friendships), 2) specialized instruction (e.g., embedded learning opportunities, activity-based intervention), 3) professional collaboration, 4) necessary supports (e.g., administrative, professional development), and 5) a philosophy that all children may benefit from inclusion.

State of Preschool Inclusion

Preschool inclusion has had legislative support, at least with respect to least restrictive environment (LRE) (IDEA, 2004); public policy support (cf. Turnbull, Stowe, Turnbull, & Schrandt, 2007); empirical support (e.g., Buysse & Bailey, 1993; Odom et al., 2004); and parental and professional support (e.g., Division for Early Childhood, 2009; Hurley & Horn, 2010) for many years. Although a number of early childhood educators have argued cogently for preschool inclusion (e.g., Bricker, 1995; Brown & Conroy, 1997; Guralnick, 2001; Odom et al., 1996; Wolery & Wilbers, 1994), unfortunately, the proportion of children served for at least some part of their school day in inclusive settings has not changed appreciably in the last several decades and has remained about 50% of the children served in Part B 619 services (Lazara et al., 2010). Moreover, as Odom and colleagues (2011) noted, with recent changes in definition and when children are analyzed who have their primary placements in general education settings (i.e., receiving both general and special education services in regular education settings), preschoolers represent only about 30% of the children with IEPs in the United States. We find this state of affairs disheartening given that the vast majority of children served with Part B 619 services have been preschoolers with speech or language impairments (47%) or developmental delays (36%), and presumably most of those identified children have relatively mild developmental delays and might benefit greatly from educational and social integration with same-age peers without disabilities (Individuals with Disabilities Education Act Data, 2009). This static trend has continued for a number of years in spite of the continued advocacy and leadership of prominent professional organizations such as the Division for Early Childhood and the National Association for the Education of Young Children (e.g., Division for Early Childhood, 2009) and federally funded national centers focusing on promoting preschool inclusion (e.g., Early Childhood Research Institute on Inclusion, 2000; National Professional Development Center on Inclusion, 2011).

RESPONSE TO INTERVENTION IN PRESCHOOLS

Since the passage of the Education for All Handicapped Children Act (PL 94-142) in 1975 and through subsequent reauthorizations of IDEA (the Individuals with Disabilities Education Improvement Act of 2004, PL 108-446), the IEP process has been a fundamental component of special education law and services. The core functions of IEPs continue to be communication, management, accountability, compliance, monitoring, and evaluation of children's special education services (cf. Yell, 2012). Moreover, measurable goals for involvement in general education classrooms and in other specified educational settings related to children's disabilities are legally required. The Individuals with Disabilities Education Improvement Act of 2004 included significant changes to federal special education law (Yell, 2012). The change most relevant to this chapter was in RTI regulations. Specifically, state education agencies (SEAs) can no longer require local education agencies (LEAs) to use discrepancy models to identify children with disabilities, and SEAs and LEAs are encouraged to employ research-based procedures to serve and identify children with academic and behavioral problems (Individuals with Disabilities Education Act Regulations, 34 C.F.R. § 300.1). Moreover, school district personnel can use as much as 15% of their IDEA funding for early intervening services for children who have not yet been identified for special education services (*Memorandum to Chief State School Officers*, 2008). Although these changes clearly place contemporary special education services within a prevention framework (cf. Conroy & Brown, 2004), the reauthorized IDEA made no provisions for RTI prior to kindergarten.

RTI has been a well-known approach for school-age children with learning difficulties for a number of years (Council for Exceptional Children, 2008; Jimerson, Burns, & VanDerHeyden, 2007; National Association of State Directors of Special Education, 2005). RTI has been based on a continuum of interventions and supports typically arranged in three tiers, with all children involved in high-quality instruction with a core curriculum at Tier 1, some students receiving small-group interventions and supports at Tier 2, and a few children being provided with intensive and individualized interventions and supports at Tier 3. The Office of Special Education Programs of the U.S. Department of Education delineated the following core characteristics of RTI approaches: 1) evidence-based instruction in general education, 2) frequent progress monitoring, 3) screening for academic and behavioral difficulties, and 4) tiered levels of more intensive instruction. In recent years, some early childhood special educators have recommend that RTI processes be applied to preschool services (Barnett et al., 2006; Buysse & Peisner-Feinberg, 2010; Greenwood et al., 2008; Greenwood et al., 2011; National Professional Development Center on Inclusion, 2012; Peisner-Feinberg, Buysse, Benshoff, & Soukakou, 2011).

Response to Intervention Definitions

Unlike preschool inclusion and the IEP process, RTI is relatively new to the field of early childhood special education and especially early childhood education. Hence, as with preschool inclusion, recent definitions may be helpful. Coleman and colleagues (2006) defined Recognition & Response (R&R, i.e., their term for an RTI approach in early childhood) as a system with "four essential components: 1) an intervention hierarchy; 2) screening, assessment, and progress monitoring; 3) research-based curriculum, instruction, and focused interventions; and 4) a collaborative problem-solving process for decision-making" (p. 3). Similarly, Greenwood and colleagues (2008) defined RTI for early childhood programs as a "systematic problem-solving process designed to" provide early identification of children's difficulties, better align the level of teaching with preschoolers' responsiveness to instructional techniques, and provide an assessment process for evaluating teaching effectiveness and, when indicated, implementing instructional changes to promote children's behavioral and academic progress (see Center for Response to Intervention in Early Childhood, 2012). Furthermore, they noted that RTI for early childhood programs was individualized and based on evidence-based teaching and learning strategies, with an overall aim of reducing the need for special education.

Present Knowledge Base and State
of Preschool Response to Intervention

Unlike preschool inclusion and IEPs, the conceptual framework for preschool RTI has emerged only in recent years from school-age RTI (e.g., Fuchs, Fuchs, & Vaughn, 2008; Fuchs, Mock, Morgan, & Young, 2003; Torgesen, 1998; Vaughn, Linan-Thompson, & Hickman, 2003) and the current empirical foundation for RTI in prekindergarten programs has been limited (cf. Buysse & Peisner-Feinberg, 2010; Greenwood et al., 2011; Marshall et al., 2011; Odom et al., 2011; Peisner-Feinberg et al., 2011). For example, in their review Coleman and colleagues found only 14 studies, which addressed mostly emergent literacy or numeracy, that met their three review criteria—i.e., 1) age of children (4–8 years); 2) nature of disability (at risk for learning disabilities); and 3) type of intervention used (multitiered intervention components, problem-solving or standard protocol, and assessment system to guide instruction and eligibility). Most of the children involved in RTI interventions examined were enrolled in kindergarten, first-, or second-grade classes (i.e., 7- to 8-year-olds).

Recently, Buysse, Peisner-Feinberg, and colleagues at the Frank Porter Graham Child Development Institute at the University of North Carolina have developed, refined, and systematically investigated an evolving RTI model for preschoolers, R&R (Buysse & Peisner-Feinberg, 2010; Buysse, Peisner-Feinberg, & Burchinal, 2012; Peisner-Feinberg et al., 2011; see http://randr.fpg.unc.edu/ for elaborations of current model information). R&R researchers designed their model for 3-, 4-, and 5-year-old children in prekindergarten classrooms and incorporated two complementary dimensions, *recognition* and *response*. Critical to the *recognition* dimension is formative assessment by teachers, with universal screening upon entry to preschools in the fall and readministration of progress monitoring assessments at midyear and at the end of the school year. The *response* dimension consists of an evidence-based preschool curriculum, intentional teaching (cf. Epstein, 2007), and targeted interventions based on periodic formative assessments. Hence, Tier 1 consists of universal screening and follow-up assessments along with an effective classwide curriculum. Then, based on formative assessments, some children also receive Tier 2 small-group interventions (e.g., 15 minutes daily for 8 to 10 weeks). Along with Tier 2 small-group daily lessons, teachers further enhance intervention by providing embedded teaching and learning opportunities and other curricular changes throughout the day in preschool classrooms. Finally, for a few preschoolers and within the context of ongoing Tier 1 and 2 classroom interventions, teachers implement Tier 3 interventions, which consist of intensive research-based strategies such as response prompting, incidental teaching, and peer interaction instruction. Hence, the core of the R&R model is its focus on essential prekindergarten skills (e.g., language, literacy, numeracy) with appropriate and timely formative assessments and (when warranted by assessment) its use of information gathered to problem-solve and effectively intervene with preschoolers.

Buysse, Peisner-Feinberg, and colleagues (Buysse & Peisner-Feinberg, 2010; Buysse et al., 2012; Peisner-Feinberg et al., 2011) have been carefully investigating their R&R model. Based on their efforts they have advocated for further research and development of preschool RTI approaches along with careful evaluation of effective components. Given that rigorous empirical information about RTI models is only now emerging, they also have noted that preschool RTI continues to be a promising practice (cf. Buysse et al., 2012; Peisner-Feinberg & Yazejian, 2010) and not necessarily a well-established, evidence-based approach for prekindergarten children (cf. Odom et al., 2005). Moreover, the need for further research and development has been clearly indicated by the Institute of Education Sciences funding of a multisite center on early childhood RTI (Center for Response to Intervention in Early Childhood, 2012) and other contemporary research on preschool RTI (e.g., Buysse & Peisner-Feinberg, 2010; Buysse et al., 2012; Greenwood et al., 2011). The National Professional Development Center on Inclusion (2012) has also disseminated a concept paper on the importance of RTI models for early childhood.

COMMON CONCEPTUAL CORE AND ESSENTIAL ELEMENTS OF INDIVIDUALIZED EDUCATION PROGRAM AND RESPONSE TO INTERVENTION PROCESSES

Both IEP and preschool RTI approaches align with the contemporary notion that early intervening services are an established recommended practice for young children and their families (cf. Odom & McLean, 2006; Sandall, Hemmeter, Smith, & McLean, 2005). Moreover, the common conceptual core of the two processes is preventive and interventive in nature (cf. Buysse & Peisner-Feinberg, 2010; Conroy & Brown, 2004), and they share several essential elements. Specifically, both processes include the following elements (Coleman et al., 2006; Individuals with Disabilities Education Act Regulations, 34 C.F.R. § 300.1):

- Preference for services in general education settings to the greatest extent possible

- Problem-solving methods for development and implementation of educational and instructional services and supports

- Individualization of educational and instructional services and supports

- Measurement of progress toward specified goals or objectives to maximize children's learning and development

- Employment of research- or evidence-based practices

The differences in these essential elements of the two processes appear to be a matter of degree. Nevertheless, the distinctions may well be especially important when trying to implement and integrate IEP and RTI processes to make services and supports effective in serving young children.

An essential element of both IEP and RTI approaches for preschoolers should be classrooms in which children with and without developmental delays have been enrolled and engaged in high-quality early childhood activities and curricula. Many early childhood educators have recommended this essential element as the foundational base (Tier 1 universal design feature) in early childhood services (e.g., Brown, Odom, & Conroy, 2001; Hemmeter, Ostrosky, & Fox, 2006; Sandall & Schwartz, 2008; see Snyder, McLaughlin, & Denney, 2011, for a review of frameworks). Hence, we believe as an initial essential element, high-quality inclusive early childhood services are a necessary but not sufficient contextual condition to implement IEP and RTI processes.

A second essential element of both IEP and RTI approaches for preschoolers has been a problem-solving approach for planning and implementing classroom and program activities. For example, many early childhood educators have readily acknowledged that promotion of children's social-emotional development is one of their primary responsibilities and goals. Moreover, substantial evidence exists that many preschool children who are at risk for disabilities and who have developmental delays need and may benefit from well-planned interventions in their social-emotional development (cf. Brown, Odom, & McConnell, 2008). Whereas many early childhood classrooms have been arranged to support children's play, those same classrooms may require intentional teaching of social skills to promote children's peer interactions (cf. Brown, Odom, McConnell, & Rathel, 2008). Although all of the multiple difficulties that might arise in programs that institute inclusive IEP and RTI approaches to services cannot be anticipated, the fundamental point is that practitioners' dispositions ought to include their inclination and ability to develop and "test out" acceptable and feasible modifications and accommodations to serve children within inclusive classrooms. Moreover, the focus should not merely be on structural placement of children with and without developmental delays in the same classes but rather on processes that afford teachers and children multiple high-quality teaching and learning opportunities that are carefully monitored for progress, especially in the area of peer-related social competence abilities (Brown, Odom, & Buysse, 2002).

The nature of the problem-solving mechanism has been where IEP and RTI processes differ. Historically, the IEP processes have been more formal and legalistic, usually as an annual planning process (Yell, 2012). RTI processes, however, have been intended to support screenings for intervention beyond the core curriculum and for targeted instruction in either Tier 2 small-group formats or Tier 3 intensive individualized circumstances. Hence, assessment, review, and discussion of children's progress in well-specified skill areas (e.g., emergent literacy skills, mathematical abilities, peer interaction skills) should occur more frequently, and RTI as a problem-solving approach should be superior to the traditional IEP process for monitoring short-term progress and making timely decisions about ongoing instruction.

A third essential element of IEP and RTI processes and a long-standing cardinal principle of both early childhood education and early childhood special education has been individualization of services (e.g., Bredekamp, 1987; Sandall et al., 2005). Individualization, however, does not necessarily, and often does not, mean intervention for a single child or delivery of intervention in a one-to-one teaching format. We have long asserted that

> Individualized intervention has presumed that children were assessed individually (at least with respect to analyzing their assessment information) and that one or more children's individual needs require additional intervention strategies to promote their further development. In preschool classrooms with young children with developmental delays, one, or two, or all the children might be participants in and benefit from individualized interventions that are implemented to meet the needs of one or more peers. (Brown & Conroy, 1997, p. 87)

Again, the nature of individualization as it is performed within the IEP and RTI processes may differ. In the IEP process, the placements of children, objectives, and support services have been developed for the individual by the IEP team. With the RTI approach in Tiers 2 and 3, the individualized instruction has been based on student screenings and ongoing formative assessment linked more directly to day-to-day interventions and supports.

A fourth essential element of IEP and RTI procedures has been measurement of specified goals or objectives. As discussed previously, often evaluation of IEP goals has been performed across time but less often than ongoing formative assessments employed in an RTI approach. For example, RTI practitioners have used screenings to identify children in need of Tier 2 interventions. Once in Tier 2 interventions, frequent formative assessments related to the effectiveness of those interventions and supports have been employed to determine whether children should be provided with Tier 3 intensive instruction. Hence, practitioners employing RTI approaches have been required to implement frequent and regular progress monitoring to assess and, when indicated, modify their intervention efforts in a timely manner based on resultant information. Nevertheless, both processes have required collection of information related to attainment of instructional goals or objectives, followed by use of the resultant data to change instructional procedures as indicated. Whether employing RTI or IEP procedures, individualized data-based decision making has been a foundational component of special education services and has served as the framework for assessing children's learning. Recommended practice has long been to collect and analyze needed information, and we believe efficient and effective data collection has been warranted to assure children's learning whether one is involved in IEP or RTI approaches to service provision (e.g., Brown et al., 2002; Greenwood et al., 2011; Wolery, 2004). Hence, the extent of differences in IEP and RTI processes appears to involve the frequency of data collection and the practitioners' ability to respond to the information in a timely manner.

A final essential element of IEP and RTI processes has been employment of evidence-based practices (cf. Buysse & Wesley, 2006). Unfortunately, contemporary calls for evidence- and research-based educational procedures have almost become vapid rhetoric among too many educators. Equally troublesome has been the fact some educators have argued we "do not know all that we need to know" about interventions, which is a banal truth about all applied scientific endeavors, especially in the field of education (Brown & Conroy, 2011). Nevertheless, the reality remains that we do "know" several feasible evidence-based procedures (Odom et al., 2005) and we also have other "promising practices" that can and ought (in a philosophical sense) to be employed and evaluated until additional stronger evidence is forthcoming (cf. Buysse & Wesley, 2006; McCall, 2009). Moreover, which procedures and services work effectively for whom under what circumstances should be documented and evaluated systematically to achieve a better understanding of early intervening services (cf. Dunst, Trivette, & Cutspec, 2002; Guralnick, 1997).

PRIMARY CHALLENGE FOR INTEGRATING PRESCHOOL INCLUSION AND RESPONSE TO INTERVENTION PRINCIPLES

Given that the use of RTI in early childhood education is relatively new and difficult, we recognize that discussions of the implications of employing RTI in preschools are sorely needed (National Professional Development Center on Inclusion, 2012).

We also realize that some RTI "purists" might argue that the process is a primary prevention procedure for yet-to-be-identified children to avert placement in special education services. Nevertheless, prevention models have long included secondary prevention (i.e., reducing the prevalence of disabilities) and tertiary prevention (i.e., attenuating the consequences of disabilities), and these two forms of prevention are "part and parcel" to the integrated framework we propose (cf. Simeonsson, 1991; Walker, Ramsey, & Gresham, 2004).

As we argue, IEP and RTI processes share a common conceptual core and several essential elements, and those elements should be revisited and better integrated as we strive to assure inclusive environments for all young children. Moreover, changes in special education law and regulations align the two approaches and, we believe, make their procedural integration a logical and pragmatic move forward in improving inclusive early intervening services for young children and their families. The conceptual core and common essential elements are not necessarily new, but extant and convergent data have indicated that integration of the two processes might be feasible as well as beneficial. We believe that the thoughtful integration of the IEP and RTI processes might be especially beneficial for increasing the proportion of preschoolers who are *meaningfully* included in community-based programs—that is, preschoolers who not only have been "physically" enrolled in classrooms, but who also learn, develop, and thrive in community settings. Moreover, a careful integration of the two approaches may possibly provide the day-to-day mechanisms (e.g., frequent intentional teaching, effective and regular progress monitoring, data-based decision making, timely modification of interventions) and robust and functional strategies for enhancing preschool children's inclusive experiences and improving their learning outcomes. Hence, we believe the two frameworks directly relate to the fundamental programmatic issue of what constitutes necessary and sufficient educational services and supports for young children in early childhood services.

Greenwood and colleagues (2011) recently reported that state early childhood directors delineated several challenges for implementation of RTI. These challenges included 1) insufficient trained personnel to implement RTI, 2) lack of resources to develop the infrastructure, 3) lack of Tier 2 and Tier 3 intervention strategies, 4) lack of knowledge in how to create RTI models, 5) lack of evidence-based Tier 1 programs, 6) lack of administrative support and leadership, 7) lack of progress monitoring measures, and 8) difficulties in establishing collaborative relationships. Hence, we believe a primary contemporary challenge for early childhood educators is related to high-quality professional development (Winton, 2010) and integration of RTI practices into inclusive early childhood settings in particular.

We believe high-quality professional development and technical assistance should focus on strategies for practitioners to teach both preacademic skills (e.g., Buysse & Peisner-Feinberg, 2009; Greenwood et al., 2011) and peer-related social competencies that enhance children's social engagement (e.g., Brown et al., 2001; Hemmeter et al., 2006). Moreover, professional development and technical assistance should be evidence-informed and include performance-based approaches that promote adult learning (cf. Dunst & Trivette, 2009; Wesley & Buysse, 2010; Winton, 2010; and Chapter 21 in this text). If RTI practices are to be well diffused into inclusive early childhood settings, specific practitioner skills such as intentional teaching strategies, frequent and feasible data collection procedures, and collaborative consultation and problem-solving approaches will need to be taught systematically, more widely employed, and supported administratively in early childhood programs. Given the diverse nature of early childhood programs across our states and nation (e.g., state-funded prekindergartens, Head Start Programs, child care services, private preschools), this is a daunting professional challenge but one that is critically necessary for enhancing the quality of early childhood programs.

We believe that strategic employment of RTI approaches within early childhood education may promote additional preschool inclusion, especially for children whose social competence puts them at risk for exclusion (Brown et al., 2008; Conroy, Brown, & Olive, 2008). Mere enrollment of preschoolers with and without developmental delays and physical inclusion without the required universal and individualized procedures of RTI approaches will probably not benefit children's educational and developmental attainment. Given that children learn best in context (cf. Carta & Kong, 2007; Odom & Wolery, 2003), we believe that the integration of the two processes might "set the stage" and provide the mechanisms to focus on placing children who are "at promise" for school success instead of "at risk" for school failure (cf. Horowitz, 2000; Siperstein & Favazza, 2008). Nevertheless, we also believe that empirical scrutiny should prevail over logical speculation. Any such integration of the RTI processes warrants careful and systematic evaluation to determine whether the combination will be effectively and efficiently achieved (cf. Brown & Conroy, 2011). Building on our historical knowledge and past efforts to serve children with developmental delays in early childhood settings, perhaps we can move toward a more widespread, effective approach to preschool inclusion than we have achieved to date.

REFERENCES

Allen, K.E., Benning, P.M., & Drummond, W.T. (1972). Integration of normal and handicapped children in a behavior modification preschool: A case study. In G. Semb (Ed.), *Behavior analysis and education* (pp. 127–141). Lawrence: University of Kansas.

Barnett, W.S., Elliot, N., Wolsing, L., Bunger, C.E., Haski, H., McKissick, C., & Vander Meer, C.D. (2006). Response to intervention for young children with extremely challenging behaviors: What might it look like. *School Psychology Review, 35*(4), 568–582.

Barnett, W.S., Epstein, D.J., Carolan, M.E., Fitzgerald, J., Ackerman, D., & Friedman, A.H. (2010). *The state of preschool 2010.* Rutgers, NJ: National Institute for Early Education Research, Rutgers, The State University of New Jersey. Retrieved from http://nieer.org/publications/state-preschool-2010

Bredekamp, S. (Ed.). (1987). *Developmentally appropriate practice in early childhood programs serving children birth to eight.* Washington, DC: National Association for the Education of Young Children (NAEYC).

Bricker, D.D. (1995). The challenge of inclusion. *Journal of Early Intervention, 19,* 179–194.

Bricker, W.A., & Bricker, D.D. (1976). The infant, toddler, and preschool research and intervention project. In T.D. Tojossem (Ed.), *Intervention strategies for high-risk infants and young children* (pp. 545–572). Baltimore, MD: University Park Press.

Brown, W.H., & Conroy, M. (Eds.). (1997). *Inclusion of preschool children with developmental delays in early childhood programs.* Little Rock, AR: Southern Early Childhood Association.

Brown, W.H., & Conroy, M.A. (2011). Social emotional competence in young children with developmental delays: Our reflection and vision for the future. *Journal of Early Intervention, 33*(4), 310–320. doi:10.1177/1053815111429969

Brown, W.H., Horn, E.M., Heiser, J.G., & Odom, S.L. (1996). Project BLEND: An inclusive model for early intervention services. *Journal of Early Intervention, 20,* 364–375.

Brown, W.H., Odom, S.L., & Buysse, V. (2002). Assessment of preschool children's peer-related social competence. *Assessment for Effective Intervention, 27,* 61–71.

Brown, W.H., Odom, S.L., & Conroy, M.A. (2001). An intervention hierarchy for promoting preschool children's peer interactions in natural environments. *Topics in Early Childhood Special Education, 21,* 90–134.

Brown, W.H., Odom, S.L., & McConnell, S.R. (Eds.). (2008). *Social competence of young children: Risk, disability, and evidence-based practices* (2nd ed.). Baltimore, MD: Paul H. Brookes Publishing Co.

Brown, W.H., Odom, S.L., McConnell, S.R., & Rathel, J. (2008). Social competence interventions for preschoolers with developmental difficulties. In W.H. Brown, S.L. Odom, & S.R. McConnell (Eds.), *Social competence of young children: Risk, disability, and evidence-based practices* (2nd ed., pp. 141–163). Baltimore, MD: Paul H. Brookes Publishing Co.

Buysse, V., & Bailey, D.B. (1993). Behavioral and developmental outcomes in young children with disabilities in integrated and segregated settings: A review of comparative studies. *Journal of Special Education, 26,* 434–461.

Buysse, V., & Hollingsworth, H.L. (2009). Research synthesis points on early childhood inclusion: What every practitioner and all families should know. *Young Exceptional Children, 11,* 18–30.

Buysse, V., & Peisner-Feinberg, E. (2009). *Recognition & Response: Findings from the first implementation study.* Retrieved from http://randr.fpg.unc.edu/sites/randr.fpg.unc.edu/files/KeyFindingsHandout.pdf

Buysse, V., & Peisner-Feinberg, E. (2010). Recognition & Response: Response to intervention for pre-K. *Young Exceptional Children, 13*(4), 2–13.

Buysse, V., Peisner-Feinberg, E., & Burchinal, M. (2012, March). *Recognition & Response: Developing and evaluating a model of RTI for pre-K.* Poster presented at the Society on Research on Educational Effectiveness, Washington, DC.

Buysse, V., & Wesley, P.W. (2006). *Evidence-based practice in the early childhood field.* Washington, DC: ZERO TO THREE Press.

Caldwell, B.M. (1973). The importance of beginning early. In M.B. Karnes (Ed.), *Not all wagons are red: The exceptional child's early years* (pp. 2–10). Arlington, VA: Council for Exceptional Children.

Carta, J.J., & Kong, N.Y. (2007). Trends and issues in interventions for preschoolers with developmental disabilities. In S.L. Odom, R.H. Horner, M.E. Snell, & Blacher, J. (Eds.), *Handbook of developmental disabilities* (pp. 181–198). New York, NY: Guilford Press.

Center for Response to Intervention in Early Childhood. (2012). Retrieved from http://crtiec.org/

Coleman, M.R., Buysse, V., & Neitzel, J. (2006). *Recognition and response: An early intervening system for young children at risk for learning disabilities.* Chapel Hill: University of North Carolina, Frank Porter Graham Child Development Institute.

Conroy, M.A., & Brown, W.H. (2004). Early identification, prevention, and early intervention with young children at risk for emotional or behavioral disorders: Issues, trends, and a call for action. *Behavioral Disorders, 29*(3), 224–237.

Conroy, M.A., Brown, W.H., & Olive, M.L. (2008). Social competence interventions for young children with challenging behavior. In W.H. Brown, S.L. Odom, & S.R. McConnell (Eds.), *Social competence of young children: Risk, disability, and evidence-based practices* (2nd ed., pp. 205–231). Baltimore, MD: Paul H. Brookes Publishing Co.

Consortium for Longitudinal Studies. (1983). *As the twig is bent . . . Lasting effects of preschool programs.* Hillsdale, NJ: Lawrence Erlbaum Associates.

Council for Exceptional Children. (2008). CEC's position on response to intervention (RTI): The unique role of special education and special educators. Retrieved May 20, 2010, from http://www.cec.sped.org/AM/Template.cfm?Section=Home&Template=/CM/ContentDisplay.cfm&ContentID=11769

Division for Early Childhood. (2009). *Early childhood inclusion: A joint position of the Division for Early Childhood (DEC) and the National Association for the Education of Young Children (NAEYC).* Chapel Hill: University of North Carolina, Frank Porter Graham Child Development Institute. Retrieved December 2, 2010, from http://dec-sped.org/uploads/docs/about_dec/position_concept_papers/PositionStatement_Inclusion_Joint_updated_May2009.pdf

Dunlap, G., Strain, P.S., Fox, L., Carta, J., Conroy, M., Smith, B.J., . . . Sowell, C. (2006). Prevention and intervention with young children's challenging behavior: Perspectives regarding current knowledge. *Behavioral Disorders, 32,* 29–45.

Dunst, C.J., & Trivette, C.M. (2009). Let's be PALS: An evidence-based approach to professional development. *Infants & Young Children, 22*(3), 164–176.

Dunst, C.J., Trivette, C.M., & Cutspec, P.A. (2002). An evidence-based approach to documenting the characteristics and consequences of early intervention practices. *Centerscope, 1*(2), 1–6. Retrieved December 28, 2009, from http://www.wbpress.com/index.php?main_page=product_book_info&products_id=370

Early Childhood Research Institute on Inclusion. (2000). ECRII website with resources and research. Chapel Hill: University of North Carolina, Frank Porter Graham Child Development Institute. Retrieved March 2011 from http://www.fpg.unc.edu/~ecrii/

Education for All Handicapped Children Act of 1975, PL 94-142, 20 U.S.C. §§ 1401 *et seq.*

Epstein, A.S. (2007). *The intentional teacher: Choosing the best strategies for young children's learning.* Washington, DC: NAEYC.

Federal Interagency Forum on Child and Family Statistics. (2012). *America's children: Key national indicators of well-being (2006).* Washington, DC. Retrieved September 30, 2012, from http://www.childstats.gov/americaschildren/

Fox, L., & Hemmeter, M.L. (2009). A program-wide model for supporting social emotional development and addressing challenging behavior in early childhood settings. In W. Sailor, G. Dunlap, G. Sugai, and R. Horner (Eds.), *Handbook of positive behavior support* (pp. 177–202). New York. NY: Springer.

Fuchs, D., Fuchs, L.S., & Vaughn, S. (2008). *Response to intervention: A framework for reading educators.* Newark, DE: International Reading Association.

Fuchs, D., Mock, D., Morgan, P.L., & Young, C.L. (2003). Responsiveness-to-intervention: Definitions, evidences, and implications for the learning disabilities construct. *Learning Disabilities Research & Practice, 18*(3), 157–171.

Greenwood, C.R., Bradfield, T., Kaminski, R., Linas, M., Carta, J.J., & Nylander, D. (2011). The response to intervention (RTI) approach in early childhood. *Focus on Exceptional Children, 43*(9), 1–22.

Greenwood, C.R., Carta, J.J., Baggett, K., Buzhardt, J., Walker, D., & Terry B. (2008). Best practices integrating progress monitoring and response-to-intervention concepts into early childhood. In A. Thomas, J. Grimes, & J. Gruba (Eds.), *Best practices in school psychology* (Vol. 2, pp. 1–13). Washington, DC: National Association of School Psychology.

Guralnick, M.J. (Ed.). (1997). *The effectiveness of early intervention.* Baltimore, MD: Paul H. Brookes Publishing Co.

Guralnick, M.J. (Ed.). (2001). *Early childhood inclusion: Focus on change.* Baltimore, MD: Paul H. Brookes Publishing Co.

Hemmeter, M.L., Ostrosky, M., & Fox, L. (2006). Social and emotional foundations for early childhood learning: A conceptual model for intervention. *School Psychology Review, 35*(4), 583–601.

Horowitz, F.D. (2000). Child development and the PITS: Simple questions, complex answers, and developmental theory. *Child Development, 71*(1), 1–10.

Hurley, J.J., & Horn, E.M. (2010). Family and professional priorities for inclusive early childhood settings. *Journal of Early Intervention, 32*(5), 335–350.

Individuals with Disabilities Education Act Data. (2009). IDEA 618 Data Tables. Retrieved December 28, 2010, from https://www.ideadata.org/arc_toc9.asp#partbCC

Individuals with Disabilities Education Act Regulations, 34 C.F.R. § 300.1 *et seq.*

Individuals with Disabilities Education Improvement Act (IDEA) of 2004, PL 108-446, 20 U.S.C. §§ 1400 *et seq.*

Jimerson, S.R., Burns, M., & VanDerHeyden, A.M. (Eds.). (2007). *Handbook of response to intervention: The science and practice of assessment and intervention.* New York, NY: Springer.

Kauffman, J.M., Nelson, C.M., Simpson, R.L., & Mock, D.R. (2011). Contemporary issues. In J.M. Kauffman & D.P. Hallahan (Eds.), *Handbook of special education* (pp. 15–26). New York, NY: Routledge.

Kirk, S.A., & Johnson, G.O. (1951). *The mentally retarded child.* Cambridge, MA: Riverside Press.

Klaus, R.A., & Gray, S.W. (1968). The Early Training Project for disadvantaged children. *Monographs of the Society for Research in Child Development, 33*(4, Serial No. 120).

Lazara, A., Danaher, J., Kraus, R., Goode, S., Hipps, C., & Festa, C. (Eds.). (2010). *Section 619 Profile* (17th ed.). Chapel Hill: University of North Carolina, Frank Porter Graham Child Development Institute, National Early Childhood Technical Assistance Center. Retrieved from http://www.nectac.org/~pdfs/pubs/sec619_2010.pdf

Marshall, K., Brown, W.H., Conroy, M.A., & Knopf, H. (2011). Early intervention and prevention of disability: Preschoolers. In J.M. Kauffman & D.P. Hallahan (Eds.), *Handbook of special education* (pp. 703–715). New York, NY: Routledge.

McCall, R.B. (2009). Evidence-based programming in the context of practice and policy. *Social Policy Report Society for Research in Child Development, 23*(3), 3–11.

Meisels, S.J., & Shonkoff, J.P. (2000). Early childhood intervention: A continuing evolution. In J.P. Shonkoff & S.J. Meisels (Eds.), *Handbook of early childhood intervention* (2nd ed., pp. 3–31). New York, NY: Cambridge Press.

Memorandum to Chief State School Officers, 51 IDELR 49 (OSEP, 2008).

National Association of State Directors of Special Education. (2005). *Response to intervention: Policy considerations and implementations.* Alexandria, VA: Author.

National Center for Education Statistics. (2010). *Digest of Education Statistics: Table 43.* Washington, DC: Institute of Education Sciences of the United States Department of Education. Retrieved from http://nces.ed.gov/programs/digest/d09/tables/dt09_043.asp

National Professional Development Center on Inclusion. (2009). *Research synthesis points on early childhood inclusion.* Chapel Hill: University of North Carolina, FPG Child Development Institute. Retrieved from http://community.fpg.unc.edu.npdei

National Professional Development Center on Inclusion. (2011). *CONNECT modules.* Chapel Hill: University of North Carolina, Frank Porter Graham Child Development Institute. Retrieved from http://community.fpg.unc.edu/connect-modules

National Professional Development Center on Inclusion. (2012). *Response to intervention (RTI) in early childhood: Building consensus on the defining features.* Chapel Hill: University of North Carolina, Frank Porter Graham Child Development Institute. Retrieved from http://npdci.fpg.unc.edu/resources/response-intervention-rti-early-childhood-building-consensus-defining-features

No Child Left Behind Act (NCLB) of 2001, PL 107-110, 20 U.S.C. §§ 6301 *et seq.*

Odom, S.L., Brantlinger, E., Gersten, R., Horner, R.H., Thompson, B., & Harris, K.R. (2005). Research in special education: Scientific methods and evidence-based practices. *Exceptional Children, 71,* 137–148.

Odom, S.L., Buysse, V., & Soukakou, E. (2011). Inclusion of young children with disabilities: A quarter century of research perspectives. *Journal of Early Intervention, 33*(4), 344–356.

Odom, S.L., & McLean, M.E. (Eds.). (2006). *Early intervention/early childhood special education: Recommended practices.* Austin, TX: PRO-ED.

Odom, S.L., Peck, C., Hanson, M., Beckman, P., Kaiser, A., Lieber, J., . . . Schwartz, I. (1996). Inclusion at the preschool level: An ecological systems analysis. *Social Policy Report: Society for Research in Child Development, 10* (2–3), 18–30.

Odom, S.L., Schwartz, I.S., & ECRII Investigators. (2002). So what do we know from all of this? Synthesis points of research on preschool inclusion. In S.L. Odom (Ed.), *Widening the circle: Including children with disabilities in preschool programs* (pp. 154–174). New York, NY: Teachers College Press.

Odom, S.L., Vitztum, J., Wolery, R., Lieber, J., Sandall, S., Hanson, M.J., . . . Horn, E. (2004). Preschool inclusion in the United States: A review of research from an ecological systems perspective. *Journal of Research in Special Educational Needs, 4*(3), 17–49

Odom, S.L., & Wolery, M. (2003). A unified theory of practice in early intervention/childhood special education: Evidence-based practices. *Journal of Special Education, 37*(3), 164–173.

Peisner-Feinberg, E., Buysse, V., Benshoff, L., & Soukakou, E. (2011). Recognition & Response: Response to intervention for pre-kindergarten. In C. Groark, S.M. Eidelman, L. Kaczmarek, & S. Maude (Eds.), *Early childhood intervention: Shaping the future for children with special needs and their families, Vol. 3: Emerging trends in research and practice* (pp. 37–53). Santa Barbara, CA: Praeger.

Peisner-Feinberg, E.S., & Yazejian, N. (2010). Research on program quality: The evidence base. In P.W. Wesley & V. Buysse (Eds.), *The quest for quality: Promising innovations for early childhood programs* (pp. 47–67). Baltimore, MD: Paul H. Brookes Publishing Co.

President's Commission on Excellence in Special Education. (2002). *A new era: Revitalizing special education for children and families.* Retrieved December 2009 from http://en.wikipedia.org/wiki/President's_Commission_on_Excellence_in_Special_Education

Rule, S., Stowitschek, J.J., Innocenti, M., Striefel, S., Killoran, J., Swezey, K., & Boswell, C. (1987). The Social Integration Project: Analysis of the effects of mainstreaming handicapped children into day care centers. *Education and Treatment of Children, 10,* 175–192.

Safford, P.L., & Safford, E.J. (1996). *A history of childhood & disability.* New York: Teachers College Press.

Sandall, S., Hemmeter, M.L., Smith, B.J., & McLean, M. (2005). *DEC recommended practices: A comprehensive guide for practical application in early intervention/early childhood special education.* Longman, CO: Sopris West Educational Services.

Sandall, S.R., & Schwartz, I.S. (2008). *Building blocks for teaching preschoolers with special needs* (2nd ed.). Baltimore, MD: Paul H. Brookes Publishing Co.

Scheerenberger, R.C. (1983). *History of mental retardation.* Baltimore, MD: Paul H. Brookes Publishing Co.

Simeonsson, R.J. (1991). Primary, secondary, and tertiary prevention in early intervention. *Journal of Early Intervention, 15,* 124–134.

Siperstein, G.N., & Favazza, P.C. (2008) Placing children "At Promise": Future directions for promoting social competence. In W.H. Brown, S.L. Odom, & S.R. McConnell (Eds.), *Social competence of young children: Risk, disability, and evidence-based practices* (2nd ed., pp. 321–332). Baltimore, MD: Paul H. Brookes Publishing Co.

Snyder, P.A., McLaughlin, T.W., & Denney, M.K. (2011). Frameworks for guiding program focus and practices in early intervention. In J.M. Kauffman & D.P. Hallahan (Eds.), *Handbook of special education* (pp. 716–730). New York, NY: Routledge.

Torgesen, J. (1998). Catch them before they fall: Identification and assessment to prevent failure in young children. *American Educator, 22,* 32–39.

Trohanis, P.L. (2008). Progress in providing services to young children with special needs and their families. *Journal of Early Intervention, 30*(2), 140–151.

Turnbull, H.R., III, Stowe, M.J., Turnbull, A.P., & Schrandt, M.S. (2007). Public policy and developmental disabilities: A 35-year retrospective and a 5-year prospective based on the core concepts of disability policy. In S.L. Odom, R.H. Horner, M.E. Snell, & J. Blacher (Eds.), *Handbook of developmental disabilities* (pp. 15–35). New York, NY: Guilford Press.

Vaughn, S., Linan-Thompson, S., & Hickman, P. (2003). Response to instruction as a means for identifying students with reading/learning disabilities. *Exceptional Children, 69*(4), 391–409.

Walker, H.M., Ramsey, E., & Gresham, F.M. (Eds.). (2004). *Antisocial behavior in school: Evidence-based practices* (2nd ed.). Belmont CA: Wadsworth/Thomson Learning.

Wesley, P.W., & Buysse, V. (2010). Rethinking technical assistance to support quality improvement. In P.W. Wesley & V. Buysse (Eds.), *The quest for quality: Promising innovations for early childhood programs* (pp. 131–164). Baltimore, MD: Paul H. Brookes Publishing Co.

Winton, P. (2010). Professional development and quality initiatives: Two essential components of an early childhood system. In P.W. Wesley & V. Buysse (Eds.), *The quest for quality: Promising innovations for early childhood programs* (pp. 113–129). Baltimore, MD: Paul H. Brookes Publishing Co.

Wolery, M. (2004). Monitoring children's progress and intervention implementation. In M. McLean, M. Wolery, & D.B. Bailey (Eds.), *Assessing infants and preschoolers with special needs* (3rd ed., pp. 545–584). Columbus, OH: Pearson.

Wolery, M., & Wilbers, J.S. (Eds.). (1994). *Including children with special needs in early childhood programs.* Washington, DC: National Association for the Education of Young Children.

Yell, M.L. (2012). *The law and special education* (3rd ed.). Boston, MA: Pearson.

Recognition & Response
for Dual Language Learners

Doré R. LaForett, Ellen S. Peisner-Feinberg, and Virginia Buysse

I n this chapter, we illustrate the use of response to intervention (RTI) approaches with prekindergarten (pre-K) children who are dual language learners (DLLs). Although different terms have been used to describe this population (see Center for Early Care and Education Research—Dual Language Learners, 2010), we define DLLs as "children who are learning a second language (English) while continuing to acquire their first (or home) language" (National Head Start Training and Technical Assistance Research Center, 2008). We describe the Recognition & Response Instructional Support System for Dual Language Learners (R&R–DLL), an adaptation to the core Recognition & Response (R&R) framework (Buysse & Peisner-Feinberg, 2010; Peisner-Feinberg et al., 2011). As described by Buysse and colleagues in Chapter 5 of this text, R&R is a tiered model of instruction in which the "recognition" (i.e., formative assessment) and "response" (i.e., effective core curriculum, intentional teaching, and targeted interventions linked to formative assessment) components are consistent with RTI. Assessment is used at Tier 1 to identify which children may benefit from instructional supports and to monitor their progress at Tiers 2 and 3. The dual aims of R&R are to improve the quality of instructional supports for all children and to provide additional supports for some children to ensure that all children succeed in school. Thus, the R&R framework is designed to identify children who are in greatest need of additional instructional supports, to implement those supports, and to evaluate children's response to them.

As an adaptation, R&R–DLL is designed to address the particular needs of young DLLs, and was initially developed for use in programs with bilingual staff but where the primary language of instruction was English, in which there could be opportunities for strategic use of the home language (Spanish). Future applications will explore the use of this system in programs with different linguistic features. R&R–DLL promotes instructional approaches for DLLs' language and literacy development, focusing on key skills related to vocabulary, phonological awareness, letter knowledge, and early reading. The development of R&R–DLL directly responds to recommendations that instructional accommodations are critical for teaching DLLs (Castro, Peisner-Feinberg, Buysse, & Gillanders, 2010). Further, this work acknowledges that RTI-based approaches must avoid a one-size-fits-all mentality by considering ecological validity issues when targeting culturally and linguistically diverse learners (Haager, 2007; Klingner & Edwards, 2006; Orosco & Klingner, 2010). In this chapter, we first outline the need for instructional models that address the learning of young DLLs and the role of RTI-based approaches in filling this need. We then describe the adaptations to the core R&R framework spanning both the *recognition* (assessment) and *response* (intervention) components within R&R–DLL.

THE NEED FOR EXPANDED INSTRUCTIONAL MODELS FOR DUAL LANGUAGE LEARNERS

There are several reasons to focus on improving the instructional models that are used with DLLs. First, substantive changes in population demographics have resulted in both increased and more heterogeneous representation of DLLs in early care and education programs, with estimates that 27% of all children in the United States have at least one parent who speaks a language other than English (Capps, Fixx, Ost, Reardon-Anderson, & Passel, 2005). Although the majority of these children came from families that included Spanish as a home language, DLLs are a diverse population with an estimated 140 languages represented in the Head Start program alone (National Head Start Training and Technical Assistance Research Center, 2008). Large numbers of DLLs and a great variety of languages spoken in early care and education programs pose the challenge of ensuring that these programs address the learning and developmental needs of this population.

Furthermore, research suggests that DLLs are at risk for negative academic outcomes as they progress through the grades. Relative to their monolingual English-speaking peers, DLLs are at higher risk for delays in early literacy development (Páez, Tabors, & López, 2007). They are also more likely to experience future academic difficulties and related negative sequelae such as school dropout, poor employment, and increased poverty (August & Shanahan, 2006). Such developmental trajectories reinforce the importance of fostering positive academic outcomes, particularly in the areas of language and literacy, which have been intricately tied to academic success. For young children, this means focusing on instructional approaches that promote the language and literacy skills that most strongly predict success in the early elementary grades.

Finally, emerging research outlining important differences and similarities in the ways DLLs and non-DLLs learn may have implications for instruction. Research indicates that DLLs have two separate language systems, as opposed to one system. Moreover, DLLs may learn their two languages either simultaneously or sequentially (see Paradis, Genesee, & Crago, 2011, for further discussion). According to a recent review by Hammer, Gillanders, Hoff, Uchikoshi, and Castro (under review) of research involving DLLs from birth through 5 years, there are differences between young DLLs and monolingual English speakers in development of specific language and literacy skills such as vocabulary and grammar. Specifically, young DLLs' single-language vocabularies are typically smaller than those of their monolingual peers, yet total vocabulary across both languages is similar to that of monolinguals. In addition, rates of growth in vocabulary and grammar skills for young DLLs often lag behind those of monolinguals. Nonetheless, there appear to be similarities in phonological development between DLLs and non-DLLs, although DLLs' two distinct phonological systems may develop differently depending on particular aspects of the languages being learned. Continued research on the developmental trajectories of young DLLs is essential for informing educational approaches for this population.

Taken together, changing demographics and emerging evidence on the developmental trajectories of DLLs creates a need for research-based approaches that can be used in early care and education settings to foster the learning and development of DLLs.

USING RESPONSE TO INTERVENTION MODELS TO PROVIDE EXPANDED INSTRUCTIONAL SUPPORT FOR YOUNG DUAL LANGUAGE LEARNERS

A comprehensive review by the National Literacy Panel on Language-Minority Children and Youth revealed that there is surprisingly little evidence concerning the effectiveness of various instructional approaches for DLLs, including how instruction should be adapted to address DLLs' unique needs (Snow, 2006). The paucity of research in this area is even more glaring for young DLLs attending early care and education programs. A recent research review by Buysse and colleagues (under review) found relatively few empirical studies that examined instructional approaches used with young DLLs. Specifically, there is limited information on effective, empirically validated educational interventions for DLLs that support their development in English and the home language and that are matched to their unique learning needs. Addressing this gap in knowledge has been identified by the National Task Force on Early Childhood Education for Hispanics (2007) as one of the most critical needs in the early education field in order to best serve young children currently attending pre-K programs and to help mitigate DLLs' risk of experiencing additional academic difficulties as they progress through school.

RTI-based approaches represent one option for addressing needed instructional strategies for early care and education settings serving young DLLs. Although RTI-based approaches originated in school-age populations to address the needs of students with learning disabilities, the present volume illustrates the merit of these approaches when applying them effectively and in ways that are developmentally appropriate for early childhood populations. Conceptually, RTI approaches are preventive in nature when they aim to lower children's risk for developing later difficulties (Justice, 2006). During the pre-K years when children are in the emergent and early literacy stages of reading, this means explicitly providing instruction on those skills known to be associated with future reading success (e.g., alphabet knowledge, phonological awareness [National Early Literacy Panel, 2008]). Indeed, it has been suggested that the failure of schools to provide adequate core instruction, a key element of instruction conceptually aligned with Tier 1 in RTI-based approaches, may explain why certain groups of children, including DLLs, exhibit poor academic performance (Orosco & Klingner, 2010).

Furthermore, the hallmarks of RTI-based approaches (i.e., formative assessment and tiered interventions) contain elements consistent with recommendations for assessment and instruction for DLLs. Specifically, recommendations for instruction of school-age DLLs parallel RTI models through their focus on teachers' use of formative assessment data that informs the planning of instruction for all children and targeted interventions for some children identified as needing additional supports (Francis, Rivera, Lesaux, Kieffer, & Rivera, 2006). These recommendations include ongoing and frequent assessments, focused small-group interventions, and explicit and differentiated instruction—all of which have been recommended as instructional approaches for DLLs (Castro et al., 2010). A potential implication of using tiered models with DLLs is that they may serve as a means for distinguishing between more generalized learning difficulties and difficulties related to proficiency in the language of instruction (Castro et al., 2010). Moreover, given that the impact of instructional practices or interventions may be weaker for DLLs than for non-DLLs (Goldenberg, 2008), tiered approaches such as RTI offer an opportunity to provide additional supports to DLLs whose learning may lag behind that of their classmates. Thus, by supporting young DLLs early in their academic learning, RTI-based approaches may help prevent academic failure (Donovan & Cross, 2002; Vaughn & Fuchs, 2003). Indeed, data are emerging that indicate early elementary school DLLs benefit from RTI-based approaches to reading instruction (e.g., Kamps et al., 2007; Linan-Thompson, Vaughn, Prater, & Cirino, 2006). Replication of such research with younger populations of DLLs is needed.

In sum, the limited number of studies examining instructional approaches used with DLLs necessitates increased research to more explicitly address the unique needs of DLLs. Tiered approaches may be one instructional method that can address the learning needs of DLLs.

ADAPTATIONS TO THE RECOGNITION & RESPONSE FRAMEWORK: THE RECOGNITION & RESPONSE INSTRUCTIONAL SUPPORT SYSTEM FOR DUAL LANGUAGE LEARNERS

Adaptations to the core R&R framework were made to address the language and literacy development of young DLLs, thereby responding to the need for instructional strategies for this population. R&R–DLL draws from established knowledge about language and literacy development during early childhood, incorporating emerging evidence about this domain for young DLLs. Due to the limited research base on instructional practices for DLLs of this age group, when appropriate we also refer to the literature on instructional practices used with older populations of DLLs.

Adapting the Recognition Component for Dual Language Learners

The core R&R framework defines the *recognition* component as collecting formative assessment data for all children in a classroom and periodically monitoring the progress of some children identified as needing targeted interventions in key areas such as early language, literacy, math, or behavior regulation (see Chapter 8). Universal screening assessment results are used to establish a baseline in the fall and to determine whether most children are meeting key benchmarks in learning and development at Tier 1 during fall, winter, and spring. These data are also used to determine whether some children need additional instructional supports (Tiers 2 and 3). Progress monitoring results are used to assess children's responses to tiered interventions and to make decisions about when adjustments to the intervention plan are needed.

The R&R–DLL system adapts universal screening and progress monitoring aspects of RTI by employing parallel assessment procedures. Parallel assessment refers to evaluating children in English as well as their home language (Espinosa, 2008; Peña & Halle, 2011), although this is sometimes limited by the extent to which valid measures in the home language exist. There are several reasons why parallel assessment is integral when using RTI-based approaches with DLLs. First, using parallel assessment in universal screening provides information about children's baseline performance in both languages, thereby measuring children's strengths and weaknesses in both English and the home language. Obtaining information about children's skills in both languages is critical for a complete understanding of DLL children's skills and for reducing the likelihood of underestimating their knowledge. Indeed, several authors have raised concerns that relying exclusively on English-based assessments misrepresents the total fund of knowledge possessed by DLLs (e.g., Peña & Halle, 2011). Second, applying parallel assessment to universal screening creates the potential for assessing children's strengths and weaknesses in relation to their "true peers" by using local rather than national norms (Brown & Doolittle, 2008). Local norms are derived by examining the "typical" abilities of students at specific grade levels within a given classroom, school, or district. Third, because universal screening results are used to make decisions regarding the level of intensity of interventions for individual children, fuller understanding of DLLs' skills in both languages is particularly important. Data suggest that relying on DLLs' test results in one language can lead to overdiagnosis of impairment in a given skill area (Peña & Halle, 2011). This may be even more relevant for DLLs, given that "false positives" are a concern when using universal screening tools in general (Speece & Walker, 2007). Finally, using parallel assessment makes it possible to obtain information about children's growth in both languages over time (Peña & Halle, 2011), thereby giving a more accurate picture of children's response to more intensive instruction.

Application of parallel assessment procedures in R&R–DLL involves teachers conducting universal screening and progress monitoring assessments in both English and Spanish; assessments in each language are administered on different days. Parallel assessment data generate four general potential profiles of strengths and weaknesses that inform decisions about which children need more intensive supports. The first profile consists of children who evidence stronger skills (relative to other classmates) in both languages. A second profile reflects the opposite pattern, where children demonstrate lower skills in both languages. The other two profiles represent instances of "uneven" development. Thus, the third profile consists of children with skills that are higher in the home language and lower in English, whereas the fourth profile features children whose skills are higher in English and lower in the home language. These profiles illustrate the continuum of bilingual proficiency ranging from minimal or partial bilingualism (i.e., profiles two through four) to balanced bilingualism where the level of proficiency is high in both languages (i.e., profile one) (Baker & Prys Jones, 1998). By employing parallel assessment procedures, the R&R–DLL system acknowledges the diversity of language experiences and skills among DLLs as illustrated by these profiles.

From the profiles described in the preceding paragraph, it is clear that children displaying lower skills in both languages are in the greatest need of more intensive supports beyond what they already receive in the classroom (Tier 1), and therefore would receive the highest priority for selection to participate in Tier 2 interventions. Existing research indicates that these children are at greatest risk for continued language difficulties and overall poor school performance (Lindholm-Leary & Aclan, 1991). However, because there is such great diversity among DLLs in their language skills, it is possible that a classroom may contain few or no children who exhibit low skills in both English and the home language. Such classrooms may have a greater representation of children with uneven development across the two languages (i.e., the third and fourth profiles). Yet, children with such uneven development may also benefit from participating in a tiered intervention approach. In particular, a tiered approach may be beneficial for children described in the third profile, those who exhibit higher skills in the home language and lower skills in English. Participation in Tier 2 interventions may give these children an added boost along what may be a promising developmental trajectory and assist them in transitioning to an elementary school environment.

In sum, R&R–DLL extends the recognition component of the original R&R framework by adding parallel assessment to the universal screening and progress monitoring procedures. Accounting for children's skills in both English and the home language allows for more informed decisions about which children need additional instructional supports.

Adapting the Response Component for Dual Language Learners

The core R&R framework defines the *response* component as providing an effective core curriculum, intentional teaching, and targeted interventions for some children who require additional instructional supports based on the formative assessment data. As indicated in Buysse et al. (Chapter 5), the response component consists of three tiers that address the needs of all children (Tier 1), some children (Tier 2), and a few children (Tier 3). Tier 1 is defined as using an effective core curriculum and intentional teaching of school readiness skills, including empirically supported practices such as dialogic reading (Arnold & Whitehurst, 1994; U.S. Department of Education, 2007). Tier 2 involves teachers making adjustments to enhance learning for some children through explicit, small-group instruction augmented by embedded learning activities that extend learning through environmental arrangements and curricular modifications. In Tier 3, more intensive, research-based scaffolding strategies (e.g., response prompting, modeling, peer supports) are used for a few children who require further supports to learn. Teachers also meet in groups to engage in collaborative problem solving, a data-based decision-making process used to plan these various levels of instructional supports and assess how well children respond to them. R&R–DLL adapts the response component of RTI in two primary ways by using explicit instructional strategies recommended for teaching DLLs and a bilingual approach for conducting the Tier 2 small-group lessons.

The Recognition & Response Instructional Support System for Dual Language Learners Instructional Strategies

The first adaptation, the R&R–DLL Instructional Strategies, is a rubric of recommended adaptations to instruction drawn from the empirical literature on language and literacy development of DLLs as well as best practices in early childhood education. The R&R–DLL Instructional Strategies are geared toward explicitly fostering children's vocabulary, phonological awareness, and letter knowledge across all three tiers. As described by Goldenberg (2008), the combination of direct and explicit teaching with interactive (e.g., dialogic reading) approaches is consistent with recommended instruction for DLLs. In this way, R&R–DLL responds to concerns about misalignment between foundational instructional practices and DLLs' learning needs (Orosco, 2010) and recognizes the need for incorporating instructional strategies adapted for DLLs across the tiers.

The R&R–DLL Instructional Strategies consist of two core strategies: bridging and visual and contextual cuing. The bridging strategies represent instructional adaptations that are unique to DLLs. In contrast, the visual and contextual cuing strategies are examples of instructional practices that are good for all children but

Table 23.1. The Recognition & Response–Dual Language Learners (R&R–DLL) Instructional Strategies for language and literacy development

Approach	Strategies	Examples
Bridging: Use both English and the home language for strategic instructional purposes, with repetition as needed	A. Dual language use *Definition: Use and encourage the use of both English and the home language for selected instruction.*	
	1. Introduce or define words and concepts.	*Example A1:* • This is the word *cave*. In Spanish, the word for cave is *cueva*. • Esta es la palabra *cueva*. En inglés la palabra es *cave*.
	2. Teach letter names and sounds.	*Example A2:* • This is the letter *M* (em). It makes the sound "mmm." • Esta es la letra *M* (eme). Hace el sonido "mmm."
	3. Acknowledge and encourage children's responses in both languages.	*Example A3:* When asking the child(ren) questions during a lesson or storybook reading in English: • If the child answers in Spanish, respond and prompt for the answer in English. • If the child then answers in English, respond in English. • If the child does not give a response in English, provide the response in English and continue.
	B. Metalinguistic awareness strategies *Definition: Describe similarities and differences between English and the home language.*	
	1. Point out words that are cognates in English and Spanish, noting similarities and differences in spelling, pronunciation, and meaning.	*Example B1.1:* • There are some words that seem similar in English and Spanish, like *family* and *familia*. Both words mean the same thing. They have many of the same letters and sounds. • Hay algunas palabras que parecen semejantes en inglés y en español, como las palabras *family* y *familia*. Las dos significan la misma cosa. Las dos tienen muchos sonidos y letras similares.

(continued)

Table 23.1. *(continued)*

Approach	Strategies	Examples
		Example B1.2: • Sometimes there are words that seem similar in English and Spanish but mean different things, like *once* and *once*. Both have the same letters and some of the same sounds. But in English *once* means *one time,* like when stories begin *once upon a time.* In Spanish, *once* is the number 11. • Pero, a veces hay palabras que parecen semejantes en inglés y español, pero significan cosas diferentes como la palabra *once* en inglés y la palabra *once* en español. En español, la palabra *once* significa un número que sigue el número 10. En inglés, la palabra *once* significa *una vez* como empiezan muchos cuentos escribieron en inglés *once upon a time.*
	2. Point out phonological similarities and differences in English and Spanish, such as phonemes at the beginning and ending of words, and sounds that are present in English but not in Spanish (i.e., short sounds of *a, e, i,* and *u* and the consonants *j, r, v, z*).	*Example B2.1:* • Look, the English word *puppy* and the Spanish word *pato* both start with the letter P and make the sound *puh.* • Mira, ambas la palabra *puppy* en inglés y la palabra *pato* en español empiezan con la letra P (peh) y tambien hacen el sonido *puh.* *Example B2.2:* • Look, the English word *jump* and the Spanish word *jardín* both start with the letter J. But, the letter J makes the *juh* sound in English. It makes a different sound, *hauh,* in Spanish. • Mira, la palabra *jump* en inglés y la palabra *jardín* en español empiezan con la letra J. Pero, en español, la letra J hace el sonido *hauh.* Hace un sonido diferente, *juh,* en inglés.
Visual and contextual cuing	1. Use a range of visual cues when teaching and reviewing material.	*Example 1:* • Pointing • Gestures • Pictures and picture cues • Props • Facial expressions
	2. Use children's contextual knowledge to help them understand new words and concepts.	*Example 2:* • Yesterday, we read a story about going to the beach. What are some things you can do at the beach? You can swim or splash in the water. You can use a little shovel to dig holes or make a castle in the sand. What else do you do when you go to the beach? • Ayer, leímos una historia acerca de ir a la playa. ¿Cuáles son algunas cosas que puede hacer en la playa? Se puede nadar o chapotear en el agua. Una pala se puede utilizar para hacer los agujeros o un castillo en la arena. ¿Qué otras cosas haces cuando vas a la playa?

may be particularly critical for fostering the learning of DLLs. The full set of strategies is described next and outlined in Table 23.1.

Core Strategy Number 1: Bridging The first core strategy, bridging, is defined as strategic dual language instruction, with repetition as needed. The word *strategic* underscores the use of two languages during selected instruction in an intentional manner. Bridging serves to clarify and extend concepts using the home language, particularly when children's English skills are not comparably developed. Bridging approaches are consistent with other terminologies such as "English-plus-Spanish Education" (see report by the National Task Force on Early Childhood Education for Hispanics, 2007). The R&R–DLL system specifies two types of bridging strategies: 1) dual language instruction and 2) metalinguistic awareness strategies.

Dual language instruction involves teachers using and encouraging the use of both English and the home language during key points in instruction. The strategic use of the home language is a recommended instructional guideline for teaching DLLs (Castro, Espinosa, & Páez, 2011; Gersten & Baker, 2000; Goldenberg, 2008). Dual language instruction in R&R–DLL is used when teachers introduce and define words and concepts, and during activities that focus on letter names and sounds. This entails teachers explicitly providing vocabulary words, letter names, and letter sounds in both English and the home language. The emphasis on vocabulary, in particular, has been described as a "curricular anchor" for DLLs (Gersten & Baker, 2000; Haager & Windmueller, 2001). In addition, teachers use dual language strategies when they acknowledge children's responses in the home language and encourage them to attempt a response in English.

The second bridging strategy, metalinguistic awareness strategies, focuses on describing similarities and differences between English and the home language. Metalinguistic awareness refers to an individual's ability to manipulate linguistic units and reflect upon the structural properties of language independent of their communicative use (Nagy & Anderson, 1999; Paradis et al., 2011). Metalinguistic awareness skills, such as comparing and contrasting the similarities and differences between two languages, are thought to be enhanced among DLLs (Bialystok, 2002) and are therefore critical for understanding DLLs' language and literacy development. Utilizing metalinguistic awareness strategies during instruction has the potential to help DLLs make connections between what they know in their home language and what they are learning in English. The R&R–DLL Instructional Strategies draw attention to similarities and differences between the two languages during instruction, focusing on vocabulary development, letter knowledge, and phonological awareness.

The R&R–DLL Instructional Strategies employ metalinguistic awareness strategies to promote vocabulary development through teachers' intentional use of cognates, which are words in the two languages that have similar meaning, spelling, and pronunciation. The system defines the use of cognates as intentional when teachers use them to illustrate similarities and differences between English and the home language, as opposed to merely saying the cognates. The use of cognates for instructional purposes is particularly well suited for Spanish-speaking DLLs. It is estimated that approximately 30% to 40% of words in English have a Spanish cognate (Ford, 2011). The majority of cognates between English and Spanish are considered *true* cognates (see example in Table 23.1), yet a smaller percentage of "false cognates" also exist (e.g., *éxito* in Spanish translates to the word *success* in English; *exit* in English translates to *salida* in Spanish). By explicitly drawing attention to similarities and differences using cognates, this metalinguistic awareness strategy provides useful opportunities to teach vocabulary as well as phonological awareness and print concepts.

In addition, the R&R–DLL Instructional Strategies utilize metalinguistic awareness strategies to teach letter names and sounds in English and the home language. This involves teachers pointing out similarities and differences between the two languages with respect to phonemes at the beginning and end of words, and sounds that are present in English but not in the home language. For Spanish-speaking DLLs learning English, for example, there is substantial overlap between the English and Spanish alphabet and letter sounds. However, there are some important differences between the two languages, including different names and sounds for the same letter character (e.g., *J*), letters that are present in the Spanish alphabet (e.g., *ñ, ch, ll*) but not in the English alphabet, and sounds that are present in English (e.g., short sounds of *a, e, i,* and *u*) but not in Spanish. Such differences tend to present DLLs with the most difficulty (Bear, Templeton, Helmen, & Baren, 2003; Helman, 2004). By drawing children's attention to similarities and differences at the letter and sound level, teachers explicitly build children's phonological and print awareness.

Core Strategy Number 2: Visual and Contextual Cuing   The second core strategy, visual and contextual cuing, helps to facilitate children's understanding of instructional content. Visual cues can be used to reinforce concepts and vocabulary (Gersten & Baker, 2000). They may range from labeling items in English and in the home language to using pictures, props, and gestures (Guiberson, 2009). Contextual cuing involves using children's contextual knowledge to help them understand new words and concepts. Contextual cues encompass knowledge about children and their families as well as topics from past classroom activities and events. Whereas visual cues are directly related to the content being presented, contextual cues elaborate on the presented content by drawing in additional information. In this way, teachers incorporate children's past experiences to further expand on a concept or lesson, which helps children connect instructional content to their lives.

Bilingual Instructional Approaches for Tier 2

The second adaptation to R&R–DLL involves taking a strategic, bilingual approach to delivering instruction in Tier 2 small-group interventions. Employing a bilingual approach responds to emerging evidence suggesting that incorporating children's primary language in instruction is important for promoting the school readiness of DLLs (August & Shanahan, 2006; Barnett, Yarosz, Thomas, Jung, & Blanco, 2007; Castro et al., 2010; Slavin & Cheung, 2005). When it comes to reading instruction, some research suggests that bilingual or transitional approaches to language of instruction are more effective for DLLs than English-only instruction (Goldenberg, 2008; Slavin & Cheung, 2005). However, as pointed out in Buysse et al.'s review, the limited research on instructional approaches with young DLLs makes it difficult to draw conclusions about the most beneficial language of instruction. Specifically, interventions exclusively relying on English-based instruction produced positive effects on English skills. When interventions incorporated the home language, some studies showed positive effects in only one language (English or the home language) whereas other studies found positive effects in both languages. There were no negative effects of the interventions on language and literacy skills in either English or the home language. This last point is noteworthy given ongoing debates concerning English-only instruction policies.

In the absence of clear guidance on language of instruction for young DLLs, decisions about the language of instruction for Tier 2 in R&R–DLL are based on programs' language of instruction policies, the selected curriculum for Tier 2 interventions, emerging knowledge on DLLs' language and literacy development, and existing research on different approaches to language of instruction. R&R–DLL was developed in classrooms where English was the language of instruction. In R&R–DLL, an evidence-based, bilingual English/Spanish language and literacy curriculum is used at Tier 2, with specific lessons focusing on letter naming, vocabulary development, and phonological awareness. In addition, language of instruction decisions are heavily based on research evidence of the interaction between DLLs' two language systems (Hammer et al., under review), which is captured in theoretical constructs such as cross-linguistic transfer, which generally refers to the transfer of skills between different languages in domains such as oral language, phonology, reading comprehension, and writing skills (see Genesee & Geva, 2006). According to Genesee, Geva, Dressler, and Kamil (2006), the possibility of cross-linguistic transfer is enhanced when the two languages share similar features such as phonological forms or cognate vocabulary. The comprehensive review conducted by the National Literacy Panel on Language-Minority Children and Youth, which focused primarily on K–12 populations, documented evidence of transfer from the home language to the second language among domains including phonological awareness, word reading, vocabulary with use of cognates, and reading comprehension (Dressler & Kamil, 2006; Genesee & Geva, 2006; Genesee et al., 2006; Snow, 2006). Hammer et al.'s review on young DLLs suggested that the most consistent evidence of language transfer exists regarding phonological abilities, whereas there is mixed evidence of transfer of vocabulary abilities. Thus, language transfer can be weaker or stronger depending on the skill area. This evidence of cross-linguistic transfer is particularly compelling in considering the instructional needs of young DLLs and making related language of instruction decisions.

With these considerations in mind, R&R–DLL features three approaches to language of instruction that correspond to specific language and literacy skills. The three approaches are a combination of English and Spanish, a transition from Spanish to English, and English only. Lessons that focused on phonological awareness and vocabulary development were conducted in both English and Spanish, with the lesson conducted in English first and then repeated in Spanish during the same session. Conducting these lessons in English and then repeating them in Spanish in the same sitting maximizes opportunities for children to make cross-language connections between phonological awareness and vocabulary development activities. In addition, lessons targeting shared reading followed recommendations that teachers first read the story in the home language and on subsequent occasions read the book in English (Lugo-Neris, Wood Jackson, & Goldstein, 2010). Finally, lessons that primarily focused on teaching letter names were conducted in English only. Teachers' intervention curriculum materials were modified to give explicit guidance on the appropriate language of instruction for a given lesson. These R&R–DLL procedures are consistent with Genesee's (2008) recommendation to have a clear plan for the contexts in which each language will be used.

Although it may seem ideal always to use both English and Spanish as the primary language of instruction, this approach may not be the best based on feasibility or research evidence. Given the time constraints of the Tier 2 small-group lessons for pre-K children (i.e., 15 to 20 minutes, a developmentally appropriate length), it is not feasible for teachers always to use both languages in the same sitting for shared reading activities. By using the Spanish-then-English approach across lessons, R&R–DLL adapted shared reading activities for DLLs as recommended while maintaining the integrity of the Tier 2 implementation. The decision to use English only for letter-naming lessons stemmed from research findings as well as practical considerations. First, relative to the evidence on language transfer for phonological awareness and vocabulary skills, there is less support for skill transfer for letter knowledge. In addition, classroom observations and feedback from teachers suggests that at least among young, Spanish-speaking DLLs, these children are more likely to be familiar with letter names and sounds in English relative to Spanish. Finally, we were concerned that using both English and Spanish for letter naming lessons might seem redundant for both teachers and the children given the great amount of overlap. Nonetheless, the value of knowing letter names and sounds in the Spanish alphabet is represented in the R&R–DLL Instructional Strategies.

In summary, R&R–DLL adapts the response component through specific instructional strategies and dual language instruction when conducting the Tier 2 small-group lessons. Both of these additions draw from research on young DLLs' development. They also strategically incorporate the use of both English and the home language to promote the learning of all children as well as those children who are in greatest need of additional instructional supports. However, teachers' use of these adaptations may likely depend on the proportions and types of languages present in the classroom, and the teacher's experiences using the children's home language. In many ways, these adaptations reflect instructional practices that come naturally to teachers of DLLs, particularly among those who themselves are bilingual and may initially have more resources to actively incorporate the home language in instruction. Some teachers who have less familiarity with DLLs, particularly those who are monolingual English speakers, may need additional supports to help them implement these instructional adaptations. We acknowledge that DLLs are a heterogeneous population who represent a variety of languages other than Spanish speakers. Still, these adaptations illustrate a range of strategies that can be implemented by teachers with varying degrees of bilingual skills and may provide useful principles for working with DLLs with non-Spanish home languages.

CONCLUSION

Empirically based instructional models are in great demand to address the educational needs of DLLs, who comprise a burgeoning segment of children attending early care and education programs. This chapter described R&R–DLL, an adaptation to the core R&R framework designed to support the language and literacy development of DLLs attending prekindergarten. Specifically, the R&R–DLL system incorporates a dual language approach to both the *recognition* and *response* components through parallel assessment procedures, an instructional support system, and bilingual Tier 2 small-group interventions. Current efforts to validate the efficacy of R&R–DLL will provide evidence about whether tiered instructional models offer a useful framework for adapting educational practice to address the learning and development of young DLLs. Future research directions for R&R–DLL include further replication with young DLLs learning English and Spanish in classrooms where the primary language of instruction is English, examining the use of R&R–DLL in communities with lower proportions of bilingual populations, and exploring the use of tiered models with DLLs who speak non-Spanish languages and in classrooms where multiple languages are represented.

REFERENCES

Arnold, D.S., & Whitehurst, G.J. (1994). Accelerating language development through picture book reading: A summary of dialogic reading and its effect. In D.K. Dickinson (Ed.), *Bridges to literacy: Children, families, and schools* (pp. 103–128). Malden: Blackwell Publishing.

August, D., & Shanahan, T. (2006). (Eds.). *Developing literacy in second-language learners: Report of the National Literacy Panel on Language-Minority Children and Youth.* Mahwah, NJ: Lawrence Erlbaum Associates.

Baker, C., & Prys Jones, S. (1998). *Encyclopedia of bilingualism and bilingual education.* Philadelphia, PA: Multilingual Matters, Ltd.

Barnett, W.S., Yarosz, D.J., Thomas, J., Jung, K., & Blanco, D. (2007). Two way and monolingual English immersion in preschool education: An experimental comparison. *Early Childhood Research Quarterly, 22,* 277–293. doi:10.1016/j.ecresq.2007.03.003

Bear, D.R., Templeton, S., Helman, L.A., & Baren, T. (2003). Orthographic development and learning to read in two different languages. In G.G. García (Ed.), *English learners: Reaching the highest level of English literacy* (pp. 71–95). Newark, DE: International Reading Association.

Bialystok, E. (2002). Acquisition of literacy in bilingual children: A framework for research. *Language Learning, 52,* 159–199.

Brown, J.E., & Doolittle, J. (2008). A cultural, linguistic, and ecological framework for response to intervention with English language learners. *Exceptional Children, 40,* 66–72.

Buysse, V., & Peisner-Feinberg, E.S. (2010). Recognition & Response: Response to intervention for pre-K. *Young Exceptional Children, 13,* 2–13. doi:10.1177/1096250610373586

Buysse, V., Peisner-Feinberg, E.S., Knowles, M., Hammer, C.S., & Páez, M.M. (under review). *Evaluating early care and education practices for dual language learners: A review of the literature.*

Capps, R., Fixx, M., Ost, J., Reardon-Anderson, J., & Passel, J. (2005). *The health and well-being of young children of immigrants (No. 311139).* Washington, DC: Urban Institute.

Castro, D.C., Espinosa, L.M., & Páez, M.M. (2011). Defining and measuring quality in early childhood practices that promote dual language learners' development and learning. In M. Zaslow, I. Martinez-Beck, K. Tout, & T. Halle (Eds.), *Quality measurement in early childhood settings* (pp. 257–280). Baltimore, MD: Paul H. Brookes Publishing Co.

Castro, D.C., Peisner-Feinberg, E., Buysse, V., & Gillanders, C. (2010). Language and literacy development in Latino dual language learners. Promising instructional practices. In O.N. Saracho & B. Spodek (Eds.), *Contemporary perspectives on language and cultural diversity in early childhood education* (pp. 65–93). Greenwich, CT: Information Age Publishing.

Center for Early Care and Education Research—Dual Language Learners. (2010). *Terminology used to refer to dual language learners.* Retrieved from http://cecerdll.fpg.unc.edu/node/122

Donovan, S., & Cross, C. (2002). *Minority students in special and gifted education.* Washington, DC: National Academies Press.

Dressler, C., & Kamil, M. (2006). First- and second-language literacy. In D. August & T. Shanahan (Eds.), *Developing literacy in second-language learners. Report of the National*

Literacy Panel on Language-Minority Children and Youth (pp. 197–238). Mahwah, NJ: Lawrence Erlbaum Associates.

Espinosa, L.M. (2008). *A review of the literature on assessment issues for young English language learners.* Paper prepared for the NAS Committee on Developmental Outcomes and Assessment for Young Children, Washington, DC.

Ford, K. (2011). Early literacy instruction in dual language preschools (Spanish/English). Retrieved from http://www.colorincolorado.org/article/40679

Francis, D.J., Rivera, M., Lesaux, N., Kieffer, M., & Rivera, H. (2006). *Practical guidelines for the education of English language learners: Research-based recommendations for instruction and academic interventions.* Portsmouth, NH: RMC Research Corporation, Center on Instruction. Retrieved from http://www.centeroninstruction.org/files/ELL1-Interventions.pdf

Genesee, F. (2008). Early dual language learning. *Zero to Three, 30,* 17–23.

Genesee, F., & Geva, E. (2006). Cross-linguistic relationships in working memory, phonological processes, and oral language. In D. August & T. Shanahan (Eds.), *Developing literacy in second-language learners. Report of the National Literacy Panel on Language-Minority Children and Youth* (pp. 175–184). Mahwah, NJ: Lawrence Erlbaum Associates.

Genesee, F., Geva, E., Dressler, C., & Kamil, M. (2006). Synthesis: Cross-linguistic relationships. In D. August & T. Shanahan (Eds.), *Developing literacy in second-language learners. Report of the National Literacy Panel on Language-Minority Children and Youth* (pp. 153–174). Mahwah, NJ: Lawrence Erlbaum Associates.

Gersten, R., & Baker, S. (2000). What we know about effective instructional practices for English language learners. *Exceptional Children, 66,* 454–470.

Goldenberg, C. (2008). Teaching English language learners. What the research does—and does not—say. *American Educator,* Summer, 8–44.

Guiberson, M. (2009). Hispanic representation in special education: Patterns and implications. *Preventing School Failure, 53,* 167–176.

Haager, D. (2007). Promises and cautions regarding using response to intervention with English language learners. *Learning Disability Quarterly, 30,* 213–218.

Haager, D., & Windmueller, M.P. (2001). Early reading intervention for English language learners at risk for learning disabilities: Student and teacher outcomes in an urban school. *Learning Disability Quarterly, 24,* 235–250.

Hammer, C.S., Gillanders, C., Hoff, E., Uchikoshi, Y., & Castro, D.C. (under review). *Language and literacy development in dual language learners: A critical review of the research.*

Helman, L.A. (2004). Building on the sound system of Spanish: Insights from the alphabetic spellings of English-language learners. *The Reading Teacher, 57*(5), 452–460.

Justice, L.M. (2006). Evidence-based practice, response to intervention, and the prevention of reading difficulties. *Language, Speech, and Hearing Services in Schools, 37,* 284–297. doi:0161-1461/06/3704-0284

Kamps, D., Abbott, M., Greenwood, C., Arreaga-Mayer, C., Wills, H., Longstaff, J., ... Walton, C. (2007). Use of evidence-based, small-group reading instruction for English language learners in elementary grades: Secondary-tier intervention. *Learning Disability Quarterly, 30,* 153–168. doi:10.2307/30035561

Klingner, J.K., & Edwards, P. (2006). Cultural considerations with response to intervention models. *Reading Research Quarterly, 41,* 108–117. doi:10.1598/RRQ.41.1.6

Linan-Thompson, S., Vaughn, A., Prater, K., & Cirino, P.T. (2006). The response to intervention of English language learners at risk for reading problems. *Journal of Learning Disabilities, 39,* 390–398.

Lindholm-Leary, K., & Aclan, Z. (1991). Bilingual proficiency as a bridge to academic achievement: Results from bilingual/immersion programs. *Journal of Education, 173,* 99–113.

Lugo-Neris, M., Wood Jackson, C., & Goldstein, H. (2010). Facilitating vocabulary acquisition of young English language learners. *Language, Speech & Hearing Services in the Schools, 41,* 314–327. doi:10.1044/0161-1461(2009/07-0082

Nagy, W.E., & Anderson, R.C. (1999). Metalinguistic awareness and literacy acquisition in different languages. In D. Wagner, R. Venezy, & B. Street (Eds.), *Literacy: An international handbook* (pp. 155–160). Boulder, CO: Westview.

National Early Literacy Panel. (2008). *Developing early literacy: Report of the National Early Literacy Panel*. Washington, DC: National Institute for Literacy. Retrieved from http://lincs .ed.gov/publications/pdf/NELPReport09.pdf

National Head Start Training and Technical Assistance Research Center. (2008). *Dual language learning: What does it take? Head Start dual language report*. Washington, DC: Office of Head Start.

National Task Force on Early Childhood Education for Hispanics. (2007). *Para nuestros niños: Expanding and improving early education for Hispanics. Main Report*. Tempe, AZ: Arizona State University.

Orosco, M.J. (2010). A sociocultural examination of response to intervention with Latino English language learners. *Theory into Practice, 49*, 265–272. doi:10.1080/00405841.2010.51 0703

Orosco, M.J., & Klingner, J. (2010). One school's implementation of RTI with English language learners: "Referring into RTI." *Journal of Learning Disabilities, 43*, 269–288. doi:10.1177/0022219409355474

Páez, M., Tabors, P.O., & López, L.M. (2007). Dual language and literacy development of Spanish-speaking preschool children. *Journal of Applied Developmental Psychology, 28*, 85–102. doi:10.1016/j.appdev.2006.12.007

Paradis, J., Genesee, F., & Crago, M.B. (2011). *Dual language development and disorders. A handbook on bilingualism and second language learning* (2nd ed.). Baltimore, MD: Paul H. Brookes Publishing Co.

Peisner-Feinberg, E.S., Buysse, V., Benshoff, L., & Soukakou, E. (2011). Recognition & Response: Response to intervention for prekindergarten. In C. Groark, S.M. Eidelman, L. Kaczmarek, & S. Maude (Eds.), *Early childhood intervention: Shaping the future for children with special needs and their families, Vol. 3: Emerging trends in research and practice* (pp. 37–53). Santa Barbara, CA: Praeger.

Peña, E.D., & Halle, T.G. (2011). Assessing preschool dual language learners: Traveling a multi-forked road. *Child Development Perspectives, 5*(1), 28–32. doi:10.1111/j.1750-8606.2010.00143.x

Slavin, R., & Cheung, A. (2005). A synthesis of research of reading instruction for English language learners. *Review of Educational Research, 75*(2), 247–284. doi:10.3102/00346543075002247

Snow, C. (2006). Cross-cutting themes and future research directions. In D. August & T. Shanahan (Eds.), *Developing literacy in second-language learners. Report of the National Literacy Panel on Language-Minority Children and Youth* (pp. 631–651). Mahwah, NJ: Lawrence Erlbaum Associates.

Speece, D.L., & Walker, C.Y. (2007). What are the issues in response to intervention research? In D. Haager, J. Klingner, & S. Vaughn (Eds.), *Evidence-based reading practices for response to intervention* (pp. 287–301). Baltimore, MD: Paul H. Brookes Publishing Co.

U.S. Department of Education, Institute for Education Sciences, What Works Clearinghouse. (2007). *Research summary on dialogic reading*. Retrieved from http://ies.ed.gov/ncee/ wwc/interventionreport.aspx?sid=135

Vaughn, S., & Fuchs, L. (2003). Redefining learning disabilities as inadequate response to instruction: The promise and potential problems. *Learning Disabilities Research & Practice, 18*, 137–146. doi:10.1111/1540-5826.00070

24

Cross-Sector Policy Context for the Implementation of Response to Intervention in Early Care and Education Settings

Beth Rous and Rena A. Hallam

As demonstrated in this book, there is widespread interest in exploring the implications and uses of a response to intervention (RTI) framework in early childhood programs and settings. As with many emerging practices, however, policy development has not kept up with the level of interest in applying RTI principles in early childhood settings. As of 2012, there were no national policies in place to guide state or local programs in the implementation process. Therefore, we are left with policies that have framed RTI in K–12 settings to help inform policy issues at the national, state, and local levels for young children. This chapter will explore the policy context for implementing RTI in early childhood settings.

THE STATUS OF RESPONSE TO INTERVENTION IMPLEMENTATION

RTI was launched across the country in response to the Individuals with Disabilities Education Improvement Act (IDEA) of 2004 (PL 108-446). IDEA 2004 allowed local education agencies (LEAs) to allocate a portion of special education funds for RTI as one way to implement the Coordinated Early Intervening Services (CEIS) (34 C.F.R. § 300.226) component of IDEA for K–12 programs. Through the use of these funds, LEAs could conduct evaluations and implement services and supports using scientifically based curriculum. RTI has also been presented as a way to help determine eligibility for special education services for students who may have specific learning disabilities. A 2009 report of implementation of RTI across districts for school-age populations indicated that 15 states had adopted an RTI model, while 22 states were in the process of identifying or developing a model for implementation (Berkeley, Bender, Peaster, & Saunders, 2009).

A more recent study funded through the Institute of Education Sciences, U.S. Department of Education, and conducted by Abt Associates (Bradley et al., 2011) investigated the degree to which state education agencies (SEAs) and local school districts were implementing specific activities to support the implementation of RTI in schools. At the district level, a majority of districts (70.5%) reported that they were implementing RTI for school-age populations, most commonly at the elementary school level. The study included specific questions related to the implementation of RTI for preschool populations. The majority of state preschool coordinators (32 states) surveyed indicated that no statewide initiatives were underway related to RTI for preschool, with very few states (*N* = 3; 5.8%) providing state guidelines for RTI for preschool populations. Where statewide initiatives were underway, the most common activities included training (13.7%) and technical assistance to local programs interested in or implementing RTI (13.7%). A total of six states did report that they were supporting state-level work on exploring RTI for preschool populations. Adding to this overview of the implementation of RTI in preschool are findings from the Center for Response to Intervention in Early Childhood, which indicated 18 states had engaged in preliminary discussions related to the implementation of RTI in preschool settings (Linas, Carta, & Greenwood, 2009).

THE POLICY CONTEXT

As states and local programs consider the application of RTI in early childhood settings, there are several contextual factors to be considered that may ultimately impact the success of these efforts. RTI was defined by the National Research Center on Learning Disabilities as "an assessment and intervention process for systematically monitoring student progress and making decisions about the need for instructional modifications or increasingly intensified services using progress monitoring data" (Johnson, Mellard, Fuchs, & McKnight, 2006; p i.2). The overall goal of RTI is to improve student outcomes in academics by providing more intense interventions based on a child's progress, while also reducing behavioral concerns (Harr-Robins, Shambaugh, & Parrish, 2009). The key component of RTI for school-age populations is that services occur in the general education setting and include collaboration with other "specialists" such as special education teachers, school counselors, and so on.

The implementation of RTI in early care and education must be considered in light of the unique circumstances of educational services for young children and their families. Primarily, early care and education is not universally available for young children, unlike public education for older children. This means young children and families have the potential to interact with multiple programs based on varying eligibility factors, the ability to pay for services, available community options, as well as family preferences in selecting early education experiences for their children. Further, the provision of early education is not uniformly monitored or funded within or across states. Therefore, the primary assumptions of RTI do not fit neatly into an early care and education policy framework for young children, which presents a range of implementation challenges. This unique landscape requires that additional issues be addressed through policy in order to implement an effective RTI structure. The following discussion highlights these unique policy issues in relation to RTI implementation, including the programmatic options available to young children and the effects of varying quality of early education services on both pedagogical and instructional planning.

The implementation of RTI with very young children requires an understanding and systematic examination of the wide variety of contexts in which early care and education services are provided, including state-funded initiatives, Head

Start, community-based child care, and early childhood special education services. Planning for RTI requires a customization or sensitivity to the setting, as these programs vary in their approach to instructional environments, child assessment strategies, personnel preparation, and professional development support. Further, the process of planning for children's instruction across these settings varies in relationship to program configuration; e.g., public prekindergarten programs may implement district-level curriculum whereas community-based child care programs may make curriculum decisions at the program or even classroom level. Each early childhood setting needs to be considered in light of its unique programmatic structure and how this structure interacts with an RTI framework. In doing so, particular attention is needed in the areas of child assessment, curriculum planning, and population served.

Prekindergarten

The United States has no universal public prekindergarten programs and no national standards on prekindergarten curriculum. Forty states currently operate prekindergarten programs (Barnett et al., 2010). Public prekindergarten programs are designed at the state level, and little to no national guidance exists regarding many of the key issues necessary for successful RTI implementation. State-level policy dictates teacher preparation, and recent data suggest that only 27 states currently require prekindergarten teachers to have teacher certification (Barnett et al., 2010). Despite the higher teacher education requirements in public prekindergarten settings as compared with most other early education settings, multistate studies have noted differential program quality. Specifically, analysis of several large-scale studies of public prekindergarten programs indicates that the instructional quality of prekindergarten classrooms is moderate, with quality of instruction being identified as an area of particular concern (Early et al., 2006; Early et al., 2007). Further, very little is known about the curriculum models implemented in prekindergarten programs. Current compilations of prekindergarten programs primarily focus on structural features of the program (e.g., teacher qualifications, class size), with little emphasis on curriculum and instructional practice. Eligibility for enrollment in public prekindergarten varies across states; however, most states rely on income level as a primary determinant for prekindergarten eligibility.

Title I

Title I funds offer an opportunity to create early education programs in local districts. The challenge for Title I programs is the lack of program standards to outline a framework for planning and implementing a high-quality early learning program. As mentioned previously, the United States currently has no national, universal early childhood education program. The 2004 reauthorization of the Elementary and Secondary Education Act (ESEA) of 1965 (PL 89-10) provides the opportunity to embed RTI within general education rather than solely through special education law. At present ESEA primarily addresses K–12 education only. That said, guidance issued from the U.S. Department of Education in 2004 allowed for the use of Title I funds for preschool populations, defined as children from birth through school entry (U.S. Department of Education, 2004a, 2004b). A range of services were allowable through Title I, such as classroom-based instructional programs, home visiting programs, extended day programs in Head Start or community-based child care, screening, and diagnostic assessment. Further federal guidance is not available regarding appropriate standards for implementing programs in these areas.

Early Childhood Special Education

Programs for young children with disabilities outline regulations for services to individual children who have been identified as eligible for special education. However, these individual regulations do not speak specifically to broader instructional frameworks to inform curriculum planning in the settings that serve young children with disabilities. Federal regulations through IDEA provide guidance to state and local programs on services provided to 3- and 4-year-old children identified with disabilities. These guidelines provide a structure for special education and related services. This structure includes screening, assessment, transition between programs, family participation, and individualized instructional planning. Moreover, IDEA has required that states develop accountability mechanisms to monitor and document children's outcomes. Implementation of these regulations varies, depending on state-specific systems of services for young children. For example, the inclusive programming that is consistent with IDEA regulations relies on a state's capacity to provide least restrictive environments through public prekindergarten and partnerships with Head Start and community-based child care programs. IDEA does not provide a framework for the general curriculum or specify a core curriculum for children receiving early childhood special education services.

Head Start

Although RTI provides a specific framework for making assessment and instructional decisions, Head Start programs operate under a set of federal standards that mandate assessment and curriculum requirements, including developmental screening and comprehensive assessment. Head Start programs serve low-income children who qualify based on the federal poverty guidelines as well as a mandated 10% of children with disabilities. Programs operate under a federal-to-local governance structure that is framed by a set of federal performance standards. The Head Start Performance Standards address some of the key dimensions of RTI implementation. In particular, Head Start mandates developmental screening of all children within 45 days of enrollment and comprehensive developmental assessment across three time points within a given programmatic year. However, the existing assessment structure was not designed to address the needs of an RTI model and therefore may not have the necessary features for effective implementation of RTI. Further, Head Start has outlined a child outcomes framework that drives curriculum planning and assessment efforts; however, little guidance is provided regarding the specifics of curriculum implementation in Head Start programs.

Child Care

Child care programs operate under state guidelines that dictate minimum standards and regulations for program operation. The majority of these regulations do not address assessment and curriculum practices. A variety of states are investing in child care quality, which may provide an opportunity for synergy between quality improvement efforts and RTI implementation. Child care services are generally not publicly funded and are administered through a wide range of entities (e.g., nonprofit and for-profit) and through a wide array of service delivery models (e.g., family child care homes, centers, schools, and so on). Child care programs are required to meet baseline program standards defined by each state's child care licensing department. Child care licensing requirements vary dramatically by state, with some states outlining high standards for personnel qualifications and standards of practice, while other states provide minimal rules for program operation. One source of public funds available to child care programs is the Child Care Development Fund designed to provide child care assistance to low-income families. The child care subsidy program provides supports to low-income families as well as some incentive resources for child care quality improvement in states. These incentive resources, along with varied funds depending on state priorities, have resulted in a movement to enhance program quality through quality rating and improvement systems (QRIS). National data suggest that child care program quality is variable, with an array of reports indicating that most programs are of mediocre quality (Cost, Quality, and Outcomes Study Team, 1995; Raikes et al., 2003).

CROSS-SECTOR BARRIERS TO IMPLEMENTING RESPONSE TO INTERVENTION

The diversity of programs in early care and education creates challenges for the adoption of an RTI model in early learning. As states, districts, and schools explore options for implementing RTI in preschool settings, considerations of potential policy implications can help ensure more successful implementation efforts. Consistent with the definition outlined by Rous and Townley (2010), the term *policy* in this instance encompasses "formal processes such as executive orders, legislation, rules/regulations, policy memos/directives, [and] guidelines/standards" (p. 163). These policy implications should take into consideration the differences in public preschool programs and the traditional K–12 settings and services for which RTI was designed. In this section we present a modified framework for RTI that takes into account the unique features of early care and education. These issues focus on the quality of early learning programs as it relates to the implementation of Tier 1, and the availability of and access to the necessary instructional and assessment tools needed to implement an effective RTI structure.

High-Quality, Research-Based Core Curriculum

The foundation or Tier 1 of any RTI program is the core curriculum. This foundational level requires the use of an evidence-based curriculum that is implemented with fidelity and meets the needs of the majority of students in the classroom, thus promoting increasing levels of competence across key domains. In planning for RTI implementation, we cannot assume that early childhood programs meet Tier 1 expectations. The existing policy structures across early learning program types typically do not focus on or require evidence-based curricula. It should also be noted that the majority of research in early learning has focused on the concept of "quality" as the metric to determine program effectiveness, which encompasses curriculum but also includes structural quality features (e.g., teacher education and teacher–child ratios), environmental quality (e.g., availability of and access to high-quality learning materials and resources), and process quality (e.g., teacher–child interactions, quality of language modeling, curriculum). Although these constructs are relevant to curriculum, the field has even less knowledge about evidence-based curriculum for young children. Thus, foundational to identifying a set of policy issues for RTI is the need to describe a general education framework for early care and education that works across the sectors in the early learning system. In doing so, we must address two of the key contemporary debates in early learning (Zaslow, 2011): universal versus targeted access and comprehensive versus academic approach.

The implementation of RTI highlights the need for evidence-based curriculum and instructional strategies appropriate for early care and education. To date, research suggests that children who participate in high-quality programs often have favorable developmental and learning outcomes. Good policy relies on evidence-based decision making; however, very little evidence currently exists to serve as a foundation for such decisions. Given the paucity of research-based curriculum, there are several areas where policy can help support good curricular decisions by early care and education programs and staff. Suggestions for policy making include the following:

1. Embed practices consistent with RTI into existing or developing quality rating and improvement systems. Given the emphasis on expanding these frameworks to public preschool and Head Start programs, timing is good for thoughtful decision making related to the role of curriculum in these systems and how RTI efforts can be supported and/or enhanced.

2. Provide guidance on how to identify evidence-based curriculum and instructional strategies at the program and/or classroom level. There are numerous resources and efforts at the national level on identifying evidence-based practice (e.g., What Works Clearinghouse) that can be accessed and used by policy makers to develop common criteria to be used across early care and education programs within a state or locale.

3. Provide specific guidance to early care and education programs on how to meet curricular expectations. This would include guidance on expectations related to the use of developmentally appropriate and recommended practices offered through organizations such as the National Association for the Education of Young Children (NAEYC) and the Division for Early Childhood (DEC).

4. Provide guidance to teachers and providers on how to link developmentally appropriate and recommended practices to individualized instruction. This would include targeted training, technical assistance, and written information.

Screening and Assessment Practices

Clearly, the effectiveness of an RTI framework relies on common understanding and use of reliable and valid child screening and assessment data. Policy and practice regarding the implementation of RTI should be considered relative to widely accepted recommended practices in early childhood assessments (Copple & Bredekamp, 2009; Sandall, McLean, & Smith, 2000). The assessment framework that exists in many publicly funded preschools and Head Start programs commonly relies on the established framework of developmental screening followed by authentic assessment or curriculum-based assessment practices, utilizing either criterion-referenced tools or teacher-generated approaches such as portfolios. The field of early education has historically been challenged in the area of child assessment, as many instruments fail to meet technical adequacy standards. Further, norm-referenced assessments may have technical adequacy but fail to meet recommended practices standards in child assessment (Bagnato, Neisworth, & Pretti-Frontczak, 2010; National Research Council, 2008).

The push for accountability in general and special education as well as the implementation of RTI have led to increased investment in the development and enhancement of early childhood assessment strategies that meet the standard for recommended practices and also have technical adequacy. However, misuse of early childhood assessment tools and data is still common in the field. Given this context, policy development in the area of assessment should consider providing guidance to address the following issues:

1. Selecting universal screening tools that meet standards for technical adequacy related to reliability and validity and that are appropriate for the diversity of children (i.e., language, ability, culture, ethnicity) served.

2. Selecting appropriate early childhood assessment tools for use in an RTI framework for progress monitoring. This guidance would address both the selection and utilization of child assessment tools for the different assessment functions within RTI. Criteria for identifying high-quality assessment tools that are both reliable and valid for their intended purpose should also be addressed.

3. Developing processes for integrating RTI assessment strategies within the broader assessment framework of early care and education programs. For example, high-quality programs may engage in a variety of assessment strategies including developmental checklists, portfolios, developmental screenings, and so on. Specific guidance on how RTI can be embedded within this broader conceptualization will assist programs in implementing an effective and appropriate assessment model.

4. Determining how to link early childhood assessment data with instructional practice. RTI provides an opportunity for early childhood teachers to make explicit connections between child data and instructional practice. Models for how to appropriately make this connection in a developmentally appropriate classroom are also warranted.

Professional Development and Staff Qualifications

The early care and education workforce is extremely diverse in both preparation and professional development experiences. Requirements for professional qualifications vary in relation to program types (e.g., Head Start teacher qualifications versus public school prekindergarten teacher qualifications). Given these variations, effective implementation of RTI will rely on sustained, cross-sector, high-quality professional development at both the preservice (credential and degree granting) and in-service or continuing education levels. This is especially important when the implementation of RTI requires blended programming, where children in public preschool programs are served in Head Start and/or child care settings. Currently, the professional development and technical assistance infrastructure for early learning programs most often mirrors the variation in program types, so that professional development systems differ depending on relevant federal structures, state context, as well as local and regional resources. However, there is an increasing demand for and examples of coordination in professional development in the early learning field (Zaslow, 2011). Given this momentum, considerations for policy makers related to the integration of RTI into professional development systems include the following:

1. Embed key components of RTI implementation (e.g., curriculum, assessment, and screening) into state documents that outline core skills and competencies required by early childhood professionals. This should include the identification and inclusion of competencies across administrative and direct teaching/ service staff. Competencies should also take into consideration existing state-level credential and degree requirements in the early childhood field.

2. Develop guidance on how RTI components are addressed within current program requirements to support cross-sector implementation. Although some guidance will work across sectors, in some situations guidance will need to be tailored to address unique program requirements (e.g., Head Start's requirement to screen and assess young children).

3. Provide guidance on the role of related service personnel in the implementation of RTI.

4. Develop a system of ongoing professional development opportunities related to RTI. This is especially critical when RTI is implemented in collaboration with child care programs, which traditionally have struggled with retention/ turnover of staff due to low wages and educational requirements (Whitebrook & Sakai, 2003).

Transition and Continuity of Care

A common measure of quality in early care and education is the continuity of care a child receives, which includes the number of times within a day, week, or year a child has to move between providers and/or settings. Research indicates young children often participate in multiple care arrangements at any one time, especially children from low-income families (Zaslow, Acs, McPhee, & Vandivere, 2006). Most public preschool programs currently operate on a half-day schedule, which requires many children to transition between and among two or more programs in any given day. These transitions often result in a change in curriculum and instructional approaches for the child. Research indicates the alignment of curriculum across the settings in which children participate is associated with more positive outcomes, particularly for children who have disabilities and/or developmental delays (e.g., Kemp, 2003; Kemp & Carter, 2000). At the heart of RTI is the identification of students who need more intensive interventions to support their ability to access the general curriculum and improve their academic outcomes. Considerations for policy makers related to continuity and transitions include the following:

1. Guidance on how to align curriculum and assessment practices across early care and education settings.

2. Guidance on determining when a child should be referred for special education services.

3. Specific policies related to the transition of young children from early intervention (Part C of IDEA) to preschool services, including documentation of early intervening services provided as part of the individualized family service plan.

4. Guidance on how to support children with disabilities who transition into programs and are found to be no longer eligible for services. This is particularly important in states or locales that do not provide universal and/or targeted services at the preschool level.

CONCLUSION

As presented in this chapter, existing policy related to the implementation of RTI in early care and education settings is limited. As policy guidelines are developed for implementation across states and settings, consideration should be given to four major areas: curriculum, screening and assessment, professional development and staff qualifications, and transition and continuity. Although policy is limited, the conceptualization of RTI is consistent with high-quality practice in early care and education. At the foundation of quality education in early childhood is effective instruction that is responsive, intentional, and individualized (Copple & Bredekamp, 2009); however, the field of early childhood lacks a cohesive structure to support and consistently implement this type of quality practice for all children. Future efforts to support the implementation of RTI within and across early care and education programs can be enhanced by the development of policies that are situated within the cross-sector and dynamic early education context.

REFERENCES

Bagnato, S.J., Neisworth, J., & Pretti-Frontczak, K. (2010). *LINKing authentic assessment and early childhood intervention: Best measures for best practices* (2nd ed.). Baltimore, MD: Paul H. Brookes Publishing Co.

Barnett, W.S., Epstein, D.J, Carolan, M.E., Fitzgerald, J., Ackerman, D.J., & Friedman, A.H. (2010). *The state of preschool: 2010 state preschool yearbook*. New Brunswick, NJ: National Institute for Early Education Research.

Berkeley, S., Bender, W.N., Peaster, L.G., & Saunders, L. (2009). Implementation of response to intervention: A snapshot of progress. *Journal of Learning Disabilities, 42*(1), 85–95.

Bradley, M.C., Daley, T., Levin, M., O'Reilly, R., Parsad, A., Robertson, A., & Werner, A. (2011). *IDEA National Assessment Implementation Study* (NCEE 2011-4027). Washington, DC: National Center for Education Evaluation and Regional Assistance, Institute of Education Sciences, U.S. Department of Education.

Copple, C., & Bredekamp, S. (2009). *Developmentally appropriate practice in early childhood programs serving children from birth through age 8* (3rd ed.). Washington, DC: National Association for the Education of Young Children.

Cost, Quality, and Outcomes Study Team. (1995). Cost, quality, and child outcomes in child care centers: Key findings and recommendations. *Young Children, 50*(4), 40–44.

Early, D.M., Bryant, D.M., Pianta, R.C., Clifford, R.M., Burchinal, M.R., Ritchie, S., . . . Barbarin, O. (2006). Are teachers' education, major, and credentials related to classroom quality and children's academic gains in pre-kindergarten? *Early Childhood Research Quarterly, 21,* 174–195.

Early, D.M., Maxwell, K.L., Burchinal, M., Alva, S., Bender, R.H., Bryant, D., . . . Zill, N. (2007). Teachers' education, classroom quality, and young children's academic skills: Results from seven studies of preschool programs. *Child Development, 78*(2), 558–580.

Elementary and Secondary Education Act of 1965, PL 89-10, 20 U.S.C. §§ 241 *et seq.*

Harr-Robins, J.J., Shambaugh, L.S., & Parrish, T. (2009). *The status of state-level response to intervention policies and procedures in the West Region states and five other states.* (Issues & Answers Report, REL 2009–077). Washington, DC: U.S. Department of Education, Institute of Education Sciences, National Center for Education Evaluation and Regional Assistance, Regional Educational Laboratory West.

Individuals with Disabilities Education Improvement Act (IDEA) of 2004, PL 108-446, 20 U.S.C. §§ 1400 *et seq.*

Johnson, E., Mellard, D.F., Fuchs, D., & McKnight, M.A. (2006). *Responsiveness to intervention (RTI): How to do it.* Lawrence, KS: National Research Center on Learning Disabilities. Retrieved from http://nrcld.org/rti_manual

Kemp, C. (2003). Investigating the transition of young children with intellectual disabilities to mainstream classes: An Australian perspective. *International Journal of Disability, Development and Education, 50,* 403–433.

Kemp, C., & Carter, M. (2000). Demonstration of classroom survival skills in kindergarten: A five-year transition study of children with intellectual disabilities. *Educational Psychology, 20,* 393–411.

Linas, M., Carta, J.J., & Greenwood, C.R. (2009, June). *Taking a snapshot of early childhood response to intervention (RTI) across the USA.* Poster presented at the IES Research Conference, Washington, DC.

National Research Council. (2008). *Early childhood assessment: Why, what, and how.* Washington, DC: National Academies Press.

Raikes, H., Wilcox, B., Peterson, C., Hegland, S., Atwater, J., Summers, J., . . . Raikes, H.A. (2003). *Child care quality and workforce: Subsidy and quality characteristics in four states.* Omaha, NE: The Gallup Organization.

Rous, B., & Townley, K.F. (2010). Early childhood policy and implications for quality initiatives. In P. Wesley & V. Buysse (Eds), *The quest for quality: Promising innovations for early childhood programs.* Baltimore, MD: Paul H. Brookes Publishing Co.

Sandall, S., McLean, M., & Smith, B. (2000). *DEC recommended practices in early intervention/early childhood special education.* Longmont: Sopris West Educational Services.

U.S. Department of Education. (2004a). *Elementary & secondary education, Title I—Improving the academic achievement of the disadvantaged.* Retrieved from http://www2.ed.gov/policy/elsec/leg/esea02/pg1.html

U.S. Department of Education. (2004b). *Serving preschool children under Title I non-regulatory guidance.* Retrieved from http://www2.ed.gov/policy/elsec/guid/preschoolguidance.pdf

U.S. Department of Health and Human Services, Administration for Children and Families. (2006). *Head Start performance standards.* Retrieved from http://eclkc.ohs.acf.hhs.gov/hslc/standards/Head%20Start%20Requirements

Whitebook, M., & Sakai, L. (2003). Turnover begets turnover: An examination of job and occupational instability among child care center staff. *Early Childhood Research Quarterly, 18*(2), 273–293.

Zaslow, M. (2011). The prekindergarten debates: Contrasting perspectives, integrative possibilities, and potential for deepening the debates. In E. Zigler, W. Gilliam, & W.S. Barnett (Eds), *The pre-K debates: Current controversies and issues.* Baltimore, MD: Paul H. Brookes Publishing Co.

Zaslow, M., Acs, G., McPhee, C., & Vandivere, S. (2006, January 12). *Children in low-income families: Change and continuity in family context and measures of well-being.* Paper prepared for the Urban Institute and Child Trends Roundtable on Children in Low-Income Families, Washington, DC.

25

Response to Intervention in Early Childhood

The View from States

Jim J. Lesko and Thomas Rendon

Response to intervention in early childhood (RTI-EC) presents both challenges and opportunities to state and local education entities. Many elements intervene in the process of implementing RTI-EC, and effective implementation requires adequate attention to each of them. Challenges occur because implementing RTI-EC at the state and local levels is often a matter of proposing new models, procedures, and practices to replace preexisting ones. Habitual behavior does not yield easily to any intervention, which is true at an individual level and even more so at an institutional or state level. Yet opportunities exist for RTI-EC to be implemented in a way that transforms the entire structure and delivery of early childhood education in the state. We contend that RTI-EC implementation, if done thoroughly, thoughtfully, and with careful regard for the many elements that intervene in the process, can improve the quality of early education by orienting all the systems around meeting the needs of each child. This chapter will explore the elements that should be addressed and examine the essential considerations for an effective RTI-EC system at the state and local program levels.

Six key dimensions should be considered when examining RTI-EC: 1) funding, 2) instructional settings, 3) managerial supports, 4) professional development, 5) administrative issues, and 6) interagency collaboration. Each dimension brings with it further detail that presents additional opportunities and challenges for consideration. After exploring these dimensions, we will consider an interagency or cross-systems perspective to show how an RTI-EC framework can be a structure within which collaborative work can take place. We use the example of Head Start because it is a system of early childhood services that exists in every state, and because it embraces a comprehensive mix of child services and presents a unique opportunity for blending federal and state policy with local education agency involvement. We conclude with an exploration of the imperative to reframe RTI so it makes sense in the early childhood environment and is viewed as a way to address the myriad challenges of providing effective general and special education services to all young children and their families.

KEY DIMENSIONS OF RESPONSE TO INTERVENTION IN EARLY CHILDHOOD

The key dimensions reflect structural elements that support the implementation of RTI. Identifying the unique characteristics of each dimension will assist in better understanding how to effectively use these dimensions to support RTI in early childhood settings.

Funding

There are three major funding sources and one secondary source that can be used to support RTI-EC implementation: federal, state, local, and private efforts. Most funding comes with strings attached, so the benefits of using some funding sources must be weighed against the liabilities of coordination, reporting, contracting, and restricted allowable costs, especially considering the burdens placed on staff by aspects such as arduous evaluation requirements. Each source brings with it strengths and challenges. Having adequate funding available to support RTI practices is paramount. The RTI-EC model will certainly improve results for individual children and can increase efficiency, but it will not necessarily save money in the short term, especially when one considers the additional costs for professional development, staff, and sometimes new assessment instruments. Next, we will discuss the three major sources of funding and policies and examine how each plays a role in supporting RTI-EC.

Federal funding brings many options for supporting RTI-EC. The first option is Title I. Many local education agencies (LEAs) have begun to use Title I resources to support services to children below kindergarten age (Ewen & Matthews, 2007). Local education agencies offer preschool experiences for 3- and 4-year-olds, and these early childhood settings become logical and practical environments to implement RTI-EC. Within the context of a Title I early childhood program, many additional resources can be brought to the table to support the implementation of RTI-EC, especially considering Title I emphases on data-based decision making and scientifically based reading research.

The Child Care Development Fund (CCDF) can be used to support RTI-EC in child care. CCDF funds are used for three primary purposes at the state level: child care subsidies, professional development, and quality enhancement (Office of Child Care, 2011). CCDF provides opportunities for children to attend early care and education facilities, thereby providing them with environments where RTI-EC practices can be supported. CCDF funds can be used to design and implement high-quality professional development activities, enabling practitioners to work with children who need augmented instructional interventions. Funds are also used in states to improve quality through Quality Rating and Improvement Systems and similar initiatives. Such efforts could be viewed as providing foundational supports for Tier 1 practices, especially if the quality indicators are aligned with the right kinds of standards or program evaluation measures.

Individual with Disabilities Education Improvement Act (IDEA) of 2004 (PL 108-446) funds are another potential source of financial support; however, when these funds are used for services for children below the age of 5, special considerations are in order. Although IDEA funds for children ages 6–21 can be used for

RTI in the elementary through secondary grades, these funds are meant to be used to identify "whether a child has a specific learning disability" (U.S. Department of Education, 2006). The U.S. Department of Education, Office of Special Education, indicated in a memo dated June 2, 2010, that "the category of specific learning disability is generally not applicable to preschool children with disabilities" (Posny, 2010). But developmental delays are present and the benefits of intervening with individualized support are clearly known. Therefore, the use of IDEA Part B Section 619 funds targeted at services to children 3–5 years of age must be carefully planned and appropriately allocated. Similarly, IDEA Part C funds targeted for children from birth to 3 years of age must also be used judiciously, as outlined in the U.S. Department of Education memorandum. Although these funds may not be a primary source of funding for RTI-EC, they may serve as strong secondary sources of support. For example, a local education agency providing an inclusive early childhood setting for children could enroll some children targeted as needing additional instructional support to attend as a part of the nondisabled population. Through this type of structural model, children benefiting from differential instructional practices could receive these services while enrolled in an IDEA-supported early childhood classroom.

Head Start programs are supported by federal dollars. The federal guidelines allow Head Start programs to use funds to support RTI-like services in local program operations. The typical RTI processes of screening and assessment, individualization of instruction, and referral for additional services are all required in the Head Start Performance Standards (U.S. Department of Health and Human Services, 2009). More information about the role of Head Start in the RTI process will be provided later in this chapter.

State prekindergarten programs are another source of funds for RTI-EC. There is often greater flexibility in how state prekindergarten funds may be used, particularly regarding the population of children that can be served where universal prekindergarten services are available. State funds often come with fewer restrictions on how services are offered. Local education agency preschool programs have similar flexibility in funding, with fewer restrictions on how services are offered.

Local school districts are another source of funds for RTI-EC. Whether using property tax levies or parent tuition, some local education agencies operate early childhood programs for populations in their districts. These are often ideal settings for using RTI, as local funds have even more flexibility in how they may be used. Similarly, when private funds are used, they too offer great flexibility in their use.

A final aspect of the funding element is ensuring there are adequate funds to support the intervention process. For example, when working with a practitioner in a community early care and education program, it will be necessary for the practitioner to take time out of the classroom to be involved in the intervention planning process. This often means bringing in substitutes or assistants to ensure minimum coverage in the classroom while the practitioner is involved with planning. Most community early care and education programs are nonprofit organizations or small businesses and typically cannot afford the extra costs associated with RTI practices. State and local systems need to consider how financial resources can be structured to support local RTI practices. Another consideration will be obtaining the funds needed to purchase effective curricula, support professional development activities, and purchase materials and supplies.

Instructional Settings

Early childhood education encompasses diverse settings, ranging from district-run programs to community-based programs to family child care. Each of these settings reflects a variety of instructional practices that are themselves reflective of the administrative and funding resources and capacity inherent in the setting. Properly understood, RTI-EC describes a way to define and organize instructional practices. But we are also insisting that these instructional practices be considered as occurring within the existing setting in which early childhood programs are operating, whether or not these settings are ideal for RTI-EC. The opportunity here is that the benefits of systematic means of assessing children's progress and responding effectively with a variety of instructional interventions is something to which every child should have access, regardless of where they receive early learning services. The challenge is that the capacity to deliver within these settings varies widely. Capacity variation stems from the diversity of funding sources and their adequacy to shape RTI-EC implementation and practice. For this reason, implementing RTI-EC at a state or local level must be a systemic effort. As state and local systems put together RTI-EC models, it will be important to consider the setting and personnel.

Setting Early learning programs typically are found in one of two types of settings: community-based and school-based. These settings differ considerably in terms of access to resources. In the case of community settings where staff knowledge and qualification may not be required to adhere to state educational licensure, considerations must be made regarding the adequacy of staff experience, knowledge, and training to implement the interventions. School-based settings are often a richer source of instructional supports, yet expertise in services for children under 5 may be lacking. Also, school district instructional support staff may be stretched so thin that it is difficult or impossible to support additional classrooms.

Resources also extend beyond personnel to other setting issues such as physical facilities, equipment, and management. One facilities consideration is whether classrooms can accommodate individualized and small-group instructional practices. An equipment or material consideration might be whether instructional curriculum and materials are extensive enough to support teachers in providing a variety of approaches to teaching. Management and administration inherent in the settings will reflect the overall organizational capacity in the areas of hiring, training, and supervising staff as well as strength of management structures necessary for effective operations. Adequate time in a practitioner's schedule is required for the planning, data collection, and analysis that are essential parts of the RTI-EC process.

Personnel The personnel element involves the individuals who will be directly responsible for implementing interventions. Program administrators need to consider who will be expected to implement intervention practices. In programs operated by state or local education agencies, responsibility for implementation often falls to classroom teachers and intervention specialists such as speech and language pathologists, school psychologists, and other specific content specialists. For community-based programs such as local early care and education centers, determining who will implement the intervention becomes an essential consideration. Many practitioners in early care and education centers do not have postsecondary degrees and frequently have limited professional development backgrounds. However, early care and education practitioners are often the individuals who have daily and consistent contact with the children needing intervention. Effective intervention should begin with caregivers, regardless of their professional background or "readiness" for RTI-EC. It is crucial to ensure that practitioners have sufficient support to allow them to be effective instructors.

An important aspect of the personnel element is the competencies of intervention practitioners. RTI-EC requires skilled early childhood educators and interventionists. Skills should include effective classroom management, capacity to design a variety of routines and instructional strategies, and a particularly high level of sophistication when it comes to individualizing instruction. In a community-based setting, the practitioners are often the individuals who will have primary responsibility for providing support, and that is as it should be. More and more, intervention support is directed at the lead provider in the setting as much as the children. That practice strengthens the effectiveness of the natural environment but places additional demands on early childhood educators. One benefit of RTI-EC is that it creates a framework that clarifies roles and responsibilities of various professionals and combines everyone's efforts in pursuit of a collaborative goal of improving education outcomes for every child. But the practical problem remains of ensuring adequate practitioner skills to provide the intervention. Professional development beyond the basics of RTI-EC will be needed to ensure that each staff member has the skills to fulfill his or her responsibility. Ensuring those skills across settings is essential.

An important challenge is the need for community-based and district-based professionals to work as peers. Too often, a priori assumptions of who is in charge can change the atmosphere from mutuality to turf-protection in the traditional ways of delivering services, not only between outside professionals and teachers but even between teachers and assistant teachers (Sosinskya & Gilliam, 2011). Focusing on the needs of children and families first, keeping an open mind, and inviting parents into the conversation while seeking advice from an outside technical assistance specialist across the early childhood system will go a long way toward resolving conflicts. The ability of a child care provider or Head Start teacher to seek support from early intervention specialists is instrumental to providing effective services and implementing RTI-EC. Likewise, conferring with providers and using their direct knowledge of working with children should be best practice among specialists in early childhood special education. Better services in RTI-EC result when general education and special education personnel work together.

Another important question to ask is who will be responsible for identifying children for Tier 2 or Tier 3 support and whether that person has the necessary skills to do this. RTI-EC requires access to competencies of professionals in early childhood general and special education and requires them to work together at a collaborative level that is all too rare in many communities.

Addressing skill deficits is a function of professional development that we will address later, but it should also be part of how staff are hired and supervised. The extent to which expectations in hiring and supervision practices can be aligned around a common focus on tiered instruction will enhance systemwide implementation of RTI-EC.

Managerial Supports

Management supports involve four critical elements: program structures to support intervention, monitoring and evaluation, and two often neglected elements of RTI-EC design—diversity and family engagement. Each element plays an important role in providing foundational support for implementation. States and local education agencies will need to consider how each of these elements will be established so that the RTI process can be effective.

Programmatic Structures In large part, programmatic structures are the local program supports needed for intervention. These supports include the inherent setting capacities discussed previously, but here we examine time and support requirements at each tier. Practitioners need time for professional development, planning, meeting with specialists to work through intervention development, analyzing data from implementation, and most important, implementing the intervention within the context of the regular program day and routine. Regarding support requirements, specific considerations are needed at each tier or level of intervention. Tier 1 has implications for curricular supports and the components of curricular implementation that coincide with effective use of curricular practices. Are there sufficient professional development opportunities for staff to fully understand the curriculum? Are there sufficient materials and supplies to allow the practitioners to effectively implement the curriculum?

Tier 2 and 3 interventions require a substantially higher level of programmatic supports. Given the programmatic implications discussed earlier, the interventions at Tiers 2 and 3 occur with increasing frequency and intensity, which will certainly require more structural support in terms of time and personnel. Teachers will need support with intervention planning, data collection, data analysis, problem solving, and instructional adaptations. In some cases, advanced training will be needed to implement more complex intervention strategies. It would be impossible and unwise to establish concrete principles about who should do what in developing and implementing interventions and instruction because such considerations must take into account the skills and abilities of the teachers, the child's "natural environment," and parental wishes. At this point, state policy makers and implementers should emphasize proper contexts for appropriate decision making and remain open to how best to use the available expertise. Nevertheless, specialists who provide advanced levels of support need adequate backgrounds in working with other adults as well as proficient consulting and coaching skills, not to mention caseloads that are flexible enough to allow for intervention support with just-in-time alacrity.

Monitoring and Evaluation Another managerial support is monitoring and evaluation. Questions to consider include the following: Are children making progress? Are programs implementing practices with fidelity? Are children receiving timely services, referrals, and eligibility determination? What types of resources are needed to support the individuals who are responsible for implementing interventions? Are the supports that are being put into place making a difference for the children who are receiving services? Are the individuals who are providing the supports to practitioners able to implement those supports effectively? Are all state and federal regulations being followed? These are a few examples of the types of questions that need to be considered. Consideration should also be given to how monitoring or other forms of accountability can occur across agencies in which there may not be direct authority or mandatory oversight. Interagency agreements are one common mechanism for aligning accountability and guarding against duplicative monitoring.

Diversity   Given the changing racial, ethnic, linguistic, and cultural makeup of young children in our nation, any RTI-EC system will have to be responsive to this growing diversity. Consider all the specific elements of an effective RTI-EC system, such as assessment, evidence-based interventions, alignment to state standards, and the insistence of many in the education field on research-based practices and fidelity of implementation. All of these elements need to be viewed through the lens of cultural and linguistic diversity. Assessing and responding appropriately to an intervention or an instructional strategy must reflect culturally competent practices that are flexible enough to adapt to the unique circumstances of each child and family. RTI-EC as a system cannot follow a model of rigid norms and protocols but instead needs to be humanly sized and humanly responsive to address the needs of each child.

Family Engagement   Many models of RTI ignore the role of families, but to do so would be a gross oversight in an RTI-EC state or local system. Children are a focal point of the RTI process, but they live within a broader ecological sphere that includes both education-based services and home and family. The success of young children is tied to the support and active participation of their parents. RTI-EC must consider how to engage parents, and develop and implement a clear plan to do so. Parents should be invited into the planning phase, into the design of instruction, as participatory agents in the intervention or instruction, as knowledgeable partners in assessment and progress monitoring, and as the ultimate arbitrator for what is best for their children. Thus, it becomes incumbent on the system to identify professional development opportunities for practitioners to acquire the skills needed to engage families. Similarly, if families lack the skills, knowledge, or dispositions for playing their appropriate roles, it is the responsibility of RTI-EC implementers to address those shortcomings. The concept of professional development, the next dimension we examine, is important for all individuals who are engaged in RTI-EC.

Professional Development

Given the importance of having skilled intervention practitioners, we examine professional development as a separate dimension. The field of professional development is broad and ranges from supporting practitioners in community early care and education sites to providing ongoing education for specialized practitioners who hold advanced degrees. The necessary skills to support quality instruction must be identified and their presence assessed among all staff members. Needed skills for practitioners should include assessment, curriculum planning, instruction, data-based decision making, and individualization of instruction. Staff members require opportunities to understand effective instructional practice, how to plan for and implement effective practices, and how to assess and analyze the strategies used with children. Training should go beyond teachers and extend to administrators, parents, paraeducators, coaches, specialists, and generalists alike.

States would be well advised to consider professional development at both the preservice and in-service levels. That means working closely with institutions of higher education (IHEs) to ensure that adequate and effective preservice course offerings are available. It also means not ignoring the role of community colleges in providing early childhood credit-bearing coursework for child care and Head Start. Would it not be helpful to have a Child Development Associate credential that includes at least some exposure to RTI-EC practices? RTI remains a relatively new instructional practice, and it is likely that many IHE course offerings have not been upgraded to reflect the new instructional framework. One positive option in the IHE learning system could be practicum experiences in settings already implementing an RTI model.

One of the requirements for the federally funded state advisory councils is to work with IHEs in each respective state to ensure that effective and appropriate professional development offerings are available for early care and education practitioners (Improving Head Start for School Readiness Act of 2007, PL 110-134; see §642B[b][1][A][i]). States will need to work through their respective IHEs to identify the critical professional development need areas and to support the creation and implementation of updated and new course offerings that support RTI-EC.

In-service support should be offered at varying levels of complexity, depending on the background and experience of the practitioners (certified and noncertified). States will need to consider who will be offering training and ensure that the design and implementation of the training meets the needs of attendees. Location and time are two important considerations for ensuring access. Many individuals who work in early care and education settings are able to access training only in the evening or on weekends. Professional development systems need to be designed so that they can be flexible in meeting the needs of the individuals targeted for training. Onsite training has been a typical strategy for getting information out to practitioners.

The current wave of technological advances in professional development and the availability of electronic equipment such as smart phones and other similar devices allow professional development experiences to be offered in alternative formats. Internet-accessed training is becoming an economical and access-friendly method of getting training out to practitioners, one that is available 24 hours a day, 7 days a week.

Coaching has become an important component of training. Research supports coaching as a strategy that is likely to produce behavioral changes (Rush and Shelden, 2011). Additionally, there has been new information to support the strength of socially based professional development. Coaching is much more labor-intensive and expensive than other types of training. States and professional development systems will need to consider the cost of a coaching model and explore how it might be possible to identify funding streams to support this strategy. This would be a good use of IDEA (Part B-619) and CCDF funding, as both entities designate professional development as a recommended use of funds.

Working closely with Head Start state-based or regional-based training and technical assistance (T/TA) personnel to assure common understanding of RTI-EC implementation is also important. The new Head Start National Center for Quality

Teaching and Learning (NCQTL), as well as the centers for Linguistic and Cultural Responsiveness and for Parent, Family, and Community Engagement may have materials that can support training and technical assistance in areas relevant to RTI-EC implementation. Recall that the University of Washington, where an early childhood tiered instructional model called Building Blocks was developed (Sandall, Schwartz, & Joseph, 2001), and Vanderbilt University, which houses the Center on the Social-Emotional Foundation for Early Learning and its Pyramid Model, are both institutional members of NCQTL.

It should be added that the pedagogical practices essential for RTI-EC include teamwork and collaboration skills, since working together is at the root of successful RTI implementation. Knowing how to develop trust, foster transparent communication, set aside traditional boundaries of responsibility, and freely exchange information and advice are important competencies to promote in both preservice and in-service settings.

Administrative Issues

As states begin to put together their RTI-EC structures, two overarching issues must be considered. These include 1) Where does the overall administrative function of the RTI-EC practice live at the state and local level? and 2) How will the different state and local systems be linked to create an effective, integrated RTI-EC process?

There has been a shift in perspective about where the administrative function resides for RTI in the K–12 system. Although the impetus for the establishment of an RTI system was the IDEA statute and subsequent regulations, the ultimate responsibility for administration and implementation of RTI practices has fallen on the general education system rather than on special education. A similar perspective will likely be needed for the early childhood system. An unintended outcome may be that a series of individual administrative structures is established to implement intervention practices, which is currently happening in many communities. Programs such as Head Start, state prekindergarten classes, and home visitation are likely to operate their own screening, assessment, and intervention practices. How can these critical functions be coordinated so they serve a single process of addressing and readdressing the instructional needs of children?

Achieving clarity about who is responsible for which administrative tasks is critical. Where do the critical supports of the system live? Without an institutional home, RTI may be cursed to wander around the no man's land between state institutions and federally run local Head Start programs. Even with the benefit of partnerships and collaborative agreements, RTI may languish because it has no place to call home. To address this problem, we believe RTI should be *the* conceptual model for delivering instructional services. It becomes the structure for Child Find, formal evaluation, eligibility determination, and special education delivery. It becomes the meeting place for collaboration partners including intervention specialists, special education teachers, general education teachers, disabilities coordinators, and parents. Far from being just one more thing added to the plates of busy, underresourced programs, RTI-EC should be the way in which learning happens. If RTI-EC lives in everyone's mind as a way to understand what services are delivered to the child, how they are delivered, and what to do when children are not thriving as desired, it can function as a constant guide that situates the needs of children at the center while assigning adults the responsibility for addressing these needs.

We believe it would be beneficial to create general and agreed-on frameworks from which programs will operate. States can work to create supportive professional development practices that benefit the variety of practitioners responsible for providing interventions. States can provide guidance to individual programs around resources that are available to assist local programs and agencies to implement interventions. Effective referral pathways should be made available to all providers of early childhood services to assist practitioners in maneuvering through what is often a complex array of services.

Interagency Collaboration

Early care and education at the state level is often a hodgepodge of family and center-based child care, community for-profit and nonprofit preschools, Head Start programs, and school-district-based programs. For RTI-EC to be effective, thoughtful consideration should be given to the collaborative practices necessary to achieve integration and coordination among these entities. A common vision should be established for serving all children, using a tiered model to ensure needs are met as soon as they are identified. Regulations should be crosswalked to identify alignment and contradictions. Services and procedures should be uniform across settings.

In this section, we discuss why Head Start should be an important collaborating partner in developing state RTI systems, how Head Start State Collaboration Offices can play a useful role in fostering partnerships that undergird the collaborative framework that makes RTI work, and how states can conceptualize RTI as a collaborative framework in which to deliver effective services for children with and without disabilities. State systems that support RTI require keen alignment to Head Start programs and practices. The challenge has always been providing common understanding about the roles, relationships, and responsibilities of Head Start programs and local agencies supporting children with disabilities from birth through age 5.

Our focus on Head Start is just one application in one type of program in early childhood. Other sectors such as child care and public prekindergarten are equally important settings. Although they do not require federal–state alignment, these programs rely on intrastate coordination that involves relationship-building and intentionality. State efforts to engage in work through state advisory councils and to apply for the Race to the Top–Early Learning Challenge Grant are examples of the kinds of cross-system collaborations that support RTI-EC. Our discussion of Head Start may provide ideas regarding how collaboration can promote effective implementation of RTI-EC.

Working with Head Start States will want to work closely with Head Start grantees to ensure that these partners are well integrated into their efforts to address the needs of young children, especially given the importance of disabilities services within the scope of work required of Head Start programs. Conversely, Head Start programs need to work closely with their local school districts and early intervention programs to fulfill expectations from the Head Start Performance Standards as well as to ensure that these activities are being done in a way that meets state requirements and aligns with state goals and priorities. Federal legislation is vague on the roles, responsibilities, and relationships and leaves it up to states to add the precision needed for effective interagency collaboration. Why not add the precision in a way that meets the needs of the state? Using a common focus on RTI-EC practices creates an ideal raison d'être for defining roles, responsibilities, and relationships.

Head Start State Collaboration Office   Collaborative work with Head Start, especially at the state level, properly begins with the state collaboration office. These offices are responsible for addressing the complicated regulatory and procedural arrangements that exist between state and federal authorities. Head Start receives its regulatory and procedural direction at the federal level, and states generally play no direct or formal role in Head Start operation or governance. IDEA, in contrast, is operated and regulated (in conjunction with federal statutes) at the state level. These different accountability structures create challenges in aligning the two systems because no one entity is charged with overseeing activities in both realms, despite a mandate to work together. Thus, the idea of the state collaboration office to foster partnerships and collaboration was developed in 1990 and ratified with an expanded role in the most recent Head Start reauthorization. The purpose of the collaboration offices, in the words of the Head Start Act, is "to facilitate collaboration among Head Start agencies (including Early Head Start agencies) and entities that carry out activities designed to benefit low-income children from birth to school entry, and their families" (Improving Head Start for School Readiness Act of 2007, PL 110-134; see §642B[a][2][A]).

With specific regard to Head Start serving children with disabilities, the role of the Head Start State Collaboration Offices is to

> Promote better linkages between Head Start agencies and other child and family agencies, including agencies that provide . . . other child or family supportive services, such as services provided under section 619 or part C of the Individuals with Disabilities Education Act. (Improving Head Start for School Readiness Act of 2007, PL 110-134; see §642B[a][2][B][iv])

Additional guidance from the Office of Head Start has asked Head Start State Collaboration Offices to address collaboration around disabilities in their strategic plans (Office of Head Start, 2009). The guidance recommends these activities:

- Working with the state interagency coordinating councils established under IDEA to promote policies and practices that support the effective inclusion of Head Start and Early Head Start children with disabilities

- Collaborating with organizations in Head Start's training and technical assistance network to coordinate activities and resources for children with disabilities and their families

- Facilitating the inclusion of Head Start representatives, including representatives from American Indian and migrant grantees operating in their states, on statewide interagency activities addressing the needs of low-income children with disabilities

- Encouraging the coordination and participation of local Head Start personnel in the state's child identification efforts (Child Find) and other early identification activities
- Facilitating coordination between Head Start/Early Head Start grantees, local education agencies, and Part C/Early Identification for approaches that promote the timely referral, evaluation, and transition of children from Head Start into elementary school in accordance with federal, state, and local requirements (Office of Head Start, 2009)

These expectations make it clear that state collaboration offices should be directly involved in assuring the needed collaboration of Head Start grantees and state-based T/TA personnel with state and local entities working on Part B (619) and Part C services, and therefore can and should play a central role in any state implementation of RTI-EC.

Response to Intervention as a Framework for Head Start Collaboration
We believe that RTI provides a framework within which the kind of collaboration called for by federal law and guidance can take place. Indeed, a strong RTI system provides both role and procedural definitions that in turn form the basis for the essential collaboration between Head Start and agencies carrying out services through Part B (619) and Part C. It seems to us that state systems, which have clear means to deliver services, must be well integrated and aligned to Head Start. At the very least, LEAs should be interested in seeing that all children entering kindergarten in their districts are as well prepared for success as possible. The Head Start State Collaboration Office can and should play a primary role in creating this essential alignment.

As has been clear throughout this chapter, RTI has the potential to be more than simply a way to address the needs of children with disabilities. It is a model for addressing the needs of all children regardless of their eligibility for or enrollment in special education. Hollenbeck (2007) noted that while RTI emphasizes accountability in the general education environment, it is also the case that "[t]he application of RTI models that emphasize general education accountability are few" (p. 141). We want to address this deficiency by choosing to emphasize universal applications—that is, instruction and activities that are available and presented to all children—and underscoring the importance of addressing the needs of children quickly and consistently and not in a way that depends on decisions related to eligibility for special education.

The priority of meeting all children's needs is echoed in the Head Start Act, which requires grantees to develop procedures "for providing necessary early intervening services to children with disabilities *prior to an eligibility determination*" (Improving Head Start for School Readiness Act of 2007, PL 110-134; see §642[b][15], emphasis added). Clearly, the intent is to avoid making children languish without services while eligibility is determined. The process begins with universal screening of all children, continues with ongoing assessment, and finally leads to a specialized assessment and formal evaluation to determine the presence of a disability (U.S. Department of Health and Human Services, 2009; see §3408.6). An RTI-EC framework provides for screening and assessment as well as ongoing support for the needs of children; in short, it assures consistent services before and after eligibility is determined.

A Response to Intervention Framework for Head Start An RTI framework as generally understood with its three tiers of interventions can be appropriately applied to address the demands placed on Head Start programs. Universal applications typically begin in the general education classroom, which is fully inclusive of all children without regard to disability (Tier 1). It starts with a high-quality curriculum delivered by highly qualified, well-trained teachers. Any efforts by individual grantees to address needs or requirements in the area of professional development, to meet teacher qualification requirements, to promote a comprehensive approach to school readiness (Office of Head Start, 2011), and to support the Child Development and Outcomes Framework (Office of Head Start, 2011) strengthen Tier 1. Similarly, federal regional offices, Head Start state-based T/TA personnel, and the Head Start National Training and Technical Assistance Centers to improve school readiness are all doing important work to strengthen Tier 1 and establish a strong foundation for all children to succeed and be ready for school.

For children who are struggling to learn and develop at a rate or level consistent with peers or individual expectations, additional supports are provided to increase the probability of success and provide access to the general curriculum in the inclusive setting (Tier 2). Typically, this kind of work is done by teachers and by specialists coming into the classroom, including those working for LEAs. The middle level in the RTI schema requires further definition and clarification before it can align neatly with how Head Start operates to ensure that Tier 2 practices receive adequate support and attention. Good communication between LEAs and Head Start, preferably spelled out in memoranda of understanding, can define how and when parties are engaged at the classroom level. Ideally, general education teachers and special education specialists will work collaboratively to design the interventions so they can, to the maximum extent possible, be implemented by the general education teacher within the classroom in the course of normal classroom activities. Similar collaboration should also occur around progress monitoring practices to determine whether children need additional support or will continue to progress using Tier 1 interventions alone.

Individualized interventions (Tier 3) are provided for those who are not showing improvement from the additional supports. In many places these efforts are thought of as exclusively part of special education. In our understanding of the RTI framework, at Tier 3 the collaboration continues with individualized interventions that are more focused, more intense, and often delivered by specialists. Parallel to or overlapping with these activities are opportunities for referral to a full and formal evaluation to determine special educational eligibility. Assessments and progress monitoring, which are constitutive elements of the RTI framework, focus on determining and addressing the needs of children; however, they may and should contribute to the information cache needed to determine eligibility. What emerges from this process is the assurance that a child's needs are addressed immediately, irrespective of when the formal evaluation occurs and the final outcome of eligibility determination. At the same time, evaluation is conducted in a data-rich context from an array of monitoring instruments used by providers on the instructional front lines. If a child is determined to have a disability, the individualized education program–determined intervention can be designed and delivered with appropriate consideration of the RTI context established. Children can remain in a fully inclusive setting and natural environment, maintain the support they were receiving from their general education teacher, and continue their growth and development in a seamless transition from general education to special education.

This ideal description of how an RTI framework can work with Head Start is also a model for other kinds of community-based programs or even programs within districts. In Iowa, for example, the expansion of a statewide voluntary pre-school program for 4-year-old children was conceived in part as new inclusive settings for children with disabilities. School districts who operate these preschool classrooms, with or without the help of community partners, are required to meet the same program standards as they do for their early childhood special education (ECSE) classrooms. As a result, many are combining these classrooms. RTI-EC can take this collaboration one step further by using an RTI framework to design services for all the children in those settings, both those with and without disabilities. Although challenges and complexities will invariably alter actual implementation, the framework can serve as a way to conceptualize collaboration and service delivery. What must be recognized, whatever the actual RTI-EC system looks like, is the central role of interagency collaboration.

REFRAMING RESPONSE TO INTERVENTION: SOLUTIONS AND REIMAGING

We have attempted to provide a structure for states and local education agencies to consider as they create their state and/or local RTI model. RTI in early childhood need not be a mirror image for what is available in the K–12 system. Early childhood is a very different environment, with great diversity of services and supports across multiple systems and settings reflecting a broad continuum of quality. These differences create new and unique challenges but also new and unique opportunities. In comparison with the relatively closed loop of K–12 services, the early childhood system is more complex and requires broader knowledge of the array of possible resources. This is why we took pains earlier in this chapter to consider all the key dimensions of practice and their implication across a system of systems. Interventions that are planned and made available must often cross agency boundaries, making the process more complex and challenging while making collaboration essential. It is necessary to take a new perspective on what RTI looks like when implemented for children from birth to kindergarten entry.

The first step in reimaging RTI-EC is to begin to think of the "I" in RTI as representing both instruction and intervention. Instruction must be seen broadly as developmentally appropriate and developmentally focused practices across the domains of most early learning standards. Effective Tier 1 practices reflect the implementation of evidenced-based curricular and instructional programming. Effective instruction needs to be considered a practice expected in early childhood education rather than a value-added component.

Practitioners who implement effective instruction are already responding to the needs of the children in the classroom. Any efforts to connect high-quality program standards, research-based curricula, and effective instructional practices to a state's quality rating and improvement systems (QRIS) should be viewed as a Tier 1 support within an RTI-EC framework. Practitioners who implement screening and assessment protocol in their classrooms are already identifying those children who are presenting learning challenges. Practitioners use that information to adapt their instructional practices to meet the individual needs of the children in the classroom. Depending on the needs of a particular child and the required intensity of instruction, differentiated instruction can be considered a routine instructional practice as well as a tiered intervention strategy.

Viewed from an even wider perspective, the RTI framework can be a way of thinking about statewide early childhood systems. The Early Childhood Working Group has viewed early childhood systems as a set of four interlacing ovals (BUILD Initiative, n.d.). Each oval represents a major system that provides services for young children and their families: 1) early learning; 2) family support; 3) health, mental health, and nutrition; and 4) special needs/early intervention. The RTI framework can be incorporated within this view of the early childhood system as a system of systems. Early learning and special needs/early intervention become a part of the RTI-EC process. Family support practices envision the role of the family as an intervention agent in a way that complements other supports in the child's life. Health, mental health, and nutrition assure that the basic health care needs as well as the needs of medically at-risk children are met. Universal screenings, physical exams, and immunizations ensure that all children are provided the basic preventive care outlined in the state's early periodic screening, detection, and treatment protocols. All of these system elements can be considered universal interventions that are available to all children. Using these elements as the foundation, additional supports and individualized procedures can be added to develop a comprehensive system to address varied needs of children for treatment of detected concerns in a single conceptualized system.

Children and families will benefit from a system that is linked across services and settings. As states establish their RTI-EC structure, they need to consider ways to use existing resources as supports for interveners. A program dealing with a child exhibiting substantial behavioral issues, for example, needs to be able to locate available resources to assist with interventions. Are there mental health consultants who would be able to come into the center and work with staff to support the child? Are there family-level services supporting intervention practices in the home that would be complementary to services available in the center? Creating a transparent system that is easily accessed not only provides needed support to practitioners and families but also makes them more effective in carrying out the work they must do.

Creating an effective RTI-EC structure requires states and local communities to carefully consider the dimensions laid out in this chapter. It would be helpful to craft a checklist of these elements and to establish a group to work through these suggested elements before actually beginning an RTI program. Our experience implementing state and local RTI practices has helped us identify the dimensions we propose here. These are practices that are doable given the respective systems commitment to establishing such a framework. Carefully considering these dimensions is likely to lead to the establishment and implementation of an effective RTI process in early childhood.

REFERENCES

BUILD Initiative. (n.d.). *State early childhood development system*. Retrieved from http://www .buildinitiative.org/content/early-childhood-systems-working-group-ecswg

Ewen, D., & Matthews, H. (2007). *Title I and early childhood programs*. CLASP Policy Paper. (Paper No. 2). Retrieved from http://www.clasp.org/admin/site/publications/files/0379.pdf

Hollenbeck, A.F. (2007). From IDEA to implementation: A discussion of foundational and future responsiveness to intervention research. *Learning Disabilities Research & Practice*, 22(2), 137–146.

Improving Head Start for School Readiness Act of 2007. PL 110-134, 42 U.S.C. §§ 9835 *et seq.*

Individuals with Disabilities Education Improvement Act (IDEA) of 2004, PL 108-446, 20 U.S.C. §§ 1400 et seq.

Office of Child Care. (2011, June). *Child care development fund.* Retrieved from http://www.acf.hhs.gov/programs/occ/ccdf/factsheet.htm

Office of Head Start. (2009). *Head Start collaboration offices priority areas.* Retrieved from http://eclkc.ohs.acf.hhs.gov/hslc/Head%20Start%20Program/State%20collaboration/HSSCO/Collaboration%20Offices%20Priority%20Areas%2010.07.09.pdf

Office of Head Start. (2010). *Head Start child development and early learning framework.* Retrieved from https://eclkc.ohs.acf.hhs.gov/hslc/tta-system/teaching/eecd/Assessment/Child%20Outcomes/HS_Revised_Child_Outcomes_Framework(rev-Sept2011).pdf

Office of Head Start. (2011). *On the road to school readiness: GPS planner.* Retrieved from http://eclkc.ohs.acf.hhs.gov/hslc/Head%20Start%20Program/Initiatives/ohs_summit_2011/GPS_Planner_en.pdf

Posny, A. (2010). *Letter to Dr. Linda Brekken* (Special Quest Birth–Five, Head Start/Hilton Foundation Training Program). Retrieved from http://www.cde.state.co.us/cpp/download/meetings/09-028972r-CA-Brekken-RTIHeadStart-6-2-10.pdf

Rush, D., & Shelden, M. (2011). *The early childhood coaching handbook.* Baltimore, MD: Paul H. Brookes Publishing Co.

Sandall, S., Schwartz, I., & Joseph, G. (2001). A building blocks model for effective instruction in inclusive early childhood settings. *Young Exceptional Children, 4*(3), 3–9.

Sosinskya, L.S., & Gilliam, W.S. (2011). Assistant teachers in prekindergarten programs: What roles do lead teachers feel assistants play in classroom management and teaching? *Early Education & Development, 22*(4), 676–706. doi:10.1080/10409289.2010.497432

U.S. Department of Education, Office of Special Education Programs. (2006). *Identification of specific learning disabilities.* Washington, DC: Author. Retrieved from http://idea.ed.gov/explore/view/p/,root,dynamic,TopicalBrief,23,

U.S. Department of Health and Human Services. (2009) *Head Start program performance standards.* Washington, DC: U.S. Government Printing Office.

26

Setting the Stage for Sustainability

Building the Infrastructure for Implementation Capacity

Michelle A. Duda, Dean L. Fixsen, and Karen A. Blase

Many early childhood practitioners have experienced trying new interventions or promising practices that seem to show benefits to preschoolers. Typically this experience goes as follows: At first, staff and administrators are motivated or "fired up" and ready to try out this new practice. They may attend several training sessions and even receive new materials. They spend time preparing to use this new practice in their individual classrooms, or time as a group preparing to move forward with a programwide approach. They let parents and caregivers know about the latest and greatest strategies to support their young children in order to receive their support. There is an agreement that this new program is needed. A lot of time and effort is invested, but unfortunately this practice is not sustained through the following school year. What happened?

Several possible reasons may account for lack of sustainability of a new practice. From a *leadership* point of view, there may have been a change in leadership and therefore a change in commitment. There may have been major adaptive challenges such as lack of staff buy-in and support, or there may have been too many technical issues that were not managed well (e.g., inadequate time allotted for training and coaching). Looking at potential barriers from an *organizational/programmatic* perspective, there may have been challenges around providing time for teachers to embed this new practice into their day; there may have been financial challenges that had an impact on fully setting up this new program; or perhaps leadership did not have the appropriate data to use in problem solving. Finally, there may have been a number of challenges related to *staff competence and confidence* in implementing new practices if organization supports were not adequate to help staff transfer their new skills into their classroom via effective coaching and use of data to guide program development and application of the new practices.

We have described a common problem and some possible barriers to implementation and sustainability of a new practice, but there is a solution—understanding and using Active Implementation Frameworks. The information in this chapter will help staff, teachers, and administrators learn about the science of implementation and become familiar with four Active Implementation Frameworks (Fixsen, Naoom, Blase, Friedman, & Wallace, 2005) that can be applied to implement and sustain high-fidelity use of the response to intervention (RTI) framework in early childhood settings.

IMPLEMENTATION SCIENCE: THE KEY TO
SUPPORTING AND SUSTAINING RESPONSE TO INTERVENTION

Implementation science is the scientific study of variables and conditions that impact changes at practice, organization, and system levels—changes that are required to promote the systematic uptake, sustainability, and effectiveness of evidence-based programs and practices in typical service and social settings (Fixsen, Blase, Duda, Naoom, & VanDyke, 2010). The opening vignette helps articulate some common experiences and challenges educators face. In the United States, substantial funds have been invested in education and research on education. It is equally important to invest in the practice and science of implementation if the goal is to make effective use of scientifically based interventions to improve student learning and achievement. Recent evaluations of various attempts to improve or "reform" schools concluded that the interventions being studied were effective when they were fully implemented but were ineffective when they were poorly implemented or implemented in name only and not in fact (Aladjem & Borman, 2006; Vernez, Karam, Mariano, & DeMartini, 2006). Studies like these are providing convincing evidence that the implementation process itself must be given the same careful attention that is directed to the selection of which interventions to use. Fortunately, recent advances in the science and practice of implementation can help improve the outcomes of introducing innovations such as RTI in educational settings.

Commonly Used Approaches to "Implementation"

Greenhalgh, Robert, MacFarlane, Bate, and Kyriakidou (2004) conducted an intensive review of the diffusion and dissemination research literature and noted that putting science into service needs to move from "letting it happen" or "helping it happen" to "making it happen" styles of implementation. In the "letting it happen" or "helping it happen" approaches, education researchers and innovators publish their findings, or provide summaries of new findings directly to teachers and others via handbooks and web sites, as well as through training or other technical assistance. Both of these approaches hold the teacher accountable for how well the innovation is implemented and for any benefits that might accrue to students: it is up to teachers and other school personnel to access the research-based information and to figure out how to use it effectively in their individual settings. Many early childhood professionals have experienced these approaches to dissemination and implementation of new practices. Educators frequently have encountered practices or programs that seemed promising but faced the same "this too shall pass" fate as previous interventions. Some components of these practices may have been sustained, but not in a way that would ensure that all students experienced the maximum impact of these interventions.

MAKING IT HAPPEN: IMPLEMENTING
ACTIVE IMPLEMENTATION FRAMEWORKS

For several decades there have been many studies documenting the active and effective approach to moving science to service (e.g., Chamberlain, 2003; Havelock & Havelock, 1973; Wolf, Kirigin, Fixsen, Blase, & Braukmann, 1995). These groups and others "make it happen" by using thoughtful methods that include attention to evidence-based approaches for building and sustaining implementation capacity. In a more active "making it happen" approach, implementation teams take responsibility for helping teachers and other school personnel learn how to use education practices with fidelity in order to produce good outcomes for students. This approach involves intentionality and includes a process by which implementation occurs. It includes organized and evidence-based implementation frameworks, evidence-based implementation practices to support building an implementation infrastructure, and a team of individuals that is both dedicated and available to support this work. Thus, "making it happen" is not some heavy-handed approach to implementation. Rather, it is an approach that makes full use of implementation knowledge, with accountability for results resting fully with the implementation team. In order for young children across early childhood environments to reliably receive access to the multitude of benefits that the use of the RTI framework can generate, it is critical that there is a focus on "making it happen" for teachers and staff.

Achieving Sustainability: From Making Lists to Making Sense

Fixsen, Naoom, Blase, Friedman, and Wallace (2005) completed a comprehensive set of interviews of purveyors (large-scale users and disseminators of evidence-based practices) around the globe and in conjunction reviewed implementation evaluation literature across multiple disciplines to produce a synthesis of that literature. These reviews and interviews yielded lists and provided empirical evidence related to barriers for knowledge translation, uptake, and skill development, but also illuminated what facilitates reliable and sustained use of the best practices. This information led to the development of four Active Implementation Frameworks. The Active Implementation Frameworks described in the synthesis of the implementation literature offer new ways to view the methods needed to make better use of implementation science in education and other human service settings. The Active Implementation Frameworks subsequently have been analyzed in a series of reviews of current successful implementation practices (Blase & Fixsen, 2003; Blase, Fixsen, Naoom, & Wallace, 2005) and have been used to support and inform large-scale initiatives in education (e.g., positive behavior interventions and supports). Thus, the components of "making it happen" described in this chapter represent the best available evidence garnered from the implementation evaluation literature and implementation best practices. The four Active Implementation Frameworks articulated by Fixsen et al. are as follows:

1. *Implementation teams:* Organized expert assistance with implementation to reliably produce effective outcomes

2. *Implementation drivers:* Active use of implementation core components "best practices"

   - Staff selection

   - Staff training

   - Staff coaching

   - Staff performance assessment

- Organization decision support data system
- Organization facilitative administration
- Organization intervention in external systems
- Leadership—adaptive and technical

3. *Stages of implementation:* Purposeful matching of critical implementation activities to each stage of the process

- Exploration stage
- Installation stage
- Initial implementation stage
- Full implementation stage

4. *Improvement cycles:* A focus on continuous, purposeful improvement (Fixesen, et al., 2005)

The Active Implementation Frameworks are interrelated and ongoing. All components of each framework are integrated and important, from the first thoughts about using an evidence-based practice until that practice 1) has been fully and effectively integrated into "education as usual" so that it is part of the culture, 2) is available to all students who need that intervention, and 3) is providing benefits to each student.

The Formula for Success

Implementation can be defined as a specified set of activities designed to put into practice an activity or program of known dimensions (Fixsen, Blase, Duda, Naoom, & VanDyke, 2010). This definition calls attention to two critical dimensions—a program and the conditions surrounding its use. Specifically, 1) the activity or program must be well specified so we know exactly what it is that we are trying to do, and 2) the activities designed to put it into practice must be well specified so we know how to derive the best results from using the program.

There is only one formula that will ensure that successful outcomes for students can be achieved: a successful (evidence-based) intervention *and* successful (evidence-based) implementation. Thus, the formula for success is "Effective Intervention × Effective Implementation = Positive Outcomes" (Fixsen et al., 2010). If either the intervention or implementation yields a zero (i.e., does not occur), students will not experience positive outcomes.

The work of building implementation capacity includes creating the context to support the new intervention or practice, including changing the thinking and behaviors of those who interact with that preschool or program. This encompasses all staff and teachers, program directors and administrators, and system directors or decision makers at various levels, as well as parents and caregivers. Changes in organizational culture and behavior are required so that new ways of work are possible, valued, and supported.

Implementation Prerequisite: Defining What We Decided to Implement

Once the "what"—the evidence-based intervention—has been selected, the essential elements need to be operationalized. To successfully implement an effective practice or program, the essential elements of RTI need to be clearly described so that innovation fluency of staff, teachers, administrators, and key stakeholders can be achieved. *Innovation fluency* is the degree to which an individual knows the innovation with respect to the evidence related to the need as well as the program and practice features that need to be in place (Hall & Hord, 2010). Once the program and practice features have been defined, the implementation requirements also need to be defined. Essential elements are defined through activities that are both observable and measurable. To help operationalize what critical components of RTI look like in early childhood environments, one must consider the following questions:

- What will staff and teachers be saying and doing when they are effectively using RTI?

- What should parents and caregivers see?

- What does it take to teach staff and teachers to behave in this new way?

- How does one assess the performance of staff and teachers, and the overall program, to determine whether the practice or program is being delivered with fidelity or as intended?

- Who will be responsible for collecting and reporting on these data?

- Do we have evidence to suggest that outcomes for children and families will be better when families experience this new program or practice?

According to a report by Coleman, Roth, and West (2009), four essential features of the RTI framework are shared across school- and preschool-age children. In order to achieve the desired student and child outcomes, all of the following features need to be implemented with fidelity: 1) a system of tiered instruction and intervention, 2) high-quality classroom instruction, 3) ongoing student assessment and progress monitoring, and 4) family involvement. In addition, in prekindergarten environments several additional contextual elements must be considered. All of these essential components are nonnegotiable but need to be further analyzed and operationalized to translate the components into practices. There may be different implementers for different tiers, so it is essential for the leadership team to take the time to operationally define what staff and teachers should say and do to implement each tier and what they will be held accountable for with respect to implementing RTI effectively.

One way to organize this information is to develop and use a practice profile. A practice profile, which is an adaptation from innovation configurations (Hall & Hord, 2010), can be used to help teams operationally define the essential elements of RTI, define the core activities of teachers and staff, and teach those skills so that consistency is promoted across staff. The use of a practice profile begins once a team has decided to adopt an evidence-based program or practice that has multiple essential components. Engaging in the development of practice profiles helps stakeholders (i.e., families, administrators, coaches) identify observable and measureable staff behaviors that are expected or acceptable and those that are unacceptable. The three categories of a practice profile include 1) expected use, 2) acceptable variation, and 3) unacceptable variation. Observations that fall into the acceptable variation category provide good information related to the targets for additional training or coaching.

Metz, Bartley, and Blase (2011) offered some operational definitions and processes that may be helpful to completing a practice profile. *Expected use* includes activities that demonstrate that teachers and staff are able to generalize required skills to a wide range of settings and contexts. *Acceptable variation* includes activities demonstrating that teachers and staff are able to apply required skills and abilities but that they do so within a limited range of contexts and settings, that they use these skills inconsistently, or that they need supervisor/coach consultation to apply these skills. *Unacceptable variation* includes activities demonstrating that practitioners are unable to implement required skills or abilities in any context. Often when a practitioner's performance consistently falls into the unacceptable category, there are challenges related to the overall implementation infrastructure (for example, issues related to quality of staff training or administrative support for the new program model).

Summary

Once a multicomponent intervention has been adopted, it is important to begin to operationally define the essential elements that will be taught to and expected of staff. The use of practice profiles is one approach that may perform the function described previously. Investing time in operationally defining essential elements based on research helps create a program or set of practices that can be taught, coached, and measured (e.g., fidelity) and supported administratively. The benefits of this time investment include allowing all stakeholders to gain consensus on critical observable components and how those will be measured (fidelity), clearly linking functions to outcomes, and documenting the process for decision making (i.e., what are acceptable variations to the use of RTI).

ACTIVE IMPLEMENTATION FRAMEWORK 1: IMPLEMENTATION TEAMS

An important, early step is the identification or development of a functional implementation team. Once the implementation team is formed, one of its first activities may be to help create practice profiles. Implementation teams need to have the time, expertise, and latitude to do the work of implementation initially and over the long term (Klein, 2004; Rhim, Kowal, Hassel, & Hassel, 2007; Schofield, 2004; see also http://www.pbis.org and http://www.scalingup.org). Their job is to assure the full and effective use of all critical components of RTI as contextualized by the site with students whose needs are not sufficiently met by current educational practices. Without an implementation team, busy teachers, staff, and administrators are left on their own to discover what works for making effective use of RTI or other evidence-based practices. Teachers, staff, and administrators already have full-time jobs, and implementation of evidence-based practices is too important to be relegated to volunteers (Fixsen, Blase, Duda, Naoom, & VanDyke, 2010). Studies by Balas and Boren (2000) and Green and Seifert (2005) found that it takes an estimated average of 17 years for 14% of new scientific discoveries to enter day-to-day clinical practice. However, with implementation teams in place, Fixsen and colleagues (2001) found that it took only 3 years for reliable and sustainable outcomes to be achieved in 80% of the sites. The data supporting implementation teams are just emerging but offer some compelling examples of the benefits of team-based leadership.

Function

The creation and support of an implementation team is critical for ensuring that all of the components of RTI are fully developed within the site, that the infrastructure is supported for continuous improvement of all staff, and that positive outcomes are being achieved. Three core functions of implementation teams are 1) proactively assisting staff, teachers, programs, and possibly districts to implement specific practices; 2) taking responsibility for results in implementing these practices successfully; and 3) creating readiness across all stakeholders (e.g., parents, caregivers, communities, staff, teachers, researchers). The team strives to understand the existing strengths of the organization, to identify the specific challenges or vulnerabilities for sustainability, and to develop and execute an implementation action plan. These functions take time and are too important to be an add-on responsibility for hardworking teachers and staff. Implementation teams are accountable for ensuring both fidelity to RTI (intervention) and fidelity to implementation process (i.e., training and coaching are being provided as intended). They are the group of individuals who take on the active and intentional approach to implementation and "make it happen."

Form

Core implementation team members typically consist of three to five individuals with specialized expertise who have the dedicated time (full-time equivalent allocated) to do the work of implementation. Efficient implementation team development can occur by repurposing current teams and developing their skills and abilities as implementation team members. Members of the implementation team may bring unique expertise (i.e., behavioral specialist, literacy specialist) and unique perspectives (i.e., systems, family member, community member). Collectively, the core implementation team members have the following characteristics:

- Knowledge of the intervention (e.g., progress monitoring, differentiated instruction, data-based decision making, family involvement)

- Knowledge of effective implementation strategies and methods (e.g., the Active Implementation Frameworks, building capacity, systems change)

- Experience in working within the organization (e.g., may have served on various leadership teams, have experience with supporting changes that may have occurred within the preschool or program)

- Experience in implementing an evidence-based program or practice

Given the complexity of the work and the importance of ensuring stakeholder engagement and support, the core implementation team may solicit the support of others on a short-term basis to provide specific expertise. For example, if a new data collection system needs to be developed, the implementation team may invite individuals with information technology expertise, site administrators, and others with an interest in data collection and technology to problem-solve on how to create this system.

Summary

Implementation team members represent a group with a new set of competencies, roles, and functions. They work with staff, teachers, schools, and districts to help inform and prepare them to make effective use of RTI and other innovations. Once readiness has been created, the implementation team efficiently and effectively helps teachers and schools make full use of RTI to provide demonstrable benefits to students. Building this implementation capacity consumes precious time and resources in the beginning, but it also brings a substantial return on that investment in terms of more effective educational practices; more efficient programs, schools, and districts; and aligned educational systems.

ACTIVE IMPLEMENTATION
FRAMEWORK 2: IMPLEMENTATION DRIVERS

Once the core and essential elements of RTI are operationalized at the classroom, program, preschool, and/or district levels, then it is time to consider how to implement the chosen interventions to produce good outcomes for students. The core implementation components consist of the implementation drivers needed for successful use of RTI core components through all stages of implementation (exploration, installation, initial implementation, full implementation). The appendix following this chapter illustrates key activities to support each of the implementation drivers, depending on the current stage of program implementation.

The implementation drivers are shown in Figure 26.1. These implementation components or drivers compose the infrastructure needed to develop, improve, and sustain the skills articulated though the practice profiles. The implementation drivers can be classified into three broad domains: 1) building staff and teacher *competence,* 2) creating the *organization supports* that represent the necessary environment to do this work, and 3) providing *leadership* at all levels to support and sustain the new way of work.

In many early childhood environments, the use of implementation drivers is not new. What may be new is the systematic and intentional approach used to ensure that all of the implementation drivers are in use and aligned to support the core components of RTI. Each driver represents a series of interactive processes, and the integration of these processes helps develop the supports needed to sustain the new way of work. The drivers are also compensatory, meaning that a weakness in one driver can be compensated for by the strengths of other components (i.e., strong coaching may help to compensate for weak or inefficient training).

Competency drivers are activities that help ensure that personnel at all levels have the skills necessary to effectively deliver the core and essential elements of RTI. They include 1) recruiting and selecting staff who possess the prerequisite skills and knowledge, 2) training staff to expand their skill capacity, 3) coaching staff to develop application mastery, and 4) assessing performance to monitor fidelity of implementation of the essential elements of RTI (i.e., to ensure that high-quality instruction is being delivered and family involvement is occurring as intended).

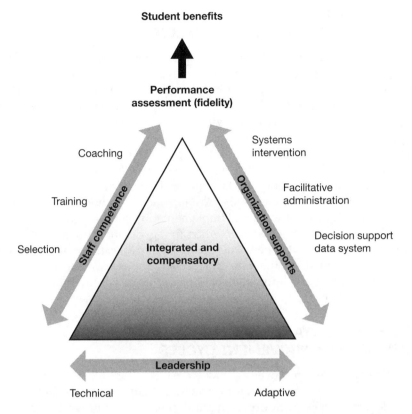

Figure 26.1. Implementation drivers. (From Fixsen, D.L., Blase, K.A., Duda, M., Naoom, S.F., & Van Dyke, M. [2008,October]. *Effectively using innovations in OASAS*. Presented at the NY Office of Alcoholism and Substance Abuse Services conference, New York; reprinted by permission.)

Organization drivers are actions, policies, and procedures that support practitioners, eliminate administrative and other barriers, and pave the way for effective implementation of the EBP. Organization drivers include decision support data system, facilitative administration, and systems intervention, accompanied by performance assessment to monitor fidelity of the implementation process to ensure implementation of the essential elements of RTI (i.e., to confirm that training and coaching are being implemented as intended).

The *leadership driver* addresses the critical leadership behaviors needed to establish effective programs and sustain them as circumstances change over time. Leadership may be provided by different people and at different levels of the system. Leadership strategies and approaches may be classified as "adaptive" or "technical," depending on the nature of the challenge (Heifetz & Laurie, 1997). Transformative leadership helps ensure that the new system is working as intended and helps remove barriers that may be getting in the way of high-fidelity implementation.

Finally, effective and sustained implementation occurs when staff competence, organization supports, and leadership are all aligned, integrated, and focused on effective education for each student and young child. Ensuring that implementation drivers are consistently used to install and implement innovations is a key to capacity building and sustainability.

ACTIVE IMPLEMENTATION
FRAMEWORK 3: THE STAGES OF IMPLEMENTATION

The activities associated with each stage of implementation are not linear, and stages often overlap. Activities related to one stage may be still occurring or recurring as activities related to the next stage begin. It is important for leadership and implementation teams to attend to activities that are stage appropriate, or else conflicts, challenges, and issues may arise that will stop the momentum of moving toward the next stage. Managing expectations, incorporating appropriate stage-based assessments, and providing a structured approach to the process of implementation are all key functions of this Active Implementation Framework.

Four stages of implementation take place: 1) *exploration*, when readiness is assessed and the decision about whether to adopt an intervention occurs; 2) *installation*, when resources are gathered and implementation supports (trainers, coaches) are identified; 3) *initial implementation*, when first-generation implementers begin using the new practice in this new way; and 4) *full implementation*, when most staff members are implementing this new practice so that assessment of student outcomes and assessment and improvement of processes can occur. Building sustainability is part of the function of the activities of each of the stages.

ACTIVE IMPLEMENTATION
FRAMEWORK 4: IMPROVEMENT CYCLES

Development and use of improvement cycles are integrated into all of the key activities of creating the implementation infrastructure to support the use of the defined essential elements of RTI. Many experts naturally engage in improvement cycles such as rapid-cycle problem solving. It is critical to document what decisions were made, how they were executed, and what was learned from each effort. This helps teams build the new system in a transparent fashion while the existing system continues to function as is. Improvement cycles include engaging in Plan–Do–Study–Act Cycles (Deming, 1986; Shewharts, 1931), conducting usability testing, and creating protocols to facilitate communication between policy makers and practitioners.

APPLICATION OF THE ACTIVE IMPLEMENTATION FRAMEWORKS

The purpose of this section is to provide examples of questions to consider and examples of activities (described in the appendix following this chapter) that can be used to install the frameworks.

Exploration Stage: "Pay Now or Pay Later"

The exploration stage is often underutilized, and its importance to a successful implementation effort is seldom fully appreciated. Launching into a decision to adopt a specific intervention without due diligence can lead to a rocky start at best, and is more likely to end in failure. For successful and sustainable implementation, taking time for activities associated with the exploration stage is critical. The exploration stage helps to clarify if there is a need for change, create buy-in from stakeholders regarding the intervention as a good way to satisfy that need, and elicit initial support from top administrators and decision makers. The exploration stage begins with recognition that there is a need for change to accomplish some purpose. The determination of need leads to a process of discovery in which information about RTI is sought from a variety of sources (e.g., literature, conferences, discussions with colleagues). An existing site leadership team will have ready access to various sources of information and will be a good resource for helping to clarify existing needs and identify the components of RTI or other innovations that are potential solutions. This team, or some of its members, may eventually develop into an implementation team, as described earlier. Early childhood education leaders and stakeholders, including parents and caregivers, are engaged in the process of determining needs and considering information to address the needs. Their understanding of and support for the use of the innovation is a key outcome of the exploration stage activities.

As the staff, teachers, building administrators, program administrators, and stakeholders learn more and build support for RTI, the implementation team will secure more detailed information about RTI's core components and will begin to help the educators plan for implementation. The following are key issues to consider during the exploration stage with regard to the potential use of any innovation:

1. *What are the core or essential components of the intervention?* Answering this question may require detailed correspondence with the researchers or developers of the innovation or may lead to a period of usability testing by the initial implementation team to identify the key components in action. Utilizing a practice profile framework will help organize this information.

   Thinking through what capacity is needed to carry out the essential components of RTI with fidelity is an activity that occurs during this stage. Will the existing infrastructure support the development of staff competence and confidence, or does capacity need to be created to systematically select, train, coach, and provide feedback on fidelity?

2. *Which teachers or staff members should be the first users of RTI?* (selection driver) As the team plans to launch RTI on a programwide level, it is important to recognize that not all teachers are well suited to be early adopters. The initial implementation team will help identify and select those who are most willing and able to initiate the use of the new intervention.

3. *How will training be done, and who will do it?* (training driver) Supporting educators in the use of new skills requires well-prepared and skillful trainers. Content expertise may already be available within the existing implementation team or within the building. However, the initial implementation team may need to bring in content experts at the beginning to help team members learn what to teach regarding a particular intervention or component of RTI.

4. *How will coaching be done, and who will do it?* (coaching driver) Training without onsite follow-up coaching has repeatedly been found to be ineffective in education, human services, business, and manufacturing. Training without coaching results in only about 5% to 10% of the trainees using the skills on the job. This means that training alone results in only 5%–10% of trained teachers demonstrating new skills in the classroom (Joyce & Showers, 2002). Coaching is important and requires knowledge of the intervention, knowledge about adult learning, and coaching skills.

5. *How will teacher/staff performance be assessed, and who will do it?* (performance assessment driver) Measuring staff/teacher performance in using the critical components of RTI as intended is an important strategy for successful and sustainable implementation. The initial implementation team needs to be very familiar with a variety of practical and useful measures of performance associated with RTI so that they can help teachers, coaches, schools, and others make constructive use of the information.

There are three organization drivers that also influence the quality and sustainability of RTI. The organization drivers include decision support data systems, facilitative administration, and systems intervention. The following questions should be considered from an organization support perspective.

1. *Do we have a robust and accessible data system in place?* Decision support data systems are processes for systematically collecting and using performance data, such as fidelity measures to the intervention and staff satisfaction data, and student outcome data. Data also can be collected and used regarding the quality of the drivers (e.g., Did training result in knowledge gains? Was coaching perceived as helpful and done as intended?).

2. *Once we have collected our data, what is our formal mechanism for using the data for informing decisions?* Data for decision making are needed at every level. At the classroom level, school staff and coaches need to know how well individual staff and teachers are implementing RTI and where they are struggling. They need access to fidelity and other performance data so that they can share data with the staff and teachers they are supporting and so they can use the data to create and monitor the effectiveness of improvement plans. At the program level, data related to effectiveness of drivers and links to student outcomes are essential for systematically maintaining strengths and addressing challenges.

3. *What are the administrative implications of using the intervention and carrying out the implementation of the intervention?* Many evidence-based practices and other innovations require changes in typical school routines. Implementation activities are new to most schools and also require changes in school structures and management (e.g., coverage for teachers while they are in training, assuring availability of skilled coaches, carrying out regular observations of teacher/staff performance).

4. *Are there external programs that are engaging in similar work, and if so, how can we pool resources and supports?* Systems alignment and intervention are critical, since even the best program will not survive if the funding, regulatory, and policy climate is not hospitable. Systems can and do regularly trump programs. This attention to systemic factors that facilitate and hinder implementation of RTI in early childhood and early learning (K–3) settings may need to occur at multiple levels (e.g., school, district, region, state).

As indicated here, successful use of RTI's essential components requires careful attention to the characteristics of the intervention *and* to planning how the intervention can be implemented successfully in each setting. Many attempts to make use of evidence-based practices never produce benefits to students because the planners did not give due consideration during the exploration stage to the factors influencing implementation. Implementation teams are an invaluable resource during the exploration stage with respect to assessing readiness of the staff to implement the new practices (e.g., answering the questions posed previously) and helping to create readiness at the teacher, program or preschool, and district levels.

The exploration stage ends with a decision to proceed (or not) with the actual use of RTI. If a decision is made to move forward, it is important to note that the consensus-building activities that began during exploration never end and will continue as the team moves forward to the next stage of implementation.

Installation Stage: Making Preparations

Although the stages of implementation are described in a logical sequence, they are not linear. For example, during the exploration stage while the decision to proceed is being made, preparations for using the components of RTI begin. The installation stage consists of activities that are further summarized in the appendix on capacity-building activities. Some core activities that will be familiar to most administrators include the following:

- High levels of communication take place among all staff and stakeholders

- Stakeholders are brought in as partners in making more detailed plans

- New functions and roles to carry out the intervention and to provide implementation support are translated into new job descriptions and pay scales

- New protocols are established to interview and select staff to perform the new functions

- Trainers are identified and training sessions are scheduled, and coaches are prepared to carry out their roles

Many attempts to make use of evidence-based practices can fail at this point because those involved are not prepared to spend the time and resources required to accomplish the functions of the installation stage. During the installation stage, preparations for implementation supports far outweigh the preparations specific to the intervention.

Two broad strategies for dealing with installation stage challenges can be very helpful. First, provide anticipatory guidance about the challenges ahead. This guidance should be provided to all involved, but this advance warning is particularly crucial for high-level supporters and champions. Apprising stakeholders of the challenges ahead and keeping them up-to-date about the project increases their confidence and ensures that they will be ready, willing, and able to step in and advocate around key issues. The second implementation strategy that will be helpful is to identify problems as they are just emerging. Already having an implementation team in place who is ready to engage in rapid-cycle problem solving will help to quickly analyze barriers, determine root causes, collect information, develop and enact solutions, and then evaluate the outcomes.

Initial Implementation: Starting to Use the Intervention and Surviving the Awkward Stage

During the initial implementation stage, the first group of teachers and staff is selected, they are provided with training, and they begin to use the intervention with students with the help of a skilled coach. The well-defined core components of RTI and implementation supports (e.g., selection, training, coaching, performance assessments) were discussed and planned for during the exploration stage, and resources to carry out these activities were skillfully and effectively secured during the installation stage. Even so, learning new skills and using those skills with real students is not easy, and things typically do not go well in the beginning (think of learning to drive a car or any other task that requires acquiring new skills).

It is during this initial "awkward stage" that coaching is so important for the following reasons:

- To encourage teachers to use their new skills in the classroom (even though they are not yet comfortable with them) and offer a variety of rationales involving the benefits to students, teachers, parents, and education systems

- To provide plenty of descriptive praise for what the staff and teachers are doing well

- To help teachers incorporate the new skills into their personal teaching styles and typical classroom management methods

- To help teachers expand their skill base by giving pleasant and constructive advice (and practice) on how to do more of the intervention more skillfully the next time. This may even include modeling the new skills.

There is no substitute for frequent in-classroom coaching during the first days and weeks after training, with continuing coaching and support thereafter (Joyce & Showers, 2002).

At this point, it is important to begin assessing the extent to which teachers and staff are using the new practices effectively. This is *not* part of staff evaluation procedures. Rather, it is more like the progress monitoring completed with students—the purpose is to see where additional training or support needs to be provided and where training and support procedures need to be improved.

For RTI to be successful in addressing current instructional challenges, all components must be implemented with a high degree of integrity. Researchers have documented that numerous "failures of education reforms and practices can be attributed to poor implementation" (Johnson, Mellard, Fuchs, & McKnight, 2006, p. 4-1). When initiatives are adopted in name only, without fidelity to essential program design and features, results are unpredictable and frequently poor. Assuming that instruction is being delivered as intended, fidelity of implementation needs to be extended to the essential RTI elements of universal screening, student progress monitoring, family involvement, and tiered interventions. RTI's effectiveness will depend upon a preschool's or program's commitment to the philosophical principles of RTI and vigilance of implementation. The success of implementation teams will depend on the skills of individual team members and coordination among them. Implementation team members will need to be frank with each other about professional development needs, funding, and evaluation of effectiveness. Periodic evaluation of universal screening and progress monitoring tools and procedures (e.g., performance assessments) should ensure that instructional interventions are being carried out with fidelity. In the event that data collected through the RTI process are to be used for eventual eligibility determination, it will be critical for eligibility teams to know that the implementation of previous interventions has been accomplished in as faithful a manner as possible.

Performance assessments of teachers' skills in using the new practices should begin soon after a teacher begins using RTI, in part to acclimate the teacher to additional direct observations in the classroom. However, the purpose of the performance assessments is to provide more sensitive and standardized information to the coach and the teacher regarding areas of strength and areas that need improvement with respect to the evidence-based practice. Performance assessment data provide us with a better understanding of how the system is working. It is good practice to have more frequent performance assessments just after training (e.g., daily, weekly) to maximize opportunities for coaching and learning.

The teacher performance assessments (or progress monitoring on implementing the component practices of the intervention) coupled with other data at the teacher, program, and preschool levels form the foundation of a *decision support data system* (another implementation driver)—a data system used to monitor performance and identify needed adjustments. These data might include

- Formative assessments

- Curriculum-embedded assessments

- Student achievement scores (outcome measures)

- Ratings from staff selection interviews

- Pre- and posttraining measures of knowledge and skills

- Teacher and staff ratings of the helpfulness of coaches

- Teacher and staff ratings of the usefulness and timeliness of performance assessment

- Cost information

This process of measuring aspects of the implementation—not just assessing outcomes—is a key feature of the new scientific approach to implementation that sets this approach apart from the common practice of simply "trying new things" in ways that weren't documented and thus couldn't be analyzed to identify contributors to the success or failure of the new practice.

Implementation teams need to be well versed in how to establish effective and efficient decision support data systems in educational settings, in preschools, and in district organizations. These teams also work with teachers, trainers, coaches, evaluators, and administrators to help them interpret and make good use of the available data as they make decisions. Implementation teams work with agency/school and district administrators to help them change policies, regulations, and practices in order to remove barriers to high-quality and effective implementation and to design new policies and regulations that will more fully support the new ways of work that define RTI. The decision support data system forms the basis for a continuous improvement cycle.

Full Implementation: Ready for Assessing Outcomes

Full implementation is defined as the point at which at least 50% of the teachers have been selected, trained, coached, and evaluated on their use of RTI, and meet the criteria for competent performance (sometimes referred to as *fidelity* or *adherence*). Thus, it is possible to reach full implementation even while some staff members are still working to reach higher levels of skill in using the new practices. Meeting this criterion is an indicator that the selection, training, coaching, performance evaluation, decision support data systems, and facilitative administrative supports are in place and are functioning well individually and collectively to routinely produce competent teacher and staff performance and bring benefits to students. It often takes 2–4 years to progress from the beginning activities of the exploration stage to the point of meeting the definition of full implementation.

Full implementation also is difficult to maintain over many years. For staff and teachers, meeting the criterion for competent performance once is no guarantee that it will be reached again. Also, turnover occurs at all levels and affects the competent performance of teachers and staff (e.g., an excellent coach leaves and the newer teachers and staff are left without competent advice and support for a period of time). With the continuing support of an implementation team, a school will get through such periods of adjustment and once again will reach full implementation.

Once full implementation has been reached and maintained, the outcomes of RTI can be assessed. Full implementation is a clear indicator that the intervention is in place and is working for students. At this point, there is a program in place, the effects of which can be assessed. Any attempts to measure outcomes prior to reaching full implementation run the risk of assessing the outcomes of an evidence-based practice that does not yet exist. Effective interventions that are implemented with competence routinely produce positive outcomes (e.g., Duda, Dunlap, Fox, Lentini, & Clarke, 2004; Landenberger & Lipsey, 2005).

Summary

As the high-fidelity use of the essential components of RTI becomes accepted practice, the implementation team remains vigilant but their work becomes more routinized. By this time, the implementation drivers are embedded in the program's or preschool's culture of conducting education and providing services, and the decision support data systems are in place to provide guidance for continual improvements in the intervention itself and in the implementation drivers. At this time, the implementation team may be able to take on other evidence-based practices waiting to be implemented to achieve further benefits to students.

CONCLUSION AND FURTHER CONSIDERATIONS

The purpose of this chapter was to provide an overview of how to utilize best practices gleaned from implementation science to develop the necessary infrastructure for creating and sustaining high-fidelity implementation of the core components of an RTI framework. By employing the four Active Implementation Frameworks (Fixsen et al., 2005)—implementation teams, implementation drivers, stages of implementation, and improvement cycles—programs that have adopted an RTI framework will be more likely to be able to sustain this process in complex early childhood environments. Supporting implementation teams to carry out their work is a critical component of creating the new system and of identifying and building upon the strengths in the early childhood setting. By using the implementation drivers to create alignment across the system, implementation teams ensure that teachers and staff receive the support they need to deliver all of the RTI components with fidelity. Implementation takes time, and working through the stages of implementation allows the implementation team and leadership to ensure readiness, manage expectations, and build a context that will support the use of RTI. Finally, by engaging in improvement cycles, implementation teams help to ensure that decision making is based on data collected to monitor progress continuously, leaving behind a clearly defined process that is both replicable and sustainable so that all young children can benefit from the interventions.

REFERENCES

Aladjem, D.K., & Borman, K.M. (2006, April). *Summary of findings from the National Longitudinal Evaluation of Comprehensive School Reform.* Paper presented at the annual meeting of the American Educational Research Association, San Francisco, CA.

Balas, E.A., & Boren, S.A. (2000). *Yearbook of medical informatics: Managing clinical knowledge for health care improvement.* Stuttgart, Germany: Schattauer Verlagsgesellschaft GmbH.

Blase, K.A., & Fixsen, D.L. (2003). *Evidence-based programs and cultural competence.* Tampa: University of South Florida, Louis de la Parte Florida Mental Heath Institute.

Blase, K.A., Fixsen, D.L., Naoom, S.F., & Wallace, F. (2005). *Operationalizing: Strategies and methods.* Tampa: University of South Florida, Louis de la Parte Florida Mental Health Institute.

Chamberlain, P. (2003). The Oregon multidimensional treatment foster care model: Features, outcomes, and progress in dissemination. *Cognitive and Behavioral Practice, 10,* 303–312.

Coleman, M.R., Roth, F.P., & West, T. (2009). *Roadmap to pre-K RTI: Applying response to intervention in preschool settings.* Washington, DC: National Center for Learning Disabilities.

Deming, W.E. (1986). *Out of the crisis.* Cambridge, MA: MIT Press.

Duda, M., Dunlap, G., Fox, L., Lentini, R., & Clarke, S. (2004). An experimental evaluation of positive behavior support in a community preschool program. *Topics in Early Childhood Special Education, 24*(3), 143–155.

Fixsen, D.L., Blase, K.A., Duda, M.A., Naoom, S.F., & VanDyke, M.V. (2008, October). *Effectively using innovations in OASAS.* New York Office of Alcoholism and Substance Abuse Services conference, New York, NY.

Fixsen, D.L., Blase, K.A., Duda, M.A., Naoom, S.F., & VanDyke, M.V. (2010). Implementation of evidence-based treatments for children and adolescents: Research findings and their implications for the future. In J.R. Weisz & A.E. Kazdin (Eds.), *Evidence-based psychotherapies for children and adolescents* (2nd ed.). New York, NY: Guilford Press

Fixsen, D.L., Blase, K.A., Timbers, G.D., & Wolf, M.M. (2001). In search of program implementation: 792 replications of the Teaching-Family Model. In G.A. Bernfeld, D.P. Farrington, & A.W. Leschied (Eds.), *Offender rehabilitation in practice: Implementing and evaluating effective programs* (pp. 149–166). London, UK: Wiley.

Fixsen, D.L., Naoom, S.F., Blase, K.A., Friedman, R.M., & Wallace, F. (2005). *Implementation research: A synthesis of the literature.* Tampa, FL: University of South Florida, Louis de la Parte Florida Mental Health Institute, The National Implementation Research Network (FMHI Publication #231).

Green, L.A., & Seifert, C.M. (2005). Translation of research into practice: Why we can't "Just do it." *Journal of the American Board of Family Practitioners, 18*(6), 541–545.

Greenhalgh, T., Robert, G., MacFarlane, F., Bate, P., & Kyriakidou, O. (2004). Diffusion of innovations in service organizations: Systematic review and recommendations. *The Milbank Quarterly, 82*(4), 581–629.

Hall, G.E., & Hord, S.M. (2010). *Implementing change: Patterns, principles and potholes* (3rd ed.). Boston, MA: Allyn and Bacon.

Havelock, R.G., & Havelock, M.C. (1973). *Training for change agents.* Ann Arbor: University of Michigan, Institute for Social Research.

Heifetz, R.A., & Laurie, D.L. (1997, January-February). The work of leadership. *Harvard Business Review,* 124–134.

Johnson, E., Mellard, D.F., Fuchs, D., & McKnight, M.A. (2006). *Responsiveness to intervention (RTI): How to do it.* Lawrence, KS: National Research Center on Learning Disabilities.

Joyce, B., & Showers, B. (2002). *Student achievement through staff development* (3rd ed.). Alexandria, VA: Association for Supervision and Curriculum Development.

Klein, J.A. (2004). *True change: How outsiders on the inside get things done in organizations.* New York, NY: Jossey-Bass.

Landenberger, N.A., & Lipsey, M. (2005). The positive effects of cognitive-behavioral programs for offenders: A meta-analysis of factors associated with effective treatment. *Journal of Experimental Criminology, 1*(4), 451–476. New York, NY: Springer.

Metz, A., Bartley, L., & Blase, K.A. (2011). *Developing practice profiles.* Retrieved from http://www.fpg.unc.edu/~nirn/

Rhim, L.M., Kowal, J.M., Hassel, B.C., & Hassel, E.A. (2007). *School turnarounds: A review of the cross-sector evidence on dramatic organizational improvement.* Lincoln, IL: Public Impact, Academic Development Institute.

Schofield, J. (2004). A model of learned implementation. *Public Administration, 82*(2), 283–308.

Shewhart, W.A. (1931). *Economic control of quality of manufactured product.* New York, NY: D. Van Nostrand Co.

Vernez, G., Karam, R., Mariano, L.T., & DeMartini, C. (2006). *Evaluating comprehensive school reform models at scale: Focus on implementation.* Santa Monica, CA: RAND Corporation.

Wolf, M.M., Kirigin, K.A., Fixsen, D.L., Blase, K.A., & Braukmann, C.J. (1995). The teaching-family model: A case study in data-based program development and refinement (and dragon wrestling). *Journal of Organizational Behavior Management, 15*(1/2), 11–68.

APPENDIX
Overview of Capacity-Building Activities

	Stages of Implementation		
	Pre-exploration **Current state**	**Exploration** **Actively considering a change**	**Installation** **Preparing for use of the innovation**
Selection	Human resource department has a generic protocol to recruit and hire staff	New job descriptions and pay scales are developed for key personnel	New interview protocols with hiring criteria specific to the innovation are established
Training	Staff selection is based on academic degrees and years of experience	Content specific to the core components of the innovation are located/developed	Specific content is developed, a workshop schedule is prepared, and space for conducting training is identified
Coaching	A current employee is appointed to supervise practitioners	A person with expertise in the innovation is recruited; a new job description and pay scale are developed	A person with expertise in the innovation has been hired, acceptable coach–practitioner ratios are established, and a coaching schedule is developed
Performance assessment	Supervisors provide their opinions regarding each practitioner's performance	Core components of the innovation are reviewed to see how they can be assessed in practice	A careful review has been conducted to align the content/criteria used in selection interviews and preservice training with areas to be assessed in practice
Decision support data systems	Information is collected regarding funding and issues related to regulations and compliance	The team outlines areas relevant to the innovation in order to evaluate processes and outcomes	Active work is done to develop/locate appropriate measures of organizational functioning; staffing is arranged
Facilitative administration	Organizational structures and functions focus on compliance and cost containment	Senior administrators examine changes needed to fully support the innovation	Specific plans are made to change organizational structures and functions, staff roles and functions, and financial allocations to fully support the innovation
Systems interventions	Meetings are held with officials outside the organization for purposes of contracting and reporting	Senior administrators examine the fit between the innovation and system requirements outside the organization	Specific plans are made to meet with officials in external systems to change current requirements to more fully align systems to support the innovation

Implementation drivers (vertical axis label)

Note: *Innovation* may refer to response to intervention or other evidence-based practice.
From Fixsen, D.L., Naoom, S.F., Blase, K.A., Friedman, R.M., & Wallace, F. (2005). *Implementation research: A synthesis of the literature*. Tampa: University of South Florida, Louis de la Parte Florida Mental Health Institute, The National Implementation Research Network (FMHI Publication #231); reprinted by permission.

Initial implementation	Full implementation
Actively engaged in learning how to do and support the doing of the innovation	**Actively working to make full use of the innovation as part of the organization's typical functioning**
Interviews are conducted by individuals with expertise in the innovation, using innovation-specific protocols and hiring criteria	Results of interviews are used to analyze data on staff performance and longevity; changes in interview methods are based on data analyses
Training is conducted by individuals with expertise in the innovation using innovation-specific content; behavior is rehearsed to criterion performance	Results of pre- and posttests of knowledge and skills are used to analyze data on trainer and staff performance and longevity and used to improve specific sections of the training
Coaching occurs at least once a week for each practitioner; a staff development plan is established for each practitioner; coaching time is divided between direct observation, behavior rehearsal, and data reviews	At least annually, practitioners rate their satisfaction with the helpfulness and quantity of coaching they have received; data on coaching frequency, duration, and helpfulness are compared with data on staff performance and longevity in order to improve coaching
The performance of each practitioner is assessed at least quarterly until performance criteria/fidelity is reached on a consistent basis; assessment methods include direct observation (live, recorded), data reviews, and consumer queries (e.g., satisfaction questionnaires)	At least annually, practitioners rate their satisfaction with the helpfulness and promptness of reporting of performance assessments; practitioner performance data are used to analyze data on staff selection, training, and coaching and are used to improve performance assessment methods; process data are correlated with consumer outcome data
The functioning of the organization with respect to the innovation is routinely measured and the results are reported monthly to practitioners, coaches, and administrators	Quarterly and annual reports display the results with respect to innovation and organizational processes and outcomes; at least annually, staff members rate their satisfaction with the helpfulness and promptness of reporting of organizational assessments; staff routinely make decisions based on the reported findings
Organizational structures and functions, staff roles and functions, and financial allocations are modified to fully support the innovation	Senior administrators make use of the decision support data system reports and other sources of information to assure integration of the selection, training, coaching, and assessment functions associated with the innovation; administrators at all levels look for ways to improve practitioner skill levels, satisfaction, and time with consumers
Organized effort is put into working with leaders in external systems to align their structures and functions to fully support the innovation	Senior administrators make use of the decision support data system reports and other sources of information to continue to educate leaders in external systems to continue to influence those systems to more fully support the practitioners' work with consumers and the organization's support for practitioners

Future Challenges
and New Directions

27

Promising Future Research Directions in Response to Intervention in Early Childhood

Judith J. Carta and Charles R. Greenwood

Where does research on response to intervention (RTI) in early childhood need to go to advance this approach to educating young children? To address this question, one must examine the research that has been carried out on the various components of multitiered systems of support in early education. The history of research in this area does not go back much farther than about 6 years. In 2006, some researchers were beginning to take a look at whether the broad concepts of RTI that had been implemented for many years in elementary and secondary grade levels could be applied to settings that serve young children. Recognition & Response was just being conceptualized, along with the first synthesis of research to examine the applicability of RTI to children in the early years (Coleman, Buysse, & Neitzel, 2006). This handbook is evidence of the variety of questions about RTI that have been answered since then. This chapter will provide a brief overview of where we've been and then examine some of the primary questions that still need answering.

RTI is an approach to instruction that has a number of "moving parts" (i.e., universal screening and progress monitoring, a decision-making model for identifying those children who would benefit from more intense intervention, and a hierarchy of intervention strategies that can be used to provide supplemental instruction and increased learning opportunities to children who are showing early signs of struggling in various areas of development) (National Dissemination Center for Children with Disabilities, 2010). The general idea behind RTI is prevention—that is, the goal is to identify children who are showing the earliest signs of falling behind and then to provide them with more intensive instructional experiences in the general classroom setting. This is an alternative to the more traditional approach of waiting until children's trajectories continue on a downward slope and only then providing additional support for learning through referrals to special education. Much of the research already carried out on RTI has focused on developing and testing the various components of an RTI model. Some of this work has focused on examining the effectiveness of individual components of RTI (Bailet, Repper, Piasta, & Murphy, 2009; Koutsoftas, Harmon, & Gray, 2009; Spencer et al., 2011); other work has focused on evaluating entire RTI models (Buysse, Peisner-Feinberg, & Burchinal,

2012; VanDerHeyden, Snyder, Broussard, & Ramsdell, 2008). Finally, as in other areas of applied research, the ultimate test of a research and development process is whether the innovation works in the real world. Work of this sort that examines how well teachers can implement RTI is just beginning (Carlis & Lesiak, 2011; Nylander, 2011).

IMPORTANT ACCOMPLISHMENTS
IN DEVELOPING TIERED APPROACHES

An important direction for future work will be to determine how well individual RTI components and entire RTI models can be implemented with fidelity in real-world settings. The translation of this model to real early education settings will depend on work verifying that measures are accurate and yield information that can be used in decision-making models, that instructional strategies work and can be implemented by early education practitioners, and that professional development can be carried out and an infrastructure developed so that new RTI implementation skills will be maintained at high levels. Although the amount of work that lies ahead is sobering, the research that has brought the field to this point is substantial. Some of that work is described next.

Development of Screening and Monitoring Measures

One of the most critical areas of research involving RTI for young children has been the development of measures for identifying children who would benefit from additional instructional support and for monitoring their progress in response to supplementary intervention. Developing these measures has been a major focus of the Center for Response to Intervention in Early Childhood (CRTIEC). Scott McConnell and colleagues at the University of Minnesota have crafted a set of measures for universal screening and progress monitoring in language and early literacy (McConnell, Rodriguez, Schmitt, Bradfield, & Clayton, 2011). Similarly, Susan Landry at the University of Texas Health Science Center's Children's Learning Institute has developed a set of measures for monitoring young children's performance in the areas of early literacy, book and print awareness, math, and social-emotional development (Landry, 2011). These measures can provide teachers with guidance in using the assessment information for planning classroom instruction using a variety of mobile devices.

Another major measurement development effort aimed at monitoring growth of infants and toddlers has been carried out by Charles Greenwood and colleagues at the University of Kansas Juniper Gardens Children's Project (Greenwood et al., 2008). Their suite of measures, called individual growth and development indicators (IGDIs), includes measures for monitoring language, problem solving, movement, and social-emotional development (Carta, Greenwood, Walker, & Buzhardt, 2010). Their online tool (Making Online Decisions [MOD]) helps practitioners identify children who need additional support and provides reports showing progress of individual children and their response to extra support (Buzhardt, Walker, Greenwood, & Carta, 2011). All of these efforts in measurement development are a starting point in this newly developing field of RTI. They help identify children who are most in need of supplementary instruction and assess how well children grow in response to that intervention. In addition, they are giving programs a first look at the proportion of children who are not developing at a pace that will put them on a path to succeed in kindergarten. This information will help programs shore up Tier 1 and target specific areas for professional development.

Teaching Strategies Development

At the heart of the RTI approach are the instructional interventions and curricular modifications for children who need the higher tiers of support. Researchers have developed numerous strategies for supporting children's learning in early literacy and language. Most work in this regard over the past several years has focused on Tier 2 or supplemental interventions, primarily in the area of early literacy and language. In early literacy, a number of interventions have been found to accelerate children's skills in the specific areas known to be important predictors of later reading success: alphabet knowledge, print knowledge, phonological awareness, and vocabulary (Hammill, 2004). Interventions in these areas that appear to be most effective for Tier 2 instructional support most often are carried out in small-group settings using a standard protocol and share the following characteristics:

- They are systematic (i.e., they expose children to a full range of instructional targets)

- They are explicit (i.e., they clearly convey to the students what is expected and how well they performed)

- They are intense (i.e., they address learning goals with sufficient frequency to support growth toward literacy outcomes) (Justice, 2006)

For example, Bailet and her colleagues (2009) have developed an early literacy intervention that provides explicit teaching of specific early literacy skills such as letter names and letter sounds, syllable counting and segmentation, rhyming, alliteration, and onset-rime. Each lesson also includes a focus on one of the skills through one literary element such as a poem, story, or song. Other Tier 2 interventions focus on instruction in new vocabulary. For example, Justice and colleagues have created an intervention in which a teacher "calls out" new vocabulary words during a story, defines the new words, helps the child learn how the words are used, and helps children understand them in the context of the story (Justice, Meier, & Walpole, 2005). Both of these strategies embody the critical features of providing multiple opportunities for children to practice specific skills embedded in a developmentally appropriate context.

While many multitiered systems of support for young children have focused on early literacy and language, an array of strategies for teaching social-emotional skills for children needing additional supports has also come to the fore in the last several years (Joseph & Strain, 2003). Probably more resources are available for practitioners in this content area because of the existence of comprehensive models such as The Incredible Years (Webster-Stratton, Reid, & Hammond, 2001) or the Teaching Pyramid Model (Fox, Dunlap, Hemmeter, Joseph, & Strain, 2003). The Teaching Pyramid Model offers strategies for children needing more intensive training on specific social skills such as identifying and expressing emotions, social problem solving, and self-regulation (Fox, Carta, Dunlap, Strain, & Hemmeter, 2010). Also, strategies specific to those children needing individualized intervention on challenging behaviors have been developed for children needing more than Tier 2 support (Conroy, Davis, Fox, & Brown, 2002).

Models—Putting the Pieces Together

Limited research has been conducted on models that include all the important aspects of an RTI model for young children. A few entire models have been developed and tested for feasibility, and a few studies have been carried out examining their effectiveness in promoting children's outcomes and preventing later delays. Notable in this regard are two models: Recognition & Response (Buysse & Peisner-Feinberg, 2010) and the Teaching Pyramid Model (Fox et al., 2003). Buysse and Peisner-Feinberg have developed a system for recognizing children who are not making progress in early literacy and language and then providing them with additional support. In the area of early literacy and language, work in tiered models has been advanced through Early Reading First (ERF) funding (Jackson et al., 2007). Probably the strongest contribution of ERF to advancing RTI has been in promoting the advancement of scientifically based Tier 1 early literacy curricula. A number of ERF models have included tiered models of early literacy support. One premier example carried out by Gettinger and Stoiber (2007) tested a three-tiered ERF model that included progress monitoring measures to support children's early literacy.

Other multitiered models for preschool programs have been developed but may not include the measures and decision-making components of an RTI model (e.g., Building Blocks [Sandall & Schwartz, 2008]) or the Teaching Pyramid Model (Fox et al., 2003). Professional development to implement these models has been carried out to a limited degree, but very little research has been focused on the types of support that early education personnel would need to learn and implement the many components of an RTI model and sustain them with high degrees of fidelity.

RESEARCH NEEDED TO ADVANCE THE RESPONSE TO INTERVENTION IN EARLY CHILDHOOD APPROACH

Even though considerable work has established a foundation for applying the RTI model with young children, numerous questions remain about the efficacy and feasibility of such an approach for young children, the long-term outcomes resulting from RTI, and how to scale-up RTI models in the variety of early education settings. The remainder of this chapter focuses on some of the major questions that we believe will advance the next generation of research on RTI in early childhood.

Models of Response to Intervention

As mentioned previously, very little work has been conducted on developing and testing full tiered models complete with a decision-making framework and measures for identifying children needing additional tiers of support, monitoring children's progress in response to increased intensity of instruction, and determining when children's needs change in their tiers of support. Although some research has been conducted in developing full models, we have no long-term data to indicate whether RTI models actually result in better outcomes for children when they reach elementary grades and whether they have reduced need for special education services. Also, numerous questions remain about the infrastructure needed to put an RTI model in place in a given setting. Among the key questions that must be addressed to advance our knowledge of RTI models are the following:

1. *What characteristics of Tier 1 curriculum and instruction must be in place in early education programs to serve as the foundation for RTI models?* In other words, how critical is the quality of the Tier 1 instruction on which the tiered supports will be built? A large study of 65 prekindergarten classes conducted by CRTIEC demonstrated that while there was considerable variability in instructional quality across classrooms and in different program types, overall the instructional quality was in the low to moderate range and the amount of time focused on early literacy was quite limited. These features of Tier 1 were highly related to the proportions of children who were low-performing in early literacy (Carta et al., 2012) and who demonstrated low rates of early literacy growth (Greenwood et al., 2012). Although these findings established the importance of Tier 1 instructional quality, programs need to know more about what content should be presented across curricular domains and how that content should be organized and presented to maximize children's growth in these content areas and minimize the need for additional instructional intensity. What aspects of instructional quality are most critical? Which curricula or combinations of curricula promote children's growth toward important outcomes and prevent delays when children reach the elementary grades? And how do instructional features interact with individual child differences such as beginning skill levels or home language to affect children's trajectories across domains? (Connor, Morrison, & Petrella, 2004)

2. *What higher tier instructional strategies are most effective and feasible to implement in early education settings?* At this juncture, only a few instructional strategies have been tested within the context of RTI models for young children. At some point, programs should be able to get information about the comparative effectiveness and feasibility of a variety of instructional strategies for providing Tier 2 and Tier 3 support in a variety of content areas. Programs should be able to select from a variety of validated standard protocol strategies that best meet the needs of their students and fit into the ecology of the classroom. For RTI knowledge to advance to this level, much more research generated from large experimental studies will be necessary to validate the strategies currently available in the areas of early literacy, language, and social-emotional development. In addition, much more development work is needed in other curriculum areas such as mathematics, science, and adaptive skills, as well as underdeveloped areas such as self-regulation and language comprehension. Finally, while some work has been carried out to develop integrated curricula that cuts across domains (Bierman et al., 2008; Children's School Success Research Group, 2009), research is needed to demonstrate how tiered instructional approaches can work within curricula that integrate multiple content areas.

3. *What are the most accurate measures for identifying children who need additional instructional support and for monitoring their progress in response to higher tiers*

of intervention? Research and development on measures that can be used by teaching staff to help them make instructional decisions is central to the advancement of RTI in early education settings. While CRTIEC researchers have generated a new set of measures to support RTI in early literacy and language, much more research and development is needed. Some of the areas needing more development include the following:

- New screening and progress monitoring measures in the important content areas of social-emotional development, mathematics, and Spanish vocabulary and comprehension

- Decision-making models that include benchmarks and standards for expected growth that allow teaching staff to use data to identify children needing additional tiers of support and determine when changes in levels of support are necessary

- Information on ways that technology (web-based and computer pad support) can assist teaching staff in administering measures with high fidelity and in making accurate interpretations and instructional decisions

Research questions about measures that need answering include the following:

- How accurate are currently available measures (i.e., individual growth and development indicators [IGDIs]) as screening measures (i.e., what is their selectivity/specificity)?

- What are the best ways to use IGDIs in combination with curriculum-based measures to guide instructional decision making?

- How well do measures and their benchmarks predict which children will benefit from effective Tier 2 and Tier 3 support across curricular areas?

- What are the best language and literacy predictors of later reading success for children whose home language is not English?

4. *What are the most effective approaches to professional development to sustain high-fidelity implementation of RTI models?* Although the field of early education has had some demonstrations of RTI models, these tiered approaches have typically been carried out under the watchful eye of their developers. If RTI approaches are to be scaled up on a national level, considerable research is needed on the type of support needed by teaching staff as they learn to implement the instructional strategies, to administer and interpret the measures for identifying children and monitoring their progress, and to use data for making instructional decisions. Annual surveys conducted by CRTIEC on the challenges of implementing RTI identified teachers' knowledge about all of these issues as critical needs to address in advancing RTI (Linas & Greenwood, 2011). Moreover, the wide-ranging level of experience and training across programs that serve young children means that much more research is needed to determine effective ways to give teachers a conceptual understanding of curriculum content and instructional strategies and how these can be individualized based on children's performance. Research must address

cost- and time-efficient ways to help teachers acquire these important skills and to obtain feedback on their fidelity of implementation. Finally, if these programs are to be sustained over time, research must be directed at the types of support programs need to build their capacity to train and monitor teaching teams' implementation of the model.

5. *What are the most effective ways of involving families in RTI models?* Although conceptual models for including families in RTI models have been developed (see Chapter 20), research is scarce regarding the range of roles family can play in RTI models, how they want to be involved, or how family engagement can enhance the outcomes of children involved in RTI models. Probably the most work on family involvement has been carried out on tiered models focusing on social-emotional outcomes, such as the Teaching Pyramid Model or programwide positive behavior interventions and supports (Fox, Hemmeter, Jack, & Doubet, 2011). As mentioned earlier (Chapter 20), family members can play a number of roles in RTI models, depending on their level of interest and availability, yet options for family involvement in RTI models are still just being defined. Parents can be involved in enhancing children's learning in the various tiers of support, they can be part of instructional decision making and provide information about the child's skills and preferences, and they can engage in progress monitoring at home and inform the program on the generalization of children's skills being targeted in the classroom. The bottom line is that families' potential as partners has received scant attention in the development of RTI models thus far. This area would benefit from much more research to exploit the potential of these partnerships.

6. *For what new populations and in what settings can RTI approaches be used?* RTI approaches in early childhood have focused primarily on preschool-age children and for the most part on kindergarten-bound children as a means of preparing them for success in the elementary grades. Yet, multitiered models can be considered for any population that would benefit from a clear protocol for identifying those who need more intensified supports and for monitoring their response to the increased assistance.

One group that could benefit from more individualization is infants and toddlers and their families. Programs that serve infants and toddlers are increasing in number as more evidence arises that the achievement gap between children in poverty and other children begins as early as the first year of life (Odom et al., in press). Federal attention to the importance of the earliest years of life is illustrated by the expansion of Early Head Start and the recent new development of the Maternal Infant and Early Childhood Home Visiting program that is part of the Patient Protection and Affordable Care Act of 2010 (PL 111-148). Although programs such as these are expanding, only limited research and development has occurred to demonstrate how these programs can identify children needing additional support and provide that additional assistance.

In the area of language development, individual growth and development indicators (Carta et al., 2010) have been developed that allow practitioners to track children's trajectories in different developmental domains and identify when a child may be falling below the expected levels of growth. In the area of communication, the Making Online Decisions (MOD) approach (Buzhardt et al., 2010), a web-based system, has been developed that allows practitioners to track children's progress so that when a child falls into a zone of potential risk, the MOD approach recommends a set of strategies that can be employed by practitioners in centers or by parents during daily routines at home to promote children's communication skills. While this is not a full-blown tiered model, it embodies the same decision-making framework using measures that can help identify risk and then monitor children's response to a higher level of instructional support.

Another tiered model (not yet named) focusing on infants and toddlers and their families, this one addressing social-emotional behaviors, is currently being developed to parallel the Teaching Pyramid Model (Carta, Hemmeter, Broyles, & Baggett, 2009). This model advances a multitiered system of supports based on evidence-based practices for supporting infant–toddler social-emotional development so that children and families will get a level of service that matches their needs and is responsive to changes over time. The model is being used in a center-based Early Head Start program that emphasizes parental involvement and maintains a close collaborative relationship with community mental health systems. Although this work is just beginning, the need for more models that help programs serving infants and toddlers to individualize the level of service based on their demonstrated need is expanding. More research is needed to develop and validate instructional strategies that can be used by infant–toddler programs to prevent delays in children's language and social-emotional growth before they enter preschool, and to design professional development approaches that help practitioners and parents implement these strategies with fidelity.

Another population that could benefit from RTI is young children who are gifted. Few instructional strategies have been validated for young children who are either gifted or who may be twice exceptional (have a disability as well as giftedness). The RTI framework provides an ideal approach for differentiating instruction in the general classroom for those young children who show exceptional talents. Research to develop measures for identifying gifted children and instructional strategies that are closely matched to their capabilities and capitalize on their talents would be a tremendous resource for the field of early education.

One final major question regarding RTI for young children is the applicability of multitiered systems of support for the variety of early education settings in which children under age 5 are educated or receive care. If the goal of RTI in the early years is to prepare children for kindergarten and minimize failure, then we should try to develop a model that can be implemented across the range of settings that serve young children: Head Start, state-funded prekindergarten programs, Title 1 programs, tuition-based early education programs, and family-based childcare programs. Of course, numerous factors must be considered to stretch the RTI approach to fit these settings. How should programs with high proportions of struggling learners be able to provide supplemental support or increased intensity to the large number of children who might need it? What personnel will be available to implement the higher tiers of support and carry out universal screening and progress monitoring? What team members will be available to engage in the decision-making model needed to ensure that children are receiving their appropriate level of instructional support? A critical need to address all of these concerns is the development of comprehensive, coordinated systems of high-quality prenatal-to-age-5 services. Such a framework would allow for closer collaboration across programs serving young children to address the important issues of professional development, availability of evidence-based practices, and the infrastructure necessary for sharing resources to support the universal screening, progress monitoring, and delivery of instructional supports that all children need.

CONCLUSION

In this chapter, we have attempted to outline some of the major research questions that should guide future work in RTI in early childhood. While much work remains to advance RTI for young children in this country, this volume attests to the wealth of information that already exists for promoting multitiered systems of support. Important work has already been carried out demonstrating the effectiveness of several components of RTI models and the professional development necessary to put them in place. Considerable effort has already been expended on extending this knowledge to early education programs around the country. Important changes are taking place at the national, state, and community levels to bring the many facets of early education together into an integrated system. We look forward to the second volume of this text to report a new generation of research describing how RTI is improving the odds of success of young children throughout the United States.

REFERENCES

Bailet, L.L., Repper, K.K., Piasta, S.B., & Murphy, S.P. (2009). Emergent literacy intervention for prekindergarteners at risk for reading failure. *Journal of Learning Disabilities, 42*, 336–355.

Bierman, K.L., Domitrovich, C.E., Nix, R.L., Gest, S.D., Welsh, J.A., Greenberg, M.T., . . . Gill, S. (2008). Promoting academic and social-emotional school readiness: The Head Start REDI program. *Child Development, 79*, 1802–1817.

Buysse, V., & Peisner-Feinberg, E. (2010). Recognition & Response: Response to intervention for pre-K. *Young Exceptional Children, 10*, 3, 17–27.

Buysse, V., Peisner-Feinberg, E., & Burchinal, M. (2012, March). *Recognition & Response: Developing and evaluating a model of RTI for pre-K*. Poster presented at the Fifth Annual Meeting of the Society for Research on Educational Effectiveness, Washington, DC.

Buzhardt, J., Greenwood, C., Walker, D., Carta, J., Terry, B., & Garrett, M. (2010). Web-based tools to support the use of infant and toddler IGDIs for early intervention decision-making. *Topics in Early Childhood Special Education, 29*, 201–215.

Buzhardt, J., Walker, D., Greenwood, C., & Carta, J. (2011). A study of an online tool to support evidence-based practices with infants and toddlers. *NHSA Dialog, 14*, 151–156.

Carlis, L., & Lesiak, M. (2011, September). *Using RTI to improve outcomes across domains in Washington DC preschools*. Paper presented at the RTI Early Childhood Summit. Santa Ana Pueblo, New Mexico. Retrieved from http://www.crtiec.org/rti_summit/2010/documents/Lesiak.pdf.

Carta, J., Greenwood, C., Atwater, J., Goldstein, H., Kaminski, R., & McConnell, S. (2012). *Relative proportions of children at early literacy and language risk in prekindergarten programs: Implications for response to intervention*. Manuscript submitted for publication.

Carta, J., Greenwood, C., Walker, D., & Buzhardt, J. (Eds.). (2010). *Individual growth and developmental indicators: Tools for monitoring progress and measuring growth in young children*. Baltimore, MD: Paul H. Brookes Publishing Co.

Carta, J., Hemmeter, M.L., Broyles, L., & Baggett, K. (2009). *The pyramid framework within early intervention programs: Promoting the social development of infants and toddlers*. Proceedings of webinar retrieved from http://www.challengingbehavior.org/explore/webinars/9.9.2009_tacsei_presentation_teleconference.htm

Children's School Success Research Group. (2009). *Children's school success curriculum (CSS)*. School of Education, Indiana University. Unpublished curriculum manuscript.

Coleman, M.R., Buysse, V., & Neitzel, J. (2006). *Recognition & Response: An early intervening system for young children at risk for learning disabilities*. Full report. Chapel Hill: University of North Carolina at Chapel Hill, Frank Porter Graham Child Development Institute.

Connor, C.M., Morrison, F.J., & Petrella, J.N. (2004). Effective reading comprehension Instruction: Examining child x instruction interactions. *Journal of Educational Psychology, 96*, 682–698.

Conroy, M.A., Davis, C.A., Fox, J.J., & Brown, W.H. (2002). Functional assessment of behavior and effective supports for young children with challenging behaviors. *Assessment for Effective Intervention, 27*, 35–47.

Fox, L., Carta, J., Dunlap, G., Strain, P., & Hemmeter, M.L. (2010). Response to intervention and the Pyramid Model. *Infants and Young Children, 23*, 3–14.

Fox, L., Dunlap, G., Hemmeter, M.L., Joseph, G.E., & Strain, P.S. (2003). The teaching pyramid: A model for supporting social competence and preventing challenging behavior in young children. *Young Children, 58*(4), 48–52.

Fox, L., Hemmeter, M.L., Jack, S., & Doubet, S. (2011). *A program-wide model for implementing positive behavior support*. Retrieved from http://www.challengingbehavior.org/explore/presentation_docs/10.05_program_wide.pdf

Gettinger, M., & Stoiber, K. (2007). Applying a response to intervention process for early literacy development in low-income children. *Topics in Early Childhood Special Education, 27*, 198–213.

Greenwood, C., Carta, J., Atwater, J., Goldstein, H., Kaminski, R., & McConnell, S. (2012). *Is a response to intervention (RTI) approach to preschool language and early literacy instruction needed?* Manuscript submitted for publication.

Greenwood, C.R., Carta, J.J., Baggett, K., Buzhardt, J., Walker, D., & Terry, B. (2008). Best practices integrating progress monitoring and response-to-intervention concepts into early childhood. In A. Thomas, J. Grimes, & J. Gruba (Eds.), *Best practices in school psychology V* (pp. 535–548). Washington, DC: National Association of School Psychology.

Hammill, D.D. (2004). What we know about correlates of reading. *Exceptional Children, 70*, 453–468.

Jackson, R., McCoy, A., Pistorino, C., Wilkinson, A., Burghardt, J., Clark, M., . . . Swank, P. (2007). *National evaluation of Early Reading First: Final report*. NCEE 2007-4007 rev. U.S. Department of Education, Institute of Education Sciences. Washington, DC: U.S. Government Printing Office.

Joseph, G.E., & Strain, P.S. (2003). Comprehensive evidence-based social-emotional curricula for young children: An analysis of efficacious adoption potential. *Topics in Early Childhood Special Education, 23*(2), 65–76.

Justice, L.M. (2006). Evidence-based practice, response-to-intervention, and prevention of reading difficulties. *Language, Speech, and Hearing Services in Schools, 37*, 1–14.

Justice, L.M., Meier, J., & Walpole, S. (2005). Learning new words from storybooks: Findings from an intervention with at-risk kindergarteners. *Language, Speech, and Hearing Services in Schools, 36*, 17–32.

Koutsoftas, A.D., Harmon, M.T., & Gray, S. (2009). The effect of Tier 2 intervention for phonemic awareness in a response-to-intervention model in low-income preschool classrooms. *Language, Speech, and Hearing Services in Schools, 40*, 116–130.

Landry, S. (2011, September). *Advancing quality school readiness programs in early childhood programs through systematic change*. Paper presented at the RTI Early Childhood Summit. Santa Ana Pueblo, New Mexico. Retrieved from http://www.crtiec.org/rti_summit/2010/documents/Landry2011summitpresentations.pdf.

Linas, M.W., & Greenwood, C.R. (2011, November). *USA snapshot: The prevalence of response to intervention in preschool classrooms*. Poster presentation at the Division of Early Childhood, Council for Exceptional Children Annual Meeting, Washington, DC.

McConnell, S.R., Rodriguez, M., Schmitt, B., Bradfield, T.A., & Clayton, K. (2011, February). *Early childhood response to intervention: Using second-generation IGDIs*. Symposium presented at annual meeting of the National Association of School Psychologists, San Francisco, CA.

National Dissemination Center for Children with Disabilities. (2010). *Response to intervention.* Retrieved from http://nichcy.org/schools-administrators/rti

Nylander, D. (2011, September). *Putting all the pieces together: How to build an integrated RTI model in two domains.* Paper presented at the RTI Early Childhood Summit, Santa Ana Pueblo, NM. Retrieved from http://www.crtiec.org/rti_summit/2010/documents/Nylander.pdf

Odom, S. Pungello, E., & Gardner-Neblett, N. (Eds.). (in press). *Re-visioning the beginning: The implications of developmental and health science for infant/toddler care and poverty.* New York, NY: Guilford Press.

Patient Protection and Affordable Care Act of 2010, PL 111-148, 124 Stat. 119.

Sandall, S.R., & Schwartz, I.S. (2008). *Building blocks for teaching preschoolers with special needs* (2nd ed.). Baltimore, MD: Paul H. Brookes Publishing Co.

Spencer, E., Goldstein, H., Sherman, A., Noe, S., Tabbah, R., Ziolkowski, R., & Schneider, N. (in press). Effects of an automated vocabulary and comprehension intervention: An early efficacy study. *Journal of Early Interventions.*

VanDerHeyden, A.M., Snyder, P., Broussard, C., & Ramsdell, K. (2008). Measuring response to early literacy intervention with preschoolers at risk. *Topics in Early Childhood Special Education, 27,* 232–249.

Webster-Stratton, C., Reid, M.J., & Hammond, M. (2001). Preventing conduct problems, promoting social competence: A parent and teacher training partnership in Head Start. *Journal of Clinical Child Psychology, 30,* 238–302.

28

Evidence-Based Practice and Response to Intervention in Early Childhood

Samuel L. Odom and Angel Fettig

Two parallel movements now are pushing the fields of early childhood and special education. The response to intervention (RTI) approach is increasingly being applied in school districts across the country, and adaptations for its use at the early childhood level have been the focus of researchers and program developers (Buysse & Peisner-Feinberg, 2010; Greenwood et al., 2011). At the same time, a movement within education, in part mandated by the No Child Left Behind Act of 2001 (PL 107-110), has been to base educational practice on scientific evidence of efficacy (Odom, et al., 2005). The logical linkage between these two movements is an examination of the evidentiary basis for the use of RTI with young children in early childhood education programs (RTI-EC). The purpose of this chapter is to provide an examination of the evidence base for RTI-EC. We will first specify a working definition for RTI-EC and its component elements, discuss the concept of evidence-based practice, and then propose criteria for determining those practices. We will provide examples of components of RTI-EC that appear to have an evidence base and discuss the issues associated with evaluations of comprehensive models of RTI-EC. In concluding, we will offer future directions for research and practice in the field.

RESPONSE TO INTERVENTION AT THE EARLY CHILDHOOD LEVEL

Although RTI in early childhood is in its relative infancy compared to its application at the school-age level (Gersten et al., 2009; Gersten et al., 2008), a considerable number of researchers and scholars have begun identifying and documenting approaches they describe as the application of RTI to early childhood programs (RTI-EC) (Buysse & Peisner-Feinberg, 2010; Coleman, Roth, & West, 2009; Greenwood et al., 2011; National Professional Development Center on Inclusion, 2012; VanDerHeyden & Snyder, 2006). The models or descriptions of RTI-EC are remarkably similar in their component parts. They employ either a triangle or pyramidal graphic representation in which high-quality environments are the bottom or foundational level, with subsequent levels of the pyramid consisting of increasingly more intense instruction or intervention for children who are not responding positively to curricular experiences or intervention at the previous respective level.

A primary feature of RTI-EC is assessment. Universal screening usually occurs for all children in early childhood education classes to identify children who may already be lagging behind developmentally and may need more intensive instruction than is provided in the standard curriculum. Also, some form of ongoing progress monitoring related to children's learning may be applied for all children or for those children who show lags in learning (this varies across models). In addition, a common and important feature is collaborative problem solving that involves practitioners (and parents, in some models) jointly contributing to decisions made about children's instruction. Several investigators (see Chapter 2 in this volume; see also Greenwood et al., 2011) have noted that the RTI-EC model is similar to the three-level model of prevention (of disease and disability) that has existed for years in the field of public health (Caplan & Grunebaum, 1967) and serves as the basis for the now active field of prevention science (see Society for Prevention Science, http://www.preventionresearch.org/).

EVIDENCE-BASED PRACTICE

Within the fields of early childhood education and special education, the evidence-based practice movement is in full force (Buysse & Wesley, 2006; Odom et al., 2005). Although one could track the interest in evidence to support scientific claims to Galileo, Newton, and the British Empiricists (Franklin, 1993), a major contemporary influence on the evidence-based practice movement in education was the evidence-based medicine movement that began in the United Kingdom and was elaborated in Canada. Frustrated by the underuse of medical science in practice, Cochrane, an epidemiologist from the United Kingdom, advocated for the use of randomized controlled trials (RCTs) to establish the scientific base for medical practice. Following this tradition, physicians from McMaster University in Canada created the term "evidence-based medicine" and established a process for incorporating scientific evidence into practice (Evidence-based Medicine Working Group, 1992), with Sackett and colleagues providing leadership for that group (Sackett, Rosenberg, Gray, Haynes, & Richardson, 1996).

The logic and processes exemplified by evidence-based medicine have been applied to the education field by scholars (Davies, 2002) and written into public policy through the No Child Left Behind legislation of the last decade. In fact, in special education there has been a long tradition of decrying the gap between research and practice (Greenwood & Abbott, 2001), and Carnine (1999) in particular was a vocal and influential proponent of incorporating scientific information in practice. The Education Sciences Reform Act of 2002 (PL 107-279) was passed with the intent of bolstering the quality of scientific research in the field of education, which would provide an evidentiary foundation for practice. The Institute of Education Sciences (IES) was established by this act.

Scientific evidence accumulates at a fast pace, and to assist practitioners in gaining access to the most current scientific evidence, organizations have been established to conduct systematic and rigorous reviews of the scientific literature. In medicine, the Cochrane Collaboration (http://www.cochrane.org), located in the United Kingdom and named after Archie Cochrane, was established in 1992 to summarize evidence on medical and health practices. Following this precedent, the Campbell Collaboration (http://www.campbellcollaboration.org/) was formed in the United States to conduct reviews related to education, crime and justice, and social welfare. The Education Sciences Reform Act of 2002 established the What Works Clearinghouse (WWC) (http://ies.ed.gov/ncee/wwc/), also with the goal of conducting rigorous reviews of the education sciences literature and making the knowledge available to practitioners. All of these organizations are potentially valuable sources of information about education practice. In fact, WWC reviews conducted by Gersten and colleagues have examined the evidence on RTI for reading (Gersten et al., 2009) and math (Gersten et al., 2008) at the elementary and high school levels.

What Counts as Evidence?

A question that naturally emerges from the evidence-based education movement involves what is considered "evidence." From their National Academy of Science Committee, Shavelson and Towne (2002) acknowledged that different types of evidence exist and are important in education, but only randomized clinical trial (i.e., randomized experimental group design) studies published in peer-reviewed journals can provide causal evidence of efficacy. The Division for Research of the Council for Exceptional Children (CEC-DR) elaborated on this definition of acceptable causal evidence by proposing that single case experimental design (SCD) is also a research methodology that could demonstrate causal evidence (Odom et al., 2005). The WWC has incorporated both RCT and SCD studies in their reviews of evidence supporting educational practice.

The second question, also quickly emerging, is "How much and what type of evidence is necessary?" In the 1990s, leaders from Division 12 of the American Psychological Association were among the first to establish criteria for types and amounts of evidence (Chambless et al., 1996). Using this precedent and working in parallel with other organizations focusing on the same task (e.g., National Association of School Psychologists), the CEC-DR formed a task force that recommended evidentiary guidelines for evidence-based practices in special education (Odom et al., 2004). They proposed that in order for a teaching method to qualify as an evidence-based practice, positive evidence of efficacy had to be established by two high-quality experimental or quasi-experimental group design studies or five single case design studies. Single case designs had to be conducted by three different groups of researchers and involve a total of at least 20 participants across studies.

The standards just identified apply to instructional, clinical, and intervention practices. However, as noted previously, the features of RTI-EC also include assessment practices such as screening and progress monitoring. The evidence substantiating assessment practices is not based on RCT or SCD studies but on measurement of psychometric quality of assessment instrumentation. The American Educational Research Association (AERA), American Psychological Association, and the National Council on Measurement in Education have collaborated in establishing (AERA, 1999) and now revising the *Standards for Educational and Psychological Testing*, which specifies necessary reliability and validity evidence for assessment instruments. In addition to measures of reliability, evidence for the viability of screening tests also includes information about sensitivity (proportion of children having a problem who are identified—true positives) and specificity (proportion of children not having a delay who are not identified—true negatives) (Meisels & Atkins-Burnett, 2005).

Evidence-Based Practices versus Evidence-Based Practice

A subtle but very important distinction must be made when discussing *evidence-based practices* (i.e., a noun) and *evidence-based practice* (i.e., a verb). Evidence-based practices are interventions that are verified as being efficacious by meeting the standards noted in the previous section. However, the use of those practices involves a decision-making process that incorporates clinical wisdom, knowledge of previous treatment history, family values, and perhaps other contextual information. Sackett et al. (1996) emphasized the importance of integrating scientific evidence of effectiveness with clinical expertise and patient choice in evidence-based medicine, and Buysse and Wesley (2006) made a similar point of incorporating information about EBPs, practitioner knowledge, and family choice in following an evidence-based practice approach in early childhood programs. We want to explicitly state that in this chapter we will be focusing on EBPs, which we propose is the place to begin when making decisions about instructional approaches for young children. Implementing evidence-based practices requires the practitioner or adopter to incorporate a wider range of information.

The Question of Unit of Analysis for Response to Intervention in Early Childhood and Evidence-Based Practice

When considering RTI-EC, the question of the unit of analysis is critical. RTI-EC is a multicomponent approach, so one may evaluate RTI-EC models as a whole, comprehensive model and make a judgment of cumulative effects. Such evaluations would most likely employ a cluster randomized clinical trial (CRCT) design because children are nested within classrooms. In such an approach, classrooms or schools are randomized into treatment or control conditions and differences in child outcomes for the two conditions are measured. One could also construct a single case design study where classrooms, schools, or districts are the cases in the study, although this approach for evaluating comprehensive models has not been used very often.

Alternatively, educational leaders may want to establish an RTI-EC model that fits the local context without adopting a comprehensive, "predeveloped" model, and may "build" a model based on components that have evidence of efficacy or psychometric quality. Tier 1, 2, or 3 approaches should themselves be established as evidence-based intervention or teaching practices through independent research. For example, a model designed to promote social-emotional development might include a well-validated early childhood curriculum at Level 1 (e.g., Dinosaur School curriculum from *The Incredible Years* [Webster-Stratton, 1990]), a more focused small-group intervention at Tier 2 (e.g., social integration activities), and a more focused teacher-directed intervention occurring in small groups or with individual children at Tier 3 (e.g., social skills training).

A Note on the Available Evidence and Purpose of the Review

As stated, RTI-EC has just emerged as an early childhood approach in the last decade, and science takes considerable time to accumulate. One would not expect to find fully validated interventions at this stage of development. The purpose of this review is to describe RTI-EC components or models that have begun to appear in the literature, and if they have not yet met the criteria for evidence-based practice, to propose future directions for research. In addressing this purpose, we will provide examples of practices and models rather than conducting an extensive review of the literature.

EVIDENCE-BASED PRACTICE IN RESPONSE TO INTERVENTION IN EARLY CHILDHOOD

Conceptual frameworks for RTI-EC have elements of assessment as well as curriculum and intervention. In this section, we will identify examples of assessments, interventions, and even comprehensive models prominent in the RTI-EC literature, and comment on the degree of evidence available. Although the examples we will select are those with the strongest evidence available, we will note when the examples do not meet the evidentiary criteria proposed in the field. In addition, RTI is often described in terms of content areas rather than as RTI-EC that is integrated across skills areas. The content areas often focus on language, literacy, math, and social-emotional skills, which is how we organize our review.

Assessment

There are at least two purposes for assessment in the RTI-EC process. First, practitioners use universal screening to identify children who may be lagging behind, who may need further assessment, and who may need more intensive intervention or instruction. When the assessment is applied to all children, practitioners use the data to make decisions about which children require more focused intervention or instructional support at the Tier 2 level. The second purpose of assessment is to provide continuous monitoring of children's learning. For example, a decision may be made about altering instruction a child receives in Tier 2 small-group math instruction or moving a child to a more intensive level of instruction if he is not making progress at Tier 2.

For the purpose of universal screening, the issues of sensitivity and specificity are relevant, as are the more basic psychometric qualities of reliability and validity. A primary mode of assessment for early childhood universal screening and progress monitoring is the set of individual growth and development indicators (IGDIs) developed by Greenwood, Carta, McConnell, and colleagues (see Chapter 9 in this volume; see also Greenwood & Walker, 2010). IGDIs have been used for screening and progress monitoring and are based on more than a decade of research to establish their psychometric qualities (Greenwood & Walker, 2010). IGDIs currently exist to monitor motor, cognitive/problem solving, communication, social, and early literacy performances (Carta, Greenwood, Walker, & Buzhardt, 2010). Buzhardt and Walker (2010) also have developed a system of web-based applications that support ongoing monitoring. In an evaluation of the psychometric quality of the IGDIs, Greenwood and Walker (2010) reported strong evidence of interobserver agreement and split-half reliability, and moderate to strong evidence of alternate form reliability. Concurrent validity (i.e., correlations with other measures) ranged from high to moderate, and social validity (i.e., evaluation by consumers) was very strong.

Another potentially useful assessment resource is an assessment system identified as the CIRCLE: Phonological Awareness, Language, and Literacy System (C-PALLS) (see Chapter 10 in this volume; see also Landry, Anthony, Swank, &

Monseque-Bailey, 2009). C-PALLS assesses phonological awareness, letter knowledge, and language and is very quick to administer. Personal digital assistant devices have been used to enter child data and to provide feedback on child performance to the teacher. Also, a math screener has recently been added to this assessment (Guttentag, n.d.). Landry et al. (2009) described a study of a previous version of the C-PALLS documenting test–retest reliability, internal consistency, and concurrent validity.

These two assessment systems are the best available tools, to date, for RTI-EC, and although much work has been devoted to their development, little has been published on the psychometric evidence itself (i.e., information is reported secondarily from conference presentations and technical manuals). In addition, neither assessment system has evidence published of sensitivity or specificity, although Landry et al. (2009) did report anecdotally that C-PALLS has been shown to be sensitive to individual differences in rates of growth.

Instructional Component Tiers

The assessment approaches just described represent one feature of an RTI-EC model. Other components of an RTI-EC approach include curricula or other quality features of a general early childhood classroom environment (i.e., Tier 1), along with more intensive forms of instruction or interventions that may be applied for a smaller group of children who may not be benefiting from the general curricula and practices provided (i.e., Tier 2 approaches). Children who are not making progress in the Tier 2 instruction may then receive more intensive, individualized intervention or instruction (i.e., Tier 3). In this section, we provide examples of curricula or instructional approaches at each tier in order to highlight the research (or lack thereof for commonly used practices) used as evidence for efficacy. These sections are not designed as definitive or exhaustive reviews of the literature.

Tier 1 Curricula that are geared toward Tier 1 of the RTI-EC models should be composed of broad concepts, skills, and developmental milestones that are set as standards for all children. The assumption is that these curricula will have positive developmental or learning effects for most children in an early childhood program. *Creative Curriculum* (Dodge, Colker, Heroman, 2002) and *High Scope* (Hohmann & Wiekart, 2002) are two examples of broad curricula that are often used, but little evidence exists from randomized or quasi-experimental efficacy studies that show strong support for these curricula (see the Preschool Curriculum Evaluation Research Consortium, 2008a).

In the absence of clearly documented, efficacious curriculum models in early childhood, program providers may opt for curricula that focus on specific domains. *Literacy Express* (Lonigan, Clancy-Menchetti, Phillips, McDowell, & Farver, 2005) is an example of a curriculum that is designed for use at the Tier 1 level to increase children's language and literacy skills, and three studies (Farver, Lonigan, & Eppe, 2009; Lonigan, Farver, Clancy-Menchetti, & Phillips, 2005; Preschool Curriculum Evaluation Research Consortium, 2008b) have used RCT methodology to examine the efficacy of this curriculum. For the mathematics domain, *Building Blocks— SRA Real Math, Grade PreK* (Clements & Sarama, 2007) and *Big Math for Little Kids* (Ginsburg, Greenes, & Balfanz, 2003) are two examples of math curricula that are developed to help preschool children learn mathematical concepts. Several studies used cluster-randomized design and curriculum-based assessments to attest to the effectiveness of the *Building Blocks* program (Clements & Sarama, 2007; Clements, Sarama, Spitler, Lange, & Wolfe, 2011). Pilot research and field tests indicated that *Big Math for Little Kids* is effective for lower socioeconomic status (SES) children, and indeed for children from all social backgrounds, helping them to achieve high levels of mathematics learning (Ertle, Ginsburg, & Lewis, 2006). For social-emotional development and behavior, the Dinosaur School feature of the *Incredible Years* program (Webster-Stratton, 2000) has a preschool prevention model that is well suited for Tier 1. Two CRCT group evaluations of the child training series indicated significant increases in children's appropriate cognitive problem-solving strategies and more prosocial conflict management strategies with peers, increased social competence and appropriate play skills, and reduced conduct problems at home and school (Webster-Stratton, Reid, & Stoolmiller, 2008).

It is important to note that using domain-specific curricula requires program providers to make a choice about the domains that are most important for the children in their programs. It should be acknowledged that it is a challenge to implement several domain-specific curricula effectively. Conversely, implementing a broad developmental curriculum that has little or no evidence of efficacy would be inconsistent with an evidence-based approach to RTI-EC. To address this issue, curriculum developers have attempted to develop "integrated" curricula that address more than one domain in their curriculum model. The Head Start REDI Program incorporated early literacy and social-emotional content in their curriculum model and found significant effects in a CRCT for children enrolled in Head Start programs in Pennsylvania (Bierman et al., 2008). Working with early childhood programs in Philadelphia, Fantuzzo, Gadsden, and McDermott (2011) integrated literacy, math, science, and social-emotional content in the Evidence-Based Program for Integrated Curricula (EPIC) curriculum, employed a CRCT research design, and found significant positive effects for children in the EPIC group. Although these curricula have shown positive effects for some child outcomes in large CRCTs, there have only been single studies documenting their efficacy and little information about replication.

Tier 2   Tier 2 focuses on children who are not making progress in Tier 1, and the instructional strategies aim to increase opportunities for children to respond in small-group instructions. Tier 2 may include planned, teacher-directed activities that are designed to provide a stronger focus on the skills taught in Tier 1 (Gettinger & Stoiber, 2008). For example, Justice, Chow, Capellini, Flanigan, and Colton (2003) used structured teaching activities to target the emergent literacy skills of children who demonstrated multiple risk factors for reading achievement. Results showed a significant increase in children's scores on emergent literacy skills following the intervention. Koutsoftas, Harmon, and Gray (2009) implemented Tier 2 type instruction that was based on Tier 1 scope and sequence to increase the phonemic awareness skills of low-income preschoolers who were already receiving quality Tier 1 instruction. Results show that this intervention was successful at improving children's phonemic awareness skills.

The *Pre-K Mathematics Curriculum* (Klein, Starkey, & Ramirez, 2002) is a math curriculum that teachers could potentially use as a Tier 2 intervention. The curriculum includes 29 small-group preschool classroom activities employing manipulatives and 18 home activities for parents to use with their children. The content of the program involves number and operations, space, geometry, pattern, measurement and data, and logical reasoning. Evaluation research employing cluster-randomized design and curriculum-based assessments showed impressive gains for low-SES children in the treatment group (Clements & Sarama, 2006). A second example of a potential Tier 2 approach is a more naturalistic intervention approach developed by Arnold, Fisher, Doctoroff, and Dobbs (2002). They examined a process in which teachers incorporated math concepts into natural routines and activities occurring across the day in Head Start classes and found positive effects in an RCT efficacy study.

In the area of social-emotional development and social competence, one Tier 2 type approach is the use of social integration playgroups (Frea, Craig, Odom, & Williams, 1999; Jenkins, Odom, & Speltz, 1989), in which children with limited social and play skills and/or who are socially isolated participate in organized, small-group structured play activities, with support from the teacher. The application of incidental teaching and naturalistic interventions to promoting social competence and increased social interactions has also been discussed as a Tier 2 type approach (Brown, Odom, McConnell, & Rathel, 2008), but to date there have been few empirical demonstrations of the effects of this technique. Also, several authors have conducted social skills training for groups of preschool children (Guglielmo & Tryon, 2001; Odom et al., 1999).

It is important to acknowledge that we describe a range of strategies that would apply at Tier 2 (i.e., elaboration of Tier 1, domain-specific activities through small-group instruction, application of naturalistic interventions that embed learning opportunities for Tier 2 children in routines and activities), which follow the common theme of providing more intense, but not the most intense, additional instruction for children initially identified through universal screening. These interventions have not been evaluated within an RTI model, but rather are given as examples of intervention approaches that could potentially fill that role. Currently investigators with Recognition & Response (R&R) and the Center for Response to Intervention in Early Childhood (CRTIEC) are directly examining Tier 2 interventions within the RTI-EC context. Also, for many potential Tier 2 interventions only single case design studies have been reported and/or conducted by a single group of investigators, so replication is limited. This would place them below the criterion level that many organizations follow for classifying intervention or instructional approaches as EBPs, making this a fertile area for future research.

Tier 3 Within Tier 3, the content focuses on foundational skills and/or prerequisite skills that are tied to a common expectation or standard (i.e., tied to Tier 1 scope). For academic content areas such as early literacy and math skills, individual or very small ($n = 2$) instructional programs may focus on specific skills development. For example, in Dutch preschool programs for children from low-income families, Kegel and Buss (2012) described an individual instructional program that included a web-based literacy feature and verbal feedback on children's performance from a computer tutor and documented positive effects on decoding skills in an RCT. There have been few other reports of individualized, Tier 3 early math interventions.

Tier 3 interventions to promote social skills and address challenging behavior have frequently appeared in the literature. Peer-mediated approaches, which have various names such as "peer buddies," have included instruction for typically developing peers to engage individual children with social competence needs in peer interactions, which provides opportunities for the "target child" to acquire and practice social skills. Evidence for peer-mediated intervention has come from group (Odom et al., 1999) and single case design research (Owen-DeSchryer, Carr, Cale, & Blakeley-Smith, 2008). For children who have persistent and severely challenging behavior and do not respond to the typical preventive practices, interventions that are based on functional behavior assessment information and that incorporate specific behavior modification techniques are associated with reduction in challenging behaviors (Duda, Dunlap, Fox, Lentini, & Clarke, 2004).

Using research-based scaffolding strategies such as response prompting, modeling, peer supports, and corrective feedback is another Tier 3 approach that has been conceptualized within the early childhood RTI model (see Buysse et al., this volume). This approach allows teachers to individualize instruction and provide intensive support within various classroom settings to those who need it, without working one-on-one with the children. Although this approach within RTI-EC is fairly new, the effectiveness of using these types of scaffolding strategies with children who have developmental delays is well documented in the research literature (e.g., Craig-Unkefer & Kaiser, 2002; Ross & Greer, 2003).

Comprehensive Models

Although comprehensive models of RTI-EC are beginning to emerge, this area is so early in its development that no models could be called efficacious, based on most common criteria of evidence-based practice or efficacious treatment. However, examination of several tiered models, in anticipation of the efficacy studies that will be conducted, may be useful for highlighting the features of the models that could contribute to efficacious models that will doubtless be validated in the future.

Recognition & Response The R&R model has focused primarily on literacy and, currently, math skills. It includes clearly articulated procedures for universal screening and progress monitoring, specifies that a high-quality core curriculum be implemented at Tier 1, small-group instruction in Tier 2 for children who are low performers in the core curriculum, and individualized intensive scaffolding in Tier 3 for children whose low performance persists despite small-group instruction (Buysse & Peisner-Feinberg, 2010). Results from two unpublished quasi-experimental pilot studies provided evidence of the feasibility of implementation and the usability of this model (see Chapter 5). To date, CRCT or single case design efficacy studies have not been conducted for the model to guide its use and determine its efficacy.

Pyramid Model The Pyramid Model approach is designed to promote social-emotional development and reduce challenging behaviors of young children. Two national technical assistance centers, the Center on the Social and Emotional Foundations for Early Learning (CSEFEL) and the Technical Assistance

Center on Social Emotional Intervention for Young Children (TACSEI), employ the Pyramid Model. The Pyramid Model approach has many of the characteristics of RTI-EC in that it is a tiered approach with high-quality general classroom practices at its base and a progressive degree of support for children with social competence and behavioral challenges (Fox & Hemmeter, 2009). The developers have designed an implementation measure that assesses the degree to which programs or professionals adopt and implement the model (i.e., the Teaching Pyramid Observational Tool [TPOT; Hemmeter, Fox, & Snyder, 2008]), and the authors appear to be building reliability and validity evidence for the measure (Hemmeter & Fox, 2008).

The Pyramid Model approach differs from other RTI-EC conceptualizations in that there are no standard screening or progress monitoring measures. For children who exhibit the most severe behavioral challenges and who would benefit from Tier 3 types of intensive intervention, service providers develop individualized data collection systems based on functional assessment and individual child behaviors. Although positive effects have been reported by programs in which the model was adopted (Fox, Jack, & Broyles, 2005), the project has not yet conducted single case design or CRCT efficacy studies of the entire model.

Building Blocks   The Building Blocks program (see Chapter 7 in this volume; Sandall & Schwartz, 2008) is also a tiered approach to supporting young children with disabilities in inclusive settings. The current model could be seen as a precursor for emerging RTI-EC models in that it has some common elements but is missing others. The progressively more intense tiers of the model move from the provision of a high-quality early childhood curriculum to classroom modification to accommodate children's needs and increase participation, embedded learning opportunities focusing on individual skills, and child-focused instructional strategies, also focusing on individual child skills. The Building Blocks model does not have a standard screening or progress monitoring measure nor a measure of implementation. To date, the authors of *Building Blocks* have not published studies examining efficacy.

Evidence-Based Comprehensive Response to Intervention in Early Childhood Models: What It Will Take

The three examples of comprehensive tiered models reflect well the current state of development of the field. The models are comprehensive in that they have a conceptual framework in which provision of high-quality early childhood environments represents the foundation, and they build progressively through secondary and tertiary intervention strategies based on individual child needs. Individually, they contain features that will be essential for future implementation and evaluation of the models, such as screening and progress monitoring tools (e.g., the C-PALLS used by R&R), reliable fidelity/implementation measurements (e.g., the TPOT), and procedural manualization widely available to the field (e.g., IGDIs, *Building Blocks*). It is important to note that none of these models contain all of the necessary features of RTI, at least in their published descriptions of the models. As the work on RTI-EC extends across future years and into efficacy and effectiveness trials, incorporating these necessary features will be essential.

CONCLUSION

The application of RTI to early childhood programs is at an early stage of development. Originating in school programs for older children, the application of the RTI concept has required adjustment, modification, and procedural development, as reflected by the chapters in this book. The scientific basis that will establish RTI as a viable and effective approach for young children is emerging. For each of the tiered levels and also for the assessment processes that tie these levels of service together into a system of care, there are curricula, interventions, and assessments that have varying levels of scientific evidence that would support their use. Importantly, active and well-supported work to continue building efficacy at the component level is ongoing (e.g., CRTIEC). Also, comprehensive models of RTI-EC have been developed and utilized broadly in some cases, and they individually have features that will be important for future efficacy evaluations.

Given the current state of the practice, should one be concerned that RTI-EC has become such a pervasive movement within the field of early childhood special education and early childhood education when the models for practices fall short of most agreed-upon criteria for evidence-based practice? That is, few of the RTI-EC components and none of the comprehensive models would meet the criteria that the Cochrane Collaboration or the WWC have established for evidence-based programs. In their description of evidence-based medicine, Sackett et al. stated, "if no randomized trial has been carried out for our patients' predicament, we must follow the trail to the next best external evidence and work from there" (1996, p. 72). Adhering to these words of wisdom, district policy makers, service providers, and families cannot wait for the science to catch up to the need, but instead must move with the best evidence available. That does, however, place a great imperative on teachers and other practitioners to evaluate carefully the outcomes for individual children and for program providers to evaluate the impact of their program on the broad array of their constituents.

REFERENCES

American Educational Research Association. (1999). *The standards for educational and psychological testing.* Washington, DC: Author.

Arnold, D.H., Fisher, P., Doctoroff, G., & Dobbs, J. (2002). Accelerating math development in Head Start classrooms: Outcomes and gender differences. *Journal of Educational Psychology, 94,* 762–770. doi:10.1037/0022-0663.94.4.762

Bierman, K.L., Domitrovich, C.E., Nix, R.L., Gest, S.D., Welsh, J.A., Greenberg, M.T., . . . Sukhdeep, G. (2008). Promoting academic and social-emotional school readiness: The Head Start REDI Program. *Child Development, 79*(6), 1802–1817. doi:10.1111%2Fj.1467-8624.2008.01227.x

Brown, W.H., Odom, S.L., McConnell, S.R., & Rathel, J.M. (2008). Peer interaction interventions for preschool children with developmental difficulties. In W. Brown, S. Odom, & S. McConnell (Eds.), *Social competence of young children: Risk, disability, and intervention* (pp. 141–166). Baltimore, MD: Paul H. Brookes Publishing Co.

Buysse, V., & Peisner-Feinberg, E. (2010). Recognition & Response: Response to intervention for pre-K. *Young Exceptional Children, 13*(4), 2–13. doi:10.1177/1096250610373586

Buysse, V., & Wesley, P.W. (2006). Evidence-based practice: How did it emerge and what does it really mean for the early childhood field? In V. Buysse & P. Wesley (Eds.), *Evidence-based practice in the early childhood field* (pp. 1–34). Washington DC: ZERO TO THREE.

Buzhardt, J., & Walker, D. (2010). General guidelines for IGDI training and certification. In J. Carta, C. Greenwood, D. Walker, & J. Buzhart, J., *Using IGDIs: Monitoring progress and improving intervention for infants and young children* (pp. 145–158). Baltimore, MD: Paul H. Brookes Publishing Co.

Caplan, G., & Grunebaum, H. (1967). Perspectives on primary prevention. *Archives of General Psychiatry, 17,* 331–346.

Carnine, D. (1999). Perspective: Campaigns for moving research into practice. *Remedial and special education, 20*(1), 2–6. doi:10.1177/074193259902000101

Carta, J., Greenwood, C., Walker, D., & Buzhardt, J. (2010). *Using IGDIs: Monitoring progress and improving intervention for infants and young children.* Baltimore, MD: Paul H. Brookes Publishing Co.

Chambless, D.L., Sanderson, W.C., Shoham, V., Bennett Johnson, S., Pope, K.S., Crits-Christoph, . . . McCurry, S. (1996). An update on empirically validated therapies. *Clinical Psychologist, 49,* 5–18.

Clements, D.H., & Sarama, J. (2006, June). *Scaling up the implementation of a pre-kindergarten mathematics curriculum: The Building Blocks curriculum.* Paper presented at the Institute of Education Sciences Research Conference, Washington, DC.

Clements, D.H., & Sarama, J. (2007). *Building Blocks—SRA real math teacher's edition, Grade PreK.* Columbus, OH: SRA/McGraw-Hill.

Clements, D.H., Sarama, J., Spitler, M.E., Lange, A.A., & Wolfe, C.B. (2011). Mathematics learned by young children in an intervention based on learning trajectories: A large-scale cluster randomized trial. *Journal for Research in Mathematics Education, 42*(2), 127–166.

Coleman, M.R., Roth, F.P., & West, T. (Eds.). (2009). *Roadmap to Pre-K RTI: Applying responses to intervention in preschool settings.* New York, NY: National Center for Learning Disabilities. Retrieved from http://www.ncld.org/images/stories/OnCapitolHill/PolicyRelated Publications/RoadmaptoPreKRTI/RoadmaptoPrekRTI.pdf

Craig-Unkefer, L.A., & Kaiser, A.P. (2002). Improving the social communication skills of at-risk preschool children in play context. *Topics in Early Childhood Special Education, 22,* 3–13. doi:10.1177/027112140202200101

Davies, P. (2002). What is evidence-based education? *British Journal of Education Studies, 47,* 108–121. doi:10.1111/1467-8527.00106

Dodge, D.T., Colker, L.J., & Heroman, C. (2002). *The Creative Curriculum for Preschool* (4th ed.). Washington, DC: Teaching Strategies.

Duda, M.A., Dunlap, G., Fox, L., Lentini, R., & Clarke, S. (2004). An experimental evaluation of positive behavior support in a community preschool program. *Topics in Early Childhood Special Education, 24,* 143–155. doi:10.1177/02711214040240030201

Education Sciences Reform Act of 2002, PL 107-279, 20 U.S.C. §§ 9501 *et seq.*

Ertle, B., Ginsburg, H., & Lewis, A. (2006). *Measuring the efficacy of* Big Math for Little Kids*: A look at fidelity of implementation.* Paper presented at the annual meeting of the American Educational Research Association, San Francisco, CA, April 9, 2006.

Evidence-based Medicine Working Group. (1992). Evidence-based medicine. *Journal of the American Medical Association, 268,* 2420–2425.

Fantuzzo, J.W., Gadsden, V.L., & McDermott, P.A. (2011). An integrated curriculum to improve mathematics, language, and literacy for Head Start children. *American Educational Research Journal, 48,* 763–794. doi:10.3102%2F000283121038544

Farver, J.M., Lonigan, C.J., & Eppe, S. (2009). Effective early literacy skill development for young Spanish-speaking English language learners: An experimental study of two methods. *Child Development, 80*(3), 703–719. doi:10.1111/j.1467-8624.2009.01292.x

Fox, L., & Hemmeter, M.L. (2009). A program-wide model for supporting social-emotional development and addressing challenging behavior in early childhood settings. In W. Sailor, G. Dunlap, G. Sugai, & R. Horner (Eds.), *Handbook of positive behavior support* (pp. 177–202). New York, NY: Springer.

Fox, L., Jack, S., & Broyles, L. (2005). *Program-wide positive behavior support: Supporting young children's social-emotional development and addressing challenging behavior.* Tampa: University of South Florida, Louis de la Parte Florida Mental Health Institute.

Franklin, A. (1993). The epistemology of experiment. In D. Gooding, T. Pinch, & S. Schaffer (Eds.), *The uses of experiment: Studies in the natural sciences* (pp. 437–460). Cambridge, United Kingdom: Cambridge University Press.

Frea, W., Craig, L., Odom, S.L., & Williams, D. (1999). Differentiated effects of structured social integration and group friendship activities for promoting social interactions. *Journal of Early Intervention, 22,* 230–243.

Gersten, R., Beckmann, S., Clarke, B., Foegen, A., Marsh, L., Star, J.R., & Witzel, B. (2009). *Assisting students struggling with mathematics: Response to intervention (RTI) for elementary and middle schools* (NCEE 2009-4060). Washington, DC: National Center for Education Evaluation and Regional Assistance, Institute of Education Sciences, U.S. Department of Education. Retrieved from http://ies.ed.gov/ncee/wwc/publications/practiceguides

Gersten, R., Compton, D.L., Connor, C.M., Dimino, J., Santoro, L., Linan-Thompson, S., & Tilly, W.D. (2008). *Assisting students struggling with reading: Response to intervention and multi-tier intervention for reading in the primary grades. A practice guide* (NCEE 2009-4045). Washington, DC: National Center for Education Evaluation and Regional Assistance, Institute of Education Sciences, U.S. Department of Education. Retrieved from http://ies.ed.gov/ncee/wwc/publications/practiceguides

Gettinger, M., & Stoiber, K.C. (2008). Applying a response-to-intervention model for early literacy development in low-income children. *Topics in Early Childhood Special Education, 27,* 198–213. doi:10.1177/0271121407311238

Ginsburg, H.P., Greenes, C., & Balfanz, R. (2003). *Big math for little kids.* Parsippany, NJ: Dale Seymour Publications.

Greenwood, C.R., & Abbott, M. (2001). The research to practice gap in special education. *Teacher Education and Special Education, 24,* 276–289. doi:10.1177/088840640102400403

Greenwood, C.R., Bradfield, R., Kaminski, R., Linas, M., Carta, J.J., & Nylander, D. (2011). The response to intervention (RTI) approach in early childhood. *Focus on Exceptional Children, 43*(9), 1–22.

Greenwood, C., & Walker, D. (2010). Development and validation of IGDIs. In J. Carta, C. Greenwood, D. Walker, & J. Buzhart, *Using IGDIs: Monitoring progress and improving intervention for infants and young children* (pp. 145–158). Baltimore, MD: Paul H. Brookes Publishing Co.

Guglielmo, H.M., & Tryon, G.S. (2001). Social skill training in an integrated preschool program. *School Psychology Quarterly, 16*(2), 158–175. doi:10.1521/scpq.16.2.158.18701

Guttentag, C. (n.d.). Progress monitoring: A conversation with Dr. Susan Landry and Dr. Mike Assel. *A Closer Look: Research in Action.* Retrieved from http://www.childrenslearning institute.org/our-programs/program-overview/TX-school-ready/newsletter/documents/09Oct-CG.pdf

Hemmeter, M.L., & Fox, L. (2008). *Teaching Pyramid Observational Tool for Preschool Classrooms, Research Edition.* Nashville, TN: Center on the Social and Emotional Foundations for Early Learning.

Hemmeter, M.L., Fox, L., & Snyder, P. (2008). *Teaching Pyramid Observation Tool.* Unpublished assessment instrument.

Hohmann, M., & Wiekart, D.P. (2002). *Educating young children: Active learning practices for preschool and child care programs* (2nd ed.) Ypsilanti, MI: High/Scope Press.

Jenkins, J.R., Odom, S.L., & Speltz, M.L. (1989). Effects of integration and structured play on the development of handicapped children. *Exceptional Children, 55,* 420–428.

Justice, L.M., Chow, S.M., Capellini, C., Flanigan, K., & Colton, S. (2003). Emergent literacy intervention for vulnerable preschoolers: Relative effects of two approaches. *American Journal of Speech-Language Pathology, 12,* 320–332. doi:10.1044/1058-0360(2003/078)

Kegel, C.A., & Buss, A.G. (2012). Online tutoring as a pivotal quality of web-based early literacy programs. *Journal of Educational Psychology, 104,* 182–192. doi:10.1037/a0025849

Klein, A., Starkey, P., & Ramirez, A.B. (2002). *Pre-K mathematics curriculum.* Glenview, IL: Scott Foresman.

Koutsoftas, A., Harmon, M., & Gray, S. (2009). The effects of tier 2 intervention for phonemic awareness in a response-to-intervention model in low-income preschool classrooms. *Language, Speech, and Hearing Services in Schools, 40,* 116–130. doi:10.1044/0161-1461(2008/07-0101)

Landry, S.H., Anthony, J.L., Swank, P.R., & Monseque-Bailey, P. (2009). Effectiveness of comprehensive professional development for teachers of at-risk preschoolers. *Journal of Educational Psychology, 101*(2), 438–465.

Lonigan, C.J., Clancy-Menchetti, J., Phillips, B.M., McDowell, K., & Farver, J.M. (2005). *Literacy express: A preschool curriculum.* Tallahassee, FL: Literacy Express.

Lonigan, C.J., Farver, J.M., Clancy-Menchetti, J., & Phillips, B.M. (2005, April). *Promoting the development of preschool children's emergent literacy skills: A randomized evaluation of a literacy-focused curriculum and two professional development models.* Paper presented at the biennial meeting of the Society for Research in Child Development, Atlanta, GA.

Meisels, S.J., & Atkins-Burnett, S. (2005). *Developmental screening in early childhood: A guide* (5th ed.). Washington, DC: National Association for the Education of Young Children.

National Professional Development Center on Inclusion. (2012). *Response to intervention (RTI) in early childhood: Building consensus on the defining features.* Chapel Hill: The University of North Carolina, Frank Porter Graham Child Development Institute.

No Child Left Behind Act of 2001, PL 107-110, 115 Stat. 1425, 20 U.S.C. §§ 6301 *et seq.*

Odom, S.L., Brantlinger, E., Gersten, R., Horner, R.D., Thompson, B., & Harris, K. (2004). *Quality indicators for research in special education and guidelines for evidence-based practices: Executive summary.* Arlington, VA: Council for Exceptional Children Division for Research.

Odom, S.L., Brantlinger, E., Gersten, R., Horner, R., Thompson, B., & Harris, K. (2005). Research in special education: Scientific methods and evidence-based practices. *Exceptional Children, 71,* 137–148.

Odom, S.L., McConnell, S.R., McEvoy, M.A., Peterson, C., Ostrosky, M., Chandler, L.K., . . . Favazza, P. C. (1999). Relative effects of interventions for supporting the social competence of young children with disabilities. *Topics in Early Childhood Special Education, 19,* 75–91. doi:10.1177/027112149901900202

Owen-DeSchryer, J.S., Carr, E.G., Cale, S.I., & Blakeley-Smith, A. (2008). Promoting social interactions between students with autism spectrum disorders and their peers in inclusive school settings. *Focus on Autism and Other Developmental Disabilities, 23*(1), 15–28. doi:10.1177/1088357608314370

Preschool Curriculum Evaluation Research Consortium. (2008a). *Effects of preschool curriculum programs on school readiness* (NCER 2008-2009). Washington, DC: National Center for Education Research, Institute of Education Sciences, U.S. Department of Education. Washington, DC: U.S. Government Printing Office.

Preschool Curriculum Evaluation Research Consortium. (2008b). *Literacy Express* and *DLM Early Childhood Express* supplemented with *Open Court Reading Pre-K*: Florida State University. In *Effects of preschool curriculum programs on school readiness* (pp. 117–130). Washington, DC: U.S. Department of Education, Institute of Education Sciences, National Center for Education Research.

Ross, D.E., & Greer, R.D. (2003). Generalized imitation and the mand: Inducing first instances of speech in young children with autism. *Research in Developmental Disabilities, 24,* 58–74.

Sackett, D., Rosenberg, W.M., Gray, J.M., Haynes, R.B., & Richardson, W.S. (1996). Evidence-based medicine: What it is and what it isn't. *British Medical Journal, 312,* 71–72. doi:10.1136/bmj.312.7023.71

Sandall, S.R., & Schwartz, I.S. (2008). *Building blocks for teaching preschoolers with special needs* (2nd ed.). Baltimore, MD: Paul H. Brookes Publishing Co.

Shavelson, R.J., & Towne, L. (Eds.). (2002). *Scientific research in education.* Washington, DC: National Academy Press.

VanDerHeyden, A.M., & Snyder, P. (2006). Integrating frameworks from early childhood intervention and school psychology to accelerate growth for all young children. *School Psychology Review, 35*(4), 519–534.

Webster-Stratton, C. (1990). *Dina dinosaur social skills and problem-solving curriculum.* Seattle, WA: Incredible Years.

Webster-Stratton, C. (2000, June). The incredible years training series. *Juvenile Justice Bulletin,* 1–23.

Webster-Stratton, C., Reid, M.J., & Stoolmiller, M. (2008). Preventing conduct problems and improving school readiness: Evaluation of the Incredible Years Teacher and Child Training Programs in high-risk schools. *Journal of Child Psychology and Psychiatry, 49,* 471–488.

29

Building Consensus on the Defining Features of Response to Intervention in Early Childhood

Heidi Hollingsworth and Camille Catlett

Despite the evolutionary nature of evidence related to response to intervention (RTI) in early childhood, programs are making decisions every day about how to move forward. To offer a framework for thinking about RTI in early childhood, the National Professional Development Center on Inclusion (NPDCI) produced a concept paper to articulate important considerations for early care and education programs that choose to implement RTI. An important aspect of developing the concept paper was gathering input from a wide array of consumers within the fields of early education and intervention (e.g., teachers, practitioners, faculty and professional development providers, administrators, specialists, researchers, policy makers). This chapter describes the process for developing the concept paper. The concept paper itself, *Response to Intervention (RTI) in Early Childhood: Building Consensus on the Defining Features* (NPDCI, 2012a), is provided at the conclusion of the chapter.

NEED FOR GUIDANCE ON RESPONSE TO INTERVENTION

RTI is an approach that is increasingly being used to ensure student success in K–12 education by improving the quality of instructional practices for all children and providing additional instruction and supports for some children. Current provisions within the Individuals with Disabilities Education Improvement Act (IDEA) of 2004 (PL 108-446) address the use of RTI for school-age children, particularly for children in kindergarten through third grade. Furthermore, there is research evidence supporting the effectiveness of RTI for school-age children, particularly in the areas of targeted reading and math interventions. The use of RTI practices *prior* to kindergarten (particularly in programs for 3- to 5-year-olds) has generated widespread interest in the early childhood field, and a number of programs throughout the United States have begun to implement RTI for 3- to 5-year-old children. However, a lack of familiarity with and understanding of RTI, along with a lack of federal policies and research evidence on RTI in early childhood, has led to a number of questions about its use with young children. There are no specific provisions within IDEA or any other federal legislation addressing RTI for children in prekindergarten (pre-K), child care, and early intervention, and only general references to the concept of early intervening within Head Start legislation. There is little consensus in the early childhood field about how RTI is defined and what constitutes recommended practice related to RTI for this age group. Thus, there is a need for reliable information on RTI and for common language about and understanding of key features of early childhood RTI. Both are needed to guide the implementation of RTI, to provide effective professional development on RTI, and to design policies that will support RTI with young children.

In response to these needs, NPDCI led a multifaceted effort to develop guidance for the field on RTI in early childhood. This work involved input and feedback from multiple sectors and colleagues, including a panel of national experts, a work group of representatives from three national professional organizations—the Division for Early Childhood (DEC) of the Council for Exceptional Children, the National Association for the Education of Young Children (NAEYC), and the National Head Start Association (NHSA)—and a series of listening sessions at national conferences. One of the goals of this process was to utilize knowledge mobilization approaches (e.g., electronic discussion platforms) to make the process of developing and refining guidance for the field transparent and participatory.

THE DEVELOPMENT PROCESS

The process of developing and refining *Response to Intervention (RTI) in Early Childhood: Building Consensus on the Defining Features* incorporated multiple rounds of input, feedback, review, and revision involving conference attendees, national experts, and work groups. Web-based platforms were utilized in multiple steps of this process. Table 29.1 outlines the steps used to develop and validate the concept paper. Details are provided in the following sections.

Seeking Input from the Field Through Listening Sessions

Between December 2009 and November 2010, seven listening sessions at national conferences and one online webinar were conducted. Dates and locations of the listening sessions are provided in Table 29.2. The purpose of these listening sessions was to obtain input on key issues related to RTI in early childhood from stakeholder groups and to use this input to inform the development of guidance for the field. Participants from 44 states, the District of Columbia, and Puerto Rico representing a variety of disciplines, professional roles, and organizational affiliations attended the listening sessions. Facilitators posed similar questions at each session (e.g., How much is RTI occurring in your state, community, or program? What do you think are the key features of an early childhood RTI system? What do you already have in place to implement RTI effectively in your state, community, or program? What do you think is still needed to implement RTI effectively? What do you think is important to include in guidance on RTI in early childhood?). Notes were taken at each session to provide a record of attendees' input, and these notes were later summarized and organized around key themes (summary available at http://npdci.fpg.unc.edu/resources/rti-summary-listening-sessions).

Table 29.1. Time line and activities for development of concept paper on RTI in early childhood

Time line	Activities
Fall 2009	• NPDCI established a plan for developing national guidance on RTI in early childhood • NPDCI began to seek input from the field in listening sessions at national conferences; listening sessions continued throughout the following year
Spring 2010	• Existing source materials on RTI in early childhood were gathered • 12 national experts were identified
Summer 2010	• National experts convened to identify key issues and additional source material for developing guidance on RTI in early childhood • A work group of 12 members was established with representatives of DEC, NAEYC, and NHSA
Fall 2010	• Work group members convened to provide input on key issues related to RTI in early childhood
Spring 2011	• NPDCI generated a first draft of guidance, using relevant sources and results from summaries of the listening sessions, national expert meeting, and work group meeting • National experts and work group members reviewed the draft and provided written feedback via electronic platform on a web site provided by NPDCI • NPDCI generated a second draft, incorporating feedback and providing a table delineating changes • National experts and work group members reviewed the revised draft and provided written feedback via electronic platform on a web site provided by NPDCI
Summer 2011	• NPDCI generated a final version of the concept paper providing guidance on RTI in early childhood
Fall 2011	• NPDCI prepared the concept paper for release and distribution

Key: DEC, Division for Early Childhood; NAEYC, National Association for the Education of Young Children; NHSA, National Head Start Association; NPDCI, National Professional Development Center on Inclusion; RTI, response to intervention.

Table 29.2. Listening sessions

Date	Conference
December 8, 2009	OSEP National Early Childhood Conference, Washington, DC
May 6, 2010	NHSA Annual Conference, Dallas, TX
May 18-19, 2010	National Inclusion Institute, Chapel Hill, NC
June 6-9, 2010	NAEYC National Institute for Early Childhood Professional Development, Phoenix, AZ
July 19-21, 2010	OSEP Project Directors' Conference, Washington, DC
October 14-17, 2010	DEC Annual Conference, Kansas City, MO
October 27, 2010	National Association of Early Childhood Specialists in State Departments of Education, *webinar*
November 3-6, 2010	NAEYC Annual Conference, Anaheim, CA

From National Professional Development Center on Inclusion. (2012b). *Summary from listening sessions.* Chapel Hill: University of North Carolina, Frank Porter Graham Child Development Institute; reprinted by permission.
Key: DEC, Division for Early Childhood; NAEYC, National Association for the Education of Young Children; NHSA, National Head Start Association; OSEP, Office of Special Education Programs.

The following four key themes emerged from these listening sessions:

- How much RTI is occurring across the country varies widely, but participants reported that many people in early childhood are talking about it, if not implementing it . . .

- Participants noted the need for a definition of RTI in early childhood that includes the key components of this approach . . .

- Participants mentioned some supports already in place for implementing RTI in early childhood as well as resources that are lacking in this regard . . .

- Participants stressed that guidance on RTI should offer specific guidelines about how to implement RTI, build on available resources, and improve the quality of programs (NPDCI, 2012b, p. 1)

Seeking Input from National Experts

In June 2010, 12 national experts were convened to identify key issues related to RTI in early childhood. Table 29.3 provides a list of the national experts. These experts represented diverse content expertise in areas such as early childhood program quality, curricula and instruction in academic learning and social-emotional development, assessment, culturally and linguistically diverse learners, and tiered models of instruction and intervention in pre-K and the early elementary grades. The discussion was documented and summarized around key themes that emerged (summary available at http://npdci.fpg.unc.edu/resources/rti-summary -national-expert-meeting). The following key themes informed the development of the concept paper:

- There was general consensus among the national experts on the need for national guidance on RTI in early childhood . . .

Table 29.3. National experts

Name	Affiliation
Sue Bredekamp	Consultant
Judith J. Carta	University of Kansas
Marijata Daniel-Echols	High Scope Educational Research Foundation
Douglas H. Clements	University at Buffalo
David K. Dickinson	Vanderbilt University
Linda M. Espinosa	University of Missouri, Columbia (retired)
Mary Louise Hemmeter	Vanderbilt University
Gail Joseph	University of Washington
Scott McConnell	University of Minnesota
Rollanda O'Connor	University of California, Riverside
Ellen Peisner-Feinberg	University of North Carolina at Chapel Hill
Carolyn Webster-Stratton	University of Washington

From National Professional Development Center on Inclusion. (2012c). *Summary from national expert meeting.* Chapel Hill: University of North Carolina, Frank Porter Graham Child Development Institute; reprinted by permission.

- National experts agreed on the need for a definition of RTI in early childhood that identifies key features of this approach . . .
- National experts agreed on the need to provide guidance on how RTI should be implemented in early childhood programs and contexts (NPDCI, 2012c, p. 1)

Seeking Input from Members of National Organizations

In November 2010, a daylong meeting of a work group comprising representatives of DEC, NAEYC, and NHSA was convened to obtain input on key issues related to RTI in early childhood. Work group members represented diverse perspectives, including faculty, early childhood teachers and administrators, parents, and state-level coordinators, and are listed in Table 29.4. As with the meeting of national experts, the discussion was documented and summarized (summary available at http://npdci.fpg.unc.edu/resources/rti-summary-decnaeycnhsa-work-group-meeting). The following key themes emerged from the work group meeting and informed the development of the concept paper:

- The topic of RTI was new for most work group members . . .
- Work group members nominated a variety of features that should define RTI in early childhood . . .

Table 29.4. Work group members

Name	Role (State)
DEC	
Bill Brown	Faculty (SC)
Samtra Devard	Parent, Hope Center Network for Families (DE)
Jim Lesko	619 Coordinator/State EC Administrator (DE)
Donna Nylander	Early Childhood Administrator (IL)
NAEYC	
Marica Cox	Administrator (DC)
Ida Rose Florez	Faculty (AZ)
Diane Tunis	Head Start Teacher (MD)
Bea Vargas	Early Childhood Administrator (TX)
NHSA	
Heather Brown	Parent, Community Action Program (NH)
Mary Ann Cornish	Head Start Director (VA)
Regina Harrell	Family and Community Services Director (NC)
Connie Robers	Head Start Director (WI)

From National Professional Development Center on Inclusion. (2012d). *Summary from the DEC/NAEYC/NHSA work group meeting.* Chapel Hill: University of North Carolina, Frank Porter Graham Child Development Institute; reprinted by permission.

Key: DEC, Division for Early Childhood; NAEYC, National Association for the Education of Young Children; NHSA, National Head Start Association.

- Work group members mentioned that some foundational elements for building an RTI approach are already in place in many early childhood programs, but these are overshadowed by the challenges of implementing this approach (NPDCI, 2012d, p. 2)

Developing and Refining the Initial Draft

NPDCI staff, national experts, and work group members were involved in the process of refining the initial draft of the guidance on RTI in early childhood. To begin with, NPDCI staff reviewed data from initial listening sessions and gathered relevant resources to inform the development of an initial draft. Such resources included publications and web sites on RTI for school-age children and for younger children, although fewer publications related to younger children exist. Next, NPDCI staff reviewed the summaries of key themes from the national expert meeting and the work group meeting. With information from all of these sources, NPDCI staff developed an initial draft providing guidance for the field on RTI in early childhood.

Review and Revision via Electronic Platform

The work of the national experts and work group members was conducted on a transactional platform (also known as a "landing pad") on the Web. The landing pad was a specific online location at which resources could be posted and a threaded conversation could occur for a specified period of time. Comments and opinions offered by national experts and work group members were visible only to the members of those groups and NPDCI staff. Members were provided with a Uniform Resource Locator (URL) for the web-based platform at which they could review drafts and respond to one another's comments. At the end of the specified comment period, NPDCI staff systematically reviewed all comments and engaged in a series of meetings to discuss the feedback and reach a consensus on revisions of the initial draft. Adjustments to the initial draft were made accordingly. The national experts and work group members were then provided with the revised draft, along with a summary table outlining how NPDCI staff had responded to each of the editorial suggestions made in feedback provided by national experts and work group members in response to the first draft.

The same process was repeated with the revised draft, with national experts and work group members again providing feedback on a web-based landing pad. This iterative process of review, feedback, and revision resulted in the concept paper *Response to Intervention (RTI) in Early Childhood: Building Consensus on the Defining Features.* The entire concept paper is provided on the pages that follow.

The concept paper offers recommendations for its use by families, practitioners, administrators, researchers, and policy makers to guide and inform future efforts related to RTI in early childhood. This concept paper could 1) help professionals and families to better understand RTI, 2) assist early childhood programs in thinking about important planning and decision-making processes prior to adopting RTI, 3) guide the provision of effective professional development on RTI, and 4) inform public policies designed to support RTI.

REFERENCES

Individuals with Disabilities Education Improvement Act (IDEA) of 2004, PL 108-446, 20 U.S.C. §§ 1400 *et seq.*

National Professional Development Center on Inclusion. (2012a). *Response to intervention (RTI) in early childhood: Building consensus on the defining features.* Chapel Hill: University of North Carolina, Frank Porter Graham Child Development Institute.

National Professional Development Center on Inclusion. (2012b). *Summary from listening sessions.* Chapel Hill: University of North Carolina, Frank Porter Graham Child Development Institute.

National Professional Development Center on Inclusion. (2012c). *Summary from national expert meeting.* Chapel Hill: University of North Carolina, Frank Porter Graham Child Development Institute.

National Professional Development Center on Inclusion. (2012d). *Summary from the DEC/NAEYC/NHSA work group meeting.* Chapel Hill: University of North Carolina, Frank Porter Graham Child Development Institute.

APPENDIX

Response to Intervention (RTI) in Early Childhood

Building Consensus on the Defining Features

BACKGROUND AND PURPOSE

Response to Intervention (RTI) is an approach that is gaining acceptance in kindergarten-Grade 12 in many schools throughout the U.S. RTI has a dual focus—improving the quality of instructional practices for all students, and as providing additional instructional and behavioral supports for some students to ensure that every student succeeds in school. Although there is not a single definition or agreed-upon way of implementing RTI, the key features of this approach generally involve gathering information on students' skills to help teachers plan and organize instruction, providing evidence-based interventions and supports, and monitoring student progress in learning. A growing body of research indicates that RTI is effective for addressing learning difficulties among school-age children, with strong evidence for the effectiveness of targeted reading and math interventions for this age group.[1,2]

In recent years, the use of RTI practices to support learning and development in children prior to kindergarten has generated widespread interest in the early childhood field. However, there is considerable variability in how familiar people are with this approach, ranging from individuals having little or no awareness or understanding about RTI to some programs beginning to implement this approach with three-to-five year-olds.[3] Furthermore, there is little research evidence at this time to guide the use of RTI with children prior to kindergarten. As a result, a number of questions about RTI in early care and education programs have emerged—what practices define RTI, who implements it, which children and families are affected, who benefits, and how does RTI fit within existing practices and services?[4]

In response to the critical need for reliable information on RTI, and with input from national experts and key stakeholders, the National Professional Development Center on Inclusion (NPDCI) created this concept paper on RTI in early childhood. This paper offers a framework for thinking about the meaning of RTI in early childhood. In addition, it outlines important considerations for early care and education programs that choose to adopt and implement RTI. Finally, it provides recommendations for how the concept paper can be used by families, practitioners, administrators, researchers, and policymakers to guide and inform future efforts related to RTI in early childhood.

RESPONSE TO INTERVENTION: A FRAMEWORK FOR LINKING ASSESSMENT WITH INSTRUCTION

RTI practices for school-age children are shaped by the following defining principles: (a) the use of formative assessment and learning standards to guide

From National Professional Development Center on Inclusion. (2012a). *Response to intervention (RTI) in early childhood: Building consensus on the defining features.* Chapel Hill: University of North Carolina, Frank Porter Graham Child Development Institute; reprinted by permission.

instructional decision-making, (b) the use of effective instruction as well as evidence-based interventions and supports that are matched to students' learning needs, (c) a focus on maximizing student achievement as well as preventing learning difficulties and behavior problems, and (d) an emphasis on collaboration and problem-solving to plan instruction and interventions and assess how well students respond to them.[5,6]

The principles that serve as the foundation for RTI are consistent with those widely acknowledged in early childhood. These include, for example, the emphasis on high quality curriculum and intentional teaching, the use of valid and reliable assessments aligned with early learning and program standards to make sound instructional decisions, the need for collaboration with families and professionals to guide decision-making, and the importance of intervening early with children who need additional instructional or behavioral supports.[7] RTI provides a comprehensive, systematic approach for instructional decision-making that complements and extends recommended practices in early childhood, for example, by helping practitioners use assessment to determine the intensity of interventions and supports that children need.

RTI is a framework that can be used in early childhood to help practitioners connect children's formative assessment results with specific teaching and intervention strategies. RTI is designed to improve instructional practices for all children and includes foundational instructional practices as well as the provision of additional supports for children with varying learning needs such as those with learning difficulties, challenging behaviors, disabilities, or who are dual language learners.

RTI: KEY COMPONENTS

The key components of an RTI approach in early childhood are: (a) formative assessment, (b) instruction and tiered interventions/supports, and (c) collaboration and data-based decision-making.

Formative assessment. Assessment within RTI is formative which means that information is gathered on children's behavior and skills and used to inform instructional decisions. To guide decisions regarding the effectiveness of instruction and children's responsiveness to interventions, formative assessment should reflect measurable and relevant learning goals for young children. Universal screening and progress monitoring are particular types of formative assessment used within RTI. Universal screening involves gathering information periodically on *all* children in a classroom or program to monitor their development and learning, and to determine whether *some* children might need additional interventions to acquire key skills in academic learning or behavior regulation. Progress monitoring is designed to gather additional information on the children who receive targeted interventions to determine their responsiveness to these interventions. Together, universal screening and progress monitoring represent one component of a comprehensive assessment plan which also should include developmental screening, diagnostic assessment, and program evaluation.[7]

Instruction and tiered interventions/supports. An effective core curriculum and intentional teaching are the foundation of instructional practices for RTI in

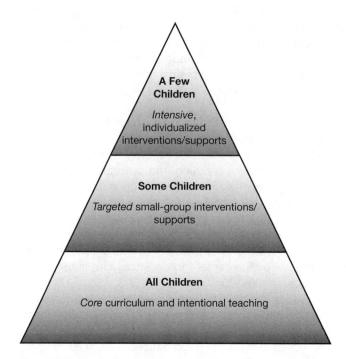

Figure 1. The Continuum of Instruction and Interventions/Supports within Response to Intervention in Early Childhood

early childhood. Intentional teaching means the purposeful organization of the early learning environment and developmentally appropriate learning activities within a comprehensive curriculum to help children develop and acquire important skills. In RTI, the concept of intentional teaching is expanded to include targeted interventions for some children who require additional academic or behavioral supports, generally provided through small-group instruction, embedded instruction/interventions, or individualized scaffolding. Instructional strategies and behavioral supports are arranged by tiers from least to most intensive to show the level of adult involvement needed to help individual children learn. The targeted interventions for some children provide instructional supports in addition to those provided to all children through the core curriculum and intentional teaching. Figure 1 shows the continuum of instruction, interventions, and supports within an RTI framework.[8] The figure is intended to show how educators can organize instruction, interventions, and supports within an RTI framework as opposed to labeling children or placing them in tiers.

Collaboration and data-based decision-making. RTI includes methods that practitioners can use to collaborate with families, specialists, and others to plan and organize learning and behavioral supports and to assess how well children are responding to them. Broader, system-level supports also are needed to support an RTI approach. These include ongoing professional development, methods for gathering and reporting assessment results, and strategies for documenting and sharing information with families and others.

CONSIDERATIONS FOR IMPLEMENTATION

Because RTI is a framework that involves a set of related instructional practices (e.g., formative assessment, instruction, and tiered interventions and supports), a number of decisions must be made to support its implementation in early care and education programs serving children prior to kindergarten. Many of these decisions will need to be made at the program-level with input from key stakeholders such as administrators, practitioners, and families. The following are important considerations for early childhood programs planning to adopt or implement RTI practices.

1. **Early care and education programs that choose to adopt RTI should engage in a strategic planning process prior to implementation.** Key considerations related to this activity include determining who will be involved in the planning effort and how decisions will be made, identifying how RTI fits with existing program policies and practices, and addressing logistics such as determining the need for administrative approval and resources, and creating a time frame for implementation.

2. **Important decisions related to implementing RTI will need to be made.** Several decisions that should be addressed early in the planning process are related to the context and scope of implementation (e.g., determining whether RTI should be used with children ages birth to five or limited to pre-kindergarten children); deciding whether the focus of RTI will be on academic learning (e.g., language, literacy, math, science), behavioral supports and social-emotional development, or a combination of these; choosing to implement RTI in a few demonstration sites versus implementing it more broadly across an entire system. Other critical decisions include identifying valid and meaningful assessment approaches and benchmarks to inform instructional decision-making, selecting research-based curricula and tiered interventions linked to curriculum goals and program standards, and specifying how early childhood practitioners will collaborate with families, specialists, and administrators to support data-based decision-making.

3. **Systemic supports are needed to ensure that RTI is implemented appropriately and is beneficial for young children and their families.** Planners should identify RTI assessment and intervention practices, consider how to define the roles of teachers and specialists, and provide ongoing professional development and support for implementing RTI; determine agreed-upon methods for sharing information about children's developmental progress with families and professionals; determine how to provide time for collaboration and allocate resources related to using RTI; and make provisions for evaluating the implementation and effectiveness of RTI for young children and families.

RECOMMENDATIONS FOR HOW TO USE THIS CONCEPT PAPER

Reaching consensus on the meaning of RTI in early childhood and identifying key considerations related to its implementation are important first steps in articulating the field's collective wisdom on this issue. The following recommendations address ways in which this paper can be used by families, practitioners, administrators, higher education faculty, and professional development providers, researchers, and policy makers to guide future efforts related to RTI in order to:

- **Advocate for family involvement and engagement in early childhood programs in which RTI is implemented.** Building on ways that families already use to communicate and collaborate with practitioners, RTI presents new opportunities for families to share their unique perspectives and participate in data-based decision-making in collaboration with early childhood program staff. Families, in turn, can help the early childhood programs understand what additional information and guidance would be helpful to families as the field gains experience in implementing RTI. Programs should consider ways of sharing information on RTI that are accessible and understandable to families who vary widely with respect to culture, language, and experience with educational issues.

- **Promote professional development on RTI to ensure that practitioners acquire the knowledge, skills, and ongoing supports needed to implement this approach effectively in practice.** Ongoing professional development is vital to helping practitioners learn new skills related to using formative assessment and linking instructional strategies and specific learning goals. Practitioners also need new skills in interpreting assessment results and selecting appropriate interventions and supports. As practitioners apply these skills in practice settings, they will need ongoing professional support using approaches such as coaching, mentoring, consultation, and communities of practice.

- **Guide strategic planning and decision-making about whether and how to implement RTI in early childhood settings.** To use RTI effectively, practitioners will need to participate in strategic planning and obtain the full support of administrators, specialists, and families as part of a problem-solving process. In most cases, administrators will take the lead in organizing strategic planning efforts, securing resources, and making provisions for ongoing professional development to ensure that RTI practices are implemented appropriately. In some cases, it may be beneficial for strategic planning to occur at a community-wide level to ensure that various types of early care and education programs build consensus and a shared vision of how RTI can enhance services and supports for young children and their families.

- **Identify gaps in knowledge regarding the implementation and efficacy of RTI in early care and education programs.** Research is needed to advance knowledge about the best way to implement RTI to enhance academic learning and social-emotional development in young children with diverse learning characteristics in various types of programs. Research is needed to provide evidence that this approach is acceptable, feasible, and effective for these children and families.

- **Identify policy gaps and the need for additional resources to support implementation of RTI on a broader scale.** Additional resources and policies are needed to guide the adoption and use of RTI in early care and education programs and to support its implementation on a broader scale.

FUTURE DIRECTIONS

The use of RTI with children prior to kindergarten entry is an emerging practice. RTI holds promise for supporting learning and development prior to kindergarten, but additional research is needed to provide direct evidence of the effectiveness of this approach with younger children. Although there is now a body of evidence on the effectiveness of RTI for improving the academic performance of school-age students, the early childhood field is only beginning to gather research evidence on RTI to guide its implementation with children prior to kindergarten. Furthermore, unlike the use of RTI with school-age children, there are no specific provisions within federal legislation or national policies addressing RTI for younger children in pre-kindergarten, child care, Head Start, and early intervention programs to guide the professional and program standards needed to support these practices. In light of the widespread interest in RTI, the early childhood field needs additional policies, guidelines, and resources to support its implementation in the future. Furthermore, early educators who choose to implement RTI will need to ensure that this approach complements effective practices and services already in place and adds value by providing additional supports for children who need them; that early childhood programs continue to address all developmental domains (including social-emotional development and academic learning); and that all practices reflect the cultural, linguistic, and developmental diversity of children and families served within the early care and education system.

ENDNOTES

1   Gersten, R., Beckmann, S., Clarke, B., Foegen, A., Marsh, L., Star, J.R., & Witzel, B. (2009). *Assisting students struggling with mathematics: Response to Intervention (RTI) for elementary and middle schools* (NCEE 2009-4060). Washington, DC: U.S. Department of Education, Institute of Education Sciences, National Center for Education and Regional Assistance. Retrieved from http://ies.ed.gov/ncee/wwc/publications/practiceguides/

2   Gersten, R., Compton, D., Connor, C. M., Dimino, J., Santoro, L., Linan-Thompson, S., & Tilly, W. D. (2008). *Assisting students struggling with reading: Response to Intervention and multi-tier intervention for reading in the primary grades.* (NCEE 2009-4045). Washington, DC: U.S. Department of Education, Institute of Education Sciences, National Center for Education and Regional Assistance. Retrieved from http://ies.ed.gov/ncee/wwc/publications/practiceguides/

3   See summaries of discussions on RTI in early childhood from eight listening sessions conducted at national conferences and meetings of a national expert panel and a DEC/NAEYC/NHSA work group related to the formulation of this concept paper available at http://community.fpg.unc.edu/resources/articles/RTI-EC

4   In 2010, the Office of Special Education Programs in the U.S. Department of Education issued informal guidance on issues regarding the use of RTI to determine eligibility for special education for three-to-five year-olds, RTI

procedures for referrals from Head Start to local education agencies (LEAs), and parental rights related to requests for evaluation of children's development and learning in the context of RTI. The guidance is available at http://www.nectac.org/idea/clarfctnltrs.asp

5   For additional information on how RTI is defined and implemented with school-age children, see National Center on Response to Intervention (March 2010). *Essential components of RTI – A closer look at Response to Intervention.* Washington, DC: U.S. Department of Education, Office of Special Education Programs, Author. Available at http://www.cldinternational.org/Articles/rtiessentialcomponents.pdf

6   Sugai, G. (May, 2009). *School-wide positive behavior support and response to intervention.* Storrs, CT: University of Connecticut, OSEP Center on Positive Behavioral Interventions and Supports available at http://www.pbis.org/common/pbisresources/presentations/Sugai_2009rSWPBS_RtI%20final_May25_2009.pdf

7   For information on core principles and recommended practices related to assessment and instruction in early childhood, see the following sources:

DEC. (2007). Promoting positive outcomes for children with disabilities: *Recommendations for curriculum, assessment, and program evaluation.* Missoula, MT: Author. Available at http://www.naeyc.org/files/naeyc/file/positions/PrmtgPositiveOutcomes.pdf

NAEYC/NAECS/SDE. (2003). *Early childhood curriculum, assessment, and program evaluation: Building an effective, accountable system in programs for children birth through age 8.* A Joint Position Statement of the National Association for the Education of Young Children (NAEYC) and the National Association of Early Childhood Specialists in State Departments of Education (NAECS/SDE). Available at http://www.naeyc.org/files/naeyc/file/positions/pscape.pdf

Sandall, S., Hemmeter, M. L., Smith, B. J., & McLean, M. E. (2005). *DEC recommended practices: A comprehensive guide for practical application in early intervention/early childhood special education.* Missoula, MT: Division for Early Childhood (DEC) of the Council for Exceptional Children (CEC).

U.S. Department of Health and Human Services, Administration for Children and Families, Office of Head Start. (2010). *The Head Start child development and early learning framework: Promoting positive outcomes in early childhood programs serving children 3–5 years old.* Washington, DC: Author. http://eclkc.ohs.acf.hhs.gov/hslc/tta-system/teaching/eecd/Assessment/Child%20Outcomes/ revised-child-outcomes.html

8   The conceptual framework for the continuum of interventions and supports within RTI in early childhood is consistent with the way this has been conceptualized for school-age children, although the content and implementation of instructional practices will vary depending on the age group.

Index

Page numbers followed by *f* indicate figures; those followed by *t* indicate tables.